Trespass Against Us
Dow Chemical & The Toxic Century

Jack Doyle

Common Courage Press
Monroe, Maine

A publication of the
Environmental Health Fund
Boston, Massachusetts

Environmental Health Fund

The Environmental Health Fund (EHF) is an education and advocacy organization working to protect people's health through reducing toxic chemical exposures. EHF is one of the founding members of Health Care Without Harm, the Campaign for Environmentally Responsible Healthcare (*www.noharm.org*). EHF is also working to hold the chemical industry accountable for its global contamination, and has published a report entitled "Beyond the Chemical Century: Restoring Human Rights and Preserving the Fabric of Life." The Environmental Health Fund is presently collaborating with several United Nations agencies (including UNDP, UNIDO and WHO) to involve civil society organizations in implementing the Stockholm Convention on persistent organic pollutants (POPs). The Environmental Health Fund can be reached at 41 Oakview Terrace, Boston, MA 02130; phone (617) 524-6018; fax (617) 524-7021.

Library of Congress Cataloguing-in-Publication Data is available from the publisher on request.

ISBN 1-56751-268-2 paper
ISBN 1-56751-269-0 hardback

Common Courage Press
121 Red Barn Road
Monroe, ME 04951
(207) 525-0900; fax (207) 525-3068
info@commoncouragepress.com
www.commoncouragepress.com

First Printing

Printed in Canada

This book is set in ITC Cheltenham, with page layout by Elizabeth Doherty and Jack Doyle.

Cover: Photos and images, clockwise from top left: aerial herbicide spraying during Vietnam War, 1960s, U.S. Air Force photo; pesticide barrels on airport tarmac in Stuttgart, Arkansas, April 1983, *New York Times*/David P. Fornell; female image, "Woman," art by Greg Spalenka, *www.spalenka.com*; Dow Chemical complex at Terneuzen, Netherlands, photo by Greenpeace/Bas Beentjes, 2003-01-07, *www.greenpeace.org*; and "Vietnam Napalm," June 1972, AP/Wide World Photos, photo by Huynh Cong 'Nick' Ut. Cover concept by Jack Doyle, design and layout by James Lee, JML Design, Potomac, MD, *www.jmldesign.com*.

Contents

Acknowledgments

Books are enterprises of many people, and this one is no exception. A good number of generous people helped along the way, providing sources or perspective that improved the final product. They are owed my most sincere thanks. They include: Shelley Alpern, Greg Bates, Jim Brophy, Barry Castleman, Gary Cohen, Pat Costner, Charlie Cray, Dave Dempsey, Peter Diamond, Elizabeth Doherty, Tracey Easthope, Willie Fontenot, Alex, Dana, and Noah Fruzynski, Mike Gilbertson, Krishnaveni Gundu, Casey Harrell, Diane Hebert, Rick Hind, Michelle Hurd-Riddick, O. D. Kenemore, Dorothy Kew, Sanford Lewis, Ed Luchessi, Robert E. Martin, Marc Messing, Fred Millar, Paul Orum, Bill Ravanesi, Wayne Schmidt, Dick Schneider, Keith Schneider, Peter Sills, Sharron and Vaughan Stewart, Wilma Subra, Mark Van Putten, and Carol Van Strum. Several individual reviewers and sources who requested anonymity are also acknowledged here for their help, comments, and/or information. For financial support, I am indebted first and foremost to the Environmental Health Fund (EHF) of Boston, and to Gary Cohen and Peter Diamond at EHF for making this endeavor possible, and to anonymous donors and supporters.

I am especially indebted to a number of journalists and historians who have traveled some of this same ground before me, leaving a rich trove of material from which I have liberally drawn. Chief among these are the authors of Dow's corporate history, Don Whitehead, whose excellent 1968 book, *The Dow Story*, lively and well written, provided important insights. E. N. Brandt's exhaustive 1997 work on Dow, *Growth Company*, is clearly the company's definitive history, and enlightened this reader considerably along the way. Special thanks to Cathy Trost for her remarkable 1984 book, *Elements of Risk*, which is highly recommended to any student of Dow and the modern chemical industry. Ms. Trost's work is very thorough, reliable, and most telling without polemic, bombast, or exaggeration. It is one of the best single works on Dow's 2,4,5-T and DBCP history that I had the pleasure of discovering in this 14-month sojourn. I have excerpted from it in several chapters and for drawing individual profiles in two long sidebars. Thomas Whitesides' early and eloquent writing on 2,4,5-T and dioxin, *The Pendulum and the Toxic Cloud*, is also recommended, as are Carol Van Strum's *A Bitter Fog* (and *No Margin of Safety* with Paul Merrell) and Lewis Regenstein's *America the Poisoned*. Joe Thornton's *Pandora's Poison* has been most helpful, as have any number of Greenpeace reports and studies, including those written and or edited by past and present staffers there, including Charlie Cray, Dave DeRosa, Rick Hind, Pat Costner, Sandra Marquardt, Bonnie Rice,

Joe Thornton, Bill Walsh, Jack Weinberg, and others. Dave Dempsey's history of conservation and environmental policy in Michigan, *Ruin & Recovery*, helped in corroborating some Michigan and Canadian parts of the story. Eileen Welsome's excellent series on the Rocky Flats complex in *Westword* was drawn upon quite heavily in Chapter 9, as was John Byrne's *Informed Consent* and Susan Zimmerman's *Silicone Survivors* in the silicone chapter. *Deceit and Denial* by Gerald Markowitz and David Rosner, also helped, as did *War on Waste* by Louis Blumberg and Robert Gottlieb; and *Toxic Deception* by Dan Fagin and Marianne Lavelle. Among other works cited are: Marc Lappe's *Chemical Deception*; Michael Brown's *Laying Waste* and *The Toxic Cloud*; Russell Mokhiber's *Corporate Crime and Violence*; and Lois Gibbs' *Dying From Dioxin*, to name a few. Others are listed in each chapter's notes. Front-line journalists from daily newspapers—whether in Midland, Michigan; Brazosport, Texas; or New York city's financial district—provided important, first-hand historical reporting on Dow, as did those from more specialized trade publications such as *Chemical Week* and *Chemical & Engineering News*. On the web, there were a number of helpful sources, among them, the good sites of the Pesticide Action Network in San Francisco and the Tittabawassee River Watch in Michigan, to name just two.

Special thanks are due Charlie Cray, Tracey Easthope, and Diane Hebert for generously sharing their files and years of research on Dow Chemical, without which this project would still be at square one; Liz Doherty for her patience, good cheer, and fine professional work and attention to detail in layout and typesetting; Gary Cohen for standing by the project and providing consistent moral support; and Greg Bates for creative suggestions and taking the book to market.

The Dow story that follows is not a strict business history, told in a dollars-and-cents way, or from a process engineer's perspective, or that of chemist. For those accounts, there are other books, such as Dow's more or less official biography mentioned above. Rather, the book that follows here looks at Dow through a different, more critical lens—that of Dow neighbors, workers, public health advocates, and those harmed by its chemicals. The opening pages provide an introduction to the reality of persistent chemicals—those found, uninvited, in the environment and in the human body, contributing to a "body burden" that we all carry: a quantity of synthetic substances in our persons as a consequence of the chemical revolution. Subsequent chapters tell of Dow's business and history with various chemicals, from World War I warfare gases and Vietnam's Agent Orange defoliant, to dry cleaning chemicals, pesticides, and polyvinyl chloride. A chapter on Union Carbide, a company now owned by Dow, covers some of that firm's past as it relates to Dow, with attached concerns of asbestos liability and the 20-year-old problems left at Bhopal, India. Dow's political history and corporate philosophy are also explored, as are the company's environmental and public-relations strategies. There are separate chapters covering Dow in Canada, Louisiana, Texas, New Zealand, and Michigan. Added to these are profiles of Dow as government contractor managing the Rocky Flats nuclear complex in Colorado; its involvement in the Dow Corning silicone breast implant fiasco; and some accounting of its record with chemical plant accidents, toxic gas releases, and chronic pollution. Altogether this is not a flattering profile of the Dow Chemical Company, though it recognizes and acknowledges Dow's ingenuity and business acumen. Rather, this is a work directed at bringing more public attention to the very real problems of invasive synthetic chemistry and toxic chemicals, and to changing corporate behavior in that arena.

Jack Doyle
Washington, DC
March 2004

Introduction

The Dow Chemical Company has been trespassing on private property for decades, crossing private boundary lines without the owner's permission. The boundary lines being crossed are unseen for the most part and the property is personal, even sacrosanct. For what is being violated is the biological common, or rather, "all of us," one-celled and many-celled; paramecium and orangutan; Mom, Dad, and the kids.

The trespass in this case is harmful and it is toxic. For the transgressors at issue are man-made synthetic chemicals, more than 100,000 of which have been "invented" and let loose in the world since the 1930s. These are the chemicals that make up the good life, we're told, for products that make our lives better. Yet many of these chemicals are toxic to life and have been doing harm for years, insinuating themselves into blood, body tissue, sperm and egg. On that course, they have been trespassing: invading biology's inner sanctum, violating life-sustaining processes, and creating undesirable changes that last not just for a day, but in some cases, generations. The guilty parties in these transgressions, however, have not been brought to account, and they have not been stopped. To this day, "toxic trespass" continues, and it is poisoning all of us.

This book is one account of that trespass; a story of how one company's chemical products and byproducts have damaged, and continue to damage, public health and the environment. It is not a pretty picture; there are cancers, birth defects, deformed babies, healthy lives turned unhealthy, broken people, injured and sickened workers, and poisoned communities.

The central character in this story is the Dow Chemical Company of Midland, Michigan. Dow is a century-old company and currently the world's largest chemical corporation. By most conventional yardsticks, Dow is a terrifically productive and inventive company, with a growth and prosperity record envied the world over. On Wall Street, Dow's stock is found in many investment portfolios, and on Main Street, in many retirement accounts. Dow Chemical is also a "founding father" of the synthetic chemical revolution, and today, one of its most determined boosters. Yet there has been, and continues to be, a major flaw in that revolution. Despite the benefits that have poured forth from modern chemistry's Golden Horn, too many of its substances have been found to pose grave risks to public health and safety.

Not every single chemical is a problem, of course. But the damage wrought by some—especially those that persist, accumulate, and magnify in the biota—is especially worrisome. And the latest revelations are even more

ix

troubling. For some synthetic chemicals intrude into the developing fetus, create havoc with hormones, and/or lodge in the DNA—there, in effect, for generations. Complicating this picture historically is the fact that synthetic chemistry's most obvious damage did not emerge until some years *after* the prosperity—after the capital investment, after the profits, and after the embedded uses and dependencies. This lag effect is owed, in part, to disease latency, the time it takes for diseases to reveal themselves and take their toll. It is also owed to poor industry testing of chemicals prior to their use. In addition, proving cause and effect—a disease/chemical link—hasn't always been possible or definitive. In this process, vested interests like Dow, have moved to keep things in play, using the due process of law and regulation to guarantee protracted contests, chemical by chemical. This maneuvering and politics is also part of the story.

At The Headwaters

Dow Chemical, it turns out, is an especially important player in the synthetic chemical revolution. For Dow has been at the headwaters of modern chemical development from practically day one; a key "first source" generator of building-block chemicals that allowed a frenzy of combinational wizardry to proceed with few questions asked. Dow's chlorinated compounds, in particular, became first-source chemicals for a major part of the modern synthetic revolution. Once known for its *Saran* wrap and *Ziploc* bags, Dow is today the world's largest chemical company with $32 billion in annual sales. It is also the world's largest chlorine producer and one of the world's leading plastics producers. Dow's chemistry is deeply embedded throughout the global economy, found in countless products—from plastic toys and compact discs, to vinyl siding, shower curtains, running shoes, and automotive dashboards, to name a few. Every day, the company handles upwards of 7,000 chemicals and chemical products in its research, manufacturing, and marketing. Yet much of what Dow makes and sells goes unnoticed. For Dow—known at times as "a chemical company's chemical company"—sells in bulk, in truck-load and train-car lots, to other companies which in turn make a vast array of products. Dow's chemistry then, is often a "behind-the-scenes" type of chemistry, though key in stoking a burgeoning chemical commerce—and global chemical proliferation.

About *every ten seconds*, a new chemical substance is discovered; new chemical compounds enter commerce at an average rate of about *three per day*. Tens of thousands of chemicals have been released into the environment—and because of their persistence, hundreds today are found still lodged in biological food chains, in birds and wildlife, and in human beings. New chemicals continue to be released without adequate testing, amounting to a grand chemical experiment on all of us—a global toxic trespass; what some see as a fundamental violation of human rights. As this book will show, Dow Chemical has been and continues to be at the headwaters of that process.

"Better Living ... "

Since the 1890s, Dow has had a fairly dramatic and prosperous ride—from brine-derived bleach and medicinal bromides through the early 1900s; magnesium and gasoline additives in the 1930s and 1940s; to a booming world pesticide and plastics market through the 1950s and 1960s. During those times and today, Dow has been in a more or less constant formulating and expansionist mode, always developing new chemicals. Dow even became a pharmaceutical power for a time, producing all manner of products, from cholesterol drugs to artificial kidneys. It also became an energy company, involved with oil, gas, and even nuclear power. In fact, it appeared there was little Dow couldn't do. Supremely confident in its abilities—owing in part to the Horatio Alger-style rise of its independent founder and inventor, Herbert Dow—the company took on any charge, whether producing mustard gas for the government in World War I, napalm and Agent Orange in Vietnam, or running a government factory for making nuclear bomb triggers. Yet these missions were loaded with risk, and as will be shown, some peril for people and planet.

In the 1950s and 1960s, "Better Living Through Chemistry" was the touchstone philosophy that informed and molded the world view at Dow and other chemical companies. Dow's managers, scientists, and executives believed their products were promoting better living and economic growth. Substantiated by the success and booming chemical growth of the 1950s and early 1960s, Dow's outlook for the next half century was also built on this philosophy. A manifest, beneficent chemistry became bedrock at Dow, shaping a corporate culture that was imbued at times with patriotic overtones. What could possibly go wrong? Dow became a bit intoxicated with itself and its science. It got into the habit of thinking it was always right.

By the late 1960s, however, that world view began to change. Dow soon discovered it could be held accountable for the things it made, especially if those things created harm. Its wartime contracts supplying napalm and Agent Orange during the Vietnam War had more light shed on them than earlier, anonymous work in World War I and World War II. Its domestic pesticides drew fire too, and a few bad drugs put Dow on the defensive as well. When federal agencies such as the U.S. Environmental Protection Agency (EPA), the Food and Drug Administration (FDA), and the Occupational Safety and Health Administration (OSHA) were created or given broader mandates in the 1970s, Dow's unfettered world of turning science into products was suddenly put upon. But rather than developing a new strategic model and business plan that built in more precaution, Dow decided to fight. In a number of confrontations, Dow dug in its heels and insisted that its science was correct, its products safe, and that workers and communities had nothing to fear. The 1980s, however, produced a decade of revelations about things Dow was hiding; about its workers, the safety of its products, and the real toxicity of some of its chemistry—particularly that revolving around a family of byproduct chemicals called the dioxins. These revelations did not come willingly from Dow, but rather were forced into public light by litigation, journalists, and government officials. Dow's science was not all Dow claimed it was.

Toxic Trespass

Granted, many of Dow's chemicals today are beneficial to society and do improve the quality of life. Yet some have and are creating egregious harms. The harms created are not typically catastrophic, acute, or highly visible—though there is some of that with ongoing emissions, spills, and chemical plant accidents. Rather, the chemicals of continuing concern are those that cause damage over time; those that plant the seed for cancer or a mutation. These are chemicals that can do damage even after one fleeting exposure, at levels that seem impossibly small—at the trillionth- and quadrillionth-part levels; where angels dance on the heads of pins. Still, at the same impossibly tiny levels—and within the exquisite biochemistry that is a seal pup, a lioness, a blue whale, or a human being—there is the delicate dance of life going on within cells, within DNA, and among biochemical messaging molecules. When these processes are invaded, if only for a moment in time, the balances and messages can be disrupted; the normal formings and joinings can be set askew, and a birth defect or health effect is set in motion—in the gene, in the sperm, in the hormone, in the reproductive cycle. This is toxic trespass at the sub-obvious level; at a level perhaps not conventionally recognized by courts as a tort trespass, such as when a factory's toxic emissions damage a neighbor's land, or a pesticide spray drifts onto an adjacent vegetable field. Yet clearly, this is a kindred damage, and potentially far worse in consequence since it can live beyond the initial assault, as in birth defects or chemically-induced mutations. It is also, as in any trespass, an uninvited intrusion. And the damage created, in the aggregate, is an alteration of the global common; a subterfuge of public health and environmental safety. As long as such toxic chemistry persists, the public health and safety is placed in continuing danger.

Altering the global common with dangerous chemistry is certainly not the planned intention of any good chemist working hard at his or her craft. Nor is it the intended design of any good business manager or CEO. Yet modern commercial chemistry has too often been an experiment on unwitting subjects—launching products with too little precaution and too much marketing enthusiasm. What *is* the fault and intention of Dow and its industry trade groups on too many occasions, is holding back information on the chemicals developed, promoted, and sold. Dow's knowledge about its chemicals and products, it turns out, was often different from that which the public had, or even some of its best customers. The first signs that something was amiss with Dow's chlorophenol products—an early indication of the embedded dioxin problem—emerged nearly 70 years ago, in the 1930s when Mississippi lumberman and Dow workers in Midland began to have rashes and other problems. Dow's early knowledge of potential health effects from other chemicals—pesticides such as 2,4,5-T, DBCP, and chlorpyrifos; plastics and plastic ingredients such as polyvinyl chloride and bisphenol-A; silicone and silicone ingredients; benzene and epichlorohydrin in the workplace; and war-time products such as Agent Orange—wasn't always shared promptly, and in fact, was sometimes held back. And in the absence of complete and perfect evidence that a chemical was harmful, but suspected as such, or even shown fairly strongly to pose a risk—as in the case of 2,4,5-T—Dow would push out the legal appeals or stretch out the regulatory process as far as possible to ensure more marketing time. This is perhaps the unforgivable trespass; the mortal sin of commercial synthetic chemistry: the after-the-fact defense of chemicals known to do harm.

The Big Experiment

"Very few people had even been trained in toxicology at that time," explained Dow scientist Dr. Ted Torkelson, describing the early 1950s when he first came to Dow as a 22-year-old biochemist. "Fact is, when I was hired, I didn't know what toxicology was."[1] But Dow did undertake testing—some dating to the 1930s when it first set up its own laboratories. Still, in the 1950s, once some cursory lab tests of a chemical had been finished, companies often put chemical products on the market while continuing to investigate their effects. This happened with the herbicides 2,4,5-T and 2,4-D, and with the fungicide DBCP, made by Dow and others—and many other products and their derivatives. At times, in fact, it seemed the preferred way to fully and finally "test" chemicals was to begin marketing them, wait and see what problems emerged, and then deal with the consequences. Today, world regulators are still playing "toxicological catch-up" with many thousands of chemicals that remain inadequately tested.

But this was the way of the toxicological world in the 1950s and 1960s; a time when patterns and methodologies were set and cast; a time when synthetic chemistry exploded on the world and became embedded in thousands of industrial and consumer products. Dow's Torkelson offered this explanation in one 1980s interview after trouble over DBCP had broken:

...I think science oversold itself, or maybe it was an overzealous press. It goes back to "Better Things for Better Living Through Chemistry" and that kind of thing. All you had to do was wait a day, and there'd be a new food additive or a new whitener for your clothes or a new floor polish or a new paint or a new weed killer, a new this, a new that—you know, chemistry will take care of us. And finally the pendulum just went the other way, and people started to see bad things about chemistry, and that's all they saw. But I don't think the people here at Dow have lost faith in technology.[2]

Indeed, the people at Dow for the most part, did not lose faith in their technology or their hard-charging corporate approach, even after they were taken to task for some toxic problems in the 1970s and 1980s. In fact, like Torkelson, they became more determined to validate their model. Dow became imbued by the infallibility of its own mission; a company whose "we-can-do-no-harm" culture gave it a wrongly self-centered air of entitlement. Dow dug in too deeply on more than a few occasions to make sure its brand of chemistry and/or management style prevailed, damn the consequences. And perhaps that's one reason why Dow today remains one of the most sued companies in existence.

Toxic Torts

Litigation aimed at Dow for its wayward chemistry—whether of the leaking and polluting varieties, or the longer-term invasive kind—has been with the company from practically the beginning. Neighbor- and worker-filed lawsuits dating to 1900 were filed against Dow's Midland, Michigan operation. Since the 1960s, Dow has been in court almost constantly, beginning with pesticide cases, as well as those involving some pharmaceutical products. Agent Orange claims by Vietnam veterans, and litigation with Dow and Dow Corning over silicone breast implants, have resulted in some of the largest and most controversial mass toxic tort cases ever. Today, with Union Carbide, Dow faces still more litigation, with cases pending on matters related to asbestos, old Carbide mining operations, and Bhopal. Neighbors continue to sue Dow, too—for vinyl chloride drinking water contamination and adverse health effects in Plaquemine, Louisiana; for leaking chemicals in an underground storage cavern and an old landfill in two Texas communities; and for pesticide exposures ranging from 2,4-D to *Dursban*. With *Dursban*, in fact, there have been some 270 lawsuits since 1990. Workers' widows have sued Dow in wrongful death actions in several states, and fisherman in Brazil have sued Dow for pesticide contamination of fishing waters. Dow, along with Shell, is also mired in current litigation in Nicaragua and the U.S., filed by banana workers alleging health effects, including sterility, suffered from the use of the fungicide DBCP. In New Zealand and Vietnam, lawsuits are being filed or prepared for Dow and/or Dow subsidiaries alleging continued health effects and damages of Agent Orange chemicals. In 2003, the U.S. Supreme Court found that Agent Orange litigation is still ripe for U.S. Vietnam war veterans, despite previous attempts by manufacturers and some judges to close it off. And as this books goes to press, nearly 2,000 potential plaintiffs along the Tittabawassee River in Michigan await word on their standing to sue as a class in dioxin-related litigation aimed at Dow. These actions amount to much more than frivolous lawsuits; they are actions speaking to real and aggrieved losses, and in total add up to a substantial pattern of Dow's continuing toxic trespass.

Hard-Nosed Dow

In its litigation and courtroom dealings, Dow is a hard-nosed player, not above using intimidation or outside influences to move the process in its favor. In Michigan recently, Dow deposed potential witnesses for hours trying to intimidate and confuse them. In one Louisiana breast implant case, Dow was accused of jury tampering and using advertising to influence prospective jurors. Still, a few juries have made some not-so-flattering findings of Dow conduct, verdicts which Dow typically appeals and appeals, until in most cases, they are overturned or watered down. Like other corporate litigants, Dow prefers out-of-court settlements where possible, meaning most case details and proceedings are sealed from public view.

Dow's lobbyists, too, are ready to nip "trouble" in the bud, wherever it may appear. In the fall of 2002, Dow spent $90,000 in a few weeks during a special session on tort reform in the Mississippi legislature to make sure caps were placed on punitive damages—with no exceptions for jury awards in environmental cases. In 2003, along with two other companies, Dow hired former Clinton and Reagan administration officials to repeal Nicaragua's DBCP victims law. As homeland security legislation worked though the U.S. Senate in 2002, Dow lobbied against key provisions of the Chemical Security Act, including one to require inherently safer technologies to help minimize and eliminate hazardous risks at chemical plants. Yet with the other hand, Dow's advertising money is used to tell the public it is doing "great things" or "improving life daily."

Still, a few who have studied Dow for years conclude there is no intentional wrongdoing at the company. "... I found no case where the corporation (as contrasted with an individual within the corporation) knowingly engaged in wrongdoing of any nature," writes E. N. Brandt, in his Dow biography, *Growth Company*. "If there is such as thing as a 'corporate' conscience, I am convinced Dow has one."[3] Yet, the accounts of people and places subjected to Dow chemicals that follow in this book, tell a somewhat different story.

Real People

There is Billie Shoecraft, the spunky 53-year-old wife and mother who was sprayed in 1969 with a Dow 2,4,5-T herbicide by the U.S. Forest Service near her home in Globe, Arizona. Shoecraft, perfectly healthy at the time of the spraying, began a long and painful ordeal with cancer shortly after the incident, and died in 1977. Similarly, stories of 1970s miscarriages and birth defects in heavily sprayed areas of Oregon implicate Dow herbicides—the same herbicides used in Agent Orange and Agent White defoliant concoctions in the Vietnam War. Accounts of returning Vietnam veterans before Congress are here too, telling of their herbicide poisonings—such as that of Michael Ryan's and his daughter Kerry, born with severe birth defects. North Vietnamese veterans too, have horror stories of what Agent Orange and other herbicides continue to do to their homeland and people. The Agent Orange legacy, in fact, continues to surface today, with some horrific birth-defects stories coming out of locations such as New Zealand, where a Dow subsidiary helped supply war needs. Back in the U.S., a parade of individuals tell tales about how Dow's insecticide and termite killer, *Dursban*, changed their lives through toxic exposure—among them, a high school student, a pest exterminator, an office worker, and two children with various maladies attributed to possible pre-natal *Dursban* exposure.

In the national travail over silicone breast implants—still ongoing with pending lawsuits and appeals as this book goes to press—Dow Chemical is implicated as a partner and owner of Dow Corning, the implant maker. Amid the abbreviated history of that story in Chapter 12 are the personal accounts of Colleen Swanson and Charlotte Mahlum; women irreparably harmed and made ill by Dow Corning implants that Dow Chemical claims it had no role in making. Yet a trail of silicone research between the two firms over the years, plus shared reports, scientists, and executives, appears to suggest otherwise.

Mike Trout, an Occidental Chemical worker in Lathrop, California and young family man in the 1970s, became afflicted with a brain cancer from which he initially rebounded, but was also made temporarily sterile after working with the Dow-supplied chemical, DBCP. The fungicide was turned out in quantity at the Occidental plant and sold in various remixed formulations. Trout died in 1979 of his brain cancer when he was 27 years old. There are also other workers' stories here too, but these are told more anonymously in groups, as in vinyl chloride workers suffering health effects of vinyl chloride monomer; dry-cleaning workers and nearby residents suffering the ill effects of the solvent perchloroethylene; Dow workers of the 1970s handling benzene and epichlorohydrin found to have chromosome damage; and plutonium workers suffering various maladies and dangers at Dow's poorly-managed Rocky Flats nuclear complex.

Dow's workers, in fact, stand out in these pages, emerging as some of the most important heroes in the struggle to move Dow to improved safety and environmental responsibility. Repeatedly, from Canada to Texas, organized labor stands up to Dow, and in some ways, workers are the first to raise the larger environmental and public health issues. Labor leaders such as Ivan Hillier at Sarnia, Ontario, or O. D. Kenemore from Brazoria County, Texas, while representing their members' interests economically, also pushed the envelope on community health and safety and environmental protection. Dow, however, appears to be no friend of organized labor, and is often found trying to break unions.

In Dow communities, too, there are more people stories. Central Michigan landowners in the vicinity of Dow's old brine wells and pipeline system—such as Erich and Edna Tessin of Saginaw County, Michigan—have stories about leaks, spills, property damage, and contaminated drinking water. Some believe there was more in the brine than just brine, with reports of deformed and diseased farm animals and some unexplained cancers. In Plaquemine, Louisiana, Dow's sprawling 1,500-acre complex has leaked chemicals from toxic waste dumps into the underground aquifer—a leak some charge has contaminated the drinking water of Myrtle Grove residents with vinyl chloride, suspected of contributing to a number of miscarriages there. Spills, fires, explosions, and toxic gas releases occurring at Dow operations—in Arkansas, California, Florida, Louisiana, Michigan, Texas, West Virginia, Canada, Italy, Germany, Switzerland, and various other locations—suggest it is dangerous to live near Dow. Dow plants in the U.S. and Canada are still among the top industrial polluters, and the company has a long record of fines and citations in the United States and abroad for violating environmental, health, and worker safety laws.

Some of this Dow history has been covered before, and a number of the stories included here have appeared elsewhere. Yet they are important to tell again and compile in one place, "old news" or not. For taken together, these incidents show a pattern of performance and reveal a corporate resume that is not always seen at initial reporting.

No Trespassing

In business, however, Dow Chemical is an impressive company, no question. Dow's rise from Michigan's Tittabawassee River basin of the 1890s to become the world's largest chemical company is a story with many admirable qualities. Imbued with the persistence and ingenuity of young Herbert Dow, the new Dow Chemical Company made its mark, and after a few setbacks, rose to considerable success. One hundred years of jobs, prosperity, and economic growth followed, bringing value to workers, local communities, and the larger society. Dow Chemical, on this level, has made the world a better place. Yet still, there is a substantial reality of chemical consequence that must be laid squarely on Dow's doorstep; an unpleasant reality of people and communities poisoned; of disease, birth defects, and ruined lives.

Dow's liabilities and failings are not simply matters of a few passing pollution episodes or neglected toxic waste dumps. Rather, they involve broadly an entire branch of toxic, persistent chlorinated chemistry that has permeated much of the world's economy. It is this toxic chemistry that is creating daily very real and ongoing public health effects for millions of people, altering the entire living world. It is a toxic legacy that may soon affect Dow's balance sheet as well.

We have been sold a bill of goods with the wonder products of the synthetic chemical revolution—not all of which have proven so wonderful. We are now up to our necks in the stuff, with hundreds of substances permeating our living fiber in detrimental ways. This toxic chemistry is so intricately woven into our lives and economies, that separating from it will become a major economic undertaking. But separate we must—and soon.

Dow Chemical, a dominant firm in its industry with $32 billion in 2003 sales, is still in toxic denial; the company appears to believe it can continue business as usual. Yet a new accounting is coming to Dow and companies like it. Those harmed are not sitting still. New coalitions of victims, workers, investors, and public health leaders are now forming. They are pursuing legal and economic strategies to bring toxic trespassers to account. There is still time for Dow to take the high road, of course. Dow could commit to inventing the safer course, leaving the damaging and persistent branches of chemistry behind; shedding its most toxic lines immediately. For that is the course of action that more people and governments the world over see as necessary—and will be demanding. No more toxic trespass; that is the message—a new kind of property rights revolution is taking form.

1.
In The Blood

For the first time in the history of the world, every human being is now subjected to contact with dangerous chemicals, from the moment of conception until death.

Rachel Carson, *Silent Spring*, 1962

It was a bright, spring day in Midland, Michigan on May 8, 2003. Hundreds of automobiles, SUVs, and minivans streamed into the huge parking lot at the Midland Center for the Arts off Eastman Avenue. The annual shareholders meeting of the Dow Chemical Company was scheduled to begin at 2 p.m. in the center's auditorium. It was a big event for Midland, Dow's corporate headquarters. Nearly 1,000 stockholders, retired employees, and representatives of pension funds and brokerages would attend.

Midland—located in the "palm of the mitt" as locals will tell you, pointing to the center of their hand as surrogate Michigan map—is where Dow Chemical began its enterprise more than 100 years ago. Some call Midland a company town, as Dow's presence looms large in buildings, in the arts, and in the economy. Dow Corning, a part-owned Dow company, is also here. But Midland is known most as the place where Herbert Dow began "mining" the huge underground deposits of brine in the 1890s, fashioning a new kind of chemical commerce. As if by a sorcerer's apprentice, Dow Chemical grew upon the proliferating magic of bromine and chlorine to become the global colossus it is today—the world's largest chemical company. With Union Carbide, acquired in 2001, Dow's global reach now extends to more than 170 countries.

Dow's shareholders are, for the most part, a happy lot. They typically get their dividend. Dow's business has been enormously prosperous; one of the most profitable companies of all time. But not all of Dow's shareholders filing into the Midland Center for the Arts were smiling on May 8, 2003. In fact, a small group of them—dissidents, some might say—were quite concerned about Dow's chemistry, or at least a portion of it. These shareholders wanted to know more about a special group of chemicals that Dow made—the ones that were showing up in the blood and body tissue of polar bears and people.

Inside the Midland Center for the Arts, a resolution on this very topic awaited Dow shareholders—a resolution requiring Dow to prepare a public report on those chemicals. Variously labeled "persistent organic pollutants" (POPs) and/or "persistent, bioaccumulative toxic substances" (PBTs), more than 500 such chemicals have been found in human blood and body tissue in the last decade or so. Few of these chemicals existed in the 1920s. Many have come on the scene since the 1940s and 1950s. Some, like the pesticide DDT, or the former electric insulating chemicals, polychlorinated biphenyls, PCBs, have been banned in the United States in recent years. Yet they are still found in the remotest regions of the planet and in most people's blood or body fat. Others have been found insinuating themselves into animal and human reproduction, causing birth defects and other problems. Still others cause cancer, or are believed to be mimicking and tricking hormones, causing varying kinds of developmental and/or metabolic havoc throughout the biological world. All of these concerns have cast a new, hard scrutiny on the synthetic chemical revolution—that seemingly unstoppable cornucopia of thousands and thousands of "new and better" chemical products.

More than 500 chemicals have been found in human blood and body tissue in the last decade or so.

Dow's small group of dissenting shareholders came to Midland to raise pointed questions about POPs and PBTs, and about Dow's role and responsibilities as a "first source" producer. For Dow Chemical is a company that has been there from the beginning; a progenitor of the synthetic chemical revolution and key inventor of its techniques and ingredients—a company still at the manufacturing headwaters of a global chemistry that is both prosperous and poisonous.

As Dow's shareholders continued to stream into the Midland Center for the Arts, some passed by the silent vigil and banner of a small group of protestors from Bhopal, India. The protestors were assigned a designated area for their demonstration; off to the far side of the main entrance, on a small grassy area at the edge of the parking lot. They were seeking Dow's attention for the still-festering contamination and health problems left behind by Union Carbide 20 years earlier after a chemical plant there released a toxic gas, killing more than 3,000 people and injuring tens of thousands. These quiet protestors, some of whom were on a hunger strike to draw attention to their plight, would later make their way to the microphones inside, imploring Dow to clean up Bhopal. Dow formally acquired Union Carbide in 2001, but maintains it is not responsible for the current problems. However for some, Bhopal wasn't just an anomaly or another part of the "side effects"* ledger of the synthetic chemical revolution; it was sym-

---

*Some argue that use of the term "side effects" is misleading, especially since the effects that do occur on people and in the environment are—in their lives and place—"main effects."

bol and reality of its inherent dangers. But not for Dow. Dow's managers typically celebrated the chemical revolution at its annual meetings, and the May 2003 gathering was no exception.

Upbeat Dow

The message Dow shareholders would take away at the end of the day on May 8 was a reassuring and upbeat one. Dow was doing just fine, its leaders would tell them, despite a few bumps in the road here and there. When 63-year-old Chief Executive Officer Bill Stavropoulos strode onto the stage in the spacious and comfortable auditorium of the Midland Center for the Arts, he was backed by a huge drop-down screen which had already pumped out a short promotional film on the products, people, and future of the Dow Chemical Company. On stage, the decor was patriotic, with red and royal blue curtains framing the picture. The "Dow Diamond"—company symbol and trademarked logo—was prominently featured, displayed behind the speakers on the big drop-down screen. The word "Dow," set in white lettering in the middle of the red diamond, stood out against a blue background. A large America flag, falling unfurled from its pole, stood silent sentinel on one side of the stage, though clearly in the picture. Behind Stavropoulos, in two tiers of box seats arrayed quiz-show-like, were Dow's board members, some with prominent political pedigree, like former U.S. Senator, John C. Danforth (R-MO), and former President George H.W. Bush's Secretary of Commerce, Barbara Hackman Franklin.

The New York Times / March 31, 1983

During the pre-business warm-up, Stavropoulos played knowingly to his hometown crowd. He singled out former Dow executives in the audience, asking them to rise for special recognition as he called their names. He then asked those in the audience who were former Dow managers, Dow retirees, or Dow employees to stand for recognition. Nearly the entire audience stood up. It was a Dow love-in. Stavropoulos and Dow appeared to be reminding any outsiders in attendance just where they were: on Dow's turf. Was it intentional intimidation? Hard to say. But within minutes of that exercise,

Dow called for the presentation of the one bit of potential controversy on the docket: the toxic chemicals shareholder resolution. What had taken proponents and company officials months and months of prep time and negotiation, move and counter move with the U.S. Securities and Exchange Commission over whether to allow or disallow the resolution, took Stavropoulos and Dow less than 15 minutes to dispense with. Shelley Alpern of Boston's Trillium Asset Management, the brokerage representing the Dow shareholder offering the resolution, delivered the proponent's position. Alpern reeled off all the reasons and supporting data on behalf of the resolution and why Dow shareholders should want to know more about these toxic chemicals and the future of their company—including matters of potential shareholder liability. Dow's corporate secretary, Tina Van Dam, delivered management's position and the case against the resolution, essentially saying that Dow was handling the situation, spending a lot of money on the problem, and was already reporting on the chemicals in company publications and government reports. The vote was then called for, with most proxies submitted in advance of the meeting in any case. When the vote was later reported, Dow had won handily. No surprise. Just over 93 percent of the shareholders had supported their company, or more than 580,000 shareholders voting to oppose the report on toxic chemicals. However, 6.9 percent, or roughly 50,000 Dow shareholders, cast their vote in favor of the proponents' resolution, agreeing that Dow should do the report. Although Dow "won" the popular vote and defeated the resolution, the proponents also "won" on technical grounds, having successfully crossed the 3 percent threshold, which entitled them to bring their resolution back the following year. So for the moment, the untidy unpleasantness—as far as Dow was concerned—had been dealt with quickly. But the issue would not go away.

When Stavropoulos made his financial report and review of the previous year, he indicated that 2002 had been "difficult," given the economy. But there were bright spots, too. "Our organization is focused and energized," he said, in his best CEO cheerleaderese, Dow "beat Wall Street expectations by a mile," he proclaimed, earning 9 cents per share while the mavens expected losses of up to 10 cents a share. In a slumping economy with rising energy prices, "this was a 'bravo' performance by Dow people," he said, adding, "that's not to say our job is even close to being done." Still, things were improving, he assured. Speciality chemicals had a growth rate of 9 percent a year. Asia was looking good, and the recent acquisitions Dow had made—Ascot, a U.K. chemical maker; Rohm & Haas' agricultural products division; and Union Carbide—all looked promising, too. There was some problem with asbestos liability inherited with Union Carbide, he acknowledged, but he assured his listeners there was little to worry about. The liability was being quantified, he explained, bringing some certainty to the matter. And it also appeared that Congress might establish a trust fund to deal with the payout.* Dow's plans going forward were to reduce structural costs and capital expenditures by a combined $800 million. Underutilized and non-competitive assets would also be shut down. At the same time, growth would accelerate through increased production and managed price rises. In addition, "new geographies" and "new products" were looking good for Dow. Among them, the company's *Incite* technology, a new catalyst technology that had spawned 15 new products and $1 billion in sales, and other chemistry, such as polyurethane dispersions, spawning a new line of synthetic leather.

> **"It is not just my family and our yard that is contaminated, but nearly 2,000 families living all along a 22-mile stretch of river."**
>
> Betty Damore

All of the business reporting was textbook and straightforward. No surprises—as one might expect from any *Fortune 500* company. Then came the "open mike" segment, where Dow allowed short questions from the audience.

Stavropoulos personally fielded all the questions, most of which were anticipated, with some of the CEO's replies no doubt practiced in advance and likely run by the lawyers as well. Still, Stavropoulos took questions on Bhopal, genetically-engineered farm seed, toxic chemical dangers, and the possibility of chemical plant accidents. He handled the questions politely and deftly, careful to avoid controversy and legal ensnarement. Dow had previously dealt with the Bhopal issue at other shareholder meetings and was well aware of the current legal situation. However, in that day's edition of the *Wall Street Journal*, a story bearing the headline "Bhopal Haunts Dow Chemical" had appeared.[1] Nevertheless, Stavropoulos, offering perfunctory sympathies for those in India still suffering at the site, stuck to the legal script: the Union Carbide matter is settled and Dow was not involved. "It was a horrific event," he acknowledged, quickly adding that "a separate corporation"—Union Carbide—"accepted moral responsibility. The responsibility ends there," he said. "Dow inherited no responsibility...the responsibility clearly lies with the state and federal governments in India." Indian authorities also held the remainder of the $450 million settlement paid by Union Carbide years earlier, which the Indian Supreme Court reviewed and found reasonable, Stavropoulos noted. The site is also owned by the Indian government. Still, litigation aimed at Dow was pending, and while Stavropoulos may have dealt with the issue at the annual meeting, Dow Chemical may yet be tied to Bhopal and its victims.

Closer to home, Michigan resident Betty Damore rose with a question

---

*More on the asbestos issue in Chapter 20.

about dioxin contamination along the Tittabawassee River—the river along whose banks Dow grew to become a global colossus and whose waters flow through Midland. Beyond Midland, the Tittabawassee flows east to the Saginaw River, Saginaw Bay, and Lake Huron. Damore came from a family that had long roots along the Tittabawassee, stretching back more than 100 years. In late 2001, Damore and other residents along the Tittabawassee received notices from the Michigan Department of Environmental Quality informing them about elevated dioxin levels in floodplain soils that could pose possible health threats. Damore was alarmed and angry about the reports, as her children had spent many hours playing outside and at community parks along the river. Her family also planted a yearly garden raising the typical garden vegetables, consuming that produce every season. "It is not just my family and our yard that is contaminated," she explained, "but nearly 2,000 families living all along a 22-mile stretch of river and floodplain running all the way to Saginaw Bay. All of it is contaminated with dioxin and other toxic pollutants." Dioxin, an infinitesimally tiny contaminant with a very potent profile, making it one of the most toxic substances on earth, has been a suspected problem at Dow for at least 40 years. First surfacing as an unwanted "byproduct" in the making of other chemicals, dioxin appears to be bound up in the business of making chlorinated chemical products and is also a pollutant in their disposal, especially when chlorinated substances or wastes are incinerated.* The science and politics of dioxin have a long, unresolved, and continuing history and will occupy a number of pages in the remainder of this book. Suffice it to say here that dioxin is a matter very much at the center of Dow's business in Michigan and elsewhere, and potentially, a huge liability for Dow and others.

As Damore continued her statement, she noted that most scientists, according to what she had read, found dioxin to be a very potent poison. "It can cause cancer," she said. "It can harm the development of babies. It is toxic to the immune system, the hormone system, and the reproductive system. It has been linked to conditions like endometriosis and diabetes. It is toxic in tiny amounts.... Every exposure increases our risk...," she said. But Damore was not optimistic that Dow would clean up the dioxin in the Tittabawassee floodplain, charging that the company had avoided responsibility for problems in the past and would likely "spend a lot of money" to show that dioxin was safe this time too. "They will fight cleanup every step of the way," she said. "That is what they have done in the past. Just a few months

---

*Actually there is more than one dioxin, so it should be *dioxins* plural. Technically, dioxins are a "chemical family" of 75 polychlorinated dibenzo-p-dioxins and 135 polychlorinated dibenzofurans. One particular dioxin, 2,3,7,8-tetrachlorodibenzo-p-dioxin (also abbreviated as TCDD), has been described as the most toxic synthetic chemical known to science. And dioxins are not commercially produced chemicals, but rather chemical "byproducts"—the unwanted chemical spawn of making, using, and burning chlorinated chemicals. See also Chapter 4.

ago they tried to get a deal with the previous [Michigan governor] that would have made our area a dioxin hot zone permanently." Dow wanted to raise the allowable dioxin levels in Midland residential soils to 831 parts per trillion (ppt) compared to the state clean up standard of 90 ppt. Damore was angry. "Imagine how you would feel if one day you woke up to this nightmare. You learn that you have raised your children with a highly toxic chemical all around and inside you. Imagine how angry and frightened you would be...."

Dow, in fact, has been fashioning chemicals from a particularly active and dangerous region of the periodic table.

Damore closed by saying the problem wouldn't go away, but would just keep getting bigger until Dow took responsibility and addressed it. "Will you do that," she asked. "Will Dow take responsibility?"

"We are a responsible company," Stavropoulos replied. "We will get to the bottom of this. We're doing a river study and a health study, including the areas downstream... We will do the right thing here, when we learn what the right thing is."* But as much as Dow tried to reassure its petitioners about the company's handling of dioxin and persistent toxic chemicals, these concerns were not going to fade away. For the central question facing Dow and the global chemical industry is the "invent-first-ask-questions-later" approach to developing and selling chemicals; an approach that has typically introduced new substances into commerce and society without the benefit of full and thorough toxicological study. Dow, in fact, has been fashioning chemicals from a particularly active and dangerous region of the periodic table—the halogen region, using primarily chlorine, fluorine, bromine, and iodine. Halogens have seven electrons in their outer shells, making them ready partners for many elements. When halogens are combined with carbon to make organohalogens, the results can be, and have been, catastrophic. Commercially-produced organochlorine compounds alone—those combining hydrogen, carbon, and chlorine—number more than 11,000 or so at last count. Dow, for most of its 100-plus years, has been a major organochlorine producer and a key purveyor of bulk chlorine and other halogens for further chemical combination throughout industry. Dow, in other words, is and has been a key chemical enabler and developer, helping to spread synthetic chemistry throughout global commerce.

Today, Dow continues its business at the headwaters of some of the most troubling chemistry on the planet. In fact, in many ways, Herbert Dow is the "founding father" of chlorinated and brominated products. By inventing and perfecting the electrolysis of brine to harvest bromine and chlorine in the 1890s, Dow and his company helped set the stage for the synthetic

* Chapter 19 covers the issue of dioxin in the Tittabawassee River floodplain in more detail.

chemical revolution and a near endless manipulation of molecules to produce new compounds. The resulting explosion of toxic and persistent organochlorine products, for example, is only part of the resulting legacy—one which today's world is only now beginning to deal with.

Pandora's Poison

A vast river of products and processes commences from the making of chlorine—a highly toxic gas released in the breaking apart of sodium chloride. About one-third of all U.S. chlorine is used to make plastics such as polyvinyl chloride, found in shoe soles, shower curtains, automobile components, and vinyl siding. Chlorine also plays a major role in synthesizing thousands of commercial chemicals, such as carbon tetrachloride found in non-stick frying pans, and chlorosilanes used in making semiconductor components, or chlorinated solvents. In fact, today, chlorine is used in about 60 percent of all modern chemical products. To illustrate the wide-ranging influence of chlorine in the chemical industry, Dow and others, including Euro Chlor, an affiliate trade group of the European Chemical Industry Council, have sometimes used chlorine product charts or "chlorine trees" to show the vast array of products and processes that derive from, or begin with, chlorine.[2] The chlorine tree displayed on the opposite page, for example, illustrates the four major industrial uses of chlorine: 1) direct applications as in pulp and paper making, metallurgy, and titanium dioxide production; 2) organochlorine product manufacturing—from plastics and detergents to pharmaceuticals and refrigerants; 3) intermediate chemicals used to make nonchlorinated plastics, pharmaceuticals, and other products; and 4) inorganic chemicals such as iron and aluminum chlorides.[3] Dow Chemical is involved in all four, either as supplier, intermediary, and/or manufacturer.

Yet, the very qualities that have made chlorine such an industrial wunderkind also make it problematic in the environment, in the workplace, and for public health. Chlorine gas, the progenitor medium for making chlorinated products, is highly reactive, making it effective in bleach or for synthesizing other chemicals. But chlorine's reactive quality also makes it capable of creating incidentally—within the manufacturing process or in the environment—hundreds, if not thousands, of organochlorine by-products like dioxin. Chlorination also affects stability, making chemicals useful in producing products like plastics or refrigerants, but also making them stable over time, and therefore persistent and capable of resisting biodegradation—sometimes for decades. Reactive organochlorines are often converted into highly toxic and cancer-causing forms. "The chemical effect of chlorination," explains Joe Thornton, author of *Pandora's Poison*, "is therefore to increase, in one way or another, the hazard that a chemical poses." Chlorine atoms also give their compounds the ability to dissolve in oils, which is why many

A Global Products "Chlorine Tree"

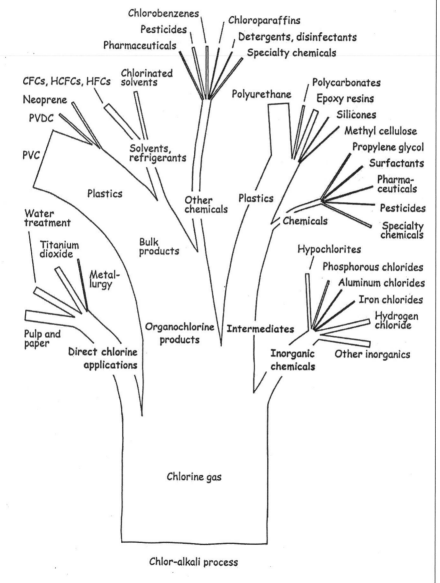

Source: Joe Thornton, *Pandora's Poison*, Cambridge: MIT Press, 2000, Figure 6.4, p. 248.

organochlorines make excellent solvents and grease-cleaning agents. The same feature, however, makes them "fat loving," or gives them an affinity for lodging in animal tissue. Many organochlorines are also "bioaccumulative," which means they can build up or accumulate in the tissues of living things over time.

The suite of characteristics that makes organochlorines persistent, reactive, and oil-soluble, also makes them apt to do damage in human beings.

They can also be magnified in their concentration through food-chain dynamics—whether plankton-to-blue whale, algae-to-fish-to-eagles, or to humans at the top of many plant and animal food chains. Organochlorine levels in such chains may start out in tiny amounts, but over time—through bioaccumulation and biomagnification—wind up to be quite substantial and harmful, at thousands of times their ambient levels in some cases.*

Generally for organochlorines, the suite of characteristics that makes them persistent, reactive, and oil-soluble, also makes them apt to do damage in human beings. And the damage can occur at crucial times—including in the womb—disrupting key natural processes involving basic physiology, developmental processes, and/or hormonal activity. In fact, many pesticides, pharmaceuticals, and antibiotics are *intentionally designed to be biologically disruptive* in some way. So it should not be surprising that in addition to killing or disrupting the unwanted biological target, such chemicals are also doing collateral damage to the rest of the living world. "Virtually all organochlorines examined to date," observes Joe Thornton in *Pandora's Poison*, "cause one or more of a wide variety of adverse effects on essential biological processes, including development, reproduction, brain function, and immunity."[4]

Chemical Roulette

Synthetic chemistry first emerged in the mid-19th century, initially in European laboratories seeking anesthetics and disinfectants. DDT was first synthesized, for example, in 1874, but not developed as a pesticide until the 1930s. Plastics were first synthesized from wood cellulose in the 1890s. Around 1900, however, things really started to get interesting when oil-based

---

*For example, "TCDD [dioxin] accumulates in the tissues of fish to levels 159,000 times greater than in the waters in which fish swims," explains Joe Thornton. That number is known as a "bioconcentration factor." Such factors have also been calculated for other dioxins, furans, PCBs, hexachlorobenzene, and octachlorostyrene—all at 10,000 or more. Chlorinated pesticides have bioconcentration factors in this range as well. Hexachlorobutadiene has a bioaccumulation factor of up to 17,000. See Joe Thornton, *Pandora's Poison*, pp. 35–36.

synthesis of dye production began. By the 1930s, Germany became a leader in the early commercialization of synthetic chemicals. About this time too, companies like Dow and DuPont were also synthesizing new chemicals, manipulating and combining molecules in new ways. With World War II and post-war expansion, the synthetic chemical revolution exploded, resulting in some 50,000 to 100,000 chemicals brought into commercial production. Between 1935 and 1995, according to the Worldwatch Institute, the production of all synthetic organic compounds in the United States rose 1,000-fold. By 1998, biochemists had identified the *18 millionth synthetic chemical substance* known to science.[5]

A new chemical substance is discovered approximately every nine seconds.

Today, a new chemical substance is discovered approximately *every nine seconds*. Granted, many new chemicals don't go much beyond the curiosity stage. Still, new compounds are introduced into global commerce at an average rate of about three per day. That's about 90 per month, or more than 1,000 new chemicals every year. Global chemical production is now about 400 million tons annually.[6] In the United States alone, annual production of carbon-based synthetic chemicals is roughly 1,600 pounds per capita.[7] While much of this inventiveness and productivity are welcomed for generating jobs, economic value, and generally improving things, environmental and public health analysis of these same chemicals has typically come as an afterthought. As a result, detailed toxicological and health-effects knowledge of many chemicals has lagged well behind their commercial use. Even today, only about 700 of the existing registered 100,000 chemicals used in global commerce have complete toxicological profiles. Most have not been studied in-depth for potential ecological problems or

New compounds are introduced into global commerce at about three per day.

reproductive effects. Of the 2,500 "high production volume" chemicals—those used most heavily and regularly in global commerce—roughly half have been profiled from a hazards standpoint. Science and society continue to play a game of "catch up," taking a chemical-by-chemical approach, which is laboriously slow and often prone to lengthy reviews and/or litigation. But the problems are real now, manifest in the environment and human populations.

Most alarming, of course, is the fact that many synthetic chemicals are now routinely found in human blood, body fat, and/or breastmilk—more than 500, as already mentioned, have been found to date. No one knows for sure how many others may have lodged in human biology since tests for detecting many chemicals do not exist. The discovery that chemical substances could invade the human body and do harm is not new. In 1775 or so, British surgeon Percival Pott concluded that London's chimney sweeps were having a high incidence of cancer of the scrotum because they were accumulating chimney soot in their genitals.[8] Problems with worker deaths and illness in the manufacture of tetraethyl lead in the 1920s and 1930s— made as an additive for gasoline—raised the level of awareness that such substances could kill and invade the blood of the general population, with lead emissions and residues proving especially harmful to children. Still, leaded gasoline wasn't banned in the United States until 1972, and is currently used in some regions of the world. Synthetic pesticides began to be identified as potential problems in the 1950s by a few medical researchers using anecdotal evidence. The American Medical Association raised its voice in 1951 about the growing concentration of pesticides in human body fat.[9] But it wasn't until 1962, when Rachel Carson, focusing on pesticides, brought the synthetic chemical issue home to a broader public with her book, *Silent Spring*. Still eloquent more than 40 years later, Carson's book foresaw the chemical "body burden" problem:

> ...The chemicals to which life is asked to make its adjustment are no longer merely the calcium and silica and copper and all of the rest of the minerals washed out of the rocks...; they are the synthetic creations of man's inventive mind, brewed in laboratories, and having no counterpart in nature.
>
> To adjust to these chemicals would require time on the scale that is nature's; it would require not merely the years of a man's life, but the life of generations. And even this, were it by some miracle possible, would be futile, for the new chemicals come from our laboratories in an endless stream; almost five hundred annually find their way into actual use in the United States alone [*Note: today it's more like 1,000 annually*]. The figure is staggering and its implications are not easily grasped—500 new chemicals to which the bodies of men and animals are required somehow to adapt each year, chemicals totally outside the limits of biologic experience.[10]

In the 1960s, Carson chose the chlorinated hydrocarbon insecticides such as DDT, chlordane, aldrin, and endrin to make her case. DDT, for example, had been shown by tests from 1947 through Carson's time and beyond to be carcinogenic to animals. Yet it continued to be used, despite its persistence in the environment, long retention in fatty body tissue, and its ability to kill wildlife. It was banned in 1974 after three years of litigation. Today, DDT still shows up in human blood samples.

Throughout the 1970s, lab animal testing and wildlife studies produced revelations about a range of other chemicals. Polychlorinated biphenyls (PCBs)—a family of synthetic chemicals used in electrical transformer coolants, in hydraulic fluids, lubricants, plasticizers, coatings, sealants, and pesticide extenders—were found in the mid-1970s to be entering the human food chain through fish, cheese, eggs, and animal feed. Persistent, bioaccumulative, and "fat-loving"—i.e., stored in fatty tissues and fluids such as breast milk—PCBs were linked to a number of cancers, birth defects, and brain damage. They were banned in 1976, but are still found today in blood samples of the general population. In 1975 and 1977, the National Cancer Institute (NCI) published evidence that ethylene dibromide (EDB)—a chemical Dow sold for years as a gasoline additive and later as a soil fumigant—induced cancer in lab animals. It was later banned by the EPA. In the 1970s, NCI also found cancer problems with a widely used hair dye compound, 4 methoxy-mphenylenediamen, as well as a bromine/phosphate-based chemical called Tris, used as a flame retardant in textiles, fabrics, clothing, furniture and toys, and infant sleepwear.[11] And so it went, chemical by chemical, battle by battle, decade by decade.

One 1997 survey of supermarket foods found PCBs, DDT, and dioxins present in foods from chicken and pork to butter and ice cream.

By the mid-1980s, chlorofluorocarbons, or CFCs—a family of chemicals initially discovered for use as refrigerants, and subsequently manipulated for an array of others uses, were shown by dramatic satellite photography to be degrading the earth's protective ozone layer. CFCs were later banned. Yet prohibiting harmful chemicals didn't always mean they were removed from circulation. One 1997 survey of supermarket foods, for example, found PCBs, DDT, and dioxins present in foods from chicken and pork to butter and ice cream.[12] Meanwhile, one 1992 study reported that sperm counts in Europe and the United States had declined by about half since World War II. Another found that rates of testicular cancer had soared in the United States between 1973 and 1994. Chemical additives used in the making of plastics, such as phthalates and bisphenol-A, were gaining scientific notice, too: female rats whose mothers were exposed to phthalates gave birth to male pups with single testes or sacs of blood in place of testicles; and pregnant mice given tiny does of bisphenol-A gave birth to male offspring with abnormally large prostates.

Hormonal Havoc

By the mid-1990s, more was being learned about the persistent and invasive nature of chemicals. The *timing* of chemical exposure in human and all biological development began to get more attention, and some new insights and theories were advanced. Only in the last 10 years or so, have scientists discovered that some man-made chemicals are playing havoc with human and animal endocrine systems, disrupting critical hormone messengers, and altering developmental biology in the womb. Researchers have identified more than 120 chemicals currently found in the environment that are reported to have reproductive and/or endocrine-disrupting effects.[13] Hormone disruptors, as they are also called, include some large chemical families such as the 209 compounds classified at PCBs, 75 dioxins, and 135 furans.[14] Some of these substances can cross the placenta, reaching the unborn, and can be passed along to infants in breastfeeding. Others cause mutations, affect intelligence, or lodge in the ·DNA. Several studies in Europe and North America have linked reduced intelligence and/or behavioral effects with a child's exposure in the womb to PCBs and co-contaminants. With regard to dioxin and dioxin-like PCBs, the World Health Organization noted in 1998 that subtle effects may already be occurring in the general population of developed countries at current background levels.[15]

More than 120 chemicals currently found in the environment are reported to have reproductive and/or endocrine-disrupting effects.

Immunity Down

New scientific findings in the 1990s were also revealing that contaminated water, food, and air in some locations appeared to be suppressing human immune systems, lowering an individual's resistance to viruses, bacteria, and tumors they would normally fend off. One disturbing report came from the Inuit people of Arctic Canada, far removed from industrial society, but in a location where pollution is circulated and deposited by global air and ocean currents. The contaminants had migrated into the Arctic food chain, resulting in dangerously high levels, particularly in marine mammals and other creatures the Inuit used for food. As a result, Inuit women's breast milk built up contaminants like PCBs to very high levels—measured at 1,052 ppb in one Quebec Public Health report, nearly twice that of the seal blubber they ate (527 ppb) and ten times that of arctic fish (152 ppb)—a classic food chain-biomagnification effect. Pregnant and nursing Inuit women passed these high doses of magnified poisons directly and unknowingly on to their children, born with depleted white blood cells and doomed to life of suppressed immunity. Some Inuit children have suffered excessive bouts of disease, including a 20-fold increase in life-threatening meningitis compared to other Canadian children. The findings in the Inuit community provide a powerful message to the rest of the world.

"We're probably all—and I mean the whole...planet—immunosuppressed," says Steve Holladay, an immunotoxicologist at Virginia-Maryland Regional College of Veterinary Medicine in a 1996 interview. "Simply, it means we're not quite as healthy as we could or would be. Our risk of developing (diseases) is slightly higher."[16] British scientist, Dr. John McLaren-Howard of Biolab agrees, noting "we are all blitzed with a load of toxic chemicals," the effects of which we don't fully understand." He also believes toxic chemicals hamper the immune system making individuals more susceptible to colds and other bugs. "The toxic chemicals in our system put a burden on us because our body has to work hard to get rid of them," he says. "So fighting off a cold will be much harder, because it's yet another thing for the body to have to cope with."[17]

"We're probably all—and I mean the whole planet—immunosuppressed."

Dr. Steve Holladay

In addition to suppressing immunity, toxic chemicals are also implicated in stimulating the immune system in the wrong way; in effect, triggering human immune cells to attack the body's healthy tissue as if it were a foreign agent, giving rise to various auto-immune disorders. Among chemcials that have been linked to various auto-immune conditions, for example, are carbon tetrachloride, mercury, perchloroethylene, PCBs, silica, trichloroethylene, and vinyl chloride. In fact, in recent years, lupus and other auto-immune diseases have increased internationally and appear to be popping up in clusters within communities tainted with toxic chemicals.

Cleaned Up?

Today, the general perception, in the United States and Europe at least, is that pollution is being cleaned up and that exposure to toxic chemicals is lower than it used to be. But other data suggest the clean-up might be somewhat superficial, or at least not reaching the larger universe of what's out there. For example, the U.S. Geological Survey released a study in March 2002 of 139 U.S. waterways that

The U.S. Geological Survey recently found trace amounts of chemical and pharmaceutical products in 139 U.S. waterways.

found trace amounts of many chemical and pharmaceutical products in those streams. Among the findings, 74 percent of the streams had residues of the insect repellent DEET; 69 percent had degraded detergent residues, 66 percent had disinfectants, 60 percent had residues of fire retardant chemicals; 45 percent had insecticide residues, and 24 percent had residues of the solvent tetrachloroethylene. Prescription drug residues and steroidal compounds were found in more than 80 percent of the streams.[18] Although there has been apparent progress over the last decade in reducing reported chemical pollution and wastes under various environmental laws, these laws fall short in covering the vast universe of chemicals now used in daily commerce. Thousands of chemicals are still not reported or regularly tracked in the environment. And the chemicals that are tracked haven't gone away. In October 2003, for example, the Virginia Department of Health issued fish consumption advisories after mercury and PCBs had been found in several of the state's rivers and swamps.[19] Given the large number of regulated and unregulated chemical substances still found in the environment—in soil, air, water, waste emissions, not to mention those leaching out of products themselves—it's no wonder they are routinely found in the human body.

Body Burden

Although various government health agencies have collected human chemical exposure data in the past, such efforts have typically been sporadic, not well funded, and focused on one or two substances at a time. In addition, such information has not been routinely presented to the public. But that changed in March 2001, when the U.S. Centers for Disease Control

In Bill Moyers' Blood

Dioxins & Furans	Bill Moyers	U.S. Average
	(in picograms per gram, pg/g, or parts per trillion)	
2,3,7,8-TCDD (tetra dioxin)*	5.38*	5.38
1,2,3,7,8-PeCDD (pentadioxin)	11.60	10.70
1,2,3,4,7,8-HxCDD (hexadioxin)	9.26	75.10
1,2,3,7,8,9-HxCDD (hexadioxin)	7.32	11.70
1,2,3,6,7,8-HxCDD (hexadioxin)	58.30	—
1,2,3,4,6,7,8-HpCDD (heptadioxin)	125.00	110.00
1,2,3,4,6,7,8,9-OCDD (octadioxin)	1,104.00	724.00
2,3,4,7,8-PeCDF (pentafuran)	9.76	9.70
1,2,3,4,7,8-HxCDF (hexafuran)	7.43	7.42
1,2,3,6,7,8-HxCDF (hexafuran)	7.54	5.78
2,3,4,6,7,8-HxCDF (hexafuran)	3.76	0.54
1,2,3,4,6,7,8-HpCDF (heptafuran)	18.90	15.30
1,2,3,4,7,8,9-HpCDF (heptafuran)	1.84	0.73
1,2,3,4,6,7,8,9-OCDF (octafuran)	30.50	2.28

Source: PBS, Trade Secrets—"Bill Moyers' Test Results"

*The sample volume was insufficient for analysis of TCDD levels. The value given is the average that EPA has found in U.S. citizens. TCDD is not included in the total of 84 chemicals counted in Mr. Moyers' results.

and Prevention (CDC) in Atlanta committed to more regular reporting of chemicals found in the human body. At that time, CDC reported that most Americans carried detectable levels of plastics, pesticides, and heavy metals in their blood and urine. Health officials cautioned, however, that just because people had chemicals in their blood or urine did not necessarily mean those levels would cause disease. Still, some scientists believe that any level of industrial chemicals in the body is unacceptable. "For human beings to carry the burden of industrial chemicals is commonplace, but it's not normal," said Michael McCally, vice chairman of the Department of Community and Preventative Medicine at Mount Sinai School of Medicine, "...and we shouldn't accept it as normal. It represents a mass experiment by the chemical industry on us."[20]

> **"It represents a mass experiment by the chemical industry on us."**
>
> Michael McCall, Mount Sinai School of Medicine

In addition to the CDC, some prominent journalists and citizens, with the help of recognized public health agencies, also began preparing and reporting on the "body burden" issue. Nationally-known journalist Bill Moyers—a former speech writer for President Lyndon Johnson—had his body burden measured for a March 2001 PBS television special he hosted on the chemical industry. Those tests revealed that Moyers had 84 chemicals in his blood and urine—many of them carcinogens and worse.[21] (See sidebar, opposite.)

In March 2003, CDC released the second *National Report on Human Exposure to Environmental Chemicals*, the largest and most extensive assessment of the U.S. population's exposure to environmental chemicals. The report presented human exposure information for 116 environmental contaminants—ranging from lead and tobacco smoke, to pesticides and heavy metals.[22] As the CDC released its report, another "body burden" blood and urine study was made public, this one led by Mount Sinai School of Medicine in New York, and completed in collaboration with the Environmental Working Group in Washington, D.C. and Commonweal, a California-based public health organization. Using a small group of nine environmental health professionals as volunteers, this study found an average of 91 industrial compounds, pollutants, and other chemicals in the volunteer's blood and urine. None of the volunteers worked with chemicals in their job or lived near an industrial facility. In total, some 167 chemicals were found in the volunteers. Of these, 76 were known

> **"This was completely outside my control. Dow put this chemical into me without any assistance on my part."**
>
> Charlotte Brody on her blood test

to cause cancer in humans or animals, 94 were toxic to the brain and nervous system, and 79 caused birth defects or abnormal development.[23] Some of the chemicals were specifically traced to the Dow Chemical Company.

Charlotte Brody, executive director of the Boston-based nonprofit group, Health Care Without Harm, was one of the public health professionals participating in the Mount Sinai-led survey. In Brody's blood and urine, the Mount Sinai researchers found 85 chemical contaminants, including more than two dozen types of PCBs, seven dioxins and the Dow Chemical insecticide *Dursban*. *Dursban*, whose active chemical agent is chlorpyrifos, is known to cause neurological damage at high doses in animals and humans, and the federal Environmental Protection Agency has banned its indoor use.* Brody, a nurse, activist and gardener, has taken great pains to avoid commercial pesticides in her gardening and tries to eat organic produce. Which is why she was quite surprised to find *Dursban* in her blood. "It was the biggest insult of all," she said, after learning the results. "This was completely outside my control. Dow put this chemical into me without any assistance on my part."[24]

Chemical Trespass

So these are the chemicals—the *Dursbans,* the POPs, the PBTs, the endocrine disruptors, the carcinogens, and mutagens. They are the chemicals that the dissident Dow shareholders in Midland, Michigan were talking about on May 8, 2003. They are also the chemicals that Dow workers, Dow neighbors, and Dow activists have questioned and continue to question.

On one level, the questions are not new. Yet the way they are being framed *is* new. For the basis of the charge today is *chemical trespass*: that "body burden" chemicals are an invasion of personal property; a transgression on inherent rights to health. Such invasive chemicals are causing biological and/or genetic damage to persons and life processes. Dow, a global corporation with more than 200 plants operating in 38 countries, has a specific chemical burden in many living things, say its critics; burdens that result in real costs and damages. For these, Dow is a responsible party, and may soon face a new kind of legal and social liability that will profoundly affect its bottom line.

In the meantime, "the writing is on the wall," say Dow's critics. A global consensus is emerging on toxic chemistry. The U.S. and Canadian governments have signed the Great Lakes Water Quality Agreement, establishing a goal to "virtually eliminate" the discharge of persistent toxic substances into Great Lakes. And more than 150 nations have signed the

---

* For more on *Dursban* see Chapter 5.

Stockholm Convention on Persistent Organic Pollutants (POPs), an international agreement ratified in February 2004 that commits ratifying nations to eliminate certain "bad actor" POPs and their byproduct chemicals. A dozen of the dirtiest chemicals are now listed, with more to follow. Dow should heed these messages.

The charge today is *chemical trespass*: that "body burden" chemicals are an invasion of personal property; a transgression on inherent rights to health.

The goal for Dow—for the good of its business, its shareholders, and society—should be to move away from the chemistry that makes POPs, PBTs, endocrine disruptors, and other such substances. Yet the resistance to that course within the company has been striking, demonstrated repeatedly in the chemical-by-chemical fighting of the last three decades—a resistance rooted in Dow's founding chemical trove and its corporate culture. That part of the story is next.

2.
House of Wonders

In this century Dow has grown to be a $20 billion-a-year firm, with operations pole to pole and an impact, in one way or another, on most of humanity.

E. N. Brandt, *Growth Company*

Herbert Dow arrived in Midland, Michigan just as the state's big timber boom was winding down. It was August 1890. A frenetic four decades of taking down Michigan's rich stands of big White Pine had preceded Dow's arrival. The gold rush to timber began in the late 1840s, and Central Michigan's Saginaw Valley was part of the frenzy. Huge flotillas of logs streamed down the Tittabawassee River past Midland to the mills in Saginaw Bay, and from there, out over the Great Lakes to Eastern and Midwestern markets. Enormous fortunes had been made. Now in 1890, as Herbert Dow rode the train to Midland, he was running against the tide. The fortune seekers were heading in the opposite direction—they were leaving Midland. All that remained around Midland, and what young Dow saw as he stepped off the train, were stumps. But Dow hadn't come for the timber in any case. What he wanted was under the ground; the remains of an ancient inland ocean, baked by eons of sun, leaving huge deposits of brine, nicely preserved by the preceding Ice Age.

Herbert Dow had heard about the brines in Michigan. For years, men had been pumping salt water in the Saginaw Valley and evaporating it for salt. In fact, Michigan in the late 1800s was the leading salt-producing state in the nation. But neither Dow nor anyone else fully realized just how big the underground cache of mineral- and chemical-bearing brines were. But young Dow, picking Midland, had an incredibly good stroke of fortune—locating over the geologic center of a nearly inexhaustible source of underground brine. "The sea of brine was his raw material waiting to be processed," writes Don Whitehead in *The Dow Story*, of Herbert Dow's coming to Midland in the 1890s. "It cost him nothing except the expense of pumping it. The earth was his storage tank to be drawn on any time he chose. The Michigan brine was rich in bromides, and in calcium, magnesium, and sodium chloride. And with his revolutionary process (using electricity to separate the bromine and chlorine from the brine...) his early manufacturing costs were lower than his competitors..."[1]

Young Dow was fully an Horatio Alger-type character, charging into projects with complete confidence and endless energy. Initially, he failed with a start-up business in Canton, Ohio before coming to Midland. Eventually, with the help of backers in Cleveland, Herbert Dow established the Dow Chemical Company in 1897. He soon saw chlorine as the bigger prize, with bleach as the first big possibility—the demand for which was then substantial from the textile, cotton, and paper industries. The invention of the rotary press helped power the demand for printing and paper—and for bleach in the paper industry. "About $2,000,000 worth of chloride of lime or bleaching powder is consumed here each year in the U.S.," he told a group of investors in Cleveland, "but none is now made here on a commercial scale.... We propose to manufacture it by a new electrical process...."[2]* Within months of that claim, Dow was producing chlorine from brine at Midland. But Dow would later leave the bleach business, believing that chlorine had more valuable uses. Soon, other new chemicals such as phenol and chloroform began flowing from Dow's new business, building upon the original brine chemicals, but combining them with others to form a much broader chemistry.

> **It soon became clear to Dow that chlorine was the bigger prize.**

Salt, Savvy & Synthesis

In many ways, salt is the cornerstone ingredient of the Dow Chemical empire—salt and Herbert Dow's electrochemical savvy in separating and exploiting salt's primary components: chlorine and sodium. Dow unlocked salt's chemical potential. "Dow's first generation products were bromine-based," explains author William Boddie in a company publication titled, *Salt, The Mysterious Necessity*. "His second generation products were chlorine-based. His third generation products were based on magnesium chloride and calcium chloride salts that were also components of the Midland brine." Further along, Dow also worked with iodine salts in brine and mined the ocean for bromine and magnesium. As Dow's empire grew, each expansion involved an affiliation with a brine deposit of some kind—or a way to get at

---

*Traditionally the brines were worked in a multiple-step process to get at the bromine. Dow changed that by running an electric current through the brine that released the bromine, then blowing air through the bromine to vaporize it into a direct-collection system. He later devised a similar system for chlorine.

the elements of salt.* But from the beginning, the Dow empire was built in a step-wise, building-block fashion—linking one chemical to the next.

From the basic compounds made from the brine in Dow's early years—mostly salts such as sodium chloride, calcium chloride, magnesium chloride—it was possible, in further reactions and combinations with other chemicals, to fashion new synthetic compounds. By the early 1900s, for example, Dow was making chloroform in a process that used, among other ingredients, sulfur chloride as a raw material. Chloroform, sold chiefly for medicinal purposes, became the first Dow product other than bleach to use chlorine. Carbon tetrachloride was also produced in the same process, but at an earlier stage in the reaction, and by 1908, had become more valuable to Dow than the chloroform, sold largely for use in fire extinguishers. Carbon tetrachloride, in turn, was also used as a starting material for making other chemicals. But Herbert Dow—always on the lookout for new ways to use bromine and chlorine—also had his eye on the constituents of petroleum for making new compounds as early as 1911. By 1913, his company was "cracking," or heating, gasoline in the lab to yield a gas that had "quite a percentage of butadiene," later to become important in plastics. Dow's scientists were also successful around the same time in making ethylene dibromide by cracking pentane. Explain Dow biographers Murray Campbell and Harrison Hatton: "[Herbert Dow] was looking for a cheap and plentiful source of such unsaturated hydrocarbons as butadiene and ethylene, which he knew could be treated with chemicals like chlorine to make almost an infinitude of new compounds."[3] Dow would later become a leader in making chlorinated petrochemicals. And when Dow scientists around 1915 moved to improve the making of phenol in a process using caustic soda, chlorobenzol, and hydrochloric acid, the process also yielded four useful by-product chemicals that helped reduce the cost of making phenol and more. Two of the by-product chemicals—orthophenylphenol and paraphenylphenol—were never-before-seen chemicals, and became the base of a line of Dow pesticides. Paraphenylphenol also was used to make a varnish for boat hulls. Another phenol by-product was diphenyloxide, later converted to a material for manufacturing that could hold high temperature at low pressures with great stability, a product that became known as *Dowtherm*.[4] And on it went,

---

*Dow's expansion to Pittsburg, California in 1938 used salt produced by solar evaporation from the waters of San Francisco Bay. In Freeport, Texas in 1940, an underground salt dome was tapped for magnesium and bromine, as was the Gulf of Mexico. In Sarnia, Ontario during the early 1940s, salt was involved. In Plaquemine, Louisiana, in the 1950s, again salt and ethylene became key. In the 1960s, salt deposits were important in Europe—in the formation of Dow Unquinesa in Spain (1960); Terneuzen in the Netherlands (1964); and Stade, Germany (1972). Fifty years later, in 2002, Dow was still acquiring brine deposits, opening a field in Western Canada. See Mark Batterson and William W. Boddie (eds.), *Salt, The Mysterious Necessity*, Dow Chemical Company, 1972, pp. 110–12.

from chemical to chemical, product to product, a pattern that would stoke Dow inventiveness and chemical serendipity for the next century.

Autos & Gasoline

Herbert Dow had always thought there might be a way to link the fortunes of his business with those of the nascent automobile industry. His first idea was to use magnesium in automobiles—the magnesium he had begun extracting from brines. In 1919, using the DowMetal brand name adopted for its magnesium, the company began making DowMetal pistons for automobile engines. By 1921, a national advertising campaign began on behalf of DowMetal, and on Memorial Day that year, race car driver Tommy Milton won the Indianapolis 500 in a car using DowMetal pistons. Despite the notoriety, DowMetal pistons never caught on. But Dow's fortunes in the auto business were about to change.

The gasoline of that day was poorly refined and of low octane, causing engines to knock and run rough. The fuel, rather than exploding in the engine's cylinders smoothly and rhythmically, burned erratically or fired too fast, causing a jerky, uneven acceleration, and loud engine knocking noise. The poor performance was also hard on the engine. General Motors (GM), had been on the hunt for an additive to address the engine knock problem since about 1916, and GM's Thomas Midgley discovered in 1920 that tetraethyl lead did the trick. But the leaded gasoline left behind a metallic deposit that fouled the cylinders and spark plugs, resulting in a clogging action that was worse than the knocking problem. GM then sought a cure for the deposit problem. Herbert Dow, learning of GM's search, sent some samples of chlorinated compounds to GM's laboratories in Dayton, Ohio. Among the samples was ethylene dibromide (EDB), a derivative of bromine. At GM, Midgley had in fact already found that EDB had worked—using a mixture of two parts EDB to every three parts of tetraethyl lead. Dow had been producing EDB for some time, but had no real market. Now it did, as GM was satisfied that Dow and its favorably-located Michigan brine deposits could fill the bill. This was a huge development for Dow, and indeed, a project so big in its potential demand that Herbert Dow worried it would throw his company's production out of kilter and present a huge waste brine disposal problem. Nevertheless, Dow began supplying GM with bromide at a pilot level of about 100,000 pounds a month. Soon GM returned, and asked Dow to supply 600,000 pounds a month, sending the material to the tetraethyl lead company, then named Ethyl Gasoline Company. But two months after the deal was made with GM and Ethyl, tetraethyl lead came under suspicion as a dangerous substance. Workers handling and breathing the tetraethyl lead at the Standard Oil Company (today, Exxon) in Elizabeth, New Jersey, and later at a DuPont plant in Deepwater, New Jersey, had died. Questions surfaced over the safety of the new lead anti-knock additive, to be used widely by the motoring public and in cities. New York banned the sale of leaded gasoline, and some other cities followed. State and federal investigations were begun into the worker deaths, and production was halted for more than a year. But in what many believe was a short-sighted ruling, even at that time, government reports found that leaded gasoline itself was not harmful and that faulty laboratory and safety procedures had caused the worker deaths, not the lead.[5] With this government blessing, leaded gasoline—and Dow's production of ethylene dibromide—

By the late 1930s, Dow was supplying 30 million pounds of ethylene dibromide for leaded gasoline from one plant alone.

boomed. Back in Midland, Herbert Dow's son, Willard was put in charge of building out the new bromine production capacity—the new wells and pipelines that would now be required to supply the bromine for ethylene dibromide production. "...We pushed out twenty to thirty miles from the plant with our wells and pipes...," Dow's Dutch Buetel would later recall.[6] For years thereafter, Dow's ethylene dibromide would be mixed with the tetraethyl lead in millions of gallons of gasoline, year after year.

By 1928, Dow built its first plant outside of Midland to exploit brines, this one in Louisiana to produce iodine from waste brines, forming another Dow company in the process—the Jones Chemical Company. But the demand for Dow's brine-derived products was growing, especially for EDB in leaded gasoline, exceeding Midland's capacity. In June 1930, Dow had sent one of his men to scout the East Coast for a location where a plant could be built to extract bromine from seawater. By 1933, Dow and the Ethyl Gasoline Company had built a plant at Kure Beach on North Carolina's Cape Fear peninsula to extract bromine. At the time, Dow anticipated that its yearly production of 6 million pounds of EDB would meet the need for several years to come. But two years later, the plant capacity had to be nearly doubled to 10 million pounds, and then doubled again by 1937, reaching 20 million pounds. A year later it was expanded again, adding another 10-million-pound production unit. Dow by this time was supplying 30 million pounds of ethylene dibromide for leaded gasoline from this one plant alone.[7] Years later, after Dow had begun extracting minerals and chemicals from seawater in Texas, the company exited the Michigan-based brine business, leaving a network of more than 100 brine wells and miles of pipeline strewn through Midland, Bay, and Saginaw counties. These wells proved to have ongoing environmental problems during their operation and for years after Dow officially left the brine extraction business.*

*See Chapter 19 for more detail on Dow's brine pollution problems.

Dow's business in the 1930s, however, went well beyond the brines and the auto industry. Dow's Midland operation by 1930 was producing over 800 rail-car loads a month of some 150 chemical products.[8] Dow was also beginning its early moves into wood cellulose-based plastics, and in 1935 formed the Cliffs Dow Chemical Co. at Marquette, Michigan to manufacture wood chemicals. By June 1936, Dow Chemical was listed on the New York Stock Exchange. In 1938, in what would later prove to be a key acquisition for its research and production capabilities, Dow acquired the Great Western Electrochemical Co. at Pittsburg, California. By the end of the 1930s, Dow was America's fastest growing chemical company, then ranked as the fifth largest, behind DuPont, Allied, Union Carbide, and American Cyanamid.[9] But soon, with World War II on the horizon, Dow was about to change and grow in some fundamental new ways.

World War II

Dow played a key role during World War II producing strategic materials for the Allies—magnesium, a key ingredient for bombers and fighter planes; silicone, produced and supplied through Dow's new joint venture, Dow Corning; and styrene for synthetic rubber. As early as 1909, Dow chemists had been searching for a synthetic rubber but had not found a viable substance. In 1941, Dow teamed up with Goodyear and proposed to the government the two companies build a synthetic rubber plant, but the government turned them down. After Pearl Harbor, and the Japanese takeover of Southeast Asia's rubber plantations, the government changed its tune and launched a crash program to make synthetic rubber. Dow, as the only company producing styrene on a commercial basis, was soon enlisted to help lead the effort, building styrene plants for the government at Velasco, Texas and Los Angeles, California. Dow scientists had also been exploring silicone, and in 1940, teamed up with a group of scientists from the Corning Glass Works in New York, also then working on silicone. By 1942–43, the Dow-Corning company was formed, a 50–50 venture that was soon supplying silicone sealants for the ignition systems of Allied aircraft.* *Dow Corning 4*, an engine grease, enabled B-17s to fly at 35,000 feet, which gave the Allies an important advantage in the air war. Stateside, in Texas, the Dow Company had set its sights on expansion, and had purchased land near Freeport, Texas where it began to build. By January 1941, Dow began its magnesium-from-seawater venture at Freeport, and had already been producing the light metal for years in Michigan. With WWII, however, and the need for lighter and faster warplanes, Dow was perfectly positioned as one of the few magnesium producers in the world. Supplying both British and American forces

*See Chapter 12 for more on silicone and Dow Corning.

with magnesium for aircraft—rising from 80 pounds to about 2,000 pounds per American plane for example—Dow became the global leader in magnesium production during the war, and continued to supply about 75 percent of the world's magnesium for many years thereafter.[10] Dow's other ventures also prospered after the war. In 1945, *Dow Corning 35,* an emulsifier used in tire molds, and Pan Glaze, which made baking pans stick-proof and easier to clean, were instant successes on the home front. Within a decade, in fact, Dow Corning alone had developed more than 600 products.[11] But Dow's talents and capabilities after the war were tapped for other purposes, too.

> **Within a decade, in fact, Dow Corning alone had developed more than 600 products.**

In 1949, after the Soviet Union had exploded its first atomic bomb, the U.S. Congress authorized a major expansion of American nuclear weapons capability, and Dow Chemical was asked by the government to help build and manage a top secret nuclear weapons research and production project. By 1951 Dow was running a new $45 million plant at Rocky Flats, Colorado that would make plutonium triggers for America's nuclear bombs. Dow scientists worked in uranium chemistry, and its workers dealt with one of the deadliest substances on earth, plutonium.[12] Dow would operate the Rocky Flats complex under contract with the Atomic Energy Commission (AEC) for more than a decade, through the 1960s, a tenure marked by a series of incidents and some controversy (see Chapter 9). Dow would also become involved in a controversial nuclear power generating project with Detroit Edison and several other companies—a project that ultimately died. But the Dow of nuclear weapons and nuclear power was not the Dow most Americans would come to know. Rather, Dow became one of America's heartland companies, plugging away at commodity chemicals, and fashioning the ingredients of the American good life to come.

"House of Wonders"

In July 1950, the *Detroit Free Press* described the Dow Chemical Company in a most flattering way as inventive and essential to America's every product. "The fabulous Dow Chemical Company opened its doors to the working press for the first time and revealed itself as a hitherto hidden house of wonders," gushed the paper. "The clothes you are wearing, the ice cream you had for lunch, your wife's permanent wave [hair style], the pharmaceuticals in your medicine chest, your children's toys and your automobile all most likely have ingredients in them which came from Dow."[13] By 1958, Dow was the fourth largest chemical manufacturer in the United States, turning out "several hundred products," predominantly chemicals and plastics. By then, about one-third of its total sales derived from plastics, including *Styron*, Dow's polystyrene brand, *Ethocel*, Dow's brand of ethylcellulose, saran, used in a number of applications, including *Saran Wrap*, polyvinyl chloride, polyethylene, *Styrofoam*, and various latexes used in paper coating and the production of latex paints. Dow was also the world's largest producer of magnesium, and still a leading producer of chlorine and bromine, consuming most of its own production of those chemicals internally to make other compounds. In addition to its extensive home-base operations at Midland, Dow had operations, subsidiaries, and associated companies throughout the United States and abroad. A refining operation in Bay City, Michigan handled products of petroleum refining. The Dobeckmun Company Division in Cleveland, Ohio and Berkeley, California worked in transparent packaging, gift wraps, metallic yarns and products from plastic films. The James River Division in Williamsburg, Virginia handled Dow's synthetic staple fiber *Zefran* for textiles. Its Western Division in California produced iodine at Seal Beach, plastics at Torrance, and chemicals at Pittsburg, Venice, and Inglewood. Dow's Hanging Rock Plant in Ironton, Ohio produced plastics, and its Dowell Division in Houston, Texas serviced oil wells and other industrial equipment. Other Dow subsidiaries included the Adams Paper Company in Wells River, Vermont, Ben-Mont Papers in Bennington, Vermont, and Cliffs Dow Chemical Company in Marquette, Michigan.

By 1958, one-third of Dow's sales were from plastics.

Dow Abroad

In 1950, Dow Chemical was pretty much a home-grown American company with a somewhat parochial focus. Only about 5 percent of its sales were in the export market, roughly about $10 million. Canada was then the extent of Dow's foreign expansion. But Dow's managers and planners soon saw the light of international opportunity, especially in 1951 when U.S. tax concessions were offered to American companies establishing foreign trade subsidiaries. Dow Chemical International and Dow Chemical Inter-American were formed that year, and by 1952, Dow's first overseas subsidiary was established in Japan in a partnership with Asahi Chemical Co.—a venture named Asahi-Dow Ltd., which would produce the plastic, saran.[14]

In the United Kingdom, Dow built a small polystyrene plastics plant at Barry, South Wales in 1954, and an agrichemical plant at King's Lynn in Norfolk, England in 1958. About 40 percent of the production from both of these plants would come to be exported, including much of the grass herbicide *Dowpon*, produced at Kings Lynn, and sold in quantity to Malaysian rubber plantations to kill tropical grasses that menaced slow-growing rubber

Saran Wrap

In the 1930s, Ralph Wiley, a research chemist, was working away at his post in the Dow Chemical research labs in Midland. He was focused on a process to make a chemical called perchloroethylene. This chemical, like many others, was made from chlorine. But in the making, Wiley kept confronting another chemical, a problematic byproduct. It was a bothersome substance that was sticking to the bottom of his flasks and beakers. And it was tough, too. If he left his beakers exposed to the substance overnight, he would have to use steel wool on them the next morning to remove the scum. Wiley's boss, however, got to thinking about the troubling substance, and encouraged Wiley to keep at it, which he did for another 10 years or so. Along the way, they tried using the substance to make battery casings and special-use tubing for chemical reactions, but nothing of consequence came to pass. By then, upper management thought this avenue was a waste of time, with little payback, even though Wiley by then had acquired 20 to 30 patents on the material. Wiley, in fact, threatened to quit if Dow canned the project. The head of the patent department supported Wiley's work, thinking there would be a payback. Just before World War II, the material was made into a film-like substance. Dow then began selling the film—then oily, green-colored, and of thicker composition—to the armed forces for wrapping military equipment being shipped overseas. The film protected the machinery from salty sea spay and moisture. Still, with the war's end, nothing much became of the material. Dow did develop a transparent version, and began selling it to industrial firms as a protective wrap in big 40-inch rolls. In 1947, two Dow employees bought the product from Dow and began packaging it in smaller rolls. They called it "Clingwrap" and began selling it locally in Midland as a food wrap, for which it was ideally suited since it blocked most air molecules. "It sold like hotcakes because women liked to put it over bowls," recounted inventor Ralph Wiley some years later. By 1948, Dow had bought back the new plastic wrap from the fledgling employee venture in Midland, and began selling *Saran Wrap* nationally in 1953. "Dow at that time was sort of resistant to the retail market," explained Wiley. "They liked to sell things by the ton and let other people worry about the retail market." But now, Dow was stepping into the retail business, and that meant a major change in the way it did business. Dow began its venture with *Saran Wrap* in October 1953, just as the Korean War was ending. New people were brought in to help move the product. One of those was William R. Dixon, Dow marketing manager who set his sights on TV as the vehicle for Dow's new products and the launch of *Saran Wrap*. "You had to show the housewife how to use the stuff," he said, "and TV was ideally suited to that purpose." Dow began its product launch for *Saran Wrap* with Dave Garroway, the host of the original *Today* morning TV show. In those days, TV ads were often done live on the shows, and at one point, Garroway and a group of ad agency and TV officials visited Dow's Midland plant so Garroway could become acquainted with the product and how it was made. But Saran Wrap was also advertised on the *Kate Smith Show* and the Sid Caesar/Imogene Coca comedy *Your Show of Shows*. But in those times, big shows were often cast around one featured product, so Dixon set out to have "the Saran Wrap show." What Dow and Dixon pulled together took form in a new TV series, *Medic,* which presented for the first time dramatized medical cases based upon actual cases of the Los Angles County Medical Association. It would run evenings on NBC in prime time, and would star then unknowns, Richard Boone, Lee Marvin, and Beverly Garland, each of whom would rise to stardom. In August 1954, Dow invited press, medical leaders, food brokers, and others to a special closed circuit preview of *Medic.* Dow's Lee Doan told the special audience this was new ground for the company, but said that with *Medic,* "I believe we have found a vehicle of such caliber that it will not only serve our necessity but will additionally satisfy our sense of social responsibility." That may have been overstatement, but *Medic* did its job even though it was cast opposite CBS's *I Love Lucy,* then the most popular show on TV. "The little screen did its work," explains Dow historian E.N. Brandt. "By 1958 the 200 millionth roll of *Saran Wrap,* enough to go around the world 38 times, was on its way to someone's kitchen."

Saran Wrap, in fact, became the cornerstone product in a new Dow Brands consumer products enterprise, which by 1994 would include *Ziploc* bags, *Yes* detergents and *Dow Bathroom Cleaner* accounting for $930 million in annual sales. *Saran Wrap* alone by that time was a $30 million-a-year product. By the 1990s, *Saran Wrap,* a polyvinylidine chloride, could be found on the grocery store shelves along with other plastic food wraps like Reynolds *Plastic Wrap,* made of polyvinyl chloride, and DowBrand's own *Handiwrap,* made of polyethylene.

The tough stuff that researcher Wiley had discovered, and Dow later parlayed into a major product, was not without long-term consequence, however. Like other of its chlorinated brethren, products made with vinylidene chloride polymers, when burned in waste incinerators—or "pyrolytic decomposition," as the scientists call it—would yield, as emissions, some not-so-healthy substances, including the full range of highly toxic dioxins and furans. These little nasties, unseen and in seemingly harmless microscopic quantities, would add to the daily stream of other problematic chemicals wafting into the air, land, and sea—all covered in more detail later.[15]

seedlings. The Kings Lynn plant also came to produce glycols for antifreeze and latex for paints and carpet backing. In 1955, Nederlandsche Dow Maatschappij was organized in Rotterdam, with a chemical terminal established in the Botlek area for warehousing Dow products. Rotterdam became Dow's window on Europe. By 1959, Dow established an overseas headquarters in Switzerland.[16]

In Spain, Dow had "meteoric growth" in the 1950 to 1973 period, according to company biographer E. N. Brandt, starting from zero and becoming the largest chemical firm in the country. There, in 1960, Dow acquired half interest in Unquinesa, later named Dow-Unquinesa, which built a polystyrene plant at Bilbao by October 1963 and a polyethylene plant at Tarragona near a new government refinery in 1966. Spain's legendary leader, Franco, came to Tarragona in 1967 to dedicate the new Dow plant. By the 1990s, Dow's Spanish operations employed about

1,600 people with annual sales at $400 million.[17]

In Greece, Dow incorporated Dow Hellas to build and run a plastics plant at Lavrion about 33 miles from Athens. By late 1962, the plant—also a deep-water port that brought styrene in from the Netherlands—was operating and producing *Styron*. A sales office in Athens also served as a Dow "jumping-off point" to the Middle East. Dow salesmen there in the 1960s, for example, were selling: jet fuel additives to the Arab American Oil Company in Saudi Arabia; refrigerator insulating material in Israel; plastics and polyvinyl chloride in Tehran; and plastics for packaging and polyethylene for film in Turkey, among other products and markets.[18] Dow also moved rapidly in Asia and South America.

In Zurich, Dow established the Dow Banking Corporation in 1965, the initial purpose of which was to make medium- and short-term loans to the company's European customers in a market where money was usually tight. Dow's bank made a profit from day one, and by 1979, had become the eighth largest bank in all of Switzerland and the largest foreign-controlled bank there. Dow for a time flirted with the idea of becoming an international banking institution, and by 1980, its bank had branches in Hong Kong, Buenos Aries, Bogota, London, Singapore and Miami. But in 1986, the Dow Bank was sold to the Royal Trust Bank of Canada.[19]

In central Italy, Dow built a plastics plant on the coast at Livorno in 1963, and bought partial interest in the Milan-based drug company Lepetit, among the largest such companies in Europe with 21 subsidiaries selling products in 100 countries. Dow acquired full ownership in 1975, and its Italian market grew rapidly. By the late 1980s, annual sales there leapt to $650 million.[20] Back in the States, as Dow was setting up shop abroad, the company was also undergoing significant change in its business direction, looking for ways to diversify.

Drugs & New Chemistry

In the 1960s, Dow began to move away from an exclusive dependence on old process chemistry and into more sophisticated realms of chemical R&D. It was not enough for Dow to be a major player in bulk chemicals with a loyal base of industrial customers. Dow managers saw that a new business world was on the horizon, and they had to move both to protect themselves and get their share of the expanding pie. They saw that international expansion was not only a growth opportunity, but a way to produce the revenues necessary to finance research—research needed to produce a continuing parade of new, exclusive, patent-protected products. "Building new positions, each as exclusive as possible," is how Dow's president Ted Doan put it in 1960, seeing this strategy as "the answer to the disappearing exclusiveness of the historical chemical industry."[21]

In December 1960, for example, Dow entered the pharmaceutical business in a big way when it acquired Allied Laboratories, a $30 million business with research labs, products and operations throughout North America and several other countries. Allied was then one of the country's largest manufacturers and distributors of human health products. In all, Dow acquired more than 600 products in the Allied deal, and a long line of drugs, including those developed by Allied subsidiary Pitman-Moore. It also acquired a manufacturing capability for the Salk polio vaccine, and a new 4-in-1 vaccine named *Compligen* for protection against tetanus, diphtheria, whooping cough and polio myelitis. Pitman-Moore also had a line of animal health drugs and biologicals sold to veterinarians. Pitman-Moore labs became Dow labs in Indiana, South Dakota, Illinois, Canada, Italy, and Mexico. Allied labs and properties were also added to Dow in Canada and Panama. But the deal was significant for Dow in that it moved the company into a more sophisticated realm of chemistry. Dow's Ted Doan clearly saw the new reach and new synergies that might be possible:

> ....We have not only a large amount of biologically-oriented work to contribute to the Allied Division," he said, "but also the chemical synthesis people to turn up thousands of new chemicals each year, some of which may fit pharmaceutical or veterinary needs, whether or not this was their original aim.... Allied obviously offers us not only skill in the unique marketing methods of the pharmaceutical industry, but such things as pharmacology and clinical work, pathology, virology, and pharmaceutical product development and other areas which we of course had not developed to any extent.[22]

But Dow was not, by any means, throwing over its old chemistry. In fact, by 1962, Dow was the world's largest producer of chlorine and caustic soda, and "ranked at the top or near the top in supplying industries with vinyl chloride, propylene oxide, glycol, phenol, synthetic glycerine, hydrochloric acid, methylene chloride, bromine, aspirin granules, magnesium, and plastic monomers." Overseas, meanwhile, Dow "was pouring money into new plants and expanding at a faster clip than any of its competitors."[23] By 1964, Dow's sales had surpassed $1 billion for first time. That year, Dow's diversified offerings included 24 new products, among them, *Rovana* drapery fiber, *Zoalene* coccidiostat for poultry farmers, and *Handi-Wrap* for kitchen use. In February 1965, Dow's one-shot measles vaccine, *Lirugen*, was introduced, and would dominate the market by year's end. Two years later, the U.S. Public Health Service launched a campaign to eradicate measles in the United States, and most of the vaccine used was Dow's. The U.S. Agency for International Development

From Ramie to Plastic

In 1951, according to Dow's account of how the company's first Japanese venture began, two executives from Asahi Chemical came to Midland to talk to Dow's Lee Doan about fishing nets. The Japanese had always made their nets of cotton and ramie, a flax-like fiber produced from a woody Asian plant used in making fabrics and cordage. But at the time, Japan imported both cotton and ramie. Asahi had been experimenting with filaments made from saran and found them to possess great advantage over ramie. Would Dow build a plant in Japan to provide the raw material for such nets, asked the Japanese? Asahi would provide the capital, and Dow the know-how. The company would be jointly owned. Dow accepted the Japanese proposal, and in 1952, a plant was built at Nobeoka. Four years later, styrene and *Stryon* polystyrene were added to the production mix. By 1979, Asahi-Dow was the largest polystyrene producer and the most profitable petrochemical company in Japan, operating nine plants across the country. However, by 1982, parent Asahi Chemical wanted a bigger share of the venture and Dow sold out to them for $231 million. But by 1991, Dow and Asahi teamed up again, this time in a joint venture named Styron Asia Ltd., formed to market polystyrene in Asia beyond Japan. By 2002, this new venture had opened a large, 120,000 ton-per-year polystyrene plant in Zhangjiangang, China.

Source: Dow Chemical Co., "Dow and Union Carbide Have Merged," *Around Dow*, Special Commemorative Issue, 2001, p. 26.

also chose Dow's *Lirugen* vaccine to inoculate more than 24 million children in 15 West African nations.

During the 1960s, Dow was also involved with the federal government in the space program and in fact, years earlier, had fashioned magnesium "Dowmetal" gondolas for U.S. Army Corps high-altitude balloons in the pre-satellite era of space testing. At Cape Kennedy in the 1960s, a Dow Aerospace Services team helped with the firing of a Saturn booster rocket. In 1965, when astronaut Edward H. White made his historic space walk, the 27-foot hose which supplied his oxygen was made of Dow Corning *Silastic* silicone rubber. And by 1968, as Apollo 8 orbited the moon and splashed down in the Pacific, the heat shield on the vehicle was made from Dow epoxy resin. Back on earth, Dow's new Oyster Creek Division near Freeport, Texas, designed to mass-produce chemicals featuring the world's largest phenol plant, came on-line in 1969.

But in the 1960s, Dow had a major wake-up call, as it began producing napalm, a jellied, chemical explosive, for use in the Vietnam War. Protests against the war also focused on Dow's production of napalm, made from a combination of benzene, gasoline, and polystyrene. Between 1966 and 1969, hundreds of demonstrations occurred, many on college campuses aimed at

Dow college recruiters. Other protests targeted Dow facilities and offices with noisy pickets, some of which were televised in national newscasts. Napalm, and also Agent Orange, a herbicidal defoliant Dow supplied to the U.S. military during the Viet-nam War, left long-lasting scars on Dow and affected the company's public image for years (see Chapter 3 and below). Still, Dow had its successes in the 1960s, and continued making chemicals and new products as it always had. By 1971, Dow sales would surpass $2 billion annually.

By 1968, as Apollo 8 orbited the moon and splashed down in Pacific, the heat shield on the vehicle was made from Dow epoxy resin.

Dow in the Oil Patch

Dow Chemical was also in the oil business, dating to the 1930s when it created an oil-well servicing subsidiary named Dow Well Services, later shortened to Dowell, Inc. This company was soon pulling in $75 million a year improving oil flow at wells across the country.[24] But Dow not only serviced the oil industry, it also established its own oil and gas business. From its earliest days, Dow was a company that used prodigious amounts of oil and gas to power its plants and to make its products. As the company became more immersed in synthesizing chemicals, it became more energy- and petrochemical-intensive. Dow officials in Texas during the 1940s, especially Dutch Beutel, pushed the idea that Dow should not be dependent on the oil industry for its energy and petrochemical feedstock. Operations like Dow's Freeport plant in Texas were then receiving their energy by contract, not all of which was delivered in a timely fashion. At Freeport, for example, Dow needed upwards of 30 million cubic feet of natural gas per day to fuel its magnesium-from-seawater plant alone. Ethylene and propane pipelines were also feeding the Freeport plant.

By the end of World War II, Willard Dow established the Brazos Oil and Gas Company in Texas, and by 1947, the new company had 265,000 acres of oil and gas leases in Texas and California. Brazos soon became a growing part of Dow and took on a life of its own. By 1950, the company was drilling oil and gas wells in Texas and Michigan and soon built a pipeline system in California. In Texas, Brazos pipelines covered 1,000 miles in nine counties transporting natural gas, ethylene, and liquefied petroleum gas to Dow's Freeport plant. Brazos became the Oil and Gas Division of the Dow Chemical Company, and soon had operations in Ohio, Louisiana, Wyoming, Oklahoma, Colorado, Kansas, Nebraska, Florida, and New Mexico. By 1965 it was even drilling in the Netherlands and Libya. Dow's Oil and Gas Division also subcontracted out to other oil drillers, such as Texas Oil & Gas and MacMorran, companies that helped Dow boost its oil and gas reserves going into the 1970s. Dow would also pick up smaller energy companies or pipeline systems on occasion. In the early 1970s, Dow had purchased the Wanda Petroleum Company from Ashland Oil, a gas liquids processor. It also became a 30 percent owner of the Oasis Pipeline Company, operator of a big 36-inch natural gas line from west Texas that kept gas flow-

Brazos Oil & Gas Co. soon became a growing part of Dow and took on a life of its own.

ing to Dow's plant at Freeport. In the 1970s, Dow also dabbled in coal, lignite, nuclear, and geothermal. In 1972, it was issued a license by the Atomic Energy Commission to build a nuclear power plant at Midland, Michigan—an endeavor that embroiled the company in controversy and a long battle with anti-nuke activists. The plant never operated. In 1974, Dow acquired a partial interest in Magma Power Company of Los Angeles, a geothermal energy developer.[25]

But in the 1970s, Dow planners had correctly predicted rising natural gas prices, and were better prepared than many other chemical companies for the energy price shocks that came. On supply too, Dow was well situated. When the energy crisis of 1973–74 arrived, Dow plants continued to hum, as the company then controlled 50 percent of the pipelines that carried fuel and feedstock to its plants and produced 80 percent of its own power. In Europe, Dow became active in North Sea oil exploration off northern England through the Sovereign Oil Company. Dow bought some North Sea oil properties, funded oil exploration there through Sovereign, and also acquired a landing site for pipelines it expected to bring ashore. In Canada, Dow teamed up with Dome Petroleum to develop oil and gas in Western Canada to help supply natural gas to Dow's Fort Saskatchewan plant, which came on line in 1980. By the end of 1981, Dow had proven oil and gas reserves of 40.5 million barrels of oil and 702.5 billion cubic feet of natural gas in the United States and Canada. However, in September 1982, under pressure to reduce its debt load, Dow exited the major part of its oil and gas business, selling its U.S. holdings to Apache Petroleum Co. for $402 million. Still, in that deal, Dow managed to secure first rights to feedstock supply and agreed to purchase 75 percent of the gas Apache produced from the properties.[26]

The "Go-Go" Years

The 1970s were generally a tremendous growth period for Dow Chemical. In 1970, the company launched a complete line of products for automotive applications, even though in 1971, with lead-free gasoline coming on the market, Dow would soon lose its lucrative market for ethylene dibromide, used for years as an anti-fouling additive with leaded gasoline. By 1972, the year President Richard Nixon established the U.S. Environmental Protection Agency, Dow would issue its first set of pollution control guidelines, the year it also launched its *Lorsban* insecticide—a soon-to-be top-seller that would later become controversial for its toxicity (see Chapter 5). Still, the money rolled in for Dow as business was better than ever; sales reached $3 billion in 1973. For the next four years running, Dow became the world's most profitable chemical company. Overseas, it became the first foreign industrial firm to be listed on the Tokyo Stock Exchange.

Dow's corporate profile continued to become more pharmaceutical, with drugs playing a bigger role in the company's bottom line.

At the opening of the 1980s, a recession took its toll on Dow for a time, causing a 30 percent drop in income. But soon, the company was back on track, expanding and growing. Dow's corporate profile continued to become more pharmaceutical, with drugs playing a bigger role in the company's bottom line. Dow acquired the Merrell pharmaceutical business of Richardson-Vicks in 1981, for $260 million. Building on Merrell's prescription drug business, Dow introduced *Seldane* (terfenadine), a nonsedating antihistamine in 1985 that produced nearly $400 million in worldwide annual sales. In 1989, Dow went further into the drug business by merging its existing pharmaceutical lines with Marion Laboratories of Kansas City, Missouri, forming Marion Merrell Dow, which Dow headquartered in Kansas City. Doctors across the country at the time were writing more than 1 million prescriptions monthly for Marion's *Cardizem* heart drug, which alone accounted for nearly 60 percent of Marion's $930 million in sales. Dow's new drug empire would soon exceed $2 billion in annual sales, with products such as *Lorelco*, a cholesterol-lowering drug, *Nicorette*, an anti-smoking drug, *Gaviscon*, a heartburn medicine, *Citrucel* a laxative, and *Cepacol*, a mouthwash. With these and other products—such as *Texize* cleansers which it bought from Morton Thiokol in 1985—Dow was becoming more of a consumer-products company.[27]

Bad Drugs

Dow's entry into businesses with more direct consumer products also presented the company with new kinds of risks and potential liabilities, especially with drugs. In February 1980, for example, research on a Dow's *Lorelco* cholesterol drug—also known as probucol, and then taken by 25,000 people—was found to cause fatal heart abnormalities in laboratory monkeys. Dow was required by the FDA at the time to send letters to 115,000 doctors warning them to check for abnormal heart rhythms in patients then taking the drug.[28] But a bigger problem for Dow came with another drug that

Dow inherited in the acquisition of the Merrell drug business—a drug named *Bendectin*. Widely prescribed to pregnant mothers for morning sickness since the mid-1950s, by the time Dow was marketing the product in the early 1980s, more than 33 million women had used it. But *Bendectin*—a drug that combined two chemicals with unwieldy names, doxyalimne succinate and pyridoxine hydrochloride—was suspected of causing birth defects. By

By 1983, Dow was facing some 300 lawsuits over its morning-sickness drug, *Bendectin*.

1983, in fact, Dow's Merrell-Dow unit was facing some 300 lawsuits over the product, and FDA was looking closely as some troubling animal studies. But by June 1983, Dow decided to quit selling the drug worldwide, citing the rising costs of lawsuits. "Although we have no doubt of its safety and effectiveness," said Merrell-Dow president David B. Sharrock in June 1983, "the burdens of continuing to market *Bendectin* have become just too heavy..." He said the firm had to increase prices to cover the costs of litigation. But others said Dow was simply moving in advance of an expected FDA action on the drug after reviewing studies on birth defects. "The company knew that these studies were going to be released soon, and they pulled their drug off the market in advance of an FDA recall," said J. Douglas Peters, an attorney with Charfoos, Christensen, Gilbert & Archer in Detroit then representing several *Bendectin* plaintiffs. Merrell-Dow had indeed been in intensive negotiations with FDA over the drug. In fact, it agreed at one point in June 1983 to send a "dear doctor" letter alerting physicians to the drug's problems. But then a month later, Merrell-Dow reversed course and refused to send the letter. Merrell-Dow reversed itself, it said, because of another study, using a larger database, that found no association between birth deformities and the drug. FDA, preparing a bulletin on the drug at the time, had also acknowledged the same study in its bulletin: "Nevertheless, the reported association...is of concern because it represents the first observation of a possible adverse fetal effect of *Bendectin* that had been reported from more than one study....It is therefore important that all who may prescribe or receive *Bendectin* be kept as fully informed as possible about factors that might influence a decision to use it." It appeared from internal memos and reporting by *Washington Post* writer Morton Mintz, that Merrell-Dow officials had, after some debate, first agreed to the "Dear Doctor" letter and to FDA language in the letter citing all the studies. But then Dow Chemical headquarters became involved and instructed Merrell-Dow officials to inform FDA it would not agree to the letter, with a message from Dow Chemical saying "our research executive staff... concluded that the data do not support a finding that [the] association [re: the drug and fetal effects] exists." FDA tried again to persuade Merrell-Dow to send the letter, but the company said it would not yield. FDA then issued its bulletin to doctors, which cited increased rates of a stomach deformity among infants whose mothers took *Bendectin*. The defect, called pyloric stenosis, constricts the stomach outlet soon after birth, reducing ability to eat, and can cause severe dehydration and malnutrition. Untreated, the condition could prove fatal in weeks. A short surgical procedure could fix the defect, which was estimated to occur one to three times in each 1,000 live births. But that wasn't the only problem. By 1987, other *Bendectin* birth defects cases were also coming to light, resulting in a few unfavorable verdicts against Merrell-Dow, many of which were later reversed on appeal. Still, some of the cases reveal a look at the issues involved at the time and how Dow handled them. One such case is offered in the sidebar opposite.

Dow headquarters instructed Merrell-Dow officials to inform FDA it would not agree to the "dear doctor" letter.

The Image Problem

By the mid-1980s, Dow was getting a little too much publicity it didn't like, and was developing a negative image among consumers. So it embarked on a public relations campaign to fix the problem. Dow's image woes had been bubbling up in the company for more than a decade, since the 1960s in fact, when the Vietnam War had thrust the company into the public spotlight over two controversial military products: napalm, a jellied gasoline explosive, and Agent Orange, a herbicidal defoliant.*

Dow's experiences with napalm and Vietnam War protestors moved the company in the 1970s to consider its social responsibilities. The company crafted a statement of corporate objectives, written by Dow's president Ted Doan and Ben Branch—an official who would follow Doan as president in 1971. As Doan recalled in an interview with author Cathy Trost:

> "They [the corporate objectives] were cribbed from a book of John Gardener's called *Excellence*." A lot of stuff about people doing things well and honestly. It was real motherhood and it was real good motherhood. The last statement was: "We'll do business in a way that leaves the world better because we were in business." That was [Ben] Branch, direct quote. That was the way he felt. He couldn't stand having a product go out if he thought it was going to do anybody harm. He would go a long way toward putting a company out of business and restructuring it in some way if he thought he was really doing damage. Let me not be so modest. I think all of us were the kind of guys who would say, "If we have

---

*See Chapter 3, "Dow Goes to War," for more details.

Kids Made Fun of Him

In July 1987, an 8-year old Washington, D.C. boy named Sekou Ealy, son of a State Department employee who took the Merrell-Dow drug *Bendectin* during her pregnancy, was awarded $20 million in compensatory damages for permanent deformities of his hands and arms. Punitive damages of $75 million were also awarded in that case, determined by a jury trial panel of six women. In the five-week trial, argued before U.S. District Court judge June L. Green, the proceedings included one session where the young boy was presented to the jury to see that he could not raise his arms high enough to button his own shirt, could not tie his shoelaces in a tight knot, and was made fun of by his 2nd-grade classmates because he couldn't straighten out his arms or throw a football normally. Barry J. Nace, attorney for the boy, argued that Merrell-Dow "played a form of Russian roulette" with the 1.34 billion *Bendectin* pills sold in the U.S. since 1956. "They didn't have anything that said the drug was safe," Nace contended of the company. "All they had was [the position that] you can't prove the drug is not safe." In the proceedings, Judge Green had divided the trial and the jury's considerations into two phases—one on whether Merrell-Dow had caused the child's deformities and had engaged in wrongful conduct that led the mother to use the product, and a second, in which the amount of damages was considered. The polled jury answered yes to 10 written questions which found, among other things, that Merrell-Dow had been negligent in testing, making, selling, and distributing *Bendectin*; had failed to warn physicians; that the negligence was "a proximate cause" of the young boy's injuries; and that the *Bendectin* tablets taken by the boy's mother were "unreasonably dangerous." The boy's attorney, Barry Nace, concluded the jury's message was that Merrell-Dow "knew, and had to know, of the dangers associated with taking any drug in pregnancy, yet did not take any active steps to prove that *Bendectin* was safe, and instead, went so far as to ignore all the signs that were there." In the damages phase, Merrell-Dow's attorney, Mark L. Austrian, told the jury that Merrell officials "may have been negligent" or "wrong," but that there was nothing in the record to show that any of them acted with "reckless indifference," engaged in "malevolent or malicious conduct," or believed *Bendectin* "would hurt children." Still, the jury thought otherwise and called for $20 million in compensatory damages and $65 million in punitive damages. Merrell-Dow's Donaldson called it "incredible" that the jury blamed *Bendectin* for the boy's deformaties, and awarded what he called "grossly excessive" damages. "We can only conclude that the jury was motivated by emotion and sympathy for the child," he said. Merrell-Dow appealed to the D.C. Circuit Court of Appeals, which in March 1990, overturned the jury case based on other litigation that had found the weight of scientific testimony offered on behalf of injured children was not enough to justify verdicts in their favor. The plaintiffs, however, pledged to appeal. By this point, Merrell-Dow had been the target of hundreds of such cases, with only one 1983 case resulting in an award of $750,000. Five other cases had ended in favor of injured children, but most of those were also appealed by Dow.

Source: Morton Mintz, "Deformed D.C. Boy Awarded $95 Million," *Washington Post*, July 15, 1987, p. A-1.

to go out of business, fine, we'll go out and we'll find a way to rebuild the damn thing some other way. We won't put arsenic in babies and kill 'em." You know, that kind of thing.[29]

Yet it was Dow's string of problems in the early 1980s that really focused the company's attention on the image problem and how to change it. Dow's dioxin controversy in Michigan, and its role in altering an EPA report on the subject, were also part of the mix.* But there were other factors, too.

Dow was then approaching $1 billion in direct sales to consumers for household and healthcare products. Dow's CEO at the time, Paul Oreffice, a hard-nosed executive in his late 50s who had little patience with critics, was nonetheless more attuned to the value of public communications than his predecessors. Oreffice became president and CEO in 1978, and he had already set some of Dow's makeover in motion:

> In the late '70s we took a look at our company—not from a public standpoint at all, more from a standpoint of how it was going to grow and thrive—and we decided that we've always been very good at marketing large quantities of basic chemicals and plastics which are sold to industry, and that [the bulk chemicals] business had been hurt very badly by the fact that every country in the world wanted to have petrochemical plants; it became the buzzword....
>
> We needed to move further downstream, and that meant moving into more things like pharmaceuticals, like consumer products, like agricultural chemicals, like insulation materials, like *Styrofoam*. At the time, 85 percent of the profits of the company were in the basics and only 15 percent were in what we call the specialties. I set a goal that by 1987 we would have 50–50, and that's about where we are today [September 1986].
>
> We had a good reputation with the industrial buyers, but we did have problems with the general public. So there was a business reason for better public relations too, no question about it, because we're moving closer to the consumer.[30]

But Dow's environmental problems in the late 1970s, its confrontations with EPA over a plant inspection, its dioxin woes, and its negative publicity over altering the EPA dioxin report in 1981, all began to take a toll. In the mid-1980s, a Dow task force under the direction of Keith McKennon, then Dow's head of U.S. operations, government and public affairs, surveyed 213 employees, managers, directors, and government and outsiders about how Dow was then perceived by the outside world.

The results were not good: "The current reputation of Dow with its many publics may be at an all-time low," explained the internal report. "We

---

*These and other issues are discussed in more detail in subsequent chapters.

are viewed as tough, arrogant, secretive, uncooperative and insensitive."[31]

"It was a very difficult time," recalled Richard K. Long, Dow's manager of external communications in late 1985. "We got accused of things that we felt were inaccurate." Even some of Dow's employees at the time viewed the company as arrogant and secretive, Long acknowledged. "Management began to look at ways in which we could change the perceptions of several key audiences," he said.[32] So in 1985, the company began a series of television advertisements built around the theme, "Dow Does Great Things."

> **In 1985, the company began a series of television advertisements built around the theme, "Dow Does Great Things."**

It was Dow's attempt to boost internal company morale and woo back the public. Three 30-second TV ads made their national debut in late September 1985. Print ads in the same genre also began appearing in *USA Today, Time, Newsweek, Business Week*, and *U.S. News & World Report.* Dow's intent was to use positive and buoyant themes—which according to Richard F. Dalton, Dow special projects manager in communications—were intended to connect the company to the optimistic attitudes of the 1980s. "Those are the kind of positive feelings we are trying to generate toward Dow," he explained to *Chemical Week* in October 1985. "We want the public to see that we're not a bunch of ogres."[33]

In 1985, Dow spent about $7 million for producing the ads and air time, but planned a much bigger commitment of $40 million over the next four years for the total campaign, which included other outreach and "good cause" undertakings. "We recommended that Dow get involved in a national social issue that would be humanitarian and not have to do with the company's business," explained Dow's Richard Long. Dow chose organ donation and transplantation and gave $1 million to the America Council on Transplantation.

In Dow's TV and magazine ads, young, bright-eyed college students had the starring roles. "It sounds like my kind of research," says one student in an ad showing the student at his dorm room desk writing home to his

Now, I'm about to join a company that's committed itself to helping people preserve our wildlife...

...and to finding new ways to protect the earth.
SING: Yes, you can make a difference...

HER (V.O.): I can't wait.
SING: 'Cause Dow lets you do...

Dear Dad,
Just got back from my Dow interview.
It sounds like my kind of research.
Finding new ways to grow more food.
Ways to help sick people.
I'm going to go for it, Dad. And I'm
going to try to make you proud.
                                    Love, David

**Dow lets you do
great things.**

DOW

father about an interview he has just had with the Dow Chemical Company. "It sounds like my kind of research. Finding new ways to grow more food. Ways to cure sick people." (See ad, left.) In another ad, a young woman in cap and gown waiting to receive her diploma, recalls how "Mom made me clean my plate 'cause there were places where kids were starving." But now, as a college graduate, she was "about to walk into a Dow laboratory to work on new ways to help grow more and better grain for those kids who so desperately need it."[34] These images were quite a change from the 1960s, when Dow was pilloried on many campuses for its role in the Vietnam War. Dow's testing of viewer responses in 1985 showed the ads to be effective in "making Dow a highly regarded company among its key publics," explained communications specialist Dalton. Back in Midland, however, some environmental activists such as Diane Hebert remained skeptical. "I'm not convinced that there really is a new Dow," she said.[35]

But Dow had other audiences in mind, too. "We found that if we were perceived as not running our business in the public interest," explained Dow chairman Robert W. Lundeen to *New York Times* reporter Phil Shabecoff in January 1985, "the public will get back at us with restrictive regulations and laws. That is not good for business." Dow was then selling about $1 billion worth of products directly to consumers. "Our reputation has a real dollar sign on it," added Lundeen.[36] Two years later, Dow's Richard Long, then the company's public affairs manager in Washington, put more of a fine point on the same observation. "We had made a lot of enemies who could influence our future. We recognized we had to clean up our act."[37]

"In fact," wrote *Wall Street Journal* reporter John Bussey in November 1987, describing Dow's efforts at that time, "the company is seeking nothing less than public redemption through an extraordinary image-makeover campaign." Other ingredients in Dow's program included: a performance review system that took into account a manager's public relations skills; sharing more information with regulators; support for environmental legislation; and extra efforts with the media.[38]

> **"We had made a lot of enemies who could influence our future."**
>
> Richard Long, Dow Chemical

Yet by 1989, there had come a whole new set of revelations and environmental concerns—ranging from new EPA data on the extent of toxic chemical pollution in the U.S., to the *Exxon Valdez* oil spill and Earth Day 1990, touching off a new round of public concern about the environment and corporate responsibility.* Dow would be in the thick of these matters, coming under considerable public scrutiny in the years ahead, and would continue to use public relations to address controversy and mend its corporate image.

Business As Usual

Apart from its image problems, Dow continued to pursue its business interests and expand its operations through the 1980s. It continued, for example, to acquire companies that fit into its business plan. In 1988, Dow added to its auto supply business, acquiring Essex Chemical, a leading producer of auto sealants and adhesives. Dow was always looking for new chemical niches to fill. By the late 1980s, Dow was not only selling its normal menu of bulk chemicals, but also a range of speciality chemicals and other products, including surfactants, antimicrobials, glycol ether products, superabsorbents, coatings and binders, plastic-lined pipe products, heat transfer fluids, brake fluids, deicing fluids and pellets, compressor lubricants, membrane systems, gas separation products, window film, insulation, adhesive films, electronic grade epoxies, epoxy hardeners, rigid foam products, carpet backing, herbicides, insecticides, nitrogen stabilizers, soil fumigants, gas fumigants, detergents, bleach, hair care products, plastic bags, stain removers, hybrid seed, mouthwash, a fiber laxative, cough and cold remedies, antibiotics, antihistamines, an intravenous cardiostimulant, and artificial kidneys.[39] In agricultural chemicals, Dow formed a major joint venture in 1989 with Eli Lilly—DowElanco—which quickly became one of the world's largest pesticide makers (see Chapter 5). By 1989, overall profits at

---

*See Chapter 11, "Dow Environmentalism."

Dow were running about $2.5 billion a year. Stockholders who took a chance on Dow in the1980s and stuck with it had made some money too. Dow stock bought for $1,000 in 1980, sold for $5,405 on January 2, 1990.[40] But Dow was not without its problems. In 1992, Dow posted a net loss of $496 million—its only loss in the century. Dow also faced new troubles, and thousands of lawsuits, as its Dow-Corning venture, the number one producer of silicone breast implants, had stopped making the devices following allegations the company had put the implants on the market without proper testing.* Dow plastics business faltered a bit in the early 1990s. But even with the difficulties, Dow's overall corporate sales by 1994 had surpassed $20 billion.

Back To The Future

By the mid-1990s, Dow began to change its corporate strategy in a couple of ways. First, it began to move away from two decades of diversification, most dramatically by selling its 71 percent stake in its Marion Merrell-Dow pharmaceutical business to Hoechst A.G. for $5.1 billion. Between 1995 and 1996, Dow also began selling off speciality businesses, including acrylamides, boride products, gas separation lines, membrane filtration systems, industrial cleaning, aspirin, and personal care businesses. "In the 1970s and '80s diversification was the means to growth," explained Dow's CEO William S. Stavropoulos in August 1996, "but we found we couldn't diversify enough to make a difference to cyclicity." But in the post-Cold War era there were some new opportunities, and Dow especially liked what it saw. With the opening of formerly closed economies, explained Stavropoulos, "the potential consuming market for chemicals has increased fivefold"—much of this in Dow's traditional line of businesses.[41] So Dow began buying up some bargain-priced European companies, such as three formerly state-run East German firms southwest of Berlin known as BSL. In this case, Dow announced that it planned to revitalize East German chemical production, starting with polypropylene, acrylic acid, and polyethylene terephthalate. It also expected to add and expand specialty lines at the new German companies (see sidebar). Dow had also acquired Enichem's Inca International subsidiary, giving Dow a good position in the European polypropylene and polyethylene terephthalate markets.

Meanwhile, Dow's agricultural chemicals business, DowElanco, acquired a stake in biotech seed developer Mycogen, and planned to push Mycogen's line of insect-resistant corn hybrids. DowElanco, said CEO Stavropoulos in August 1996, was at "the forefront of biotechnology" and had "a good pipeline" of products. Dow was also planning to double its plant

---

*See Chapter 12, "Silicone."

"Cleaning Up" in Germany

After the Berlin Wall came down in the late 1980s with the fall of Communism, the big three West German chemical makers—BASF, Bayer, and Hoechst—were offered a chance to acquire the huge East German chemical works at Schkopau, a sprawling and crumbling 2,100-acre complex near the Polish border that was built in the 1920s and 1930s. The West German firms said no thanks, as the complex was a mess and highly contaminated. The costs of cleaning it up appeared prohibitive, and the German chemical makers saw no real strategic value in the deal. Dow Chemical, however, jumped at the chance, seeing the location as an opening to future East European markets. The German government was also dangling some attractive inducements: it would give Dow 80 percent of the project and $4.8 billion in cash and subsidies to cover the cost of the cleanup and new construction. There was a catch, however: Dow had to do the job in five years, between 1995 and June 1, 2000, or lose the subsidies. Dow jumped in. By late May 2001, Dow had transformed the place, demolishing more than 2,300 buildings and factories, rebuilding more than 65 miles of roads, pipes, canals and rail lines, and erecting 14 entirely new chemical plants. The complex, known in German as Buna Sow Leuna Olefinverbund, or BSL for short, was transformed. Dow had tackled some very nasty pollution and contamination—including mercury contamination from an old mercury-based chlorine works and a coal-based acetlyne operation that spewed 30,000 tons of ash a year that fed a perpetual yellow-brown haze in the region—and cleaned it up. Dow dug out toxic soils down to a depth of 9 feet in some locations. In all, more than 5 millions tons of wastes and rubble were hauled out, with hazardous wastes treated or otherwise disposed. The conversion and clean up were not without their difficulties, and local traffic was a mess for a time. But Dow met the government's deadline, even if it did spend over $100 to $200 million more than it planned. Still, Wall Street viewed the Dow-refurbished BSL as a good deal, and projected that BSL would be generating more than $2 billion in revenue and more than $1 a share in profit for Dow by 2003. Dow says there are 22 "world-scale plants" operating there today, with several of them producing products or using technologies that are new for Dow—such as acrylic acid, synthetic rubber, dispersion powders and hydrocarbon resins. BSL is now one of Dow's largest production sites outside of North America, which Dow sees as well-positioned for booming European growth. "The whole enterprise is a technological trendsetter," says Dow, "the nucleus for industrial regeneration in the region; the area's biggest industrial employer and one of the greatest hopes for new job creation."

Irish Fight. But Dow wasn't always welcomed everywhere. In July 1988, when Dow announced it was planning to build a Merrell-Dow pharmaceutical plant to produce the antihistamine terfenadine about 23 miles from the small Irish village of Killeagh not far from Cork and Waterford, it soon confronted local opposition that grew to include farmers, citizens, and some politicians. Through 1989, the fight was front page news in Ireland, regularly featured on evening TV broadcasts. But before a final decision on the merits could be made, Dow decided the factory no longer economically fit its plans, since during that time, in

August 1989, Dow had made the Marion Laboratories/Merrell-Dow merger. The controversy, however, is credited with helping create Ireland's Environmental Protection Agency in 1990.

Source: Susan Warren, "For Dow, A Dirty Job In Germany Presented A Chance to Clean Up," *Wall Street Journal*, May 19, 2000, p. A-1;, Dow Chemical Co., "BSL—Restructuring A Piece of History," *Around Dow*, Special Commemorative Issue, pp. 33–34; and E. N. Brandt, *Growth Company*, pp. 387–93.

capacity at the Peroquimica Bahia Blanca plant in Argentina, and hoping to build an ethylene and chlor-alkali project in China with a then-unnamed partner.[42] But in 1997, Dow still had its bread-and-butter customers—among them: Electrolux, the Swedish kitchen appliance and refrigerator manufacturer using Dow plastics at its plants throughout the world since 1981; Reynolds Metals, the Richmond, Virginia maker of aluminum foil and other products, using Dow polyolefins, magnesium, and caustic soda since the late 1960s; and Eastman Kodak, the Rochester, New York photo giant and Dow customer since 1908, using Dow's polyethylene, polystyrene resin, allyl chloride, organic intermediates, formulation products, and antimicrobial, among others.[43]

> **"[B]iotechnology is an important growth platform for Dow, and we will continue to invest in it."**
>
> William Stavropoulos, CEO, 1998

In 1998, continuing its move back to basic chemicals, Dow sold off its consumer brands unit, including its bathroom cleaners, and its *Ziploc* and *Saran Wrap* lines, to S.C. Johnson. But Dow's leaders also continued talking up the prospects for biotechnology. "Every sign points to the fact that the biotech revolution is ushering in an entirely new economic era, comparable to the age of the transistor," said CEO William Stavropoulos at the company's 1998 shareholders' meeting. "In the future, biotechnology will touch nearly all aspects of our lives: food, medicine, electronics—and chemicals and plastics," he continued. "The important fact is biotechnology is an important growth platform for Dow, and we will continue to invest in it."

Dow was by this time a $20 billion company with 43,000 employees, selling chemicals, plastics, and agricultural products in 164 countries. It was also a company increasingly concerned about its image, and was spending money to make sure the public saw the kind of company Dow management had in mind. Stavropoulos told his shareholders in May 1998 that Dow needed to increase its "public presence," and to that end was launching some new advertising around the theme: "Look at All the Good Things a Little Good Thinking Can Do." The Dow TV ads would portray a company deeply involved in everyday things—"from the clothes we wear to the food we eat to the computer and telecommunications products that have come to define the Information Age," explained Stavropoulos. "We want to be known as a science company that is trying to help solve problems," he said.[44]

Union Carbide

In August 1999, Dow announced it would spend $9.3 billion to acquire Union Carbide—a company then ranked as the world's 28th largest chemical firm. The combination with Carbide would push Dow ahead of Bayer, then making it the world's No. 2 chemical company. The new Dow-Union Carbide would have $24 billion in annual sales with operations in 168 countries. Adding Carbide would immediately make Dow a much bigger global player in basic and intermediate chemicals—the "building block" chemicals like polyethylene, ethylene glycol, and propylene oxide; chemicals found in products from computers to food wrapping. Dow-Union Carbide would be No. 1 in ethylene production, a primary component of most plastic products; No. 1 in low-density polyethylene, used in plastic bottles, food wrapping and dry cleaning bags; No. 1 in linear low-density polyethylene, used in garbage bags and tops for butter and coffee containers; and No. 3 in high-density polyethylene, used in plastic garbage cans, cereal box liners, and grocery bags. The new company would also be a leading supplier of solvents and other chemicals to the paint industry. The deal also brought new plants to Dow where it had none or few—in the Middle East and Southeast Asia.[45] But aside from all the business synergy and new markets that Dow would gain, there was something else: the 1984 Bhopal toxic gas leak, the most horrific chemical accident in modern times (see Chapter 20). Why would Dow acquire a company that was still mired in the seemingly endless liability of the Bhopal victims' litigation and compensation claims?

> **Why would Dow acquire a company mired in the liability of Bhopal?**

In May 2000, *Business Week* put some of those very questions to Dow's CEO, William Stavropoulos. "Carbide was involved in the 1984 chemicals spill at Bhopal, India, that killed or maimed thousands. Will that create an image problem for Dow?" asked *Business Week*. "It could," replied Stavropoulos, who also noted he couldn't comment directly because Carbide and Dow were then still separate companies. But he did say that "Union Carbide settled with the Indian government," indicating that was Dow's understanding at the time. "But our whole drive," he said, "no matter what business we're in or acquire, is to be an absolute leader in environmental health and safety performance. Yes, people might tag us with it [Bhopal]. But we're looking to improve the situation, to bring it to the next level."[46]

In early February 2001, after the merger was approved, Dow ran full-

page ads announcing the new company in selected newspapers under the
banner, "Today Is a Big Day For Us."

> Today, we're proud to say Dow and Union Carbide have come togeth-
> er. Our two companies have rich histories for innovation—a combined
> 217 years to be exact.
> We're enhancing medicines for human health. Producing more
> abundant and nutritious foods. Improving insulation for more comfort-
> able homes. And helping create faster, more powerful computers. From
> health and medicine to electronics and entertainment, starting today,
> we're better together.
> Uniting to improve the essentials of life.
>   ...**Dow**. Living. Improved Daily.[47]

By early 2002, Wall Street analysts were generally giving Dow high marks
for the Carbide deal—focusing mainly on financial savings. Environmentalists
and human rights activists, however, kept pointing to the damages and victim
compensation tab yet to be paid by Union Carbide for its 1984 Bhopal chemical plant disaster. And there were still festering toxic wastes at the site. Carbide also had its own environmental baggage, ongoing emissions and waste
problems, and significant asbestos liability. But none of that appeared to matter much to the deal makers or Dow management.

In addition to Carbide, Dow also made other acquisitions in the late
1990s—deals that involved at least $3 billion beyond the $9.3 billion shelled
out for Carbide. Among these were: Bassel's Cologne polypropylene plant;
Cargill's hybrid seed business; Enichem's polyurethane lines; two foam makers, Flexible Products and General Latex; Integral Compounding, a manufacturer of an engineering plastics compound; Reichhold's latex business for
paper and carpet; Rohm and Haas's agricultural chemicals business with its
line of fungicides, insecticides and herbicides; and Zeneca's herbicide, ace-
tochlor.[48] Although Dow had divested its drug businesses in the mid-1990s, it
did not sell the chemical basis for making the basic pharmaceutical intermediates vital to the drug industry. By the late 1990s, Dow acquired several
chemical-specialty companies that fit into its pharmaceutical-supply business, turning out "custom and fine chemicals." It also added a company in
fermentation technology. Explained Dow's Andrew N. Liveris in February
2002, then a performance chemicals manager, "Even if you have just a few
drug company customers, it can easily be a $1 billion business."[49]

Dow Chemical Today

Today, Dow Chemical is a company with $28 billion in annual sales. On
the *Fortune 500* list for 2003, Dow stood at No. 51, outranking companies
such as: Lockheed-Martin, Intel, Motorola, Disney, DuPont, Georgia Pacific,

Bell South, Alcoa, Caterpillar, Aetna, Coca-Cola, Cisco Systems, Weyer-haeuser, and Bristol-Meyers Squibb. Dow operates 208 manufacturing plants and has 50,000 employees worldwide, selling 3,200 products in more than 170 countries.

Although Dow is still a company close to it traditional businesses, and still makes much of its money selling basic commodity chemicals in bulk, it is gradually shifting to more speciality lines. And like the rest of the chemical industry, it is always inventing new things. Dow's researchers have designed a new polymer film which can be used in semiconductors. The product, called SiLK, increases the chips' speed by protecting copper circuits from extraneous electronic noise. IBM, using semiconductors built with Dow's SiLK, has announced 30 percent faster computing speeds. A new electronics polymer market is already booming. According to *Forbes* magazine, Dow is also working on "polymeric light-emitting diodes," semiconducting polymers made of fluorine that give off colored light and can be used to make vivid, wide-angle display screens. Dow's first diode, which gives off green light, went on the market October 1999 (red and blue diodes were expected to follow). Cell phone displays using the diode are 40 percent to 60 percent thinner than ones made with previous materials, says Dow's manager for electro-active polymers.[50]

Using biotechnology, Dow researchers hope to manipulate crop plants to make fuels and supply new kinds of bio-materials for next-generation Dow products and processes. In early 2000, Dow AgroSciences and Dow Chemical joined forces with four academic centers in a $10 million initiative called the Oilseed Engineering Alliance. The aim, in part, is to turn green fields into bio-factories that produce commodity chemicals and raw materials for plastics. Some crop plants "perform complicated synthetic reactions that are impossible for chemists to do in the lab," explains Michael Pollard, a scientist at Michigan State University working with Dow on the project. Crop plants also produce hundreds of different oils and coaxing some of them to make just one kind of oil in quantity could prove very valuable to Dow, and much cheaper than petroleum.[51] Yet the reality of Dow's business and business expansion continues to be built around its chlorinated products. That chemistry is at the root of much of this company's culture and history, and continues to mold its future.

3.
Dow Goes to War

If Saran Wrap hadn't done the trick of making Dow a household name, napalm surely did.

Cathy Trost, *Elements of Risk*

One image of the Vietnam War still prominent in public memory is the 1972 photograph, "Vietnam Napalm," taken by Associated Press photographer Huynh Cong "Nick" Ut near the war's end. It recorded a tragic scene near the village of Trang Bang, Vietnam. At the photograph's center is a crying, Vietnamese girl, about eight years old or so. She is nude and her arms are extended bird-like as she runs down the middle of a country road. She is flanked by other children, also running and crying. Behind them on the road, are a few soldiers, and further in the background, is a sky filled with smoke from a freshly bombed village. The nude girl had shed her clothes after being hit with napalm—the jellied, liquid explosive used in combat. Napalm stuck to the skin, continuing to burn through muscle and bone, frequently killing its victims through the excruciating pain inflicted. Ut's photograph, winner of a Pulitzer Prize that year, leaves a painful reminder about the particular horror of that unpopular war, and some of the nasty weapons used.

General Earle Wheeler, chairman of the U.S. Joint Chiefs of Staff, explaining why napalm was important in the war, said it helped penetrate dug-in Viet Cong and North Vietnamese positions. Conventional bombs were not as effective, he said. "Napalm, by nature of its splashing and spreading, can get into such defensive positions. It's also especially effective against antiaircraft positions, because normally the enemy digs a hole—... and puts his machine gun in that hole.... The napalm splashes in and incapacitates the crew and sometimes destroys the weapon."[1]

Jellied gasolines for use in warfare were not a new invention for Vietnam. They were used in the flamethrowers of World War I, World War II, and Korea. But for napalm, there were some new twists in the chemical formula. In 1964, the U.S. Air Force developed Napalm "B"—50 percent polystyrene, 25 percent benzene, and 25 percent gasoline. Napalm's delivery was also improved, developed as a bigger and more awesome aerial firebomb delivered from air-craft. Dow Chemical, then the leading manufacture of polystyrene, was one of 17 American companies asked by the government to submit bids on produc-ing napalm. The orders were to be filled in 25-million-pound lots. By 1966, Dow became a government contractor to produce napalm for the U.S. military. Napalm was relatively easy to make: a simple mixing of the ingredients—gaso-line, benzene, and polystyrene. Dow set up a small production line and tank-age system combining the three chemical ingredients at its Torrance, California plant. With a small group of workers, Dow proceeded to meet its napalm contracts over the next four years. Napalm was never a big business for Dow, and according to one estimate, the company never made more than $5 million worth of napalm in any one year. Yet it became an infamous prod-uct for Dow, and thrust the company into the public limelight as never before. Napalm became a focus of the1960s anti-war activists, and with it, Dow was cast as the government's handmaiden in the war.

Weapons Producer

Dow Chemical was no stranger to weapons production and govern-ment contracting. From World War I on, Dow did what the government asked, and repeatedly served as its wartime chemist and producer of muni-tions, strategic materials, and weapons—from mustard gas in WWI to pluto-nium triggers for nuclear weapons during the Cold War and beyond. During WWI, Dow's phenol provided the basis for making explosives. It also pro-duced tear gases bromacetone and xylyl bromide,* and was involved in the development of mustard gas, also known as blister gas for the effect it caused on the skin. The Germans first used mustard gas in the war without much effect in 1915, but in 1917, they used it successfully in a five-mile breach of British and Canadian front lines. It soon became the Germans' preferred gas weapon, which they further refined and perfected. By Febru-ary 1918, Dow officials were among a handful of key people summoned to Washington to come up with a way to produce and manufacture large quan-tities of the gas for the Allies. Midland soon became the Army's base for making the needed mustard gas compound—dichlorethyl sulfide. The Army then estimated its need at 40 tons per day. The G-34 plant in Midland, Michi-gan was built to produce half that amount. By war's end, there was a com-bined military and civilian production force of about 3,000 workers in

---

*One of the principle scientists working at Dow laboratories recalled that in the frantic crash effort to ramp up production of xylyl bromide at Dow in Midland in the winter of 1917–18, "con-siderable" amounts of it were spilled in the ice and snow. Upon the spring thaw, however, one area of the plant "became a very uncomfortable place" for several weeks as the spilled chem-icals warmed and vaporized, producing their intended teary effects on unfortunate workers.

Midland turning out the gas and other products. There were also spills and accidents, and some soldiers detailed to Dow's production operations during the war died from exposures after cleaning out machinery that had gummed up. But in the end, the gas manufactured at Midland was shipped to France but was not used by the Allies, according to Dow biographer, E. N. Brandt.[2] Still for Dow, WWI was a bountiful time, even if the lethal gases only played a small role in the company's burgeoning chemicals list. More importantly, new knowledge and position were gained for the post-war world to come. The company's work with wartime gases, had given it valuable insight into ethylene, a key building block of incalculable value.

During WWII, Dow again played a key role in producing strategic materials, especially light-weight magnesium used in the production of long-range bombers, and styrene and butadiene, two key chemicals used in making synthetic rubber. Phenol production—now revamped in a new process since WWI—also made Dow the leading producer of this explosives ingredient for U.S. and Allied forces. Hexachloroethane, the principal ingredient in smoke screens, was also produced by Dow at its Midland, Pittsburg, and Freeport plants.[3] Dow's chemicals were used in a wide range of products shipped to the military, including "...incendiary bombs, flares, and tracer powder, camouflage paints, germicides, fungicides and preservatives, gun muzzle covers, water purifiers, greases and oils, dyes, shoe polish, shaving cream, shell casings, map protectors, soaps, explosives and other products too numerous to list."[4] A top-secret substance called impregnate, or "CC2"—a material used to treat combat clothing to make it resistant to gas warfare agents such as mustard gas and *Lewisite*—was also made by Dow in Midland. During the years 1937–41, explains E. N. Brandt, "Dow was by far the fastest growing of the nation's large chemical firms, averaging 26 percent in annual growth during a period when one expert estimated growth for the top ten firms in the industry at an average of 3.2 percent yearly, and much of Dow's growth was in products that were to be key to the war, such as magnesium and styrene."[5]

'60s Protests

But in the Vietnam War of the 1960s, it was napalm that made Dow a target of activist protests. One of the first such protests aimed at Dow occurred in late May 1966 at Dow's New York headquarters at Rockefeller Center. Peace groups, including some 75 protestors from groups such as Citizens' Campaign Against Napalm and Women Strike for Peace, handed out leaflets on the street. In their street taunts and protest literature, the protestors charged, "Napalm Burns Babies!" and other such slogans. They called on consumers to boycott Dow products such as *Saran Wrap*. Between 1966 and 1970, Dow was the focal point of more than 200 major anti-war demonstrations on American college campuses. Dozens of other protests and incidents aimed at Dow also occurred—ranging from the bombing of the company's office in Frankfurt, Germany and protests at various Dow plants around the world, to the trashing of the company's Washington, D.C. offices. By the fall of 1967, the Dow protests were occurring so frequently—133 campus demonstrations aimed at Dow employment recruiters in that year alone—that the company began publishing a newsletter for key managers and campus recruiters to keep them informed of where protests might be expected. It was called *Napalm News*, and it ran from November 1967 to late March 1969.[6]

The legacy of napalm for Dow, however, was that it pushed the company into the national limelight. Well known and admired in central Michigan as a symbol of economic prosperity and new products, Dow was fairly obscure elsewhere. Napalm and Vietnam changed that. "In the time of the flower children," as Dow biographer Brandt put it, using a common 1960s counter-culture descriptor, "Dow became a household word." In 1965, one public opinion survey found that only 38 percent of the American public had heard of the Dow Chemical Company. Four years later, 91 percent "knew something about" the company. "What made [Dow] famous," says Brandt, "was the war protests in which it was involved, which were front page newspaper and TV news fare throughout that period."[7] Long after the protests disappeared, however, people continued to associate Dow with napalm. Wrote one *Wall Street Journal* reporter in 1987, "Dow still gets questions about napalm, even though it stopped making the flammable gas gel 17 years ago."[8] But there was also something else from the 1960s that clung to Dow in an unflattering way: Agent Orange, a herbicidal defoliant made by Dow and also used in Vietnam. Unlike napalm, the Agent Orange chemicals came home to America with returning Vietnam veterans—in their blood, body tissue, and DNA.

Agent Orange

From late 1961 to 1970, the U.S. military in Vietnam undertook a massive chemical spraying campaign to defoliate Vietnam's forests. The chemical most extensively used was called Agent Orange, owing to the orange band on the drums the herbicide was shipped in. The main ingredients in Agent Orange were two agricultural herbicides—2,4,5-T (2,4,5-trichlorophenoxyacetic acid) and 2,4-D (2,4-dichlorophenoxyacetic acid). Other herbicides, in mixtures designated Agents Purple, Pink, Blue, and White, were also used.*

---

*2,4,5-T was used in Agents Orange, Purple, and Pink, but not Blue or White. Agent White, for example, contained a mixture of 2,4-D (2,4-dichlorophenoxyacetic acid) and picloram (4-amino-3,5,6- trichloropicolinic acid), concocted in an approximate ratio of 4 to 1; and Agent Blue, was code named for cacodylic acid (dimethyl arsenic acid). But Agent Orange was the most widely used Vietnam defoliant.

Dow became the largest of nine government contractors supplying herbicides for the war. At a price of $7 a gallon, Dow eventually supplied about one-third of the nearly 13 million gallons of Agent Orange the government used in Vietnam.[9] But Dow did not invent the chemicals used in the Agent Orange concoction. That happened elsewhere, 20 years before.

In 1941, scientists at the botany laboratories of the University of Chicago were conducting research on plant hormones and plant growth, and had synthetically produced chemicals that affected various kinds of plant growth. The substances were then called "plant growth regulators," not herbicides. However, the Chicago researchers became frustrated in their work by the lethal action of the chemicals they were testing. All the plants were dying. That's when one scientist got the idea that the chemicals might in fact be put to that very use—specifically to kill weeds that plagued most crop farms. With some experimentation, they found their idea worked quite well. That's when the government stepped in. About that time, the Chicago chemicals had come to the attention of the National Academy of Sciences' War Research Committee and the U.S. Army. The Army was then becoming interested in biological warfare research, and shortly recruited the leader of the University of Chicago botany lab to begin secret military research on the herbicides at Fort Detrick, Maryland. Between 1944 and 1945, the Army tested the effects of more than 1,000 different chemical compounds on living plants at Fort Detrick. Among these were 2,4-D and 2,4,5-T. The use of the compounds in warfare was seriously contemplated at the time, but never actually unleashed in the war.[10]

With the end of WWII, herbicides soon made their way to U.S. agricultural experiment stations, private companies, and farmers. In 1945, the American Chemical Paint Company (later named AmChem, which subsequently became a part of Union Carbide) began selling the first systemic herbicide—2,4-D—under the brand name *Weedone*. Two years later, 30 different preparations of herbicides containing 2,4-D were being sold in the United States, including brands sold by Dow. By 1949, more than 23 million acres of agricultural land were being treated with herbicides of all kinds. 2,4,5-T by then was also registered under the federal pesticide law, known as the FIFRA, the Federal Insecticide, Fungicide and Rodenticide Act, then administered by the U.S. Department of Agriculture (USDA). In 1950, Dow began producing 2,4,5-T at its Midland, Michigan operations. By 1959, nearly 60 million acres of U.S. agricultural lands were being treated with herbicides of all kinds.[11] 2,4-D and 2,4,5-T were among the most widely used, with 2,4-D even reaching the lawn care market.

In the Vietnam War, the U.S. military first authorized the use of herbicides in November 1961 to improve visibility along roads and waterways and to clear camp perimeters. But that soon expanded to clearing areas suspected of harboring North Vietnamese or guerrilla base camps, then to supply routes, and also for destroying crops. By the mid-1960s, 2,4,5-T and 2,4-D were being dumped by the planeload over thousands of acres in Vietnam.

The U.S. Air Force created the 309th Air Commando Squadron to conduct the spraying. Originally code named "Operation Hades," the spraying campaign later became known as "Operation Ranch Hand." On the ground, American soldiers would see vegetative death by super growth—giant bananas and luxuriant jungle growth; growth that quickly wilted and became dying forests. Some soldiers, told the spray was harmless, would even engage in spray fights occasionally, while a few would even ingest the chemical to show reporters how safe it was.

Yet, even as the U.S. military was beginning its Vietnam spraying in 1962, back home, Rachel Carson was raising a lone voice of warning about pesticides with her book *Silent Spring*. Noting that 2,4-D and 2,4,5-T had become widely used agricultural herbicides, she reported on some of the early lab results and health-effects then beginning to appear. "People spraying their lawns with 2,4-D and becoming wet with spray have occasionally developed severe neuritis and even paralysis," she noted. 2,4-D, said Carson, "has been shown experimentally to disturb the basic physiological process of respiration in the cell and to imitate X-rays in damaging chromosomes." Other research, she warned, "indicated that reproduction of birds may be adversely affected by these and other herbicides at levels far below those that cause death."[12]

There were some indications that the U.S. military wanted a safe defoliant—or at least a few of its key people at the time made statements to that effect. In 1963, at the Defense Department's First Defoliation Conference reviewing Vietnam spraying operations, Brigadier General Fred J. Delmore alerted chemical company representatives, including those from Dow and Monsanto, that there was a need for the defoliants to work in a quicker fashion, and that the material used for the defoliants must be both "perfectly innocuous to man and animals," but able to "do its job." Additionally, Albert Hayward, chief of the Fort Dietrich program coordination office told those attending the conference, "It goes without saying that the materials must be applicable by ground and air spray, that they must be logistically feasible, and that they must be nontoxic to humans and livestock in the areas affected."[13] Dow officials then extrapolated from the company's experience with its agricultural herbicides, advising General Delmore in 1963: "We have been manufacturing 2,4-D and 2,4,5-T for over ten years. To the best of our knowledge, none of the workmen in these factories have shown any ill effects as a result of working with these chemicals."[14]

In 1963, the Advanced Research Projects Agency did hire the Institute for Defense Analysis (IDA) to review the toxicity of all the herbicides proposed for use in Vietnam. The IDA reported that it couldn't guarantee if any of them would be safe for military use, also noting the military penchant for over-kill concentrations, with possible effects on the exposed population and domestic animals. The IDA recommended that the military take extra precautions. But the military didn't follow this advice. In the war, if safety protocols existed, they were mostly ignored. "The methods for transporting, load-ing, and spraying these chemicals were haphazard and sloppy," observes Peter Sills, working on a book about Agent Orange. "Stuff leaked everywhere, and nobody cared very much."

Sills also explains that Agent Orange was sprayed at much higher concentrations than any of the domestic uses of 2,4,5-T or 2,4-D. "Dow and the other manufacturers knew all of this," he explains, "and must have realized that the risks were much greater than normal." And while the Army Chemical Corps scientists approved Agent Orange as safe, "the Corps got most of its data straight from V. K. Rowe, Dow's chief toxicologist," says Sills. "Rowe is even quoted in the press release announcing the Corp's decision."[15]

While the Army Chemical Corps approved Agent Orange as safe, the Corps got most of its data straight from V. K. Rowe, Dow's chief toxicologist.

By 1963–64, Dow was producing 2,4,5-T for the military at full throttle. In 1964, there were incidents of Dow workers contracting chloracne, a severe skin rash. But little of this surfaced publicly at the time, as the herbicidal mix-tures were pretty much known only to the chemical industry and the U.S. mil-itary. Nor was any government agency then connecting the dots between what some may have been finding in agricultural pesticides used domestical-ly and what was being dropped on Vietnam. The U.S. military, meanwhile, had not undertaken any Agent Orange toxicological testing of its own before order-ing and deploying the chemical. Observed Thomas Whitesides in his book *The Pendulum and The Toxic Cloud:* "... [T]he American military, having developed 2,4,5-T as part of its biological warfare program in the years follow-ing the Second World War, unhesitatingly employed it during the war in South-east Asia, spraying twenty thousand tons over both populated and unpopulated areas of South Vietnam, without the Pentagon's scientists ever having taken the precaution of systematically testing whether the chemical caused harm to the unborn offspring of as much as an experimental mouse...."[16]

In 1964, reports began to circulate in Vietnam of increased miscar-riages, stillbirths, and birth defects among exposed Vietnamese women and farm animals. These reports came to the attention of scientists at the Nation-al Cancer Institute. The reports from Vietnam, plus other findings on the use of 2,4,5-T and 2,4-D domestically, convinced some U.S. scientists they ought to take a closer look at the chemicals, including the Agent Orange mixture. As it happened, the National Cancer Institute had already contracted Bio-netics Research Laboratories of Bethesda, Maryland in 1963 to conduct can-cer studies on a number of pesticides, including 2,4-D and 2,4,5-T. Bionetics' studies were then to be reviewed by a blue ribbon commission of scientists. In the summer of 1965, Bionetics' tests on female mice and rats showed that

2,4-D and 2,4,5-T caused a significant number of deformities in unborn off-spring. A preliminary report on these findings was prepared in 1965 and 1966, but was not made public.

Bionetics' tests had found that a production impurity in 2,4,5-T known as dioxin* was a powerful teratogen—a substance that caused birth defects in the rat offspring. A number of the offspring were born dead or deformed, some with cleft palates, no eyes, cystic kidneys, and enlarged livers. Dow Chemical, then the principal American producer of 2,4,5-T, objected to the findings, saying the 2,4,5-T sample Bionetics used was a "dirty sample" and unrepresentative because it contained abnormal amounts of dioxin. No decisive action was then taken by the government; the Bionetics study remained under wraps and 2,4,5-T continued to be used both domestically and in Vietnam. Some critics suggested that Dow, the nation's leading producer of 2,4,5-T, simply pressured the government to hold back the report. In addition, observes author Carol Van Strum in her book, *A Bitter Fog*, "the White House apparently feared that disclosure of the Bionetics report would encourage international criticism of American chemical warfare in Vietnam and feed growing antiwar sentiment at home."[17] However, in July 1969, Ralph Nader received a leaked copy of the Bionetics report and made it available to Dr. Matthew Meselson, a Harvard University biologist. Meselson was concerned about the Vietnam spraying and helped to gather the signatures of 5,000 scientists petitioning Lyndon Johnson to stop the use of herbicides in Vietnam. The United Nations adopted a Swedish resolution that declared the use of herbicides a violation of the Geneva Protocol of 1925. President Nixon, however, drew a different interpretation.[18]

Meanwhile, in places like Oregon and Arizona, Louisiana and Arkansas, and Pennsylvania and North Carolina, some of the same Agent Orange chemicals—2,4,5-T and 2,4-D—in various combinations and mixtures, were being sold and sprayed regularly. In these applications, too, Dow was a leading purveyor, promoting their use practically everywhere—in American forests, along railroads, highways, and transmissions lines, and on farms, rangelands, lawns, and golf courses.

Back at the White House, Nixon administration science advisor, Dr. Lee A. DuBridge, reacting to public criticism over the leaked Bionetics test results, decided to take some action and ordered "restrictions" on the use of

---

*2,4,5-T is manufactured by chemically combining 2,4,5-trichlorophenol sodium salt and chloroacetic acid at elevated temperatures and pressures under alkaline conditions. The substance 2,3,7,8-tetrachlorodibenzo-p-dioxin (TCDD)—or "dioxin" for short—is an inevitable byproduct of 2,4,5-trichlorophenol and 2,4,5-T production. Dioxin is the key toxic substance in these and other compounds, and would later be discovered as a much wider problem throughout the chemical industry as well as other industries. Dioxin will be explored in more detail in the next chapter. Here, for the moment, suffice it to say that dioxin was beginning to be understood by a small circle of government and industry scientists as a very potent toxic chemical.

"Viet Cong Poison the Water"

During the Vietnam War, as charge and counter-charge flew back and forth about Agent Orange's use and effect on the civilian population and environment, the American military engaged in a bit of its own propaganda, using helicopter-mounted public address megaphones blaring messages to South Vietnamese villages. One episode, in Binh Dinh province, recounted below by Carol Van Strum in her 1983 book, *A Bitter Fog,* is based on the account of a Vietnam veteran who took part in it:

... Late in 1969, a young man [Paul Merrill, the Psychological Operations Combat Loudspeaker Team leader] crouched beside a 1,000-watt trumpet loudspeaker mounted on a frame that had been lifted into the helicopter. Beside him, another man readied boxes of leaflets, and just behind them, crew chief and gunner manned the machine guns on either side of the craft. The pilot brought the helicopter low over a small village at the mouth of a valley where two rivers met. A single two-story cement building dominated a cluster of mud and thatch houses. Buildings, paths, palm trees, banana trees, and dirt roads were contained within a concertina-wire perimeter, separating them from surrounding rice paddies.

As the helicopter circled the village, the young soldier swung the hinged speakers out the cargo door and tinkered with the control panel of tape recorder and amplifier. Grasping the strut of the seat, he leaned out the open doorway to throw the leaflets his partner handed him, while the loudspeakers blared their message in Vietnamese, in a voice clearly audible 7.6 kilometers away:

"The Viet Cong have been saying the sprays make the people sick and are making them sad, and that the sprays are killing the elders and the children. The Viet Cong are lying. They are poisoning the water, so the people will believe their lies. The Viet Cong do not like the sprays because they let the soldiers see where they are hiding."

2,4,5-T. DuBridge announced, by White House order, that government agencies would stop using 2,4,5-T in populated areas, and that pesticide registrations for 2,4,5-T on food crops would be canceled by January 1970 unless the government could establish safe tolerance levels. The Department of Defense would also restrict the use of the herbicide to remote areas in Vietnam. "It seems improbable that any person could receive harmful amounts of this chemical from any of the existing uses of 2,4,5-T," said DuBridge at the time of the announcement. "While the relationships of these [Bionetics] effects in laboratory animals to effects in man are not entirely clear at this time," he continued, "the actions taken will assure safety of the public while further evidence is sought." But journalist Cathy Trost writes that DuBridge's move "was a hollow announcement. None of the promises was kept," she says. "The Pentagon announced the very next day it would not alter its use of the herbicide in Vietnam because it believed its present policy conformed to the White House directive...." Meanwhile, scientists such as Yale University's Clement L. Markert, chairman of the biology department, were speaking out about the possible effect of 2,4,5-T. He told *Science* magazine that 2,4,5-T unquestionably exhibited a high order of toxicity and posed an unacceptable risk to the people of Vietnam, where it might cause hidden, if not overt, birth defects, such as lessening of brain capacity.[19]

By November 1969, a U.S. Department of Health, Education and Welfare panel named the Mrak Commission—reviewing the latest National Institute of Environmental Health Services findings—concluded that 2,4,5-T, some forms of 2,4-D, and several other then-registered pesticides, were found to be teratogenic and "should be immediately restricted to prevent risk of human exposure." Dow, meanwhile, continued to object to the findings. According to Dow biographer Brandt, "On December 27, 1969, the federal office of Science and Technology summoned a group of Dow scientists to Washington to tell them all they knew about 2,4,5-T. The Dow group told a panel of distinguished scientists among other things about a new methodology to determine [dioxin] level recently developed by Rudy Stehl of Dow." At this time, Dow appears to have continued to argue that the Bionetics samples were dirty, coming from another company which Dow charged had a very high impurity level in its manufacturing. "If Bionetics had selected a Dow material or that of almost any other manufacturer, the teratogenic effects would not have been detected," said Warren B. Crummett, one of Dow's experts, in a 1994 interview.[20] Yet, in 1970, after new tests were conducted using "cleaner" 2,4,5-T, the results from the National Institute of Environmental Health Sciences and the Food and Drug Administration—using samples that contained less than one part per million dioxin as Dow had requested—still showed 2,4,5-T to have significant teratogenic effects in test animals, including cleft palates, missing limbs, and skull defects.[21]* Dow conducted its own tests and did not find the birth defects detected in the government tests. The federal government, by this time however, was ready to act.

In April 1970, at U.S. Senate hearings on the health effects of 2,4,5-T conducted by Senator Phillip Hart (D-MI), U.S. Surgeon General Dr. Jesse Steinfeld, presented a chronology of research dating back to 1966 that also showed the chemical to be teratogenic. Dr. Steinfeld and David Packard, Secretary of Defense, announced formally on April 15, 1970, the government's

---

*Other tests in 1970 were also conducted, including those of Dr. Jackie Verrett of the FDA Toxicology Lab in Washington. Dr. Verrett used a 0.50 parts per million dioxin solution obtained from chemicals used in Vietnam and applied them to chick embryos and found cysts, necrotic livers, slipped tendons, cleft palates and beak deformities in the resulting broods. She also used a 0.25 parts per trillion solution and observed similar effects. Further tests of 2,4-D and 2,4,5-T without dioxin still produced dead and deformed offspring. Some tests in England at the time had also found that Agent Orange contained as many as 17 or more contaminants.

action limiting the use of 2,4,5-T in the United States and suspending Agent Orange use in Vietnam.*

By 1971, when the Vietnam spraying program ended, over 11 million gallons of Agent Orange containing some 50 million pounds of 2,4,5-T had been used in the spraying program.** In total, including other agents and other herbicides, more than 100 million pounds of herbicides were sprayed over at least 6 million acres of Vietnam between 1962 and 1971.[22]

The Home Front

As the spraying of Agent Orange came to a halt in Vietnam, the use of 2,4,5-T and related herbicide formulations at home seemed to increase markedly in some applications. Even though the USDA, under White House orders, had moved by May 1970 to cancel registration of 2,4,5-T on food crops, gardens, recreation areas, and locations where it might contaminate water supplies, the herbicide still had a wide berth. It continued to be used in forests, along powerline rights-of-way, on rangeland, and other areas. In fact, by the mid-1970s, 2,4,5-T spraying across America *exceeded annually* in acreage the total 5 to 6 million acres that had been sprayed in Vietnam over more than eight years. Meanwhile, chemical producers, led by Dow, waged their own war against the federal agencies trying to rein in 2,4,5-T. The fighting began almost from the moment the first 2,4,5-T restrictions were announced in April 1970—a time when the federal government was also re-defining its environmental and public health responsibilities, shifting pesti-

---

*Also testifying at the 1970s hearings was Dr. Julius Johnson, a vice president at Dow Chemical and director of research and development. Johnson reported on Dow's 1964 episode of chloracne among workers who handled wastes from 2,4,5-trichlorophenol at the company's 2,4,5-T plant. Johnson described chloracne as "a skin disorder mostly prevalent on the face, neck, and back." It is similar in appearance, he said, "to severe acne often suffered by teenagers," leaving the impression, in Thomas Whitesides' opinion, that "chloracne might seem…a transient cosmetic problem…." But there were indications even then that chloracne—and dioxin—were associated with maladies beyond the skin rash that Dr. Johnson described for the committee. In fact, Dr. Benjamin Holder, director of Dow's medical department, had only two months earlier told a group of government chemists that the early symptoms of the chloracne included fatigue, lassitude, depression, the appearance of blackheads on the face and back, and weight loss. He also reported that heavy exposure to dioxin-contaminated trichlorophenol waste caused damage to internal organs and disorders of the nervous system. (see Whitesides, pp. 24–25). But at the time, most of this went unnoticed, as the government's announcement limiting 2,4,5-T was what made the headlines.

**These were the numbers used for the next 30 years or more. However, recent investigations suggest the amount of land sprayed and chemicals used may have been greater. Researchers at the Columbia University School of Public Health, for example, have suggested amounts 10 percent higher than previously reported.

cide authority away from the USDA and toward a new agency called the U.S. Environmental Protection Agency (EPA). Amid these changes, Dow and other herbicide producers dug in their heels.

In May 1970, Dow, Hercules, and Amchem Products appealed USDA's decision to cancel the use of 2,4,5-T on rice. Under the law at the time, the continued use of the contested substance was permitted to proceed during the appeal process. By January 1971, the newly formed EPA was ordered by the courts to uphold the restrictions on 2,4,5-T. Several months later however, in May 1971, EPA's Science Advisory Panel found that 2,4,5-T did not create any health hazard and proposed to lift the ban around homes, although the panel

Dow's maneuver in the Arkansas courts had gained the company nearly two years of continued 2,4,5-T sales for rice.

acknowledged the chemical's teratogenic potential and proposed language for a warning label: "This compound may be dangerous to pregnant women." In August 1971, after scientists, including Barry Commoner of Washington University, Matthew Meselson of Harvard, and Samuel S. Epstein of Case Western Reserve, and the U.S. Food and Drug Administration objected to EPA's Science Panel findings on 2,4,5-T, EPA administrator William Ruckelshaus, conducting his own review, decided to keep the 2,4,5-T cancellation order in place while calling for further hearings. Citing the known facts about lab animal birth defects stemming from dioxin in 2,4,5-T, Ruckelshaus warned of the possibility that even "pure 2,4,5-T" containing the lowest amount of dioxin, might be a hazard to man and the environment. He also asserted the chemical companies had failed to establish that either dioxin or 2,4,5-T did not accumulate in body tissue, as was then known for other chlorinated hydrocarbons.[23]

Dow Chemical, meanwhile, had sent its lawyers to U.S. District Court in Arkansas—in the heart of the rice production belt where 2,4,5-T was then used heavily. There, Dow sought an injunction against EPA's ruling to continue the cancellation on rice. The court granted Dow's request and also required Ruckelshaus to issue a new ruling on the cancellation, which Ruckelshaus continued, declaring it was "abundantly clear" that Dow had not met the burden of proof to show 2,4,5-T was harmless. EPA then appealed the Arkansas ruling to the U.S. Court of Appeals in St. Louis.[24] But during the appeal, 2,4,5-T continued to be sold and used. Nearly two years later, in April 1973, the St. Louis Appeals Court sided with EPA, reversing and overturning the Arkansas decision that had allowed 2,4,5-T to be used on rice. Yet Dow's maneuver in the Arkansas courts had gained the company nearly two years of continued 2,4,5-T sales for rice.

EPA, however, still had its scheduled hearings on 2,4,5-T—on whether the herbicide should be banned for all uses. EPA staff had been preparing their materials and arguments. Dow was preparing too, and spared no resources or affiliations in its attempt to keep the herbicide on the market, as Environmental Defense Fund's (EDF) Bill Butler recounts:

> As the time for the hearing approached, EPA got more and more shaky as to what the evidence against 2,4,5-T was. The agency had only one lawyer on the case, and one, less than full-time staff scientist preparing the evidence. The outside interested parties such as the environmental groups, had formidable opposition. Dow had enormous scientific and financial resources at its disposal. Although we could consult with people like [Drs. Meselson, Robert Baughman, and Samuel Epstein] we had only one part-time scientist of our own to work on a very complicated issue. As we did our best to pursue the subject, Dow tried to bring as broad a coalition as possible against us, including the Department of Agriculture and the Department of Transportation. The agriculture people were solidly ranged against EPA. The Dow people wanted the Department of Transportation to testify about the importance of using 2,4,5-T to clear railroad and highway rights-of-way. Unfortunately for Dow, the Department of Transportation had a couple of people in the office of its general counsel who knew something about 2,4,5-T. These people had a study made of the experience of several state transportation agencies. The agencies who were questioned on the subject minimized the need for using 2,4,5-T to clear rights-of-way.
>
> ...Dow and the Department of Agriculture [about a month before the expected EPA hearings] put together what I can only call a sham conference on 2,4,5-T. It was supposed to bring together the biggest experts on 2,4,5-T and produce the definitive word on the subject. However, it turned out that the invited parties were mostly Dow employees and USDA folk, who proceeded to give as formal papers what in essence was their forthcoming testimony at the EPA hearings. We suspected that they were doing this so that if there were any conflicts in their proposed testimony these conflicts could be ironed out... In other words, it was a dry run to make everybody feel comfortable—a psychological ploy by Dow's attorneys, in my opinion.... [25]

Dow Shifts The Burden

Then in June 1974, EPA surprised environmental and other interests by calling off the long-planned 2,4,5-T public hearings. EPA also withdrew its cancellation order on the use of 2,4,5-T on rice. "EPA just got cold feet," said EDF's Butler at the time. "They were saying, in effect, that the agency would assume the burden of proving, through further research, that 2,4,5-T was harmful, rather than requiring Dow to show the herbicide was harmless." [26] This change, noticed first by lawyers and those involved closely with regulatory matters, was a key shift in the "burden-of-proof" battle that many thought had been established in government policy—with *manufacturers* bearing the responsibility to prove chemical safety. Shifting the burden to the *government*—requiring a finding of harm in order to remove a pesticide from the market, rather than requiring the *manufacturer* to prove the substance was safe—was a seminal shift in regulatory philosophy. Dow had won an important precedent not only for itself, but for the rest of the chemical industry, and one that went well beyond 2,4,5-T.

As for 2,4,5-T, Dow continued to maintain—without full, independent toxicological proof, using essentially its 1940s pesticide registration—that the herbicide was safe to use. Although the company acknowledged dioxin's toxicity, Dow scientists and salesman insisted dioxin's low levels in 2,4,5-T formulations was not a problem.

"So, in effect, we are playing Russian Roulette."

Sen. John Tunney, 1974

When 2,4,5-T was applied to vegetation, Dow claimed, the dioxin was broken down by sunlight and bacterial action. Dow also claimed 2,4,5-T did not leach out of soil and was nearly insoluble in water and therefore did not tend to be taken up in watercourses. And finally, when 2,4,5-T was sprayed, Dow said, the spraying itself helped to diffuse the chemical—and the dioxin—over such large areas that the risk to human health was infinitesimal and essentially not a practical concern. Many of these claims would later be challenged and disproved, but at the time, there was little effective challenge to Dow.

In 1974, Congress undertook another round of congressional hearings on the woes of 2,4,5-T. Still, the herbicide emerged under a use restriction rather than a total ban. "So in effect," said a frustrated Senator John Tunney (D-CA), witnessing government officials reluctant to ban a toxic herbicide, "we are playing Russian Roulette... We know it is harmful, and it is just very difficult at the moment to tell how harmful it is, and therefore we will just put our heads in the sand and pretend it doesn't exist."[27] 2,4,5-T continued to be used widely across the United States, sprayed on millions of acres. And Dow was its leading marketer.

Dow, in fact, had been selling the herbicide since the spring of 1948, the same year the company's scientists began early trials of combinations of 2,4-D and 2,4,5-T. Dow's Dr. Mullison had patented some of these new products, which were formulated in a way that made them somewhat less volatile and better plant penetrators. "The results look exceptionally promising," said Dow in one 1949 promotional piece. Dow later extolled the results of one test application of the new mixture along 742 miles of the Delaware, Lackawanna & Western Railroad in Pennsylvania, credited with killing 85 percent of the brush. "Chemical weed killing," concluded Dow, "is here to stay." Dow soon added a new formulation called silvex, a slower acting form of the herbicide, marketed under the *Kuron* tradename, that was targeted to tougher weed species, even oak-type vegetation.

Miscarriages in the Forest

In the 1960s and 1970s, Dow and other herbicide producers had pitched their new weed killers hard to farmers and ranchers,* state highway departments, railroads, utility companies, and the timber industry. The U.S. Forest Service, in fact, became an important Dow customer, buying the company's herbicides in bulk quantities. Forest Service lands were sprayed with Dow herbicides containing 2,4,5-T, 2,4-D, silvex, and other ingredients in Oregon, North Carolina, Arizona, and a number of other states. Between 1972 and 1978, for example, over 7,000 acres of Oregon coastal forests were sprayed with 2,4,5-T. But like Vietnam, anecdotal and medical reports started coming in during the 1970s about birth defects and miscarriages, some of the earliest from the Pacific Northwest. One such case was that of Patty Clary, who had moved with her husband to Days Creek, Oregon in 1974. She lived in an area sprayed frequently by timber-company helicopters using the herbicides as part of their forest management practice. Mists from the sprays would occasionally waft down on the land where they lived, or drain into streams. Once, Clary was sprayed by a passing helicopter. Still, she didn't think much about it at the time. Her husband, in fact, worked as part of a "hack and squirt" forestry crew, using some of the same herbicides, residues from which were sometimes still on his clothes. Then Patty Clary had two miscarriages and also some serious hemorrhaging over a three-month period that sent her to the hospital. "Here I was, 29 years old, perfectly regular my whole life, and suddenly I had a 'hormonal imbalance.' Five doctors could not tell me what happened."[28]

Patty Clary had two miscarriages and also some serious hemorrhaging over a three-month period that sent her to the hospital.

The coastal, forested Pacific Northwest is a well-watered environment, with lush growth and steep, irregular terrain. Helicopter spraying of timber company clear-cuts was being routinely used to wipe out weeds and keep new underbrush from taking hold before new Douglas Fir could be planted. But the runoff from those lands went right into streams, along with the sprayed chemicals. Drifting spray would also settle into streams and onto non-target lands—as it had near Allegany, Oregon in the 1970s. "The spraying goes on continually," explained Allegany resident Rose Anna Lee, describing her community to visiting *Environmental Action* editor Deborah Baldwin in late 1979. "Within one drainage system, maybe they'll hit the southeast unit one season, the northeast unit the next...I lived a quarter

---

*See Chapter 5 for a review of Dow's agricultural pesticide history.

mile downstream. My neighbors and I could smell the stuff. I could see it..."
Lee's young daughter, Angie, became ill. As her mother explained: "When
Angie first got sick she didn't feel that bad, but she was bruised all over. The
doctor did blood tests and put her in the hospital. They found 2,4,5-T and sil-
vex in her bloodstream. Angie was in the hospital for eight or nine months.
Her spleen was removed. She came

In 1979, EPA declared 2,4,5-T and *Silvex* to be imminent threats to human health.

close to spontaneous hemorrhaging." Angie was diagnosed with
something called ITP, idiopathic
thrombi-cytopenic purpurea, a rare
blood disorder that lowers the
platelet count and prevents proper blood clotting. "Idiopathic" means the
exact cause of the disease is not known, but some doctors at the time suspected it may be caused in part by exposure to toxic chemicals. "Angie was
only seven," continued her mother. "She was given massive doses of corti-
sone. She was in and out of a hospital in Seattle." But after Angie's platelet
levels climbed back up, they would drop again on her return home. A year
and half after the last hospital visit, Angie's mother, Rose Anna Lee, decided
it was time to move away from Allegany, Oregon. Others who remained
there would soon report massive crawfish kills in the river.[29]

In the Alsea, Oregon area, where 2,4,5-T spraying had gone on
between 1972 and 1978, a small group of women who had experienced miscarriages following spraying began keeping personal diaries detailing the
dates of spraying and their miscarriages. In the six-year period, nine women
had suffered 13 spontaneous abor-

"2,4,5-T is about as toxic as aspirin," said one Dow rep-resentative in a 1979 televi-sion broadcast.

tions. This data, anecdotal and
unscientific as it was, got EPA's
attention. It was first reported to the
agency in April 1978 by one of the
Oregon women. Follow-up investigations and others studies were
undertaken by EPA. By then, the
agency had also started a process that would de-register 2,4,5-T. That meant
it would be phased out unless a pressing need for it could otherwise be
shown. Dow Chemical dug in to fight the proposed de-registration, and continued working to undo the existing restrictions.[30]

In late February 1979, EPA declared 2,4,5-T and silvex to be imminent
threats to human health and issued an emergency ban, temporarily prohibiting the use of the herbicides on forests and rights-of-way. At a March 1st
news conference on the emergency ban, EPA Deputy Administrator Barbara
Blum noted that "dioxin, even at very low levels, causes severe reproductive
effects—miscarriages and birth defects—and tumors in laboratory animals..." Noting the new studies in the Alsea basin of Oregon, Blum
explained, "there is a statistically significant relationship between the spray

season and the high miscarriage peak," which followed the application of 2,4,5-T by two to three months. "It's a remarkable correlation," said Blum.[31] Yet even with the new emergency ban, other agricultural uses on 2 million acres of rice and rangeland were allowed to continue. Silvex was still permitted for use on apples, prunes, sugarcane, pears, fence rows, storage areas, and parking lots. Dow, meanwhile, maintained the product did not pose a health threat. "2,4,5-T is about as toxic as aspirin," said one Dow representative in a 1979 television broadcast of *Plague on Our Children*, a PBS documentary.[32] Dow Chemical, by this time, was preparing to sue EPA over the proposed ban.

Dow's president, David Rooke, noted at the time that Dow "believes in fighting." Explained Rooke: "We hung in on napalm when it didn't mean anything business-wise. The government asked us to make it and we did. We believed in the principle."[33] In its legal and regulatory deliberations, Dow

The Audubon Response

In the early 1970s, as spraying in the Pacific Northwest was proceeding, Carol Van Strum and others in her area sought the help of scientists, journalists, and national environmental organizations to aide their efforts and bring broader public attention to the use of herbicides. One of the groups they wrote to was the National Audubon Society and its magazine, *Audubon*. Van Strum explains:

…Hoping to add other voices to our own, we wrote to environmental groups and publications. Only one responded—indirectly. *Audubon* magazine had referred our letter to the Dow Chemical Company. Dow sent a thick package of company literature, including an elegant brochure on phenoxy herbicides. The brochure was illustrated lavishly with color nature photographs by Eugene Kenega, an assistant scientist for Dow who was also president of the Michigan Audubon Society.

The cover letter, explaining that Audubon had referred our letter to Dow for reply, was signed by Dr. Kenaga. He praised us for our concern and repeated what he had already heard from USDA. The herbicides were safe. No harm could result if the EPA label instructions were followed.…

Source: Carol Van Strum, *A Bitter Fog: Herbicides and Human Rights*, p. 9.

would take a methodical, strictly corporate and legal course in attacking EPA's actions, going after its methodology and weak studies, while attacking uncertain science and the credibility of witnesses. Anticipating Dow's line of defense and attack, Deborah Baldwin, editor of *Environmental Action*, observed at the time:

…Dow will also argue that the levels of dioxin in current batches of 2,4,5-T are so minute as to be inconsequential and that, in any event, the toxic contaminant breaks down in soil and "disappears" from the environment. Exposure to dioxin, the company will say, can pose only short term hazards, since the body "excretes" the chemical. The unusually

Shoecraft v. Dow

In the 1960s, Billie Shoecraft was a housewife and mother in her forties living with her husband and family in the canyon lands of the Tonto National Forest near Globe, Arizona. A spunky 5-foot-4, weighing 100 pounds or so, Shoecraft wore her hair in a bouffant flip and was a bit eccentric in her ways. In fact, some people around Globe called her just plain crazy. But Billie Shoecraft loved the canyon lands and the Arizona environment—she adopted them as home after going there from Indiana in 1948. But Shoecraft was no Barbie doll; she could ride a horse, handle a rifle, and helped build her own house. Nor was she an activist or environmentalist, though she loved nature and animals. On women's rights, she was characterized as "closer to Phyllis Schlafly than to Betty Frieden." But in the 1960s, Shoecraft embarked on a new career. Accidentally doused with a herbicide spray in June 1969, Shoecraft—then perfectly healthy—became ill and died from cancer at the age of 53. She attributed her illness to the continuing spraying of herbicides in the area, and while alive, fought furiously to stop it. For more than a decade, she and her neighbors took on the U.S. Forest Service and the herbicide establishment, ultimately bringing a lawsuit against Dow Chemical and others for their respective roles in the spraying.

Shoecraft had always been suspicious of the spraying in the national forest near her home. She was not alone. Other neighbors in the rural area also had experiences with the spraying, some reporting dead birds, sick domestic animals, damaged plants, and incidents of their homes and family members being sprayed. In fact, from 1965 to 1969, the U.S. Forest Service sprayed thousands of acres in the Pinal Mountains area of the Tonto National Forest with various mixtures of 2,4-D, 2,4,5-T, and 2,4,5-TP or Silvex. A large portion of the product was supplied by Dow Chemical. In 1966, Shoecraft once asked a local Forest Service ranger about a dying pine tree near her land, unaware at the time it had been sprayed. She was told it had a "mysterious disease." But it was the June 8, 1969 spraying in the Pinal Mountains area that pushed Shoecraft and her neighbors into an activist mode. Roused in the early morning hours of Sunday June 8 by the sound of a helicopter approaching her home, Shoecraft rose from her bed and went outside in her nightgown to have a closer look. Minutes later, when the copter flew over her house, she was sprinkled with something wet. She then phoned the local ranger's office for information, and not getting much help, decided to jump in her car and try to flag down the pilot. At one point, the pilot did pass over and hover near Shoecraft, who by then was out of her car and waving at him from the ground. There, Shoecraft was accidentally drenched again by the pilot, who blamed the release on a defective spray nozzle. After that incident, the pilot departed for repairs to his helicopter base. Later that day, however, the helicopter spraying continued, with several other residents in the area also reporting being sprayed.

By July 1969, Shoecraft and her neighbors started to press the Forest Service on the spraying program, calling for among other things, an analysis of all the hazards to plant and animal life. One Forest Service agent dismissed their reports of plant and animal damage as "a bunch of malarkey." The spraying, which helped clear watersheds of water-clogging vegetation, was also supported by the giant Salt River Valley Water Users Association. Local ranchers supported it too, since it made more pasture. But some angry residents said they would shoot down aircraft flying over their property. Shoecraft and her neighbors had their land and plants tested and levels of 2,4,5-T and silvex were found. They soon began compiling documents, talking to the press and petitioning their congressmen and senators. More than 90 residents had come together to claim damage to their health, property, and animals. Shoecraft and her allies were not always well regarded by their neighbors, thought of as "on the fringe" or "crazies"—and they used protest-theater tactics on occasion, such as a mock funeral at the Forest Service office—that rubbed some locals the wrong way. Still, newspaper stories and radio shows began covering the issue. By mid-July 1969, Dow Chemical had a man go to the scene to assess the public relations situation. He pegged Shoecraft as the key player.

Shoecraft, meanwhile, had broken out with a blistery rash after the 1969 spraying incidents, and she'd been to local hospitals twice—once for difficulty breathing and swallowing, and another time for chest pains and pains in her extremities. Tests found nothing out of the ordinary. Shoecraft had some emotional strains, and some stress in her marriage at the time, but she was otherwise a very healthy person with no history of illnesses or health problems. But Shoecraft began piecing together past incidents of problems in her family—with herself, her children, family pets, and local plants and animals—correlating those with previous spraying dates. Some of her neighbors had done the same, finding what they believed was something more than coincidence. Shoecraft and friends upped their activism, and they continued to get notice, not all of which was flattering. Billie Shoecraft had samples of her fatty tissue tested in February 1970 and learned she was carrying all kinds of chemicals—DDT, lindane, endrin, and chlordane, among others. Silvex was also in her tissue at 35 ppm, and 2,4-D at 2.5 ppm.

In the spring of 1970, Shoecraft and 20 others in Globe, Arizona filed suit against Dow and three other chemical companies that made the herbicides sprayed in the area, as well as the helicopter company that did the spraying, the state agency that helped finance them, and separately, the federal government's U.S. Forest Service program. She also wrote a book on the spraying, called *Sue The Bastards*, which was published in Phoenix in 1971. Shoecraft's activism grew beyond Globe, and she was soon speaking to other activists. But by then, Shoecraft's health was deteriorating, according to records of her California doctor—she didn't trust the doctors in Globe. By 1971, Shoecraft was greatly fatigued, and taken to spending time in a cabin apart from her homeplace, which she believed contaminated and the source of her woes. By 1972, she was continuing to loose hair, had numbness on one side of her body, and extended periods of menstrual bleeding. Similar effects were reported through 1974. But during the legal proceedings with Dow and others, Shoecraft persisted despite her failing health, answering lawyers' questions in at least seven depositions between the fall of 1970 and the summer of 1974.

By the fall of 1974, the court case against the companies had been transferred out of state court into federal district court. A case against the federal government remained on a separate track. Over time, most of the chemical companies and the helicopter company had settled out of court. Dow, however, remained. Dow, for its part, hired Dr. Charles Hine, a San Francisco toxicologist who had served as a pesticide consultant to industry and had done some of the original research on DBCP. Dow hired Hine to perform a medical examination on Shoecraft. She had to fly to San Francisco for the session, which did not go well. She resisted some of the testing, having a pap smear done by another San Francisco lab rather than Hine. But Hine did get a blood sample from her, which was sent to Dow's lab in Midland for analysis. That analysis took more than year to complete, with no traces of herbicide or dioxin detected.

Through 1975, Shoecraft's health went into further decline, with continuing weight loss, depression, fatigue, menstrual bleeding, and difficulty swallowing. By then she was wearing adult diapers for incontinence. In early 1976, a Phoenix urologist found some nodules in her breasts and armpit. X-rays from another doctor showed collapsing vertebrae. By now, Shoecraft, with help from her family, was traveling to Tijuana for *Laetrile* to ease her pain. In July 1976, exploratory surgery by a family doctor found tumors throughout her abdomen, her liver, and her pelvis. "She's just full of it," her doctor was reported to have said, with no way to operate. Biopsies later showed the cancer in her ovaries. A sample of fatty tissue taken from Shoecraft and sent to GHT Laboratories in California also found traces of 2,4-D, 2,4,5- T and silvex . To be close to the *Laetrile,* Shoecraft and her husband Willard took up residence in San Diego for a time, then went back to Globe, where another Dow attorney visited for more fact-finding discovery. Right before Christmas 1976, the Shoecrafts went to Salem, Oregon for a doctor who could administer *Laetrile*. By December 28, Shoecraft was admitted to Salem Memorial Hospital where on January 6, 1977, she died. Cause of death was listed as malignant tumor in the ovaries and carcinomatosis—the spread of cancerous tumors throughout the body.

The litigation that Shoecraft and her neighbors had initiated seven years earlier, had proceeded. Some new attorneys had been added, and after a time, they assembled a prospective lineup of scientists to testify to help their case. Scheduled for a jury trial in October 1980, the case was later postponed until March 1981. Still, the Shoecraft lawyers felt they had a good case. Twenty-one formerly healthy people had been exposed to a herbicide containing dioxin. Dow had not done the long-term effects studies on Silvex. Dioxin was a known contaminate of 2,4,5-T, but Dow continued to claim 2,4,5-T was absolutely non-toxic to humans or animals. Dioxin was found in the herbicides sprayed in Globe at levels of least 0.15 ppm. Dow's warning label on the Silvex sprayed in Globe did not warn the Forest Service about the danger of spraying it in populated areas. The Shoecraft plaintiffs were suing for wrongful death, physical injuries, fear of cancer, and fear of birth defects. Dow's attorney, for their part, were planning to defend the company's products by playing up their importance to agriculture and minimizing the effects of dioxin exposures. They would admit that both 2,4,5-T and silvex contained trace amounts of dioxin, and like any other compound, from aspirin to zinc, in sufficient quantities it could produce adverse health effects. The compounds were well studied, the amounts of contaminant tiny, and that no more than minor health hazards—covered by the product labels—were likely involved. As the trial date approached, both sides readied their final documents. Jerry Sullivan, one of the Shoecraft lawyers, said "no one is ever gonna have a better chance against Dow than you people." Just as jury selection process began, however, Dow made a settlement offer. The Shoecraft litigants rejected it, and jury selection proceeded. But then, just as the judge was about to call for the trial to begin, Dow's attorney telephoned him with another settlement offer—this time with a bigger pot of money, more, in fact, than the plaintiffs had asked for. Although there was some disagreement, and those who felt the case should continue on principle, the Shoecraft litigants settled and the case did not go to trial. There was no admission of guilt or wrongful activity on Dow's part; no formal legal findings. Jerry Sullivan, one of the Shoecraft attorneys, wanted the trial. "We get doctors to testify. We get epidemiologists to testify. I had people calling me to testify. And they settle... You throw some money at people and they cave.... And Dow started throwing money at them. We would have had a jury finding of proximate cause, I know that. We would have had a finding that dioxin causes cancer..." But even Sullivan, in the end, did not blame the plaintiffs for settling. Some had been through a grueling decade-long struggle; and a few of them were now in bad personal health and just wanted it all to be over with. Still, Billie Shoecraft, some observed, would not have settled.

Sources: Adapted from Cathy Trost, *Elements of Risk*, pp. 95–195, and Carol Van Strum, *A Bitter Fog*, pp. 35–46.

high level of miscarriages and birth defects... will be cited as an irrelevant, if troubling, coincidence. Timber companies such as Weyerhaeuser will protest the suspension... as an intolerable restraint on reforestation efforts and as an economic impediment that will cost the Northwest jobs. Dow will say the burden of proof in such controversies lies with EPA; government lawyers will say just the opposite...

Conclusive proof that 2,4,5-T causes birth defects, miscarriages and a host of related health problems can never be shown in court, and that's something Dow is banking on. At best, EPA can put forward laboratory experiments on monkeys and rats and a troubling if inconclusive array of "anecdotal evidence"....[34]

By April 1981, EPA had backed off its attempt to ban 2,4,5-T, and began negotiating a settlement with Dow on more restrictive labeling requirements.[35] Dow would continue to sell the herbicide under selected restrictions. Gradually, however, the scientific record built against 2,4,5-T to the point where Dow finally quit making it in the United States in 1983. But the company had spent at least $10 million defending its prized herbicide, keeping it on the market, at least in some form, for more than a decade after its first challenges. In fact, since 1969 when the very first restrictions were suggested for 2,4,5-T, Dow was determined to fight. As Dow biographer Brandt

"Chemical McCarthyism"

In April 1979, a PBS documentary produced by San Francisco television station KRON entitled the *Politics of Poison* began airing in California and around the country. The film focused on several small, Northern California timber towns that had received herbicide spraying, the residents of which had reported various health problems, including miscarriage and birth deformity rates in the 40- to 60-percent range. The film included interviews with officials from EPA and Dow Chemical—which the documentary reported had spent millions fighting government pesticide regulations. In the film, Dow's spokesman, Cleve Goring, called the campaign against 2,4,5-T "chemical McCarthyism." He defended Dow's use of the chemical. Calling 2,4,5-T "a very important symbol," Goring said if Dow were to lose on this issue, "it would mean that the American public has been really taken back a couple of hundred years to an era of witch-hunting, only this time the witches are chemicals, not people." But *San Francisco Examiner* columnist Bill Mandel, had a different take on the film, noting among other points, that commercial interests were "spraying populated areas with herbicides considered too deadly for use as chemical weapons." More than 40,000 letters from the film's viewers were generated in California. The film was also shown in Washington during Congressional hearings. In June 1979, two weeks after the film was aired, Mendocino County voted overwhelmingly to ban aerial spraying of phenoxy herbicides such as 2,4,5-T and 2,4,-D.

Source: Lewis Regenstein, *America The Poisoned*, 1982, p. 25.

put it: Dow "stubbornly attempted to defend the product, contending that 30 years of science had shown 2,4,5-T to be a safe and useful product. . . . " Dow claimed it had greatly improved its manufacturing process for 2,4,5-T, and that its dioxin content was negligible.

Some years later, Dow CEO Paul Oreffice would say of the company's ten-year 2,4,5-T battle: "If we let them ban a product that has 30 years of studies behind it that says it's safe, what happens to the next product, and the next product, and the next? How many products would have been banned with no good reason if we hadn't fought for 2,4,5-T. . . ?"[36] In October 1983, Dow closed its U.S. 2,4,5-T plant. Several years later, in August 1987, Dow announced in New Zealand it would close what was then believed to be the last 2,4,5-T production factory on the planet. Yet the decade of fighting over 2,4,5-T's safety and use as a domestic product was only the opening salvo.

Vietnam Veterans Sue

Following the Vietnam War, returning American veterans began reporting illnesses of mysterious origin, and began to point to Agent Orange as the suspected culprit. By 1977 or so, Vietnam vets began filing medical disability claims at the U. S. Veterans Administration (VA). They filed for a long list of problems, including skin rashes, nervous disorders, dizziness, chronic coughing, impotence, liver and kidney disease, loss of sex drive, cancer, and birth defects in offspring. In most cases, the VA refused to acknowledge any of the illnesses were connected to Agent Orange. In June 1979, calling the government's failure to adequately investigate Agent Orange and its

Some 9,000 vets filed lawsuits against Dow and other Agent Orange producers, seeking $44 billion in damages.

effects on Vietnam vets "a national disgrace," Congressman Bob Echardt (D-TX) held hearings that produced some dramatic witnesses. One of those testifying was Michael Ryan, a Long Island, NY policeman who had been exposed to Agent Orange in Vietnam and had suffered extreme weight loss and other illnesses. Accompanying Ryan that day were his wife and daughter Kerry—a daughter conceived after Ryan had returned from Vietnam, and who was born with severe deformities. Neither Ryan nor his wife had any family history of birth defects. "... Kerry, a frail child with short brown hair, sat in her wheelchair gazing wide-eyed at the television cameras, the Congressman high on the wood-paneled dais, and the roomful of lobbyists and reporters," wrote Margot Hornblower for the *Washington Post*. "... Kerry was born eight years ago with 18 birth defects: missing bones, twisted limbs, a hole in her heart, deformed intestines, a partial spine, shrunken fingers, no rectum... "[37] Michael and Maureen Ryan would later write, in a 1982 book entitled *Kerry: Agent Orange and an American Family:* "Some of these executives from the chemical companies belong in jail. We have veterans and children who have spent years trying to cope with catastrophic disabilities without help. Now that we know who is responsible, we want help for the veterans and we want the people who sold them out to go to prison for it. They're criminals. They knew."

By 1982 there were more than 12,000 vets who had filed Agent Orange-related claims at the VA, some 852 of which were allowed—but only for other causes, not Agent Orange. Soon there were lawsuits brought by the veterans aimed at both the government and the chemical manufacturers. Some 9,000 vets filed lawsuits against Dow and other Agent Orange producers, seeking $44 billion in damages. The cases were eventually consolidated, and at the time became the largest product liability case in U.S. history, and one of the first mass tort class-action cases. The veterans' case raged in argument for months in the Brooklyn, New York, U.S. District courtroom of Judge Jack Weinstein. It was finally brought to a settlement in 1984. The settlement established a $184 million compensation fund for the vets, funded by the seven major producers of Agent Orange—Dow, Uniroyal, Monsanto, Hercules, Agricultural Nutrition, Diamond Shamrock, and Thompson Chemical. The payments were to be distributed to the vets and their families over ten years. Disabled vets received from $256 to $12,800, and families of deceased vets from $340 to $3,400. Eventually, about 39,000 vets received money from the fund, with an additional 28,000 claims denied. By January 1995, more than $160 million had been paid out, with some $21 million still remaining in the fund.[38]

In 1996, studies by the National Institute of Medicine found that exposure to Agent Orange might be linked to higher rate of spina bifida in veterans' children.

However, a number of veterans and those following the case felt the 1984 settlement was a bad deal, and that vets really didn't get their due. The judge played a key role in pushing both sides to a settlement, which excluded all future claims. Nevertheless, in 1989, the widow of a Vietnam veteran filed a second class-action lawsuit on behalf of other veterans. That case was filed in Texas state court. However, the chemical companies requested that the federal courts transfer the case back to its last jurisdiction in New York, under Judge Weinstein, who had presided in the last case, and had ruled, in the view of many, in industry's favor. The widow's attorney argued the chemical companies really had no legal ground for sending the new case back to the former judge, and that his client was being denied the right to an impartial decision-maker. But the case went back to Weinstein, and in April 1992, as the chemical companies had hoped, he dismissed it. The widow then appealed Weinstein's dismissal.[39]

Congress, meanwhile, had passed the Agent Orange Act of 1991. Among other things, that law called on the National Academy of Sciences to review new Agent Orange and herbicide studies every two years to determine whether fresh research shed any new light on additional diseases. The latency period of some cancers can be 20 to 30 years. In March 1996, a second evaluation of studies by the National Institute of Medicine, found that exposure to Agent Orange might be linked to higher rate of spina bifida in veterans' children. The report also found a possible new association between Agent Orange and a nerve disorder known as transient peripheral neuropathy, that can result in temporary numbness, pain, and weakness in the arms and legs. In earlier studies, the institute found sufficient evidence to strongly link Agent Orange exposure to chemical acne and three types of cancer—non-Hodgkin's lymphoma, Hodgkin's disease, and soft-tissue sarcoma.[40]

Back in court, veterans who had developed diseases since the 1984 settlement and were being denied compensation, had filed lawsuits. One was Daniel Stephenson, who discovered in 1998 that he had a deadly form of cancer. Another was Joe Isaacson of New Jersey. By the time Stephenson and Isaacson developed their diseases, however, the money from the 1984

Herbicidal Horrors Remain

In a tiny office at the Hue Medical College in Vietnam, Dr. Viet Nahn has some photocopies of U.S. Air Force maps sent to him by a U.S. veterans' organization. The maps show the number of herbicide spraying missions carried out over the Central Highlands region of Vietnam during the war—in particular, those in the province of Quang Tri, a province adjacent to the former DMZ, or Demilitarized Zone, a priority defoliation target. Dr. Nhan says it is this area where almost all his patients come from—places with names Americans may recognize, such as Khe Sanh, Hamburger Hill, Camp Carroll and the Rock Pile. At least 741,143 gallons of herbicidal chemicals were dropped in the central highlands area where Dr. Nahn is working, more than 600,000 gallons of which were Agent Orange. His office and its 21 volunteers try to do what they can for Vietnamese children afflicted with various diseases and heath problems believed to be rooted in Agent Orange. Dr. Nhan, studying the impact of Agent Orange as a medical student, found numerous afflicted Vietnamese families when he went out to the villages. He soon established his small office and began performing operations on afflicted children—operations for hernias and cleft palates, open-heart surgery, and kidney transplants. The Vietnamese Red Cross estimates that one million Vietnamese have been disabled by Agent Orange.

Cathy Scott-Clark and Adrian Levy, reporters for London's *Guardian* newspaper, visited Vietnam in 2003 and found some of those victims. Some were adults, some were teenagers, some were young children—even grandchildren. All were connected somehow to the herbicide spraying. The reporters saw adults suffering from skin lesions and goiters; children with various birth defects, including large heads, enlarged, bubble eyes, altered limbs, and others with severe depression or no control over themselves. They were also told of women who spontaneously abort or give birth to genderless babies "that horrify even the most experienced midwives." According to former vice-president of Vietnam, Madame Nguyen Thi Binh, returning veterans in Vietnam were eager to have children and build families to repopulate their devastated country. However, many of the first-born children in these families had birth defects, so the veterans tried again and again. As a result, according to Madame Binh, there are a number of Vietnamese families that now have four or five disabled children.

In 2003, Ngo Luc turned 67 years old. He is former captain and sole survivor of his unit, which served in the Vietnam War as a North Vietnamese guerrilla unit. Today he lives with his two granddaughters, both born partially paralyzed, near the Vietnamese city of Hue in the country's Central Highlands. It was in that region during the war that Ngo Luc remembers the planes that circled overhead one day: "We expected bombs," he says, recounting one incident to the *Guardian*, "but a fine yellow mist descended, covering absolutely everything." Mr. Luc remembers being "soaked" in the spray, "but it didn't worry us, as it smelled good. We continued to crawl through the jungle." The next day, he remembers, "the leaves wilted and within a week the jungle was bald." Mr. Luc and his men "felt just fine at the time." But years later that would change not only for Mr. Luc's family, but for hundreds of thousands of Vietnamese—ex-soldiers, farmers, and their offspring.

"Cancer, miscarriages, and birth defects in the sprayed areas are always higher than in the areas not sprayed," said Tran Manh Hung of the special committee on Agent Orange in Vietnam's Ministry of Health. "It might take another 50 years before those rates become equal." Vietnamese scientists, recently working with Hatfield Consultants, a team of Canadian environmental scientists, suspect their country may be contaminated with herbicidal residue for years, with a number of severe hot spots. In the Aluoi Valley, for example, an area adjacent to the Ho Chi Minh trail, and once home to three U.S. Special Forces bases where Agent Orange was both stored and sprayed, the scientists' analysis has shown that, rather than naturally disperse, dioxin has remained in the ground in concentrations 100 times the Canadian safety levels for agricultural land. It has also spread into the area's ponds, rivers, and irrigation systems, and into the food chain through fish, shellfish, chicken, and ducks that store dioxin in fatty tissue. Samples of human blood and breast milk in the area reveal that villagers have ingested dioxin, and that pregnant women pass it through the placenta to the fetus, and through breast feeding, to newborn babies. More than 15,000 children and adults from this region have been registered as suffering from an array of chronic health problems. "We theorize that the Aluoi Valley is a microcosm of the country, where numerous reservoirs of TCCD still exist in the soil of former U.S. military installations," says Dr. Wayne Dwernychuk, vice president of Hatfield Consultants. There may be as many as 50 of these "hot spots" throughout the country. Some, such as the former U.S. military base of Bien Hoa, also had spills—including one 7,500-gallon Agent Orange spill which occurred on March 1, 1970. In addition, former Ranch Hand pilots allege that there were also some 26,000 aborted spraying operations during the war in which some 260,000 gallons of herbicide were simply dumped on the countryside. One former pilot based at Bien Hoa during 1968–69, claims he regularly jettisoned his chemical into the Long Binh reservoir. Military regulations required spray planes and helicopters to return to base empty.

Source: Cathy Scott-Clark and Adrian Levy, "Spectre Orange," *The Guardian*, March 29, 2003.

settlement had all been paid out. In fact, by 1997, all the settlement money was gone, leaving veterans such as Stephenson, Isaacson, and others without any compensation. And their claims had been denied by lower courts. In early 2003, however, these cases were brought for review before the U.S. Supreme Court. In a rare 4–4 tie, the Court's action resulted in allowing veterans who missed the original settlement to sue. "A lot of veterans have been waiting ten years to hear this," said Gerson Smoger, Oakland, California attorney representing the two veterans. Smoger and his plaintiffs had been working to show that the Agent Orange class-action settlement was inadequate since it was not helping the injured Vietnam veterans. "Their rights are vindicated," he said, of his clients' opportunity to now seek compensation. However, Dow and a number of industrial colleagues, including insurance companies and trade groups such as the Product Liability Advisory Council, had filed friend-of-the court briefs in the case, and did not want any reopening of class-action settlements or further litigation. Dow's New York attorney, Andrew Frey, expressing frustration with the Court's tie vote, predicted the issue would eventually be brought before the high court again.[41]

To this day, researchers continue to find links between Agent Orange and various illnesses in Vietnam veterans. In January 2003, for example, it was reported that researchers at the Institute of Medicine, after reexamining past research on cancer rates in agricultural workers and residents of farm communities, had found a link between a type of leukemia and Vietnam soldiers exposed to herbicides such as Agent Orange. That finding prompted the U.S. Veterans Administration (VA) to extend benefits to Vietnam veterans with the illness. Veterans diagnosed with chronic lymphocytic leukemia, would start receiving improved benefits from the VA within a year, the agency said, which expects to find about 500 new cases a year among Vietnam vets. The VA reported at that time that 10,000 Vietnam veterans were receiving disability pay for illnesses related to exposure to Agent Orange and other herbicides used during the Vietnam War.[42]

Worse Than Thought

Further study of U.S. military data on herbicide spraying in Vietnam has also turned up new information. In fact, the amount sprayed, the area sprayed, and toxicity of the sprays involved all appear to have been greater than previously reported. A study team at Columbia University led by Jeanne Mager Stellman undertook a historical reconstruction of the herbicide spraying using earlier National Academy of Sciences reports based on a U.S. military record of flight paths and sprayings known as the Herbicide Report System. The Columbia team's findings, published in *Nature* in April 2003, reveal that far more herbicides were used during the early years of the war than had been previously reported—including more dioxin-rich herbicides such as Agents Purple and Pink. In fact, the Columbia team found that more than 9.4 million liters of sprayed herbicide had not been previously counted, and some 200 missions flown during the war prior to 1965 were also missed. Those missions alone reveal that about 1.9 million previously unaccounted for liters of Agent Purple were sprayed between 1962 and 1965. And Agent Purple, according to the researchers, was likely to have had a dioxin content of as much as 45 parts per million (ppm). Agent Orange, in contrast, is thought to have contained 13 ppm dioxin, revised upward from an earlier estimate of 3 ppm. Others say such numbers can be misleading, as dioxin content in the sprays varied widely, and could have been much higher than the 13 ppm estimated for Agent Orange. Still, the Columbia recalculations indicate that the amount of dioxin sprayed was almost double that of previous estimates. And on the ground in Vietnam, the data reconstruction also revealed more detail—that some 20,585 towns were within the spraying regions and that as many as 4.8 million people could have been present in these towns when the herbicides were sprayed.[43]

So today, the Vietnam "war" is still being waged. The military hostilities are long gone, of course, but some "battles" still rage daily and hourly. These battles are fought quietly, individually—mostly in the blood and body tissue of too many living things—in Vietnam, America, and other far-flung places seemingly unconnected to the war. Yet they are connected—as are the Vietnamese citizens and America's Vietnam veterans, who have more in common with one another than not. In fact, these former enemies are now on the same side. They are allies in league against a common enemy: the left-behind toxic timebombs ticking inside them and their families—and in the environment too. For whether in Vietnam's highlands, Michigan lakes and rivers, or New Zealand's cattle, the enemy is the same—the toxic 2,4,5-T and 2,4-D residues of the Agent Orange spraying and production frenzy. No one knows for sure how much or how widespread this left-over toxic chemistry is—as some of it still shows up occasionally in global commerce, not to mention continued legal uses of the herbicides in many places. But the health effects and human toll are becoming increasingly clear. Dow Chemical, of course, isn't the only source. But from Michigan to Vietnam, there is one continuing common thread and chemical marker that keeps pointing back to Dow—a poison called dioxin.

More herbicides were used during the early years of the war than had been previously reported—including more dioxin-rich herbicides such as Agents Purple and Pink.

4.
Dioxin in the Dark

[I]f you feed a guinea pig one-billionth of its weight with dioxin, this will kill the guinea pig. One part per billion.

Dr. Matthew Meselson, Harvard University, 1979

In the 1980s, dioxin—an obscure substance that most people had never heard of—began to emerge as the toxicological time bomb of the synthetic chemical revolution. Yet dioxin was, and still is, a difficult piece of chemistry to understand, aiding both its politics and its longevity. For dioxin is not a store-bought commodity or a packaged good; you can't buy "a dioxin" off the shelf. Along with its chemical associates—a cadre of dioxin-like elements that form throughout the modern industrial world, especially around chlorine*—a kind of "neutron bomb effect" has been insinuating itself throughout the biological world. Property remains intact, but soft tissue and DNA—in frogs and people—are in some jeopardy. For dioxin and its chemical associates are among the most toxic substances known to science. These chemistries can do nasty things to biology at very, very low levels. But learning this has been a difficult labor for the modern world, resisted in fact, by the

---

*Dioxin is not manufactured or used as a product. Rather, it is an unwanted by-product of a variety of industrial processes that involve chlorine in some form, as in the production of some pesticides and plastics. Dioxin is also formed when materials that contain both carbon and chlorine are burned, as in the inceineration and open burning of household waste that contains some plastics and other chlorine sources. "Dioxin" singular, is the term used initially, years ago, when scientists principally referred to one form of dioxin—2,3,7,8-tetrachlorodibenzo-p-dioxin, or TCDD, dioxin's most potent form. But dioxin today means dioxins plural, since there are many dioxins. In fact, there are 75 forms of dioxin; that is, 75 polychlorinated dibenzo-p-dioxins. There are also 135 polychlorinated dibenzofurans (PCDFs) that are members of the "dioxin family." In addition, there are other dioxin-like chemicals, including: some of the 209 polychlorinated biphenyls or PCBs; polychlorinated diphenyl ethers; and polychlorinated naphthalenes. Beyond these, there are brominated analogues of all of these substances. All of these groups have many members that may have dioxin-like toxicity, but 7 dioxins, 10 furans, and 11 PCBs are known to have dioxin-like toxicity in humans, all determined by how successfully these chemicals "fit"or "bind" to certain receptors in cell tissue.

commercial apparatus that has built multi-billion dollar empires upon the very chemicals that generate the poisons. Dow Chemical is part of that story; a company whose chemical choices place it at the very beginnings of the dioxin headwaters.

Prior to the 1970s, most people hadn't heard much about dioxin—and only a very limited circle of scientists had any idea of how toxic and dangerous it was. Barry Commoner, a scientist at Washington University in St. Louis, had raised the specter of dioxin in the early 1970s. "Synthetic chemicals, specifically chlorinated organic compounds," he said in one interview at the New York offices of *Modern Plastics* magazine, "are responsible for the appearance of dioxins in the environment." Yet few people were on Commoner's level. In 1976, an industrial accident at Seveso, Italy had spewed dioxin into the local environment, and a year or two later, there were reports in the press about its effects. But Seveso, in the public mind, was associated more with chemical plant safety than it was dioxin. Love Canal too—the New York community discovered in 1976 that it was built over a toxic waste dump contaminated with dioxin and evacuated because of the dangers—was more associated with toxic waste than dioxin per se. A few journalists, namely Thomas Whitesides of *The New Yorker* magazine, were also writing about dioxin in the 1970s, though little noticed by most Americans. Dioxin had yet to hit mainstream America. However that began to change in the 1980s for two reasons. First, Agent Orange litigation began in the courts. And second, discoveries of dioxin contamination at Times Beach, Missouri, soon led to major media coverage. At Times Beach, the contaminant was first found in a used-oil concoction that had been sprayed on roads as a dust suppressant, which was then spread throughout the entire town by a 1982 flood. The EPA-ordered evacuation that followed received a lot of attention and *Nightly News*-type TV coverage. Still, even with this, most people thought of dioxin as an end-of-the-pipe problem or a toxic waste issue. But dioxin was much more than that. It was woven into major parts of the economy, and was being slowly released in persistent form from thousands of locations, permeating air, water, food, blood, body fat, breast milk, placenta, and DNA.

As scientists began looking, dioxin started showing up everywhere, from the wastes and "by-products" of chemical manufacturing and pulp- and paper-making, to municipal incinerators burning trashed *Saran Wrap*, old bathtub Donald Ducks, and things generally made with plastics like polyvinyl chloride. Still, the general public impression was that even the scientists dealing with dioxin didn't know much about it, and that industry and government were just starting to understand it. But the fact was, the chemical industry, including Dow Chemical, had by that time, more than 20 years' experience with dioxin, had considerable files on it, and knew it was a bad actor long before the public really understood how dangerous it was. Whenever dioxin did come into public view, Dow and other companies stood by a fairly standard line. "There is absolutely no evidence of dioxin doing any damage to humans except for causing something that is called chloracne," said Dow CEO Paul Oreffice in a March 1983 *Today Show* appearance. "It's a rash," he said. Dow's chairman Robert Lundeen, about a month later on CBS' *Morning News* show in April 1983, was even more emphatic. "We stand on 30 years of producing and using the material, and either in our plants or in the people used [making it], there is no indication that there were any adverse health effects," he said.[1] Yet, even as Oreffice and Lundeen made their remarks in early 1983, there was a swirling controversy engulfing them in Washington and Michigan about just what Dow officials knew and when they knew it. By May 1983, the dioxin story broke more dramatically at the national level—with Dow Chemical at the center.

Trail of Trouble

In 1983, during the Vietnam veterans' Agent Orange litigation, some previously confidential chemical industry memos and other documents on dioxin—and the role of several chemical companies including Dow—began to surface publicly. *Chemical Week* and the *New York Times,* in particular, appear to have been among the first to present the new findings.[2] Coupled with earlier overlooked historical information, a revised picture of just what Dow and the chem-

Dow, it turned out, had known about the extreme toxicity of dioxin since at least the mid-1960s.

ical industry knew about dioxin began to take form. Dow, it turned out, had known about the extreme toxicity of dioxin since at least the mid-1960s, and appears to have been aware of other health effects in related chemicals in earlier products, some dating to the 1930s.

In 1933–34, Dow introduced a line of chlorophenol wood preservatives called *Dowicides*. The company had barely begun making the new product when reports of severe chloracne began reaching the medical literature. One case in 1936 reportedly involved 300 to 400 Mississippi lumber workers stricken with ulceration, severe pimpling and/or thickening of the skin, urinary disturbances or leg cramps.[3] Back home in Midland in 1937, Dow also had an outbreak of chloracne among its workers—an incident involving 21 men who worked sacking chlorophenol products containing 2-(2-chlorophenyl) phenol and tetrachlorophenol. Marked skin rashes with an enormous number of blackheads appeared among the workers—"some cases so numerous as to produce a black discoloration," reported Dr. Milton G. Butler in a 1937 published paper. Butler, a medical consultant for Dow, stated that the chemicals should not be used as biocides until the mechanisms causing chloracne were understood. Dow's plant was temporarily closed. Fifteen months after the workers had been removed from the plant, none had completely recovered. A number of the men had lost weight and complained of being easily fatigued. Butler sought to conduct further experiments with animals to gain a better understanding of the toxicity, but Dow refused his requests.[4]

In the 1940s, other cases surfaced, including reports following a 1949 industrial accident involving 228 workers at a Monsanto Company plant at Nitro, West Virginia then producing 2,4,5-T. Chloracne was again the major symptom in the exposed workers. However, other reported symptoms also included, "severe pains in skeletal muscles, shortness of breath, intolerance to cold, palpable and tender liver, loss of sensation in the extremities, demyelination of peripheral nerves, fatigue, nervousness, irritability, insomnia, loss of libido, and vertigo."[5]

In 1955, a German chemical company, Boehringer, sought information about chloracne from another company, the Givaudan Corporation, a maker of hexachlorophene, which was later also found to form dioxin in production. Givaudan referred the Boehringer query to Dow. Dow responded to Bohringer "describing the hazards and precautions for safe handling of 2,4,5-trichlorophenol." Bohringer, meanwhile, began its own investigation and testing, and two years later, in 1957, sent Dow and other trichlorophenol makers a summary of its research. That letter described the "danger points in the process and the limits which had to be observed in order to avoid producing [the] acne exciter in trichlorophenol and in 2,4,5-T acid." The "acne exciter" or irritant Boehringer identified was 2,3,7,8-tetrachlorodibenzodioxin, or TCDD. Dow later claimed this "remarkable letter"—sent to all makers of trichlorophenol in 1957—was somehow "filed and forgotten."[6]

In the 1960s, chloracne outbreaks occurred at other plants making herbicides, including one owned by Diamond Alkali (later named Diamond Shamrock) in Newark, New Jersey (see sidebar). Dow itself had another outbreak of chloracne among 50 workers at its Midland, Michigan plant in 1964 as it was stepping up production of trichlorophenol, a precursor for Agent Orange. Dow's medical director, Dr. Benjamin B. Holder wrote some years later reviewing Dow's 1964 chloracne outbreak: "The clinical picture of the disease is one that primarily affects the skin. In extreme exposures to certain chlorinated compounds, a general organ toxicity can result. This is primarily demonstrated in the liver, hematropoietic [blood-forming] and nervous systems." Holder further explained, regarding the skin disease, that the chemicals at issue stimulated the skin glands to produce the acne and blackheads, and that "many patients" demonstrated a continuation of the skin lesions for several years, even after being removed from the exposure. He also noted that "fatalities have been reported in the literature," and that there was no specific treatment for the disease.[7]

"It's Only A Rash"

In the 1960s, dermatologists from Newark, New Jersey's Beth Israel Hospital were called into Diamond Alkali's herbicide plant to treat workers who had chloracne outbreaks following two accidents. The doctors came in every Thursday to lance and drain the workers' boils and give them vitamin and vaccine shots after the rash had spread throughout the plant. Several men had the tips of their blister-ravaged ears removed. The chloracne began after explosions occurred in the manufacturing reactor in 1955, and again in February 1960. Cathy Trost, reporting in her 1984 book, *Elements of Risk*, explains that the Beth Israel doctors in the *Archives of Dermatology* in June 1964, described the chloracne they found in 29 workers. Nearly half of the workers exhibited hyperpigmentation, or a darkening of skin on the head, neck, and hands. Eleven had porphyria cutanea tarda, a disease of the body's blood-forming elements characterized by a darkening of the urine. That was caused by one of the chemicals in the plant, the doctors speculated, which exerted a toxic effect on the liver. In one case, several years after a 48-year-old man had come to work in the factory, his skin darkened, his face, ears, and hands erupted with blisters; his forehead and eyelids sprouted tufts of hair the consistency of his eyebrows; and his urine turned "the color of Coca-Cola." In another case, a welder who had "frequent and prolonged contact" with the herbicidal chemicals was admitted to the hospital after his skin had darkened, his eyebrows had thickened, and his urine had taken on a dark, reddish color. His face, chest, and shoulders were covered with blackheads and boils, and some of his skin had a purplish cast. His feet developed a fungus disease, and his hands were covered with boils. A third worker had dark and blistered skin, hairy temples, dark urine, and chloracne so severe that company officials removed him from contact with the chemicals. The dermatologists speculated in 1964 that both diseases, chloracne and porphyria cutanea tarda, were caused by either the finished chemicals in the plant—2,4-D and 2,4,5-T—or one of the intermediate chemical ingredients, including trichlorophenol. The doctors, however, were not aware of the dioxin contaminant. A Diamond Alkali manager, meanwhile, had also discovered that by 1962, several large Diamond customers were experiencing chloracne problems, and in one case he wrote, "we have definitely lost them as a customer."

Source: Cathy Trost, *Elements of Risk: The Chemical Industry and its Threat To America*, New York: Times Books, 1984, pp. 77–78.

Dow's 1965 Meeting

By the mid-1960s, complaints and inquiries from some of Dow's industrial customers—and word that government officials were looking into the matter—appear to have prompted Dow to hold a meeting with its chemical-industry colleagues. On March 19, 1965, Dow invited officials from Monsanto, Diamond Alkali, Hooker Chemical, and Hercules to come to Midland to discuss "problems of health" associated with findings of "highly toxic impurities" in 2,4,5-T and related materials. At the meeting a few days later, Dow officials discussed their 1964 outbreak of chloracne at the Midland plant, and the company's 25 years of experience in laboratory work and animal testing. But Dow also had another agenda. "Like a Mafia sit down, at which the ruling don settles disputes among rival families so as to preserve the whole," wrote Cathy Trost in *Elements of Risk*, "Dow wanted to convince the rest of the herbicide makers to institute 'self-imposed controls' on dioxin production before the government smelled trouble."[8] Dow had discovered there were ways to reduce the amount of the dioxin contaminant produced in making herbicides and other products, and wanted its industrial colleagues to follow suit.

E. L. Chandler of Diamond Alkali, in file memos he later wrote on the meeting, concluded that Dow's purpose "was obviously designed to help us solve this problem before outsiders [i.e., government regulators] confuse the issue and cause us no end of grief." He also recorded that Dow believed that repeated exposures to 1.0 ppm dioxin were hazardous. Dow scientists had described their laboratory tests of exposing rabbits' ears to 1.0 ppm dioxin, and after 11 applications there was a severe skin reaction. "They concluded therefore, that 1 ppm with repeat exposure can create a real problem." (In fact, Dow by then had found as much as 40.0 ppm dioxin in other companies' commercial 2,4,5-T products.)

Dow, however, was holding its cards close to the vest, as they say. Dow scientists and managers did not tell their competitors everything at the March 1965 meeting. They didn't explain, for example, that Dow had quietly made a deal with Boehringer Chemical to use that company's low-temperature trichlorophenol process, which had been found to lower the level of dioxin. On the one hand, Dow was trying to browbeat its competitors to lower their dioxin output so as not to draw government attention to the lucrative herbicide industry, while at the same time, behind their backs, carve out a better competitive position for themselves using the new Boehringer process that none of the others had. Observes Cathy Trost:

> The rationale for the meeting was transparent. Dow was the biggest producer of herbicides in the United States. It also knew more about their dangers than anyone else. And it had a secret, albeit expensive method of making 2,4,5-T with [safer] levels of dioxin. Instead of calling down certain government controls on its head, throwing itself wide-open to product liability and workers' personal injury lawsuits, and jeopardizing the industry's multimillion-dollar herbicide market, Dow devised a plan whereby the industry would police itself and keep quiet about its problems until they were worked out.[9]

Internally, however, within the "Dow family," Dr. V. K. Rowe, the company's toxicology director at the time, was offering perhaps a truer picture of

A sampling of newspaper headlines Dow faced on the dioxin issue in the early 1980s.

Dow's concerns. On June 24, 1965, Rowe wrote to a Dow manager in Canada, outlining the dangers of dioxin and the implications for Dow:

> As you well know, we had a serious situation in our operating plants because of contamination of 2,4,5-trichlorophenol with impurities, the most active of which is 2,3,7,8-tetrachlorodibenzodioxin. The material is exceptionally toxic: it has a tremendous potential for producing chloracne and systemic injury.
>
> One of the things we want to avoid is the occurrence of any acne in consumers. I am particularly concerned here with consumers who are using the material on a daily, repeated basis such as custom operators may use it.
>
> If this should occur, the whole 2,4,5-T industry will be hard hit and I would expect restrictive legislation, either barring the material or putting very rigid controls on it. This is the main reason why we are so concerned that we clean up our own house from within, rather than having someone from without do it for us.
>
> ...I trust you will be very judicious in your use of this information. It could be quite embarrassing if it were misinterpreted or misused.[10]

Meanwhile, Dow's attempt to push its competitors to voluntarily hold down their dioxin contamination didn't work. The other chemical makers simply continued producing as they always had, raising Dow's worry that government would be drawn into the fray. By September 1965, Dow was no longer playing the role of mafia don, trying to preserve the whole. "Dow officials stopped phoning their competitors and adopted a low profile, keeping silent about the dangers of dioxin for the next four years while simultaneously continuing to supply the defoliation and crop-destruction needs of the Vietnam War and the myriad of domestic uses," explains Cathy Trost. "Dow did not inform the Agriculture Department because it did not believe the dioxin in its consumer products was hazardous. The silence even extended to pleas of chloracne-plagued rival companies for help."[11]

"The material is exceptionally toxic: it has a tremendous potential for producing chloracne and systemic injury."

Dr. V. K. Rowe, Dow Chemical, June 1965

In terms of Dow's disclosures to the U.S. military while the company was selling it Agent Orange, G. E. Lynn, director of registration for Dow's Bioproducts Department, wrote to one Army general on April 22, 1963: "...[W]e have been manufacturing 2,4-D and 2,4,5-T for over ten years. To the best of our knowledge, none of the workmen in these factories has shown any ill effects as a result of working with these chemicals."[12] True, this was before Dow's 1964 Midland outbreaks, but well after other reported

Dioxin: How Toxic?

In the late 1970s, when dioxin was tested for health effects by the federal government in laboratory animals, researchers could not find a level at which there was no effect. In other words, every dose they used, no matter how small, produced an effect. Thus, many would argue in later years, there was no point in setting acceptable tolerance levels, period—that exposure standards set at one part per million or one part per billion were still too high. For dioxin, they maintained, there was no safe level. In July 1983, Congressman James Scheuer (D-NY), then chairman of the House Subcommittee on Natural Resources, Agriculture Research, and Environment, thought it important enough in opening hearings on dioxin to highlight exactly how toxic the chemical was. EPA, the Congressman explained, had found dioxin to be the most toxic substances it had ever tested and was likely a carcinogen in humans. In the air, he explained, EPA had estimated that a trillionth of a gram of dioxin in a cubic foot of air could be expected to result in 9 additional cases of cancer in every 100,000 people. In water, EPA suggested it was unacceptable to have dioxin concentrations of more than 2.1 parts per quintillion—a quintillion being equal to a billion billion.

Today, the accumulated knowledge about dioxin confirms earlier concerns. All American children, for example, are born with dioxin in their bodies. "Dioxins are passed transgenerationally with great efficiency," explains author Joe Thornton. "A typical nursing infant in the U.S. receives a daily dose 92 times greater than that of the average adult." Epidemiological and laboratory studies have established that dioxin is a human carcinogen. The lifetime risk of getting cancer from exposure to dioxin is 1 in 10,000 for the general American population and 1 in 1,000 to highly exposed members of the population. These risks are 100 and 1,000 times higher, respectively, than the one-in-a million "acceptable" cancer risk. Dioxin is a potent endocrine-disrupting hormone, capable of altering or disrupting the action of gonadotropin, retinoic acid, steroid hormones, thyroid hormone, and growth factors at extremely low doses. Dioxin is also a powerful immune suppressant, increasing susceptability to disease. According to some experts, the current body burden of the general human population is already at or near the level at which dioxin has been found to cause a variety of effects in laboratory animals and human populations, including cognitive defects, endometriosis, hormonal changes, immune system suppression, reduced sperm count, and impaired development of male and female reproductive systems.

Sources: Opening Statement, Rep. James H. Scheuer, Chairman, Subcommittee on Natural Resources, Agricultural Research, and Environment, U.S. House of Representatives, Washington, DC, "Dioxin Hearing," July 28, 1983; Tracey Easthope, "Even More Dangerous Than Previously Thought," *From The Ground Up* (Ecology Center, Ann Arbor, MI), Aug–Sept 2000; Center for Health, Environment, and Justice, "The American People's Dioxin Report;"Joe Thornton, PhD, *Environmental Impacts of Polyvinyl Chloride Building Materials*, Healthy Building Network, Washington, DC, November 2002, pp. 82–83; and U.S. Environmental Protection Agency, Office of Research and Development, *Exposure and Health Assessment for 2,3,7,8-Tetrachlorodibenzo-p-dioxin (TCDD) and Related Compounds* (review draft), June 2000.

knowledge of chloracne and earlier incidents related to these chemicals, some dating to at least 1955, and others to the 1930s.

In 1970, five years after it had been meeting with its industrial colleagues on the matter, Dow met with the military to share at least generally what it knew about dioxin and Agent Orange production. When Defense Secretary Melvin Laird indicated the Pentagon was thinking about re-instituting the defoliation program in Vietnam, Dow wrote: "There is abundant evidence that [dioxin] occurring as an impurity in 2,4,5-T is highly toxic." If the Pentagon did decide to reinstate the program, Dow suggested that specifications be set to insure that products with very low levels of dioxin be used. Some military officials who had met with Dow officials months earlier, complained that what Dow was then saying about dioxin's effects "represented information that we were receiving for the first time...."[13]

However, during the Agent Orange litigation in May 1983 when Dow claimed immunity as a government contractor, it offered a more detailed history. Dow, arguing that its role as a military contractor protected it from Vietnam War related liability and veteran claims, acknowledged that industry and the military knew quite a lot about dioxin's toxicity by the mid-1960s, including that dioxin might cause liver damage and birth defects. Dow's papers in federal court said that "undisputed evidence" showed that by the mid-1960s the government had "substantial knowledge of potential occupational health hazards to workers engaged in the production of herbicides containing 2,4,5-T and also was well aware of the evidence suggesting possible adverse health effects, including teratogenicity [malformation of a fetus] with the use of finished products."[14] For itself, however, Dow lawyers claimed there was no record prior to 1969 indicating that the company had similar knowledge—which appears to have been either an outright lie or a gross oversight, since Dow was aware of the Bionetics and other research data around the same time the government was. Dow had also held the March 1965 meeting with its industrial colleagues discussing the danger of dioxin formation in the 2,4,5-T making process.

Lawyers for Vietnam veterans in the case, represented by Victor Yannacone and Associates, were incredulous at Dow's claim. "Since the mid-1960's, Dow had information that Agent Orange supplied to the Government contained large levels of dioxin, far in excess of anything Dow considered safe or necessary," they said. "Dow also knew that its own product would be mixed with that of the others and used in this manner on the battlefield."

"What did Dow do with this information?" the lawyers asked in their motion. "It concealed it from the Government and asked others, its co-defendants, to do the same."[15]

In July 1983, *New York Times* reporter Ralph Blumenthal, summing up the revelations he had discovered from the court-released documents, concluded: "The Dow Chemical Company knew as early as the middle 1960s about evidence that exposure to dioxin might cause people to become seriously ill and even die, but the company withheld its concern from the Gov-

The Holmesburg Experiments

In January 1981, a *Philadelphia Inquirer* story revealed that Dow Chemical had paid a University of Pennsylvania dermatologist to test dioxin on prisoners at Holmesburg Prison in Philadelphia. The tests were conducted in 1964, and Dow paid Dr. Albert M. Kligman $10,000 to conduct them. In all, some 70 inmates were tested, each of whom signed a form that neither informed them of the risks involved, nor specified what chemical was to be used. At that time, the drug, cosmetics, and chemical industries sometimes used prisoners to test various substances, but the practice was not generally known by the public. Such experiments later became illegal. "You can't do it now—it's against the law," explained Dow's Perry J. Gehring, director of health sciences in January 1981, who acknowledged that Dow had authorized the tests. "The courts have decided these people are a captive audience, and are not really volunteers," he said. Still, the tests were offensive in any case, and smacked of a serious ethical lapse at Dow. The experiments were motivated by Dow's experience with its workers contracting the skin disease chloracne while making 2,4,5-T and Agent Orange in 1964. According to Gehring, Dow asked Dr. Kligman to test dioxin at 16 micrograms on the prisoners, a level slightly above that which chloracne had been observed by Dow using the "rabbit ear test." After testing the dioxin on the prisoners at the Dow-specified levels, Kligman reported to Dow that he found no chloracne. Then, without Dow's knowledge, according to Gehring, Dr. Kligman proceeded to test dioxin on the prisoners at a higher level, administering dioxin doses of 7,500 micrograms to one-square-inch patches of skin on each prisoner's back. Eight of ten of the inmates in this experiment did develop chloracne, and Kligman reported these results to Dow in a January 1968 letter. Dow, apparently concerned with the unauthorized testing, appears to have requested a letter of liability waiver from Dr. Kligman, as in March 1965 he wrote to Dow's V. K. Rowe at the Biochemical Research Lab in Midland:

> ... *This letter will indicate that The Dow Chemical Company is released from liability in case of adverse effects developing in human volunteers in the course of certain studies in which The Dow Chemical Company is interested. I assume full responsibility for any liabilities which may arise in connection with human testing. I might add that we have never encountered a problem in this respect. These are the terms which are obtained in all of our contracts with industry.*
> *Very sincerely yours, Albert M. Kligman, M.D.*

In May 2002, a group of former Holmesburg inmates appeared before a Philadelphia City Council committee to testify about the experiments—which not only included Dow's dioxin testing, but also testing of infectious diseases, radiation, and psychotropic drugs. The inmates were seeking an official apology from Philadelphia and compensation for serving as "guinea pigs." A lawsuit filed in October 2000 on behalf of 298 former Holmesburg inmates claims they were subjected to the testing without informed consent from the 1950s to the 1970s. Named as defendants in that suit were the City of Philadelphia, Dr. Kligman, Johnson & Johnson, and Dow Chemical. One federal judge ruled that the statute of limitations for the lawsuit expired two decades ago, but a U.S. Circuit Court of

Appeals was expected to review the case on appeal.

Nor was Kligman the only doctor to conduct such tests for Dow, as in the 1950s, apparently, Dow had asked another Philadelphia dermatologist, Joseph V. Klauder, to conduct a series of human experiments to gauge the potential health effects of herbicides based on 2,4,5-T. One internal Dow report on Klauder's work noted, for example, that a herbicidal compound containing 55 percent Silvex (2,4,5-T) proved irritating in concentrations exceeding 5 percent.

Sources: Letter of Arthur M. Kligman, M.D., Hospital of the University of Pennsylvania, Philadelphia, PA, to V. K. Rowe, Biochemical Research Laboratory, The Dow Chemical Company, Midland, Michigan, March 2, 1965; Aaron Epstein,"Human Guinea Pigs: Dioxin Tested at Holmesburg," *Philadelphia Inquirer*, January 11, 1981; Paul Rau, "Dow Confirms TCDD Experiments on Prisoners," *Midland Daily News*, January 12, 1981, p. A-1; "Medical Testing: Former Philadelphia Inmates Seek Payments," *American Health Line*, May 10, 2002; and, "Agent Orange Finally Gets Its Day in Court," *Chemical Week*, May 18, 1983, pp. 44–45.

ernment and continued to sell herbicides contaminated by dioxin to the Army and the public."[16]

The Michigan Connection

In the early 1980s, as the dioxin riddle played out at the national level with the disclosures from the Agent Orange papers, there was another important thread of dioxin-related developments occurring in central Michigan and the Great Lakes region. Much of this would point back to Dow's Midland chemical works. At first, the discoveries were not front page news outside of Michigan, or they were otherwise buried in scientific arcana. But some of it bubbled up into national political controversy, and all of it figured into the calculus of Dow's actions around dioxin. The first troubling evidence came from Dow's own front yard—the Tittabawassee River, where Herbert Dow, back in the 1890s, began his new venture.*

In 1976, native catfish taken from the Tittabawassee below Dow's wastewater discharge were found to contain from 70 to 230 parts per trillion (ppt) dioxin. Dow also reported in 1977 that various species of Tittabawassee native fish it collected had dioxin levels ranging from not detectible to 240 ppt—most in the 20- to 170-ppt range. Then in June 1978, Dow reported to the Michigan DNR and the Michigan Department of Public Health that rainbow trout exposed to a mixture of Dow's treated wastewater had accumulated up to 50 ppt dioxin in the edible portion of the fish, and up to 70 ppt in the whole fish. These findings prompted the Michigan Department of Public Health to issue a fish consumption advisory in June 1978 for

---

*See Chapter 19 for more on Dow and central Michigan.

any fish from the Tittabawassee River downstream of the Dow dam at Midland. EPA followed with their own action in September 1978 making a preliminary determination that concentrations of dioxin in Tittabawassee River fish represented a substantial risk to public health.[17]

Two months later, in November 1978, Dow began propounding its "Trace Chemistries of Fire" theory about dioxin—a "finding" that dioxins were ubiquitous in the environment, and formed as a result of a wide variety of combustion processes, including fire. "The family of toxic chemicals known as chlorinated dioxins are formed in minute amounts by normal combustion processes that occur everywhere," stated Dow's November 15, 1978 press release, citing its own scientists as the source. Dow claimed that research to date "verified the following sources of dioxin: refuse incinerators, fossil-fueled powerhouses, gasoline and diesel powered automobiles and trucks, fireplaces, charcoal grills and cigarettes." Dow said its findings came after "a four-month search to explain the presence of 2,3,7,8-TCDD in fish taken from the Tittabawassee River...." Robert R. Bumb, research director at Dow Midland and head of the Dow dioxin study, said: "We now think dioxins have been with us since the advent of fire." Dow's "Trace Chemistries of Fire," however, proved misleading as an explanation for industrial-level dioxin pollution.*

Dow's own scientists by this time had made some rather disturbing discoveries in lab tests. Dow's Richard Kociba led a 1976 team that found liver cancer in laboratory rats exposed to 210 ppt dioxin, revealing the substance to be the most potent animal carcinogen ever tested to that point. The Kociba study, published in 1978, was verified in similar testing by the National Institutes of Health in 1982.

Back on the Tittabawassee, meanwhile, follow-up studies by EPA and the U.S. Food and Drug Administration (FDA) in 1979 and 1980 determined that dioxin persisted in native fish at levels of concern in the Tittabawassee, the Saginaw River, and Saginaw Bay, despite the fact that by this time Dow had closed the manufacturing facilities thought to be most associated with dioxin formation—those that made 2,4,5-trichlorophenol and the 2,4,5-T herbicide.[18] Then in December 1980, the Canadian government released a report on dioxin contamination of Great Lakes herring gull eggs. The report included data on high levels of dioxin in gull eggs and tissue from Saginaw Bay and others areas of the Great Lakes. All of the herring gull eggs and muscle tissue analyzed by the scientists contained detectable levels of dioxin, with the highest concentrations occurring in the gull colonies at Saginaw Bay.[19]

---

*For example, core samples taken from lake bottoms, revealing no dioxin until around 1940, and the absence of dioxin in body tissue of Andean Indians mummified for more than 2,800 years, tend to refute the contention that modern chemistry played no role in dioxin formation. Although it is true that dioxin can be formed by natural combustion, man-made sources of dioxin have been shown to exceed the natural variety by a ratio of 100 to 1. See Thornton (2000).

Dow Edits EPA

After the December 1980 dioxin-in-gull-eggs revelations, EPA's Midwest regional office in Chicago began its own study of dioxin in the Great Lakes area. A draft report concluded: "Dow Chemical... has extensively contaminated their facility with PCDDs and PCDFs [dioxins and furans] and has been the primary contributor to contamination of the Tittabawassee and Saginaw Rivers and Lake Huron." EPA also cited the gull egg contamination. Since the gulls' dioxin contamination came primarily from eating fish, and high levels were also found in fish, the draft report recommended that "the consumption of fish from the Tittabawassee River, the Saginaw Bay, and possibly other sites in the Great Lakes should be prohibited." Although the report was still a draft, some of the report's findings surfaced in a June 1981 Canadian newspaper story, noting Dow's role and the recommendation to ban Great Lakes fish. Dow soon called EPA, asking about the study. In Washington, EPA headquarters rejected the draft, saying it would "inflame the public... implicate industry, and suggest that a health problem is evident...." Under further review, EPA's assistant administrator, John Hernandez, gave the draft report to Dow and instructed EPA's Chicago staff to take comments from Dow in preparing the final draft. Dow reviewed the report in detail. In a conference telephone call, according to one EPA participant, Dow made clear "what lines and what sections are acceptable to the company and what should be preferably deleted." In the final report, all mention of Dow as a source of dioxin— and in fact, *all* reference to Dow—was deleted. The recommendation to prohibit public consumption of fish was also removed, as were the assessments of the human health hazard posed by dioxin in the Great Lakes.[20] The special editing opportunity given Dow in the Great Lakes dioxin study soon became the subject of Congressional hearings. By early 1983, the whole episode was front page news, eventually leading to the dismissal of EPA's Hernandez while drawing more attention to Dow and dioxin.[21]

Back in Michigan, meanwhile, Larry E. Fink, a former analyst at the Michigan Department of Natural Resources, had checked local cancer statistics in the Midland area and found they had increased above the national norm. Fink would later cite a National Cancer Institute study indicating that certain cancers were found at twice the national level in Midland County from 1950 to 1969. Fink, in effect, had found statistically significant increases in soft tissue sarcoma that had been overlooked by local, state, and federal agencies. In March 1983, Fink—who was also director of a local watchdog group called The Foresight Society—together with another local group, the Environmental Congress of Mid-Michigan, charged that high levels of dioxin contamination in the soil at a Dow plant might be contaminating the city of Midland and downwind areas. Fink asserted that Dow had carried out some major plant dismantling and product changeovers during the 1960s that might have led to a release of dioxin byproducts of the Vietnam War defoliant Agent Orange. Dow officials did recall that when one of its dioxin producing plants "was demolished in 1968," the equipment was decontaminated, dismantled, and buried on the plant grounds and covered with a clay cap. Deep wells were also used to dispose of some material. But Dow added it had also completed a 24-year health study of 8,000 employees that revealed a lower mortality rate among

Dow made clear "what lines and what sections are acceptable to the company and what should be preferably deleted."

Dow employees than among white American men generally. "Based on Dow employee health studies such as this, as well as soil and fish tests," said Dow in a prepared statement, "Midland is not atypical from other industrial communities." But Larry Fink discounted Dow's reliance on its study since it had not been made public and subject to outside scrutiny. Dow said the study was part of a doctoral dissertation and therefore subjected to peer review and would be released later.[22] Fink and his colleague citizen groups then filed a petition with the EPA under TSCA calling for a full field investigation of Midland and surrounding counties.

Now at the center of the dioxin storm on several fronts, Dow decided to take the offensive. On June 1, 1983—just before some big stories were about to break on what Dow and the chemical industry knew about dioxin—Dow CEO, Paul Oreffice, held a press conference. At Dow's television studio inside the company's Midland headquarters, Oreffice announced that Dow would spend $3 million on independent studies. *Washington Post* reporter Ward Sinclair, attending the press event, noted that Oreffice conceded the program was aimed as much at quieting public fears as it was producing new science. "Our perspectives and judgements about the dioxin controversy remain unchanged," said Oreffice. "What has changed is that with all the publicity dioxin has received, the general public cannot be expected to take our word for it without corroboration. We invite and are encouraging third-party evaluation and verification of our own scientific conclusions." Dow's $3 million would cover a state and federal study of soil contamination inside the plant and around Midland; a state study of soft-tissue cancer; and a University of Michigan research study on ways to reduce dioxin in Dow's wastewater. Dow also planned to expand its analytical laboratory, doubling its ability to detect dioxin in the regional environment, and would authorize a study by an independent scientific organization to determine if trace amounts of dioxin posed a health hazard to humans. Oreffice also said Dow supported the proposed national dioxin study by EPA. However, he indicated he expected no surprises, anticipating the studies would show "that all our science is correct and that there is no danger.... We will accept the results."[23]

But then came the July 1983 *New York Times* stories on the Agent

Orange papers revealing Dow's early history with, and knowledge about, dioxin. These stories were soon being reported in newspapers all over the country. Dow and dioxin, it seemed, were joined at the hip, despite the company's best efforts to bury the issue with more study.

Then there was the 2,4,5-T situation at EPA.

The 2,4,5-T Maneuver

During 1983, Dow was still in the thick of a formal pesticide review fight with EPA over its herbicide 2,4,5-T—a long and involved process that generally involves opportunities for both sides to make their case, with public hearings, appeals, and the possible disclosure of new information. In March 1979, during the Carter administration, EPA had issued an emergency suspension of 2,4,5-T and Silvex, prohibiting many uses of the herbicides after the chemicals appeared to be linked to spontaneous abortions among women living in the Alsea Basin of Oregon—an area sprayed heavily with the herbicides by the Forest Service. Dow, though filing and losing an appeal on the suspension, and then fighting in the courts for specific exceptions—such as continued use of 2,4,5-T on rice, discussed earlier—had turned off its manufacturing of the herbicides, but was still selling them for permitted uses from its inventory. Dow was also working hard to reinstate the prohibited uses in the EPA review process. By 1981, Dow and EPA, in fact, had begun private negotiations to settle the 2,4,5-T review, and by the spring of 1983, it appeared 2,4,5-T was headed back to market, with an announcement to that effect anticipated later that summer. But in October 1983, Dow made a surprise announcement: it would give up the fight with EPA to continue selling 2,4,5-T and Silvex, both known to be contaminated with dioxin. In bowing out, however, Dow still made the same adamant statements it had always made, standing by its herbicides. "The great weight of scientific evidence confirms that 2,4,5-T can be used safely without undue risk to people or the environment," said Keith R. McKennon at the time. "Our commitment to this position is firm, unwavering, and unequivocal."[24] Hours after the Dow announcement, EPA announced it would cancel all remaining uses of 2,4,5-T and Silvex. With the surprise announcement by Dow that it was folding its tent on 2,4,5-T, followed by EPA's cancellation, environmentalists generally cheered, with some surprised that Dow had quit after vowing to overturn EPA's restrictions. But behind the scenes, there was something else.

EPA had held back some old sampling data on 2,4,5-T from the 1979 Alsea Basin study in Oregon; information that revealed the harmful dioxin-related health effects of 2,4,5-T and 2,4-D. Alsea Basin residents and attorneys in litigation—including Agent Orange attorneys who had first filed their case in 1979—had long sought the data. However, the lid was on. "[T]he Reagan EPA buried the most incriminating data on the Alsea study and ordered the scientists conducting the study not to publish their data nor discuss the study in any public forum," charges author and EPA litigant Carol Van Strum.[25] By August 1983, at a time when Congress was typically in its summer recess, EPA and Dow had been moving toward their planned settlement over 2,4,5-T, with the herbicide to receive a qualified bill of health for marketing with an unspecified allowable level of dioxin. But that's about the same time when some of EPA's Alsea Basin data was leaked—raising the visibility of dioxin and 2,4,5-T health effects. Some believe that Dow's "voluntary" October 1983 withdrawal and EPA's near simultaneous cancellation, were more than what they appeared to be. Though never proved, these actions may have been designed to keep the Alsea Basin data—and the bad news on dioxin—from receiving further public scrutiny; from formally entering the EPA pesticide review process; and/or from making its way into other legal proceedings. For the damaging data leaked from the 1979 Alsea Basin study was known as "Table VII," which contained the results of EPA's dioxin sampling. Explain Carol Van Strum and Paul Merrell in their 1987 report, *No Margin of Safety*:

> . . . Table VII put the lie to EPA's statements in court that no such study existed. Furthermore, the TCDD [dioxin] levels recorded suggested why EPA had covered up and denied the existence of the study. The results were in fact the "smoking gun". . . EPA had found TCDD in drinking water sediment at levels up to 5800 parts-per-trillion—nearly six times EPA's "level of concern" for *residential soils*—and had found low TCDD levels in tissues from wildlife and from a human baby born without a brain, supporting the statistical correlations of the Alsea Study. Most significantly, these levels resulted not from waste dumping or from manufacturing, but from routine use of a chemical widely used in agriculture, for timber and rights-of-way management, and by the military. The missing TCDD causal link, human exposure, had been made. The implications of Table VII for the Agent Orange veterans' class action lawsuit were obvious. . . .
>
> . . . Within months of the [EPA-Dow] 2,4,5-T settlement, Dow and EPA also settled EPA's lawsuit to gain access to Dow's Midland plant for dioxin sampling, and Dow engineered the involuntary "settlement" of the Agent Orange veterans' class action lawsuit over the vehement objections of many veterans. Repeatedly referring to the suppressed results of Table VII and to "widespread fraud" in herbicide health testing, in January 1984, the Ninth U.S. Circuit Court of Appeals banned federal use of all herbicides in the Alsea study area until they are adequately tested for human health effects. . . . [26]

EPA claimed it was all a mix-up; that the Table VII/Alsea samples weren't really from Alsea, but some other place, which EPA would not name initially, and was never fully disclosed to critics' satisfaction. EPA also didn't bother to order a retest of the dioxin-laden specimens, ten of which contained dioxin in the 0.03 ppb to 5.8 ppb range.[27]

In any case, Dow's withdrawal on 2,4,5-T in October 1983, followed by

EPA's cancellation, may have helped to keep the wraps on any further airing of the Alsea dioxin data—and further agency and public probing of dioxin, 2,4,5-T, and 2,4-D. "With the death of 2,4,5-T," says Carol Van Strum, "the smoking gun evidence of dioxin's human effects were quietly buried in EPA archives." Also buried, contends Van Strum, "were the EPA's steadily increasing data on the dioxin content of 2,4-D."[28] Only years later, did this information get the full airing it should have had in 1983.

Shift to Chlorine

By the mid-1980s, however, two significant dioxin-related developments occurred that began to shift more attention to the "root cause" chemical involved in dioxin's formation: chlorine. First, EPA, in response to public concerns over Times Beach, Love Canal, the Great Lakes, and other dioxin "hot spots," had been charged by Congress in 1983 to begin a National Dioxin Study, which it completed in 1985. With this study, EPA moved to establish an exposure standard for dioxin with a level it described as an "acceptable" daily dose.* That sparked a major political and scientific debate over standard-setting which led EPA to commit to a subsequent study, known as the first dioxin reassessment, begun in 1988, which subsequently evolved into a second dioxin reassessment in 1991—a process which is still ongoing to this day, awaiting a final report.**

The second key development in the mid-1980s—which also figures into the EPA political battles and delay—was dioxin's 1986 discovery in fish and rivers downstream of paper mills due to chlorine bleaching of white paper. Greenpeace subsequently released documents in 1987 revealing dioxin to be present in everyday consumer products such as diapers, sanitary napkins, tampons, paper plates, toilet paper, coffee filters, and office

---

*0.006 picograms per kilogram of body weight per day (pg/kg/day).

**The "dioxin reassessment wars" at EPA and elsewhere would take a separate book to explain adequately, and cannot be included here. Among the reasons the dioxin study process became bogged down, for example, is that the Chlorine Institute sponsored "scientific" gatherings aimed at challenging EPA's standard-setting and assessments, using a public relations firm at one point to paint an industry-favored "scientific consensus" that in fact was no consensus at all. The pulp and paper industry had also entered the fight in a major way, and had quietly joined with EPA in a secrecy agreement to obtain a reassessment favorable to its interests. A long and heated court battle was necessary to uncover this and other revealing and suppressed information—a fascinating story which is adequately covered elsewhere. Carol Van Strum and Paul Merrell, for example, recount much of this in *No Margin of Safety*, as does Lois Gibbs' *Dying From Dioxin*. But suffice it to say here that delaying the outcome—to establish a standard that EPA and other agencies would then use for regulatory purposes—appears to be the goal of the paper, chemical, and chlorine industries.

copy paper. The revelations about dioxin in the paper industry not only brought a giant industrial player into the fray, it also helped foment activist targeting of chlorine as the dioxin "root-source" chemical, generator of thousands of problematic organochlorine compounds and dioxin-like toxicity. Soon thereafter, the first calls for phasing out chlorine began to be heard, and Dow—with a huge portion of its empire built on chlorine—began girding for a long battle.

Dow Digs In

In September 1990, Dow began a top-down reorganization of resources to deal with chlorine-related issues, announcing the formation of a "Global Chlorine and Chlorine Derivatives Issues Team." Presented in the hedged language of a corporate communication in its newsletter, *Dow Today,* it was clear where Dow was heading. "Foremost among the new team's role," explained the newsletter "will be the effort to determine the scope and potential impact of issues affecting chlorine and chlorine derivatives businesses on an international basis and to develop global strategies addressing these issues." The team, said Dow, "will assure the deployment of resources necessary to successfully manage the issue both globally and in each geographic area." Among examples of chlorine and chlorine derivatives-type issues Dow listed were: dioxin, global warming, ozone depletion, chlorinated solvents, indoor air, air toxins, groundwater, waste disposal, recyclability, chlorofluorocarbons substitutes, and polyvinyl chloride. "The new team's primary goals" were:

> To clearly understand, by business function and geographic area, the potential effect of an issue on Dow, and then to devise a global strategy to minimize the impact.

> To assure that each area has plans of action for managing the issue consistent with Dow Core Values and then to provide oversight during both the development and implementation of these plans.

> Provide an industry leadership position by maintaining a solution-oriented, proactive position in key countries.

> Determine business and reputation improvement opportunities for the corporation and for each Dow geographic area.

> Develop and assure the Dow's position and strategies are actively and consistently used throughout the Dow organization and with key external audiences (coalition, associations, government, media and special interest groups).[29]

In the outside world, meanwhile, more scientific and government bodies were drawing a bead on chlorine. "The dynamic growth of chlorine chemistry during the '50s and '60s," said the German Council of Environmental Advisors in 1991, "represents a decisive mistake in twentieth century industrial development, which would not have occurred had our present knowledge as to environmental damage and health risks due to chlorine chemistry then been available."[30]

In 1992, the U.S.-Canadian International Joint Commission, called for a phase out of chlorine... "It is prudent, sensible and indeed necessary to treat these [chlorinated organic] substances as a class rather than as a series of isolated individual chemicals. Further, in many cases, alternative production processes do exist.... The Commission concludes that the use of chlorine and its compounds should be avoided in the manufacturing process.... The Commission therefore recommends that the Parties, in consultation with industry and other affected interests, develop timetables to sunset the use of chlorine and chlorine-containing compounds as industrial feedstocks."[31]

In 1992, the U.S.-Canadian International Joint Commission, called for a phase out of chlorine.

By this time, the Chemical Manufacturer's Association (CMA), the chemical industry's chief trade association and lobbying arm, had created a new subsidiary trade group called the Chlorine Chemistry Council (CCC) to do industry's bidding in the chlorine wars. Its chief responsibilities were to handle public relations, lobbying, and scientific initiatives on behalf of the chlorine industry. "From its origin," says one Greenpeace report, "the CCC was a Dow-led effort. The Council's first managing director was Brad Lienhardt, a career-long Dow employee."[32] The CCC soon had a multi-million-dollar annual war chest, with a significant public relations component. In 1993, for example, after the U.S.-Canadian International Joint Commission (IJC) proposed a chlorine sunset provision, the CCC hired Charles River Associates to prepare a report on the economic importance of chlorine. The report cataloged the entire range of chlorine, organochlorine, and caustic soda uses, stretching the chemical's reach to include far downstream users and adding in their value. The numbers in the Charles River were very dramatic: the IJC's recommendation would cost U.S. and Canadian economies $102 billion per year, said the CCC paid-for study. It would also result in the loss of 1.4 million jobs and prevent society from meeting basic human needs including nutrition, health care, and clean water. The CCC/Charles River report also used an immediate ban of chlorine as the calculator, not a gradual sunset as the IJC had called for.

Carol Browner's Remarks

Then on February 1, 1994, EPA Administrator Carol Browner lit a match. At a press conference in Washington, Browner said that within three years EPA wanted to find a way to "substitute, reduce or prohibit the use of chlorine and chlorinated compounds." The reaction from Dow and others was quick and vitriolic. Letters, speeches and Op-Eds began flying. "We're dumbstruck at the prospect of losing 15,000 chemical compounds vital to medicine, the food supply and, yes, clean water," wrote Dow's Enrique Sosa, president of Dow North America and Larry Washington, vice president of Dow North America, in one editorial. "If there was ever a time for us to make our voices heard loud and strong in Washington, this is it."[33] By February 8, Frank Popoff had done just that, sending a testy letter to President Bill Clinton, which was copied to key Cabinet members and more than 200 members of Congress. Popoff's letter brought a rejoinder from among others, Jay Hair of the National Wildlife Federation, who took exception to Popoff's arguments and other material that Dow had been sending to Congress and the media. (See sidebars with both letters.)

The reaction to Browner and EPA's proposal was overblown. EPA essentially proposed to study the viability of a national strategy to "prohibit, substitute, or reduce" the use of chlorine in four major sectors—PVC, solvents, pulp bleaching, and water treatment. The CCC—as it had done with the IJC recommendation—mounted a campaign in Congress and in the media which emphasized chlorine's role in the economy, the jobs at stake, and annual payrolls. The Vinyl Institute charged that EPA's proposal "declares war on modern society." The White House soon withdrew the EPA proposal. Two years later, in 1996, an industry-funded report from the Competitive Enterprise Institute delivered essentially the same CCC message: "The end of chlorine would spell the end of modern civilization itself."

In 1994, the CCC also hired public relations firm Mongoven, Biscoe and Duchin (MBD) to gather intelligence on environmental and public health organizations involved in the chlorine issue. MBD was also retained to recommend strategies to counter environmental activists. MBD's main recommendations to the CCC were: "to mobilize science against the precautionary principle.... Engage a broad effort on risk assessment within the scientific community...and take steps to discredit the precautionary principle within the more moderate environmental groups as well as within the scientific and medical communities."[34]

In 1994, the CCC and CMA began putting their collective spin on the dioxin issue, sounding very much like Dow's 1978 "Trace Chemistries of Fire" theory. One selection from the CCC/CMA "Dioxin Reassessment Briefing Packet," for example, stated: "Among the natural sources of dioxin are forest fires, volcanoes, and compost piles. Man-made sources of dioxin

Dear Mr. President

The Dow Chemical Company, as well as the entire chemical industry and related industries, was startled and deeply troubled by Administrator Browner's announcement on February 1 that the Environmental Protection Agency intends to pursue a strategy to "prohibit, reduce or substitute the use of chlorine." This statement has created concern among our employees about their jobs, our customers about their product needs, and out communities about the safety of their drinking water supply.

This strategy to phase out the use of chlorine is both scientifically unjustified and economically unsound. It would be irresponsible to pursue a policy that presumes all chlorine compounds are bad without considering either the weight of scientific evidence on chlorine chemistry or the economic ramifications of a chlorine ban.

The EPA's announcements on chlorine is unnecessary and contradictory. With the possible exception of a limited number of chlorinated compounds, chlorine has not been found to cause adverse effects on humans or the environment. The safety of chlorine is supported by an array of third-party and peer-reviewed studies in the United States, Canada and Europe.

We support further studies that will help identify the adverse effects of persistent, bio-accumulative and toxic compounds some of which are chlorinated. We also agree that pollution prevention is the ultimate answer and must be increased in intensity. On this issue, Dow and EPA share common ground and have the greatest opportunity for progress. However, extending concerns to the entire class of chlorinated products is absurd.

Chlorine is a vital component of approximately 15,000 widely and safely used compounds. The EPA is proposing to ban an element from the periodic chart. Such a policy directly contradicts the EPA's statement last October that the Untied States does not support the sunsetting of chlorine and that would instead pursue a weight-of-the-evidence approach to regulates specific chlorinated compounds.

A chlorine phase out will impact virtually every industry in every region of the Untied States. A Charles River study conducted in 1993 contained these findings:

- 1.3 million U.S. jobs depend on the chlorine industry. That's equal to the number of jobs in Oregon.
- Industry wages and salaries total more than $30 billion annually.
- 40 percent of all U.S. jobs and income depend in some way on chlorine or the product of the chlorine industry.
- 212 industries use chlorine and related compounds, generating 45 million jobs and $1.6 trillion in economic activity.
- Chlorine-based products represent nearly $3 billion in net trade surplus.
- Chlorine and chlorinated compounds are used in 85 percent of all medicines and 96 percent of crop protection chemicals.

Finally, industry has been left out of the decision-making process. The decision to pursue such a sweeping approach to this very complicated issue was reached without industry's participation. We believe that the impacted parties in a decision of this magnitude must be involved in the process. The Dow Chemical Company is committed to constructive participation. We hope that the Environmental Protection Agency and your Administration reciprocate this sentiment and will work with us to resolve this matter.

Sincerely, Frank Popoff

Dear Mr. Popoff

Dear Frank:

On behalf of the members of the National Wildlife Federation (NWF), I want to take this opportunity to directly respond to misrepresentations you have made to the President, Congress and your customers about the Administration's recent chlorine proposal. We are very disturbed that you are misstating the proposal and, furthermore, that you would have your customers perpetuate these misstatements through the sample letter to Congress. It is particularly egregious that in your letter to President Clinton you state that "EPA is proposing to ban an element from the periodic chart." This is simply not true.

In both the letter to President Clinton and the letter to your customers you have inaccurately characterized the Administration's proposal as "a strategy to phaseout the use of chlorine." The truth is that the Administration's proposal is limited to four industries and one of the control strategy options proposed is to require the reduction in the use of chlorine, not phaseout or substitution. In addition, the study would specifically look at the safety and availability of substitutes for chlorine and involve all stakeholders, including industry and labor, before the Administrator would finalize the strategy. If the available science demonstrates that safe substitutes for chlorine are not reasonably available, the Administrator would presumably require the chlorine use in that sector be reduced, but not banned.

Your letters have also characterized the Clinton proposal as a threat to continued manufacture of critical medicines and to our food supply, by emphasizing how vital chlorine is to both of these industries. The truth is that the proposal does not even address chlorine use in pharmaceuticals or pesticides, despite our concerns about risk from exposure to some chlorinated pesticides. The study and strategy proposed are specifically limited to four key industries: pulp and paper, solvents, plastics, and drinking water systems.

Your letter to President Clinton states "[w]ith the possible exception of a limited number of chlorinated compounds, chlorine has not been found to cause adverse effects on humans or the environment." The truth is that growing scientific evidence indicates that chlorinated compounds are causing devastating health effects in both humans and wildlife. These health effects include increased incidence of breast, prostate and testicular cancer as well as reproductive abnormalities associated with infertility, such as low sperm counts and endometriosis.

Chlorine is an essential ingredient in about half of the nearly 50 common chemicals now known to have reproductive- and endocrine-disrupting effects. This relatively short list reflects the inadequate scientific study of such effects, not the scope of the risk to society. Dioxin (2,3,7,8-TCDD), for example, continues to be released into the environment as a by-product of chlorine-based chemistry and products. We are deeply concerned about growing evidence of dioxin's role in wildlife and human health impacts. *[Note: In this paragraph and the following two, Hair provided footnoted citations.]*

The list of studies linking dioxin to various fish and wildlife health effects, including reproductive abnormalities, is extensive. The potential effects of dioxin exposure are well-documented in studies by Dr. Richard Peterson and colleagues at the University of Wisconsin. A link also increasingly appears likely between dioxin and endometriosis in women.   *(continued)*

> Perhaps most troubling, reputable scientists now are suggesting that levels of current everyday exposure to dioxin and dioxin-like compounds has the potential to cause population-wide adverse effects, with particular risk to nursing infants and certain high-risk sub-populations. Your letter to the President also states that it is "irresponsible to pursue a policy that presumes all chlorine compounds are bad without considering either the weight of scientific evidence on chlorine chemistry or the economic ramifications of a chlorine ban." The truth is that the control strategy proposed by the President would take into account both science and economics.... Further, requiring the Environmental Protection Agency (EPA) to regulate the hundreds of chlorinated compounds individually would take decades that the human race does not have to spare if we are to continue to reproduce successfully. The control strategy would also take into account economic ramifications through consideration of the availability and feasibility of alternatives and participation... of industry representatives such as Dow.
>
> In addition, your letter to the President contains economic forecasts of a chlorine phase out based on work done by Charles River Associates last year. These figures are fundamentally flawed and misrepresentative.... First, they assume that all chlorine use would be banned immediately, instead of phased out gradually.... Second, most of the costs attributed by Charles River to this ban are from eliminating pharmaceuticals, which is not addressed in the President's proposal.... Finally, these figures make no assumptions about what the alternatives to chlorine would be, or who would produce them.
>
> We expect that your company and other chlorine producers would also supply many of the alternatives and whoever produces the alternatives will provide new jobs. Right now, any costs to industry from the President's proposal are purely speculative since no one knows what the control strategy will require.
>
> Your letters state Dow supports "further studies that will help identify the adverse effects of persistent, bio-accumulative and toxic compounds some of which are chlorinated" for pollution prevention. We agree and are pleased that this is exactly what President Clinton has proposed. You also state that Dow is committed to "constructive participation" in the process of addressing the continued use of these chemicals. Again, this is exactly what the President has proposed. We trust, however, that you will be accurate in your dealings with the public and policymakers on what the President's proposal does and does not do.
>
> I hope we can work together productively, with our policymakers, to address these issues under the framework President Clinton has proposed.
>
> Sincerely, Jay D. Hair
> April 15, 1994

include municipal, hospital and hazardous waste incinerators, motor vehicles, residential wood burning and a variety of chemical manufacturing processes. With so many sources, it is not surprising that scientists have detected dioxins virtually everywhere they have looked."[35]

Into The Light

By the mid-1990s, dioxin was certainly no longer in the dark—even if effective strategies for controlling and/or eliminating it were still being held back. Although the dioxin issue by then had been broadened to implicate a range of industries and industrial processes, Dow Chemical was still at the center of the storm. In 1995, for example, Greenpeace published a highly charged report, *Dow Brand Dioxin*, in which it identified Dow as "likely the world's largest root source of dioxin," responsible for more man-made dioxin than any other company. Greenpeace arrived at this conclusion, in part, by noting that: 1) Dow is the world's largest producer of chlorine, holding more chlorine production capacity than any country in the world except the U.S., and accounting for nearly 12 percent of annual global chlorine production; 2) Dow is, and has been historically, one of the world's largest producers of chlorinated pesticides—having made at least 27 pesticides known or suspected of dioxin contamination, ranging from 2,4,5-T, now banned, to 2,4-D, currently on the market; 3) Dow is the world's largest producer of the chemical feedstocks used to make polyvinyl chloride (PVC) plastic—which through its life cycle is associated with more dioxin formation that any other product; and 4) Dow is the leading U.S. producer of chlorinated solvents, including carbon tetrachloride, chloroform, methyl chloride, methylene chloride, trichlorethane, trichloroethylene, and perchloroethylene—chemicals which also result in the formation of dioxins, furans, and dioxin-like toxicity in their manufacture and product life cycles.

Today, Dow Chemical continues to be at the center of the dioxin issue globally, facing continuing litigation and/or government scrutiny in Michigan, New Zealand, Vietnam, and elsewhere. Some of these cases—and the ongoing dioxin controversy in Dow pesticides, plastics, and solvents—are covered in subsequent chapters.[36]

5.
Dowicides

They all go to town for Dow weed killers!

Dow advertisement, 1951

In January 1995, the CBS television network broadcast a report on *Eye to Eye with Connie Chung* about a pesticide called *Dursban*. The show was based partly on information and files at the U.S. Environmental Protection Agency (EPA). Among those appearing with reporter Roberta Baskin, were three individuals who alleged *Dursban* had poisoned them. Jack Kahn, who had a short career as a termite exterminator, claimed he was poisoned and made ill by *Dursban*. "I'll get dizzy, I'll get muscle and joint pain very strongly, and it almost feels like you're going to blow up," he said in the show's opening segment. Next came Joe Cotazino, a civil servant who worked for the New York state government in Albany and charged that *Dursban* spraying there had changed his health. "I would go into seizures and convulsions," he said. Third, came high school student Jim Geralds of rural Lewisburg, Ohio, who ticked off the ill effects he encountered after his school was sprayed with *Dursban*: "Nauseousness, dizziness and I just couldn't concentrate." Following the opening statements of the three alleged victims, Roberta Baskin led into the main body of the show with her introduction: "These people are part of a growing army of walking wounded. They share mysterious symptoms; symptoms that bewildered their doctors—in some cases for years—until, they say, they solved the mystery."[1] *Dursban*, these and others on the show would conclude, changed their health, or made them more sensitive to other chemicals, altering their lives. *Dursban* is made and sold by the Dow Chemical Company.

* * * * *

In the late 1890s at his home in Midland, Michigan, Herbert Dow was a part-time gardener, orchardist, and back-yard experimenter, applying various substances to his fruit trees to improve their growth and keep the bugs away. So it was only natural that his company, Dow Chemical, became a player in the upstart agricultural chemicals business. In 1907, Dow's company began manufacturing lime sulfur as a fruit tree fungicide. Dow also sold lead arsenate sprays. A formal agricultural chemicals division took shape at Dow in 1910.[2] By the 1930s, Dow scientists were combining two basic chemicals—chlorine and phenol—into various compounds which targeted fungi and mold. Several by-product chemicals from the phenol process were also put to use as pesticides, among them, orthophenylphenol and paraphenylphenol, the basis for one of Dow's first line of pesticides, trade-named *Dowicides*. Soon, the *Dowicides* included a number of germicides, fungicides, and insecticides. Some were sold to kill pests like termites. Others were sold to the paper, leather, and glue industries, plagued by various fungus problems and other pests.[3] One line of wood preservatives included fungicidal chemicals developed from a chlorophenol formulation. Pentachlorophenol, or simply penta, was one of these, promoted by Dow as "life insurance" for lumber, preserving its use and protecting it from fungus. All manner of lumber products were treated—whether used for building barns, homes, carports, or backyard toolsheds. Penta was also used at amusement parks, fence posts, utility poles, railroad ties.[4] *Dowicide-H* was another of the wood preservatives, consisting primarily of tetrachlorophenol, sold to saw mills and lumber operations. In 1935 and 1936, Dow obtained U.S. patents for the use of alkali metal salts of 2,4,5-trichlorophenol as fungicides. These and other *Dowicides* were described in a company prospectus of December 1936.[5] That same year, the company established its first agricultural experiment station at South Haven, Michigan.

Pentachlorophenol was promoted by Dow as "life insurance" for lumber.

Following World War II, the full force of synthetic chemistry began to reach agriculture with a whole range of new products. And Dow was in the lead. One of the first popularly known pesticides was DDT, an insecticide. Invented by the Swiss in 1939, DDT was used with much success in combating a typhus epidemic in Naples, Italy in 1943, as well as by the U.S. Army in fighting mosquitoes and malaria in the Pacific. DDT, by late 1944, was receiving rave reviews in advance of its first domestic marketing. Dow did its part to sing the praises of DDT. One ad in 1947 announced: "Freed From Flies, Stock Thrives—Most Pests Surrender to Dow DDT." (See opposite page.)

Meanwhile, in California, at Dow's Seal Beach agricultural research labs, company scientists had discovered in 1942 that ethylene dibromide (EDB), the chemical Dow was selling successfully as an additive to leaded gasoline, had been shown to be an effective poison for nematodes and wireworms, microscopic pests that ravaged crop roots. Use of the chemical in some tests was so successful in killing the worms, that crop yields in some cases, as with sweet potatoes, shot up dramatically. Word spread, and the

Dow Chemical pesticide advertisement for DDT, circa June 1947 (top), and a Dow ad for fungicides from September 1950 (bottom).

chemical, marketed under the trade name *Dowfume W-10*, became one of the hottest items in the California pesticide market of 1945.[6] Dow also began selling 2,4-D that year as a herbicide, first to home gardeners, then to farmers, ranchers, utility companies, and railroads.*

By the spring of 1948, Dow began selling the other major war-research herbicide, 2,4,5-T. By then, Dow had also begun experimenting with combinations of 2,4-D and 2,4,5-T. Dow's Dr. Mullison had patented some of these new products, which were formulated in a way that made them somewhat less volatile and better plant penetrators. "The results look exceptionally promising," said Dow in one 1949 promotional piece. Dow later extolled the results of one test application of the new mixture along 742 miles of the Delaware, Lackawanna & Western Rail Road in Pennsylvania that killed 85 percent of the brush. "Chemical weed killing," concluded Dow, "is here to stay." Dow soon added silvex, a slower acting form of the herbicide, marketed under the *Kuron* trade name, targeted for tougher weed species. Dow by this time was marketing more than 50 kinds of insecticides and herbicides.[7] Dow magazine ads for its various pesticides appeared

---

*See Chapter 6 on 2,4-D for more detail.

regularly during the 1950s and 1960s in publications such as the *Progressive Farmer*. Dow ads for herbicides such as *Premerge*, a dinitro chemical, and fungicides, such as *Ferradow*, appeared in the early 1950s, as did Dow ads pitching *Dowfume MC-2*, a methyl bromide pesticide aimed at killing weed seed and soil insects, to tobacco and truck farmers. (See ads.)

Dow Chemical ad for weedkillers in Progressive Farmer, May 1951.

As the new pesticides tumbled out of American chemical labs during the late 1940s and 1950s, there was little attention paid to the possibility of any problems. The first extensive field tests and government-required toxicological tests for 2,4-D, for example, weren't begun until after the chemical was put on the market. And once on the market, 2,4-D's boosters assured users it was safe, even to the point in a few cases of individual promoters eating or otherwise dosing themselves with the chemical to demonstrate its safety. When pesticide tests were done, they were typically rudimentary safety screens, not going much beyond "lethal dose" testing levels on laboratory animals. When *Silvex*—Dow's special formulation of 2,4,5-T for woody and tough weed species—was brought to market, there were a few caveats offered, with some warning about possible skin irritation from repeated contact with concentrated doses, and that the spray might drift and affect other crops. "Silvex possesses some unique properties which warrant further investigation," explained Dow in a January 1954 technical bulletin distributed to agricultural schools and farmers. ". . . It should be emphasized that the practical field hazard from drift to cotton and other crops has not been fully evaluated."[8] Nevertheless, Dow put *Silvex* on the market.

Some observers of that period,

such as Cathy Trost, author of *Elements of Risk*, say the cavalier approach to new products at the time was just a part of the culture, the generally-accepted industrial and social creed:

> ...There was little room in the 1950s for the advocates of the slow, thoughtful approach in any portion of life—business, science, or politics. The country was so firmly in control of itself and had tied technology so tightly to patriotism that to be skeptical, to be Robert Oppenheimer working to "retard" the hydrogen bomb program or an "alarmist" scientist warning of potential dangers of radioactive fallout, was to be a traitor. Nationwide publicity linking cigarettes to heart disease for the first time in 1954 was countered by advertisements that pointed out reassuringly that "More Doctors Smoke Camels Than Any Other Cigarette." "The deadliest sin was to be controversial," observed William Manchester in describing a generation that wanted "the good, sensible life" and that was "proud to be conservative, prosperous, conformist and vigilant defenders of the American way of life." The largest group of college undergraduates were business majors, and industry leaders were lionized (General Motors president Harlow Curtice was *Time*'s Man of the Year in 1956). A free market, left to its own devices, was thought to be the most efficient path to productivity. In 1957 the Soviets simultaneously launched *Sputnik 1* and the space race by taunting Americans with the specter of Russian superiority. Obeisance to technocracy took on patriotic as well as religious overtones.[9]

By the early 1960s, however, there were some new voices on the scene—discordant voices as far as the chemical industry was concerned; people raising questions and concerns about the new wonder products that no one dared to challenge. One of those voices belonged to Rachel Carson, a marine biologist who had worked for the U.S. Bureau of Fisheries. Carson was among the first scientists to raise popular concern about chemical pesticides. In articles she wrote in the *New Yorker* in 1961, and then with her famous book, *Silent Spring*, published in 1962, Carson warned generally that the killing effect of chemical pesticides wasn't limited to target pests. Rather, pesticides were indiscriminate in their collateral damage, including that done to human health. She singled out a group of insecticides—those that did their handiwork by attacking the central nervous systems of bugs and pests—which is what made them effective bug killers. Many insecticides were, in effect, nerve agents, although dispensed at low dose levels and later regulated. Still, Carson's point, and that of others in subsequent years, was that the use of nerve agents, period, was a bad idea.

Dow's Dursban

One of the chemical pesticides that came on the scene in the 1960s, even as Carson's message was first emerging, was chlorpyrifos. Dow began selling the new insecticide in 1965 under the trade name *Dursban*.* It soon became a multi-million-dollar-a-year product globally for many years; a product that proved to have the very nerve-agent effects that Rachel Carson warned about.** Nonetheless, chlorpyrifos was a chemical that Dow fought to continue using for many years after the first warning signs were raised— even in Dow's own labs.

Chlorpyrifos has its roots in 1930s Germany, in the firm of I.G. Farben, recruited by Hitler's government during WWII to design chemical warfare agents—among them, organophosphates such as tabun and sarin. Chlorpyrifos, described by chemists as "an organophosphate attached to a chlorinated pyridinol ring," became somewhat unique among pesticide compounds, having both organophosphate and organochlorine components, as well as a sulfur component. But it would take nearly 40 years before the full toxicity of this chemical, in all of its hundreds of uses and permutations, would be finally revealed and challenged. Dow Chemical played a key role in that process—and while going through the motions of compliance and safety testing, some believe the company used the regulatory system to prolong chlorpyrifos' market life, agreeing to restrictions over time, but continuing to fight for its use, insisting every step of the way it was safe when used as directed.

As pesticides generally came under modest public and regulatory scrutiny in the late 1960s and early 1970s, Dow quietly undertook some studies of chlorpyrifos—using human subjects. In 1971, Dow began tests on 16 "volunteer" prisoners at the Clinton Correctional Facility in Dannemora, New York. The subjects were split into four groups. Three of the groups received pills containing different doses of *Dowco 179*, made with chlorpyrifos. The remaining groups received placebos. The prisoners were monitored and their blood and urine analyzed. The results found that none of the 12 inmates who were fed chlorpyrifos became violently ill. One volunteer in the highest-dose group had complained of a runny nose, blurred vision, and a feeling of faintness. He was treated for a cold and recovered. But all four members in the highest-dose group also experienced something else: a

---

*The pesticide has been marketed under a number of trade names depending on its use, which could range from termiticide to pet care products. Among the many trade names used have been the following: *Dursban TC, Dursban LO, Dursban HF, Dursban 2E, Dursban 4E, Dursban 6, Dursban 30 SEC, Dursban 50 W, Dursban ME, Dursban Turf, Lentrek 6, Lorsban, Empire, Killmaster II, Duratrol,* and *Equity*.

**On its web page (www.dowagro.com/chlorp/about/ profile.htm, March 2003), Dow's technical definition of the chemical includes some description of its nerve action: "Chlorpyrifos is an organophosphate insecticide. Like other organophosphates, its insecticidal action is due to the inhibition of the enzyme acetylcholinesterase resulting in the accumulation of the neurotransmitter, acetylcholine, at the nerve endings. This results in excessive transmission of nerve impulses, which causes mortality in the target pest."

sharp drop in levels of an enzyme called plasma cholinesterase. That was evidence of some toxic insult to the human system. However, the readings returned to normal four weeks after the testing. Dow, meanwhile, continued to market its product, but also continued the safety testing.[10]

In 1972, when the widely-used insecticide DDT was banned, *Dursban* filled the void and replaced it. Sales took off. *Dursban* and related formulations did well through the 1970s. Soon Dow was selling *Dursban* and other formulations globally. "We had a big *Dursban* insecticide business in Indonesia," recounted Dow's Colin Goodchild. "We were supplying $10 million of *Dursban* to the rice industry in Indonesia."[11] By the early 1980s, Dow's agricultural chemicals business was bringing in about $500 million a year. The company then produced some of the leading lines of herbicide, including 2,4-D and *Tordon*. *Dursban* by then was the world's best-selling broad-range insecticide, and *Plictran* was a leading miticide. But Dow CEO, Paul Oreffice, felt that the company's agricultural chemicals business could do better, and in 1982, he tapped Keith McKennon, Dow's corporate public affairs director, to put the business more fully on a global footing. Recalls McKennon: "...We went from a bunch of people around the world thinking first about their region to a bunch of people around the world thinking first about Dow's global ag business...."[12]

Poison Reports

Back in the U.S., government officials in California and EPA had been tracking the use of chlorpyrifos, and noticed an uptick in the number of reported pesticide poisoning cases involving the chemical, then also used for killing termites in homes and office buildings. "Chlorpyrifos was the seventh most common cause of hospitalized pesticide poisoning in California...," reported EPA Health Statistician, Jerome Blondell in a June 1987 memo, citing the chemical's use during the 1981–85 period. Chlorpyrifos was also the second most commonly inquired-about pesticide on EPA's hotline, after chlordane, reported Blondell. "Although I do not have hard data," he continued, "I have heard many reports of serious allergic-type reactions to chlorpyrifos from people who have become sensitized to this chemical. Effort should be made to minimize exposure to the public." Blondell also added that the main source of California poisonings was the use of chlorpyrifos in the workplace, "typically in office buildings," he said. "How many of these cases involved termite application is not known."[13]

In a one-page summary of his findings attached to the memo, Blondell cited several reports and studies of poisonings in which chlorpyrifos was implicated. From the 1981 PIMS report, he noted 113 incidents alleging chlorpyrifos-caused adverse health events—including two fatalities. The Consumer Product Safety Commission had conducted six investigations of chlorpyrifos pesticide applicators who had become ill either at home or in their yard. One was seriously poisoned after a gust of wind blew the chemical on him from a nearby spraying operation. Blondell also cited another incident reported in summaries appearing in both the *New England Journal of Medicine* and the *Journal of Occupational Medicine.* In that case, five office workers became ill when the outside of their building—a 40-foot by 40-foot cement bunker with one door and one air intake port—was treated for termites with chlropyrifos and bendicarb. "Chlorpyrifos drawn through the air intake was believed to be the responsible cause for the illnesses," reported Blondell. The authors of the studies cited by Blondell recommended that such pesticides only be applied to empty buildings and that reentry to such buildings be delayed for some time after spraying.[14]

> **"Chlorpyrifos was the seventh most common cause of hospitalized pesticide poisoning in California...," reported the EPA.**

By 1986, some state health departments, such as that in New Jersey, included the following statements about chlorpyrifos in their "hazard summary" paragraph issued in a state hazardous substance fact sheet typically aimed at workers and the general public:

- Chlorpyrifos can affect you when breathed in and quickly enters the body by passing through the skin. Severe poisoning can occur from skin contact. It is a moderately toxic organophosphate chemical.
- Exposure can cause rapid, severe poisoning with headache, sweating, nausea, and vomiting, diarrhea, loss of coordination, and death.
- Chlorpyrifos may damage the nervous system and liver with repeated exposure.[15]

New Jersey also reported that chlorpyrifos had not then been tested for its ability to cause cancer, but noted there was "limited evidence that chlorpyrifos may damage the

developing fetus." That was in 1986. The following year, EPA banned chlordane, a chemical widely used for killing termites. Chlordane was sold by a Dow competitor, Velsicol, and its ban opened the door wider for Dow's chlorpyrifos. *Dursban* soon captured chlordane's market share, becoming the leading termite poison. Also then used in a number of other farm and household applications, *Dursban* was well on its way to becoming a $1-billion-a-year product for Dow.

Safe Pesticides?

In 1988, Congress amended the nation's pesticide law—known as FIFRA, the Federal Insecticide, Fungicide and Rodenticide Act—to require EPA to re-examine the toxicological information it used for assessing pesticide safety. More than 800 compounds had been registered prior to 1984, and the new amendments meant that all of these compounds, plus the continued flow of new ones, had to be evaluated. Needless to say, this was a enormous task for EPA, one which would take years, if not decades, to complete satisfactorily. One of the chemicals getting a closer look was *Dursban's* chlorpyrifos.

By June 1989, EPA had complied a draft guidance for the re-registration of chlorpyrifos whose "science chapters" alone—embracing past and present lab studies and other reports—spanned 732 pages. But still, there were gaps in the data and a lack of health-effects testing. In September 1991, EPA initiated what is known as "a data call-in" to fill in some of the information needed to evaluate chlorpyrifos. "The agency has concluded that additional data on chlorpyrifos are needed in all discipline areas," EPA wrote in its certified mail notice to all those using chlorpyrifos-containing products. That meant a range of things would be examined—product chemistry, residue chemistry, toxicology, environmental fate, and ecological effects would all be evaluated using the latest science. Health-effects testing would also be undertaken. In addition, EPA indicated it also sought a specific analysis of chlorpyrifos "for potential impurities structurally related to dibenzodioxins." Offering its rationale for this testing, EPA explained that it was "concerned that an impurity structurally related to TCDD (2,3,7-8-tetrachloro-p-dioxin) may form during the manufacture of chlorpyrifos, based on starting materials used and other impurities known to occur." All of the new data were needed, EPA explained, "to conduct a comprehensive review of chrorpyrifos for re-registration, including a reassessment of tolerances."[16] Among other field and scientific reports on chlorpyrifos in the 1989–91 timeframe, were findings that a major biological metabolite and environmental breakdown product of chlorpyrifos was 3,5,6-trichloro-2-pyridinol, or TCP. EPA had determined, by way of monitoring, that some Cape Cod, Massachusetts golf courses where chlorpyrifos was applied to turf, showed TCP present in the groundwater. Elsewhere, USDA's Southern Forest Experimental Station noted that certain termite formulations of chlorpyrifos were effective for more than 15 years, which underscored the chemical's persistence.[17] But despite the findings and EPA's data call-in during the late 1980s, nothing much happened on chlorpyrifos. The agency had already banned chlordane.

The chlorpyrifos empire of products for Dow, meanwhile, had become enormous. It was not only the primary ingredient in *Dursban* and *Lorsban*, but was also found in more than 800 other products, ranging from flea collars to bug sprays, such as *Raid*, *Hartz* flea sprays, and *Black Flag* roach and ant killer. It was also used widely on farm crops from citrus

Household use surveys of 1992 showed that 17 percent of the nation's homes then used chlorpyrifos-containing products.

to vegetables, on residential lawns and gardens, and by various pest and termite exterminators in office buildings, schools, and day-care centers. Household use surveys of 1992 showed that 17 percent of the nation's homes then used chlorpyrifos-containing products, applied millions of times each year in kitchens, bathrooms, bedrooms, living rooms, lawns, gardens, porches, and pets. In all, about 200 million household-related applications were being made each year. Agricultural uses then were variously estimated at between 10 and 20 million pounds per year, with termite exterminators using more than 1 million pounds a year. Dow by this time had also merged its agricultural operations with those of Eli Lilly, becoming DowElanco (and later, Dow AgroSciences), giving the firm additional political and economic influence in certain states and congressional districts.

Reports of *Dursban* poisonings, however, continued, with some surfacing in the case files of private attorneys either bringing lawsuits or considering them. Among such incidents in the files of one Oneida, New York law firm, for example, were those from an April 1992 list of individuals allegedly injured by *Dursban*, offered below in the law firm's anonymous shorthand:[18]

"Mr. R."—37-year-old male, married with 2 children. Sprayed with *Dursban L.O.* at work. Treated approximately 1 month for symptoms of flu and sore throat. After second application of *Dursban* at place of employment caused acute symptoms, illness was properly diagnosed. DX: Reactive airways dysfunction syndrome, secondary to acute organophosphate poisoning. Prognosis: Totally and permanently disabled.

"Ms. B."—63-year-old female, married... Employed in a facility where *Dursban L.O.* was sprayed every Friday night. Developed chronic symptoms of pesticide exposure. Doctor ordered [her] to be removed from the building before spraying. Fill-in applicator sprayed with Ms. B. present, causing acute reaction. DX: Chronic obstructive airways disease; chronic bronchitis. Prognosis: Totally and permanently disabled.

DowElanco—1989

In April 1989, Dow and Eli Lilly, the Indianapolis, Indiana pharmaceutical giant—agreed to merge their pesticide businesses in a new joint venture called DowElanco. Focused on crop-based chemicals, the new venture—60 percent owned by Dow and 40 percent by Lilly—would become the world's sixth largest ag-chem company with projected sales of about $1.5 billion annually. Wall Street analysts were generally positive on the deal. Anantha Raman, a chemical industry analyst in Parsippany, New Jersey, called it a "super deal and a good marriage." The *Wall Street Journal* described the venture as fitting "Dow's long-term strategy of moving into speciality markets to balance its plastic and industrial chemical businesses."[19] Dow's ag business alone, explained Clay Williams, a Dow vice president, "could have remained a good second-tier company." But adding DowElanco, he said, "offers us an opportunity to be a world-class player in the top tier." Dow would hold the CEO seat in the venture, with headquarters located in Indianapolis. About 45 percent of Dow's ag chem business at the time was based in the U.S., compared to 55 percent for Lilly's Elanco. The new venture also planned to build a $35 million research center in Indianapolis, and would have some 2,800 employees in marketing, sales, and research with another 4,500 in related production operations. An internal company assessment of the new DowElanco in November 1989, saw a company with a burgeoning stable of products. The new company's pyridine pesticides, which had their roots in Dow's 1930s chemistry, included *Dursban* (chlorpyrifos), *Tordon* (picloram), *Garlon* (triclopyr), *Starane* (fluroxypyr), *Lontrel* (clopyralid), and *Gallant/Verdict* (haloxyfop-ethoxyethyl). These alone accounted for 70 percent of Dow's agrichemical sales. Dow's phenoxy herbicides, including 2,4-D, added another 10 percent of sales. Fungicides coming from the Lilly side of the operation, included *Beam* (tricyclazole), *Rubigan* (fenarimol) and *Trimidal* (nuarimol). By 1990, this stable of products was effectively covering industrial and agricultural markets in numerous countries. *Dursban* by then was one of the most widely used insecticides globally. *Treflan,* or trifluralin, had been a wildly successful dintoraniline herbicide for Lilly, used on corn and soybeans, and despite coming off patent in 1985, was still going strong. *Tordon, Gasolne* and *Spike* (tebuthiuron)—all herbicides—were used for rangeland brush control. *Spike* was also used on sugar cane in Brazil. *Starane* herbicides were doing well in the U.K., France, and West Germany, and were also being sold in Romania and the Soviet Union. They were also being targeted for "plantation crops" in the Pacific region. *Gallant/Verdict*, technically a graminicide, or grass herbicide, was registered for use on broad-leaved crops, but was most widely used on soybeans, registered in 38 countries, including Italy and the former Soviet republics. *Flexidor* (isoxaben), a herbicide, was marketed in Europe for small grain cereal crops, and was also being used in the U.S. under the trade name *Gallery* for turf, ornamental, and non-crop uses. *Flexidor* was also being sold in Australia. *Rubigan*, a fungicide used on vineyard, orchards and vegetable crops, was being sold in the United States, Europe, Latin America, and Japan. *Trimidal*, another fungicide for cereal and other crops, was being marketed in a number of European countries. *Cut-

less (flurprimidol), a plant growth regulator, was being sold in the U.S. for use on turf such as golf courses in order to reduce mowing. The new DowElanco also had a research pipeline full of expectant new herbicides, insecticides, fungicides in various stages of development. The company's principal manufacturing locations at the time were: Midland, Michigan; Lafayette, Indiana; Pittsburg, California; Freeport, Texas; Kings Lynn, U.K.; Stade, Germany; Comopolis, Brazil; Aratu, Brazil; New Plymouth, New Zealand; and Kuala Lumpur, Malaysia.

Sources: Gregory Witcher and Frank E. James, "Dow, Eli Lilly To Join Forces In Agrochemicals," *Wall Street Journal*, April 19, 1989, p. A-8; Milt Freudenheim, "Lilly and Dow to Combine Farm Chemicals Divisions," *New York Times*, April 19, 1989, p. D-1; and Ellen Goldbaum with Langdon Brockinton, "An Ag Venture is Born," *Chemical Week*, April 26, 1989, p. 9. Company Feature: "DowElanco Moves In And Plans Ahead," *Agrow*, June 1, 1990, No. 112, pp. 8–9.

"Ms. L."—25-year-old female, married, no children. Exposed to regular applications of *Dursban L.O.* at work place. Developed chronic bronchitis, pneumonia and asthma. Has returned to work but suffers fatigue, shortness of breath and hypersensitivity to cleaner, smoke, perfume, etc. DX: Reactive airways dysfunction syndrome. Prognosis: Permanently partially disabled.

"Ms. M."—31-year-old female, married, no children. Exposed to regular applications of *Dursban L.O.* at work place. Developed asthma and hyperactive airways dysfunction. Forced to change employments to limit exposure to exhaust, fumes, perfumes and smoke. DX: Reactive airways dysfunction syndrome. Prognosis: Employed but has permanent lung damage and permanent reactive airways dysfunction syndrome.

"Ms. W."—25-year-old female, married, one child. Exposed to *Dursban L.O.* at work place. Developed chronic bronchitis, recurring pneumonia and asthma. DX: Reactive airways dysfunction syndrome. Prognosis: Has returned to work. Suffers continued fatigue, shortness of breath and hypersensitivity to perfume, odors, smoke and exhaust.

People Getting Sick

In Montgomeryville, Pennsylvania in 1992, Connie Eash, her husband, and their six-year-old son, Michael, were living a comfortable suburban life north of Philadelphia. Connie was a former scientist employed by the pharmaceutical firm, Squibb. In the fall of 1992, Michael began to come home from first grade with a low-grade fever and other ills. Connie thought he might be having recurring flu bouts or that "he just didn't like school." But over the summer of 1993, Michael became healthy again and even joined a swimming team. Then in the fall of 1993, Michael and 16 other children at his school became sick. Michael's problems persisted, and Connie Eash went looking for answers. She found that the North Penn School District was using chlorpyrifos to keep its buildings pest-free. When she had Michael tested, the results showed that he was suffering from pesticide poisoning. Tests conducted at Michael's school by the Montgomery County Health Department failed to show there was a pesticide-related problem, according to the department. Connie Eash, however, remained convinced that chlorpyrifos was causing Michael's problems and pulled him out of school. She tutored him at home for five months. Michael did go back to school, shook off some of his health problems, but still has difficulties. "Michael has developed chemical sensitivity as a result of the poisoning," she says. He also had to quit swimming because he became sensitive to chlorine.[20]

By 1994, a survey of 1,000 Americans found 82 percent of them had residues of chlorpyrifos in their urine.

In 1993, a *McCall's* magazine article featured suspected effects of a *Dursban* treatment for Lyme disease at the Burke family residence in Suffolk Country, New York. The Burkes had three children. When their oldest daughter was a toddler, the Burkes began regularly treating their carpets with *Dursban* to kill Lyme-disease carrying ticks that their dog might have carried. The Burke's second child was born with cerebral palsy, cataracts, and suffered from seizures. When their third child was born with similar problems, doctors agreed that the children might have been damaged prenatally by the *Dursban* treatments.[21]

By 1994, a survey of 1,000 Americans found 82 percent of them had residues of chlorpyrifos in their urine. But not all people—as the cases of young Michael Eash in Pennsylvania and others in New York seemed to show—are affected the same way by chemicals. A certain number of people, scientists began discovering, were "hypersensitive." Others might be exposed one time to a particular chemical without incident, and then at a second exposure, have very dramatic reactions and subsequent health problems. Consider the case of Joey Walker, who used a chlorpyrifos-containing product named *Green Light*, described by reporter Jim Morris for *U.S. News & World Report*:

> ...[O]n the afternoon of July 31, 1993, Joey Walker applied a granular fire-ant killer called *Green Light* to his yard in Liberty Hill, Texas. Dressed in a T-shirt, jeans, and boots, Walker was using a hand-held spreader—just as the label instructed—and inhaled the compound, absorbed it through his sweaty skin, or both. That evening, he collapsed on the sofa, complaining of flu-like nausea, fatigue, and headache. In April 1994, he suffered a grand mal seizure while watching his oldest son play Little League baseball. "He turned blue," his wife, Margaret, recalls. "All his muscles drew right up, like the Incredible Hulk." Walker was in and out of hospitals

for 15 months. In August 1995, he was admitted to a nursing home, where he remains in a vegetative state. Walker had used *Green Light* without incident the year before he got sick....Walker, now 43, is oblivious. "He can look around," his wife says, "but we're not sure what he sees."[22]

Failure to Report

Meanwhile, it turned out that Dow Chemical and DowElanco were not always reporting to EPA the full picture of chlorpyrifos and *Dursban* adverse reactions they were receiving from the field. Under the federal pesticide law, known as FIFRA, pesticide makers are required to submit any information on the adverse effects of their pesticides to EPA promptly. These include "adverse incident reports"—in effect, poisoning reports—that occur with agricultural workers or consumers for one or more reasons. Dow Chemical and DowElanco had reported some but not all incidents in the 1989–94 period. In May 1995, EPA charged that DowElanco failed to report in a timely manner some 288 claims of "adverse effects," most from *Dursban*, but also some from other Dow or DowElanco pesticides, including trifluralin, triclopyr, picloram, and 2,4-D. Nearly 250 of the claims were for *Dursban*-related incidents. The claims involved nervous system effects, neurotoxicity, and other problems.[23] In its investigation of DowElanco's practices, EPA had requested and received from DowElanco additional information on some of the alleged poisoning incidents—"factual information concerning unreasonable adverse effects" of the pesticides on human health or the environment; information "that was not reported to EPA prior to December 27, 1994." DowElanco, it appears, was being selective about which effects it was reporting.[24] EPA considered DowElanco's withholding of documents a major infraction and assessed a record fine of $732,000. The company then appealed, but an administrative law judge found Dow's withholding of information so serious that the fine was actually increased to $890,000 in August 1995. DowElanco then settled for $876,000. Dow had argued that the late submissions of the 288 cases occurred because the company and the EPA had different interpretations of federal law. A year earlier, New York's attorney general had brought an action against DowElanco for making deceptive claims in a *Dursban* brochure. DowElanco agreed to discontinue the practice, but said its statements in the brochure were not deceptive, but grounded in science.

EPA by this time had compiled an analysis of chlorpyrifos-related "adverse incident" case summaries supplied by DowElanco. The agency

was focusing in particular on a condition known as delayed peripheral neuropathy, in which the sensory and motor nerves to the arms and legs are
impaired, with the victims experiencing muscle weakness and inability to
coordinate movement. "Available evidence from case reports suggests that
chlorpyrifos may be a cause of delayed peripheral neuropathy," wrote EPA
health statistician, Dr. Jerome Blondell in a January 1995 memo. The memo
included 30 case profiles of adverse incidents related to chlorpyrifos.[25]

Eye-to-Eye, 1995

As EPA was conducting its analysis, CBS aired its report on *Dursban* in
January 1995 on *Eye to Eye with Connie Chung,* a report based partly on EPA's
files. Among those appearing on Chung's show with reporter Roberta Baskin,
as mentioned earlier, were the three individuals who alleged *Dursban* poisoning—Jack Kahn, the termite exterminator; Joe Cotazino, the New York civil
servant; and Jim Geralds, the high school student from Lewisburg, Ohio.[26]
Dursban, these and others on the
show would conclude, changed
their health, or made them more
sensitive to other chemicals, altering
their lives.

> **"These are nerve agents akin to the chemicals that were used in Iraq."**

Baskin also interviewed Dr.
Ronald Gotts, an environmental
toxicologist who consulted with Dow. "*Dursban* is a valuable agent or it
wouldn't be used in 7 million homes and thousands of farms every year," he
said. "...It prevents crop damage. It prevents our homes from being infest-
ed by termites. It kills fire ants, it kills bees, it kills fleas." On the other side,
Baskin spoke with Dr. Janette Sherman, a scientist who has written widely
about organophosphates, including chlorpyrifos. "*Dursban* kills insects by
interfering with their nervous system," Sherman explained, "and it interferes
with humans' nervous systems just the same way," she said. "...These are
nerve agents," she reiterated later in the show, "...akin to the chemicals that
are—were used in Iraq. These are the same families of chemicals that are
used to kill people."[27]

Dow sent CBS a letter for the show, apparently in answer to some questions. In the letter, Dow stated, that from an acute standpoint, *Dursban* was
about as toxic as caffeine. Baskin asked EPA's Dr. Lynn Goldman, the
agency's top pesticide official at the time, if Dow's assessment was a fair
statement. "...[T]hat's not the way I would characterize the toxicity of *Dursban* at all," Goldman replied. "We have information that this product might
be causing long-term neurological effects." Goldman explained on camera
that "in some of these cases, people didn't even have symptoms of acute
pesticide poisoning. They are reported to have instead developed more sub-

Dursban Goes To India

Even as chlorpyrifos was under increased scrutiny in the U.S., DowElanco was moving forward with business plans to produce and sell more of it in India and elsewhere. In 1995, Dow had plans to form a new company near Bombay to produce pesticides, *Dursban* among them. The new company would be a joint venture with Bombay's National Chemicals Industries Ltd., called DE-NOCIL Crop Protection. DE-NOCIL would produce chlorpyrifos, the active ingredient in *Dursban*, as its first product at the Lote manufacturing site, south of Bombay. Startup was planned for 1996. DE-NOCIL's plant would have expansion capacity to produce up to 8,800 metric tons of product each year. "DE-NOCIL is one of India's top five chemical companies and is recognized for its leadership role, especially in its commitment to health, safety and the environment," said G. L. Jerry Ytzen, DowElanco Pacific manager in March 1995.

Source: Doug Henze, "DowElanco Plans New Product Plant in India," *Midland Daily News*, March 6, 1995.

tle symptoms that then turned into chronic problems—problems with memory, problems with coordination, difficulty concentrating—very serious neurological effects."[28]

Baskin was later shown in the telecast with Jim Geralds, the schoolboy from Lewisburg, Ohio. "I couldn't concentrate," he said. "I couldn't get my homework done, so my grades slipped and I was a very good student." Tri-County North, Geralds' school in rural Lewisburg, was sprayed with *Dursban* on a regular basis. DowElanco instructions on its product warned against people entering an area that had been sprayed for at least four hours. But Jim Geralds was one of dozens of students who regularly came in only a half-hour later. "... [E]verybody had the same symptoms," he told Baskin. "Headaches, nauseousness, dizziness, tiredness, leg cramps—a range—tons of symptoms." These were symptoms similar to flu, explained Dr. Sherman to Baskin, following up. "It sounds like the flu," said Baskin. "Yes, and that's why it doesn't get diagnosed," said Dr. Sherman. Baskin then concluded the segment: "Jim Geralds transferred out of Tri-County North. So did children from some 50 other families. The school stopped spraying *Dursban* and renovated its faulty ventilation system. DowElanco points to a government report that blames the ventilation system problem, not *Dursban*."[29]

Protect The Children

In 1996, Congress enacted the Food Quality Protection Act, which amended existing pesticide law and required strong new health protections for children. One EPA analysis found that more than half of the 17,771 suspected chlorpyrifos poisoning incidents reported to U.S. poison-control centers between 1993 and 1996 involved children under the age of six. Chlorpyrifos was still being widely used across the country. In New York, one formulation of *Dursban Pro* was the state's most popular bug killer in 1997—3.5 million pounds and 665,000 gallons were applied throughout the state that year. The chemical was still being used extensively in schools, too. In 1997, a survey of 46 California school districts found that almost half routinely applied pesticides containing chlorpyrifos.

EPA did move against *Dursban* and DowElanco in 1997—but not against the pesticide's big markets for residential and agricultural uses. Under pressure from the agency, DowElanco agreed in 1997 to withdraw the compound from a few specialized markets, such as indoor total-release foggers and pet shampoos. "The agreement with Dow is inconsequential in terms of the overall risk to public health," said Jay Feldman, executive director of the National Coalition Against the Misuse of Pesticides.

In October 1998, Dow tested *Dursban* on 60 men and women at a lab in Lincoln, Nebraska.

DowElanco, meanwhile, realizing that it would soon be facing tougher threshold levels for chlorpyrifos under the 1996 law, moved to update its testing data. Dow decided to do some tests on human subjects. In October 1998, Dow tested *Dursban* on 60 men and women at a private lab in Lincoln, Nebraska. The lab targeted students at the University of Nebraska as potential test subjects, advertising for volunteers who could "earn extra money," as one ad claimed. Dow's test subjects in Nebraska were given pills containing chlorpyrifos and were paid about $200 each. Gary Hamlin, a spokesman for Dow AgroSciences, said Dow sought the human research as a complement to some 3,600 previous studies on the pesticide. Direct testing on human volunteers, Hamlin explained, could help clear up uncertainty that exists between animal studies and the eventual impact on people. Previous research guided the dosage levels for the human subjects, said Hamlin, so that the tests "would not cause any harm to the volunteers." Ken Cook, president of the Environmental Working Group in Washington called the testing questionable. "Would you want your kid to participate in a study like this?" he asked.[30] The incident fed into the debate then raging over the ethics of testing pesticides on humans, which continues as this book goes to press.* But Dow's efforts in Nebraska were for naught, as the *Dursban* study using the human subjects was thrown out by EPA scientists. The agency's Scientific Advisory Panel had already concluded that the small sample sizes

---

*EPA is currently weighing the matter of human testing, as Dow and others in the industry want to retain the practice. See, for example, *www.ewg.org* and Tennille Tracy, "Spoon-Feeding Poison," *The Village Voice*, July 9–15, 2003.

and limited data evaluated in such studies gave them little scientific value.

Through 1999, Dow had spent more than $100 million on 3,600 studies that suggested chlorpyrifos was harmless when properly applied. Why then, asked *U.S. News & World Report* journalist Jim Morris, was the company the target of 274 lawsuits since 1990? "It's been the biggest kid on the block for a long, long time," replied Guy Relford, the company's global legal counsel. "Historically, [*Dursban* has been] one of the most prevalently used insecticides in the world, and when you're out there in the marketplace like that, then you're going to be a target."

Two studies suggested the pesticide inhibited the body's ability to create plasma and red blood cells.

However, in October 1999, a panel of pesticide experts reviewing chlorpyrifos and reporting to EPA recommended tighter controls on *Dursban*. Among the studies the panel considered were two human studies which suggested that people may be more sensitive to the product than animals. Both of the studies suggested that the pesticide inhibited the body's ability to create plasma and red blood cells. The panel noted that the chemical was so widely used throughout the U.S. that a majority of the nation's population had been exposed to it. At the time, EPA identified 822 products containing the pesticide, ranging from flea collars to agricultural sprays and pest control at schools and day-care centers. But the review panel noted that health risks were greatest among workers who applied the chemical to homes and lawns. EPA said the report was the first step in a long process of hearings and policy judgments. Dow Chemical, however, stood behind its product, saying that "three decades of use have shown chlorpyrifos products can be applied safely by homeowners, gardeners, pest-control operators and others."[31]

Dow soon began placing full-page ads in a number of farming magazines depicting farmers going out of business because of restrictions on *Lorsban*, the agricultural version of *Dursban*. "The World Without Dursban," was the headline Dow used on one ad. A friendly-looking, family-farm style pickup truck was featured, its roadside vegetable bins empty, sitting behind a homemade sign that normally read "Fresh Fruits and Vegetables," now plastered over with a placard that read "Fresh out of business." Dow's text explained:

> It's not just the back of the pickup truck at the local farmers' market. Without *Lorsban-4E* insecticide, packing houses, processing plants, maybe even grocery stores would run a little short. That's because for 20 years, *Lorsban* has been a crucial part of IPM [integrated pest management] programs, actually becoming the most widely used insecticide in the West. And with its help, growers have produced quality fruit, vegetables, and fiber unparalleled anywhere in the world. With continued support, we'll keep this truck rolling.

EPA Acts

In June 2000, EPA announced an agreement with the manufacturers of chlorpyrifos to sharply limit the uses of the pesticide, eliminating uses around homes, schools, and other places where children might be exposed. By then, there were six manufacturers, of which Dow AgroSciences was the largest. The chemical would also be limited in agricultural uses on apples, grapes, and tomatoes to limit children's exposure to the chemical in fruit juices. "Organophosphates are a World War II class of chemicals," said EPA's Carol Browner at the announcement. "We can do better today." Dow officials, however, stood by the safety of their product when properly used. "The rules have changed, but the safety of chlorpyrifos hasn't," said Elin Miller, a Dow Agro-Sciences vice president.[32] In making the announcement, Browner said the scientific evidence of unacceptable risk was clear, justifying the agency's action. She also noted that poison control centers had received about 800 calls a year for incidents related to chlorpyrifos-containing products and that "too many" of the incidents were among children. Browner, in fact, took special pains to show the agency's concern for protecting children:

> This action is good news for the protection of the country's public health, it is good news for the environment, and it is particularly good news for children, who are among the most vulnerable to the risks posed by pesticides.
> ...Children are not just small adults. Their bodies are still developing, and they are more susceptible to risk from toxic chemicals. They play on the floor. They play in yards where pesticides have been applied... When our health and safety standards protect children, the entire public is protected.[33]

Some environmentalists and public officials, however, while lauding the deal, felt the timeline was too generous and urged retailers handling the product to move on their own. New York Attorney General Eliot Spitzer said the federal ban did not go far enough, and urged retailers to pull chlorpyrifos products off their shelves.[34] Some big retailers handling the product, such as Wal-Mart, announced they would stop selling the products by the end of October 2000, more than a year ahead of EPA's deadline. But the battle over chlorpyrifos, and with Dow Chemical, didn't end there.

New York Sues

In April 2003, New York Attorney General Eliot Spitzer announced his intent to sue Dow AgroSciences for violating a previous agreement the company had made with the state regarding *Dursban* advertising. Spitzer alleged that Dow had made repeated violations of its 1994 agreement governing the advertising of the pesticide. Dow was supposed to stop making claims that *Dursban* was "safe," but continued to make the claim despite the fact that chlorpyrifos had been linked to severe health problems, including nerve damage, asthma, and birth defects. In addition, the safety claims were expressly prohibited by state and federal law.

An investigation in the early 1990s by Spitzer's office found that Dow engaged in false and misleading advertising that violated both state and federal laws. In exchange for not paying fines for its illegal advertising claims, Dow signed an agreement with the state in 1994, in which it pledged to reform its advertising and marketing practices. However, since the 1994 agreement, Dow AgroSciences continued to advertise *Dursban* products, claiming they had no "long term (health) effects," and that the pesticide exhibited "no evidence of significant risk to the environment." Spitzer's lawsuit, filed in New York State Supreme Court in Manhattan, sought a court order directing Dow to cease its deceptive advertising. It also sought substantial monetary penalties for the company's violations of its agreement with the state. "Consumers must not be lulled into a false sense of security by misleading safety claims," Spitzer said. "They should be urged to use pesticides only with the utmost caution."

Spitzer prevailed in his action. In mid-December 2003, Dow AgroSciences agreed to pay a $2 million penalty to resolve the dispute over its *Dursban* advertising. Dow said it was making the payment to avoid protracted litigation, while retaining its right to defend false claims made against its pesticide. Spitzer's office reiterated that Dow had been in violation of the 1994 agreement almost from its inception, making misleading safety claims about chlorpyrifos-containing products in print, TV, video, and internet advertisements. "Pesticides are toxic substances that should be used with great caution," Spitzer said in a written statement. "By misleading consumers about the potential dangers associated with the use of their products, Dow's ads may have endangered human health and the environment by encouraging people to use their products without proper care."[35]

Under the December 12, 2003 consent judgment, signed by Manhattan Supreme Court Justice Joan Madden, Dow agreed to pay a $2 million penalty and is barred from making safety claims about its pesticide. Dow must also meet three other stipulations: conduct an internal review of all advertisements published by Dow or its agents in New York State and remove any that make safety claims about pesticide products; appoint an attorney who will be responsible for reviewing and approving advertisements; and institute an employee training program for advertising agency workers who create or review Dow advertising.

Spitzer investigated Dow ads from 1995 to 2003. Among the advertised claims he found Dow making was: "No significant adverse health effects will likely result from exposures to *Dursban* even at levels substantially above

Circle-of-Poison

Two other DowElanco pesticides that brought criticism in the early 1990s were those that failed to meet U.S. registration standards for health and/or environmental reasons, but were marketed abroad by DowElanco and used on a wide variety of crops and feed grains. Some of those pesticides came back to America in the form of imported foods in classic "circle-of-poison" style. The two chemicals at issue, with their jaw-breaking names, were haloxyfop and nuarimol, the former a herbicide and the latter a fungicide. Activists argued that not only did the use and sale of these pesticides overseas place DowElanco in a category of "below-best-standard practices," but that residues of the "never-registered-in-the-U.S." pesticides in imported foods, meats, and beverages put American consumers at risk. First, consider haloxyfop.

Sold under the tradenames *Galant, Gallant, Verdict*, and *Dowco 453 ME*, haloxyfop is a "systemic herbicide," meaning that the chemical is taken up by the crop plant it is used on, and that residues can remain in the edible plant tissue or fruit. In 1988, EPA upgraded haloxyfop from a Class C, or "possible" human carcinogen, to a Class B-2, or "probable" human carcinogen. The World Health Organization classifies haloxyfop as a "moderately hazardous pesticide." In 1988, when EPA upgraded its classification of haloxyfop to a "probable" human carcinogen, studies showed "significant increases in benign and malignant liver tumors in male and female mice" and also "a strong structure activity relationship with other biphenyl ether herbicides" which could cause tumors. Health effects observed in lab animals included harm to the liver, testes, red blood cell components, serum blood cholesterol, and cornea. If liquid haloxyfop entered the lungs—called aspiration—researchers found, it could cause lung damage or even death due to pneumonia. In addition, the *Verdict* and *Gallant* formulations of haloxyfop contained xylenes as inert ingredients in the mixture. Xylenes are known to damage the liver, kidneys and bone marrow, are toxic to the fetus and the nervous system, and cause a low blood cell count. It is also known that haloxyfop can potentially leach into groundwater following application, and is toxic to fish.

Still, with all of this known about the chemical in the U.S., haloxyfop was being used in the early 1990s in at least 36 foreign countries—a number of which were U.S. food exporters. Haloxyfop herbicides were then being used overseas on alfalfa, beans, cabbage, carrots, chickpeas, coconut, cotton seed, cucumbers, fruits, mungbeans, onions, potatoes, peanuts, peas, soybeans, sugarbeets, sunflowers, pears, rape and tobacco. In 1990, more than 360,000 metric tons of Australian beef were imported to the U.S., representing about 47 percent of all U.S. beef imports. Haloxyfop herbicides were used on Australian soy, chickpeas, rapeseed, lupines, field peas, navy beans and sunflowers, all of which were fed to Australian cattle. Argentina—also an exporter of beef to America, with 1991 exports exceeding 57,000 tons—fed haloxyfop-treated soybeans to its cattle. Haloxyfop was also being used on palm oil plants in Indonesia, the No. 2 exporter of palm oil to the U.S. Palm oil, in addition to its use in frying and cooking, is often added to margarine, spreads, and frozen foods. France—which used haloxyfop-methyl herbicides to treat its grapevines in 1991—then accounted for more than one-fourth of U.S. wine imports.

Nuarimol is another DowElanco pesticide sold abroad under the trade names *Gauntlet, Trimidal,* and *Criminal.* Known in chemical argot as a chlorinated pyrimidine fungicide, nuarimol is used as a seed-treatment and a spray. It is also a systemic pesticide, whose residues can travel throughout a plant, including its edible parts. EPA rejected a DowElanco food tolerance petition for the fungicide's use on bananas in 1983 after it found cancer and birth defects in lab animal tests. DowElanco testing data showed that a single oral as well as inhalation exposure of the chemical to laboratory rats caused them to exhibit reduced activity, muscle contraction, loss of balance and coordination, labored breathing, reduced weight gain, and coma. Laboratory animals also exhibited increases in liver weight and enzyme activity and microscopic liver cell changes when repeatedly exposed to the product. The fungicide is classified as a "slightly hazardous" Class III pesticide by the World Health Organization and is also an eye irritant. In the environment, nuarimol is moderately hazardous to fish, falling in EPA's Class III toxicity category.

Although DowElanco's 1983 banana petition remained active and pending for eight years, it never pursued any other U.S.-based food-tolerance applications for nuarimol. Internationally, however, nuarimol is used in at least 19 countries, many of which use it as a fungicide, seed treatment or foliar spray on apples, artichokes, barley, bush beans, chicory, cucumbers, fruits, grapes, melons, nectarines, peaches, peanuts, pears, peppers, strawberries, sugarbeets, wheat, and zucchini. In Germany and the U.K.—two major exporters of malt beverages to the U.S.—nuarimol is applied to barley seed. In Italy, France, and Spain, nuarimol is used extensively on grapevines, those counties being the top three exporters of wine to the U.S.

Source: Sandra Marquardt, Laura Glassman, and Elizabeth Sheldon, *Never-Registered Pesticides: Rejected Toxics Join the "Circle of Poison,"* Five Case Studies of Pesticides Manufactured by DowElanco, FMC Corporation, Mobay Corporation, and Monsanto Agricultural Company. Greenpeace USA, February 1992.

those expected to occur when applied at label rates." Meanwhile, scientists, like Dr. Philip Landrigan of the Department of Community and Preventative Medicine at Mount Sinai Medical Center in New York City, continued to stress what was known about chlorpyrifos. "Excellent studies conducted by independent scientists have clearly shown that chlorpyrifos, the active ingredient in *Dursban,* is toxic to the human brain and nervous system and is especially dangerous to the developing brain of infants," he said.[36]

A glimpse into how Dow may have been marketing the pesticide, and splitting fine hairs in the process, came in the retort from Dow's head attorney, Guy A. Relford: "The 1994 agreement restricted our ability to support and defend our products, even if our statements were true," he said. "For instance, the old agreement was interpreted by the New York attorney general as prohibiting our informing people that the U.S. Environmental Protection Agency had registered one of our products as a Reduced Risk Pesticide." Spitzer's office was also looking at a wider range of Dow communications, such as labeling and other non-advertising Dow statements—to which Dow objected. So under the penalty, Dow retained the right to make company statements in response to "product-related public concerns," according to Dow. The penalty paid by Dow was the largest pesticide enforcement penalty ever in New York state.[37]

Hot Compost

Composting is a centuries old practice of taking decaying organic matter such as leaves, grass clippings, garbage, and other material and allowing time and nature to work their magic. Composting turns biological discards into "gardener's gold"—that is, a soil-enriching material that backyard gardeners and farmers use to improve their flowers, vegetables, and crops. In the last few decades, composting in the U.S. has enjoyed a popular rebirth of sorts as the organic farming and gardening movements have grown. Composting has also become a major business for some, now involving sizeable contracts for collecting and recycling biological wastes on a municipal-wide scale in some cities, generating large amounts of usable compost while saving considerable sums of money for what would otherwise be landfill waste.

Dow Chemical, however, has become something of an unwanted guest in the composting world since 1999–2001, when one of its lawn-based herbicides named *Confront*, was found contaminating compost used by backyard gardeners and some farming operations. "Composting is one of the oldest and easiest types of recycling," said Bill Shee-

"Dow's toxic products . . . are killing financially successful compost programs that keep thousands of tons of organic material out of landfills."

han, executive director of the Grassroots Recycling Network in September 2002. "Dow's toxic products not only kill weeds, they are killing financially successful compost programs that keep thousands of tons of organic material out of landfills."

Confront is the popular trade name for a Dow herbicide with the chemical name clopyralid methyl, or simply clopyralid. Clopyralid is the active chemical ingredient in the herbicide, also known as a "chlorinated pyridine carboxylic acid herbicide."* Originally sold by Dow in Europe in the 1970s,

---

*Technically, this chemical is written as 3,6-dichloro-2-pyridinecarboxylic acid.

Confront was approved for use in the U.S. in 1987 and soon appeared in 50 states under as many as 37 brand names including, *Stinger, Reclaim, Transline*, and *Lontrel*. In short order, *Confront* became a very popular herbicide in the commercial lawn-care business, where hundreds of companies made it their favorite because it rid lawns of unsightly dandelions, thistles, and other unwanted growth without killing the lawn-grass. Known in the trade as a selective herbicide, *Confront* is a chemical that will kill or damage some plants but not others. In the commercial lawn-care business, applicators loved it: one treatment would last a year, whereas rival products would have to be applied two or three times. However, *Confront* remained potent in the grass clippings, leaves, and other materials hauled off for composting. The first place to experience the toxic side effect on a large scale was Spokane, Washington.

> **Dow was imposing the duty of safety on the consumer and recyclers rather than on itself and its product.**

In 1993, Spokane initiated a regional compost facility that became a successful operation. By 1998, the city initiated a curbside collection program for lawn clippings in an effort to reduce landfill wastes. In 2000, however, Spokane discovered its regional waste system composting operation was contaminated with *Confront*. By July 2002, Spokane moved to close a 72-acre compost facility because of the contamination. The composting operation, which normally handled 40,000 tons of Spokane's yard waste a year, was then unable to take the area's grass clippings and other material because Dow's *Confront* made the compost unusable.[38]

But Spokane was not alone. In California, grass recycling facilities in San Diego and Los Angeles also found clopyralid residues in 2001. By 2002, the California compost industry estimated that as many as two-thirds of the state's facilities had some sort of contamination, and that prompted the California Department of Pesticide Regulation to issue an emergency ban on the herbicide. Further cases of contamination were recorded in New York, Ohio, Oregon, Pennsylvania, New Zealand, and Canada.

Dow, for its part, did take action. In Spokane, it voluntarily suspended sales to residential areas pending an evaluation of the product. But Dow also pointed to homeowners contributing to the composting stream who had not read the herbicide label. Some Dow critics, meanwhile, felt this was a cop-out; that Dow was imposing the duty of safety on the consumer and recyclers rather than on itself and its product. One Dow spokesman, in fact, blamed the composting process as interfering with the Dow product. "Clopyralid has a very favorable toxicological and environmental fate profile," explained Bryan Stuart of Dow AgroSciences in Sacramento. "Beneficial organisms break down clopyralid in soil at a rate consistent with similar products; however, *composting disrupts this natural degradation process* (emphasis added)."[39]

It was well known by Dow and others that clopyralid was "phytotoxic"—toxic to certain plants that could be harmed or killed by the chemical. Although clopyralid is generally not regarded as a threat to people or the environment, and will break down in time, researchers discovered that in compost, it broke down very slowly over a year or more. Soil scientists from Washington State University traced

"Dow is trying to...undercut legislation that would go a lot further to cure the problem."

damage to "non-target" plants such as tomatoes and petunias to compost made from *Confront*-treated lawn clippings. Residues of the chemical at levels of 10 parts per billion (ppb) or less were found to be toxic to some popular backyard garden crops, such as sunflowers, tomatoes, and potatoes.

As the reports of clopyralid contamination emerged in Washington state and California, recycling activists and municipal officials began focusing on the Dow product, with some calling on the company to pull it off the market. In California, a bill was introduced in the Assembly in the spring of 2001 calling for a ban on almost all turf use of the chemical. The measure was approved by the Assembly shortly thereafter, and the state Senate was expected to follow suit that summer. Then, in July 2002, in an effort to preempt a possible ban in California, Dow AgroSciences asked EPA to ban clopyralid from the shelves of hardware stores and garden centers nationwide. The "ban" however, would apply only to the retail trade, and would not prevent professional lawn-care companies or local gardeners from applying the chemical to residential or public lawns. "Dow is trying to put itself in the role of a responsible citizen," said Stephen Grealy, San Diego's recycling program supervisor. "But in effect what they are trying to do is undercut legislation that would go a lot further to cure the problem. Half of the lawn in California is commercial lawn, and that's where most of it is used. Dow is only removing it for sale for treatment of residential lawn."[40] The California bill, however, was adopted in September 2002.

Spokane, meanwhile, agreed to pay $950,000 to buy out its 10-year composting contract with Norcal Waste Systems because of the contaminated compost. As of September 2002, the city was considering a lawsuit against Dow to recoup the money it had to pay out. "It is an option that we're exploring,"said Damon Taam, system contract manager for Spokane Regional Solid Waste System. "We've obviously had a significant amount of damage here." Norcal, the composting firm, was also looking at its legal options. "Dow should pull this product off the market," said Norcal spokesman Robert Reed in September 2002—"and it should have done it a long time ago."[41]

In California, the emergency ban that went into effect after clopyralid was discovered, appears to be working. According to recycling supervisors in San Diego and Los Angeles, compost there is either getting a clean bill of health or clopyralid levels are falling. But elsewhere, the herbicide is still a problem. A 2003 University of Oregon study confirmed that compost at state-permitted facilities in Oregon "contain significant levels of the herbicide clopyralid." The level of herbicide residue being found there varied, and depended on the seasonality of the materials going into the composting operations. But "lawn clippings collected with yard debris appears to be the major contributing source of the residue...," according to the study.

As of November 2003, the Grassroots Recycling Network (GRRN), which has led the campaign demanding that Dow take responsibility for its damaging herbicide, continued to charge that "Dow's toxic herbicide threatens taxpayer investments" in municipal composting programs. GRRN continued its call for Dow to remove *Confront* and other such products from the market until they are proven safe.[42]

6.
"Saving" 2,4-D

2,4-D is the most widely used herbicide in the world.

Industry Task Force II on 2,4-D Research Data, 1996

The visitor's lobby at Dow Chemical's headquarters building in Midland, Michigan, is full of Dow memorabilia. There is history on the walls and a corridor full of various everyday products highlighting Dow's contributions to the good life. One display of a cut-away automobile, reveals all the various parts that Dow contributes. A wall panel focuses on Dow's contributions to medicine, and another, its past consumer products. In one corner of the lobby, opposite the guard desk, there is a large Dow "trophy case" of sorts, with various Dow awards, historic objects, photographs and Dow drawings. Inside the case, among the items displayed, is a small square of *Lucite* containing an award announcement commemorating Dow's 50th anniversary year for selling the phenoxy herbicide 2,4-D.

Dow is proud of its long history with 2,4-D, and has been producing, selling, and singing its praises practically since the chemical's inception. Although Dow did not invent 2,4-D, the company has been right alongside the herbicide's development every step of the way; there at every possible new use or opportunity, be it agricultural, industrial, or military. As noted earlier, 2,4-D and 2,4,5-T came into considerable notice after researchers at the University of Chicago used them to promote rapid and destructive plant growth. The two chemicals then became the focus of early 1940s war research at Fort Dietrich, Maryland. 2,4-D, in fact, was specifically considered as a potential agent to kill Japanese rice crops, and had been stockpiled with that intent in mind, but the war ended before the planned action could be carried out. (A few years later, however, the British did use 2,4,5-T as an agent to kill the crops of Chinese guerrillas in Malaysia.) 2,4-D, as a commercial weed killer, appears to have begun in Britain, first used in wheat farming, soon reformulated by the USDA for turf and the U.S. lawn-care market.

Dow began selling 2,4-D in 1945 as a herbicide, first to home gardeners to kill dandelions, poison ivy, and poison oak without damaging lawns. It had been tested prominently in 1944 on the National Mall in Washington and on the White House lawn by Fanny Fern Davis, then in charge of the U.S. Golf Association's greens section. Davis also tested the compound at the Chevy Chase (Maryland) Country Club, zeroing in on the unsightly dandelions and other rough grass, leaving the desired grasses untouched. So Dow pitched the new chemical as a lawn-care product. It also sold 2,4-D in bulk to rice, sugarcane, and sorghum farmers; to cattlemen and for rangeland; and to railroad and utility companies for clearing rights of way along rail tracks and transmission lines. In Iowa, for example, the Northwestern Bell Telephone Company was spending as much as $1 million a year in the 1950s for brush control. Dow promoted 2,4-D through its sales literature and the helpful endorsements of local agricultural agents. It also produced at least one film on the product called *Death to Weeds*, a color production that played to "extremely heavy bookings" among farmers and others. Extolling the benefits of Dow's 2,4-D, the film featured success stories from Michigan grain farms, California rice and sorghum fields, on Texas rangeland, and from rights-of-way managers in Pennsylvania. "Like any chemical it has its limitations," Dow observed, "but the results on the whole are nothing short of miraculous."[1]

Dow spared no expense in promoting and advertising 2,4-D. And when the need for a more potent form of the herbicide was called for, Dow tested new concoctions until it found them. In fact, by 1948, Dow experimented with combinations of 2,4-D and 2,4,5-T that yielded herbicides that were less volatile, better plant penetrators, or slower acting. Yet the first extensive field tests and government-required toxicological tests for 2,4-D weren't begun until *after* the chemical was put on the market. And once on the market, 2,4-D's boosters assured users it was safe, even to the point in a few cases of individual promoters eating or otherwise dosing themselves with the chemical to demonstrate its safety. By the 1950s, Dow was marketing more than 50 kinds of insecticides and herbicides. In the 1960s, Dow used 2,4-D in making the Vietnam War defoliant Agent Orange, in a potent mix with 2,4,5-T, and in Agent White, mixed with Picloram, another herbicide, sold domestically under the trade name *Tordon*.

Today, Dow is still selling 2,4-D, and along with several other companies, is fighting to keep the chemical on the market, as government agencies in the U.S. and Canada are now reviewing a substantial decades-long health-effects history and scientific record that appear to implicate 2,4-D as a threat to public health and safety. Some of that history, with Dow's maneuvering, is recounted below.

Dr. Ruth Shearer
2,4-D: 1982

I'd been doing basic cancer research for ten years before I was asked by Metro, a public agency in the Seattle metropolitan area, to do a world-wide literature search on four herbicides, including 2,4-D. I did this in early 1979. The report was published by Metro in January 1980. It was a study of the health effects of the herbicides on mammals, and studies that involved human exposure and injury.

I found that in the whole world's literature, only three cancer tests have been done on 2,4-D, none of them adequate by today's methodology. Two of them were done in the U.S. They used too few rats and mice, and the mouse experiment used too low a dose and too short a time for an adequate cancer test. However, both of these tests did give some statistically significant positive results.

The third test was done in the Soviet Union. They used more than adequate numbers of mice and rats. As an assay for complete carcinogenesis—the ability to induce all stages of cancer—this test was negative. But they also ran a test for cancer promotion, to see whether 2,4-D would stimulate pre-malignant cells— that had already been initiated by another carcinogen—into fully malignant cancer cells. This test was very strongly positive.

Now 2,4-D contains as a contaminant another chemical, 2,4-dichlorophenol. Also, 2,4-D is broken down into 2,4-dichlorophenol by microbial action in the environment. The 2,4-dichlorophenol is an even stronger cancer promoter than 2,4-D, and is a weak carcinogen—cancer initiator—as well.

2,4-D induces mutations in both animal and human cells in culture, and damages DNA in a manner similar to ionizing radiation—x-rays or gamma rays. It causes developmental toxicity in offspring when given to the pregnant female animal. It causes fetal hemorrhage at a low dose in rats. This is increased synergistically in the presence of its breakdown product, 2,4-dichlorophenol. That is a study done in the Soviet Union. It's the only study of fetal synergism that I've found. In other words, the question hasn't been asked in U.S. research. 2,4-D caused malformations and fetal death in the animals only at a high dose, but it caused various kinds of malfunction and growth retardation at very, very low doses.

Cancer takes an average of 20 years to develop in humans. The latent period is shorter in children. The younger the animal the shorter the latent period. It can be quite short in children....

One of the commonest misconceptions perpetuated by the chemical industry is that there's a safe level of a carcinogen—that a little bit won't hurt you. With a cancer initiator, that's definitely not true. The changes it causes in cells are irreversible. These changes are not repaired, and they are cumulative over the lifetime of the person. The idea of a "safe" amount of a carcinogen is a fallacy.

Source: Carol Van Strum interview of Ruth Shearer in Van Strum, *The Toxic Cloud: Herbicides and Human Rights,* Sierra Club Books: San Francisco, 1983, pp. 66-68. Dr. Ruth Shearer of Issaquah, Washington was a former molecular geneticist at the University of Washington. She later served as a consultant in genetic toxicology, and was often called to testify in support of citizens and workers exposed to toxic chemicals.

Dow on the Defensive

In 1980, a year after EPA suspended many uses of 2,4,5-T and silvex, an investigation of 2,4-D was begun, and a number of new studies were commissioned and completed. However, key tests for determining whether the chemical caused cancer or birth defects still had several years to go before completion. With more government attention on 2,4-D, the herbicide's two main manufacturers—Dow Chemical and Diamond Shamrock—began a "public education" effort to save the herbicide. In Chicago during the early 1980s, in a large office on Michigan Avenue, a group called the National Coalition for a Reasonable 2,4-D Policy, worked to offset public concerns. Formed in 1981, the group was bankrolled primarily by Dow and Diamond Shamrock, then with an annual budget of $120,000. "We believe that 2,4-D is among the most beneficial herbicides available," said Glenn Bostrom, the new group's director in mid-1983. "Scientists have stated that it is the single greatest advancement in weed control and one of the most significant gains in agriculture. We would have trouble feeding our people without this chemical."[2] But others had quite the opposite view. "Scientific studies show that 2,4-D causes cancer in laboratory animals," wrote Lewis Regenstein in his book, *America the Poisoned,* published in 1982. "Where people have been exposed to 2,4-D, the evidence is clear that it causes an incredibly high number of miscarriages."

EPA was then questioning some of the scientific studies that had been originally used to register the pesticide. And there were also Canadian and U.S. scientists who found several kinds of dioxin compounds in 2,4-D. Other studies were finding what appeared to be a link between 2,4-D exposure and increased cancers, as one study of Scandinavian railway workers showed. Still, regardless of what science was finding at the time, 2,4-D was enjoying robust use all across the country.

By 1983, between 70 and 80 million pounds of 2,4-D were being used in the U.S. each year on wheat farms, national forests, golf courses, and suburban lawns. Dow and Diamond Shamrock had much of the 2,4-D market—a chemical whose development costs were paid for in the 1940s by the U.S. Army. The profit by the 1980s was no doubt quite good. Dow had been selling the herbicide for more than 30 years, with its own capital costs long paid for. No surprise then, that Dow and Diamond Shamrock were determined to save 2,4-D from the clutches of its critics—touting "a 30-year record of safe and effective use." So the National Coalition for a Reasonable 2,4-D Policy went to work, spreading its message wherever 2,4-D was being challenged. "Once we provide our material to a group in a trouble spot," explained director Glenn Bostrom, "we seem able to limit concern." The 2,4-D group sent out newsletters and targeted information packets and provided funding assistance to similarly minded local groups in 10 states. The information packets included a 33-page green booklet entitled, *Public Concerns About the Herbicide 2,4-D*, written by Dr. Wendell R. Mullison, a retired Dow researcher. The booklet was published by Dow Chemical. Mullison was among the first scientists to synthesize 2,4-D, and claimed that 2,4-D was not toxic to animals and was less toxic than table salt. Although the Mullison/Dow report did acknowledge that dioxin was found in 2,4-D—no small admission—the type found, said the report, was a far less poisonous variety than the TCDD version found in 2,4,5-T. The Mullison report also challenged the Swedish studies, charging deficiencies and bias. However, the National Cancer Institute had found the Swedish 2,4-D studies "very well done" and a "cause for concern."[3]

By 1985, internal Dow memos and research presentations indicated the company was standing pat on 2,4-D. One outline memo for 1985, discussing "goals and key tasks" listed three elements under an "R&D" heading:

1) continue to develop specialty products, such as the IPA salt of 2,4-D for Monsanto, whenever the need is identified;
2) continue registration activities [i.e., studies, etc., related to regulatory activity] in support of the phenoxy business;
3) provide technical support in the public and private arenas to support phenoxy herbicide, while minimizing direct Dow involvement. Continue support of the 2,4-D Industrial Task Force, the MCPA Task Force, and the MCPP group.[4]

Sick Farmers

In 1986, a study published in the *Journal of the American Medical Association (JAMA)*, found that Kansas farmers and crop workers who had applied 2,4-D had a heightened rate of non-Hodgkin's lymphoma, a cancer of the immune system. The study, conducted by researchers for the National Cancer Institute, Kansas State University, and the University of Kansas found

Farmers exposed to 2,4-D at least 20 days a year had six times the normal rate of non-Hodgkin's lymphoma.

that farmers exposed to 2,4-D at least 20 days a year had six times the normal rate of non-Hodgkin's lymphoma, a tumor that develops in the lymph system. Occurrence of the same cancer was eight times higher than normal for farmers who personally mixed batches of the herbicide, the study found. Terry Witt, a spokesman for Dow and a multi-company task force on 2,4-D at the time, said the new study was done by reputable scientists, but had to be considered in the context of "an astronomical amount of data" on the chemical. Sheila Hoar, a National Cancer Institute senior researcher who helped write the Kansas study, said about half of those diagnosed with non-Hodgkin's lymphoma survived for five years. Lois Rossi, who then oversaw 2,4-D for the EPA, said the report had "raised quite a concern" within the agency.[5] The Kansas study, in fact, prompted the first EPA review of 2,4-D since the chemical's introduction in the 1940s. In March 1987, Dr. Sheila Hoar, the National Cancer Institute researcher, gave a talk on her findings at Michigan State University, reiterating the "dramatic association" she had found with 2,4-D and the 170 non-Hodgkin's lymphoma victims she studied. But Hoar counseled protective equipment and applicator caution rather than dramatic regulatory action. Dow's Nick Hein, a public affairs director, asked to comment on Hoar's study, reiterated that it was a well conceived study, but was in "substantial conflict" with other studies. "There is overwhelming evidence to prove that 2,4-D is a safe product to use." he said. He explained that Dow and an industry task force had conducted 31 studies on 2,4-D, which confirmed no links between 2,4-D and cancer, and were submitted to EPA.[6] Although 2,4-D continued to be reviewed by EPA and other agencies, its status on the market was unchanged.

In 1991, the National Cancer Institute suggested that 2,4-D might cause a lymphatic cancer in dogs. It also calculated that diagnosis of non-Hodgkin's lymphoma among farm workers had been increasing 75 percent in the past 20 years. It attributed part of the rise to better diagnoses but also considered 2,4-D a possible contributor. Another study found higher than normal levels of the disease in lawn service applicators.[7] Still, 2,4-D continued to be sold widely. By 1993, an estimated 20,400 metric tons of 2,4-D were consumed in the United States, making it one of the top 10 pesticides.

Birth Defects?

In 1996, as the cancer risk argument rolled on, University of Minnesota pathologist Vincent Garry published a study in *Environmental Health Perspectives* showing that 2,4-D might also cause birth defects. Garry found almost twice the number of birth defects among children of pesticide applicators than that of a control population. The children had been conceived in spraying season in a Minnesota potato and sugar beet farming region predominantly using 2,4-D.[8]

Dow and its colleague companies, meanwhile, were not sitting idly by. They were sponsoring and submitting their own studies. In June 2002, Don Page was executive director of the industry's task force on 2,4-D research— "industry" in this case consisting primarily of Dow, BASF, an Australian producer, New Farm, Inc., and one U.S./Argentinian firm named Agro-Gor. Page was using the industry's standard line to defend 2,4-D at this date: "As long as label instructions are followed, [2,4-D] certainly poses no unreasonable risk." The only verified examples of 2,4-D poisoning in humans, he said were suicides. "If you drink enough of it, you can kill yourself," he said.[9] Part of Page's job was to round up industry's research on 2,4-D, and use it to counter other studies that might be critical of 2,4-D. Page and his task force had already helped coordinate some 270 industry studies and $30 million on

Toxic Shell Game?

In the early 1980s, Dow Chemical entered a curious business relationship with a company in Arkansas named Vertac; a company, like Dow, in the agricultural chemicals business. Vertac had been formed quite independently of Dow in 1976 from the merger of four small companies—Vicksburg, Eagle River, Transvaal, and Agricultural Chemicals—taking each company's first initials to form the name, Vertac. Although there is much more to the Vertac odyssey than can be included here, the company initially ran into problems and went into bankruptcy. In 1978, as Vertac began coming out of bankruptcy, Dow Chemical struck up a business deal with the company—a venture some believe was designed as a calculated move by Dow to create a liability shield for herbicides then under federal scrutiny. Wrote journalist Dick Russell in March 1988 after doing an extensive investigation of Vertac for *In These Times*: "In retrospect it appears that Dow was using the smaller company [Vertac] as a kind of 'shell' to handle some of Dow's more controversial products. On paper, the two companies were competitors. Both, for example, made substantial quantities of 2,4-D herbicides—which recent studies have linked to cancer. But even though Dow continued to manufacture 2,4-D, in 1983 it sold all of its registration rights, inventories, formulation recipes and marketing data for 2,4-D to Vertac."

Former Vertac official David Simmons told Russell: "Dow knew 2,4-D was a dirty business, with a lot of environmental hazards associated. So they wanted Vertac to take front-line responsibility for it." Curiously, just as the Dow-Vertac 2,4-D deal was occurring, Vertac had received permission from EPA to put some wastes containing TCDD-dioxin back into its 2,4-D products. "Some of these wastes may have come directly from Dow," wrote Russell, citing Paul Merrell, who had written a dioxin report for Greenpeace. Merrell found that among Dow employees, "the scuttlebutt was that part of its dealings with Vertac involved transferring a bunch of Dow's 2,4,5-T [dioxin-contaminated] waste to the Jacksonville plant."

Vertac, meanwhile, had made a mess in Jacksonville, both inside its plant and in the environment. Although all production ceased there in 1986, EPA found enough contamination to designate three Superfund sites and estimate a total plant and off-site cleanup bill of some $400 million, including disposal of nearly 30,000 drums of hazardous wastes, some with the highest dioxin readings ever detected. For 30 years, wastes were dumped into the city's waterways, sewer systems, and landfills, severely contaminating the area and leading to a number of health problems among residents and workers. The first any of this came to public light for the local residents was in 1979. Two decades of lawsuits, incineration "solutions," and toxic waste fights would follow, which cannot be adequately covered here due to space limitations. But in 1987, when EPA and the Justice Department were trying to collect money from Vertac to pay for toxic waste clean-up, Vertac revealed that it couldn't meet those costs. Yet Vertac and Dow, it appeared, had made another arrangement. Again, Dick Russell explains:

> ...In December 1986, two months before Vertac pulled out of Jacksonville, company officials held a series of meetings with Dow execu-

tives in Great Britain, Washington, D.C., and Michigan. At the time Vertac was feeling considerable heat from the government. Although it had ceased operations in Jacksonville in February 1986, the company was being sued by the Justice Department (on behalf of the EPA) for continuing to discharge contaminated wastes water into a creek adjacent to the plant site. The department was seeking a $10,000-a-day fine. Vertac wanted out from under—and in a complex back-handed way, Dow was about to provide the opportunity.

Dow, which contracted trademarks and products to Vertac, privately informed its "supply partner" that the smaller company had breeched one or more of their agreements. Thus, Dow declared Vertac in default, with a debt of $5.3 million owned Dow for goods sold and delivered.

Vertac could cover the debts, but its money was tied up in a trust fund and letter of credit; the company had earlier agreed with government agencies to set aside $11 million for initial on-site cleanup at the Jacksonville plant. After consulting with Dow, Vertac quietly established three new companies in Memphis, Tennessee, where Vertac's corporate headquarters were located.

Then on Jan. 31, 1987, Vertac President J. Randal Tomblin called representatives of the EPA, the state of Arkansas and Hercules to a meeting in Dallas. Without mentioning Vertac's meeting with Dow or Vertac's newly formed companies, Tomblin said that the company could no longer meet its legal obligation to maintain the corroding waste drums in Jacksonville. He seemed to be implying that Vertac was broke.

But it wasn't. Nine days later, Vertac transferred all of its assets (which claimed were $12.7 million) into Inter-Ag, under the umbrella of two other newly formed companies in Memphis.

The next day Inter-Ag gave Dow Chemical nearly $1.7 million of the money Vertac owed the chemical giant. Dow also received claim to both the interest payments from the Jacksonville cleanup trust fund and any uncontaminated equipment from the Arkansas plant. And Dow took title to the remainder of Vertac's inventory, along with all product formulas and trademarks. This was a strange turn of events, because Dow had sold those three areas of its 2,4-D herbicide business to Vertac back in 1983.

By the late 1990s, however, a U.S. District Court judge ruled that the state of Arkansas could pursue natural resources damage claims against Dow for alleged water pollution near the Vertac plant site in Jacksonville.

Source: Dick Russell, "Dioxinville III: The Toxic Trail," *In These Times*, March 23–29, 1988, pp. 8–22.

2,4-D research submitted to government agencies. He'd been rebutting the earlier critics, too. When the National Cancer Institute suggested that 2,4-D might cause a lymphatic cancer in dogs, Page attacked the institute's canvassing methods. Then he attacked the institute's interpretation of the results, and accused it of scaremongering to raise research funds. Page said that industry's 270 toxicity studies, submitted in 1995, show that the amount of 2,4-D it takes to harm lab animals is far higher than anything that could be encountered in the environment.[10] What about University of Minnesota's Vincent Garry and his 1996 findings on birth defects? Page had an answer there, too, pointing to a new study show-ing that "none of Dr. Garry's findings were significant." He adds: "Dr. Garry himself will not defend that study." But Dr. Garry can speak for himself.

People who spray 2,4-D have shown higher levels of the chemical in their urine, and also more frequent chromosomal changes.

The problem with 2,4-D, Dr. Garry explained to *Los Angeles Times* reporter Emily Green, might come in the mixtures, formulations, and additives. By itself in the lab, 2,4-D might not show anything. But mix 2,4-D with other chemical ingredients in any one of the 1,500 formulations now on the market, and the story changes. Commercial-grade 2,4-D, explained Dr. Garry, is mixed with "adjuvants," and things that aid the chemical's penetration. "When you move to commercial grade of the product," he said, "then you begin to see stuff." People who regularly spray the herbicide have shown a higher level of 2,4-D in their urine than any other group, Dr. Garry said. They also show more frequent chromosomal changes than people not in contact with 2,4-D.[11]

In 1997, during EPA's review of 2,4-D, the agency's Carcinogenicity Peer Review Committee stopped short of ranking the chemical a probable cause of cancer. But three years later, one of its own statisticians and one of Dr. Garry's collaborators in the Minnesota study, linked many cancers—of the esophagus, stomach, rectum, throat, pancreas, larynx, prostate, kidney, and brain—to heavy wheat growing regions notable for 2,4-D use.[12]

But it's not only cancer. "2,4-D is unusual among herbicides," writes Caroline Cox of the *Journal of Pesticide Reform* in a 1999 review, "in that it causes an array of adverse effects to the nervous system." Maturing nervous systems may be particularly vulnerable, observes Cox: "In laboratory tests, juvenile rats exposed to 2,4-D developed smaller brains than unexposed rats."

And then there's dioxin.

2,4-D Neglected

In the 1970s and 1980s when 2,4,5-T and Agent Orange had the lime-light for their suspected dioxin connection, similar concerns about 2,4-D were overshadowed and neglected. Yet the two phenoxy herbicides are in the same chemical family and only differ by a few molecules. In the Alsea River area of Western Oregon in 1979, after 2,4,5-T was suspended under the federal government's emergency ban, 2,4-D was then used in its place in forest spraying programs, with similar health effects reported for a period of several years thereafter. Author and activist Carol Van Strum explains what she and others found after the substitution:

> ... The emergency ban of 2,4,5-T [in 1979] did not end the suffering of [Irene Durbin and family, who lived along Oregon's Alsea River] and their equally devastated neighbors, who became unwitting guinea pigs.... The government substituted 2,4-D in subsequent defoliation spraying over the valley. In the wake of this spraying, every first trimester pregnancy in the valley spontaneously aborted, three children nearly died of spinal meningitis, one baby was born without a brain (anencephalic), a kitten was born with four eyes, and nearly every household reported outbreaks of rashes, uterine hemorrhaging, intestinal disorders, and respiratory diseases.
>
> Following this disaster, a preliminary study by the U.S. Centers for Disease Control found a 13-fold increase in neural tube birth defects in the Alsea study area, and post 2,4-D sampling identified dioxin in valley water supplies, wildlife, and tissues of the anencephalic baby. Sediment from the Durbin's water supply, resampled four years after 2,4-D replaced 2,4,5-T, contained 79 parts per trillion 2,3,7,8-TCCD, four times the 1979 level. Nevertheless, the EPA informed residents that this level presented no "immediate health hazard" and ended all further investigation.... [13]

Little of this information surfaced publicly at the time, as there was a concerted effort at EPA during the Reagan years to keep the Alsea study findings under wraps. Today, however, there is a long scientific record of studies and government reports—from the early 1980s through the mid-1990s—that have found dioxin-contaminated 2,4-D.*

Lawn to Dinner Table

Meanwhile, in one November 2001 report, researchers from Battelle Memorial Institute and EPA's National Exposure Research Laboratory, examining how 2,4-D makes its way from the innocent lawn application to the dinner table in one small study, raised some troubling questions about human exposures to the herbicide, particularly children. The researchers' abstract offers a fairly straightforward summary:

---

*For example "... Low levels of PCDD/Fs have been found in some samples of 2,4-D ... As of 1989, 20–30 million kg were used annually in the U.S. PCDD/F levels have been measured to be about 0.2ppm (200ug/kg) or less. On this basis, about 5 kg of PCDD/F are contained in the 2,4-D used annually in the U.S." V. M. Thomas and T. G. Spiro, "An Estimation of Dioxin Emissions in the United States," *Toxicol. Environ. Chemistry*, Vol. 50, 1995, pp. 1–37.

One Man's Protest

"Lake Weed-A-Way" is the name of a Michigan weed control company that does its business by spraying chemicals on hundreds of Michigan's lakes. In the early 1990s, Lake Weed-A-Way had contracts from various Michigan towns and private landowners to control weeds in at least 200 Michigan lakes. The weed-control technique of choice for the company—and which it intended to use that year on all 200 lakes—was 2,4-D. But when word got out that Lake Weed-A-Way was coming to Arbutus Lake near Traverse City to dump a ton of 2,4-D in the lake to kill a noxious water weed called *Euranism milfoil*, a lone, middle-aged Vietnam veteran named Larry Butcher didn't think that was such a good idea. Butcher and a friend decided to stage a small protest and block the company from spraying the lake. So one Thursday morning about 11:30 at the Lake Arbutus dock, Butcher stood in the way of the Lake Weed-A-Way boat loaded with 2,4-D ready for launch. Butcher and friend Bill Seater would not let the company owner, Greg Cheek, pass. "You people should be put in jail for putting this in the lakes," Butcher said. "Stop killing people. This stuff is toxic." Butcher explained that he worked with children that had birth defects. "I'm tired of seeing what happens because of these chemicals." Cheek, who also said he served in Vietnam from 1966 to 1967, said, "If I thought this was harmful I wouldn't use it." Still, a stand-off ensued for a few hours while the authorities were called. Two Michigan DNR officers arrived and informed Butcher he would be arrested unless he gave way. Butcher held his ground, and then was hand-cuffed by one of the DNR officers. About 20 acres of the lake were then treated with 2,4-D. Swimming and bathing in the lake were prohibited for one day following the application, and warning signs were posted around the lake in the areas where the chemical was dispersed. The DNR permit issued for the spaying indicated that water from the lake should not be used for household purposes, irrigation, or animal watering for an "indefinite" period. One reporter at the scene noted that the 2,4-D bags said the herbicide was toxic to fish, but Cheek informed him that the dosage used in the lake would not kill the fish. One local fisherman, however, said while he had fished Arbutus Lake for 14 years, this year he would fish elsewhere when bass season opened.

Source: William Scott, "Arbutus Lake Protestor Arrested," *Record-Eagle* (Traverse City, MI) (after 1991).

We collected indoor air, surface wipes (floors, table tops, and windowsills), and floor dust samples at multiple locations within 11 occupied and two unoccupied homes both before and after lawn application of the herbicide 2,4-D. We measured residues 1 week before and after application. We used collected samples to determine transport routes of 2,4-D from the lawn into the homes, its subsequent distribution between the indoor surfaces, and air concentration as a function of airborne particle size. We used residue measurements to estimate potential exposures within these homes. After lawn application, 2,4-D was detected in indoor air and on all surfaces throughout all homes. Track-in by an active dog and by the homeowner applicator were the most significant factors for intrusion. Resuspension of floor dust was the major source of 2,4-D in indoor air, with highest levels of 2,4-D found in the particle size range of 2.5–10 μm. Resuspended floor dust was also a major source of 2,4-D on tables and windowsills. Estimated post application indoor exposure levels for young children from nondietary ingestion may be 1–10 μg/day from contact with floors, and 0.2–30 μg/day from contact with table tops. These are estimated to be about 10 times higher than the pre-application exposures. By comparison, dietary ingestion of 2,4-D is approximately 1.3 μg/day.[14]

In November 2003, federal regulators in Canada found traces of dioxin and furans in 10 pesticides currently used in that country. Dioxins were found in over-the-counter pesticides, such as 2,4-D, the active ingredient in most lawn-weed killers. 2,4-D is widely used in Canada by homeowners to kill dandelions and by farmers to control weeds in wheat fields. The information was compiled by Health Canada's Pest Management Regulatory Agency, conducting a review of 2,4-D safety. Although Canada has a limit on the amount of dioxin allowed in 2,4-D, there are no standards for other pesticides. The Canadian federal review didn't find the most toxic varieties of dioxin in 2,4-D, but they did in some other pesticides. However, environmentalists said the government shouldn't allow any pesticides containing dioxin on the market because the chemical is a potent cancer-causing agent and its application on crops gives the contaminant a potential route to enter the food supply.[15]

Much of the research by Canadian authorities on dioxin in 2,4-D was conducted in the mid-1990s, and the samples tested then frequently had dioxin. But government scientists concluded the amounts detected weren't an environmental threat, and expressed more concern about dioxin levels in other pesticides.*

Canadian records show that the 2,4-D sold in Canada in the early 1980s was laced with higher levels of dioxins. A total of 70 percent of samples tested at the time contained the compound, with concentrations typically around 3,000 parts per billion. New control measures adopted in the 1980s led to a sharp drop in dioxin contamination. By 1989–94, the percentage of 2,4-D samples containing dioxin had fallen to 6 percent and typical concentrations had fallen to 10 ppb. But no federal testing for dioxin has been done by the Canadian government since then. However, the Industry Task Force on 2,4-D Research Data, a lobby group of 2,4-D manufacturers, sent the Canadian

---

*Among the other pesticides in Canada found to contain dioxin was pentachlorophenol, used extensively as a wood preservative and sold for many years in Canada and the U.S. by Dow and others. Observed the Canadian authorities in one 1996 document: "Pentachlorophenol appears to remain a significant anthropogenic source of dioxins in the environment despite a significant reduction in sales volume and in level of contamination during the last 15 years."

Toxic Lawns & Gardens

It has long been suspected that suburbia is probably more contaminated with lawn and garden pesticides like 2,4-D than America's agricultural heartland. Owing to this problem is the fact that the concentration of chemicals used on lawns is likely much higher. In fact, in 1989, the National Academy of Sciences estimated that homeowners were likely to use 10 times more chemicals per acre on their lawns than farmers used. Suburbia is also increasingly among the top conveyors of toxic contaminants to streams and rivers. "Residential streets are the worst possible place for pesticides," explained Phil Renfrow, of Seattle's Parks Department to *L.A. Times* reporter Emily Green. "There is a lawn, a sidewalk and gutter and a catch basin all within a couple feet of each other. The entry into the water supply is right there." And 2,4-D is among the biggest polluters coming from those areas. The U.S. Geological Survey confirms that 2,4-D is routinely found in urban watersheds. In testing between January 1999 to April 2000 of southern California's Santa Ana River in the Los Angeles area near Imperial Highway, 2,4-D was detected in more than a fourth of the samples.

Source: Emily Green, "Concern Grows In Weed War," *Los Angeles Times*, June 1, 2002, p. A-1.

authorities a letter in early 2003 playing down the recent discovery of trace amounts of a highly toxic form of dioxin in one of 42 samples being tested as part of the U.S. EPA's review of the herbicide. The traces were well within regulatory limits and the industry group said the finding was not a cause for concern. But many environmentalists see it quite differently. "Because of the nature of these chemicals, because they're persistent and

Canadian records show that the 2,4-D sold in Canada in the early 1980s was laced with higher levels of dioxins.

bioaccumulative, any amount is too much," said Julia Langer, a pesticide expert with the World Wildlife Fund. "We should not be spreading any dioxins." However, Canada's re-evaluation of 2,4-D, first announced in October 1980, is years late and isn't expected to be completed until the spring of 2004.

In the U.S., too, the re-registration process for 2,4-D at EPA grinds forward nearly 60 years after the first 2,4-D formulations were used. In 2004, there may be a final decision. In any case, the herbicide is still being sold globally. And Dow Chemical, for one, is still turning out new 2,4-D formulations. *Frontline 2,4-D* is Dow AgroSciences' "new selective post-emergent herbicide." It is presently being sold in Canada and other markets to control "a wide range of broadleaf weeds in all varieties of spring wheat and durum wheat." *Frontline 2,4-D*, says Dow, provides a wide spectrum of weed control knocking out pesky weeds from wild buckwheat to Russian thistle. Stay tuned.

7.
Plastic

The year was 1967. A popular American movie, *The Graduate*, starring Dustin Hoffman, had struck a chord with young people. In the film, with the innocence-meets-reality music of Paul Simon and Art Garfunkel running in the background, Hoffman plays a befuddled, returning-home college graduate, Benjamin Braddock, being propositioned by his girlfriend's mother, Mrs. Robinson, played by Anne Bancroft. The movie's most famous, enduring line comes at a neighborhood party when young Ben receives some unsolicited career counseling from family friend and businessman, Mr. McGuire. Taking Ben aside, McGuire guides him out of the house to a more private setting in the backyard by the swimming pool, where the following exchange takes place:

> "I just want to say one word to you, Ben—just one word," says McGuire.
> "Are you listening?" he says, pausing intentionally to get Ben's attention.
> "Yes I am," says Ben.
> "*Plastics*," says McGuire, staring intently into the boy's face, arm around his shoulder.
> The two men look at each other for a long moment.
> "Exactly how do you mean?" asks Ben, somewhat perplexed.
> "There's a great future in plastics," McGuire replies. "Think about it. Will you think about it?"
> Young Ben dutifully replies, "Yes sir, I will."
> "O.K. Enough said. That's a deal," concludes McGuire, who then turns and walks back into the house.

Mr. McGuire's enthusiasm for plastics captured a piece of Americana at the time—a material place where inventiveness held a profitable TomorrowLand, and plastics were the latest wonder product to flow from the Golden Horn. But Ben was a 1960s child, trying to get free of things artificial and hypocritical. Pink flamingoes and plastic dinnerware didn't seem to be in his future. Yet, to McGuire's generation, plastics had become emblematic of the good life and the promise of unending opportunity and growth. McGuire could have worked for Dow Chemical, and most certainly held its stock. For Dow Chemical was a company whose name had become practically synonymous with plastics—from *Saran Wrap* to *Styrofoam*. In fact, by 1967, half of Dow's entire business was in plastics with annual sales at about $500 million. That year, Dow produced well over 1 billion pounds of plastic.

Creating Plastic

Dow's entry into the plastics business was more by accident than design. In the 1930s, the company's key chemical harvesting process—the electrolysis of salt brines that yielded chlorine and caustic*—had accumulated more caustic than Dow could use or sell. The two substances had become core commodity chemicals for Dow by then, key to making other chemicals, and were sold in huge quantities to other chemical and industrial firms. But in harvesting these two key starting chemicals, the company tried to manage a "chlorine-caustic balance," never getting too much or too little of either. But the market wasn't always cooperative. In the early 1930s, Willard Dow—Herbert's son, and now in charge—was faced with an excess of caustic soda. He asked his chemists to come up with ways to use the substance, along with ethyl chloride which Dow also had in excess at the time. One of the product possibilities was ethyl cellulose, which Dow soon began making in quantity in combination with wood pulp. The new plastic, introduced in 1935, was called *Ethocel*, and by World War II, it began to be used in a number of wartime products, including canteens, telephone headsets, control knobs, dust goggles, and airplane parts. It was also used as a spray to waterproof tents, sleeping bags, clothing, and other gear. After the war, there were also plans to use it as fiber in a product to be called "Ethorayon," as Dow had set up pilot weaving operations and was testing some of the new material with its employees, especially women trying out new underwear made of the silky-like fiber. But cotton then dominated the scene, and synthetic fibers generally did not come into public acceptance as fabric ingredients until DuPont invented nylon.[1] Dow's *Ethocel*, meanwhile, settled into a variety of niche markets that were generally not well known by the public. Still, to this day, the *Ethocel* brand survives for Dow as a viable plastics line.

Another plastic that grew out of Dow's chemical excess was polystyrene. By 1931, as Dow was building a new ethylene plant, it became clear

---

*Also known as sodium hydroxide

the company would soon have an excess of ethylene. Willard Dow again turned to his chemists to come up with a way to use the excess ethylene. Soon the path became clear: ethylene would react with benzene to produce ethylbenzene. Ethylbenzene, in turn, could be hydrogenated to form styrene monomer. And finally, the styrene could be polymerized, or strung together in long chains of itself, and in that form became a valuable property. By September 1935, Dow was making styrene of 98 percent purity, later to

Styrene could be polymerized, or strung together, in long chains of itself, and in that form became a valuable property.

become a key ingredient in styrene-butadiene rubber—synthetic rubber—a key strategic material for World War II. Dow's styrene monomer was also polymerized into another new plastic called polystyrene. Trademarked by Dow as *Styron* in 1937, polystyrene became a huge product. It initially found uses in radios, clock cases, electrical equipment, and wall tiles. Over the years, *Styron* became Dow's number one product in sales volume and earnings, holding that distinction through the company's first century. Dow's scientists also developed other plastics and key feedstock chemicals during the1930s, including the plastic film *Saran*, which became a huge consumer product following its successful World War II uses protecting military equipment and key war materials (see *Saran* sidebar, Chapter 2).[2]

During the war years, Dow also developed an expanded white plastic that trapped millions of air bubbles, making it light, rigid, water-resistant, and buoyant. The substance, known as *Styrofoam*, became one of Dow's most successful plastics, initially used by the U.S. Coast Guard in flotation devices. In water, *Styrofoam* could support 25 times its own weight. Yet a cubic foot of it only weighed between 1 and 2 pounds. *Styrofoam* proved adaptable to many forms and uses. "It was three times as light as cork," wrote Don Whitehead in *The Dow Story*. "Its multicellular structure made it useful as a nonconductor of electricity and an insulation material. It could be cut, sawed and shaped into a giant-sized toy panda, a stage setting, or a Christmas tree bauble. And it could be installed in boats, making them virtually unsinkable, or used as floating supports for boat docks." *Styrofoam* was soon found in these and others less-noticed markets, such as wire insulating boxes on Bell Telephone Company antenna towers from New York to Chicago.[3] From 1948 on, *Styrofoam* became a ubiquitous material at residential and home construction sites, used as rigid foam insulation. By 1975, more than 100 million board feet of it were used in the Alaskan pipeline. In 1980, it was found in the Winter Olympic skating rinks and spectator facilities at Lake Placid.[4]

Dow's growth in plastics was meteoric—climbing from 2 percent of sales in 1940 to one third of revenues by the late 1950s. The post-war plastics revolution, in fact, spawned a whole array of new smaller businesses that formed, molded, and extruded the plastics into all kinds of products.

New plants sprang up for molding styrene polymers into cabinets for television sets, refrigerator parts, wall tile, radio cabinets, and various housewares. As these businesses grew, so did the demand for Dow plastics.[5]

Creating the Market

Overseas, meanwhile, as Dow was busy penetrating new markets with agricultural pesticides, plastics were not far behind. In Colombia, for example, Dow had done quite well with pesticides in the early 1960s and had built production lines to turn out those products. Soon it found there was also potential there for polystyrene and built at plant at Cartagena in July 1965. Dow received a generous deal from the Colombian government, which restricted polystyrene imports and raised tariffs on the plastic once Dow had built its plant. But initially, Dow had to overcome a temporary oversupply of polystyrene as Colombian marketers anticipated the government's action by stockpiling imported polystyrene. So Dow sent in the marketing calvary. "Dow told us 'you have to create a market,' and sent us a guy named Joseph J. Rabideau, who knew all about polystyrene uses," explained Rafael Pavia, a Colombian chemical engineer who became a key Dow manager there. "He [Rabideau] showed them how to produce new things... because the plastics industry in Colombia was being born in those days. It was kind of a garage industry, the plastics converters. He came from the outside and taught them how to use polystyrene—not theory, but how to do things.... [Y]ou could see how the new applications improved sales, and the market was growing and growing and growing. The participation of a fellow like Joe Rabideau was vital to the market in Colombia." By 1985, the Cartagena plant had gone through its fourth expansion and had become one of Dow's top plants in Latin America. By then, it was producing 45,000 tons of polystyrene annually, about half of which was shipped to other South American countries.[6]

> "Dow told us 'you have to create a market,' and sent us a guy who knew all about polystyrene uses. He showed them how to produce new things."

Back in the U.S., stagnant growth and heavy price-cutting in plastics during the early 1990s hit Dow's bottom line hard. The company's plastics division went through the requisite belt-tightening and plant efficiency upgrades to help improve its position. But Dow also sought ways to expand the use of plastics throughout the industrial world and in the general economy. In 1994, it helped develop a combination hot water-home heating system sold by Lennox International that included a heat-resistant plastic cover and pipes. It also provided plastics parts that replaced metal hardware in windows sold by Ashland Products. In Houston, Dow sold plastic sewer-pipe lin-

Making Plastic

Today's plastics are derived from fossil fuels, typically oil or natural gas. They are made by combining petrochemicals with oxygen and various other chemicals. Plastics are manufactured in a four-part process: conversion of raw materials into intermediate compounds or polymers; transformation of those compounds into resins; converting the resins into secondary products; and finally manufacture of end products. In the plastics business, a handful of corporations, Dow among them, dominate the first two processes—from raw material to polymer to resin. But resins are key. Although there are thousands of plastic processes and end products, there are only two main types of resin: *thermosets*, which are ultimately used in strong and durable plastics, such as those used in car parts; and *thermoplastics*, which are used for a variety of packaging materials as well as industrial and consumer products. Thermoplastics can be molded when they are hot. Thermosets, on the other hand, do not melt, and can't be remolded. They are used to make things that need to be really strong and heat resistant. Of the two, thermoplastics is by far the largest category, accounting for as much as 80 percent of all plastic produced. Dow Chemical is essentially a key supplier of plastic ingredients—a big one—to thousands of small and large businesses which dominate the end-products phases of the plastics industry.

<u>Sources</u>: Louis Blumberg and Robert Gottlieb, *War On Waste: Can America Win Its Battle With Garbage?* Washington, DC: Island Press, 1989, p. 265.

ers to be used throughout the city's sewer system to help the city forego digging up its streets to make repairs. The company also gained market ground with plastic shoe soles that were lighter, less slippery, and more flexible at low temperature than other brands. As a result, Dow's plastics sales grew by 15 percent in 1994, rising to about $7 billion for the year. "We are extremely optimistic about the future of the plastics industry and particularly the role Dow Plastics will play in that future," said Dennis McKeever, a Dow Plastics senior vice president, in December 1994.[7] Overseas, meanwhile, Dow teamed up with Zhejiang Pacific Chemical Co. in 1994 to build a joint-venture propylene oxide plant in Ningbo, China—Dow's first production in China.

By the mid-1990s, Dow boasted it ranked "among the world leaders in the production of plastics," offering the "broadest range of thermoplastic and thermoset materials of any manufacturer." By then, Dow plastics were used in appliances, automobiles, building and construction, electronics, flooring, furniture, health care, housewares, packaging, and recreation products and structures.[8] However, the environmental underside of the plastics revolution was already quite apparent by then—from trash accumulation and ozone depletion, to worker health problems and dioxin contamination. And Dow Chemical's products and processes were at the headwaters of these and other problems.

Big Mac Trash

By the 1970s, packaging, including plastic packaging, was becoming a major contributor to the nation's solid waste problem. The waste, initially going into landfills and later incinerators, wasn't necessarily Dow Chemical's products per se, but the *plastic resins*—i.e., the upstream chemistry—used to make the packaging and throw-away items were from Dow. Like several other modern products that had their initial base in the chemical industry, Dow and its resins were again found at the chemical manufacturing

Dow used CFCs, compounds found to degrade the earth's protective ozone layer, in making styrofoam.

headwaters of the throw-away packaging problem. But solid waste was only part of the trouble, since other later-discovered contaminants, like dioxins, resulted when incineration was embraced as an "end treatment" to the trash problem. But for the moment, consider only solid waste.

By the mid-1980s, fast-food packaging waste, and in particular, the McDonald's clamshell container surrounding its hamburgers—a container made of foamed polystyrene—came in for a round of activist campaigning. McDonald's was then the single largest consumer of foamed polystyrene containers in the U.S., contributing some 70 million pounds of foam packaging to the national waste stream every year. In fact, by 1988, there were at least 21 states with measures pending to ban fast-food containers. At the same time, concerns had also emerged over the chemical blowing agents used in making the foam—chlorofluorocarbons or CFCs, compounds found to degrade the earth's protective ozone layer. CFCs were used to inject the air into the plastic when making styrofoam containers. Dow was involved in both problems—it produced the resins for the styrofoam containers and it used CFCs in making styrofoam. But it was McDonald's, at least initially, that bore the brunt of activist campaigning and public criticism.

By late 1990, McDonald's decided to discontinue the clamshell-style containers it used for *Big Macs, Quarter Pounders*, and other sandwiches at its 8,000 restaurants nationwide. The Society of the Plastics Industry, a Washington trade group said that McDonald's clamshells accounted for less than 1 percent of the $5 billion-plus market for polystyrene. Karl Kamena, a spokesman for Dow, said at the time he didn't think the McDonald's move would have a negative ripple effect on the industry. He also disputed the environmental threat posed by the product. "People tend to forget that foam polystyrene is 95 percent air," Kamena said. "We've found a clever way of using air as a package." Kamena said the average American uses between three and four pounds of polystyrene each year—the equivalent of up to 888 foam cups.[9] Still, more than "just air" was being sent out into the material world and the environment.

Indeed, by 1990, Dow was the third largest producer of polyethylene resin and largest producer of polystyrene, both at the center of modern packaging. In 1990, for example, Dow produced 930 million pounds of low-density polyethylene (LDPE), used primarily as plastic film wrap; between 240 million to 1.6 billion pounds of high-density polyethylene (HDPE), used in plastic milk jugs and another 1.3 billion pounds of polystyrene used in dairy containers, egg cartons and clamshell take-out containers. These three lines of plastics packaging alone were worth between $1 billion to $1.6 billion a year to Dow. No wonder then, that when the Oregon Recycling Act, also known as Ballot Measure #6, was offered that year in Oregon, Dow Chemical was in the forefront of companies opposing it. Measure #6 would have required that 60 percent of plastic resins used in packaging be acquired from recyclers, not from virgin plastic producers like Dow. Dow spent at least $50,000 opposing the measure, and with four other plastics producers helped form a front group—the Oregon Committee for Recycling—to confuse voters and kill the initiative.[10]

Dow spent at least $50,000 opposing the Oregon Recycling Act.

Pieces of Dow

Today, plastic trash litters the world's coastlines, oceans, lakes, streams, and forests. Even in the world's remotest regions, plastic trash is found. A portion of this trash, it could be argued, is another form of Dow trespass, as "bits and pieces of Dow"—in proportion to its upstream and end-product plastics production—are found everywhere. In the U.S., civic and environmental groups regularly collect tons of discarded plastic in the environment. For example, "during one three-hour sweep by volunteers along 157 miles of Texas beach front in 1987," reported Louis Blumberg and Robert Gottlieb in *War On Waste*, "31,773 plastic bags, 30,295 plastic bottles, 15,631 plastic six-pack rings, 28,540 plastic lids, 1,914 disposable diapers, 1,040 tampon applicators, and 7,640 milk jugs were collected."[11] In January 2004, the CBS television network sent news correspondent John Blackstone out on the Pacific Ocean aboard the research vessel *Algalita*. Blackstone, along with the ships's captain, Charles Moore, were more than 1,000 miles from land, but they saw lots of plastic in the ocean. "Day after day after day, when I came on deck," explained Captain Moore to Blackstone, "I saw objects floating by: toothbrushes, bottle caps and soap bottles." The trash was found in a patch of ocean called the North Pacific Gyre where the currents can trap floating debris for years. "I have no doubt that some of these things that we're discovering out there have been there since the dawn of the plastic era in the 1950's," said Moore. As plastic ages it crumbles, leaving many tiny fragments behind. Moore found that seawater in the North Pacific Gyre contained more plastic than plankton, the tiny sea life that many ocean creatures feed on. To jellyfish, the plastic particles seem like food, Moore explained. "It's like putting them on a plastic diet. It becomes part of their tissue." In his lab, Moore studies jellyfish embedded with plastic. "I saw that it had brightly colored plastic fragments inside," he said of one—pieces like blue monofilament fishing line. One jellyfish shown by CBS was so entangled in a scrap of synthetic net that its tentacles had grown around the plastic strands. The CBS spot closed with a shot of a swollen Los Angeles river culvert meeting the sea after a heavy rain. Discarded plastic items were flowing from the river into the Pacific in torrents, despite the best efforts of giant shovels trying to scoop out trapped material.[12] Dow, as one of the world's largest plastic producers and leading proponent of new plastic uses, is at least partially responsible for a share of this plastics trashing.

One researcher found seawater in the North Pacific Ocean that contained more plastic than plankton.

Fire & Fume

Another problem that some lay at the doorstep of plastics manufacturers is toxic fire. For decades, little was known about the special toxicity that comes with accidental fires in homes, office buildings, cars and trucks, and other materials that have come to be made of or filled with plastic. For example, even after thorough investigation of the famous catastrophic 1943 Coconut Grove nightclub fire in which 300 people were killed, only a handful of scientists and investigators knew that the nightclub's copious decor of nitrocellulose coconut fibers were a contributing cause of death and injury. During the 1960s and 1970s, airplane crashes in which victims survived the crash but died in a toxic fire also raised questions about the plastic material inside planes. And the 1969 New York Harbor fire aboard the *USS Enterprise* killed many sailors after plastic-coated electric cables burned. Following these incidents, even a White House report on fire in 1972 noted that plastics were being sold and used without adequate attention to the special fire hazard they presented. But when the National Fire Protection Association tried in 1975 to require by code that material used in construction be no more toxic than wood, the Society of the Plastics Industry blocked the move. In 1974–75, some plastics manufacturers advertised that urethane foam was fireproof and self-extinguishing, a claim the Federal Trade Commission challenged, but only resulted in industry's "rehabilitating the product" to improve its public image.[13]

In her eye-opening 1990 book, *In The Mouth of the Dragon*, Deborah Wallace describes the "plastic effect" in a number of tragic fires, among

Plastic Infernos

... That burning plastic could release noxious gases equal to any biochemical weapon ... was dismally proven in January 1970 when an elderly resident of the Harmar House nursing home in Marietta, Ohio carelessly tossed a lighted cigarette into a polypropylene wastebasket filled with waste paper. The burning paper caused her plastic basket to flare up, throwing out flames that rapidly consumed her polyurethane foam mattress, touched off her nylon wall-to-wall carpet, and instantly ignited the carpet's styrene-butadiene foam underlayer. By the time rescue workers arrived on the scene to evacuate the ward, they were met by a dense, black wall of smoke that obscured their view of survivors still trapped inside. The billowing smoke not only blinded the firemen but was so viciously toxic that it overcame scores of enfeebled patients who might otherwise have been able to escape on their own. By the time the fire was brought under control five hours later, twenty-two elderly people had died. The vast majority, coroners concluded, had been felled by the toxic fumes, not the flames.

Eight months later, on a steamy day in August 1970, a twelve-alarm fire broke out on the thirty-third floor of One New York Plaza, a modern high-rise office building in Manhattan's financial district. A stray electrical spark ignited a welter of computer cables concealed within a dropped ceiling in a telephone equipment room, which was itself filled floor to ceiling with mile after mile of exposed polyethylene-insulated cable. As the heat intensified, flammable and toxic gases were distilled from the polyurethane foam padding cushioning office furniture in the suites below. As the toxic gases burned, the blaze exploded, as if shot from an aerosol can. Fed on this rich diet of toxic, flammable gas, the fire consumed two entire floors covering over forty thousand square feet of office space in under twenty minutes. During the six hours it took to extinguish the flames, two firemen died of smoke inhalation. Thirty more were hospitalized with potentially life-threatening lung injuries—as the result of inhaling burning, noxious plastic fumes.

Only three weeks later, at 8:30 on the morning of August 26, a third blaze broke out in the recently completed British Overseas Airways terminal at New York's John F. Kennedy Airport. As flames licked across six hundred polyurethane foam-padded benches clustered by the gate entrances, clouds of toxic gas distilled from the benches' foam padding caused the fire to gallop off down the 35-foot-wide, 330-foot-long corridor at lightning speed ... As the roaring fire leapt wildly from seat to seat, blowing out dozens of large plate-glass windows in its wake, it took a mere fifteen minutes to consume the entire west gallery of the newly completed airline terminal, at an estimated cost of $2.5 million in damages. Awestruck insurers would later term it "the shortest large-loss fire in the history of mankind." [A] flammability expert retained by BOAC's insurance company to investigate the blaze, delivered the bad news to plastic manufacturers on ... the issue of plastic fire safety: "Plastics ignite like excelsior, contribute heat like kerosene, and produce four to thirty times the amount of smoke as nonsynthetic materials."

Excerpted from Stephen Fenichell, *Plastic: The Making of A Synthetic Century*, Harper-Collins: New York, 1996, pp. 308–11.

them: the 1975 New York Telephone Exchange fire that injured 239 out of 700 firefighters who battled a blaze fueled by polyvinyl chloride (PVC); the Beverly Hills Supper Club fire of 1977, in which 165 people were killed in an electrical and PVC-fueled blaze; the 1978 Cambridge, Ohio Holiday Inn fire in which 10 died from smoke from burning PVC and nylon; the 1978 Younkers Brothers Department Store fire in which 10 people died in another PVC-electrical fire; the 1980 MGM Grand Hotel fire in which 85 died in a fire largely fueled by plastics; the 1980 Stouffer's Inn fire in which 26 people died in a blaze fueled by PVC and nylon/wool; the 1983 Westgate Hilton fire in which 12 died from smoke that came mainly from PVC and urethane foam; and the 1983 Fort Worth Ramada Inn fire in which five died from PVC and nylon fumes.[14] Add to these the toxic fires that came during and after the September 2001 terrorist attack on the Twin Towers at the World Trade Center, and the February 2003 fire at The Station nightclub in West Warwick, Rhode Island. Burning plastic material played a role in the death and injury in both of these catastrophes. Individual homes are vulnerable to the plastic effect of toxic fires too, as everything from urethane-filled sofas and mattresses to PVC siding, wall coverings, plumbing lines, and molded furniture can provide toxic fuel. "No one thought to test [the] early synthetic polymers for their combustion toxicity," observes Deborah Wallace. "These products were virtually untested when they were put on the market. Instead, the public became the test animals."[15]

Toxic Life Cycle

Plastic, however, not only presents fire hazards and trash problems, its *production process* is also a problem—for workers, the environment, and nearby communities. By the mid-1980s, EPA had found that five of the six most hazardous chemicals—propylene, phenol, ethylene, polystyrene and benzene—were commonly used by plastics producers. At the upstream end of the process, where plastic resins are made, more than 5 million tons of hazardous waste were generated in 1984. At the processing end, where final products are made, another 88.7 million tons of hazardous wastes were generated. "Life cycle" analysis of some plastic materials—that is, looking in detail at the toxicity and fate of the materials, from manufacturing creation to final product disposal—reveals major public health risks. And perhaps no other plastic drives home that problem more dramatically than does polyvinyl chloride, or PVC.

> **By the mid-1980s, EPA had found that five of the six most hazardous chemicals were commonly used by plastics producers.**

The PVC Peril

Polyvinyl chloride is found everywhere in modern society—from building and construction materials such as vinyl siding, to furniture, cars, and toys. PVC today is a multi-billion-dollar global business, with markets still expanding, especially in developing economies. Cheered as one of many "wonder substances" in the plastics firmament of the 1940s and 1950s, PVC today has also become a **PVC is a "life cycle polluter," leaving its toxic residues in the environment—and in people—at every stage of its production, use, and disposal.** quiet public health and environmental crisis. First suspected, but covered up, as a workplace hazard by manufacturers after 1950s animal tests revealed potential health problems, PVC was later found to be a much broader environmental and public health threat. In fact, the PVC life cycle is toxic from beginning to end—in its manufacturing and generation of production wastes; in the additives used in making various PVC products soft, pliable, tough and/or resistant; in the products themselves during normal use, including "leaking" toxins that endanger consumers; and in the final disposal of both consumer and industrial products made with PVC.

PVC, in other words, is a "life cycle polluter," leaving its toxic residues in the environment—and in many cases, in people—at every stage of its production, use, and disposal. Among the leavings are an assortment of some of the most toxic substances on earth—all persistent and bioaccumulative. They include: chlorinated dioxins and furans, PCBs, hexachlorobenzene, octachlorostyrene, and some chemicals yet to be identified or tested. Of the known PVC-related toxins, the health effects include: cancer; endocrine, reproductive, and immune system effects; neurotoxicity and birth defects; and child development impairment.

The toxic dangers in the PVC life cycle do not come from PVC per se, but in how it's made and what's put into it. The main problem with PVC—and the one central to all its corollary impacts throughout its life cycle—is that it is made with chlorine. That is, chlorine is the starting material. In fact, making PVC consumes 40 percent of the world's chlorine gas production, with most PVC products in their final form consisting of about 45 percent chlorine by weight. Following chlorine are the two "feedstock chemicals" needed to make PVC. They are ethylene dichloride and vinyl chloride monomer—known by their acronyms, EDC and VCM. These chemicals are among the chief generators of PVC's toxic problems—the dioxins and furans, PCBs, HCB, and others. Dow is a major producer of both EDC and VCM, and is also the world's leading producer of chlorine.

Although not the inventor of PVC per se, Dow was more or less present at the creation of its key ingredients. At the company's California Physics Lab in the 1930s, Dow scientists developed vinyl chloride,[16] and Dow's animal research in the 1950s made the company one of the first knowledgeable about PVC's toxic downsides, especially in VCM.

From the 1950s onward, PVC plastic was increasingly used in construction and home building to replace wood, metal, and ceramics.* Soon, it was showing up in pipes, window frames, exterior siding, floor tiles, and even wall coverings. It was also used in furniture, upholstery, appliance casings, shower curtains, and toys. By 1965, bottles made from polyvinyl chloride were gaining market share. Grocery bags made of a PVC formulation appeared in the 1970s.

Dow is very much at the chemical headwaters of the PVC production process.

Today, polyvinyl chloride is the second most common plastic in the world after polyethylene.

To produce polyvinyl chloride, EDC is made first, 98 percent of which is then used to make VCM. Most of this chemical, in turn, is used to make PVC. This two-step process, however, generates huge amounts of waste and toxic byproducts. One 1994 internal memo from British chemical maker ICI concluded that the formation of dioxins and furans during the manufacture of EDC was unavoidable. The production of VCM is also believed to generate dioxins and furans, as well as a range of other chemical byproducts—in fact, several hundred thousand tons' worth globally.[17] In some of these wastes, sizeable quantities of what were supposed to be banned chemicals have been found. In 1990, Dow Chemical analyzed its EDC "heavy end" wastes and found that they were 65 percent chlorine, including 302 parts per million PCBs, 0.3 percent hexachloroethane, 1.2 percent haxachlorobutadiene, and 30.6 percent unidentified compounds. "If this analysis is representative of heavy ends in general," observes Joe Thornton in his book *Pandora's Poison*, "then EDC oxychlorination results in the worldwide production of a stunning 20,000 pounds of

---

*Plastic products generally, and PVC in particular, have replaced other materials that once performed their tasks in perfectly good form. Plastic may have offered some added durability and lower maintenance, or helped to "dumb down" certain uses, but one effect was to replace craft and workmanship in trade for convenience and/or ease of installation. "Not so long ago," observes Joe Thornton, "virtually all products now made from PVC were made from other traditional material that functioned perfectly well. Home siding was once wood, stucco or aluminum; now it's increasingly vinyl. Window frames were wood or metal. Floors were wood, ceramic tile, linoleum or carpet. Clothing and upholstery were cloth or leather. Pipes were cement or metal. Many containers were glass, metal or cardboard. Packaging, when necessary, was paper or cardboard..." Joe Thornton, *Pandora's Poison*, pp. 386–87.

PCBs each year, even though these compounds were banned from intentional production in the late 1970s."[18]

Additive Toxicity

At the end of the PVC-making process, VCM is polymerized into "raw" PVC resin, which is then formulated with various combinations of additives. The additives stage, it turns out, is problematic too, as the chemicals used to make PVC soft and pliable are also bad actors. These "plasticizers," or softening agents, make PVC suitable for use in roofing materials, floor tiles, and wall coverings. The dominant group of plasticizers are the phthalates (pronounced "tal – ates"), used at a rate of about 5 million tons annually, accounting for about 90 percent of all plasticizers. Phthalates have been found everywhere on earth—in arctic sediments, in the air over the Atlantic and Pacific oceans, and in deep-ocean jellyfish.[19] More than 80 million tons of phthalates are believed to be bound up in PVC products and materials found in buildings, appliances and other products. The problem with phthalates is that they are known animal carcinogens and have been found in human body fluids and tissue. They are also moderately persistent in the environment. Phthalates leak out of landfills and are released in incineration. They also leach out of PVC products and materials, from furniture coverings to plastic drinking straws. In laboratory animals, phthalates have been found to damage the reproductive system, causing infertility, testicular damage, reduced sperm counts, and suppressed ovulation.[20]

Scientists at the CDC have detected phthalates in urine of child-bearing-age women—at levels that cause fetal abnormalities in lab animals.

As early as the 1970s, scientists found that chicken embryos died when subjected to a 0.4 percent solution of one of the most common phthalates, diethylhexylphthalate or DEHP. Hospital patients receiving intravenous treatment have been shown to be at risk of exposure to DEHP, which can leach directly out of intravenous tubes and into the patient's bloodstream. Scientists at the Centers for Disease Control (CDC) have also detected phthalates in urine of child-bearing age women—at levels that cause fetal abnormalities in lab animals. Other studies have shown that children chewing on PVC toys as well as pacifiers and teething rings, can absorb phthalates into their bodies. One Norwegian study in 1999 concluded that young children may absorb phthalates from vinyl floor coverings.[21] In addition to the phthalates, other additives, including lead, cadmium, and organotins—the "metal stabilizers"—are also added to some vinyl products to make them tough and resistant for construction and extended-life applications. All of these additives are toxic and problematic, both in production and incineration—and also in fires.*

Although Dow is a relatively minor player in making actual PVC products—save for a few industrial-type products such as polyvinylidene chloride films[22]—the company is very much at the chemical headwaters of the PVC production process, and many believe, responsible for a major share of its toxic problems. Dow is the world's largest chlorine producer, accounting for roughly 11.5 percent of all global production from its plants in the U.S., Canada, Germany, and Brazil. It is also a leader in the two PVC feedstock chemicals—EDC and VCM. In the United States, Dow produces about 26 percent of the EDC, and about 17 percent of the VCM—all from its Texas and Louisiana plants. In Canada, Dow produces 1.8 billion pounds of EDC annually at its Fort Saskatchewan, Alberta plant—100 percent of the Canadian production. At these plants and others, Dow is not without its troubles, having occasional to chronic releases of chlorine, vinyl chloride and other toxic chemicals. Longer-term problems involving toxic waste have also plagued the company, such as vinyl chloride groundwater pollution in Plaquemine, Louisiana (see Chapter 15).

> **"...the life cycle of PVC accounts for more dioxin than any industrial source."**
>
> *Pat Costner*

Dioxin is also a main worry with PVC production. Dioxins are present in high concentrations in EDC and VCM as they are produced. More dioxin is generated when chlorine-rich wastes from the manufacture of EDC and VCM are incinerated. At Dow's plants, there are more than 100 incinerators operating, with 25 at the Freeport, Texas plant alone. In recent years, Dow has pledged to reduce its dioxin emissions, and has made some progress, but the company also ships a lot of waste off-site for contract incineration. "The evidence is becoming clear," explained Greenpeace scientist Pat Costner in early 1995 after compiling a report that analyzed Dow and other waste samples, "that the life cycle of PVC accounts for more dioxin than any industrial source."[23] Additional dioxin emissions in the PVC life cycle occur in post-consumer use, when discarded PVC products are disposed of in various waste streams. Both PVC and products such as *Saran Wrap*, for example, form dioxins when burned. Municipal and hospital waste incinerators, capturing PVC waste

---

*For much more detail on PVC's environmental and public health effects, see, for example, any number of Greenpeace (*www.greenpeaceusa.org*) publications, including *The PVC Life Cycle: Dioxin, From Cradle to Grave*, April 1997, and, *This Vinyl House: Hazardous Additives in Vinyl Consumer Products and Home Furnishings*, May 2001. See also, Joe Thornton, PhD, *Environmental Impacts of Polyvinyl Chloride Building Materials*, published by the Healthy Building Network (*www.healthybuilding.net*), Washington, DC, 2002. For PVC-related concerns from medical and hospital materials see *www.noharm.org*, the web site of the Boston-based, Health Care Without Harm, and also *www.ourstolenfuture.org*.

Dow In ToyLand

"Uses of Dow plastics by the toy industry are across-the-board," boasted Dow Chemical in an internal company newsletter one Christmas season—"and more and more are our materials found under the Christmas tree and on the birthday table, making some child, some toy company, and Dow, very happy indeed." Among the chemicals Dow described and sold at the time, used in making one or more toys, sporting goods, game boards, and other items, were the following:

Polystyrene—noted for its low cost, easy fabrication, excellent colors and good impact in a rigid material, and sold to toy manufacturers as *Styron*, polystyrene "is widely used" in road race track boards, game boards and pieces, musical instruments, hobby kits, toy dishes, blocks, gun sets and boats.

SAN—a chemical composite of styrene and acrylonitrile, results in a rigid plastic having better strength and chemical resistance than polystyrene. Dow's *Tyril* brand SAN is used in paint pots, pen holders, toy cars, and toy truck windshields.

ABS—the chemical shorthand for acrylonitrile-styrene-butadiene, produced as a rigid plastic stronger and more chemical resistant than SAN, and sold to toy makers under the trade name *Typrene*. These Dow plastic resins are found in car racer bodies, microscope and telescope bodies, luggage, doll parts, blocks and toy seats.

Polyethylene—is sold to toy makers by Dow in both high- and low-density grades. High density material is used to make semi-rigid flexible molded items, while low-density poly has major uses in the clear, flexible film that is wrapped around hundreds of toys, dolls, and games. Dow's high-density polyethylene is used in pails, buckets, safety hammers, toddle carts, wheels, dolls, golf games, bats, and hula-hoops.

Ethylene copolymer resins—billed by Dow for their "rubbery behavior" and their "excellent weatherability and outstanding flex at low temperatures," are sold as *Zetalin* brand-name resins, and are molded into squeeze toys, instrument bellows, balls, pool covers, toy sports equipment and goggle rims.

Saran resins—made into thin films, fibers, and molded items, are extruded into wigs and doll hair, Christmas tinsel and toy furniture webs.

PVC resins, or vinyls—are made into soft and flexible films and sheets and into semi-rigid and rigid molded shapes. Billed as having good chemical resistance and easily processed into fire-retardant and highly durable items, Dow PVC resins are found in artificial Christmas trees, toy luggage, flexible covers, and toy place settings.

Polystyrene beads—sold to toy manufactures under the Dow brand-name *Pelaspan*, are molded into resilient, light-weight foam shapes. Toy makers use them in safety building blocks, game display bases and packages, gliders and large model aircraft, dart game boards, special games, and swim flotation toys.

Ethyl cellulose—one of the toughest, most inert plastics in existence, Dow's brand *Ethocel* is used by toy and sporting good manufacturers to make batting helmets, football helmets, and a range of other sports equipment and tools.

The major toy makers, explained the newsletter, "are now sophisticated enough in their evaluation of plastics to use two and sometimes three and four different plastics in the several parts of a given toy." The world of toys, concluded this account, "is fast becoming a plastics world." And the Dow thermoplastics used by the toy industry "are helping make it a 'good' world for the small-middle-old fry whom it serves."

Source: LA V.F., "Dow Provides Toy, Hobby Manufacturers With a Wide Variety of Plastics."

streams in medical and household products, have been among the largest generators of dioxin. Dow, as an originator of chlorinated chemicals in at least a portion of these PVC-incinerated wastes, is also seen as responsible for a share of that dioxin.[20] But Dow has presented other dangers in the PVC process, most notably those involving vinyl chloride in the workplace.

Danger on the Job

As early as the 1950s there were documented cases of European vinyl workers suffering from a wide range of maladies such as gastritis, skin lesions, and dermatitis. In 1958, Dow began some experiments testing vinyl chloride on rats, rabbits, guinea pigs, and dogs at the company's Biochemical Research Laboratory in Michigan. Those tests revealed that rats exposed to vinyl chloride monomer (VCM), and inhaled at levels as low as 100 ppm, had developed liver defects and tumors. Chemical workers at the time were inhaling VCM at levels many times that amount. Industry then more or less subscribed to some loosely set standards for worker chemical exposure called "threshold limit values," or TLVs. Established only for a small group of chemicals, TLVs were set by a voluntary organization of scientists called the American Conference of Governmental Industrial Hygienists (ACGIH), (see also Chapter 12). The TLV for VCM was 500 ppm. Dow's V. K. Rowe, one of the scientists conducting the Dow rat tests that found problems at 100 ppm, sent a letter on May 12, 1959 to B. F. Goodrich Co.'s industrial hygiene director, in which Rowe outlined the experimental findings. Rowe concluded that vinyl chloride could produce "rather appreciable injury" among workers routinely exposed to 500 ppm, the voluntary standard. In concluding his letter, Rowe noted, "...this opinion is not ready for dissemination yet and I would appreciate it if you would hold it in confidence...."[21] Dow did not widely disseminate its evidence of a vinyl-cancer causation pattern, explains Stephen Fenichell in *Plastic: The Making of A Synthetic Century*, "preferring instead to do what little it could to protect its own workers without raising a national cancer scare."[22]

In the late 1950s, Dow was also considering using VCM as a propellant in hairsprays, insecticides, room deodorants, and spray paints, and apparently joined with other chemical companies in producing and selling vinyl chloride for such uses through the 1960s,* generally believing the voluntary 500 ppm VCM standard was adequate.[23] In 1961, Dow researchers did publish their earlier data on the animal experiments in the *American Industrial Hygiene Association Journal*, recommending a vinyl chloride exposure limit of 50 ppm. But few in the industry heeded this recommendation in practice, including Dow. In 1966, when the 50 ppm vinyl chloride recommendation was first proposed as a TLV, Dow scientist Dr. Theodore Torkelson moved in committee at the ACGIH to "put off" the recommendation and await further accumulating experience. Dow claimed to have taken steps to tighten VCM exposure levels at all its vinyl plants in 1961—to averages as low as 100 ppm, then five times lower than the accepted 500 ppm level. But some, including occupational health analyst Barry Castleman, maintain that Dow "knowingly exceeded" this level, and in effect, still had 300 ppm levels at their plants up to 1968 or later.[24]

In the mid-1960s, the chemical industry also discovered that VCM was linked to a degenerative bone condition that appeared in workers at a number of its plants; a condition called acroosteolysis, causing the bones in the tips of fingers to wither and become painful to the touch. Some workers, for example, would complain they couldn't open their own lunch boxes. The condition had never been seen before; it was a totally new occupational hazard. Industry later verified the problem and debated the matter internally, hearing some reports that VCM exposure levels should be reduced to 50 ppm. Worried of negative publicity and that the vinyl- and *Saran*-using pub-

---

*By 1969, however, B. F. Goodrich noted that people in the cosmetics trade had become concerned about the possible toxicity of vinyl chloride propellents and that measurements of vinyl chloride in the air of some hair salons had found VCM at 250 ppm. In some cases, when the duration of spraying was 3 minutes or so, the VCM concentration could go as high as 1400 ppm, leading Goodrich observers to conclude that some beauticians and other customers could be exposed to VCM levels at or greater than those found at chemical plants. In any case, vinyl chloride continued to be sold and used as an aerosol propellant until sometime in 1974. See Gerald Markowitz and David Rosner, *Deceit and Denial*, pp. 184–85.

lic would hear of such problems, industry did its best to bury the problem, with very muted 1971 reports calling the bone-disease agent "unknown" with no suggestion that the 500 ppm standard be changed.[25]

But soon, the industry had more bad news about VCM: it was cancer-causing. In 1970, an Italian researcher, Dr. Pierluigi Viola found carcinogenic effects in lab rats exposed to 30,000 ppm VCM gas. The rats had developed tumors of the skin, lungs and bones. The chemical industry, briefed on Viola's findings in 1971, did not revise its position, believing the experiment was not a good predictor of what

By 1970, an Italian researcher found that rats exposed to high levels of VCM developed angiosarcoma, a rare cancer affecting the liver's blood cells.

might happen in humans, as some of the cancers occurred in rat glands that did not exist in humans. Viola repeated his experiments, found tumors at 5,000 ppm level, and recommended that further research be conducted at levels of 50 ppm. PVC production in the U.S. meanwhile, had doubled between 1966 and 1971. Little of Viola's findings were broadcast by the American chemical industry. Europe's chemical industry, meanwhile, secretly employed another researcher to follow up on Viola's findings. This researcher, Cesar Maltoni, found rats developing angiosarcoma—a rare cancer affecting the liver's blood cells—at VCM exposures of 250 ppm. Maltoni expressed the view that VCM gas was likely to cause cancer in workers exposed to it over extended periods. By the time Maltoni's results came to the American chemical industry in 1972, there was concern that the results would become public, and some cited a secrecy agreement with the European producers sharing the new findings. Dow, for one, felt "honor-bound to make sure that information received from the European producers remains within our own company until formal permission has been granted for its release." Dow, in fact, instructed that no one "discuss the European work" even within the company unless such persons "have a need to know." And even then, such discussions were to be cleared in advance.[26]

Gerald Markowitz and David Rosner, authors of *Deceit and Denial*, explain industry's bogus claim to the need for secrecy:

> While it is common practice for researchers to jealously guard their findings until they are published, in cases where human lives are at stake, most researchers accept that they have an obligation to share knowledge about potential harm. Further, the insistence on confidentiality [on the European cancer findings] was not coming from the scientific researcher, but from the vinyl manufacturers. The secrecy was not entered into at the beginning of the experiments, but only when it became apparent that vinyl chloride monomer was carcinogenic at half the accepted TLV. Secrecy, in this case, was not to protect product infor-

mation, patent secrets, or even innovative experimental procedures. Rather, its sole aim was to avoid a public relations and legal nightmare.[27]

By early 1973, a couple of related developments bearing on PVC toxicity had occurred. The U.S. Food and Drug Administration (FDA) had learned that the Treasury Department's Bureau of Alcohol, Tobacco and Firearms had been testing plastic liquor bottles since 1968, finding that the bottles were leaching VCM into the liquor. FDA confirmed the "migration" of VCM to alcohol in the PVC bottles through its own tests. FDA, in light of the Italian findings from Viola, plus its charge for protecting the public from dietary exposure to carcinogens under the law, began to move on banning the use of vinyl chloride in liquor bottles. It later did so, finding no studies that established a safe level of consumption when VCM is leached from the liquor bottles.

Misleading NIOSH

Also in early 1973, the National Institute of Occupational Safety and Health (NIOSH) published a notice that it was seeking public input in a process to establish a workplace standard and safe exposure level for vinyl chloride. The chemical industry's trade group, the Manufacturing Chemists Association (MCA), immediately began to consider how they would brief NIOSH and what public posture they would assume on the whole matter of vinyl chloride's emerging occupational health problems. NIOSH was not fully aware of the Italian cancer studies, especially those of Maltoni, still under wraps by both European and American chemical industries. After some wrangling with lawyers and others, it was agreed by industry they would only inform NIOSH of certain things. They would not tell the government, unless asked directly, about the Maltoni studies. Nor would they tell NIOSH of any need to reduce the VCM standard below the 500 ppm level—and in fact, the MCA struck all reference to Dow's earlier recommendation that the TLV be reduced to 50 ppm. In mid-July 1973, an MCA delegation that included Dow's V. K. Rowe, convened at the NIOSH office in Rockville, Maryland. Rowe made the formal presentation, and described the industry's efforts to address health concerns, including acroosteolysis and cancer. European representatives at the meeting told of exhaustive studies of PVC workers that revealed no indication of hazard. Some of Viola's findings were offered and discussed by the Europeans, but the results, said the Europeans, were based on findings in rats, not humans, and at high exposures of 30,000 ppm. No firm conclusions were yet drawn, said the Europeans. Not mentioned by anyone in the delegation briefing NIOSH that day was Maltoni, or anything about liver or kidney cancers, or the fact that tumors had been found at 250 ppm. Near the end of the meeting, Dow's V. K. Rowe went to a separate office and privately spoke with the NIOSH director about the cancer findings, apparently assuring him industry was on top of the situation. At the meeting's conclusion, NIOSH felt it had been fully apprised on vinyl chloride in the industry, and brought up to date on the state of knowledge to that point. Back at MCA, there was general agreement that the industry delegation to NIOSH had likely forestalled any precipitous action on vinyl chloride. "In short," observe Gerald Markowitz and David Rosner, "the industry's trade association had succeeded in preventing NIOSH from learning about the danger to workers and consumers from vinyl chloride."[28] But that would soon change.

A few months later, reports coming out of Europe indicated that dozens of workers had already died as a result of vinyl chloride exposure, and that a larger exposure problem loomed from the chemical leaching from food and beverage containers, filters used in artificial kidneys, and cardiac valves. In the U.S., one report in November 1973 noted meat wrappers developing respiratory problems as a result of breathing fumes created by the heating of PVC film. But the real blockbuster was the news from B. F. Goodrich.

Dead Workers

B. F. Goodrich, a profitable U.S. tire manufacturer, had become a major player in PVC production. In January 1974, however, Goodrich reported that one of its workers died of the rare liver cancer, angiosarcoma, and that another employed at the same plant had died of the liver disease a year earlier. Shortly thereafter, a third Goodrich worker died of the same disease, while eight others were diagnosed with the same fatal cancer. B.F. Goodrich notified NIOSH, which quickly issued an emergency VCM standard of 50 ppm.[29] Shortly thereafter, the larger story began to emerge.

By June 1974, the American Chemical Society reported that American and European chemical companies had purposely withheld information linking vinyl chloride with angiosarcoma, nervous conditions, skin problems, and softening of the finger bones. A heated policy debate then ensued at the national level, with some calling for, and NIOSH formally proposing, a "zero tolerance" standard. The Society of the Plastics Industry protested, charging that costly measures would be needed to protect workers. Some of its members threatened to pull out of the vinyl business altogether. AFL-CIO countered: "The men and women we represent will not countenance the barbaric attitude which seems to dictate that death and disease are all just part of the sacrifice that must be made for food, clothing and shelter!"[30] Later in 1974, OSHA and NIOSH issued a "no detectable level" regulation—i.e., below 1 ppm—which the Society of the Plastics Industry promptly challenged in court, but lost. Dow, Union Carbide, and Goodrich then took steps to assure stockholders they were not pulling out of the PVC business. But that wasn't the end of the vinyl chloride matter.

Brain Cancers

In February 1979, NIOSH had found a cluster of brain cancers at a Union Carbide plant in Texas City, and vinyl chloride was strongly suspected as the causative agent. After a victim of brain cancer at Union Carbide had filed a complaint in 1979 with the U.S. Department of Labor, the department's Health and Human Services division began an investigation of petrochemical plants, including Dow's plant at Freeport, Texas. In July 1980, the investigators reported

The investigators also discovered 25 brain-tumor cases among workers at Dow's Freeport plant, 24 of which were fatal.

finding "excessively high" incidence of brain cancer in at least seven petrochemical plants in Texas, West Virginia, Kentucky and California. At a Union Carbide plant in Texas City, 18 fatalities had already been discovered. But the investigators also found 25 brain-tumor cases among workers at Dow's Freeport plant, 24 of which were fatal. That incidence of brain cancer among

Worker Sues

Lloyd Glen Smith of Denham Springs, Louisiana worked on the marine dock at Dow Chemical's Plaquemine plant handling vinyl chloride from 1970 to 1974. He was in his late 20s when he started the job. Smith later came down with arthritis, and also had several other conditions, including pulmonary dysfunction, and neurobehavioral and neurophysiological problems. In the late 1980s, he filed a lawsuit against Dow claiming that his exposure to vinyl chloride while working at Dow resulted in his various illnesses. In late November 1991, District Court judge Jack T. Marionneaux, issued a judgement ordering Dow to pay Smith $2.5 million for health problems connected with overexposure to the chemical. "This court is impressed with the clear evidence from all physicians, including Dow's, that Smith is at sufficient risk of contracting liver, lung, or brain cancer within the next decade as a direct result of the overexposures," wrote Marionneaux in his judgement. "He has already suffered physical injuries specific to the exposure, which caused mental deterioration and lung problems."

Marionneaux ruled that Smith was entitled to $496,036 in lost wages, future medical costs of $41,832, and $2 million in "general damages, representing physical and mental pain and suffering and fear of contracting cancer." At the time of the ruling, Dow said it planned to appeal, noting that Smith had elected to take long-term disability in 1987 because of rheumatoid arthritis. Dow did appeal, but the case was later settled.

Source: "Dow To Appeal Judge's $2.5 Million Settlement to Worker," *Post/South* (Plaquemine, LA), November 21, 1991, p. 1-A.

workers was twice that of the general population. At the time, the Labor Department investigators cautioned that the results were still tentative and that no firm scientific conclusions should be drawn. Still, they believed what they found was significant. "With varying levels of proof, we believe each of them [Dow and Carbide] represents an excessively high" incidence of the disease, said Dr. Victor Alexander, a medical officer with the Labor Department. "We don't have much information about chemicals causing brain cancer," Dr. Alexander added. "'This is a new area for us, and that is one of the reasons we're interested."[31] The deaths among the Dow workers occurred between 1951 and 1977, and most of the cancers were of two strains: astrocytoma and glioblastoma. The average age at death was 55, and eight of the victims were under 50. The conclusion—with which Dow strenuously disagreed—was "an increased risk of death due to brain tumor" among the ex-Dow workers.[32]

Bisphenol-A

Bisphenol-A is one of those hidden chemical ingredients in the plastics empire that most people never hear about, or have much reason to. Yet it is everywhere in modern products, from computer keyboards to food-can linings. Chemically, bisphenol-A is known as 2,2-bis (4-hydroxy phenyl) propane, but is commonly known by its acronym, BPA. Dow Chemical sells and uses BPA extensively. In fact, Dow is among the world's top five producers of BPA, about 90 percent of which is used for making polycarbonate and epoxy resin. Polycarbonate, however, accounts for the lion's share of BPA's end-uses, at 63 percent, a share that is growing yearly.

Polycarbonate is the tough, durable, shatter- and heat-resistant plastic found in thousands of everyday products, from compact discs to lightweight eyeglass lenses. In 1953, scientists from Bayer and General Electric, working independently, discovered polycarbonate, so named for the carbonate chemicals in its backbone chain. By the late 1950s polycarbonate began to be used for electrical applications, such as distributor and fuse boxes. A wide range of other uses soon followed. By 1982, the first audio CD was made with polycarbonate, followed by CD-ROMs in 1992, and DVDs in 1997. Today, polycarbonate plastic is found in Ray Ban sunglasses, Apple iMacs, Williams-Sonoma dishware, cell phones, sporting goods, household appliances, food storage containers, and bottles.

Polycarbonate, however, is made from a process that combines phosgene and BPA. Phosgene, a highly toxic gas derived from chlorine, and once used as a nerve agent in World War I, is still a toxic threat to chemical workers who deal with it today (see chapters 16 and 17). BPA, the other polycarbonate ingredient, was recently found to cause endocrine disruption in laboratory rats at very low doses. U.S. consumption of BPA, meanwhile, has more than doubled during the past decade, driven primarily by heavy demand for polycarbonate resins for automotive parts, compact discs, and sheet and glazing applications. Worldwide, BPA has a projected growth rate of 7 percent per year.

Dow Chemical initially developed its BPA during the1960s for use in the production of epoxy resins—for which it is still used today. By the late 1960s, Dow began producing a poly-carbonate-grade BPA, and by 1972, started its first commer-cial BPA plant using a new resin technology at Freeport, Texas. Today, Dow has a total

BPA was found to cause endocrine disruption in laboratory rats at very low doses.

production capacity of 300,000 metric tons of BPA annually at four plants in two locations—Freeport, Texas, and Stade, Germany. Dow's polycarbonate-grade BPA is known under the trade name *Parabis*.

Dow has had at least one run-in with the EPA over its polycarbonate production. In June 1989, EPA proposed $1.13 million in civil penalties on Dow for failing to notify the agency it was producing a new chemical, as required under the Toxic Substances Control Act of 1976. According to EPA, for a period of about two years, dating to 1986, Dow had produced and sold 227 batches of a polycarbonate without informing the agency. In the sum-mer of 1988, two years after the fact, Dow did inform the agency it had been producing and selling the chemical. Dow blamed its failure to notify EPA on "a clerical error." But EPA found the incident to be a substantial offense. "The significance of a case like this," said EPA's Michael J. Walker, assistant enforcement counsel, "is that the EPA was precluded from reviewing the chemical in advance before manufacture to see if there was a risk to health and the environment." Dow and EPA later settled the charges, with Dow paying a reduced fine of $400,000 due to allowances made for coop-eration with the agency, preparation of a video on the

BPA is also suspected as a possi-ble link to an increase in testicu-lar cancer and low sperm counts.

chemical for use by other companies, and the completion of an environ-mental audit on the substance.

In addition to being a known endocrine disruptor, BPA is suspected as a possible link to an increase in testicular cancer and low sperm counts. Male mice exposed in the womb to low levels of BPA were shown to have increased prostate weights and decreased daily sperm production.* And

---

*In the late 1990s, industry-sponsored research found no evidence of biological effects from low-dose exposures to BPA. Industry says the results are consistent with other bisphenol-A studies that also failed to find any evidence of biological effects. However, these assertions contradict widely publicized findings suggesting that the chemical can cause developmental abnormalities.

because BPA has been found to leach out of certain products, its presence in the linings of food cans and also in baby feeding bottles, has generated the most urgent concern. Evidence from an unpublished study commissioned by the U.K. Department of Trade and Industry found that BPA is released from babies' bottles following bottle brushing, dishwashing, or sterilization. Bisphenol-A is also used as an antioxidant in polyvinyl chloride. Since it is used as an additive in PVC and not as a polymer ingredient, BPA can leach out of the plastic at a faster rate from PVC products than from polycarbonate products. The World Wildlife Fund in the U.K. has charged that current legal limits for BPA are not set at low enough levels to protect human health, and advocates eliminating human and wildlife exposure to BPA where practicable.[33] In the United States, Dow Chemical in recent years has emerged in the thick of the debate over BPA's health-effects science.

Strong-Arming Science

Dr. Frederick vom Saal is a professor and researcher at the University of Missouri at Columbia. He is a leading scientist in the field of developmental biology. He has studied the action of both natural and synthetic hormones and their effects at extremely low doses. His studies with mice have shown that small shifts in hormones before birth can matter a great deal and have consequences that can last a lifetime. He has also studied how man-made chemicals, including plastics, can mimic hormones at extremely low doses.

In 1997, vom Saal had been working on bisphenol-A, and had prepared a draft paper on the effects of fetal exposure to bisphenol-A on sperm production in mice. The findings were not all that flattering of bisphenol-A. Dr. vom Saal had made copies of his draft paper available to everyone in the plastics industry who had attended a February meeting earlier that year. He intended to publish his paper in the *Journal of Toxicology and Industrial Health*. And within weeks it was being prepared for final publication. Then on April 25, 1997, Dow Chemical's Dr. John Waechter came to Missouri and held a meeting with vom Saal and some of his colleagues. What Dow's man had to say was not well received. "We were surprised that Dr. Waechter came here with the task of asking us to withhold publication of a paper on bisphenol-A which is *in press* in the *Journal of Toxicology and Industrial Health*," explained Dr. vom Saal and his colleague Dr. Wade V. Welshons in a June 12, 1997 letter they wrote to the Society of the Plastics Industry in Washington, D.C. "...Dr. Waechter began by stating that it was the hope of Dow Chemical that there could be 'some mutually beneficial outcome' as a result of withdrawing the paper and postponing its publication...." Dow wanted a replicate study of effects of bisphenol-A in mice to be conducted by MPI Research of Mattawan, Michigan, whose representative had accompanied Waechter at the meeting. Dow also wanted vom Saal and Welshons to withhold their paper until the new study had been completed and *approved for publication*." Drs. vom Saal and Welshons said they would not withdraw the paper "unless Dr. Waechter could provide a scientific basis as to why it should not be published.... "[34]

The PBS television show, *Frontline*, interviewed vom Saal in 1998. Here's a portion of that interview in which vom Saal describes his experience with Dow:

> **Scientists simply don't put away their findings until industry lawyers decide it is appropriate for them to publish.**
>
> Dr. Frederick vom Saal

> **vom Saal**: ...Dow Chemical sent a representative down to my lab a number of months ago and essentially asked if there were a mutually beneficial outcome that we could arrive at where I held off publishing the information about this chemical until they had repeated my studies, and after repeating my studies approval for publication was received by all the plastic manufacturers.

> *Frontline*: They were trying to buy you off?

> **vom Saal**: We didn't get to anywhere beyond that. My response was, "Do you have a scientific criticism that would justify not publishing this paper?" Because if anybody can ever provide a valid scientific criticism on the research that I've done, that would be a reason not to publish an article. But this was research funded through the National Institutes of Health. I have an absolute obligation to take public money and report the findings from research conducted with those public funds. To not do so would be a gross violation of professional ethics, and ... would be totally inappropriate.
>
> So I don't know what mutually beneficial outcome they were thinking about, but there was no beneficial outcome that I would have found acceptable and so I simply shut that conversation off. But clearly that was an example where they would have preferred that the information not be seen by the general community, and not be discussed about in this format.

> *Frontline*: Dow Chemical said this didn't happen. There may have been a misunderstanding, or whatever, but they certainly weren't trying to influence your research.

> **vom Saal**: Well, if you say that Dow says this didn't happen, there were a number of other people in the room during this conversation and I wrote a letter to the Food and Drug Administration documenting the conversation in detail. Quite a detailed letter that was sent to the government with copies all through my university hierarchy.

I never received a letter back from anybody at Dow suggesting that there was anything in that letter that wasn't exactly as it had happened which, again, was also witnessed by numerous other people. If they have any problem with what I am saying here, they can deal with that however they want. What I am saying is exactly what happened and could be corroborated by a number of other people who were in the room and heard this.

Frontline: Why would they do this?

vom Saal: I was stunned. I can't answer for the people who would have made that decision. It was a stupid decision as far as I am concerned. I can't imagine how they would have thought I would do something like that. It was totally inappropriate. Scientists simply don't put away their findings until industry lawyers decide it is appropriate for them to publish.

But it does raise an absolutely critical issue that when an industry funds "science"—I put "science" in quotes there because there is an inherent contradiction. Science is the pursuit of knowledge and the dissemination of that knowledge. Industry typically puts constraints on the ability to disseminate that information.

The chemical industry has shown an absolute unwillingness to give any money not attached to strings where they control the process of putting together the experiments and then publishing the experiments. And that is just unacceptable. And this is a perfect example of what would happen if I had a contractual arrangement with them that allowed them to shut me down in terms of providing you with the information I am providing to you.

What we have been calling for, in the scientific community, for a number of years is for the chemical industry to set up a mechanism to give money to address the basic issues of how chemicals work without controlling the design of the experiments and the ability to publish the work once the research has been done...[35]

Plastics Trespass

One of the premier fallacies that dominated the making of plastics in the 1950s, as Marc Lappe explains in his 1991 book *Chemical Deception*, was the notion of nonreactivity. By making long chains of otherwise highly reactive chemicals, scientists made plastics of every kind. This chain-building and plastics-making nirvana, called polymerization, worked fine as long as all the reactive molecules remained trapped in the polymerized chains. But as Lappe explains, this was not always the way things worked. Polystyrene, polyethylene, polybutylene, PVC, and a plastic known as ABS—a combination of acrylonitrile, butadiene and styrene—were "all touted as non-reactive plastics ideally suited to carrying beverages, wrapping food, and transporting water." However, each was proven, in their early formulations, to pose unforeseen problems. "[A]lcohol carried in acrylonitrile bottles was found to extract residues of carcinogenic monomers still present in the plastic, leading to the hasty recall of all alcohol-containing plastic bottles... Plastic pipes made of polyethylene or polybutylene are suspected of allowing solvents or gasoline constituents such as benzene to cross their

Plastics production is guilty of toxic trespass; its ingredients cross the placenta, infiltrate the blood, and/or enter human body tissue.

walls, thereby contaminating the water carried inside... "[36]

In the late 1990s, especially in the rural areas of Kansas and Texas, there were cases documenting vinyl chloride leaching out of plastic pipes used in rural water districts and getting into drinking water. In pre-1976 PVC pipe, vinyl chloride could separate from the pipe and leach into the water under certain conditions.[37]* And of course, today, come the additional revelations about the toxic dangers in PVC softening and plasticizing ingredients, such as the phthalates, used in products from toys to blood bags. But even as new applications and new markets for PVC are being created, many of the old endangerments remain real and unaddressed.

Dow, for one, continues to push for new uses of plastic and PVC throughout the global economy, featuring various "case studies" of new product ventures on its website to show potential buyers how PVC and plastic can be used to replace steel and other traditional materials.[38] True, Dow has made a major bio-plastics venture with Cargill, and is sponsoring other research into bio-plastics and new bio-polymers—developments which promise safer products. These are all to the good, if limited in the range of applications they offer. More safe substitutes and alternatives are needed, though many already exist in the traditional materials that have been pushed out by PVC.

Yet throughout the plastics era, Dow has been one of the leading cheerleaders for, and principal beneficiaries of, a key line of chemicals that have

---

*In February and March of 1998, EPA asked a number of states from Nebraska to Texas to assess their rural water supply systems that contained the PVC piping, and in at least one northeast Kansas water district, ordered the piping replaced. In EPA's Dallas, Texas Office, the states of Texas, Oklahoma, Arkansas, New Mexico, and Louisiana were asked to assess all water districts, not just rural districts, for the potential PVC leaching. At the time, the PVC pipe industry in Texas estimated there were nearly 1,000 rural water districts that contained PVC pipe, though it was unknown how many had the pre-1976 pipe. For some residents in northeast Kansas where the piping was ordered to be replaced, bottled water was being supplied to reduce the residents exposure to vinyl chloride.

been inadequately tested for their long-term health effects, and whose toxic effects and trace chemistries today infiltrate every living being on the planet. Plastics production today is guilty of toxic trespass; its ingredients and byproducts cross the placenta, infiltrate the blood, and/or enter human body tissue. Dow management and Dow culture, allowing such products and manufacturing to persist even when the dangers have become apparent, have also trespassed, and continue to trespass, on all of biology.

But now, a global grassroots movement that has been building over the last decade or so, is calling for a phase-out of PVC and related plastic ingredients in buildings, toys, furniture, automobiles, and other products. The resulting initiatives and actions are not only coming from "environmental radicals," but from elected officials, business leaders, and international policy makers. An impressive list of major companies, large and small, including BMW, Nike, General Motors, IKEA, the Body Shop, Sumitomo Electric, Sharp Electronics, Evian, and others have either quit using PVC in their products, materials, and/or packaging, or have announced plans to phase it out. City councils and parliaments all over the world have passed resolutions or adopted laws aimed at eliminating PVC or their related toxic byproducts.[39] The city council of Boston, Massachusetts, for example, adopted a resolution in October 2003 that directs city purchasing agents to favor materials that do not generate dioxins when they are manufactured or burned.[40]

It's long past time that Dow Chemical joined the bandwagon, phase out its toxic production, and end its plastics trespass.

8.
Taken to the Cleaners

Because of its safe handling characteristics, efficient solvency and ease of recycling, perchloroethylene has become the most widely used dry-cleaning solvent in the world.

"Drycleaning," Global Chlorinated Organics Business
www.dow.com, December 2003.

It was in France around 1825, that an accidental spill of paraffin from a lamp onto a soiled tablecloth revealed that a chemical might work to clean clothes.[1] Early cleaning establishments tried a succession of substances, from camphene, a distilled version of turpentine, and benzene from coal tar, to various derivatives of oil and gasoline. Yet many of these had obvious dangers—particularly of the volatile variety—for workers and the public. However, in the 1920s, a substance called perchloroethylene was being used by the Germans as a metals degreaser. Soon it became clear that what was good for cleaning metal would also remove everyday dirt and grime from clothing. And if properly dried, perchloroethylene-treated clothing would not have the gasoline smell of old. Soon the new chemical was on its way to a long and prosperous career in the dry cleaning industry.[2] But as science would later learn, perchloroethylene—also known as "perc"—was not a benign substance.

By the 1950s, in cities everywhere, there were tens of thousands of dry cleaning establishments, the vast majority of which were small, family-owned businesses. Most of these businesses used perc, which by then had become the dominant dry-cleaning solvent. And Dow Chemical, a major manufacturer of the substance, was selling tons of it. By the late 1950s, one month's production of perc at Dow's Freeport, Texas plant, for example, was estimated to be enough to clean 12 million men's suits.[3] Dow's market for perc soon grew to include the 40,000 or more "mom & pop" dry cleaning stores all across America. Here was an industry on practically every street corner in every major city; an industry doing business with millions of consumers. But these consumers—then and now—unwittingly trafficked in a dangerous chemical, carrying home what they thought were "clean" products to their closets in protective plastic bags. But clean they weren't.

In 1991, EPA found that dry-cleaned clothes put into a bedroom closet did some "out gassing"—leaving airborne perc levels of 2,900 parts per billion (ppb) in the closet, 195 ppb in the bedroom, and 83 ppb in an adjacent den.[4] These concentrations exceeded the New York guideline for chronic exposure to perc in indoor air by as much as 190 times.[5] Worse still, is the daily consequence for workers at dry cleaning businesses and those who live near or above them.

Workers exposed for one year to solvents experienced memory and concentration impairment for at least six years after the exposure had ceased.

According to the National Institute for Occupational Safety and Health (NIOSH), accumulated clinical evidence "clearly demonstrates that [perc] is toxic to the liver and kidneys in humans." Other studies have found that dry cleaning workers exposed for one year to organic solvents, including perc, experienced memory and concentration impairment for at least six years after the exposure had ceased.[6] By the early 1970s, perc had been found to cause liver cancer in laboratory mice. On the basis of those studies, EPA classified the chemical as a carcinogen at high doses. Despite such findings, however, little was done on the regulatory front—for workers, consumers, or the environment. In fact, until the mid-1980s, dry cleaners in most states simply got rid of their waste perc by pouring it down the drain.[7] As a result, 75 to 90 percent of all U.S. dry cleaners have costly site contamination, much of it in groundwater.

The Solvents Biz

Perchloroethylene is a chlorinated solvent—a member of a family of compounds used extensively for industrial degreasing, furniture stripping, and high-tech equipment cleaning. For more than 50 years, Dow Chemical has been producing and selling a number of chlorinated solvents in addition to perc—carbon tetrachloride, methylene chloride, methyl chloroform, and trichloroethylene among them. Dow has been selling these chemicals to a broad base of industrial and commercial customers for various uses for many years.

Industrial-scale cleaning and degreasing, for example, is a major ongoing task for many businesses, particularly in the metals fabricating and metal parts industries supplying aircraft, appliance, automotive, electronics, and railroad manufacturers. These industries typically encounter the dirt and grime of their everyday operations, which include various oils, metal fines, chips, and fluxes from operations that stamp, machine, weld, solder, mold, and die-cast metal and other material. On the high-tech end too, industries making tiny transistor parts, printed-circuit assemblies, precision surgical equipment, aircraft components, and spacecraft assemblies need regular cleaning and degreasing. All of these businesses use chlorinated solvents in these and other tasks, and they represent a sizeable customer base for Dow and other companies. But chlorinated solvents, are problematic from the start, beginning with production, which is generally by one of three methods.

Producing solvents by *direct chlorination* combines chlorine gas with etheylene or other hydrocarbons. This process produces large amounts of toxic by-product, including hexachlorobenzene, hexachloroethane, and other organochlorines. In a sec-

Every butter sample from stores near the dry cleaners contained elevated levels of perc.

ond method, where existing organochlorine compounds have formed in other production processes, more chlorine can be added. Trichloroethylene is often formed by this method when ethylene dichloride is *oxychlorinated* with hydrochloric acid in the presence of oxygen. In this particular process, huge quantities of what are called "tarry wastes" result, containing as much as 10 to 15 percent of the carbon and chlorine used. A third method, *chlorinolysis*, also begins with existing organochlorine waste from other production processes that already have higher degrees of chlorination. The chemicals in this process are then heated in the presence of oxygen, and as they degrade, the desired chemical is harvested along with huge quantities of by-product. When perchloroethylene is produced by this method, for example, up to 10 percent of the total yield is hexachloroethane, hexachlorobenzene, and hexachlorobutadiene.[8]

In the dry cleaning industry, perchloroethylene is a special concern as a toxic emission, for it is by inhalation and ingestion that perc does its damage. In the air, perc will migrate into fatty foods like dairy and meat products. In one study, the U.S. Food and Drug Administration compared the levels of perc in butter purchased from grocery stores near dry cleaners to that in butter from control grocery stores not located near dry cleaners. Every butter sample from stores near the dry cleaners contained elevated levels of perc, with several having concentrations 20 times or more the levels found at the control stores.[9] By the mid-1980s, not surprisingly, perc was being found in people. Studies of U.S. and Canadian populations found perc in blood, breath, fatty tissue, and breast milk.[10] Perc also accumulates in the liver and kidneys, can travel to other organs, such as the brain,[11] and can cross the placental barrier, carrying its toxic effects to the fetus. Exposure to high perc levels can result in unconsciousness and even death. One study found that exposure to perc at levels of 100 ppm for seven hours—the current Permissible Exposure Level, or PEL, for U.S. workers—resulted in difficulty speaking, dizziness, sleepiness, and headaches.[12]

Studies in major cities have found perc in apartments located directly above dry cleaning stores, including some as high as 12 stories above the stores. A 1990 investigation by the New York State Department of Health

found an extremely high level of perc (197,000 ug/cu.m.) over a 12-hour period in the air of a residence above a dry cleaning facility. This concentration
exceeds the standard of 170,000 ug/cu.m. set by OSHA for an eight-hour
workplace exposure. A joint investigation by the New York Department of
Environmental Conservation and New York Department of Health found elevated perc levels throughout a 12-story New York City building that contained
a dry cleaning facility. Other New York city studies have found elevated levels
of perc in the air of resi-

By the mid-1980s, perc was being found in people. dences above dry cleaning
facilities that have exceeded
the New York indoor guideline for perc by up to 550
times. In a California study, elevated levels of perc were found even with
"well-operated, new dry-to-dry, non-vented machines." A Consumers Union
study in 1995 found 24 of 29 apartments above shops with modern equipment had average perc levels above the New York Department of Health
guideline.[13]

Perc accumulation in the body is demonstrated by a study that exposed
subjects, by inhalation, to perc levels of up to 100 ppm for seven hours a day
for five days. The concentration of perc in exhaled breath increased as the
five-day week progressed, and was still present after exposure to perc ended.
A German study that examined blood samples of dry cleaning workers
showed that perc levels in workers rose throughout the week, peaking at the
end of the week. Levels decreased during the weekend, when workers were
not exposed to perc. On Monday, the cycle began again upon re-exposure.
Central nervous system effects including headaches, vertigo, nausea, fatigue,
and irritability have been well documented in dry cleaning workers exposed
to perc. Numerous studies of perc's effects on the reproductive system have
shown an association between perc and increased risk of menstrual disorders. The main metabolite of perc in humans is trichloroacetic acid which
has been linked to cardiac

Blood samples of dry cleaning workers showed that perc levels in workers rose throughout the week. birth defects in animals and
humans. The ability of
humans to metabolize perc,
however, appears to be limited. One study found that uri-
nary excretion of trichloro compounds reached a plateau at 50 ppm in
workers exposed to perc concentrations. This metabolic limit results in higher levels of perc accumulation in the body. The time necessary to completely eliminate perc from the body is estimated to be approximately two weeks.
Adds Greenpeace: "humans are continually re-exposed to perc and will
therefore never be free from its toxic effects as long as the production and
use of perc continues." The good news, says Greenpeace, "is that hundreds
of cleaners are perc-free today and as many as 3,000 offer safe water-based

The K2r Flap

In California in 1990, Dow Chemical's subsidiary, DowBrands, Inc., was selling a perc-containing spot-remover named *K2r Spotlifter*. Under California's Proposition 65, a law enacted in 1986, businesses are required to provide a warning when exposing the public to a "significant risk" from chemicals known to cause cancer or birth defects. Dow's product, it turned out, contained perc in amounts about 3,000 times the level considered safe by the state. In July 1990, the Environmental Defense Fund (EDF) and the Sierra Club filed an enforcement action against Dow charging the company with violating the warning requirements of Proposition 65. Dow maintained that the amount of perc in the *K2r Spotlifter* would not pose a significant risk to those who used the product. Richard Parry, then vice president of public affairs for DowBrands, said the company was in the process of reformulating the product when the action by EDF and the Sierra Club was filed. David Roe of EDF, one of the authors of the Proposition 65 measure, said the new law was having a major effect on company attitudes toward toxic chemicals. "If you can protect your customers from a chemical risk," he said, "it's good business now to do it instead of arguing about it." By January 1991, DowBrands decided to settle the *K2r* matter with EDF and the Sierra Club, agreeing to pay $50,000 for the infraction, the money to be placed in an environmental enforcement fund to be set up by EDF and the Sierra Club. "There was a cloud on the name perchloroethylene," explained DowBrands' Richard Parry at the time of the settlement. "We weren't going to get into a squabble with someone over a small product." Parry also explained that the settlement was agreed to by Dow to avoid costly litigation, not because the product was unsafe. Still, if the company had not settled, it could have faced fines of $2,500 per day for each case of chemical exposure.[14]

Source: Richard C. Paddock, "Firm Settles Complaint on Carcinogen," *Los Angeles Times*, January 17, 1991, p. A-3.

'wet cleaning' in their shops."[15] The bad news is that Dow and others continue working to keep perc in use.

In the political and public relations arenas, the influence of Dow Chemical is not always apparent as coming from Dow per se, as the company's preferences are sometimes carried out through various trade groups. Dow is a member of the Halogenated Solvents Industry Alliance (HSIA), based in Washington, D.C., which states on its letterhead that it is "an affiliate of the Chlorine Institute." In mid-1994, HSIA battled EPA over the reassessment of perc's potential carcinogenic risks. The International Fabricare Institute (IFI)—which has sponsored informational breakfasts for members of Congress on pending regulatory and legislative issues, perc among them—is financed by Dow Chemical and related manufactures, as well as the dry cleaning industry. IFI has worked to derail perc alternatives research at EPA.

Following one October 1994 Capitol Hill "dry cleaning" breakfast, IFI success-fully urged members of Congress to intervene at EPA on its behalf. At least one of the obliging congressmen on perc matters had also received campaign contributions from a Dow political action committee a few months prior to an EPA meeting.[16] But Dow is perfect-ly capable of doing its own direct bidding in the lobbying wars, whether in Congress or with the executive branch.

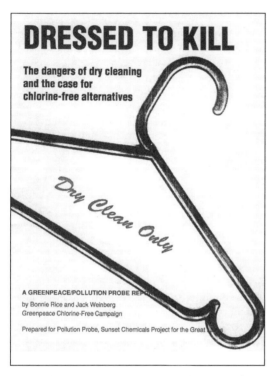

A 1994 Greenpeace report on the dangers of perc that also offered alternative cleaning solutions.

In April 2001, Dow Chemical sent out a letter to small business dry cleaners across the country urging them to send a Dow-drafted letter to Congress attacking the Small Business Pollution Prevention Opportunity Act of 2001 (H.R. 978). This bill would allow a 20 percent tax credit to dry cleaners who switched to safer perc-free alternatives, such as wet cleaning or liquid carbon dioxide. Dow's letter urged Congress to vote down the legislation unless it was changed to include perc cleaning equipment. Dow got what it wanted; the bill wasn't enacted even though it had bi-partisan support in the House and the Senate.

In the United States, there are three perc producers—Dow, Vulcan, and PPG. All three are facing a dwindling perc market in the dry cleaning business, especially with the wider use of dry-cleaning machines that use less perc and more careful dry cleaning practices. And this has been precisely the tact taken by the perc producers—adopting a "less-perc-is-better-than-no-perc" strategy in their politics and lobbying. Greenpeace and some garment unions favor a more aggressive policy of phasing out perc. Regulations have resulted in some beneficial changes, but have also contributed to continued investment in perc-using equipment at the retail end, and new production systems by the manufacturers. Both Vulcan and Dow reconfigured their perc production in 1996 so as to not co-produce carbon tetrachloride, an ozone-depletor banned under the Montreal Protocol. Unfortunately, Dow moved to the oxychlorination process, long known to create dioxin. Indeed, one perc producer outside the U.S. that used oxychlorination stated the process could not be made diox-in-free.[17] As for other perc-related problems, all three U.S. producers—Dow, Vulcan, and PPG—have been named as responsible parties in perc ground-water contamination cases.

Regulatory Wars

In 1954, Dow came up with a new chemical solvent using the name chlorothene. In advertisements, Dow presented the chemical as a safe alternative to other chlorinated solvents. But by the 1980s, chlorothene—known more commonly today as methyl chloroform or 1,1,1-trichloroethane (TCA)—had become indicted for a range of environmental and health-effects problems, cancer, and ozone depletion among them.

The Clean Air Act Amendments of 1990 required the phase-out of TCA as an ozone-depleting substance by December 1995. TCA was also regulated as a volatile organic compound, contributing to ground-level pollution and smog. In addition, three other Dow solvents, methyl chloride (MEC), perchloroethylene, and trichloroethylene (TCE), came to be regulated under the Clean Air Act as hazardous air pollutants. As of 1997, however, a complete set of specific regulations had not been issued for all uses of the solvents, but the national goal of EPA's hazardous air pollutant program was to reduce overall solvent emissions by 50 to 70 percent. Other environmental laws also regulate chlorinated solvents, including the Clean Water Act,

Taking Care of Business

Dow Chemical takes care of its business customers. It hates to lose them—for any reason. So it caters to them, offers them good technical advice, publishes newsletters on their businesses to keep them informed, and works with them closely in various trade groups, especially in the political arena. When the small business dry cleaners become upset over proposed environmental regulations, Dow Chemical is there to lend a shoulder, and will even dig into its wallet on their behalf. In February 1995 when the dry cleaners sought a $1 million war chest to do battle with Greenpeace—because they were "tired of getting kicked around by the media"—NCA director Bill Seitz, discussing the war chest, said there were some "deep pockets" around, such as Dow Chemical, that would likely make matching grants to the effort. Dow, no doubt, expects the favor to be returned when legislation comes around that may not be to its liking.

Source: Dave Johnston, "'Truth Squad' Proposed To Take On Greenpeace," *Drycleaners News*, February 1995, p. 1.

Dow advertisement of January 1959 extolling safety features of chlorothene (also known as methyl chloroform and 1,1,1-trichloroethane), later found to be a carcinogen, an ozone- depletor, a workplace hazard, and a contributor to ground-level smog. Source: *American Industrial Hygiene Association Journal,* January 27, 1959.

which treats them as toxic pollutants requiring discharge permits; the Resources Conservation and Recovery Act (RCRA), which classifies them as hazardous waste; and finally, the "right-to-know" and community notification sections of the Superfund law, known formally as the Comprehensive Environmental Response, Compensation and Liability Act (CERCLA), requires that releases of more than 1,000 pounds of these chemicals must be reported to local, state, and federal authorities within 24 hours.

"Still Your Best Choice"

After methyl chloroform was phased out under the Montreal Protocol because of its suspected role in ozone depletion, Dow made a special effort to reassure its customers that all of its other solvents were still available. Methylene chloride, perchloroethylene, and trichloroethylene, assured Dow in one 1997 brochure, were not being phased out under the Montreal Protocol and were not a threat to stratospheric ozone. In fact, according to Dow, "the overall regulatory climate" for these three solvents "remains positive." At the time, all three of the solvents were accepted into EPA's Significant New Alternatives Policy, as well as Germany's recognition of closed-loop chlorinated solvent systems as "state of the art technology." In addition, explained Dow, "both methylene chloride and perchloroethylene have low chemical reactivity and do not create ground-level ozone." In fact, these two solvents were exempt from regulation as volatile organic compounds in many areas. "Over the decades," continued Dow, still reassuring its customer base, "methyl chloride, perchloroethylene and

Dow ad of May 2001 assuring solvents customers that Dow would be their partner in "product stewardship."

trichloroethylene solvents have been subjected to extensive health studies and toxicological reviews. Consequently, their health profiles are well known and safety procedures have been standardized."[18]

In addition, Dow also uses the trade press to take much the same message to its customers, as it did with one ad in the May 2001 *Chemical & Engineering News* (see ad on page 181), which ends with the tag line, "Chlorinated solvents are *still* your best choice." Out in the environment, however, Dow's chlorinated solvents are still leaving their mark.

Solvents In The Bay

In 1997, the nonprofit environmental organization, San Francisco Bay-Keeper, sued Dow Chemical, alleging that the company's Pittsburg, California plant, 35 miles east of San Francisco, was unlawfully discharging chlorinated solvents into groundwater and contaminating San Francisco Bay. The plant had long been known as a source of bay and groundwater pollution, with ongoing battles with the California Regional Water Quality Control Board and local municipalities. Land beneath Dow's Pittsburg plant, in fact, was known to harbor a large underground plume of contaminants, including suspected cancer-causing chemicals such as carbon tetrachloride, perc, methylene chloride, and trichloroethylene. Dow first identified the plume in the 1980s and had been under the scrutiny of EPA and the San Francisco Bay Regional Water Quality Control Board. The city of Antioch and the Contra Costa Water District have intakes for drinking water within four miles of the plume.[19]

Dow's Pittsburg, CA plant was known to harbor a large underground plume of contaminants, including suspected cancer-causing solvents.

By 1999, Dow agreed to build a plant to pump the contaminated water out of the ground, clean it up, and return it. But that option promised to be very costly—as much as $100 million—and would still leave some waste behind for further treatment and disposal. Clean up was delayed and negotiations continued. In the meantime, with little progress made, Dow was fined nearly $200,000 by the California Regional Water Quality Control Board for failing to follow through with its plans. A year or so later, sometime in 2000, a more low-tech option emerged as a possible solution—a biological method, using a bug named *dehalococcoides ethenogenes*. The one-celled bacteria, it turns out—discovered by scientists at Cornell University in 1997—feeds on chlorinated solvents, which are typically very difficult to clean up using conventional techniques. By enhancing the bugs's ability with nutrients in the right environment, it's possible to use them to degrade certain oil and chemical spills. Dow began experimenting with the bugs on a small part of the plume, and the technique appeared to work. Dow then proposed to use the "bioremediation" technique to clean up its entire solvent plume. Nutrients would be pumped 100 feet into the ground, stimulating the naturally-occurring bug population, helping them to eat away at the contaminants.

The bioremediation could take a couple of years to a couple of decades—no one knows for sure.

In January 2002, the regional water board approved Dow's new treatment method, and that cleared the way for a possible settlement of the still-pending 1997 BayKeeper lawsuit. In April 2002, Dow and BayKeeper announced a deal, agreeing to the new clean-up method, and ending the litigation. In the deal, Dow would also contribute $3 million for San Francisco Bay protection. BayKeeper, the Coastal Conservancy, and Ducks Unlimited, Inc. would receive the funds to purchase or restore wetlands at Bel Marin Keys in Marin County, and in Sonoma, Solano, and Napa counties. Dow meanwhile, is relieved of the more costly treatment plant.

But the new bioremediation technique—which speeds up the bacteria's feeding process and their cleaning ability—doesn't always work at all contaminated sites. In addition to requiring that native bacteria already be present, the ground has to be comprised of sand or loose particles so that the nutrients can circulate with the water and bacteria. The technique, used mostly to clean up spilled petroleum, has been successful at other U.S. sites, but rarely has it been attempted on a site as large as Dow's, encompassing about 1,000 acres. And there are some unknowns, too, once the microbes have finished their work and exhausted their food supply. It's unclear what effect the bugs, and any enhanced activity, might have on the surrounding environment and existing microbial ecologies. Nevertheless, with the settlement of 2002, Dow began building "bio-walls" at its site to circulate nutrients—putting sodium formate, sodium lactate, and even molasses—into the groundwater. The nutrients, it is hoped, will stimulate the bacteria to do the job. The process could take a couple of years to a couple of decades—no one knows for sure. "We realize it's cutting-edge technology and that there's some level of risk," said BayKeeper's Jonathan Kaplan. "We feel it's an acceptable tradeoff." The bay area got $3 million for bay protection and a new cutting-edge cleanup technology is given a chance to shine. "If it's successful," said Kaplan, "it will advance the ball for cleanup efforts around the nation."[20]

TCE: More Toxic?

In February 2004, Dow and a few other solvent makers received some troubling news: EPA was convening a panel of scientists to examine new evidence that the widely-used industrial cleaning solvent trichloroethylene, known as TCE, might be as much as 60 times more toxic than previously thought. Suspected of causing cancer in humans, TCE has been proved to cause liver cancer in mice and kidney tumors in rats. The long-lived chemical is capable of polluting groundwater and then seeping as a vapor into homes and buildings. Its use in heavy industry for decades, and also by the semiconductor industry through the 1960s, has resulted in a number of contaminated sites across the nation—

Trichloroethylene might be 60 times more toxic than previously thought.

from groundwater to toxic waste dumps. Billions of dollars have already been spent cleaning up sites contaminated by TCE, and some in industry fear that the new information may lead to a tougher clean-up standard. Paul Dugard, a toxicologist for the Halogenated Solvents Industry, worries that EPA is contemplating clean-up standards based on the assumption that TCE is 40 to 60 times more toxic. "I think most people who have reviewed this think EPA is being way too conservative" and overprotective, he said. Most of the TCE used in the U.S. today is made by Dow Chemical and PPG Industries.[21]

9.
Rocky Flats

Safety was big talk only. It was produc-tion first; everything else was third, fourth and fifth. If anybody brought up a safety issue, it was suggested that you ought to find someplace else to work where you wouldn't be so scared.

Jim Kelly, union leader,
Rocky Flats, Colorado[1]

It was a little after 10 p.m. on September 11, 1957, when the two security guards first noticed the smell of burning rubber.[2] The guards were a part of the security force at the Rocky Flats Nuclear Plant, a top secret operation not far from Denver, Colorado that was then managed by the Dow Chemical Company. Rocky Flats was where the triggers for nuclear bombs were made. The guards were posted at Building 71, the building where plutonium, the most deadly substance on the planet, was used to make the "pits," or triggers—hold-in-your-hand metallic balls—for hydrogen bombs. Smelling the burning rubber that night, the guards followed their noses to Room 180 where they saw a Plexiglas glovebox shooting out 18-inch long flames. A pair of neoprene gloves used and attached to the box, had all but melted, and the glass was crumbling. Room 180 was where the machining of the plutonium pits took place. In the room there were massive piles of casting residues called "skulls." The skulls were burning. The plant's fire company soon arrived to fight the blaze.

Due to the heat of the burning room, the firefighters could advance only a few feet at a time, shooting carbon dioxide into the flames, but failed to make progress. They were forced to retreat and consider another approach. Meanwhile, the building superintendent, gave the o.k. by phone to turn the exhaust fans on high to help protect the firefighters, but the move made the blaze worse. Plant officials now struggled with whether to use water to fight the blaze, which mixing with plutonium might cause it to go critical—i.e., begin fissioning and cause a nuclear explosion. As the flames moved toward the air ducts, the firemen were ordered to spray water on the ceiling and floors. The temperature dropped immediately. But then there was a small explosion, and some of those present were blown back through the doors. Some unvented gases emitted by the burning materials in the

glove boxes caused the blast. No one was hurt. The fire resumed and progressed through the ventilation ducts reaching a floor-to-ceiling bank of filters on the second floor. "This bank of filters consisted of 620 paper filters
that were each two feet high and two feet wide," explains author Eileen
Welsome recounting the incident in the magazine *Westword*. "They had
never been changed since the building had begun operating, and untold
grams of plutonium had accumulated on their surfaces. The filters burned
furiously, enveloping the area in a thick, impenetrable smoke." By about
10:40 p.m., a firefighter standing outside saw a "very dark" column of smoke,
80 to 100 feet high, pouring from the building. More firefighters arrived on the
scene with respirators to fight the blaze. At about 2 a.m., the fire was brought
under control, but it continued to flare up and remained hot for several more
hours, finally extinguished just before 11:30 that morning.[3]

At the site, monitors detected an increase of short-lived radioactivity, and
workers in buildings 776 and 777 were ordered to put on respirators. Health
officials, who swabbed the noses and throats of 88 workers and also took
three fecal samples, two blood samples and one urine sample, found "positive indications" of plutonium exposure. In the official account of the fire—not
released publicly until February 1993, some 36 years later—several reasons
were identified as contributing to the fire's severity: the room was too crowded and filled with too much plutonium; the fire detection system had been
intentionally disabled; the glove boxes and filters had been constructed from
materials that Dow Chemical knew were flammable.[4] The Dow Chemical
Company was the manager of the Rocky Flats plant, and had been there since
Day One. Dow, in fact, helped build the plant and pick the site—a location
much too close to population centers for such a potentially dangerous facility,
some would later argue.

Dow Gets The Job

In 1949, after the Soviet Union had exploded its first atomic bomb, the
U.S. Congress authorized a major expansion of American nuclear weapons
capability. Some scientists at Dow Chemical were acquainted with the government's early nuclear program. Dow's Physics Lab chief, John Grebe, had
officially witnessed the Bikini A-bomb explosion in the Pacific and worked on
the Atoms for Peace project. Dow had also been solicited for, but had turned
down, earlier projects with the U.S. Atomic Energy Commission (AEC). But
now the company was being asked to build and manage a top secret AEC
nuclear weapons research and production project. In a nine-city review
process—the hunt for an acceptable location west of the Mississippi River—
the government selected the Denver area without picking a specific site. Dow
and the AEC then narrowed down the list, settling on the desolate Rocky Flats
site northwest of Denver. At the time, Denver was a modest-size city of

415,000 people. By 1951, after a construction phase that involved 2,000 workers building the new $45 million plant, Dow became its manager, overseeing the production of plutonium nuclear bomb triggers. The operation became known within Dow as the Rocky Flats Division. Its scientists worked in uranium chemistry and its workers dealt daily with deadly plutonium and other toxic materials.[5]

After the 1957 fire, both Dow and the AEC conducted investigations. The origin of the fire **Safety practices under Dow's management were not what they should have been. Dow officials put workers in harm's way.** had been in an area where mixtures of carbon tetrachloride cutting oil were stored and the plutonium waste shavings, or "skull fines," were also found. A number of changes were recommended, among them, separating plutonium storage and production areas, improving sprinkler and other fire safety systems, eliminating flammable materials in glove box construction, and using flame-resistant filters. The investigators also asked for basic research on the properties of alpha-phase plutonium and methods for controlling radioactive metal fires. For a time, more attention was paid to reducing the plutonium fire hazard at Rocky Flats: studies were begun on safer glove box construction, combustible filters were replaced with noncombustible material, and increased provisions were made for automatic fire detection.[6]

But inside the plant, it would later be learned, the safety practices in day-to-day operations under Dow's management were not what they should have been. Dow officials put workers in harm's way, often unnecessarily exposing them to higher and longer doses of radioactive material. And though plutonium was still a relatively new material—discovered in 1941—scientists knew about its lethal nature, as journalist Eileen Welsome explains:

> By the time Rocky Flats began operating, scientists knew that one microgram, a millionth of a gram, could produce a fatal cancer. The radioactive material is particularly hazardous if breathed into the lungs, where it emits small energetic particles, called alpha particles, that can kill cells or cause them to mutate and trigger the runaway growth known as cancer. Scientists also were aware of the fact that small chips and shavings of plutonium are extremely pyrophoric—that is, they burn easily in the presence of oxygen. They also realized that plutonium has a 24,000-year half-life, which means that every 24,000 years, half of a given amount of plutonium will decay or shed some energy, gradually transforming itself into a non-radioactive material. Put another way, it takes 240,000 years for plutonium to completely lose its radioactivity.[7]

In 1952, Edward Putzier, then doing graduate work at the University of Rochester in health physics, applied for and landed a job with Dow, eventually rising to become one of Rocky Flats' first health physicists. Thirty years later, in 1982, nearing retirement, Putzier wrote a paper that provided, among other things, a look at Dow management's approach to radioactive exposures. "We had, during the late 1950s and into the middle 1960s, a general increasing trend in external radiation exposure levels," wrote Putzier. "The attitude toward such exposures up to this point in time by the manufacturing people seemed to be that this was part of the business and . . . that once in a while we would have to write reports for over-exposures, and secondly, that there were sufficient safety factors built into radiation standards so that we were not jeopardizing anybody's health by occasional over-exposure."[8]

"In those years, production was first, that was number one. So we had those bad spills."

Willie Warling, a Rocky Flats worker, recalled in an oral history that Dow supervisors often ordered workers to remain in areas where radioactive contamination was high. "They knew it was bad for you," he said. "They made us go back in there and stand by them boxes." Warling was referring to the glove boxes, where workers handled "hot," or radioactive, material. With time, the interior surfaces of the boxes became coated with radioactive materials, which increased the overall doses workers were receiving. The highly corrosive acids used in the manufacturing process also caused the boxes to leak. "We had some pretty huge spills," recalled Warling. "Leaks mostly in the boxes. The boxes were old, and everything was run with acids, and these acids eat through the lines, they eat through the valves, they eat through the gaskets, you know, and in those years, production was first, that was number one. So we had those bad spills."

According to Jim Kelly, a union leader at Rocky Flats for many decades, safety at the weapons plant was not a high priority for Dow. "Safety was big talk only," he says. "It was production first; everything else was third, fourth and fifth." An almost macho attitude pervaded the workplace, he adds. "If anybody brought up a safety issue, it was suggested that you ought to find someplace else to work where you wouldn't be so scared." Kelly repeatedly brought his concerns to management. To muzzle him or other union members, he says, plant officials ordered them to clean the "snakepit," a room filled with leaking, contaminated pumps, or the "horseshoe," an area behind some glove boxes that was equally hot. And when showering did not adequately wash off the workers' contamination, they were sent to "Hot Water Johnny," a man who scrubbed their bodies with bleach until their skin was raw and bleeding.[9]

In 1955, the AEC changed its nuclear-weapons design. Instead of solid cores, it wanted to make hollow pits that were lighter and more powerful and used more plutonium. To accommodate the change, Rocky Flats began work on two new buildings, 776 and 777. But Dow officials decided to start

The 1969 Fire

...According to the official AEC accident report, the blaze began when a plutonium briquette in a storage can ignited, but Rowland Felt, one of the officials investigating the fire, now says the fire was actually ignited when some plutonium-contaminated rags caught fire.

At the time, thousands of pounds of plutonium were sitting on the conveyor lines or in storage areas waiting to be processed. In addition to the loosely pressed briquettes, there were slabs of plutonium metal thick as steaks, as well as partially hewn hemispheres that resembled derby hats. Throughout that Sunday morning, the briquettes smoldered and glowed. A security guard on his regular patrol thought the building seemed a little warm and heard some "popping" sounds, but didn't bother to report them. Meanwhile, the heat from the burning briquettes continued to build, finally tripping the building's heat detectors at 2:27 p.m. Two minutes later, fire captain Wayne Jesser and three firefighters were on the scene. As soon as Jesser saw smoke, he went back outside, grabbed an airpack and called for help. During those few seconds, the fire gained momentum, shooting down a line of glove boxes.... The fire leapt to the overhead conveyors, then to the ceiling and the rolling mill in the center line. Soon the entire area was engulfed in thick black smoke....

Although Jesser knew full well the dangers of pouring water on the plutonium, he had no choice but to order his men to roll out the hoses.... The firemen aimed the nozzles toward the ceiling so the water would not fall directly on the blaze. When stray drops fell onto the plutonium, the radioactive metal crackled and sizzled, erupting in a shower of sparks. Little by little, the firefighters were able to douse the blaze. But this was no ordinary fire. No sooner would they knock down the bright yellow flames in one spot than the fire would break out in another. The rancid smoke was horrible, unlike anything the firefighters had ever experienced; several later said the odor seemed to linger for days in their throats and mouths. On the second floor, firemen rolling out hoses heard a loud noise and felt the floor shaking. With the airpacks strapped to their backs, the firefighters had a difficult time maneuvering in the crowded production area. They used up oxygen quickly and had to go back outside every twenty minutes to get new bottles. The smoke was so thick that they fought the blaze on instinct alone and found their way to exits by groping along the fire hoses or crawling on their hands and knees, following the yellow arrows that pointed the way out.

...As the first wave of firemen stumbled out, sweating and exhausted, a phalanx of workers stripped off their clothing and suited them up again with freshly cleaned masks, hoods, double pairs of coveralls, booties, gloves and full bottles of oxygen. Some of the fireman grew alarmingly contaminated.... Nevertheless, the firefighters staggered back into the burning building four, five, six more times before being ordered to the medical department for decontamination and as many as three showers.

An hour or so after the fire began, the bystanders saw the first puff of smoke drifting out of the building. They donned respirators and watched as the whitish cloud rolled over the buildings and south toward the Denver-Boulder Turnpike....

The roof of the burning building was a shockingly flimsy affair composed mostly of metal, plywood and Styrofoam. Parts of it had been damaged by wind and were being held in place by concrete blocks. Firefighters poured water on the surface and maintained an around-the-clock watch. The roof grew soft from the heat but managed to hold. Finally, at 8 p.m., the blaze was brought under control.

Source: Excerpted from Eileen Welsome, "Bombs Away!" Part 1 of a Series—Rocky Flats—From Cold War to Hot Property, *Westword*, July 20, 2000, New Times, Inc. See also: P.G. Voillequè, "Estimated Airborne Releases of Plutonium During the 1969 Fire in Buildings 776–777," RAC Report No. 9-CDPHE-RFP-1999-Final.

making some of the hollow pits in Building C. "Not only was more plutonium in circulation," writes Eileen Welsome, "but the plutonium itself was being handled more frequently as it was rolled, shaped and machined to rigorous specifications. Soon more workers were getting zapped with bigger doses." As Dow pushed for greater efficiency and increased production, danger in the plant escalated:

...Fires, explosions and accidents occurred frequently as Dow officials rushed to meet production schedules and collect their bonuses. Plutonium salts caught fire. Plutonium dust ignited. Plutonium chips, plutonium metals and plutonium-encrusted molds burst into flames. Incinerators exploded. Oils caught fire. Tanks burned. Lines ruptured. Furnaces blew up. Even radioactive sludge erupted in flames.

The workers soon became so inured to burning plutonium—which glowed like charcoal briquettes—that they simply dunked the material in oil or tossed it into a pan and let it burn itself out. "If it does happen, it is nothing to get excited about," a supervisor once told government officials. Radioactive debris collected in the corners of glove boxes and small crevices of machines. When workers finally got around to cleaning the 4 High Mill Pit, a milling machine that was as big as a room, they found some 74 kilograms of sludge containing 13 kilograms of plutonium—enough to make several nuclear weapons. The machine had been in operation for ten years and had never been cleaned.

The workers fared no better. They were cut, scraped, burned, scalded and exposed on untold occasions. In his 1982 paper, [Edward] Putzier chronicled a few of the more serious incidents: in 1963, a fire in a filtrate recovery box exposes workers to significant amounts of plutonium and readings of 25,000 counts per minute; in 1964, a degreasing explosion in Building 776 contaminates numerous employees and results in "amputations"; in 1965, a blaze in a lathe coolant system exposes 400 workers to high concentrations of airborne plutonium.[10]

Beyond the accidents, Dow's ramped-up production at Rocky Flats was "a major source of the exposures to foundry and fabrication personnel," according to Putzier. Batch sizes were larger, ingots were bigger, and more plutonium was present on the production lines. Overall, the place was humming at full capacity, more or less continuously, with multiple sources of radiation contributing to the overall ambient levels. At the glove-box level, instead of slowing down production, Dow simply added more *Plexiglas* and *Benelex**—in all, more than 1.1 million

On Dow's watch, more than 200 fires occurred at Rocky Flats and at least 325 workers were contaminated.

pounds. The extra shielding did help cut down exposure levels, but visibility in the boxes suffered, and so did cleaning. And then there was the fire risk.

"Incredibly," writes Eileen Welsome, "Dow officials proceeded with the installation of *Benelex*, despite the fact that one of their own engineers had warned that the material was 'combustible.'" One of the worst fires ever at Rocky Flats—"a conflagration that came within a hair's breadth of contaminating hundreds of thousands of Denver residents with potentially lethal doses of plutonium"—occurred on Dow's watch on a Sunday afternoon, May 11, 1969 (see earlier sidebar). In fact, from its opening in 1953 until 1975—when Dow quit running the place—more than 200 fires occurred at Rocky Flats— and at least 325 workers were contaminated.[11]

Prying Open The Record

In 1975, Colorado landowner and Rocky Flats neighbor, Marcus Church, a rancher who had originally sold the government some of his land for the plant, filed a lawsuit against the government and Dow Chemical, alleging they had defiled his land with plutonium and numerous other toxins. Church's litigation—and his lawyer's research and discovery, including internal reports, maps, and memos—resulted in some of the first revelations about what was really going on at Rocky Flats. Church's lawyers found, for example, that Rocky Flats' toxic monitoring practices, either after accidents or during routine operations, were notable for what wasn't measured. "Rather than make attempts to evaluate the extent of such releases through material balance calculations, environmental sampling or other means," they observed, Dow and the AEC classified whatever information did exist; assumed releases were "negligible"; made "estimates" with little basis in fact; and/or made carefully-worded, frequently misleading statements with

---

*Benelex is a trade name of the Masonite Corporation. It is composed of wood fiber and plastic and was used for radiation shielding in Buildings 776–777. *Plexiglas* is a trade name of Rohm & Haas for several types of clear polymethylmethacrylate. Plexiglas G and Plexiglas SE-3, which is flame retardant, were used for viewing ports in gloveboxes and for shielding.

a minimum of information in press releases and reports—including those to outside agencies such as Colorado Department of Health, the governor of Colorado, and members and committees of Congress.[12]

Beyond the failings inside the Rocky Flats compound, and sometimes because of them, the outside environment was also threatened. Huge amounts of toxic and lethal wastes were generated. Plutonium wasn't the only substance to worry about. In fact, more than 1,500 chemicals were used in manufacturing and ongoing maintenance, including a number of carcinogens and nerve agents.* Thousands of barrels of oil and solvents were also used and discarded, adding to a variety of contaminated clothing, wood pallets and other equipment—all of which went to landfills, some dumped in crude trenches, and some burned in open pits or standard incinerators. "Yet for decades," writes Eileen Welsome, "Rocky Flats managers had no coherent plan to deal with the toxic leftovers. They stacked barrels in hallways, then moved them outside to loading docks and concrete slabs, and from there to the fields, where the noxious-smelling liquids leaked into the soil and the groundwater. In the mid-1990s, Rocky Flats was deemed the most contaminated in the Department of Energy's network of decrepit facilities. Radioactive plutonium and americium are scattered throughout the soil. Toxic plumes of groundwater encompassing more than 300 acres sprawl beneath the ground."[13]

Dow's Waste Mess

One of the toxic waste burial sites created on Dow's watch was known as "the Mound"—where drums of contaminated solvents and oils were sent for quick disposal. As the forklifts brought more drums, each layer was covered with a few feet of dirt, building up the Mound. An estimated 1,045 to 1,600 drums of oils, solvents, and dry waste were buried there. Most were contaminated with depleted uranium, some containing bomb-grade uranium and plutonium, and others with extremely hot sludges. Many of the barrels leaked, contributing to contaminated groundwater below. In 1970, union officials sought an explanation from Dow about the Mound. "A transcript of that meeting shows that Dow officials had maintained sketchy records at best," reports Eileen Welsome. "They didn't really know what was buried in the Mound and were more concerned about the dump's existence becoming public than they were with cleaning up the mess." The drums were dug up that same year and shipped off-site.

---

*Among these, for example, were: americium, benzene, beryllium, cadmium, carbon tetrachloride, chloroform, chromium, formaldehyde, lead, mercury, methylene chloride, nickel, tetrachloroethylene, thorium, and tritium.

Around 1957, Dow officials began burning certain Rocky Flats wastes in open pits and incinerators. In one open-air earthen pit not far from the Mound waste dump, Dow burned a total of 1,082 drums—drums laden with uranium-contaminated oil. The practice was repeated more or less in 1961 and 1965. Some 10,000 cubic feet of hot, ashy residues remained from these burns, wastes that were dumped into

> **Dow used an open-air incinerator for some hot and contaminated wastes, described as the "kind of incinerator you see at Safeway stores."**

other pits and covered with dirt. Rocky Flats also burned "non-contaminated" waste in the 1950s and early 1960s—though some of this was also believed to be contaminated. Dow used an open-air incinerator for these burns, described by Edward Putzier in a court document as the "kind of incinerator you see at Safeway stores." Dow's neighbors were sure that the air they were breathing was not healthy. In the 1975 Marcus Church litigation, Church's lawyers, remarking on the outdoor incineration, stated: "A better means of contaminating the countryside with large quantities of insoluble particles of uranium oxide of respirable size can hardly be imagined." They also noted that Dow's lack of records, lack of monitoring, and the lack of separation of depleted uranium, enriched uranium, and plutonium-bearing wastes at Rocky Flats "gives little assurance no plutonium oils were burned."[14]

In fact, years later, one of Dow's own officials acknowledged that the Rocky Flats operation was routinely releasing plutonium. Being questioned in the aftermath of the 1969 fire by government investigators, Charles Piltingsrud, Dow's manager of health physics, explained: "One doesn't release or dare release the fact that we are, indeed, distributing plutonium throughout the environment. If one took the average concentration per liter of air discharged from our plant, multiplied by the vast cubic feet or meters of air that we release, we release phenomenal amounts of plutonium."[15]

Not surprisingly, the accidents, wastes, and mismanagement at Rocky Flats brought a number of lawsuits. A few were wrongful death suits. One worker, who dealt with plutonium at Rocky Flats from 1959 to 1974, died of

> **"[W]e release phenomenal amounts of plutonium."**
>
> Charles Piltingsrud, Dow manger

colon cancer. The worker's wife won a court case in 1981 against Dow when it was determined that the effective dose of plutonium in his body was "far more than enough to cause his cancer." Another worker operating a furnace treating plutonium from 1969 to 1970 died of a malignant brain tumor. His autopsy revealed "significant quantities of plutonium and americium in his lungs, liver, and bones." His wife also filed suit.[16] In January 1990, some 10,000 retired workers and 50,000 businesses and property owners in communities surrounding Rocky Flats, filed separate class-action lawsuits against Dow and the subsequent operator, Rockwell International Corporation.[17] Other suits, alleging health and/or environmental damages, were aimed at Dow, the federal government, and/or other Rocky Flats contractors.

"Not Our Liability"

Dow, for its part, claims it was simply doing responsible business with the federal government at Rocky Flats. "The Rocky Flats Plant was an important part of the nuclear weapons production capability of the United States during the Cold War," explained Ronald J. Pingel, Dow's Director of Corporate Operations, Environmental Affairs and Responsible Care in one October 1991 letter. "...Dow acknowledges that there were incidences involving radiation releases over the years of Dow's presence at Rocky Flats," explained Pingel. "Generally, these releases were contained in either the immediate work area or otherwise within the plant as a whole. Shielding devices, air-filter systems, and fire control systems were installed in buildings where radioactive materials were processed to afford worker protection in accordance with Atomic Energy Commission guidelines, and a health physics program was established to monitor worker radiation exposures." In addition, wrote Pingel, Dow installed air-radiation monitors in the area surrounding the plant, including nearby communities extending to downtown Denver, 16 miles away. Dow also conducted extensive soil and vegetation sampling before the plant start-up, he said, in order to determine background radiation levels. "The metropolitan Denver area has higher than average background radiation due to fall-out from the Nevada Nuclear Weapons Testing Program in the 1950's and 1960's," explained Pingel in 1991.

The federal government, says Dow, must pay for Dow's defense, and indemnify Dow for any claims at Rocky Flats.

"There were isolated incidents of inadvertent discharge of low-levels of radioactive material into aqueous streams," Pingel acknowledged, regarding the plant's wastewater system, "but these discharges did not exceed regulatory limits for radionuclides in water."[18] As for liability, Dow typically invoked the government shield in any and all Rocky Flats-related costs, damage claims, and litigation. "It is Dow's position," explained the company in 1991, "that the Department of Energy is obligated under its contract with Dow to either assume and pay for the defense, or pay for the defense of Dow and indemnify Dow, for any claims paid by Dow that arise from Dow's performance under its contract with the Atomic Energy Commission (and its successor agencies) to operate Rocky Flats."[19] Those costs—covering Dow's failings at Rocky Flats as revealed in subsequent claims and lawsuits—have so far been in the tens of millions of dollars, at minimum, paid for by U.S. taxpayers.[20]

* * * * *

In late November 1974, Dow handed over management of Rocky Flats to Rockwell International Corporation. By then, some of the secrecy surrounding the place had begun to lift. After the 1969 fire, the public became more aware of the potential for problems and releases from the plant. In late January 1970, the first of many protests by local peace activists from Boulder and Denver were launched on Rocky Flats. Further revelations of environmental damage and public health risks emerged through the 1970s. The Colorado Health Department in May 1973 discovered radioactive material in Walnut Creek, a tributary of Broomfield, Colorado's Great Western Reservoir. In June 1989, the FBI and EPA raided Rocky Flats' offices—then under the management of Rockwell International—looking for environmental violations. Later that year, the site was added to the national Superfund list of highly-polluted toxic waste sites. In November 1989, Rocky Flats was shut down for safety reasons, billed then as a temporary closing. But in 1992, President George H. W. Bush announced cutbacks in the nuclear weapons program, eliminating the need for Rocky Flats. By 1995, it was targeted for a federal cleanup by the Department of Energy.[21] Today, the Department of Energy and its current contractor, Kaiser-Hill, say that by 2006, Rocky Flats will be cleaned up—encompassing 394 acres in the Rocky Flats industrial area and 5,861 acres of surrounding land. Nearly 700 buildings will be demolished, multiple plumes of contaminated groundwater will be remediated, and hundreds of tons of toxic earth will be hauled off. Yet some doubt a true clean up will ever be accomplished.[22]

Dow in Court

Meanwhile, the litigation has continued. In April 1996, about 50,000 Colorado residents living near Rocky Flats were still involved in a $550 million class-action lawsuit against Dow and Rockwell seeking both compensation for diminished property values and money for medical monitoring of local residents. David Bernick, lead attorney for Dow at the time, questioned the grounds for the suit: "No one has ever found that Rocky Flats poses a health risk."[23] On the other side, representing the property owners, was Denver lawyer Bruce DeBoskey. "Dow and Rockwell came into this community and poisoned the environment and damaged the real-estate values," DeBoskey explained. "People were misled about what was going on at that

Trespass Against Us

weapons plant. People whose lives were adversely affected should be compensated for that."[24]

As the case dragged on, the courts ruled in October 1999 that 12,000 property owners were eligible for the class action and were officially notified.[25] By July 2003, a federal judge in Colorado, John Kane, agreed the property owners could proceed to a jury trial. But judge Kane rejected the homeowners' contention that they were entitled to compensation simply because of proximity to Rocky Flats. Nor were health effects now involved in this case, since studies conducted by the Colorado Health Department found no evidence of health effects damage in the area. But in Judge Kane's 78-page opinion on how the case should proceed, he said the residents could present evidence that their property lost value as part of a larger nuisance argument—i.e., that Rocky Flats was such a serious nuisance it interfered with the enjoyment of their property. "Under Colorado law, a facility does not constitute a nuisance solely because its proximity to neighboring properties causes their value to decline, but [it] may be a nuisance if actions at the facility result in a substantial and unreasonable interference with the use and enjoyment of neighboring properties," Kane wrote.[26]

The full accounting of the Rocky Flats story—and Dow's role in that venture—is still coming to light.

"We've been waiting for this for a long time," said Gary Blum, attorney for the property owners, who lived downwind from the plant and charged, among other things, that plutonium was deposited on the area during the fires of 1957 and 1969.[27] In addition to property owners, Rocky Flats workers have also filed lawsuits and government claims over the years for radiation-caused cancer or beryllium disease, and more actions could yet be filed. A University of Colorado study of workers' long-term health problems was completed in 2002, but the National Institute of Occupational Safety and Health has not released it.

Stay tuned; the full accounting of the Rocky Flats story—and Dow's role in that venture—is still coming to light.

10.
Poisoning Canada

Lake St. Clair is full of mercury, and we feel it is the result of discharges from the St. Clair River.

Charles Bellmore, June 2002,
Mt. Clemens Water Treatment Plant[1]

In the spring of 2002, Dow Chemical began dredging operations in the St. Clair River near Sarnia, Ontario. Dow was working the river bottom to clean up highly toxic mercury and other contaminants spilled there years earlier. An estimated 28,000 cubic yards of contaminated material was slated to be removed from the river.[2] The St. Clair flows south from Lake Huron, marking part of the U.S. eastern boundary with Canada, as well as the Michigan-Ontario border. Eventually, the river flows into Lake St. Clair, and with the Detroit River, connects Lake Huron with Lake Erie. Dow—whose corporate headquarters at Midland make Ontario a short car ride away—built a chemical plant along the St. Clair in the 1940s.

Canadian officials came to Dow during World War II seeking help to produce synthetic rubber. Like the other Allies, Canada needed a new source of rubber since the Japanese had taken Malaysia and other regions that produced natural rubber. Dow was then one of the few companies anywhere that had the ability to produce synthetic rubber using styrene and butadiene, two key ingredients. Dow was then selling some chemicals in Canada, but it had no manufacturing plants there. By May 1942, with the encouragement of the Canadian government, Dow agreed to build a plant at Sarnia along the St. Clair to produce styrene monomer to help make synthetic rubber. Before long, Dow was turning out styrene at more than 10,000 pounds a year, and cumene, or isopropylene, another war ingredient for high-octane aviation fuel. Following the war, Dow expanded at Sarnia, adding more plants. A polystyrene plant was built in 1947; a glycols plant in 1948; and a solvents plant in 1951. Dow also built a chlorine plant at Sarnia—a plant that used the mercury-cell method of chlorine production. It was this plant that became the source of Dow's mercury pollution of the St. Clair.[3] Dow also used mercury at a

later second plant in Sarnia, as well as another at Thunder Bay, Ontario on
Lake Superior.

Mercury Pollution

In the 1950s, however, science and industry had a "blind spot" when
it came to mercury. It wasn't known then that *inorganic* mercury—the
metallic variety and the kind used by industry—could be converted
to *organic*, or methyl mercury, the dangerous kind. This conversion
occurs with the help of microbes in a process known as "biomethylation"
or "bacterial methylation." But in the 1950s, it had been conventional
wisdom that mercury wasn't a problem: if spilled, it could be flushed
away with water. Chemical engineering texts of the day said mercury
would sink to the bottom of whatever water body it was discharged
into, and would remain there
inert and harmless. But harmless it wasn't. In fact, in the
marine environment, deposited
metallic mercury could be
"eaten" by bacteria that lived in
the sediment, then "excreted" by them as methyl mercury—thus the scientific description, bacterial methylation. In this form, mercury could make its
way up the food chain—from marine algae, to tiny marine animals, to min-
nows, to small fish, to big fish, to birds, animals, and humans—becoming
more concentrated with each step.

**In humans, or any animal,
methyl mercury lodges in the
brain and vulnerable organs.**

In humans, or any animal, methyl mercury lodges in the brain
and vulnerable organs, with devastating and debilitating consequences.
In the Japanese town of Minamata in the 1950s, about 560 miles
southwest of Tokyo, a very serious episode of mercury poisoning
unfolded. The first signs appeared in small animals and birds around
Minamata Bay. In 1953, a few cats were seen with "*kibyo*," the Japanese
word for "strange disease," later called "cat-dancing" disease, describing
the animal's jerking and bizarre movements before it died. Birds were
seen flying erratically, or simply plummeting from the sky to ground
or sea.[4] Soon, hundreds of people became ill with "Minamata disease,"
a condition afflicting adults with severe paralysis, coma, and neurological
disorders. These incidents, however, were followed by a horrifying outbreak
of severe birth defects and mental retardation in children, the result
of fetal poisoning. Minamata disease was later tied to mercury-contaminated wastes dumped in Minamata Bay by the Chisso Corporation
between 1952 and 1960. Chisso used mercury as a catalyst in the production
of fertilizer, and also, according to some reports, to make chlorine for
PVC plastic.

Back in Canada, meanwhile, Dow Chemical had been producing chlorine using the mercury-cell method since 1947. In this process, much of the mercury is recycled, but significant quantities are released into the environment through air emissions, water discharges, waste sludges, and in end products.*

The Minamata Findings

By 1959, there had been published accounts in Japan on the Minamata poisonings pointing to mercury as the most likely agent. In 1960, an English-language article appearing in *World Neurology* pointed to organic mercury in fish at Minamata. If mercury was lost as an inorganic compound, the article surmised, "it presumably would have to be converted to more complex (organic) forms by plankton or other marine life after it has reached the bay." The authors expressed concern that science find out "whether or not similar situations may occur in other areas of the world where mercury is used as an industrial catalyst." But their call went unanswered. In September 1961, methyl mercury was formally identified and the Japanese Minamata studies were published in English at the Seventh International Congress of Neurology in Rome. Similar publications repeating these findings appeared again in February 1963 at a U.S. National Institutes of Health-funded conference. However, in 1965, another outbreak of Minamata disease occurred in Japan, this time killing 25 people, the result of pollution from the Showa Denko Corporation. That same year, two Swedish scientists published a paper stating that inorganic mercury of the kind used in chlor-alkali plants could be converted to methyl mercury in muddy lake bottoms. Chlor-alkali plants were then the biggest users of mercury in the United States and Canada. Through the 1960s, in fact, there was a series of international conferences on heavy metals and mercury in particular. As early as 1966, Canadian and U.S. delegates to such conferences were warned that industrial use of mercury should be monitored for potential

---

*Observes Joe Thornton in *Pandora's Poison*: "...In this century as a whole, chlor-alkali production has been the largest single source of mercury releases to the environment. As recently as the 1980s, the chlorine industry was second only to fossil fuels combustion as a mercury source in Europe....Based on estimates by Eur-Chlor, the trade association of the European chlorine industry, the world chlor-alkali industry *consumed* about 230 tons of mercury in 1994; this is the quantity not recycled but lost from production processes each year. Exactly where the mercury goes remains controversial, but if we use Eur-Chlor's data, about 30 tons were released directly into the air and water, 5 tons remained as a contaminant in the product, more than 150 tons were disposed on land, and 36 tons could not be accounted for. The actual worldwide totals are likely to be even higher, because the well-regulated facilities of Europe are not likely to be representative of those in other regions of the world." pp. 239–40.

danger. Canada's Federal Health Department, in fact, was warned in 1966 and 1967 by at least three sources—including scientists from the University of Toronto and the World Health Organization—that mercury contamination could be a serious health hazard. In 1966, the Swedish government banned the practice of coating agricultural seed with mercury as a fungicidal treatment. In the following year, two more Swedish scientists confirmed that bio-methylation was transforming metallic mercury into the killer form, and a bacterium that performed the conversion had been specifically identified. A 1968 paper on this bacterium was published in *Nature*.[5]

Dow and Mercury

During the 1950s and 1960s, Dow Canada and other industries then using mercury were losing the material to the air and water in Sarnia and elsewhere. But there were no controls or laws aimed at mercury in the environment, and it was not regarded as a problem.* Then came a Norwegian named Norvald Fimreite, a doctoral studies candidate at the University of Western Ontario. Fimreite, aware of the 1965 Swedish papers on methyl mercury, was especially interested in studying the effects of mercury on birds and fish—birds eating mercury-coated agricultural seed, and mercury in fish near industrial water discharges. His 1967 and 1968 studies in Canada revealed high levels of mercury in fish, pheasants, and partridges in sampling areas in Alberta and Ontario, including Lake St. Clair, downstream from Dow Sarnia. Fimreite found that mercury deposited in a body of water could be taken up by fish and accumulate in them as highly toxic methyl mercury. The province of Alberta, acting on Fimreite's findings, banned the 1969 upland bird hunting season. Fimreite's surveys also moved the Ontario Water Resources Commission to launch its own study, begun in 1969. At one point in 1970, Fimreite was told by an official of the Ontario Water Resources Commission that mercury levels in St. Clair River sediment near the dumping location of Dow's Sarnia plant were 1,400 parts per million (ppm).[6]

Dow's first revelations about methyl mercury's toxic effects in fish, according to company biographer E. N. Brandt, came as a result of Fimreite's research. "This—[i.e., Fimreite's finding that mercury deposited in a body of water could be taken up by fish and would accumulate in them as highly toxic methyl mercury]—had not been known before...," writes Brandt, who also claims that "Fimreite's paper was... the first explanation of the mechanism that was causing the Minamata disease in Japan...."[7] Yet,

---

*There is some question, however, about what Dow corporate, or Dow scientists, may or may not have heard from Japanese colleagues about the mercury problem in Japan. In 1952, Dow established the Asahi-Dow joint venture and built chemical plants in the 1950s with Asahi Chemical in Nobeoka, Japan.

other earlier reporting and research on mercury, recounted above, pre-dates Fimreite's findings, indicating that English-language science had some suspicion of toxic mercury and biomethylation as early as 1960, and certainly more definitive knowledge by 1966. Dow by this time—1966— had begun a second mercury-cell chlor-alkali operation on Lake Superior at Thunder Bay, Ontario on Lake Superior, and would add another mercury-cell plant at Sarnia in 1970.[8]*

Dow's managers at Sarnia "knew they were losing quite a bit of metallic mercury into the river."

According Brandt, in the summer of 1969, "at about the time" Fimreite's paper on the fate of mercury was being published in English, Dow Canada began focusing on its chlorine production at Sarnia and its known losses of mercury into the St. Clair River. Len Weldon, then Dow Canada's general counsel, said Dow's managers at Sarnia "knew they were losing quite a bit of metallic mercury into the river." They decided to revamp the whole mercury system and put in more traps and screens and develop a comprehensive program to contain the mercury. Explained Weldon of Dow's actions:

> Back then, the government of Ontario didn't have a ministry of the environment [it created one early in 1970]. That kind of problem was supposed to be looked after by the local sewage supervisor. So there was no such organization. What was going on was going on solely on the initiative of [Dow] management, not because government had said or threatened anything.[9]

At Dow headquarters back in Midland, CEO Ben Branch told the Dow board he wanted the company to abandon all mercury cell activities and take a loss on them. That was Dow's own decision, according to Branch. "We were not going to take a chance that this could adversely impact the environment," Branch later recalled. "As far as I know, we were the first ones to take any action of this sort, and it was under no pressure from anybody except our own conscience." Dow Canada had a contractor who regularly took samples of the St. Clair River bottom, but mercury wasn't among the items checked. "We were so certain that [the conventional wisdom] was right; that mercury under water doesn't do anybody any harm, and that it is only when it evaporates into the air that it does, that it wasn't even in our minds at the time," recalled Leroy Smithers, a Dow Canada plant manager.[10]

---

*Dow's three Canadian mercury cell plants included: 1) a mercury cell chloro-alkali plant at Sarnia, operating between 1948 and 1973, using a total of 318 tons of mercury; 2) a mercury cell chlor alkali plant at Thunder Bay, Ontario, operating between 1966 and 1973 using a total of 43 tons of mercury; and 3) a second chlor-alkali plant at Sarnia, operating between 1970 and 1973 using a total 72 tons of mercury. Source: Mike Gilbertson, Ontario, Canada, December 2003.

Although Dow on its own did take some initiative on mercury, action by the Canadian government was also looming.

By March 1970, graduate student Fimreite had collected 42 Lake St. Clair fish, some of which laboratory analysis revealed contained mercury at 6 to 8 ppm. The informal Canadian health standard for mercury at the time was 0.5 ppm; Minamata fish had levels in the 8–12 ppm range. Ontario authorities pinned the blame at least partially on Dow; they determined that Dow's chlor-alkali plant at Sarnia was dumping considerable quantities of mercury into the water, on average about 65 pounds a day.[11] Soon thereafter, government officials in Ontario and Quebec laid a bead on Dow and others releasing mercury into rivers and lakes.[12] In March 1970, Ontario authorities issued restraining orders under the Water Resources Act on several companies, including Dow's plants at Sarnia and Thunder Bay, ordering them to stop discharging mercury.[13]

Don't Eat The Fish

In late March/early April 1970, Michigan citizens were told that both the Ontario and Michigan governments had detected high levels of mercury in fish in the St. Clair River, Lake St. Clair, the Detroit River, and Lake Erie. Other industrial sources along the Detroit River, south of Lake St. Clair, were also found to be releasing mercury. The Canadian government impounded 18,000 pounds of walleye because of the contamination, and separate Ontario agencies with jurisdiction over commercial and sports fishing moved to ban fishing in Lake St. Clair until mercury levels declined. At first, Michigan Governor William Milliken cautioned the public on eating fish from the St. Clair River, Lake St. Clair, and the Detroit River. But a few days later, on April 14, after hearing from officials in Ohio, Ontario, the Canadian federal government, and the U.S. Food and Drug Administration, he ordered the closing of the St. Clair River and Lake St. Clair to fishing.[14]

In Ohio, the state's attorney general brought a motion in the U.S. Supreme Court in the summer of 1970 to begin a lawsuit against Dow for mercury pollution reaching Lake Erie. There were also class-action claims brought against Dow by various groups in lower

Ohio's attorney general brought a motion in the U.S. Supreme Court to begin a lawsuit against Dow for mercury pollution reaching Lake Erie.

Michigan around Detroit; claims by fisherman from Lake Erie; and a class-action suit by fisherman in Ohio where commercial fishing had been suspended. The Ohio case, brought in the U.S. Supreme Court, was rejected. And in Canada, as an Ontario case filed against Dow in 1971 seeking $35 million in damages went ahead, Dow's lawyers found the province powerless to do much, and the company emerged more or less victorious. According to Len Weldon:

> ...We were aware that the [Canadian] government was being told by their counsel that there was no basis in law for the government's claim. As the regulatory body, the government could regulate; they could do all sorts of things. They could even take away our license to manufacture chemicals. But there was no basis in law for the government of Ontario to sue us because of fish and wildlife. They could prosecute us, but they couldn't sue us in civil court for the mercury in fish. Eventually, we became aware that the counsel for the government told the attorney general he had no place to go with the case. We finally settled for a relatively small amount of money.[15]

Dow Canada, by this time, had closed down its mercury-cell operations and "buttoned up" all its mercury outlets to the St. Clair River, according to Brandt. "That was the best thing to do, the only thing we could do," said Smithers. "We couldn't let that stuff go into the river. I'm not sure . . . that we were the only contributor around there. I think there were a lot of other sources of mercury. But we were certainly the most visible and took the brunt of it." Dow Chemical was the largest buyer of mercury in Canada, paying as much as $700 a flask for the material by the late 1960s. Dow's mercury-cell chlorine operation at Thunder Bay on Lake Superior had been built to supply chlorine to the Great Lakes Paper Company. As the mercury controversy forced the company's hand, Dow sent a small delegation of its researchers and technical people to Sweden and Finland "to get first hand knowledge of what was up-to-date" in terms of chlorine technology, according to Bert Hillary, a Dow research manager. His report, called the Hillary Mission Report, recommended a number of changes at Dow, including getting out of the mercury-cell business. Yet during its mercury troubles, Dow Canada did have a non-mercury method of chlorine production already in operation—two smaller units known as diaphragm plants. Dow later built larger versions of these diaphragm systems to replace the mercury-cell operations at both Sarnia and Thunder Bay.[16]

About 6 million people in southeast Michigan get their drinking water from water treatment plants along the St. Clair River and Lake St. Clair.

The mercury released by Dow into the St. Clair River during the company's 20-plus years of mercury-cell operations continued to dog the company long after it stopped using the substance. By the spring of 2002, as Dow began dredging operations in the St. Clair south of Sarnia to remove mercury and other contaminants, state and local officials worried that toxic pollution would spread downstream, possibly impairing the drinking water at 12 municipal water plants. About 6 million people in southeast Michigan get their drinking water from water treatment plants along the St. Clair River and Lake St. Clair. Doug Martz, chairman of the Macomb Water Quality Board in Michigan asked the state to conduct water tests. The Ontario Ministry of the Environment and Dow Canada also conducted tests, some as far as 22 miles downstream. No dangerous levels of contaminants were found. Bryce Feighner, a supervising district engineer with the Michigan Department of Environmental Quality, said he inspected the test results and was satisfied that Michigan drinking water was not in peril. "All of the sample results were within drinking water standards," Feighner said. "We will sample all drinking water plants just to satisfy public concern. I think it is worth it if the public is genuinely concerned about drinking-water safety." Charles Bellmore, plant supervisor at the Mt. Clemens Water Treatment Plant, which draws its water from Lake St. Clair, 20 miles downstream of Dow's Sarnia plant, said he was relieved to hear of the test results. "If the state is confident, I'll put my confidence in them," he said. "My primary concern was for mercury and volatile organic compounds. Lake St. Clair is full of mercury, and we feel it is the result of discharges from the St. Clair River." Other private tests by Oakland University professor Linda Schweitzer were conducted downstream from the Dow Chemical's dredge site on the St. Clair River.[17] As this book goes to press, Dow is still cleaning up the St. Clair River. Dow Canada, however, has also been involved in a range of other pollution incidents and toxic releases in Canada, among them a 1979 train wreck at a town named Mississauga.

The Mess at Mississauga

It was early afternoon on Saturday, November 10, 1979, when Canadian Pacific Railway freight train No. 54 began its journey from Windsor, Ontario to Toronto, a few hours north. But train No. 54 had a few scheduled stops along the way. First, in Chatham it stopped to pick up additional cars from another train coming in from Sarnia—tank cars from the chemical plants there carrying caustic soda, propane, chlorine, styrene, and toluene. Among the additional cars from Sarnia were two Dow chlorine tankers. The train was now 106 cars long. It left Chatham about 6 p.m. and headed northeast to its next stop at London where it made a crew change. As it continued toward Toronto, however, unbeknownst to anyone on the train, one of its cars was having a problem.[18]

As the train rumbled past Milton, some 40 kilometers southwest of Toronto and traveling at about 60 miles per hour, friction had built up in an axle wheel-bearing on Car 33. It was one of the train's older cars—an old-fashioned type needing manual lubrication for its axle box. Newer, more modern cars had roller bearings. Friction and heat continued to build as the train moved down the line. Residents living near the tracks later reported seeing smoke and sparks coming from the middle section of the train. Further on, others reported that part of the train appeared to be on fire. As the train continued, the axle heat built up to the point where the axle on Car 33 broke off. Then the car started to break apart. At the Burnhamthorpe Road crossing, Car 33 sent its glowing hot wheels flying off the train and crashing through a fence, landing in the backyard of a nearby home. It was now about midnight as the train approached Mississauga, a Toronto suburb of about 300,000 people. The train sped past an area of apartment buildings and suburban homes, now carrying the dangling and damaged undercarriage of Car 33. Just past a light industrial area, at the Mavis Road crossing, the damaged tank car with its dangling undercarriage, left the tracks. Twenty-three other cars followed it off the tracks, causing a deafening crash and metal-on-metal squealing as the iron and steel cars collided and twisted into a tangled pile. Some propane cars burst into flames. Other tankers began spilling their chemical contents, initially styrene and toluene. Within seconds, the leaked liquids and vapors ignited, causing a massive explosion. Yellow-orange flames leapt to 1,500 meters in the sky and could be seen 100 kilometers away. Soon the fire was being fed by the contents of the other wrecked tank cars, with more in danger—eleven held propane, four had caustic soda, three contained styrene, three more held toluene, two box cars were filled with fiberglass insulation, and one contained chlorine. The undamaged portion of the train, still on the track, had pulled forward and away from the derailment and fire. The sleeping town of Mississauga, meanwhile, began to rouse, as police and fire department switchboards lit up with a flood of phone calls. Within minutes, firefighters arrived at the scene while police set up roadblocks.

Just as firefighters were about to begin their battle—now early Sunday morning—a violent explosion occurred as another

Tank car 'bomb' of deadly chlorine gas forces evacuation of Mississauga area

of the propane tank cars blew up. The blast knocked police, firefighters, and onlookers to the ground, showering the surrounding area with chunks of metal. Windows were shattered throughout the area, and three greenhouses and a municipal recreational building were also destroyed. Near the explosion, a green haze was seen drifting in the air. Minutes later, a second explosion occurred. In another propane car, a "bleve" occurred—a boiling liquid expanding vapor explosion—hurling the tank car into the air, spewing fire as it went, finally tumbling into a cleared field more than 600 meters away.

Within seconds, the leaked liquids and vapors ignited, causing a massive explosion. Yellow-orange flames leapt to 1,500 meters in the sky and could be seen 100 kilometers away.

Five minutes later, another bleve occurred, sending one end of the propane car about 65 meters away. Emergency authorities and public officials from several governmental levels were being summoned to the scene by this time, as police and fire officials tried to acquire the train's cargo manifest and emergency procedures. However, the main manifest was in the front part of the train which by then had moved on to Cooksville, about six kilometers away. About an hour later, a readable copy of the manifest was delivered to emergency officials. Checking the serial numbers of derailed cars, they soon determined that the derailed cars held a mixed cargo of dangerous chemicals, including chlorine, posing a possible chlorine gas threat.

Chlorine, a deadly chemical, forms a greenish-yellow cloud when released and hovers close to the ground. A chlorine cloud will follow the terrain as it drifts and disperses—a feature that made it an ideal weapon in the trench warfare of WWI. Once chlorine gas is breathed, it saps the fluids in the linings of lungs and blood, and starts a chain reaction that ends with slow suffocation. At the wreck site, a chlorine tanker was close to a filled propane tanker, in danger of exploding. The Mississauga fire chief ordered 3,500 residents living closest to the derailment to evacuate. Police officers using loud bullhorns and knocking on doors alerted sleepy residents. Later, as winds shifted and more information about the train's cargo became known, the area of evacuation was expanded. Shortly after 2 a.m., Metropolitan Toronto Police sent sound trucks to alert residents of the broader evacuation. The Mississauga section of the Canadian Red Cross Society began setting up resident evacuation centers—one at Square One, a huge covered shopping center about 2.5 kilometers from the derailment. The provincial Ambulance Co-ordinating Center sent out a general call for ambulances in the surrounding area. Buses were summoned from the Toronto Transit Commission, Oakville Transit, and Mississauga Transit authorities.

A team of experts from Dow Chemical at Sarnia, owners of the chlorine tank car, arrived on the scene armed with specialized equipment to execute something called CHLOREP, the chlorine emergency plan. Dow's Stu Green-wood headed up this effort. But it was soon determined that it would be impossible to seal the leaking chlorine tanker until the propane fires had burnt themselves out. Firefighters, using some 4,000 meters of hose, had nearly a dozen major streams of water trained on the wreck site. Most were aimed at cooling the unexploded chemical tankers, while allowing a controlled burn of escaping gases. More evacua-tions were ordered as winds changed. At about 5 a.m., the Solicitor General of the Ontario Cabinet was notified. As dawn broke, emer-gency officials and the town's mayor met to consider their options. More evacuations followed, including a decision to evacuate Mississauga General Hospital and two adjacent nursing homes. As a few Ontario cabinet officials arrived, the evacuated areas were expanded again by early afternoon, now extending to beyond the Square One shopping center, the site of the first evacuation center. Evacuees there were transferred to other centers. A mass exodus of residents was now underway—some with packed luggage, others abandoning Sunday dinners about to be served. At the day's end, at least 218,000 residents had left their homes. Others put the number closer to 300,000. "The southern part of Mississauga, Canada's ninth largest city with a population of 284,000, was a virtual ghost town," observed one reporter in *Derailment: The Mississauga Miracle.*

The derailed cars held a mixed cargo of dangerous chemicals, including chlorine, posing a possible chlorine gas threat.

By 10 a.m. Monday, November 12, at least three propane cars were still burning. Officials feared that one might explode during rush hour, or that chlorine might waft over the area's highways, trapping thousands of com-muters in their cars. The Queen Elizabeth Way, the busiest stretch of high-way in Canada, which runs through the central part of Mississauga, was closed at its eastern and western entrances to the town. Commuter traffic to Toronto was rerouted around the evacuated area, causing massive traffic jams. Back at the burning train wreck, a manufacturer of railway tank cars had prepared a steel patch to cover a one-meter hole in Dow's chlorine tanker. Some chlorine had already escaped, but officials assumed there was more remaining. Railway crews carefully removed box cars and tankers from the area which had not derailed, and attempted to clear debris at the accident site without disturbing the piled-up chlorine and propane tank cars. Staff of the Ontario Ministries of the Environment and Labor monitored the air and found a few pockets of chlorine gas in low-lying areas, but no signif-icant hazard for the general area. Police patrolled deserted streets for looting and checked all vehicles entering the area. Officials would not consider lift-ing the evacuation order and sounding the all-clear until the fire was out and the chlorine danger ended.

On Tuesday, November 13, day four of the ordeal, the propane fire went out at about 2:30 a.m., and the focus moved to patching the chlorine tanker. By late morning, some evacuated hospital patients were being returned to their hospitals just outside the evacuated areas, but the hospital remained closed. By late afternoon that day, the evacuation zone was reduced to a smaller area after air sampling indicated no hazard, allowing 144,000 residents to return home. However, closer to the derailment, the evacuation order held, as there was still concern about chlorine. Workers had been hampered in completely sealing the leaking chlorine tanker, still blocked by another. With an incomplete seal, some chlorine continued to escape. Other tankers, however, were being drained of their contents and hauled away, even as one propane tanker flared up again.

How 250,000 lives turned upside down when a trainload of terror ran amok

The Sunday Sun: November 18, 1979

On day five, November 14, workmen made a risky maneuver lifting and draining a half-empty propane tanker to get at the problem chlorine tanker, gambling that the propane tanker would not explode. Elsewhere on the site that day, a large white cloud of chlorine and water vapor rose from debris. Pockets of chlorine gas monitored in the evacuation zone still presented a health hazard for young children, the elderly, and those with respiratory problems. Frustration grew among some evacuated residents, as a 25-square-kilometer area remained closed. Traffic was still barred at two entrances to the Queen Elizabeth Way.

On day six, November 15, crews worked through the night and early morning, as 20 to 30 kilos of chlorine per hour continued to escape. The steel patch could not be fitted tightly over the rupture. A neoprene air bag was jerry-rigged over the opening which all but completely sealed the tanker, and officials announced there was little leakage. But that did not end the ordeal. Between 7 1/2 and 10 tons of liquid chlorine still remained in the tank. Most of the tanker's 90 tons of chlorine had been sucked up into the original fire ball at the wreck, with the resulting chlorine gas dispersed over Lake Ontario, according to officials. But remaining inside the tanker was a slushy ice mixture of chlorine and water that had built up on its walls from the water poured on by the fire hoses. Scientists worried that this layer of ice might break up and fall into the liquid chlorine, exposing it to the air.

On day five, pockets of chlorine gas monitored in the evacuation zone still presented a health hazard.

This complication delayed the clean-up operation, as it was decided that pumping would not start until favorable winds prevailed. That occurred about 11 p.m. that evening. Still, the remaining 72,000 evacuated residents could not return to their homes that night since the chlorine had not been removed.

On day seven, Friday, November 16, the problem involving the layer of ice was resolved, and by noon most of the chlorine had been pumped into trucks and shipped safely away. By 3 p.m., after tests showed that no dangerous pockets of chlorine were detected in the area, 37,000 of the remaining 72,000 evacuated residents were permitted to return home. However, the 35,000 residents living closest to the derailment and the first to evacuate, waited another four hours. By 7:45 p.m. that evening, the city was reopened and police removed the remaining road blocks. Only the derailment site remained off-limits, as there still was wreckage to clean up and one remaining chlorine tank car to deal with. By late evening, the last evacuation center was closed and by midnight, police at the site finished their duties. During the following week, the remaining chlorine tanker was finally emptied and the last pieces of emergency and fire equipment were removed from the scene. The clean-up of the wreckage at the site, and of contaminated soils there, would continue for another month or more.

In the aftermath of the accident, it was clear to many Canadians that Mississauga—and nearby Toronto—had dodged a

"We were lucky.... If the derailment had happened in metro Toronto just 20 miles up the tracks, we'd have had it. Thousands would have died."

Harold Morrison, Chairman, Metro Toronto Residents Action Committee

major catastrophe. "We were lucky we escaped that one," said Harold Morrison in November 1984. Morrison was chairman of the Metro Toronto Residents Action Committee that formed shortly after the incident. "If the derailment had happened in metro Toronto just 20 miles up the tracks," he explained, "we'd have had it. Thousands would have died."[19] Indeed, luck had played a role. The derailment occurred just after the train had passed through one of the most concentrated residential areas of Mississauga. The chemically-laden tank cars just happened to leave the tracks at one of the few places where a large area of undeveloped land existed—one of the few such places in all of greater Toronto. And because of the propane explosions at the scene, much of the escaping chlorine was taken up into the fire and into the atmosphere rather than released as a toxic gas along the ground. There had been no fatalities, though some firefighters complained of chlorine exposure. But the Mississauga accident had changed the political and industrial landscape in many ways. As Dow's Len Weldon would later observe, "... It was a big event politically, socially, environmentally, and in every other way..."[20]

Danger Zones

In the post-mortem at Mississauga, the finger of blame was initially waved at the railroads, and new safety legislation was introduced in the Ontario parliament. An inquiry was ordered and Canadian Supreme Court Judge Samuel Grange headed an investigation that heard 160 witnesses over more than four months, reporting some time later with a long list of recommendations. Among the called-for changes were technical improvements, such as the use of roller bearing-equipped rail cars, and other more common-sense approaches, such as lowering train speed limits in populated areas.

However, at Dow Chemical and within the Canadian chemical industry, there were those who knew the Mississauga incident had touched a nerve about the movement of dangerous chemicals—chlorine in particular. Even as the incident unfolded, newspaper stories and editorials appeared with headlines such as "Railway Roulette," "How Safe is The Freight," and "The Road to Asphyxia." People began asking questions about rail safety and chemical safety, and there were calls to ban the transport of hazardous chemicals—especially through highly populated areas. According to Jean M. Belanger, who was president of the Canadian Chemical Producers Association in the early 1980s, the Mississauga train wreck and evacuation catalyzed the effort to advance environmental and safety principles for the chemical industry, later known as "Responsible Care." Earlier attempts to adopt a set of chemical industry safety principles in Canada had failed. "In 1979, environmental awareness among companies was only starting," explained Belanger. "Regulations were causing concerns to the degree they would limit flexibility of companies to do business..." But then, a few accidents occurred. "For Canada it was the Mississauga train derailment...," said Belanger. "It put the spotlight on chemicals: Are they creating more problems than they are solving? That gave spirit to start the movement that became Responsible Care...."[21] But years after Responsible Care had become a well-established mantra of Canadian and U.S. chemical officials (see Chapter 11), toxic spills and chemical releases, including those involving rail operations, would continue to occur. And among those was a share from the Dow Chemical Company. But back at Dow's chemical plant in Sarnia, another variety of toxic problem was getting attention.

Dow's "Toxic Blob"

In the 1980s, one of the chemicals Dow produced at Sarnia was perchloroethylene—the toxic dry-cleaning solvent known as "perc." In August 1985, Dow spilled 5,000 to 10,000 gallons of perc into the St. Clair River. Dow acknowledged the spill and within days began a clean up, sucking up the material from the riverbed with a high-powered vacuum. But the spill soon drew public attention, as some charged it had also soaked up dioxin in the river from previous spills. Shortly thereafter, Dow's perc spill was tagged the "toxic blob" by environmentalists and the Canadian press. Dow's clean-up effort continued through December 1985, and even into early February 1986, when the company was still vacuuming smaller "puddles" of chemical still forming on the river bottom. As an interim measure, Dow stored the black, tar-like material it had sucked up from the river in some of its holding lagoons, intending to incinerate the material at a later date. However, the planned incineration of the material also brought protest, as Dow's incinerator had not been tested for dioxin or furan emissions. Dow's John Musser said the incinerator was "the best technology available," but also acknowledged that it was last approved in the early 1970s, and had not been tested for emissions of dioxins or furans. There were no special terms or conditions placed on its operation, nor were any special testing or reporting measures required of Dow. As the river pollution case went to court in January and February 1986, the burning of the toxic blob in the Dow incinerator awaited the spring thaw, as the holding lagoon was frozen.[22]

In January 1986, Dow lawyers in the spill case inside the Sarnia courthouse pled guilty to four counts under Ontario's Water Resources Act, but were also trying to convince an Ontario judge that the perc they spilled into the St. Clair was a "product" spill and not a "waste" spill. A product spill meant Dow could be fined a maximum $20,000 rather than $100,000 if the spilled material were classified as waste. Outside, on the courthouse steps that January, Greenpeace Canada was holding a mock funeral for the "toxic blob," pushing for the maximum fine. Court documents later showed that 8,000 to 9,400 gallons of perc and other material were released into the river, with a lesser amount of perc, about 500 gallons, settling on the river bottom. Dow leaked the perc from a tanker loading operation. The loading area drained into a sump where any spilled material was supposed to be collected and then reprocessed. But an open safety valve on a discharge line allowed the perc to overfill a separator chamber. A capacity alarm on the separator also failed. The chemical then backed up into another chamber, where the perc found its way into a sewer line via a partially seized-up discharge valve, and from there into the St. Clair River.[23]

Inside the Ontario courtroom, Environment Ministry attorney, Linda McCaffrey, argued that the Environmental Protection Act be invoked for a maximum fine for spilling a toxic waste material. "Obviously," said McCaffrey, "a $20,000 fine or even a $100,000 fine isn't going to make a difference to Dow's pocketbook." But she argued that the maximum fine should be imposed to send a clear message to industry. Acknowledging that the spill had shown no devastating consequences to the river or to drinking water, McCaffrey still argued that the cumulative and long-term effects of continued smaller spills were unknown and similar to "a death by a thousands cuts." McCaffrey explained that Dow knew the perc should not be in the river and had set up a system to deal with that fact. "The corporation, having established a system [to keep the chemical out of the river], took no steps to make that system work," she charged. Dow, on the other had, stressed it had already spent a million dollars on clean-up, and proposed to spend more on prevention.[24]

About 100 meters downstream from Dow's sewer outlet, hexachlorobenzene was found at levels 370 times Ontario's water quality guideline.

As the courtroom battle was going on, however, new information had come to light about pollution in the St. Clair and in Ontario. For one, trace levels of dioxin had been found in treated drinking water in a number of river towns—Windsor, Sarnia, Wallaceburg, and Mitchell's Bay on Lake St. Clair, south of Sarnia. Although the levels were well below the standards then in use in Canada, Ontario Environment Minister Jim Bradley explained: "Whenever any quantity of any type of dioxin is found in treated drinking water, we are concerned." In January 1986, the Canadian government had also released a report on the environmental state of the St. Clair River. Among its findings was the fact that the St. Clair was full of cancer-causing chemicals, with Dow's Sarnia plant identified as among the major sources. The St. Clair corridor, an international waterway separating Ontario from Michigan, is sometimes referred to as "chemical valley" by its residents, given the number of oil refineries and petrochemical companies located along its banks. In ten years, 1975–85, the report found that more than 11,500 tons of material had been spilled in the river by various industrial sources in some 32 incidents, with more than 7,500 tons never recovered. About 100 meters downstream from Dow's sewer outlet, the report noted, hexachlorobenzene was found at levels 370 times Ontario's water quality guideline. Other contaminants of the St. Clair were found at elevated levels as far as 15 miles downstream from the Sarnia area. Young fish were also found to be contaminated with chemicals. And finally, the report found that small amounts of 2,4,5-T and 2,4-D were coming into the river from one of Dow's waste sites. The most severely affected area of the river, the report indicated, was that adjacent to Dow and its neighbor, Suncor. The polluted area had, however, shrunk in size compared to a report eight years earlier. Still, the report singled out some of the toxic waste sites being especially problematic as potential sources of groundwater pollution and continuing "toxic feeds" to the river. One was a large salt cavern on Dow's property where nearly 9 million gallons of waste had been buried, and which Dow had used between 1968 and 1984. Some of the same chemicals making their way into the river were those found in the waste-dump cavern. Dow pled not guilty to charges related to this site.[25] But Dow had also been under investigation for two other river spills: a January 1985 spill of 2.3 million gallons of dirty acidic water, and an April 1985 spill of more than 11,600 gallons of ethylene dichloride.[26]

Bad Air

Meanwhile, in the mid-1980s, the air around Sarnia—it was feared by some—wasn't much better than the water. Although Dow's was one of a number of chemical plants in the area, it was believed to be a major contributor to some of the more hazardous air pollution. "Regulators and scientists have not looked at the largest potential source of air pollution in the area," wrote Toronto *Globe and Mail* reporter Jock Ferguson in February 1986—"an incinerator at Dow Chemical Canada, Inc." Dow's incinerator was then burning as much as 28 tons of highly toxic chemicals every day, including "hex tars" such as hexachlorobenzene and hexachlorobutadiene, chemicals just as toxic and as difficult to destroy as PCBs. Dow's incinerator—known as a thermal oxidizer, operating at temperatures of 1,200 degrees Celsius—was licensed in 1972. However, there were no public hearings at the time, because the company was disposing of wastes created at its own plant.[27]

When Dow received approval for its incinerator in 1972, the company assured the government that the wastes would be completely destroyed. But no one was checking on dioxin emissions. Phillip Roycraft, an environmental engineer with Michigan's Department of Natural Resources observed in 1986 that burning waste solvents such as "hex tars" would almost certainly form dioxins and furans.[28] Other chemical wastes being pulled out of the incinerator's scrubber system were also being discharged into a Dow sewer that emptied directly into the St. Clair River. This sewer consistently had higher levels of chemical wastes, including the hex compounds, than did any of Dow's other sewers at the time, according to the government's St. Clair River study.[29]

In addition to hex tars, Dow was also sending other highly toxic wastes through its Sarnia incinerator. Between 1977 and 1979, for example, Dow burned 13 railway tank cars of 2,4-D waste shipped in from its Fort Saskatchewan, Alberta plant—waste known to contain dioxin. Yet, up to 1986, no Canadian government agency had ever conducted tests on Dow's Sarnia incinerator to determine whether it was emitting dioxins, furans, and other chlorinated compounds. By then in the U.S., Dow's hazardous waste incinerator at Midland, Michigan had been identified by EPA and others as a source of dioxins found in the community's soil, including 2,3,7,8-TCDD, the most toxic form of dioxin. Dow's Sarnia incinerator burned a similar diet of chemicals to those burned in Midland. Finally, in February 1986, Ontario Environment Minister James Bradley said he was ordering tests of the Dow Sarnia incinerator and of the soil around the Dow plant. Bradley also ordered tests of the scrubber water discharges for dioxins and furans.[30]

Perc Fine

Back in court on the perc spill, Judge A. L. Eddy made his sentencing decision. It was February 1986. He announced a fine of $16,000. The judge said his hands were tied in the matter, and that the legislation he was dealing with led him to fine Dow $4,000 for each of four counts, treating the offense as a product spill rather than a waste spill. Judge Eddy did not evoke the maximum amount even under the product standard, as he said maximum fines should be reserved for the worst cases, which this was not, in his view. He said Dow's quick response to the spill, its guilty plea, and the fact that Dow had no previous environmental charges against it in 43 years all contributed to his decision. He said he hoped the "notoriety" of the incident would help serve as a deterrent. Outside on the courthouse steps, however, Greenpeace Canada's Joyce McLean called the fine "a mere pittance." She charged that $16,000 "is nothing," and that Dow was "probably laughing up their sleeves." McLean said "a quarter of million for a carcinogen going into a public waterway is more like it." McLean complained that is was cheaper for Dow to pay the fine than to put in the proper technology to prevent the spill in the first place.[31]

Lyle Curran, representing Dow, told a reporter he hoped the case "would clarify for most people there is nothing hazardous in the drinking water and there never has been."[32] But Pat Davis, who lived in the downriver town of Wallaceburg, and also a member of the Citizens' Coalition for Clean Water, was disappointed with the fine and said environmental laws weren't strong enough. "I don't see any deterrent for the companies," he said. Con-

Debacle At Wallaceburg

Not long after the "toxic blob" story had broken in the media, and several St. Clair River downstream communities had their water purification plants shut down, Dow was invited to the town of Wallaceburg to explain what happened. Wallaceburg was then a town of about 11,000 people. Dow scientists and managers went to Wallaceburg to reassure the residents that everything was under control. However, "they found that their audience was not prepared, this time, to accept either their assurances or their authority," says Laurie Adkin, who interviewed local residents attending the meeting. "...These three guys came down in three-piece suits, you know, real business-like," recounted one member of the Wallaceburg Clean Water Committee (WCWC) present at the meeting. The Dow trio did a presentation, which was also being taped by cable TV. "Basically what they did was talk down to everybody," said the WCWC attendee. "You don't come in a briefcase and three-piece suit to Wallaceburg and start telling people why they don't understand what's happening. That's what they did..." Another attendee, a member of the Citizens' Coalition for Clean Water, added: "[T]hey come to a public meeting, stood up with graphs and charts, distorted out of this world, and lied to us, right on TV. The night they were there, we pretty nearly ended up in a brawl...."

"Dow management realized after this 'close encounter' with the public," observes Adkin, "that a major effort was necessary to restore its credibility, not only with opinion leaders in the communities affected..., but with politicians. The chemical companies were perceiving a rapid erosion of their old relationship with government agencies and departments, as the citizens' groups increasingly were demanding equal (or greater) representation at the policy-making tables, and environmental issues were becoming politically prominent."

Dow then hired Pat Delbridge Associates to help the company improve its public relations. (Delbridge as this time had also been hired by the Canadian Chemical Producers Association to help with larger chemical industry image problems stemming from public opinion surveys which had found the chemical industry in very low esteem.) But for Dow specifically, Delbridge held meetings with "thought leaders" in the downstream communities, including Port Huron, St. Clair, Wallaceburg, Windsor, Detroit, Chatham, and Walpole Island. Dow's hire of Delbridge for conducting these meetings was at first kept secret, as Dow would later argue that the citizens wouldn't have come or have been forthright with their reactions if they'd known it was a Dow event. In Wallaceburg, key environmental leaders, a high school teacher, a minister's wife and a few other prominent citizens were invited to dinner at The Oaks, a well-regarded restaurant. There, the selected citizen leaders were asked questions like "What do you see wrong with the industry?" Dow and Delbridge built on these meetings, "actively courting the members of newly formed citizen groups in the downstream communities," according to Adkin, bringing members of groups such as the St. Clair River International Citizens Network to tour Dow's facilities and discuss their concerns. These meetings, and other ongoing "dialogues" with environmental groups, generally became a *modus operandi* for major chemical companies like Dow in the aftermath of spills and other incidents, including larger international events such as the Bhopal toxic gas release (see Chapter 11 for further discussion).

Meanwhile, the first meeting at Wallaceburg—where Dow's "suits" barely escaped—had also been filmed by Dow and became a classic instructional management video of how not to behave with citizens.

Source: Adkin, L., *The Politics of Sustainable Development: Citizens, Unions and the Corporations*, Montreal/New York/London: Black Rose Books, 1998, pp. 198–200.

cerned about their drinking water, his coalition was calling for a pipeline to Lake Huron for their water rather than continued use of the St. Clair. Many residents in his area had already turned to bottled water, he said.[33]

A few months later, in a non-river incident at Dow's Sarnia plant in mid-May 1986, nearly 13,000 pounds of chlorinated chemical vapors—including 7,700 pounds of vinyl chloride—leaked into the atmosphere. It was the sixth toxic chemical leak to occur at the plant in nine months. Sandy Carlton, Dow spokeswoman at the time, said the vapor was released in the northeast corner of the plant and was dispersed over chemical complex. "It might have extended to the river," she

It was the sixth toxic chemical leak to occur at the plant in nine months.

said. "But if it did, its potency would have been diminished." The vapor release posed no danger to residents of Ontario or Michigan, even though the wind was blowing from the northeast toward Detroit the night of the release. "I'm sure it didn't get near Detroit," she said. However, police and disaster officials on the U.S. side of the St. Clair river were not notified of the accident. Dennis M. Drake, then a compliance official at the Michigan Department of Natural Resources, said he knew nothing about the vapor release. It was possible that one of his staff members was called by the Ontario Environment Ministry, he said, but the aide probably would have told him about it. Dow's Sandy Carlton said the incident occurred when an instrument failed, causing a pressure upset in the vinyl chloride finishing section of the plant. The pressure-safety valve dispersed the vapor, but the plant was shut down to minimize environmental impact. Dr. Ian Arnold, medical director of Dow's health center at the time, said he did not expect the vapors to be harmful to residents of the Port Huron-Sarnia area.[34]

Although Dow's Sarnia operations today are not as extensive as they used to be, the plant still has occasional incidents. For example, about 5:30 p.m. on the evening of March 22, 2001 a chemical storage tank at the Sarnia plant ruptured a safety disk. A quantity of waste oil containing styrene and butyl acrylate leaked out, later estimated by Dow to be about 10 to 20 gal-

Canada's Activist Labor

Sarnia, Canada in the 1960s and early 1970s was a humming industrial center with petrochemical companies lining the St. Clair River. Labor was making good money for the most part, and there were few complaints. Most workers were not concerned with pollution. Smokestacks symbolized progress. Although there were concerns about air and water pollution from some citizens and civic organizations, industry had the expertise, and even government deferred to the companies. Pollution was in check, industry insisted. But some Dow workers who dealt with the chemicals every day in the workplace, knew otherwise. In 1962, Ivan Hillier, a Dow worker in the Sarnia chlor-alkali plant and president of the local and district labor councils, began to agitate about worker health hazards, and specifically, mercury vapors at Dow's Sarnia plant. He prodded Canadian health officials to do inspections at Dow's plants, and when that failed after the inspections were rigged, he enlisted politicians in the fight. Hillier had also asserted on several occasions that Dow "permitted pools of mercury to lie around the plant and took inadequate measures to protect employees from it." Other Dow workers told New Democratic Party (NPD) politicians that they had been instructed not to dump mercury wastes while the river was being monitored, and that Dow knowingly dumped mercury into the sewers.

In May 1970, Ivan Hillier was among those who testified at the Queens Park hearings investigating mercury pollution of the St. Clair River. He accused government labor and environmental officials of colluding with Dow—refusing or neglecting to carry out inspections and testing and withholding results from the public. Hillier and other members of the Oil, Chemical and Atomic Workers Union (OCAW), became active in the New Democratic Party, ran in local elections, helped organize local public information seminars on pollution and public health, and helped establish a local tabloid newspaper called *The Sarnia Democrat*, which issued monthly between 1970 and 1972. The *Democrat*, often running articles on corporate pollution, became an alternative to Sarnia's established newspaper that frequently took industry's views. During the November 1970 election season, Hillier and others from the NDP called for nationalizing industries that had poor pollution records. Hillier didn't buy the argument that environmental protection would threaten jobs and tax revenue. He took the position that Dow could afford to pay a large settlement should the city of Sarnia sue the company for damages.

But in his activism, Hillier did not officially use his union credentials, and was hesitant to seek union endorsement for fear resistant and "right-wing" elements in the union would take his initiatives in the opposite direction. "Throughout a decade on involvement with the mercury and other local pollution issues," writes Laurie Adkin in her book *The Politics of Sustainable Development*, " Hillier's campaign was more or less a one-man show." During his activism, and particularly after April 1970 when the Canadian environmental group Pollution Probe formed a chapter in Sarnia and Hillier became one of its executive members, Hillier and his wife received threatening phone calls. He was also harassed at work by Dow and criticized by co-workers, received "set-up" communist literature at his union office, and was the target of at least one defamatory newspaper editorial. In 1973, a chlorine release occurred at Dow that sent 80 construction workers at a neighboring Suncor plant to the hospital. Dow came after Hillier and his union blaming a pipefitter for the incident.

But Ivan Hillier wasn't the only Dow Canada labor activist who railed against the company for its pollution and toxic waste. In the 1980s, other workers, often risking their jobs and paying a price in retribution from management and sometimes other workers, also stepped forward to challenge Dow practices. In 1980-81, "Michael," a steward for the pipefitters, discovered a foreman and another worker dumping *Dowtherm*, an insulating chemical, into the sewer that went to the river. After reporting the incident and demanding an investigation, Michael began receiving bad work performance reviews and in one grievance meeting was accused of "meddling in things that were none of his business." After a series of meetings and time spent on a "boneyard" detail where he was under heavy surveillance, Michael was backed by some of his co-workers, elected to chief steward, and reinstated to his former job. In the grievance procedure, however, Dow denied any harassment. Michael also stumbled upon another dumping incident when he found some control room operators dumping perchloroethylene-contaminated acid and caustic soda—to neutralize the acid—into a sewer leading to the river. He calculated the dumping had been going on at about a rate of 78,000 to 90,000 pounds of acid per hour. The dumping continued for five days, and according to Michael, management did nothing. Michael said he did not call the Ontario Ministry of the Environment because "it would have been like signing your own death warrant. You can't trust them. They're worse than Dow."

Dave Pretty, a national union representative at Sarnia, interviewed in the mid-1980s, explained that Dow's chlorine solvents unit had to have frequent "safeties"—emergency releases of chlorine gas to the atmosphere—to avoid a more dangerous accident or explosion. However, there were also some other factors at play accounting for the frequency of the releases: ". . .[T]hey have a scrubbing system in the solvents unit [which] was never designed to handle these things to the degree that they are [being produced], so the over-capacity goes into the atmosphere. In the [solvents] unit, they are putting up a $60,000 expansion of the scrubbing system. The unit was designed 15 to 20 years ago for a certain capacity. They keep increasing it and running at 120 to 130 percent of the nameplate of the original design."

Union workers at Sarnia in 1988 also helped expose Dow's illegal dumping of hazardous wastes at the LaSalle Road landfill—including biphenyls and hex wastes. During a strike that year, the workers used this issue to depict the company as unethical and untrustworthy.

Source: Adkin, L., *The Politics of Sustainable Development: Citizens, Unions and the Corporations*, Montreal/New York/London: Black Rose Books, 1998, pp. 160–225.

lons. Styrene and butyl acrylate are raw materials used at Dow's Sarnia plant in the production of acrylic latex, which in turn is used in adhesives, coatings, and latex paint. Inhalation of these chemicals can cause irritation to the respiratory tract. Although the liquid leaking of these chemicals was contained on the plant site, a foul odor wafted south through downwind communities and persisted for approximately four hours. The emergency telephone call-out system was activated in the communities of Corunna and Froomfield. Those downwind of the spill were advised by radio and television

"I'm sure it didn't get near Detroit," said the Dow spokeswoman of the 1986 chlorinated vapor release.

to stay inside with windows closed and ventilation shut off. According to Dow, "both styrene and butyl acrylate are extremely odorous and can be smelled at levels far below Ontario exposure limits." With the incident, local roads were blocked off as a precaution to prevent the flow of traffic into the area. The "all clear" was issued at 9:45 p.m.[35]

Elsewhere in Canada, Dow's Fort Saskatchewan operations in Alberta—with eight "world-scale" plants sprawling over more than 2,100 acres—is the largest petrochemical manufacturing site in Canada. More than 3 million tons of product leave Fort Saskatchewan every year, much of it destined for Asia by way of Canada's Pacific Ocean port city, Vancouver. Dow's Western Canadian operations are busy, handling more than 3,000 rail shipments per month or about 110 rail cars per day. Among the main production operations at Fort Saskatchewan are those for chlor-alkali, ethylene, polyethylene, ethylene oxide, ethylene glycol, and the PVC chemicals, ethylene dichloride and vinyl chloride monomer. Fort Saskatchewan, in fact, is one of Dow's largest producers of chlorine and PVC feedstock chemicals, and has had occasional toxic releases of the materials.

On June 24, 1997, for example, Dow evacuated a portion of the Fort Saskatchewan plant after a chlorine release. The leak occurred at 1:25 a.m. and forced the evacuation of both the vinyl chloride monomer plant and a nearby polyethylene plant. More than three dozen construction workers were treated for chlorine inhalation. Thirty-eight workers were treated at the company's on-site health center, and nine of those were taken to the Fort Saskatchewan Health Center for further treatment. Those workers were later released. The injured workers suffered from burning eyes and sore noses and throats, but according to plant general manager Bob Knee, none developed a cough that was symptomatic of more severe chlorine inhalation. Knee reported the leak was the result of an overpressured vent in a new ethylene dichloride reactor the plant was installing. The excess pressure caused the chlorine to escape through the vent. Knee added that preliminary investigations had shown that instrument failure and inaccurate calibration may have played a role in the leak. The incident was being investigated by Alberta Environmental Protection.[36]

Dow's Dioxin: No. 1

As of 2001, Dow's Saskatchewan operation was also Canada's largest source of dioxins and furans, which are reported annually under the Canadian Environmental Protection Act. Since 1995, the Canadian government has indicated that dioxins and furans should be "virtually eliminated" in Canada because of their impact on the environment and human health. Canada was also the first national government to ratify the Stockholm Convention on Persistent Organic Pollutants, known as the POPs treaty, a global agreement that calls for the elimination of 12 POPs, dioxins and furans among them. But according to Canada's most recent toxic chemicals reporting data, for the year 2001, Dow 's operations in Western Canada—primarily those in Saskatchewan—are the nation's No. 1 source of dioxins and furans, reporting 68 grams TEQ (toxic equivalent), double that of the next largest polluter, a Norske Canada paper mill. Dow's Western Canada operations also ranked No. 4 nationally for the total reported releases and transfers of ozone-depleting substances during 2001, reporting a total 131,759 kg for three compounds—HCFC-142b, HCFC-22, and carbon tetrachloride.[37]

11.
Dow Environmentalism

We've known for a long time that pollution is economically and environmentally wasteful. If we reduce our waste, we can increase our global competitiveness through greater efficiency.

William S. Stavropoulos, President, Dow Chemical Co., April 1996[1]

Just as there's no way to make a safe cigarette, many of the things Dow produces will never be environment-friendly.

Linda Greer, NRDC, July 1999[2]

In the 1970s and 1980s, Dow Chemical and some of its executives developed a reputation for being aggressively antagonistic toward government regulation and environmental protection. But Dow managers had not always been combative over pollution. In the 1950s and 1960s, there was a willingness by some Dow officials to adopt pollution-control measures that could be accommodated in the normal course of plant and equipment improvements. This was just common sense to some of Dow's managers, according to Robert Lundeen, Dow's chief process engineer in the company's western division during the 1950s, and later its board chairman. "Management took it as a pretty reasonable thing to do," Lundeen said, recalling the company's design of measures to meet pollution-control standards in Los Angeles. "It was a technical problem," he explained. "We were quite easy working in that environment. The issues weren't resolved on the front pages of the *Los Angeles Times* or on the morning television shows." But that soon changed. As "this thing got into the political arena," Lundeen explained, that's when "Dow began to buck."[3] In fact, in California, Dow had one very unhappy experience.

In the mid-1970s, Dow was one of the largest chemical providers in the Western U.S., but it had no major processing plants there as it did in Texas and Louisiana. By then, however, a new variable had made west coast chemical production more desirable: oil in Alaska. Cheap Alaskan oil could be floated down the Pacific Ocean by tanker to California, thus avoiding the high transportation costs of bringing feedstock across the continent. And given the huge California market, it only seemed logical that Dow should build a major complex there. So in February 1975, the company announced it would build a 13-unit, $500 million petrochemical complex in Solano County, California, across the river from its smaller existing plant at Pittsburg. Dow soon took an option on a 2,700-acre sheep farm, on which it planned a 600-acre complex that would be linked in part to its Pittsburg operations. Dow's planners envisioned building-block chemicals like ethylene and propylene being piped under the Sacramento River to the Pittsburg plant. The complex Dow was planning would be a major chemical center, capable of supplying 40 percent of the plastics feedstock then used in the West. Dow promised the new facility would not discharge wastes into the Sacramento River, but rather would be "off river," using a series of thermal ponds for plant waste that would rely on evaporation. Still, the environmental review process Dow faced was formidable, as the project would be one of the first major industrial developments reviewed under California's new Environmental Quality Act, which required an environmental impact assessment along with public hearings. Nor were environmentalists happy with the proposal.

By December 1975, the Sierra Club, Friends of the Earth, and the San Francisco-based People for Open Space had filed a lawsuit to stop the project. The deputy secretary of the California Resources Agency requested that the U.S. Army Corps of Engineers not grant a needed permit until the environmental problems were resolved. Still, Dow thought Governor Jerry Brown, a Democrat then running for president, might help them. Brown had moved the environmental impact assessment on the project through the state process, and by late 1976, he promised a yes or no decision. Dow expected Brown's decision to come within 30 days of public hearings. However, those hearings, which occurred in December 1976, became circus-like in the view of Dow's manager, Jack Jones:

> There was a vice president from Dow. He was sitting in the audience and Dennis Banks—the Indian guy—got up there and the whole hearing panel stood up at reverent attention and Banks babbled something in a singsong sort of way and the hearing officer that night—former chief counsel for the Environmental Defense Fund and at the time chairman of the Water Resources Board—looked at him and said, "Would you favor us by translating those beautiful words into English?" And Dennis Banks said, "Oh well sure—the water is blue and clean, and the sky is pretty and may the buffalo roam," or some real innocuous thing like that...
>
> Well this guy from the [Dow] home office looked at me and his eyes turned glassy and he said, "Unbelievable!" He gets up and walks out the room, so I ran out to calm him down. He said, "Jack, let's withdraw from the proceedings right now." I said, "We can't. We've got to go through with this. At least the governor hasn't reneged on his promise of a decision up or down within 30 days yet."[4]

However, Dow's hope for a favorable yes or no decision from the governor fell through in January. The governor's legal counsel sided with the [state] Attorney General, concluding that material presented in the hearings resulted in new environmental information, which meant Dow would have to begin a new EIR—environmental impact review—and start the process all over again. On January 18, 1977, Dow announced it was cancelling the project. "The permitting process for new facilities is so involved and expensive it is impractical to continue," explained the company in a press release. After Dow announced it was cancelling the project, Alan Stein, secretary of business and transportation for Brown, defended the state's tough environmental standards, and suggested Dow's proposal would likely get state approval if resubmitted—which brought a stinging reply from Dow's Paul Oreffice: "You are assuming the chemical industry is coming here to destroy the environment. No industry in the world has spent more money than the chemical industry of the United States to clean up the environment. I submit to you there is a problem with attitude in state government in California. We have other states in this country that live with the same Environmental Protection Agency rules but have an entirely different attitude."[5] Yet Dow's relationship with EPA was about to take a turn for the worse.

EPA's Fly-Over

In 1978, an EPA official came to Dow's plant in Midland, Michigan. Dow had been charged with violating the Clean Air Act and threatening public health because two power plants there were spewing dense smoke, particulate matter, and sulfur dioxide (the main ingredient of acid rain) into the air. After inspecting the plant with Dow's cooperation, EPA officials asked permission to take photographs to document whether Dow had room to install pollution control equipment at the plants, a request Dow denied. Dow said EPA officials discussed obtaining a warrant, but then without notice, hired an aerial survey service to take photographs of the Dow plant. On February 7, 1978, the Abrams Aerial Survey Corp. of Lansing, Michigan took a small plane equipped with aerial surveillance cameras and made six unannounced passes over Dow's plant, photographing every inch of it. Within days of the overflights, Dow sued the EPA claiming violation of its constitutional rights, charging that the flights were an illegal search, and were also a taking of property without due process. Dow also charged that its trade secrets could be compromised, as anyone making a Freedom of Information Act request could use the photographs to obtain technical information. In its lawsuit, Dow charged the EPA flights violated the company's Fourth and Fifth Amendment rights—the former prohibiting unreasonable searches and seizures, and the latter prohibiting the taking of property without due process of law. But aerial photography by U.S. authorities was a fact of life by the late 1970s. The U.S. Geological Survey had photographed most of the country for mapmaking by then, and the U.S. Forest Service used aerial photography to monitor vegetation changes, the Army Corps of Engineers for flood control, and the Pentagon for strategic defense. EPA had used it extensively to meet its responsibilities, including to search for and pinpoint toxic waste. All federal agencies routinely had access to the photos. Government officials say their ability to enforce federal laws would be hampered without them. "If there's an area of the United States that hasn't been photographed, it's because we can't get the clouds out of the way," said Vernard Webb, director of the EPA's Environmental Photographic Interpretation Center, which by 1978 had a staff of 50 pilots, photographers and other specialists working on aerial data and related projects. Webb said the airspace above the sites being photographed wasn't owned by the landowners, "so why would we need a warrant?" Even when flying for pleasure, he observed, you have to fly over something. "When you're in airspace, it's yours," he said. EPA said it used only a 35-mm camera to take its pictures of Dow, and that film no more sensitive than *Kodak Ektachrome* was used. EPA magnified the pictures twofold. However, Dow complained the photos could have been blown up 20 times larger, revealing pipes no thicker than a man's thumb. Because much of Dow's chemical processing takes place outside of buildings, Dow argued that the configuration of pipes constitutes a trade secret, and could be worth millions of dollars if slipped into the wrong hands. "A threat to Dow's privacy threatens its very existence and integrity as a scientific, technological and researched-based company," said Dow in its court brief. Other corporations felt the same way, prompting the Chamber of Commerce to join Dow in its case, representing petroleum and iron and steel operations, which also had outside operations, as well as the auto industry, which tests its vehicles on outdoor tracks. EPA's Webb insisted the danger was overblown, and that there were already laws on the books that required EPA to protect confidential business information.[6] In 1982, when the case went before U.S. District Court Judge James Harvey, he found that EPA had violated Dow's Fourth Amendment rights and had exceeded its statutory authority as a government agency. He prohibited EPA from further aerial surveillance. EPA appealed the decision, and it was reversed by the Sixth Circuit Court of Appeals in Cincinnati by a 2–1 vote. Dow then appealed the Cincinnati decision to the U.S. Supreme Court, which sided with EPA, upholding the Cincinnati ruling by a 5–4 vote in 1986. At the Supreme Court, however, the Dow case had been consolidated with another flyover case regarding surveillance of marijuana operations. "If it had been the Dow case alone," said Dow's attorney Jane M. Gootee, "I felt we would have won."[7]

Dow charged that the EPA flights were an illegal search; a taking of property.

Toxic Chemicals

During the 1960s and 1970s, worries about toxic chemicals and public health—principally cancer—became a powerful political force moving federal regulation forward on several fronts, from registering new chemicals to toxic wastes dumps. Several pieces of legislation took form in the U.S. Congress, including: the Toxic Substances Control Act of 1976 or TSCA, a law for new chemical registration and toxic screening; the Comprehensive Environmental Response, Compensation, and Liability Act of 1980, also known as Superfund, aimed at cleaning up old toxic waste dumps; and the Resource Conservation Recovery Act, or RCRA, for regulating current waste generation, disposal, and transportation. Dow Chemical, on its own and through the chemical industry trade association, the Chemical Manufacturers Association (CMA), figured prominently in the lobbying and final configuration of these laws—and their future effectiveness.

The idea initially behind the Toxic Substances Control Act, or TSCA (pronounced "Tah-sca"), was to give EPA the power to reject a hazardous chemical before it was brought into use. Thousands of chemical substances were being brought to market before they were adequately reviewed for safety, often resulting in various environmental and/or public health problems. Under the proposed law, companies could challenge an EPA determination that a particular chemical was unfit, but would bear the burden of proving safety. The law was also designed to register each new chemical and build an inventory of information about each one. However, the reality of TSCA once it became law was something less than its framers had hoped for, thanks in part to lobbying by Dow Chemical. Dow, unhappy about government regulation generally, did not like the idea of TSCA one bit, and became one of its fiercest opponents. "In one of its most concerted battles," explains author Cathy Trost, "[Dow] and its industry allies almost single-handedly kept [TSCA] locked up in Congress for five years, until President Ford reluctantly signed it into law in 1976." Dow's Dr. Etcyl Blair, charged with building the company's health and environmental science division in the mid-1970s, expressed the company's views on TSCA shortly after it had been passed: "There is another way to protect the public than in passing another law. It involves relying on industry's strong commitment to risk management."[8] Yet others already had serious reservations about Dow's approach to risk management.

Superfund

Next came the Superfund law. By the late 1970s, the discovery of toxic wastes at Love Canal near Niagara Falls, New York, helped to foment the debate over who would pay for the clean-up of thousands of old toxic waste sites across the country. Initially, the chemical industry characterized hazardous waste as a "broader society" problem. Robert A. Roland, then president of the CMA, offered this view:

> The solid waste disposal problem, including toxic or hazardous wastes, is not just the problem of the chemical industry. It is a result of society's advanced technology and pursuit of an increasingly complex lifestyle. Man has always been a messy animal.... Certain amounts of waste are inevitable.... Everyone should realize that the blame does not belong to a single company, or a single industry, but to all of us as individuals and as an advanced society. Rather than looking for scapegoats, we should recognize the dilemma and consider new ways to encourage the disclosure of dump site information and ways to limit the crushing liabilities that could result.

There was no crisis, the industry argued. "We are not dealing with a rash, an epidemic of Love Canals," said Roland. "There is no need to rush to the legislature. And we are not dealing with an irresponsible industry."[9] Congress and the public thought otherwise, but the debate continued for about three years, with considerable wrangling over whether the cleanup law should cover oil and chemical spills as well as hazardous waste. As the debate sharpened, the issue of establishing a large fund to finance the clean up became central, as well as other key issues, including legal liability.

Dow led a faction of chemical industry lobbyists seeking a scaled-down Superfund law dismissed by most members of Congress as inadequate.

Leading Dow's effort, and a large part of the chemical industry at the time, was Dow CEO Paul Oreffice. Oreffice "led the CMA faction that counseled all-out opposition to any proposal other than a $600 million fund, which was dismissed by most members of Congress as inadequate."[10] During the 1980 debate in Congress, after a Senate committee had approved a $4.1 billion Superfund package, it was hoped the chemical industry would begin to negotiate. However, Oreffice and a majority of the CMA were unwilling. But DuPont's chairman, Irving Shapiro, broke ranks with the rest of the industry, indicating in November 1980 that he could support a smaller $1.2 billion version the House had passed. It was Shapiro's position that became the basis for negotiations between the House and Senate, and a final $1.6 billion Superfund package that President Jimmy Carter signed into law in December 1980. Dow and the CMA caught criticism for their hard-line position. *Chemical & Engineering News* called the industry's anti-compromise posture "a gross miscalculation by some segments of the chemical industry...A bitter lesson in how not to lobby." *National Journal* criticized the CMA for working two years to oppose the measure. Paul Oreffice, however, later reflected his industry "was had" on Superfund because the tax payments in the fund were based "not on what you waste but how much material you take in." Shapiro, he charged, was the architect of that. "I think it was awful for the chemical industry.... That was a very fundamental difference [i.e., between the DuPont/Shapiro and Dow/Oreffice positions]."[11]

Oreffice, in making speeches, often had few charitable words for environmental regulation and was no friend of environmental activists. "Lenin said that capitalism would be destroyed from the inside," he offered, speaking to the Arizona Business Forum. "Well, if a weapon is needed, it was indeed found in the so-called environmentalists who have now made a profession of standing in the way of any progress.... We are facing a well-organized, often unscrupulous, professional force.... We are dealing, let me tell you again, with fiendishly clever people." Oreffice also sometimes singled out particular leaders or groups, calling the Environmental Defense Fund and Friends of the Earth, "professional merchants of doom" who practice "a deadly profession."[12]

Chemical Safety

One issue that began to turn Dow and the entire chemical industry in a new direction in the 1980s was chemical safety. Dow and other companies had always preached the virtues of chemical safety at their facilities and had extensive programs and personnel devoted to the issue. But in the 1970s and 1980s, a series of incidents and discoveries within the industry pushed the issue of chemical plant safety and toxic chemicals to a much higher level of public scrutiny. In July 1976, a Hoffman-LaRoche pesticide plant in northern Italy exploded after a runaway chemical reaction, releasing a cloud of dioxin over the city of Seveso, contaminating almost 900 acres of land and thousands of people. More than 700 residents living the most heavily contaminated areas were evacuated two weeks after the accident. Back in the United States by this time, the discovery of toxic dump sites had also become a front-burner issue. In Canada, meanwhile, events were taking a somewhat different turn.

At the time, Jean M. Belanger was president of the Canadian Chemical Producers Association (CCPA). Belanger and a member of his staff, Bill Neff, had been exploring ways to help the chemical industry get a handle on environmental issues, and with a fellow Canadian, John Kitt of Exxon Chemical, then based in Houston, they began to outline some environmental principles for their industry. When these ideas were first presented to the board of the CCPA they were rejected outright, "partly because people were not yet sensitized to the issues and partly because there were legal concerns," said Belanger.[14] But the calamitous 1979 train derailment at Mississauga, Ontario—described in Chapter 10—changed all that. It was one of the largest disasters ever in Canada, leading to the evacuation of 250,000 people. "It was a terrible mess," explained Dow Canada's general counsel, Len Weldon, recalling the mishap.[14] In any case, after the Mississauga train wreck, the Canadian chemical makers quickly adopted Belanger's principles, which would become the basis for the Canadian version of "Responsible Care," the forerunner of what was later adopted in the United States. According to Belanger, environmental awareness was only just beginning among many companies in 1979. The Mississauga train derailment "put the spotlight on chemicals" and chemical safety. That spotlight, in turn, "gave spirit to start the movement that became Responsible Care."[15] By early 1984, the Canadians had formulated a one-page list of "guiding principles" which Canadian chemical companies were asked to sign and commit to. Then came Bhopal.

A June 1986 public opinion survey revealed that 48 percent of Canadians felt the risk from the chemical industry's activities outweighed the benefits.

In December 1984, a horrific accident at a Union Carbide pesticide plant in Bhopal, India catapulted chemical plant safety to the forefront of world issues. The plant leaked a cloud of a pesticide ingredient, methyl isocyanate—a toxic cloud that killed thousands of people and injured tens of thousands more, a legacy which still festers today. (See Chapter 20.) The Bhopal tragedy was followed by several incidents in the U.S. and Europe that further tarnished the reputation and public image of the chemical industry. Back in Canada, meanwhile, a June 1986 public opinion survey—the Decima Survey—revealed that 48 percent of Canadians felt the risk from the chemical industry's activities outweighed the benefits. David Buzzelli, then Dow Canada's CEO and later chairman of the Canadian Chemical Producers Association, would later recall his industry's reaction to the survey. "It was like being hit with a two-by-four. But it made the industry sit up in its chair. It asked the public, 'Who do you trust?'—and they put the CEO of chemical companies at the bottom of their list. Decima turned the tide in the CCPA. It made us realize that Responsible Care would have to move from being a philosophical statement to something with teeth."[16*] For many critics, however, "the teeth" in Responsible Care never arrived (see sidebar).

During 1986, the U.S. Congress created a new toxic chemicals reporting requirement known as the Toxic Release Inventory, or TRI, a key statute

---

*Another chemical industry program called CAER—for Community Awareness and Emergency Response—had been developed in response to Bhopal and various U.S. accidents. The idea was to reduce risk to workers and communities in the event of chemical plant accidents, and it called on companies to develop plans to deal with emergencies and establish communications programs with plant neighbors. Some of the CAER ideas were pulled into U.S. emergency planning laws written by Congress in TRI and right-to-know legislation.

Responsible Care

Responsible Care is the name of a chemcial industry program formulated in the 1980s to help chemical companies manage chemical risks, improve environmental protection, and enhance their public and community relations. In the United States, participation in Responsible Care became a requirement of member companies in the Chemical Manufacturers Association (CMA). As the Responsible Care process took form, "codes of practice" were formulated and adopted by the CMA as guidance for member companies. Initially, six codes of practice included: pollution prevention, process safety, reducing transportation and storage risks, employee health and safety, and product stewardship. But within CMA the code-making and code-adopting process was slow, and once adopted amounted to little more than putting a management structure and plan in place for each of the codes. Performance and evaluation, however, were another story. Responsible Care—although it did create a much better management structure within many companies that had none, or at best, only limited pollution prevention and emergency response capability—was essentially a self-monitoring process, or as one observer put it, "the chemical companies talking to themselves." In April 1990, for example, as CMA moved to adopt its Waste and Release Reduction Code to encourage its members to reduce waste and pollution, compliance with the code essentially required submitting data already required by EPA. There were no new specific requirements pushing CMA member companies. No company would be forced to change practices. A non-specific code, explained Responsible Care director Lori Romanos at the time, would allow companies to reduce wastes at their own pace. Indeed, that was the headline in *Chemical Week*'s story on the new waste code: "CMA's Waste Policy: Set Your Own Pace." And that criticism of Responsible Care, plus others, would reverberate in years to follow: that it lacked specifics, had no teeth, and that its members moved at their own speed. In 1999, for example, the Working Group on Community Right-to-Know leveled a scathing criticism at Responsible Care:

> "Nothing in Responsible Care...commits any [chemical] facility to *measurable goals* for reducing chemical hazards, to *timeliness* to meet such goals, or to effective *external validation*. Without these basic elements, Responsible Care lacks accountability and credibility. Since Responsible Care is voluntary, participating companies do little more than comply with current environmental laws. Further, the industry's public posture of openness conflicts markedly with its anti-right-to-know lobbying of state legislature and Congress."

CMA, for example, lobbied against the Right-To-Know-More Act, a measure intended to expand and improve public disclosure of toxic chemicals. In a 1998 U.S. PIRG survey, more than 75 percent of Responsible Care member companies would not or could not provide answers to seven basic questions about chemicals used at their facilities." From the very beginning, whether it was the 1979 train wreck in Canada or the 1984 Bhopal gas leak, Responsible Care had its origins in the industry's public relations problems, and was formed largely to deal with that issue. CMA spent heavily on public relations and promoting Responsible

Care through the early 1990s. In June 1991, for example, it announced a $10 million advertising and communications campaign aimed at showing the public the chemical industry was "run by responsible people, concerned about safety and the environment." By July 1991, the CMA ads began appearing in *Time* and *Newsweek*. Today, Responsible Care continues to be used and stretched to cover every new environmental or public safety challenge that might confront the industry, from chlorine to the precautionary principle.

Sources: Faye Flam, "CMA's Waste Policy: Set Your Own Pace," *Chemical Week*, April 11, 1990, pp. 9–10; Working Group on Community Right-To-Know, Briefing paper, "The Responsible Care" Program, 1999, Washington, DC, and U.S. PIRG, "Trust Us, Don't Track Us: An Investigation of the Chemical Industry's Responsible Care Program," Washington, DC, 1998.

advancing the public's "right to know" about toxic chemicals and emergency planning in their communities. The TRI, however—requiring most major industries to report annually on their toxic chemical pollution—would not publish its first tabulations until 1989. In the meantime, the U.S. chemical industry continued to feel public sentiment building against it, and by 1988, followed the Canadians and began formulating their own version of Responsible Care. Dow Chemical's Paul Oreffice, for one, played a key role in the process as head of the Public Perception Committee at the CMA, helping determine the public face of the new program.[17] CMA companies were then asked to abide by a set of Responsible Care principles and codes of practices.

Dow by this time was also into a heavy round of public relations campaigning, trying to improve its battered public image after a string of problems—including its dioxin problems, the company's role in altering EPA's dioxin report, and revelations about the company that surfaced in the Agent Orange litigation. Public opinion polling in the mid-1980s had put Dow's reputation at an all-time low, and the company embarked on a multi-million dollar advertising campaign showing an upbeat and positive Dow (see Chapter 2). The company was also casting itself as much more open to the public, and willing to listen to its critics. "...We had been a proud group who felt that people who knew nothing were telling us what to do," explained Keith R. McKennon, President of Dow Chemical, U.S.A. in 1987. " It took us a long time to realize that regulators, even environmentalists had a right to ask questions...."[18] But then came EPA's Toxic Release Inventory (TRI).

"Startling" Pollution

In April 1989, when EPA reported the first tabulation of TRI data—essentially the first nationwide survey of U.S. industrial pollution—it called the results "startling and unacceptably high."[19] According to that survey, U.S.

industry at the time (for the year 1987) was releasing about 22.5 *billion* pounds of some 329 hazardous substances. Linda Fischer, EPA assistant administrator for policy and planning at the time, noted that the toxic releases were "far higher than what we thought was going to occur... Everybody here [at EPA] had the same reaction," she said—"that the numbers were bigger than anticipated and we had to do something about it... You look at these numbers and you say there must be a way this country can do its business better." In that first TRI tabulation, the chemical industry was at the top of the list, accounting for 55 percent of all environmental releases.[20] Dow Chemical that year had four locations among the top 500—

Only 15 percent of those polled agreed that "when the chemical industry states its commitment to the public, it means it."

Freeport, Texas at 9.68 million pounds; the Dow Corning plant in Midland, Michigan at 5.4 million pounds; Dow Chemical's Midland plant at 4.2 million pounds; and Dow's Plaquemine, Louisiana plant, at 4.02 million pounds.[21] Dow plants were also prominent in emissions of known cancer-causing chemicals, among them: Midland, Michigan; Pittsburg, California; Plaquemine, Louisiana; and Freeport, Texas (see table, next page).

Facing the results of the TRI, and realizing that its public image was still poor, some chemical industry leaders became proactive, pledging to cut emissions and lead their industry into a new era of responsibility. Edgar Woolard, the incoming CEO at DuPont, one of the nation's top polluters, delivered a May 1989 speech in London entitled, "Corporate Environmentalism," urging his industry to move beyond compliance while charging his own company with a leadership role.

Dow, meanwhile, had thought about dropping the word "chemical" from its corporate name, and even hired a New York image consultant to measure public opinion on the matter.[22] But after viewing the results, Dow decided to stay with "Dow Chemical." Said Frank Popoff at the time: "We are and will be, a company based primarily on chemistry. We must do a better job of helping the general public understand the contributions of chemistry."[23] But the bad news for chemicals and the industry's image kept coming. In December 1989, the CMA asked 7,500 respondents to rank a list of 10 industries from the least to most environmentally responsible. The chemical industry received the second worst ranking, lower than the nuclear or oil industries. Only the tobacco industry fared worse. In the survey, only 14 percent believed the chemical industry was going as fast as it could to make the country cleaner and safer; and only 15 percent agreed that "when the chemical industry states its commitment to the public, it means it."[24]

By Earth Day 1990, corporate environmentalism had become the new corporate fashion and part of the accepted *Fortune 500* lexicon. Trade associations competed with one another as various "business codes" and lists of

Bad Air, 1987

Dow Chemical's Cancer-Causing Air Pollution*

Plant & Location	Type Operation (SIC)	Chemical	Emissions (lbs)
Russellville, AR	misc. plastic	methylene chloride	137,000
Pittsburg, CA	pesticides, ag-chems	carbon tetrachloride	43,300
Pittsburg, CA	pesticides, ag-chems	perchloroethylene	47,700
Pittsburg, CA	pesticides, ag-chems	methylene chloride	269,000
Gales Ferry, CT	plastics, resins, elastomers	1,3-butadiene	41,300
Dalton, GA	plastics, resins, elastomers	1,3-butadiene	105,000
Plaquemine, LA	alkalies & chlorine	carbon tetrachloride	31,000
Plaquemine, LA	alkalies & chlorine	chloroform	107,600
Plaquemine, LA	alkalies & chlorine	ethylene dichloride	73,000
Plaquemine, LA	alkalies & chlorine	methylene chloride	188,600
Plaquemine, LA	alkalies & chlorine	perchloroethylene	29,200
Midland, MI	plastics, resins, elastomers	methylene chloride	1,943,729
Midland, MI	plastics, resins, elastomers	carbon tetrachloride	95,566
Midland, MI	plastics, resins, elastomers	perchloroethylene	291,426
Midland, MI	plastics, resins, elastomers	acrylonitrile	27,984
Midland, MI	plastics, resins, elastomers	1,3-butadiene	63,472
Midland, MI	plastics, resins, elastomers	chloroform	165,387
Midland, MI	plastics, resins, elastomers	ethylene dichloride	23,000
Midland, MI**	industrial org. chemicals	carbon tetrachloride	58,500
Findlay, OH	misc. plastic	trichloroethylene	40,900
Cincinnati, OH***	pharmaceutical	smethylene chloride	53,300
Freeport, TX	alkalies & chlorine	ethylene dichloride	150,000
Freeport, TX	alkalies & chlorine	1,3-butadiene	55,000
Freeport, TX	alkalies & chlorine	carbon tetrachloride	75,800
Freeport, TX	alkalies & chlorine	chloroform	56,000
Freeport, TX	alkalies & chlorine	methylene chloride	260,000
Freeport, TX	alkalies & chlorine	trichloroethylene	54,000

Source: Deborah A. Sheiman, Lisa L. Dator, and David D. Doniger, *A Who's Who of American Toxic Air Polluters*, Natural Resources Defense Council, June 19, 1989. *Emissions of known cancer-causing chemicals. **Dow Corning. ***Merrell Dow Pharmaceuticals

environmental principles proliferated. CMA touted Responsible Care; the American Petroleum Institute (API) issued ten environmental principles for its members; and the Global Environmental Management Initiative, or GEMI, was launched with the endorsement of the Business Roundtable and the International Chamber of Commerce. At Dow, there were some major changes too—including the appointment in May 1990 of David Buzzelli as

Dow's top man on the environment, named corporate vice president for Environmental Health and Safety and Public Affairs.[25]

Buzzelli had confronted environmental issues at Dow Canada, where he was appointed president and CEO in 1986, a few months before "the toxic blob" issue hit (see preceding chapter). Dow and the blob were front page news for a couple of months, and the crisis helped form Buzzelli's thinking about how to deal with environmental issues. Through the Canadian Chemical Producers Association, where Responsible Care was taking form, Buzzelli helped push the new code and its later adoption in the U.S. He was also drawn into the aftermath of a 1987 United Nations report on the environment titled *Our Common Future*, the first "sustainable development" report. Buzzelli—appointed to a panel of Canadian government, industry and environmental leaders to frame a response to the U.N. report—used the experience to shape Dow's role and outlook in working with government agencies and environmentalists.[26] Buzzelli soon became something of Dow's "Mr. Sunshine" on the environment, a guy with a positive, can-do attitude who became well-liked by many who worked with him—colleagues and adversaries. Along with Buzzelli, Dow executives were out on the stump too, visibly talking up their involvement with environmental issues, offering new ideas.

By Earth Day 1990, corporate environmentalism had become the new corporate fashion.

"Don't Trust Us, Track Us"

In an April 1991 keynote speech at the annual meeting of the American Chemical Society in Atlanta, Dow's Frank Popoff said the industry must begin working with consumer and environmental critics, but he also leveled criticism at some environmental laws. "Environmental gridlock," had taken over, he charged, citing battles between regulators, industry and activists. Effective action was being stifled. "I believe that the chemical industry should take the lead in ushering in a new era of cooperation on environmental issues," he said. Why? "Public opinion is everything. What the public believes to be true, even if it is wrong, determines what laws and regulations will be adopted and how public funds will be spent," he explained. Popoff then cited the acid rain provisions of the 1989 Clean Air Act as "sheer overkill," resulting in part from widespread scientific illiteracy. The new acid rain provisions, he explained, could bring the loss of up to 100,000 jobs,

"I want to leave my environmental bills fully paid."

Frank Popoff, 1993

boost utility rates up to 30 percent, and cost American industry up to $7 billion a year. "In a situation like this," he said, "when the stakes are so high, I submit that it is not enough for scientists to be articulate. They ought to be vociferous." Then he called for cooperation among all the stakeholders to avoid over-regulation. "We don't ask that they trust us—just that they track us and our performance," said Popoff of activists and other stakeholders. In closing Popoff was disdainful of the public's judging chemical firms on their environmental record—but "not the fact that we're the leading exporters...not the fact that we create jobs, and not the fact that we're generators of enabling technologies." As for the environment, Popoff said, Dow planned to reduce its air emissions by 50 percent by 1995.[27]

Through the 1990s, Dow was regularly fined or hauled into court by one or more state or federal government agencies.

Six months later, in October 1991, Dow was making environmental news again, this time taking the initiative in creating a panel of outside environmental advisors. By 1992, EPA began a special voluntary program for companies to cut pollution called the 33/50 program, in which companies pledged reductions of 33 percent and 50 percent in 17 chemical categories by certain target dates. Dow was one of the charter members.

But still more ideas and environmental initiatives came from Dow officials. Popoff again, in mid-October 1992 at a *Chemical Week* conference in Houston, floated a proposal suggesting that Dow might adopt a plan to price each of its products to reflect their environmental costs. The idea generally was to price goods and services "to reflect their true environmental costs," explained Popoff, "including production, use, recycling and disposal." The process would systematically identify and describe "every step of a product's life, from raw material to final disposal," he explained. Popoff compared the idea to a "value-added tax" calling it a "pollution-added cost" applied at each level of converting a raw material into a finished product. "This would be unique," said Peter Young, a managing director at Wertheim Schroder & Co, a New York investment banking concern. "I am sure customers will not be particularly happy about this." But Popoff seemed to anticipate that criticism. Full-cost pricing, he said, would actually help consumers make choices. It would force them to "understand the consequences of their purchases." But even within Dow, there were some fears that full-cost environmental pricing would make certain Dow products less competitive. "I think it's a necessary change for the industry," said Leonard Bogner, senior chemical analyst at Prudential Securities in New York. "Dow is of the belief that they don't want to leave operating costs on the table. If the market will pay more for it, Dow will extract it....Dow spends about $200 million a year on environmental types of funding. You don't get a return on that.

You just try to restructure it some way."[29]

Popoff continued pushing his idea. "I want to be more like the pharmaceutical industry and less like an extractive industry," he said in September 1993. "I want to leave my environmental bills fully paid." At the time, Popoff acknowledged that "there's been kind of a mind set in the industry that you can delay, shift, or accumulate environmental bills. And I say that's bad business." Even if consumers rejected his products because of higher prices reflecting environmental costs, Popoff said that was o.k. He would rather find out from the marketplace that a product is not economically competitive than have it banned by law or government agencies.[29]

Yet, by all indications, pricing alone would not and did not stop the production and/or release of toxic and hazardous chemicals at Dow plants, pipelines, rail cars, and waste sites. Through the 1990s, despite some progress on pollution control, Dow was regularly fined or hauled into court by one or more state or federal government agencies for workplace, environmental, and/or public health transgressions of one kind or another. Consent decrees, litigation, and/or settlements appeared a normal part of Dow's business practice in the 1990s.[30]

Low-Hanging Fruit

But Dow and other chemical companies did find that reducing pollution and waste could be achieved fairly painlessly. By making relatively simple changes in production equipment, doing preventive maintenance, or altering manufacturing practices, huge amounts of waste and pollution could be cut—waste and toxicity that was cutting into profit. For example, by 1992 a latex plant at Dow's Midland, Michigan complex had cut 60 percent of the waste that had been going to landfills, saving the company $310,000 in annual fees. The changes also improved the efficiency of latex production, worth another $420,000. Such programs obviously became attractive from a business standpoint; managers would be crazy not to pursue them. In fact, in some ways, the resulting "savings and reductions" revealed how inefficient and poorly managed many businesses were prior to the "discovery" of pollution prevention. As a group, however, these programs qualified as little more than good industrial housekeeping. In many ways, the late1980s to mid-1990s was the "low-hanging fruit" era of industrial pollution control; a time when many companies jumped on their historic inefficiencies, capturing materials, making substitutions, and cleaning up in ways that scored points for "controlling pollution." Yet these were arguably clean ups and economic improvements that should have made decades earlier.

Dow instituted its much-touted WRAP program during this time—Waste Reduction Always Pays. It also joined with environmental organizations on occasion—as it did with NRDC and other environmentalists in Michigan—to discover how it might pursue pollution and waste reductions through process and production changes. These engagements, while successful and innovative on some fronts, revealing important new ways to reduce and prevent pollution, were not pursued generally in corporate business plans (see sidebar, opposite page).

Engage & Forestall

The other key strategic goal of Dow and the chemical industry during the pro-active 1990s, was simply to keep government from further tightening regulation—the dreaded "command and control" system, as industry called it. "Better to be in the game and forestall new initiatives," went the thinking, "than be outside looking in and have new costs imposed upon you." Working with the government and teaming up with environmentalists became hallmarks of the time. After Bill Clinton and the Democrats captured the White House in 1992, Dow managed to become a player in some of the Clinton Administration's environmental programs.

Dave Buzzelli, for example, was appointed co-chair of President Clinton's Council on Sustainable Development in July 1993, a 25-member body of luminaries from industry, government and the environmental community. The Council was charged with designing strategies to move the U.S. toward sustainable development goals in line with the 1992 United Nations Earth Summit treaty. Along with co-chair Jonathan Lash of the World Resources Institute, and other prominent panel members, including EPA's Carol Browner, Interior's Bruce Babbitt, and National Wildlife Federation's Jay Hair, Buzzelli and Dow were sitting in at the very top-level discussions of the government's environmental initiatives. At the Council's opening ceremony, in fact, Buzzelli was singled out by Vice President Al Gore, who explained that the Council was the Administration's key forum to address the relationship between the economy and the environment. Gore praised Buzzelli's work in organizing roundtable discussions on the environment and the economy while at Dow Canada, calling the work "an inspiring example" of business protecting the environment. Gore said he hoped the council in its work would dispel the notion that there had to be a choice between expanding business and preserving the environment.[31] Meanwhile, on global warming, a key sustainable development issue, Dow was then a member of the Global Climate Coalition, an industry group that had lobbied against U.S. endorsement of the U.N. Global Warming Convention to reduce greenhouse emissions. But at the opening ceremony in July 1993, Buzzelli wasn't talking global warming: "We know that the economy and the environment are intertwined," he said in his remarks that day. "We know the path to sustainable development will require new policies. And we know that the path we're on today will not take us to where we want to go."[32] As the Council's

Dow & Greens Collaborate

In 1993, Dow Chemical and the environmental organization the Natural Resources Defense Council (NRDC), normally adversaries on most environmental issues, began a cooperative venture at Dow's LaPorte, Texas polyurethanes plant. In the project, NRDC sought to test the notion, popular among Dow's staff at the time, that "inflexible" government regulations worked against pollution prevention gains. In the collaboration, the partners identified a list of pollution prevention opportunities at the LaPorte plant, none of which were blocked by regulation. NRDC discovered that about 80 percent of the plant's air emissions came from the solvent monoclorobenzene. Dow's solution to reducing the releases was to vent the emissions to an on-site incinerator. In the collaboration, a less expensive solution was identified in which the solvent could be recycled at the beginning of the production process rather than incinerated. This would cut about 500,000 pounds of emissions per year and save $1.2 million, eliminating the incineration. Dow, however, passed over the recommended option in favor of other more profitable opportunities. Dow's refusal to act on the pollution prevention remedies placed a strain on the relationship with NRDC, as the group then wondered whether it was worth going forward. NRDC's Linda Greer wrote an article in *Environmental Science & Technology* detailing the failures of the LaPorte project, which made Dow recognize "there's a price to pay if they work with a group like NRDC and screw up." But the two sides continued to evaluate their differences, spent a year doing so, and finally re-tooled their arrangement. This time, they focused on Dow's Midland, Michigan complex, and NRDC recruited five longtime local critics of Dow, a step that all sides agreed was crucial to the project's credibility and impact on local managers. The five activists included Diane Hebert of Midland; Mary Sinclair, who led protests that squelched Dow's efforts in the 1970s to build a nuclear power plant in Midland; Terry Miller of the Lone Tree Council in Bay City, Michigan; Anne Hunt of Citizens for Alternatives to Chemical Contamination in Lake, Michigan; and Tracey Easthope, director of environmental health at the Ecology Center in Ann Arbor. The re-tooled effort also involved the plant's business leaders, set a specific time frame and goals, and engaged a professional facilitator. The challenge was to find big reductions at Midland that would save Dow money. Along the way, the issue of dioxin emerged, resulting from the incineration of chlorinated chemicals. Dow had long questioned the claim that incineration generates dioxin. Still, Dow vice president for environment, health and safety, Jerry Martin, convinced Dow leadership that eliminating emissions of the source chemicals would render the dioxin question moot. "Jerry said 'let's do this,'" recalls Bill Bilkovich, a pollution prevention consultant who was paid by Dow to work with the activists. That helped focus the attention of both the engineers and activists. "I don't think they've ever had that much wind at their backs before." he said. Jeff Feerer, Dow's environmental and safety manager at Midland, agrees: "It got the entire site involved in pollution prevention. It brought about a culture change." In the end, there was significant success. In April 1999, when NRDC and Dow concluded the three-year effort, the Midland project boasted a 43 percent reduction in emissions of 26 toxic chemicals—among them, several chlorinated organic compounds—with annualized savings of $5.4 million. Still, Dow had dozens of other plants worldwide. Would the same measures be applied at those plants, and would activists be involved in those locations as well? Would other chemical companies follow Dow's lead? The answer to most all of these questions—at least as of 2002—was no. NRDC's Greer tried to take the program to other companies, but found no takers, though a few expressed interest. At Dow, Greer also learned that millions of dollars in savings took on a different light in a company that had sales in the tens of billions and allocated money according to business priorities. Says Greer: "... [T]he profitability bar is set higher than I thought it was; motivating companies with 'business value' alone is not going to suffice.... I'd thought that industry would opt for cleaner production methods if doing so was a break-even proposition. But what I learned is that industry leaders have a lot of inviting things to do with their money and they don't think it makes business sense to invest dollars in pollution prevention when an investment in something else will give greater financial returns." Greer concludes that in order to be effective, pollution prevention needs to be not just profitable, but more profitable than other potential investments. "That's a real challenge," she says. The other problem Greer mentions specifically for Dow, is the company's culture: "... [W]hile I think plenty of folks at Dow do care about the environment, there's not much in the corporate culture that rewards that sort of concern. Managers don't even get bonuses or promotions for effective environmental work.... Until that changes, it will remain an uphill battle."

Sources: "Dow's Clean Air Project on Target," *Chemical Market Reporter*, October 7, 1996; *Chemical Week*, July 28, 1999, p. 8; Barnaby J. Feder, "Chemistry Cleans Up A Factory," *New York Times*, July 18, 1999; Peter Fairley, "Friend or Foe? Partnerships With Critics Yield Results," *Chemical Week*, January 12, 2000, p. 24; Barnaby J. Feder, "Dialogue on Pollution Is Allowed to Trail Off," *New York Times*, November 23, 2002; and Natural Resources Defense Council, "Environmentalists and Dow: Chemical Reduction," www.nrdc.org, as of December 2003, last updated July 17, 1999.

co-chair, Buzzelli would sign onto statements that sounded good, but typically made no date-certain commitments—such as one supporting the idea that U.S. corporations "ultimately must move to zero-discharge manufacturing."[33] In addition to Buzzelli, Dow's other senior officers also continued touting environmental values and the company's openness and dedication to improvement. It all sounded good. But not everyone was buying it.

Dow's Green Hype

"This is what we call 'Greenwash,'" explained Terry Miller, chairman of the Lone Tree Council in Michigan, describing Dow's environmental program in March of 1997, "using public relations instead of action." Miller pointed to Dow's Buzzelli as one of its key practitioners. "Buzzelli is such a prominent speaker internationally, he has done a lot to increase the green image of his company. But we have substantial disagreements." Buzzelli, in reply, would simply describe Dow's "continuing improvement" in reducing toxic pollution—and progress was being made. It was hard to ague with industry's "continuous improvement" mantra.[34]

During the time that Buzzelli served as Dow's environmental leader— roughly from 1990 through 1997—Dow went into overdrive with environmental seminars, publications, and new initiatives, generally becoming pro-active, and in many ways, "out-greening" environmental organizations, or at least appearing that way. Dow constantly churned out new programs that kept the company in motion and in the news with new commitments to

> **"This is what we call 'Greenwash,' using public relations instead of action."**
>
> Terry Miller, Lone Tree Council

reduce, or account for, pollution. The company's public relations budget for environmental purposes grew larger, into the tens of millions, projecting a "sunny Dow" to the general public. Dow took on the appearance of a company concerned about the environment. True, Dow was making progress cleaning up, but not everywhere. Behind the happy TV scenes and buoyant Dow public reports, there was still pollution and toxic chemistry released every day at Dow operations all over the world. There were also chemical accidents, worker exposures, and communities at risk.

By late 2000, the political winds had changed in the United States, as Bill Clinton and Al Gore were replaced by George Bush and Dick Cheney. Pollution prevention and environmental protection lost their luster, as industry began to see a friendlier era ahead. Successes such as those achieved by Dow in collaboration with environmentalists like NRDC became less important. Industry was generally feeling less pressure to attack pollution, as the Bush Administration began sending clear signals that it was willing to relax environmental regulations and enforcement. Voluntary pollution prevention and pollution control programs are typically embraced by industry when it feels threatened by the possibility of tougher regulation, as appeared to be the case in the 1990s. By 2002, most of the people at Dow's Midland operation who had participated in the collaboration with NRDC and the Michigan activists were gone or retired. But Dow officials claimed their company had "hundreds of projects" like the one at Midland underway to further reduce pollution. Yet clearly, the shifting political winds were a factor. "The people at the edges of the companies trying to be creative and act in enlightened self interest melt away when you get an administration not interested in enforcement," says Eric Schaeffer, a former EPA enforcement official who resigned in February 2002 when it became clear where the Bush Administration was heading.[35] Meanwhile, the concerns about chlorinated chemistry and dioxin had not gone away, even as newer revelations emerged about developmental toxicity and body burden.

More Chemical Roulette

Through the 1990s, a worrisome collection of scientific information was building on changing health patterns in wildlife and human populations. Among the data were those on certain cancers and declining sperm counts. In 1992, researchers in Denmark reported that human male sperm counts had dropped almost 50 percent between 1938 and 1990. The Danish scientists also noted an unexplained rise in testicular cancer in northern Europe. Other studies pointed to specific suspect chemicals. In 1993, at Mt. Sinai Medical Center in New York, investigators discovered that the blood of women with breast cancer had a significantly higher amount of a DDT byproduct than the blood of healthy women. In Detroit a few years later, the offspring of women who ate large amounts of fish from the Great Lakes—presumably containing high levels of PCBs—had a higher rate of disabilities than other school age children. A few scientists, including Dr. Theo Colborn, a zoologist at the World Wildlife Fund in Washington, D.C., had been ruminating on these and other data for a decade or more. Colborn and colleagues had also been re-examining studies of bird and animal reproductive problems dating to the 1950s. Colborn began to formulate a common link among these findings—what she and others would call endocrine disrupting chemicals. Synthetic chemicals such as PCBs, DDT, dioxin, and others were slipping into cellular chemistry, binding to receptor sites on a cell's membrane where hormones normally do their signaling. Some of the invading chemicals became "mimics," replacing hormones and disrupting normal hormonal activity; creating developmental and reproductive havoc.

Scientists warned in 1991 that synthetic chemicals were disrupting human hormones and threatening human embryonic development.

By July 1991, Colborn and her colleagues convened a meeting at the Wingspread Conference Center in Racine, Wisconsin to discuss the findings and concerns. They focused on reproductive hazards to wildlife and people. As a group, they issued the first Wingspread Statement, concluding that endocrine disrupting chemicals had already damaged many wildlife populations by causing thyroid dysfunction, decreased fertility, decreased hatching success, behavioral abnormalities, feminization and demasculation in males, and compromised immune systems. The scientists warned that many people around the world were being exposed to the same chemicals causing problems in wildlife and lab animals, and that unless the chemicals

Chem Spin 101

Dow Chemical and other major chemical companies do some of their best politicking and image-building anonymously through trade associations such as the American Chemistry Council, the National Agricultural Chemicals Association, the Chlorine Chemistry Council, the Vinyl Institute, and others. The chemical companies—acting alone, through their trade groups, or some ad-hoc, organizational creation-of-the-moment—also hire professional public relations firms and private investigators to assist them in designing and conducing campaigns, public or private. In the 1960s, the industry mounted campaigns attacking Rachel Carson after her *Silent Spring* raised public health and environmental concerns about chemical pesticides. But since the mid-1980s, in particular, the chemical industry's image-building and PR activities have risen to a new level. Whether it's Dow touting its own corporate image through upbeat T.V. ads, or the American Chemistry Council singing the praises of Responsible Care, public relations imagery is a very important part of what the modern chemical industry is all about. Tens of millions of dollars are spent annually, and thousands of person-hours invested in projecting the right ad campaign, the right spin on a controversial issue, or generating the right kind of grassroots support or opposition for state and federal legislation. "Chem PR" has become its own cottage industry with its own celebrities and high-paid hit men and women. Several books have appeared in recent years, including *Toxic Sludge Is Good For You* and *Trust Us, We're Experts*, detailing some of the chemical industry's PR activities.

In October 2003, the American Chemistry Council (ACC) held a major PR conference in Miami under the banner "Communicating in a Volatile World," with a range of seminars devoted to handling the media, dealing with activists, and anticipating public relations problems. In the category of "Winning the Media War," for example, participants were advised to find "a credible and comforting person" to carry the industry's message in times of disaster, or when responding to a particular environmental or health issue. "This person may not be your company CEO," explained the instructor, "it may be the fire chief, or the mayor." During chemical disasters, PR folks should also focus on "the response and coordination"—playng up the involvement of the police and fire departments, hospitals, Red Cross, etc. "Do not refer to the chemicals," advised one spokesperson—or to failures at the chemical plant or in the transportation system that might have caused the disaster. In another series of sessions titled, "What the American Chemistry Council Fears," toxic chemicals and human health were the central subject, with the industry worrying in particular about how to handle "body burden" issues—i.e., toxic chemicals accumulating in human blood and body tissue—and the prospect of "chemical trespass" lawsuits. The industry's PR maestros also worried about "worst-case" PR disasters, such as the possibility of a major chemical plant accident occurring where the industry was not prepared to handle the bad PR—accidents that could taint the entire industry. The "precautionary principle"—a look-before-you-leap idea applied to new chemical introduction that has become popular among scientists and environmentalists—also came in for a round of attention at the PR gathering. And when spin fails, there's always the next level—political warfare, spying on activists, and even dirty tricks.

In California, concerns about the gaining favor of the precautionary principle led one ACC lobbyist to draft a November 2003 memo suggesting the industry hire a Washington-based firm, Nichols-Dezenhall, to conduct selective intelligence gathering on precautionary principle "movement leadership." Nichols-Dezenhall, a firm that uses former FBI and CIA agents in its business, has been known to go to some lengths to serve its clients' interests. The memo also suggested that a precautionary principle front group be established in California to help muddy the water.

Sources: Frank Graham, Jr., *Since Silent Spring*, Boston: Houghton Mifflin Co., 1970; Monique Harden and Natalie Walker, "What The Chemical Industry Fears," *Rachel's Environment & Health News*, #779, October 10, 2003; and, Environmental Working Group, "Chemical Industry's Secret Plan To Attack California's Anti-Toxics Trend," www.ewg.org, November 2003.

were controlled, the human race would risk widespread disruption in human embryonic development, inflicting damage that could last a lifetime.

In early 1996, endocrine disrupting chemicals received more popular attention with the publication of the book, *Our Stolen Future,* written by Theo Colborn, journalist Dianne Dumanoski, and zoologist John Peterson Myers. At the book's release, Colborn observed that scientists and policy makers "had been preoccupied" about whether or not exposure to toxic chemicals caused cancer. "As a result," she said, "we've missed something else going on [in the environment] with even more wider and more disturbing implications." Co-author Myers was astounded with what they uncovered. "This is going to lead to whole new way to think about epidemiology, toxicology, risk, health and they way we do business," he predicted.[36] The chemical industry, however, didn't see it quite the same way.

"We view this book as raising a theory," said CMA's Sandra Tirey at the time. "There appears to be a fair amount of disagreement in the scientific community about the interpretation of the data." CMA also prepared a point-by-point rebuttal of what it charged were uncertainties and errors in the book.[37] Christopher Klose, vice president of communications at the American Crop Association, worried about all the hype at the time of the book's release. "Our initial impression of the book is that it basically indicts modern society since World War II. We're concerned that complicated, sensitive subjects like this in a fast-paced society with the media seeking sound-bite solutions will end in science being trammeled."[38]

Dow Chemical, which had received some of Colborn's initial writings in January 1994, had drafted a short position paper on the subject, portions of which were often incorporated into Dow letters responding to queries on the issue:

...Like others, including Dr. Colborn herself, we believe her hypothesis needs confirmation, both in well controlled experimental studies in animals and via epidemiology studies in humans.

It is imperative to note that Dow supports the need for ongoing research regarding this issue. We support the further development of a valid test for use in screening chemicals for their potential to disrupt the endocrine system. We are currently working with colleagues from the Chlorine Chemistry Council as well as other scientists, to better understand the available evidence on endocrine effects. And we are participating in the development of potential screening tools.

We would like to point out that Dr. Colborn's hypothesis raises issues that extend beyond chlorine. Scientists will need to focus on all chemicals and their potential to disrupt the endocrine system. There is no evidence to date that the presence of chlorine on a molecule makes it a greater or unique endocrine simulator. Nevertheless, we continue to take this issue and any other credible hypothesis seriously and will evaluate it further...[39]

Generally, Dow took the position that it had not been demonstrated that persistent toxic chemicals such as PCBs, dioxins, furans, DDT, and others were capable of causing endocrine effects "at the very low levels they are typically encountered in the environment."[40]

Still, subsequent meetings of scientists through the 1990s confirmed the earliest concerns about endocrine-disrupting chemicals, with more alarms being raised. By the mid-1990s, more than 120 chemicals were reported to have reproductive and or endocrine-disrupting effects. More than 80 of these were pesticides or pesticide additives, and about 40 were industrial chemicals.[41] Dioxins, furans, and chemicals such as bisphenol-A, which Dow produced, were among them. By 1996, Dow and the Chemical Manufacturers Association (now the American Chemistry Council) were working with EPA, FDA, and others on a system to prioritize which endocrine-disrupting chemicals should be tested first. But the tests themselves were not yet developed, and appeared to be several years away. After testing, exposure levels would be set—levels that would constitute for some, an acceptable risk. "Currently," said Dow's Greg Bond, global director of product stewardship in October 1996, "we believe there are safe levels of exposure."[42] By 2001, no test for endocrine-disrupting chemicals had been developed in the United States.

Testing Games

The revelations about endocrine-disrupting chemicals, and what was not known about many synthetic chemicals already in commerce, underscored once again the general lack of before-hand toxicological testing of chemicals. The testing and "tox screening" issues had been debated for years, and the chemical industry—and Dow—had always been in the forefront of that debate. In fact, Dow's people sometimes had special access to decision makers in ways that derailed efforts to develop better and more comprehensive chemical testing.

In the late 1970s, for example, a voluntary, chemical testing initiative, aimed at industry, was moving through the Organization of Economic Cooperation and Development (OECD). European Common Market countries already required a series of pre-market health and environmental tests on new chemicals. In the U.S., the Carter Administration had generally supported the OECD move to tighten chemical testing and make the initiative mandatory. But that changed in 1981 with the election of Ronald Reagan. The chemical industry then, among others, gained improved access to government policy makers.

In 1982, a Dow executive, had some private "face time" with a U.S. Ambassador helping reverse the U.S. position on a pending OECD chemical testing initiative opposed by the industry.

In June 1982, Donald D. McCollister, a Dow Chemical executive, had some private "face time" with U.S. Ambassador Abraham Katz in Paris to discuss the pending OECD chemical testing initiative, then drafted as a voluntary requirement. McCollister was a private interest representative to the U.S. delegation. But other U.S. reps to the delegation—including Kristine Hall of the Environmental Defense Fund, serving as a public-interest representative to the delegation, and Irving Fuller, EPA's official representative—were excluded from the meeting with the ambassador. McCollister had exclusive access.[43]

According to an internal EPA memo prepared for EPA Administrator Anne M. Burford, McCollister gave Katz "an earful in a private conversation" with "revealing results." Essentially, explained the memo, McCollister gave the ambassador "the chemical industry view of OECD activities." Dow's position was that the U.S. approval system for new chemicals under the Toxic Substances Control Act was sufficient to protect the public. In any case, the ambassador got the message: "[Katz] now understands the need to reverse the previous administration's drive to change U.S. laws and regulations through decisions taken in international organizations...," explained the memo. But a December 1982 vote on the matter was pending, and EPA's Anne Burford was urged to attend an October meeting of the group. "[Y]ou personally must inform your international peers of the administration approach to chemicals if we are to succeed in changing directions," wrote Richard Funkhouser, the agency's director of international affairs, in the memo to Burford. Burford subsequently met with the group in Paris six weeks before the vote, and in December the new testing proposal was effectively blocked.[44]

Rubbertown

Rubbertown is the name of an industrial area of Louisville, Kentucky, along the Ohio River. In the 1940s, some American corporations and the federal government teamed up at Rubbertown in a crash World War II effort to produce synthetic rubber. Following the war, the complex grew and attracted other petrochemical producers. Although much economic benefit came to the area as a result, so did major environmental and public health problems, some of which still fester today. Among Rubbertown's current polluters is a business named DuPont-Dow Elastomers.

In 1996, DuPont and Dow formed DuPont-Dow Elastomers, a joint venture to produce rubber-based synthetic materials known as elastomers for the automotive, chemical, construction, rubber, and cable industries. The venture combined DuPont's global market position in synthetic rubber with Dow technology. The new venture immediately became the industry leader in chloroelastomers, ethylene elastomers, and fluorinated elastomers. Among its product lines are: *Engage,* a polyolefin elastomer; *Hypalon,* a chlorosulfonated polyethylene; *Kalrez* used in perfluoro elastomer parts; *Neoprene,* a poly-chloroprene; *Nordel,* a hydrocarbon rubber; *Tyrin* a chlorinated polyethylene; and *Viton,* a fluoro elastomer. Within four years of its creation, DuPont-Dow Elastomers was a $1 billion business with affiliates and subsidiaries in more than 25 countries. Its U.S. plants, including one in Rubbertown, make rubber for shoe soles, telephone cords, electric extension cords, joint boots in automobiles, hoses, and inflatable boats. DuPont-Dow Elastomers in Rubbertown also makes pollution, some of which, in the form of wastewater, is sent to the Metropolitan Sewer District (MSD) of Louisville, one of the most heavily overworked municipal sewer systems in the nation. The MSD is charged, in part, with handling the industrial load of pollutants that comes from all the Rubbertown companies. Even though the wastewater is supposedly pretreated by the contributing companies, the MSD is frequently overtaxed by the wastes, which often arrive in violation of existing industrial standards, causing the MSD to by-pass treatment and release material directly into the Ohio River. DuPont-Dow Elastomers has been among the violators.

In 1999, "rubber masses" in the wastes sent to the Morris Forman treatment plant, were found to be 99 percent neoprene rubber—material exclusively produced by DuPont-Dow. But 1999 wasn't the first time DuPont-Dow had been cited for this particular problem. The operation had been a chronic offender with its rubbery wastewater. Since 1995, DuPont-Dow had paid the MSD a total of $447,500 in fines as a result of repetitive violations. In February 1999, a consent order was signed between DuPont-Dow and the MSD to rectify the problem. DuPont-Dow agreed to install an on-site pretreatment process at its plant, with the new process slated to go on line by December 31, 2000. Since then, however, the DuPont-Dow plant has been cited by the MSD for spills, breakdowns, and equipment failure. In May 2001, coagulated rubber was getting into the wastewater being sent to the Morris Forman plant. In June 2001, neoprene rubber was found in the waste stream after a sludge pump was blocked. In January 2001, equipment failure at DuPont-Dow caused dichlorobutene to be released into the sewer. That same month the failure of a catalyst pump at DuPont-Dow led to a

180-pound discharge of 1,3, dichlorobutane-2 into the wastewater.

Air pollution from DuPont-Dow's Rubbertown operation is also a problem. In fact, overall emissions as measured by the EPA Toxic Release Inventory in 1999 and 2000 showed an increase in total air emissions by DuPont-Dow—from 590,000 pounds in 1999 to nearly 650,000 pounds in 2000. Emissions of chloroprene, which come exclusively from the manufacture of neoprene, are of special concern. In 2001, the DuPont-Dow Rubbertown plant released more than 516,000 pounds of chloroprene—the nation's largest single source. DuPont-Dow's chloroprene emissions have included both chronic and high-spike releases, some of which have occurred in the vicinity of the Cane Run Elementary School and the Farnsley Middle School. A December 2003 report to the Louisville Metro Air Pollution Control District found potentially harmful levels of chloroprene in 2000 and 2001 coming from the plant and blowing into a nearby residential neighborhood. The high levels—nine to 14 times above what could cause health problems—were reported by a private consulting firm, Sciences International, from two air monitors near the plant on Camp Ground Road and Ralph Avenue. Even though the plant is slated to close in 2006, Art Williams, director of the Metro air district, said the risk projections at one location are high enough to trigger immediate discussions. "We'll be talking in very short order to DuPont-Dow Elastomers about what steps they can take to reduce chloroprene emissions," said Williams in December 2003. Long-term exposure to chloroprene can cause liver and cardiovascular damage, among other problems, according to EPA. Symptoms of long-term exposure in workers can include chest pains, giddiness, irritability, dermatitis, hair loss and a weakened immune system. Although EPA has not classified chloroprene as a human carcinogen, a National Toxicology Program study has found evidence that it can cause cancer in rats and mice. Toluene, a known reproductive and developmental toxin, is also emitted by DuPont-Dow operations in Rubbertown, and was found in air samples taken at the Cane Run Elementary School location.

Elsewhere, other DuPont-Dow Elastomers plants have also had substantial emissions in recent years. In 1999, the DuPont-Dow plant in Beaumont, Texas ranked in the top 90th percentile of dirtiest or worst plants for its emissions of volatile organic compounds, spewing more than 845 tons of those compounds. The DuPont-Dow Elastomers plant in LaPlace, Louisiana, also known as the Pontchartrain Works, ranked in the top 90th percentile of dirtiest or worst facilities nationally in 2000 for both total environmental releases—nearly 540,000 pounds—and emissions of recognized carcinogens, at more than 400,000 pounds. In 2001, DuPont-Dow's LaPlace and Rubbertown plants together accounted for virtually all (99.9 percent) of the chloroprene emissions in the United States—some 913,000 pounds.

Sources: Metropolitan Sewer District, Louisville, Kentucky, News Release, April 26, 1999; Wilma Subra, Subra Co., New Iberia, Louisiana, "Results of the West Jefferson County Air Toxics Study in the Rubbertown Area of Louisville, Kentucky," December 2002; Correspondence of Wilma Subra, Subra Co., September 9, 2003; James Bruggers, "Tests Detect High Level of Chemical," *Louisville Courier-Journal*, December 10, 2003; and Environmental Defense, *www.scorecard.org*.

A delegate from Sweden, Dr. Rune Lonngren, told *Washington Post* reporter Cass Peterson that the U.S. "officially acted through normal channels, but I guess McCollister had a say in the U.S. viewpoint. He has made clear to me that he is not in favor of the testing rules, believing they are unnecessarily cumbersome for industry." Lonngren said he was "surprised" when he discovered that the U.S. wanted to reverse its longstanding support for the testing rules. "More and more it came out that the United States would not like action" on the rules, he explained. "We wanted a decision paper, a binding paper. When it turned out that was not possible, we tried for a recommendation that would be morally binding but not legally binding." Lonngren said he was surprised when the United States did not support that either.[45]

In Europe, Dow and the American Chemistry Council have been doing their best to hype the costs, reduce the list, and slow down the adoption of the European REACH process.

From the late 1970s on—basically, after the Toxic Substances Control Act of 1976 was passed—Dow and the chemical industry used TSCA to discourage other testing initiatives, despite the fact that TSCA offered a very limited testing protocol. Of the 100,000 existing registered chemicals worldwide, only about 400 have complete toxicological profiles. In the more limited chemical universe of what are called High Production Volume (HPV) chemicals, there are at least 2,500 chemicals used heavily in global commerce. At least half of these were identified in the mid-1990s as being insufficiently profiled from a hazards standpoint. In 1998, U.S. vice president Al Gore, called for more risk assessment on the HPV chemicals—a program now underway at EPA. The chemical industry, and Dow, are involved in the life-cycle assessment of both HPV and other chemicals, and the industry is sharing the cost of making these assessments. Dow currently produces 177 chemicals that qualify as HPV chemicals, 35 of which are unique to Dow. As of 2001, Dow reported it was "on track" to meet its HPV testing commitments.[46]

In Europe, meanwhile, something called the REACH protocol—a new regimen for chemical safety and toxicological testing—was introduced in 2001 by the European Commission, the executive arm of the 15-nation European Union (EU). In recent years, the EU has become more aggressive in protecting public health and safety, frustrating American and other multinational corporations that need to trade with European nations, but don't particularly like their regulations. America, meanwhile, has fallen behind the Europeans on some public health and safety measures. REACH stands for Registration, Evaluation and Authorization of Chemicals. The new protocol would make it mandatory for chemical manufactures to reapply for the registration—and establish the safety—of some 30,000 chemicals currently on the market, as well as new ones introduced between now and 2006. Although U.S. companies volunteered in 1998 to screen some 3,000 HPV chemicals for environmental and health hazards by 2005, U.S. policy still allows the use of some 30,000 chemicals that predate testing requirements under the Toxic Substances Control Act of 1976.

For its part, Dow says it favors "a globally consistent system of regulating chemicals based on sound science," and that it is working through its trade associations in American, Europe, and Canada "to deliver a unified, scientifically based, advocacy position to support our point of view."[47] In Europe, however, Dow and the American Chemistry Council have been doing their best to hype the costs, reduce the list, and slow down the adoption of the European REACH process. The American Chemistry Council, for example, says REACH could cost U.S. companies some $8 billion in direct testing over the next decade—a figure certainly inflated since costs will be shared by a consortium of producers. The ACC also says that testing costs could force specialty companies out of business, raise liabilities, and stifle innovation. Ultimately, says the ACC—bordering on a kind of economic blackmail—some U.S. manufacturers might have to stop doing business in the EU.

Dow and the ACC have also recruited U.S. government agencies to their cause. "The U.S. State and Commerce departments, the Environmental Protection Agency, and the office of the U.S. Trade Representative," reported the *Wall Street Journal* in September 2003, "have sided with companies, including Dow Chemical Co., Rohm & Haas Co., and Lyondell Chemical Co., and trade groups in opposing the EU's chemical-testing initiative." This U.S.-based block of opponents pushed the EU in May 2003 to revise the testing proposal, exempting a number of chemicals from the list—those that don't come in direct contact with humans.[49] Yet many of these same chemicals, or their byproducts, make their way into the environment as pollutants and/or food-chain contaminants.

Sustainable Development?

At home and abroad, meanwhile, Dow has continues to tout its corporate environmentalism more than ever. Numerous publications, progress reports, and special initiatives come regularly from Dow corporate headquarters and many of its manufacturing locations. Dow executives too, continue to be visible on environmental topics on the speaking circuit. Andrew N. Liveris, recently named president and chief operating officer at Dow, spoke to engineering students at a manufacturing seminar at the University of Michigan in February 2002, before he became president. Here's some of what he offered:

> ...It's no secret that when it comes to reputation, the chemical industry's...is not as high as that of many other industries. Those of us who

work in chemical companies want to change this. And this is why our industry is so focused upon improving our environmental health and safety performance. We also are very committed to a concept termed sustainable development.

...Sustainable development is the new way to think about economic viability, environmental integrity and social equity as an integrated whole. It's commercial development that meets the needs of the present without compromising the ability of future generations to meet their own needs. In practical terms it means managing a business toward a goal of no accidents, no injuries and no harm to the environment. It means achieving environmental and social excellence goals while you meet financial goals. We call this the triple bottom line.

Achieving sustainable development goals is vital for every industry, but I think the chemical industry is really leading the way. We want our critics to track our results and hold us accountable as we continuously improve our performance....[49]

Yet, Dow's performance does not match this rhetoric. True, Dow may well have met its own internal goals of environmental and social excellence, but these do not necessarily mean the world is a safer place as a result. For Dow's operations today are not safe and its chemicals remain dangerous. The one constant encroachment of Dow throughout its 100 plus years of operation has been the crossing of biological boundary lines with products and byproducts that invade and do harm to living things. Some of this, obviously, has been the intentional design of products that kill by way of chemical poisoning. Yet too much of it has also been the unintended but tolerated consequence of chemical manufacturing and/or chemical products that do lasting biological harm. That is not sustainable development, no matter what spin is applied. Nor is it responsible or ethical environmentalism—or ethical or responsible business—whatever color it is painted.

Dow needs to formulate and adopt an exit strategy and business plan to move away from the chemistry of harm.

Dow needs to formulate and adopt an exit strategy and business plan to move away from the chemistry of harm. For it will only be a matter of time before the concepts of molecular and biological trespass—embracing transgressions of the damaging chemical variety—begin to permeate the legislatures, liability law, and the courts.

As of December 2003, for example, a proposed bill in the California state senate would establish a "biomonitoring" program in the state, allowing people in selected communities to volunteer their blood, urine, or breast milk for testing to determine the nature and quantity of pollutants and toxic chemicals in their bodies. Such programs—and the public health law that could flow from them—may soon expand to more states. The federal government's Centers Disease Control (CDC) is already doing limited tracking of body burden chemicals in small sample groups. CDC is tracking some 116 chemicals, and has granted funds to 33 states to plan their own programs.[50] Dow and the chemical industry would do well to help expedite these programs rather than stand in their way, helping to identify which chemicals are now resulting in harmful exposures and which ones should be phased out and/or removed from the market.

12.
Silicone

Science has invented all these new wonderful things. Why shouldn't we use them?

Carol Doda, topless dancer, mid-1960s
on silicone breast enhancement

It was in July 1991 that Colleen Swanson tried to take off the bandages. Weeks earlier, she had silicone breast implants surgically removed from her body in a three-hour operation at Mount Sinai Medical Center in Cleveland, Ohio. After a long series of illnesses, and the discovery that one of the implants had been leaking, she decided to have them removed. The implants had been in her body for 17 years. Colleen's ordeal is described by *Business Week* reporter John Byrne, who later wrote a book on the subject with the help of Colleen's husband, John Swanson, titled *Informed Consent*:

> ...Ever since her surgery, she had tried to imagine how she would look. A petite woman of 55, Colleen was always impeccably turned out, her quietly tasteful clothes reflecting her conservative Midwestern background. She had sought the implants only to bring her small, uneven breasts closer to average. Now she wondered: Would she despise her appearance? Would John? "I knew it was going to be bad," she says, "because my surgeon had told me that most of my breast tissue had been destroyed."
>
> She spent hours that morning summoning her courage. At last, she eased herself into a warm bath and gently splashed water over the bandages in hopes the water would penetrate the plastic tape and lessen the pain of its removal. But the bath failed to loosen the dressing, and for a time she gave up.
>
> That afternoon, she tried again. Alone in her bedroom, she lowered the shades and lay on the bed. She began to pull at the tape, gritting her teeth against the pain. Only when the bandages were tossed aside did she glance down. What she saw made her cry out, then shut her eyes, not wanting to see any more.
>
> She climbed out of bed and walked to the bathroom, consciously

avoiding the full-length mirror on the bedroom wall, and went to the smaller mirror over the sink. Before flicking on the light, she closed her eyes once more and tensed. Finally, she stared at her reflection.

Thick, red, six-inch scars curved across each side of her chest where the creases beneath her breasts had been. Instead of breasts, there were just ridges of folded, discolored skin—like deflated balloons that had held air a long time. The left side of her chest, where more silicone had apparently leaked into her body, was nearly concave.

Colleen stared at herself for four or five minutes. She didn't recognize the frightened and pitiful woman whose trembling body was forever disfigured. Finally, she stepped into the shower and let the water wash the dried blood from the wounds. She tried to calm herself and relax, but she couldn't hold back the sobbing. "I cried and cried and cried," she recalls. "I cried for a long time."[1]

The implants Colleen Swanson's doctors had placed in her body in 1974 were made by the Dow Corning Company. "I should have had an informed choice," she later said. "If there had been one chance in a million of something going wrong, I wouldn't have done the implants. I felt betrayed by Dow Corning."

Dow-Corning

In 1875, a company named Corning founded by Amory Houghton, provided Thomas Edison with glass for his first electric lightbulbs. Corning soon became an innovative company turning out new products based on sand and quartz. By 1915, it had developed *Pyrex* heat-resistant glass. In 1938, its inventors produced the company's first samples of silicone resin. Two years later, Corning teamed up with a group of Dow Chemical scientists who were also working on silicone products. By 1942, Willard Dow and Corning president Glen Cole had a hand-shake agreement on the idea of a joint venture, and ten months later, a new company, Dow Corning, half owned by Dow and half by Corning, was formed. It was soon producing silicone-based products to help the Allies during World War II. *Dow Corning 4*, an engine grease, enabled B-17s to fly at 35,000 feet, an important strategic factor in the Allied war effort. In 1945, *Dow Corning 35*, an emulsifier used in tire molds, and *Pan Glaze,* a substance which made baking pans stick-proof and easier to clean, were instant successes on the home front.[2]

Silicone became the new company's key product. The substance had remarkable qualities. It was stronger than plastic and more flexible than glass, could withstand temperatures up to 900 degrees Fahrenheit, and it did not react with most other chemicals. The new substance could also be changed from a solid to a fluid state, depending on temperature and pressure. In liquid forms, silicone was used to lubricate high performance machinery, to waterproof leather, and clean optical equipment. In semi-solid form, the substance was used in silicone bathtub caulk and wall treatments. Some rubber products, such as infant pacifiers, were made with silicone. In the 1960s, it also found its way into *Silly Putty*, a children's clay-like substance. In the medical arena, silicone found applications in tubing for blood and dialysis equipment, and for coating needles to facilitate injections. It was also used for prostheses for joints and cartilage replacements. And it also began to be used for cosmetic purposes.[3] Dow Corning, meanwhile, had expanded rapidly; by 1969, the company had operations worldwide. But silicone was always at its core. "Over time," wrote one *Fortune* journalist, "the company culture had instilled in its employees an almost child-like awe at the wonders of silicone."[4]

Injections & Implants

Silicone attracted the attention of surgeons who found it ideal for plastic surgery—fluid enough to inject, and becoming a near-solid material once it gelled in the body at room temperature. Not only was silicone used by cosmetic surgeons to smooth out facial wrinkles, it also began to be injected directly into women's breasts to "enhance" or enlarge them. Some breast-replacement techniques, dating to the late 1940s, had been developed using non-sili-

By 1976, a law requiring proof of safety for medical devices was passed by Congress, but lobbyists convinced FDA to make an exception for silicone breast implants.

cone-based material in implantable sponges. But the sponges proved problematic because they had no outer envelope encasing the material. Human tissue would grow into the sponges, resulting in hard formations of scar tissue. Silicone injections, meanwhile, continued to be used cosmetically. However, in 1965, after a series of medical problems developed, including death, silicone injections were classified as a drug. Still, physicians continued using the substance under "research" allowances, and Dow Corning continued to sell it to doctors who said they were continuing research, or using it for approved uses such as a lubricant for artificial joints and catheters. But the practice of silicone injections for breast enlargement continued, prompting at least one state, Nevada, to outlaw the practice in 1975. By 1976, a law requiring proof of safety for medical devices was passed by Congress, but lobbyists convinced FDA to make an exception for silicone breast implants, which by then had been on the market for about a dozen years.[5]

In the late 1950s, two doctors, Thomas Cronin, a surgeon at Baylor University, and Frank Gerow, a resident working with Cronin, were searching for a better breast prosthesis. Seeking a replacement that would produce a good cosmetic result but not pose a threat to a woman's health, Gerow came up with the idea of encasing salt water inside an inflatable silicone bag, similar to blood bags he'd experienced as a working resident. Once in position, the bags could be inflated and then filled

Dow Corning's first silicone breast implants—trade-named *Silastic*—went on the market in 1964.

with the necessary amount of saline. But after an exploratory meeting at Dow Corning's offices, Dow's public relations manager, Silas Braley, indicated that placing a valve on the bag might create deterioration problems over time, and suggested the doctors

fill the bags with liquid silicone gel—material that would "duplicate the feeling of the normal breast." Braley also later told Cronin that the silicone gel would have the same chemistry as the material used in the silicone bags and that he would expect "minimal reaction to it" by a woman's body.[6] Both doctors, however, were aware of the problems associated with liquid silicone injections, but they came to believe, with assurances from Dow Corning,* that if the silicone gel was encased within a thin envelope of silicone polymer, the substance would not migrate into women's bodies. "This assumption," writes Susan Zimmerman in *Silicone Survivors*, "was not based on clinical trials involving human subjects, nor on animal studies. At the time, FDA had no protocol for testing medical devices, nor did [it] have the jurisdiction to regulate these devices once they were in use."[7] Since silicone had been employed in other medical applications, including brain and eye surgery, without any reported complications, Dow Corning and the doctors assumed human bodies could tolerate the new contemplated silicone implants. The two doctors, working with Dow Corning's assistance and prototypes, designed their first silicone implant in 1961, and surgically implanted the device for the first time a year later. By 1963, the silicone implant was presented to the Society of Plastic Surgeons, by then patented by Dr. Cronin as the "Cronin implant," assigning the rights to the Dow Corning Corporation. The patent application described the new invention as a "totally implantable, non-reactive device" to be placed within the human body. Dow Corning proceeded to market it as safe and effective, touting its "softness, contour, and fluid-like mobility of the normal breast."[8]

---

*"Braley's assurances to Cronin and Gerow that silicone gel would be safe," writes John Byrne in *Informed Consent*, "...were not based on clinical trials involving human beings. Nor were they based on animal studies using miniature implants. Cronin did perform some rudimentary dog studies of his own, putting miniature versions of the implants in no more than six dogs—two of which were studied for 18 months. But when autopsies were done on the animals, he did not do extensive microscopic studies of their organs." When Gerow installed the first pair of silicone implants in Houston in March 1962, he and Cronin were still performing their limited dog study. See John Byrne, *Informed Consent*, pp. 47–48.

Dow Corning's first silicone breast implants—trade-named *Silastic*—went on the market in 1964. Three years later, according to one estimate, 40,000 American women had silicone breast implants. But soon the early version of this implant had problems. In order to keep in place, *Dacron* patches on the back of the device were used to adhere it to the pectoral muscle. Inflammatory reactions sometimes resulted, leading to scar tissue, **Silicone implants, placed on a piece of paper, left a greasy stain.** which made implant removal very difficult if not insurmountable. These and other complications pushed scientists during the 1970s to make modifications in the devices.[9]

At Dow Corning and other manufacturers, the outer silicone shell was made thinner, and the silicone gel inside was altered to make it less viscous and more fluid, to improve the natural feel. The new implants were so flexible in fact, that surgeons could insert them into a woman's body through very small incisions, leaving little- to barely-noticeable scarring. But these "new & improved" implants had a significant problem that would later draw much attention. Beginning in 1978, evidence in medical journals increasingly suggested the devices were permeable—that free flowing silicone gel could slowly leak out of them over time and into women's bodies. The leakage problem, apparently, was not rocket science, as silicone implants placed on a piece of paper left a greasy stain. Internal memos would later reveal that Dow Corning officials were fully aware that implants leaked even before they began marketing them.[10]

In U.S. society during the 1960s and 1970s, implants had not received much attention. However, in September 1977, that changed with a couple of articles that appeared in *Ms.* magazine, the feminist publication founded by Gloria Steinhem. One article—with a headline that warned of "A 60% Complication Rate for an Operation You Don't Need"—told of "infections, deformities, excessive hardness, painful and disfiguring scars...." The *Ms.* article also accused Dow Corning of selling "inadequately tested implants." It quoted one plastic surgeon who suggested that animal tests, such as they were, might not be enough. "You cannot compare a test of any implant on a rabbit for 18 months with a breast implant a young woman might have in her body for 30 to 40 years," said Dr. David White. "It would seem that the patients are serving as rabbits for testing these implants."[11] Also in 1977, the first lawsuit was brought against Dow Corning over a ruptured implant. Lawyers for a Cleveland woman argued in a Houston courtroom that her ruptured implants, and subsequent operations, had caused her pain and suffering. She received a $170,000 settlement from Dow Corning, but the case received little public notice. Shortly thereafter, one of Ralph Nader's Washington, D.C.-based public interest groups, Public Citizen, began warning women about possible health consequences of implants.[12]

In 1984 in San Francisco, a key lawsuit was brought on behalf of Maria Stern, the first woman to allege that her implants were linked to auto-immune symptoms and disease. After a month-long trial, the jury found that Stern's illnesses were attributable to silicone and awarded her $211,000 in compensatory damages. The jury also found Dow Corning guilty of fraud and called for $1.5 million in punitive damages. Dow appealed the case and lost, and then appealed again, but settled before the second appeal was heard. The evidence in the case was sealed and the expert witnesses involved were also bound by the seal. Stern's attorney in the case, Dan Bolton, had discovered a mother lode of internal Dow Corning documents from a Dow storage area—documents which proved to be decisive in the case, but with the court seal in place, were not made public.

In 1977, the first lawsuit was brought against Dow Corning over a ruptured implant.

On the regulatory front, implants were still exempt from the 1976 proof-of-safety requirement for medical devices. Only in June of 1988, did FDA finally order manufacturers to demonstrate the safety of silicone implants, bringing them under the law for the first time. Manufacturers such as Dow Corning were then required (by July 1991) to submit studies and data to the FDA under the FDA's "Pre-Market Approval" (PMA) process. Still, through the late 1980s, breast implantation was one of the most common procedures performed by plastic surgeons.

The general public, meanwhile, began hearing more about breast implants. In December 1990, a TV special on *Face to Face With Connie Chung* aired a program on the dangers of silicone breast implants. "It was a milestone of sorts," wrote John Byrne of the show, "because it was the first time on national television that a medical authority, Dr. Douglas Shanklin, a University of Tennessee pathologist, put the issue Dow Corning most feared out in front: 'Silicone gets right into the heart of the immune system,' he said."[13] In Washington, congressional hearings by Rep. Ted Weiss (D-NY), exploring the safety of silicone implants, raised questions about information locked up under the 1984 court seal. Dr. Sydney Wolfe of Public Citizen had already sued the FDA to obtain these and other documents, but no decision had then been rendered.[14]

In the summer of 1991, although Dow Corning had met the FDA deadline and submitted some 329 studies on implants, FDA found in August the data was flawed and incomplete. The agency then warned Dow and other implant makers that unless complete and satisfactory studies were submitted, silicone breast implants would be removed from the market. Meanwhile, another lawsuit against Dow Corning was argued in a San Francisco courtroom in December 1991 by attorney Dan Bolton—the attorney who discovered the Dow documents used in the 1984 Maria Stern case. In the new case, Bolton's client was Mariann Hopkins, who alleged her "mixed connective-tissue disease" was linked to her ruptured silicone breast implants. The jury agreed and awarded Hopkins $7.3 million in compensation, the largest such award at the time. Bolton used new studies from Dow in the case, several of which he subsequently gave to FDA—studies the agency had not seen before.

In early January 1992, FDA Commissioner David Kessler, citing some of the new information, called for a voluntary moratorium on the distribution and implantation of silicone breast implants until FDA's advisory panel could conduct a review. The manufactur-

Dr. Douglas Shanklin put the issue Dow Corning most feared out in front: "Silicone gets right into the heart of the immune system," he said.

ers, including Dow Corning, agreed to Kessler's moratorium. A few weeks later, as the result of Public Citizen's earlier FDA lawsuit previously-withheld internal studies, memos, and sealed documents were released to the public. One of the released memos was especially revealing on the implant's "oily" problem—i.e., silicone leakage—advising Dow Corning salesmen in the mid-1970s how to deal with implant samples:

> It has been observed that the new [implants] ... have a tendency to appear oily after being manipulated. This could prove to be a problem with your daily [sales presentations to doctors] where [implant] manipulation is a must ... Keep in mind that this is not a product problem; our technical people assure us that the doctor in the O.R. will not see any appreciable oiling on products removed from the package. The oily phenomenon seems to appear the day following manipulation ... You should make plans to change demonstration samples often. Also, be sure samples are clean and dry before customer detailing. Two easy ways to clean demonstration samples while traveling: 1) wash with soap and water in the nearest washroom, dry with hand towels; 2) carry a small bottle of [cleaning fluid] and rag.[15]

Damage Control

By February 1992, Dow Corning's two parent companies—Dow Chemical and Corning—began public-relations damage control on their joint venture, and some of the drama played out at an unlikely spot: Dow Chemical's airport hangar at the Tri-Cities Airport near Midland, Michigan. There, Dow Corning CEO, Lawrence Reed, was met in a small conference room by Jamie Houghton, CEO of Corning, and Frank Popoff of Dow Chemical. Popoff and Houghton told Reed he was essentially being fired. Reed would remain as president and also carry the nominal title of chief operating officer, but he would report directly to Keith McKennon, a Dow Chemical executive who would be named Dow Corning's new chairman and CEO. McKennon was then executive vice president of Dow Chemical. He was also a Dow Corning board member, having served there since December 1987. But perhaps more importantly, McKennon had helped Dow Chemical weather some other difficult public relations battles—those with napalm and Agent Orange—earning him the nickname "fireman" for his ability to extinguish controversy. Now, at Dow Corning, Popoff and Houghton were cleaning house, trying to rebuild their venture. "Neither Houghton nor Popoff thought Reed had managed the [implant] crisis effectively," wrote John Byrne of the firing. "Later, with reporters from chemical trade magazines in the room, Popoff would issue an extraordinary public rebuke. Reed, he said, 'was not emotionally equipped to handle the controversy. When the safety of implants became an issue, the company should have been in the first phase of damage control rather than the first phase of denial.'"[16] And soon enough, there would be more damage to control—by December 1992 there were more than 3,500 individual lawsuits filed against Dow. A year later there were more than 12,300.

By this time there had been a lot more publicity about implant problems. FDA had received a total of more than 14,000 reports from women alleging adverse reactions to implants.[17] In mid-October 1992, TV talk show host Jenny Jones, had came forward on air about her own problems with silicone breast implants. Newspapers increasingly reported on implant-related risk, providing details to the public about alleged manufacturer cover-ups and anecdotes from women who claimed they were harmed by the devices. A few ongoing court cases also received close news coverage.

Implant Litigation

In 1992, after some class-action lawsuits aimed at the implant manufacturers were consolidated, settlement negotiations began with Dow Corning, Bristol-Myers Squibb, and Baxter-3M. The parties agreed to establish a fund of $4.25 billion to cover class-action claims over a 30-year period. This so-called "global settlement"—with the money offered as compensation to any woman with diseases or symptoms allegedly associated with breast implants—was approved by implant manufacturers in March 1994.[18] However, by then more than 400,000 women had filed claims under the settlement, and U. S. District Court Judge Sam C. Pointer, Jr. declared that the settlement fund was underfunded by at least $3 billion. In addition, nearly 20,000 women opted to pursue individual lawsuits against implant manufacturers outside of the settlement. At the state level, a number of lawyers were still preparing and filing individual cases. In one 1992 Texas case, tried with full television coverage and running commentary, a woman with ruptured implants and flu-like symptoms was awarded $25 million. Such judgments, some believe, resulted in additional cases being filed. By May 1995, the proposed federal class action settlement included 480,000 claimants. Outside of the ongoing settlement negotiations, there had been 11 trials, most of which were brought against Dow Corning. Juries in these trials by July 1995 had awarded plaintiffs more than $80 million in damages.[19] Faced with the huge number of federal claims, and the prospect of ongoing litigation from thousands of individual plaintiffs, Dow Corning filed for Chapter 11 bankruptcy, freezing breast implant litigation against the company.

Under Dow Corning's subsequent bankruptcy reorganization plan, offered in August 1997, a fund of $2.4 billion was proposed to settle most lawsuits against the company. The plaintiffs and their attorneys immediately criticized the new proposal, claiming it was inadequate and unjust. One lawyer for the Dow Corning bankruptcy Tort Claimants Committee, estimated that under the plan women would receive on average only $5,000—not nearly enough to cover their medical expenses.[20] Under the plan, women would have the option of refusing the Dow Corning offer and pursuing litigation on their own. But Dow's new proposal also stipulated that before such trials could begin, the court would need to determine whether there was sufficient scientific evidence of a causal relationship between breast implants and disease. Dow had admitted by then to problems such as ruptures and encapsulation, but continued to argue that its implants did not cause other illnesses, such as various auto-immune diseases. Meanwhile, a federal bankruptcy judge found legal flaws in the new proposed settlement and refused to allow claimants to vote on it.

In 1998 Dow Corning upped the ante to $4.4 billion—offering $3 billion to the silicone claimants and the rest to creditors. Both sides later agreed to a $3.2 billion compensation package, and in 1999, the plan received approval from a bankruptcy judge and creditors. However, the settlement stalled when the judge ruled that women who disagreed with the settlement could still sue Dow Corning *and* Dow Chemical.

Dow Chemical's Role

Up until late October 1995, Dow Chemical had successfully dodged most of the litigation on silicone implants. All along, Dow had maintained that it did not manufacture the implants and was not liable, despite what some saw as a direct research relationship between Dow Chemical and Dow Corning. But in a Nevada jury case, Dow Chemical was hit with $14.1 million in compensatory and punitive damages. The Nevada case was brought by Charlotte Mahlum, 47, a former Elko, Nevada resident, who received implants in 1985 in Minnesota following a double mastectomy. Six years following the procedure, Mahlum began to have health problems— skin disorders, muscle pain, tremors, and incontinence. She blamed her problems on leaking fluid from the implants, which she had removed in

1993. "I was never told they were dangerous," Mahlum said sometime later, "I was told they would last a lifetime." The jury awarded her $3.9 million in compensatory damages and $10 million in punitive damages. Her husband received $200,000. The jury also found that Dow Chemical had a duty to ensure the safety of the implants made by Dow Corning. The Nevada verdict marked the first time Dow Chemical had been held solely responsible for injuries suffered because of defective implants made by Dow Corning. "If upheld," observed *Business Week* at the time, "the verdict could devastate Dow Chemical." By then, in fact, Dow Chemical was named in over 13,000 implant-related lawsuits.[21]

> **"I was never told they were dangerous. I was told they would last a lifetime."**
>
> Charlotte Mahlum

In addition to being an obvious founder and partner in the Dow Corning venture, Dow Chemical had reaped nearly 50 years of Dow Corning profits and participated in its management. Dow Chemical executives and a number of its scientists spent parts of their careers either in association with, or on separate paths, working on Dow Corning substances or projects. In fact, the entanglements of Dow Chemical and Dow Corning went well beyond those of traditional parent and/or joint venture partner,* especially when it came to the research behind their products and the commercial prospects for those products. From day one, Dow Chemical had a major controlling role in Dow Corning written into most of the venture's legal agreements. For starters, Dow Corning's physical location became Midland, Michigan, hometown of Dow Chemical. Trademark and product-inspection agreements that were made between the two, dating to the 1940s, essentially gave Dow Chemical control over the nature and quality of all Dow Corning's goods. The trademark agreement, for example, as stated in the 1940s, and further buttressed in the 1970s, gave Dow Chemical a major role in the products that were manufactured, distributed, and sold, to the point where the nature and quality of the products involved would be "acceptable" to Dow Chemical. Further, when requested, Dow Corning and its associate companies were required to submit specimens of products to Dow Chemical and make available for inspection all of their operations and facilities.[22]

Dow Chemical also appears to have played a pivotal role in defining sil-

---

*For example, in 1943, Willard Dow asked William R. Collings, then heading up Dow's Cellulose Products Division, to become the first general manager and later first president of Dow Corning. Collings worked for both Dow Chemical and Dow Corning while the new venture was forming. Collings also took a third to a half of the Cellulose Products Division with him to Dow Corning, including Shailer L. Bass, his assistant, who later became his successor and the second president of Dow Corning. In addition, the group that Collings had assembled to organize Dow Chemical's first plastics venture became the nucleus of Dow Corning's early silicone business. E. N.Brandt, *Growth Company*, pp. 229–30.

An Insider's View

In September 1995, a former Dow Corning ethics officer, John Swanson, husband of implant victim Colleen Swanson, collaborated with *Business Week* reporter John Byrne in a tell-all book, *Informed Consent*. That book told the story of Dow Corning's breast implant saga, in part from the inside, and of the Swanson family's ordeal and John Swanson's conflicted role at Dow Corning. Swanson eventually quit Dow Corning. But the book put him at the center of the controversy. He appeared on television broadcasts such as *Dateline* and Oprah Winfrey. He also recounted his Dow Corning experience in several newspaper pieces, such as the following Op-Ed he wrote for the *Chicago Tribune* in April 1997:

I worked for Dow Corning Corporation from 1966 to 1993, serving 18 of those years on the Business Ethics Committee. With the exception of the silicone breast implant debacle, I was proud of my company. Unfortunately, this single exception has proven the undoing of a once respected corporation.

Dow Corning's company line is that there was no choice but to file for Chapter 11 protection. But Dow Corning had many options—any one of which may not have led to bankruptcy. Looking at my former employer's actions over the last 20 years, stonewalling information about a defective product may turn out to be the company's ultimate downfall.

Dow Corning introduced the first silicone breast implant in 1963. At that time there were no standards to ensure product safety. However, injecting silicone directly into breast tissue had already been outlawed in some states.

There were also early warnings that implants might be problematic. Internal company memos reported liquid silicone "bleeding" through the implants. Plastic surgeons complained the devices felt oily to the touch, and ruptured easily. Early animal studies noted possible long-term health effects. Opportunities to address these problems were brushed aside.

> **"The manufacturers and surgeons have been performing experimental surgery on humans."**

No attempts were made to evaluate how breast implants performed after they had been surgically inserted into women. Despite early evidence to the contrary, Dow Corning labeled them "good for life" for nearly 30 years.

In 1976, Dow Corning employee Arthur Rathjen wrote: "I have proposed again and again that we must begin an in-depth study of our gel, envelope and bleed phenomenon." That same year Thomas Talcott, a Dow Corning materials engineer, left the company in frustration over lack of safety testing. Talcott later said, "The manufacturers and surgeons have been performing experimental surgery on humans."

When the U.S. Food and Drug Administration began requiring medical device manufacturers to conduct long-run safety studies, it should have been time for serious reflection. Had implant safety been assessed then, Dow Corning might reasonably have decided to get out of the implant business.

Instead, the company took advantage of its "grandfathered-in" status to market a new breast implant with an even thinner outer envelope. Although it felt more natural, the flimsier implant bleeds and ruptures more easily. Independent researchers subsequently found that the lining of the implant loses tensile strength over time. Among implants older than 10 years, women run a one-in-three or one-in-two risk of having them break.

Another warning sign flashed in 1984 when a California woman won $1.5 million in punitive damages against Dow Corning partly because earlier animal studies were misrepresented in court. Rather than listen to this warning, the company sealed the evidence. Following the verdict, Dow Corning's upper management was urged to purchase advertisements warning women of potential hazards. This suggestion was rejected. Production and sale of implants continued.

In 1991, the FDA required Dow Corning to provide evidence of implant safety. Several boxes of disorganized documents were shipped to Washington. The FDA decided the information was too weak to ensure safety. The best—and most honorable—course of action would have been to suspend implant sales until the devices could be fully investigated. Although media reports were increasingly challenging the company's ethics and failure to disclose the animal studies, a bunker mentality had set in.

During these tense times, I urged my colleagues to err on the side of disclosure. But the company felt legal considerations came first. Robert Rylee, a vice president who ran the company's medical business, was quoted as saying, "We don't want to be over educating plaintiffs' attorneys."

Finally in early 1992 Dow Corning's top management was summarily ousted. The new chairman and chief executive officer immediately released hundreds of previously restricted internal memos and studies. Within a few weeks he announced Dow Corning would get out of the breast implant business. Since filing for Chapter 11 protection the company has launched a multi-million dollar public relations campaign intended to blame its troubles on the American legal system.

But Dow Corning has only itself to blame, although the company could have cut its losses by heeding just one of many clear warnings over the past 20 years. Bankruptcy may have temporarily shielded the company from litigation, but it is no absolution for ultimate moral or financial liability.

icone scientifically and sanctioning it for various commercial and industrial uses. It was Dow Chemical, in fact, that christened silicone to be biologically inert, and therefore acceptable for a wide variety of applications. In 1948, two Dow Chemical scientists, Dr. Rowe and Dr. Spencer, along with a Dr. Bass of Dow Corning, published a seminal research paper which declared silicone to be "biologically inert." This put Dow Chemical in an authoritative leadership position on silicone science at the time. It also placed the company, once again, at the industrial and commercial headwaters of another class of commercial chemistry—the organo-silicones. But Dow Chemical not only helped define the industrial and commercial acceptability of silicone, it actively participated in researching its properties, discovering in that research that silicone wasn't the inert substance that Dow Chemical's scientists said it was in the late 1940s. In fact, Dow Chemical scientists would perform studies that demonstrated silicone's toxic hazards and biological activity.[23]

In September 1954, for example, one Dr. Spencer of Dow Chemical reported that Dow Corning silica it tested had "quite a high order of toxicity from dust inhalation." In March 1955, Dr. V. K. Rowe of Dow Chemical reported that a certain kind of "fumed silica" called Dow Corning Degussa Dust—a silica that would later be added to the elastomer shell of the implant to strengthen it— "caused diffuse cellular infiltrates and fibrocystic changes in the lungs and organs of animals." In 1956, Dow Chemical learned in

Dow Chemical not only helped define the industrial and commercial acceptability of silicone, it actively participated in researching its properties.

animal studies that a certain building block chemical* used in silicone gels, when administered orally or by intramuscular injection to lab animals, led to traces of siloxane being found throughout the animals' bodies. That study also found the compound caused a "slight initial weight loss and moderate liver pathology." A similar Dow Chemical study found biological effects on the eyes and conjunctival membranes. Other Dow Chemical reports on Dow Corning Silicone Fluid found some irritation to the eyes and skin. One particular report indicated the silicone fluid caused hyperemia, edema, and general skin rawness in all cases. In 1956, Dow Chemical initiated a research project with the University of Miami on behalf of Dow Corning. Dow Chemical negotiated the price of the project and determined what testing would be performed. When the test results found that a Dow Corning silicone compound entitled Z-4141 caused fat or silicone deposits in the livers of laboratory rats, Dow Chemical, not Dow Corning, retested the results. The retests indicated that the deposits found in the rats' livers represented silicone, not fat. Some research was done by Dow Corning and sent to Dow Chemical, apparently in accord with the agreements between the two companies. In 1957, Dow Corning sent Dow Chemical reports that Dow Corning's 200 Fluid was "absorbed through the skin by the adrenal and kidneys of a rabbit." In 1961, Dow Chemical tested a Dow Corning silicone fluid that when heat-treated had different effects, causing death in some laboratory rats, apparently because of "irritation of the respiratory tract." In 1970, Dow Chemical discovered that Dow Corning 360 Fluid caused spontaneous death in several rats, pulmonary deposition, and cavities to develop in the

---

*The chemical, octamethylcyclotetrasiloxane, also known as D-4, became the building block of the gel used in silicone breast implants from the 1960s until they were taken off the market in 1992.

liver, heart, kidney, spleen, pancreas, ovary, adrenal and stomach mucosa. Also in 1970, Dr. Olson, a Dow Corning scientist newly transferred from Dow Chemical, reported that "if there is any leakage of the [breast implant], by diffusion, rupture, or by any means, some frequency of allergic reactions of patients will occur. In some cases, the problems posed are likely to be serious." A 1975 study by a Dr. Lake, which showed significant silicone bioreactivity, was presented to a joint conference of Dow Corning and Dow Chemical scientists. Other 1976 Dow Corning and Dow Chemical studies found that subcutaneous implantation, as performed in mammary augmentation or reconstruction, changed the physical properties of medical-grade silicone rubber.[24]

Observed attorney Richard Alexander in 1994 after compiling much of this record: "Although it is clear...that Dow Chemical knew as early as the 1950s that the silicone used in breast implants was not biologically inert, neither Dow Chemical nor Dow Corning ever published the results of any of this research. In fact, Dow Chemical indicated just the opposite to the public— that silicone was [biologically inert] and safe for human use. In 1954, and again in 1959, Dow Chemical promoted the suitability of silicone products for medical uses. In October of 1974, product inserts indicated that silicone breast implants were 'nonreactive to body tissue.'..."[25]

Silicone Gel 555

Dow Chemical and Dow Corning also worked together on joint silicone research and new product ventures, as they appear to have done in the 1960s and 1970s with a substance known as "555 silicone gel," or simply gel 555. The gel initially was explored for potential pharmaceutical uses, and in one experiment with monkeys the results did not appear promising. The monkeys' reproductive systems were suppressed by the gel. Dow Corning, apparently then selling the substance as a topical ointment, pulled it off the market. The researchers, however, saw something else—since the gel suppressed certain activity, perhaps it might work as a suppressant of cancer cells, in the male prostate, for example. They set up a Biosciences Divisions to test the biological properties of a number of various silicone compounds, thinking they might be on the verge of discovering a whole new family of drugs. In the research, they found that gel 555 both suppressed and enhanced immune system activity and that it also had sedative effects. At this point, Dow Chemical appears to have joined the party, contributing $200,000 to underwrite research on silicone 555. At a 1968 meeting on the research, one of Dow Chemical's top scientists, V. K. Rowe, offered comment on the methodology being used. By 1971, Dow Chemical and Dow Corning had signed an agreement to split profits from any silicone-based drugs they developed. Much of this research was conducted by a Dow

Chemical subsidiary, Lepetit Pharmaceutical Co., located in Italy. The Dow Chemical/Dow Corning silicone research also explored some possible insecticidal applications of the silicone compounds, including those for mites and cockroaches. Dow Chemical also tested silicone compounds for the government as a possible riot-control gas. Dow Chemical chairman and CEO, Frank Popoff, would reveal in a deposition that the two companies had an agreement

Dow Chemical also tested silicone compounds for the government as a possible riot-control gas.

designed to protect the Dow trademark, and that Dow Chemical had the right to inspect all Dow Corning products. But perhaps most damaging for Dow Chemical, was the revelation that its own Italian subsidiary, Lepetit Pharmaceutical, had sold silicone breast implants throughout Europe, and likely had knowledge of implant problems on that basis.[26]

Jury Tampering?

In Louisiana, meanwhile, as one of the implant cases was nearing jury selection in 1997, Dow Chemical sought to set up a meeting with officials at Tulane University. A consultant then working for Dow sent an e-mail to a Tulane University doctor in April indicating the chemical company wanted to meet with university and medical school department heads. "Dow is very anxious to perform major 'damage control' in New Orleans at their expense," the consultant wrote—substituting the dollar sign for the "s" in the word "expense."[27]

The Tulane Medical School, it turned out, was also the home of researcher Robert Garry. Garry co-authored a controversial study published two months earlier about an experimental test claimed to detect certain antibodies in the blood of some women with silicone implants. The Louisiana women suing Dow believed Garry's study showed a link between implants and disease, and hoped to have him appear as an expert witness in the case. Dow thought Garry's research flawed and too new to be widely accepted among other scientists. However, the women plaintiffs believed the company's entreaties to the Tulane medical community, and its sponsorship of a hospital lecture so close to jury selection in their case, amounted to a form of jury and witness tampering. They charged the attempted Tulane meeting was "an unconscionable, and possibly illegal, effort to place pressure upon Dr. Garry"—and the hospital lecture, an attempt to influence potential jurors. Additionally, Dow had indicated Tulane was at the top of its list for possible conferences, seminars, and forums on topics such as women's health issues and silicone breast implant research. The women plaintiffs filed a court action and asked a judge to investigate. In court papers, the plaintiffs said they had evidence of Dow's attempts to tamper with wit-

Tort Wars & Big Money

"Mass tort" is a term of art known mostly by lawyers and legal journalists. In shorthand, a mass tort is a personal injury lawsuit that eventually is filed by many individuals—thousands and tens of thousands in some cases. When tort cases get to this level, billions of dollars in costs and awards are involved, with some consolidated cases essentially becoming a small industry operating for years at a time. Dow Chemical and Dow Corning have both had experience in mass tort cases—Agent Orange in Dow Chemical's case, and the silicone implant litigation involving both companies. For most corporations in mass tort situations, the prospect of litigating thousands of individual cases is a daunting challenge, and settling such cases can and has driven major companies to seek bankruptcy protection, as it did with Dow Corning. Corporate interests, typically—given negative publicity, over-hanging liability, and Wall Street pressures—want to settle such cases quickly. Among the advised legal strategies in emerging mass-tort cases is to nip them in the bud before momentum gets rolling—to crush plaintiff's lawyers in early cases that might otherwise send out large award signals to other potential litigants.

When companies like Dow Chemical and Dow Corning get into major tort trouble, they look for the best lawyers money can buy. Such attorneys can save their corporate clients millions in costs, damages, legal time, and negative publicity. In the 1980s, when Dow Chemical got into liability trouble with a product known as *Sarabond*, a mortar additive that allegedly weakened brick structures and corroded steel, Dow hired David Bernick, then a 30-something attorney described by *Fortune* as a "whip smart" national litigator for the Chicago firm of Kirkland & Ellis. When Bernick was brought on to help Dow in its *Sarabond* fight, the company had lost the only two lawsuits that had been tried and had spent more than $100 million in settlements. "Bernick's first trial," explained *Fortune* writer Joseph Nocera, "resulted in a verdict for the company so convincing that no *Sarabond* case was ever tried again." Bernick also became a star player in some of the Dow Corning and Dow Chemical implant cases.

But in the implant litigation, the federal government sent the most powerful signal to potential victims and plaintiff's lawyers, based in part upon Dow documents discovered in plaintiff's litigation. FDA Commissioner David Kessler's January 1992 moratorium on implants, coupled with a series of successfully litigated cases that won large awards for individuals, helped propel the silicone implant litigation into the mass-tort realm. Once at that level, the litigation—and then, behind the scenes, the often more important negotiation—spawns a whole new style of maneuvering. Big-gun, big-name lawyers who specialize in such matters, commanding huge fees, are brought into the process to either litigate or negotiate, and generally work the settlement process to the advantage of some finality. For that is what the corporations want most—to end the uncertainty and do it as quickly and as cheaply as possible.

Class actions—putting thousands of litigants who allege similar harm together in one case—are obviously one way that plaintiffs try to leverage companies with defective products to agree to big settlements. But class actions can also be purposely manipulated and expedited by corporations to save them money—by making a deal that excludes all future litigation. This was the basis for the 1984 Agent Orange settlement, which has not withstood the test of time, as Vietnam veterans with alleged harms emerging since that settlement have been permitted by the Supreme Court to pursue their cases. In mass tort litigation, judges can and do play important roles in moving settlements along—settlements like the Agent Orange case that aren't always popular. In that case, Judge Weinstein pushed both sides along for his own reasons—not clogging up his court.

In the Dow Corning implant litigation, the federal courts and numerous litigants on both sides of the process came together in a global settlement process designed to expedite damage awards and consolidate many of the cases. This process had its difficulties, with many plaintiffs opting out in favor of their own litigation. Still, damages were paid by Dow Corning to thousands, and the company continued to operate under bankruptcy protection. Yet today, the litigation continues. The maneuvering by corporate strategists and big-name negotiators only worked in part. Plaintiffs' attorneys kept coming at the companies.

But in the end, what most corporations want and continue to work for—including Dow Chemical and Dow Corning—is tort reform. And what they mean by "reform" is capping awards, especially the punitive and large penalty awards sometimes assessed guilty parties for their egregious behavior. In 1995, while Dow Corning's silicone implant woes were still very much a national issue, the company's CEO, Richard Hazleton, went lobbying in Washington to try to rally support for tort reform legislation then pending. Republicans at the time were pointing to the implant litigation as Exhibit A. Hazleton described the plaintiffs' bar—i.e., lawyers bringing personal injury cases—as "Litigation, Inc." Both Dows are also members of the American Tort Reform Association, the corporate trade group created in 1986 which has a long list of items it wants to change, including one proposal for doing away with the jury system and replacing it with a tribunal and non-discretionary awards.

Dow Chemical is also paying attention to tort reform at the state level. In the summer and fall of 2002, as a special legislative session on tort reform in Mississippi was coming to a close, Dow put on a full-court press, spending some $90,000 on lobbying in a few weeks' time. Dow, which does not have a plant in Mississippi, raised some eyebrows with their involvement. "They get sued, like most chemical companies do in many states because they distribute chemicals," explained Ronald Peresich, a Gulf Coast lawyer who represented Dow during the Mississippi special session. "They're getting sued in Mississippi in a number of chemical exposure and asbestos cases," he said. Peresich, a well-connected lobbyist who knows his way around the legislature, is a close ally of the Mississippi Senate leadership. In June 2003, Lt. Governor Amy Tuck, who presides over the Senate, named him to be her statewide campaign chairman. But during the special legislative session on tort reform, Peresich went to work for his clients.

Late in the special session, the generally anti-tort reform House was trying to compromise with the pro-business Senate. House members say they found themselves in private negotiations across the table from Dow's lobbyist, Peresich, more or less working for the Senate position. Peresich at first declined to identify his client, sparking a heated exchange with one House negotiator. Peresich later acknowledged working for Dow and advocating on behalf of the business community. Dow and other business interests were especially interested in placing caps on punitive damages and were worried in particular about an environmental exception proposed for the punitive cap. The exception would have allowed that jury awards against environmental polluters would not be capped. This exception was not adopted, and Dow's lobbyist obviously helped insure that it wasn't. In the end, the Mississippi legislators did adopt caps on punitive damages at $20 million, or 4 percent of a company's net worth. They also enacted other changes limiting where lawsuits could be filed and how financial responsibility for jury verdicts would be assessed in cases with multiple defendants.

Sources: Joseph Nocera, "Fatal Litigation" (Part I), *Fortune*, October 16, 1995, p. 60, and "Dow Corning Succumbs—Fatal Litigation" (Part II), *Fortune*, October 30, 1995, p. 137, and Reed Branson, Associated Press, "Lobbying Spending Hits Record High in Mississippi During Tort Reform Year," July 15, 2003.

nesses and jurors. They asked Judge Yada Magee to take testimony from the woman working on Dow's behalf, Monique Ellis, and Dow's chief public relations executive, John Musser. The judge agreed to a deposition of Ellis.[28]

Dow responded that the tampering charges were unfounded, and countered with its own filing that the Louisiana women were trying to deny the company free speech. The plaintiffs, Dow Chemical charged, were themselves attempting to sway the public and potential jurors in their direction. Dow also claimed in court papers that the company's e-mail "was doing nothing more than seeking to initiate scientific dialogue and scrutiny." And as for Garry, "whether Dr. Garry wished to participate in the scientific discourse was his decision to make at his pleasure," said Dow, "unintimidated, unthreatened." Both sides by then had retained national public relations firms to help make their respective cases outside the courtroom. In all, about 10,000 Louisiana women were then seeking damages for illnesses they say silicone implants caused.[29]

Another form of jury influence, some plaintiffs charged, was a barrage of Dow Chemical advertising that hit the airways in the months immediately preceding the Louisiana trial and jury selection. From about January 1997 through April of that year, Dow ran a flurry of TV ads and radio spots that played up its corporate citizenship. Another spot, curiously not linked to Dow and run courtesy of a nonprofit group, highlighted the benefits of silicone products. It featured a little girl with a life-saving silicone device in her brain called a shunt. In the ad, the girl's mother rails against greedy personal-injury lawyers. "Silicone is not the problem," she says. "The personal-injury lawyers and their greed is the problem." Dawn Barrios, a New Orleans attorney for the breast-implant plaintiffs, said the ads and their sponsors were "trying to pollute our jury." Barrios had appealed to the state judge for limits on the ads, but the judge refused.[30]

In 1995, state court judges in Texas declared mistrials in two separate implant cases when Dow Corning took out newspaper ads during jury selection, holding up the latest studies as proof of the devices' safety. The same year, a Nevada state court judge banned Dow from running similar ads before a trial—but then reversed herself, citing First Amendment concerns. In Louisiana, implant plaintiffs and

Dow Chemical's TV ads, said one New Orleans attorney, were "trying to pollute our jury."

their lawyers began noticing the Dow Chemical TV ads—one for household cleaning products featuring a sympathetic company scientist and her kids, another promoting Dow Chemical's environmental record, and another featuring volunteer Dow workers helping to build homes for American Indians. Then came the silicone-shunt ad sponsored by a group calling itself Citizens Against Lawsuit Abuse. That ad, however, was produced and made available by the American Tort Reform Association, whose members include Dow Chemical. Spokesmen for the two groups said they were unaware of the Dow trial, and that the timing of their ad was coincidental. As for Dow Chemical's own self-promotional ads, company spokesman John Musser said the Dow corporate citizenship spots were run nationally, and that Dow had a big plant in Louisiana (see Chapter 15), but was also attempting "to rectify damage to our public image" caused by the implant cases. Meanwhile, although Judge Yada Magee in 1997 declined plaintiffs' request to limit ads, she did allow them to question Dow about the shunt ad and the company's ties, if any, to the lawsuit-abuse group. Dow declined to answer, and spokesmen for Dow and the lawsuit-abuse group declined to say whether the company contributed to the group.[31]

The Mahlum Case

Back in Nevada in the Charlotte Mahlum implant case—where a 1995 jury had awarded Mahlum and her husband $4.1 million in compensatory damages plus $10 million in punitive damages—further litigation ensued. In April 1997, lawyers for Dow Chemical asked the Nevada Supreme Court to overturn the entire $14 million judgment. Dow lawyers Thomas Wilson and Michele Odorizzi said the Reno jury award to Mahlum should be thrown out because Dow Chemical didn't design, test, or sell the implants. Dow's Odorizzi said there was no evidence Dow Chemical—which over the years had done various tests on other uses of silicone gel—knew of problems that might occur if it was used in breast implants. The other Dow attorney, Wilson, argued that the Reno trial wasn't fair because the judge, among other things, excluded evidence of safe medical uses of silicone but allowed evidence of toxic uses. Wilson added that arguments against Dow Chemical during the Reno trial focused on allegations of criminal conspiracies, deliberately skewed studies, and other claims that resulted in "a portrait of an inflamed jury."

Rick Ellis, a Boston attorney, representing Charlotte Mahlum, told the court that his client should be awarded the judgment because the company was responsible for her ruptured silicone breast implants that made her sick. "We have a 47-year-old woman who must wear diapers," stated Ellis. Dow attorney Odorizzi said scientific evidence had not concluded that liquid silicone causes disease.

Dow Chemical, said the plaintiff's attorney, had known since the 1960s that liquid silicone affects the immune system.

"People do get sick, and not everything is the result of a toxic chemical," she said. Ellis said Dow Chemical had conducted studies since the 1940s proving that liquid silicone was hazardous. Tests had determined the fluid migrates in the body. "You don't need to be a rocket scientist to know what's going to happen when it gets to the heart, the liver, the brain," Ellis said. According to Ellis, Dow Chemical had known since the 1960s that liquid silicone affects the immune system. Mahlum suffered numerous immune disorders, and had "brain lesions" and "rashes all over her body," he explained, and was entitled to the money because she was disfigured when the ruptured implants were removed. At various times during the court hearing, Ellis held up a sample implant or showed color photographs of Mahlum before and after the implant removal. For Dow Chemical, Odorizzi argued that the company's early tests were conducted when silicone was an industrial product used in pesticides and other items. She said Dow Chemical didn't manufacture breast implants or test liquid silicone's "long-term" effect on the human body. Those tests were conducted by Dow Coming, whose officials never alerted the parent company to any problem, she said.[32] But in fact, the relationship between Dow Chemical and Dow Corning over the years left a lot more murky questions than clear answers.

In the end, in a December 1998 ruling, the Nevada Supreme Court upheld the award for Charlotte Mahlum, but it overturned the $10 million punitive award. Elsewhere, in other state litigation, Dow Chemical had fared better, as in Louisiana where an appeals court in December 2002 threw out a 1997 jury verdict that had found Dow Chemical liable for failing to alert women to the potential dangers of silicone implants. The Louisiana jury in that case made some especially pointed findings.

Originally brought in early 1997 as a state class-action lawsuit on behalf of 1,800 Louisiana women, the case before Louisiana District Judge Yada Magee, was planned to proceed through several phases. The first phase yielded a jury verdict which found that Dow Chemical for years had negligently conducted research on silicone and misrepresented the safety of the silicone that later went into the implants made by Dow Corning. The jury, responding to questions put to them by Judge Magee, found that Dow Chemical did "knowingly or intentionally remain silent, conceal, or suppress information about the harms and dangers of using silicone in the human body." The jury heard and evaluated evidence about animal tests showing silicone as an irritant to rabbits and that injected silicone fluid migrated through animals' bodies. The jury determined that Dow Chemical had failed to conduct enough safety tests and had made "false or misleading statements" about silicone safety.[33] The verdict—essentially that Dow Chemical was negligent in testing silicone

> **The Louisiana verdict—that Dow Chemical was negligent in testing silicone for breast implants, lied about the possible risks, and conspired with Dow Corning—made national headlines.**

for breast implants, lied about the possible risks, and conspired with Dow Corning to hide potential health effects—made national headlines. It was also the first case to go to trial as a statewide class-action lawsuit.[34]

Dow appealed the Louisiana verdict, and the appeals court in December 2002 sided with Dow, throwing out the case, but did so citing Judge Magee's handling of the case and procedural missteps rather than the merits.*[35]

But another state case in Nevada had gone the other way on appeal, keeping Dow Chemical in the picture for 55 women who had opted out of the Dow Corning global settlement process in favor of going after the chemical parent.[36] By 2003, Dow Chemical was telling its shareholders it thought the company's litigation strategy would prevail, though adding qualifiers that a "material adverse impact" on the company might still be possible.**

---

*Judge Magee had moved to decertify the case as a class action, which Dow had requested, but allowed it to proceed after verdict, selecting eight plaintiffs to continue the case and keeping the verdict intact for the larger class. The appeals court ruled this inappropriate and also found Judge Magee's plan for dividing the trial into separate phases for conduct and causation was in violation of Louisiana law, making the first-phase findings "highly prejudicial against Dow."

**"...The Company's management believes that there is no merit to plaintiff's claims that the Company is liable for alleged defects in Dow Corning's silicone products because of the Company's alleged direct participation in the development of those products, and the company intends to contest those claims vigorously. Management believes that the possibility is remote that a resolution of plaintiff's direct participation claims, including the vigorous defense against those claims, would have a material adverse impact on the Company's financial position or cash flows. Nevertheless, in light of Judge Pointer's April 25, 1995 ruling, it is possible that a resolution of plaintiff's direct participation claims, including the vigorous defense against those claims, could have a material adverse impact on the Company's results of operations for a particular period, although it is impossible at this time to estimate the range or amount of such impact." Dow Chemical Co.,"The Way Forward," *2002 Annual Report*, February 12, 2003, p. 58.

Silicone Knowledge

Among the lessons of the silicone breast implant story—and there are many—two stand out: first, the history and general knowledge of observed silica and silicone health effects, and secondly, what was known and learned about immune-system reaction. Silica-bearing dusts have long been known to do damage to the lungs. Silicosis—the lung disease suffered by miners and sand blasters—has a long health-effects record, with crude cause-and-effect relationships surmised centuries ago, dating to the 1700s. Sand-blasting projects in the 1930s, such as the Gauley Bridge tunnel project in West Virginia (managed by an early Union Carbide company; see Chapter 20) contributed to hundreds of worker deaths, providing more evidence.

Japanese reports in the 1960s and 1970s found chronic stimulation of the immune system after breast augmentation or following silicone-based injections.

Dow Chemical appears to have done its own toxicological studies on silica and silicone since the 1940s, though pronouncing silicone safe for industrial use in the late 1940s. The 1950s came full of findings from animal studies that silica, in addition to lung disease, might also have central nervous system and neuromuscular effects. Dow Chemical scientists found that Dow Corning silica was capable of causing "diffuse cellular infiltration and fibrotic changes" not only in lungs but other organs as well. Animal lab tests by Dow Chemical utilizing radioactive tracers testing a Dow Corning silica—a "200 fluid"—found the silicone in all manner of organs and body parts, from hair, heart, and skull bone, to spleen, thyroid, and pancreas. According to more than one account, Dow Chemical never disclosed important research findings that silicone gel migrated to major organs in the body.

In addition, the role of silicone implant fluid as an *adjuvant*—a substance that can elicit, heighten, or prolong immune responses—appears to be especially instructive. As Marc Lappe observes in his book *Chemical Deception*: "Adjuvants are any chemical that resist the body's efforts to tear antigens down and take them away, thereby providing a constant stimulus to the immune system's response.... Since an exaggerated response can be provoked by any chemical that the immune response defines as an antigen, such chemicals need not be toxic in and of themselves. Other chemicals need only serve as adjuvants (without being antigenic themselves) to goad the body into mounting a profoundly damaging reaction...."[37]

For nearly 40 years, researchers had indications that silicone was a possible adjuvant in the immune system. Japanese reports in the 1960s and 1970s found chronic stimulation of the immune system after breast augmentation or following silicone-based injections. Similar Western reports of

the mid-1970s also found that breast augmentation with silicone-based fluids could cause autoimmune-like phenomenon. "But the Western medical
community was lulled into complacency by the assurances of Dow Corning
and some of their own colleagues that U.S.-made silicones were a 'pure,'
totally biocompatible product that could not and did not provoke immune or
chronic inflammatory reactions," explains Marc Lappe. These assurances,
he says, were clearly mistaken.[38]

Silicone and its associated effects on the human body, observes Lappe,
passed undetected in the normal range of toxicological tests and screening.
He draws these lessons from the silicone implant fiasco: "[O]ur understanding of toxicity must embrace immunological provocative reactions,"
and that we pay attention "not only to the structure of material in question
but to its reactivity in the human body."[39]

Trespass In Women

The silicone implant tragedy is also another kind of chemical trespass.
Silicone's invasion of the body, and its provocations and associations, however clear or unclear, proved or unproved, were nonetheless uninvited, invasive, and life-altering for thousands of women. And for those women, the
line crossed was very clear; the violation unforgivable. Mary White Stewart,
in her book, *Silicone Spills*, has likened the travesty to a kind of corporate
pollution, or toxic dumping, in women:

> ...The women who have silicone in their bloodstreams are the human
> counterparts to the rivers of carcinogenic chemicals running through
> Texas barrios. Their bodies, ravaged by silicone spills reflect the chemi-
> cal dumps in New York and New Jersey. Not only are women the dump-
> ing grounds for corporations with their eyes on the profit margin, they are
> experimental animals for the manufacturers of silicone gel breast
> implants, as they were for the Dalkon Shield IUD and DES. This attitude
> toward women's bodies is not just cavalier; rather, it reflects a deep dis-
> regard for women. Just as the land and the fish and animals are
> destroyed by the strafing and dumping of industry, women's bodies are
> being systematically devastated by corporate use of them as dumping
> grounds for dangerous, untested, and potentially fatal, but highly prof-
> itable products, here and abroad. If we were talking about one company
> or one year, we might simply blame an irresponsible CEO or a perverse
> policy. But we are talking about a process that has been in existence for
> over thirty years; years during which hundreds of thousands of women
> have been damaged....[40]

In late 2002, a California company, Inamed Corp., applied to FDA to
begin selling silicone breast implants in the United States, a move that if

approved, would reverse the 1992 FDA ruling restricting implant use. By October 2003, an FDA advisory committee had recommended approval, despite the fact that little progress had been made since 1992 in answering even basic questions about how often implants rupture. Long term follow-up studies of implant recipients were also still lacking. However, in January 2004, the FDA continued the ban on silicone breast implants, concluding that there was not enough information to tell women that the implants were safe to have in their bodies for many years. The information was still limited, an FDA spokesman said, on why some implants rupture and what then happens to the silicone gel.[41]

Silicone's invasion of the body, and its provocations and associations were uninvited, invasive, and life-altering for thousands of women.

Dow Corning, meanwhile, operating under bankruptcy protection and no longer making silicone breast implants, currently produces over 7,000 other kinds of silicone products for various uses in the automotive, aerospace, electronics, and medical devices industries. In 2002, it had sales of $2.5 billion, contributing millions in profits to its founding partners, Dow Chemical and Corning. Dow Corning expects to emerge from bankruptcy in 2004.

13.
Men at Work

Why should we have a no-risk workplace?

Paul Oreffice, Dow CEO,
Press conference, 1980s

From the earliest days at Dow's Midland, Michigan operations, the process of extracting and refining chemicals was something of a risky enterprise. In the 1890s, Herbert Dow's experimental plants blew up on more than a few occasions. By the early 1900s, after the Dow plants became more of an established presence, daily operations still presented hazards to workers and nearby residents. In those days, however, concern for worker health and safety was more or less governed by foremen and plant managers exercising common sense, utilizing visceral clues like smell, sound, or direct inspection. Herbert Dow himself—very much a hands-on manager concerned with keeping things running—recalled one incident of reluctant workers fearful of bromine gas after one operation became plugged:

> ...A good many years ago I went out to the bromine plant and saw it was shut down. I found most of the men were on the roof. I went up and found they had a trap door open at the top of a coke tower that was plugged with iron hydrate ... [T]his layer of iron hydrate was only on the top layer of coke and they understood the necessity of getting in there and taking out a few inches from the top of the coke. I stuck my head through the door and there was considerable odor of bromine and the men claimed they were waiting for the air to clear up. I was satisfied that the amount of bromine was not more than it had been customary for me to soak up on many occasions, and I presumed the foreman ... was equally familiar with the amount of bromine the men could absorb without injury. So I told him I thought it was up to him to set the example by going down and taking out the first pail of coke. He started to climb down the ladder and when his head got inside the door he immediately changed his mind and came out again. He said there was too much bromine in the tower. So I took my coat off, threw it to one side, went down myself and

told them to pass down the tools. I filled one pail full of coke and they pulled it out, and by that time the ladder was full of men trying to get down to help me, and very promptly enough coke was removed to permit free access of air... and the trap door was closed and the plant started again. If I had not gone up on the roof, and if I had not known by experience how much bromine irritation a man can stand before it becomes a serious matter, that plant might have been shut down all day and several hundred dollars lost thereby....

Again, around 1908, when Dow's new chloroform plant was not producing up to par, a Dow engineer and plant manager, E. O. Barstow, resorted to the "smell test" to decipher where pipes were leaking. Recounts Dow historian, E. N. Brandt: "...He went around the plant and sniffed at the pipe joints, and as soon as he smelled chloroform he called in the plumber and ordered the pipe repaired. He quickly discovered that he could smell the chloroform only for a short time before his nose 'wore out,' so he got a pipe blowtorch and went around applying it to pipe joints; when he saw a peculiar blue color it meant chloroform was leaking. He soon discovered that the plant was one vast leak. Barstow then had the whole piping system ripped out and put in an entirely new system with tight joints. Within three weeks after he had taken over the plant, it was operating in the black..."[2]

Toxic Exposure

Prior to the mid-1920s, there was little attention paid to worker safety or worker exposure to toxic chemicals. By the mid-1920s, a series of worker deaths by way of exposure to tetraethyl lead in a few incidents at one DuPont plant and a Standard Oil plant, both in New Jersey, momentarily caught the nation's attention. At DuPont, in addition to lead poisonings, more than a dozen cases of bladder cancer occurred at a dye plant using beta-napthylamine. And at Dow, there were incidents attributed to worker exposure to phenol. In the 1930s, there were a handful of companies, Dow among them, that did set up investigative labs in the aftermath of worker deaths and poisonings. The new investigative labs, however, were not necessarily established to be preventative screens to help eliminate toxic risks, but rather, became guides for the best ways to build plants and deploy equipment given particular chemical processes or products. The objective was more to manipulate the workplace for acceptable worker exposure than it was hazard elimination. The labs also had a public relations component, as one DuPont lab manager put it: "to keep the company out of trouble by producing valid information on toxicity of chemicals."[3]

Industrial safety in those days generally fell under the rubric of "industrial hygiene." Protecting workers on the job was essentially voluntary, done individually, company to company. There were no government workplace

OSHA Wars

In the 1970s, the U.S. Occupational Safety and Health Administration (OSHA) sought to rank cancer-causing chemicals in the workplace and establish corresponding worker exposure standards and restrictions. Essentially, two broad categories were proposed: those defined as human carcinogens, about 260 chemicals, and those defined as animal carcinogens, about 200 chemicals. Dow, by this time, was generally opposing most government regulation, and in this case believed the government's perception of workplace cancer was skewed and inaccurate. In this particular battle, Dow and the chemical industry created the American Industrial Health Council, run as an arm of the Chemical Manufacturers Association with an annual budget of at least $1 million. Dow's CEO at the time, Paul Oreffice, was the Council's first chairman. The Health Council took issue with an OSHA advisory council prediction that workplace chemicals could play a role in up to 38 percent of all future cancer deaths. The Council put the figure at 5 percent, emphasizing that cancer was on the rise largely because of cigarettes and diet. Longer life also meant more cancers were being recorded, said the council. Still, even at 5 percent, 20,000 would die each year.

safety standards. However, there were some private bodies and industrial trade associations that tried to advance the notion of safety standards, testing, and safe chemical exposure levels. One such organization established in 1938, was the American Conference of Industrial Hygienists (ACGIH), comprised mostly of academics and some state, local, and federal officials. During the mid-1940s, the ACGIH developed what it called "threshold limit values," or TLVs, for a number of chemicals and other substances then known to be in the workplace environment. TLVs were intended as exposure limits for workers, but they were rudimentary at best, since there was very little toxicological testing or data available.

"The industry knew that TLVs were a benchmark of what was achievable, although not necessarily what was safe," write Gerald Markowitz and David Rosner in their book, *Deceit and Denial*. Liability was a factor, too. "From the 1930s on, the establishment of safety standards was a central concern of industry worried about liability suits," they observed. "But the question of standards was misleading. Most of the established standards were only vaguely dependent upon experimentation and epidemiological study. More often they resulted from bargains struck between industry leaders and public health officials."[4] Acting on knowledge of hazards and worker health risks was often painfully slow.

By the 1960s, however, as ACGIH moved to update its standards, some companies responded by supplying data from their own industrial hygiene programs. But generally, even through the late 1960s, this was a minimal effort on the part of industry, as there was a concern among some that a data depository would be subject to subpoena in damage suits. By 1969, the chemical industry's contribution to the TLV process for new substances was described by one expert as "pathetic." Even animal study data were in short supply because the studies did not exist for the most part, and where they did exist, companies were reluctant to publish or otherwise share the information. But in 1970 all that suddenly changed. The U.S. Occupational Safety and Health Administration (OSHA) was created and the existing list of TLVs was used to form OSHA's federal standards. The ACGIH committee on TLVs suddenly took on a new cache.[5]

At least one scientist from Dow Chemical had participated in the TLV process during the 1960s, providing data on some half dozen or more of its chemicals. Dow had also made comments and suggestions and shared some of its published work on toxicology. Dow had struck up a pretty good relationship with the ACGIH and its TLV committee that worked on and set the standards—

Dow Chemical appears to have played a substantial role in influencing the TLVs for at least 40 chemicals.

now of new importance given OSHA. In the 1970s, in fact, Dow's chief toxicologist at the time, V. K. Rowe was enlisted as a "liaison member" of the TLV committee, and his co-worker Theodore Torkelson, designated alternate. Similar positions were gained by DuPont. In fact, Dow's Torkelson and DuPont's man became two of the four members on a new "carcinogenic substances" subcommittee established in 1972. Through the mid-1980s, the documentation that was used to establish and update TLVs—standards that continued to be used as guidance by OSHA—came increasingly from ACGIH's industry representatives. Dow Chemical, according to one source, appears to have played a substantial role* in influencing the TLVs for at least 40 chemicals.[6] By the early and mid-1970s, however, the chemical industry was implicated in a series of occupational illnesses and cancers linked to specific chemicals—among them, vinyl chloride, kepone, DBCP, and bichloromethyl ether (BCME). These controversies and others contributed to an increased focus on OSHA standards and the passage of the Toxic Substances Control Act

---

*In 1973, for example, OSHA proposed to regulate ethylenimine as a carcinogen, as Barry Castleman and Grace Ziem explain: "Dow's Dr. D. J. Kilian provided the basis for the TLV committee observation, that despite this chemical's toxic carcinogenic effects in animal studies, 'industrial experience has been good.' The entire basis for this was . . . [a] second-hand report of a telephone conversation between two manufacturers [i.e., Dow and BASF] . . . It does not appear that any study was subsequently published. Ethylenimine was removed from the TLV booklet's appendix list of 'experimental carcinogens' after 1974, presumably upon the recommendation of the subcommittee on carcinogens, which included Torkelson of Dow Chemical (sole U.S. producer)." Barry I. Castleman, ScD, and Grace E. Ziem, MD, DrPH, "Corporate Influence on Threshold Limit Values," *American Journal of Industrial Medicine*, Vol. 13, 1988, p. 551.

(TSCA) in 1976, which would establish "new chemical" notification and basic screening requirements. But getting to that point often involved chemical-by-chemical battles over standard setting. And Dow was involved in more than a few of the battles—among them vinyl chloride, discussed earlier in Chapter 7.

Damaged DNA?

In the early 1970s, Dow Chemical had instituted one of the nation's more sophisticated medical tracking programs to monitor the potential carcinogenic or mutagenic effects of the company's chemicals on workers. One program Dow initiated and refined over a 13-year period was to detect chemically-induced chromosomal abnormalities. By 1974, in fact, more than 43,000 such studies were carried out on 1,689 Dow workers. Among these programs was a 1970s survey of workers exposed to

By the summer of 1977, Dow's scientists had found clear-cut evidence of chromosome damage, particularly in men over 40.

benzene and epichlorohydrin—both believed to be carcinogenic at high exposure levels. Soon the scientists discovered what appeared to be increased chromosome breakage among employees exposed to relatively low levels of the chemicals. Such changes in the chromosomes—the rod-shaped structures in the DNA that carry the genes—could be signs of cancer and/or birth defects. That's what Dow's chief researcher at the time, Dr. D. Jack Kilian who directed the studies, believed might be possible (see sidebar). At Dow headquarters, the company first accepted—then rejected—the validity of the study. Dow also resisted the suggestion that workers exposed to the chemicals should be shifted to other duties.[7]

Benzene is a chemical that can have toxic effects on bone marrow, which in turn can induce a wide range of effects, especially aplastic anemia, characterized by fatigue, and sometimes other associated conditions as well as increased susceptibility to infection. Benzene has also been associated with leukemia and reproductive effects. In the early 1960s, several European studies had shown there was a relatively high incidence of chromosomal abnormalities in white blood cells of workers who had varying degrees of marrow damage following benzene exposure. Abnormalities were generally found in workers intermittently exposed to benzene at levels between 25 and 150 ppm. Lower levels of exposure left a less clear pattern.

Dow's chromosome tests at Freeport, Texas, were made with workers exposed to "low" levels of benzene, believed to be under 10 ppm. By the summer of 1977, Dow's scientists had found clear-cut evidence of chromosome damage, particularly in men over 40.* Dow initially decided not to disclose the results, for among other things, industry was then fighting a proposed OSHA move to tighten the benzene standard to 1 ppm. However, news of the Dow findings leaked out, and in late 1977, NIOSH sent two letters to Dow and another in January 1978, requesting the results of the study. In March 1978, Dow released the results which confirmed the occurrence of chromosome damage in workers at average benzene exposure levels of 2 to 3 ppm.[8] Apparently, according to Barry Castleman and others, Dow's data on chromosomal abnormalities among workers exposed to benzene below 10 ppm were withheld by Dow during OSHA's benzene hearings in 1977. This prompted one of the researchers, Dr. Dante Picciano, to quit his job in 1978 in order to release the results. Because of the company's delay in releasing the findings Picciano denounced Dow as "unethical" and "immoral."[9]

At Dow meanwhile, Dr. Kilian, who had done the chromosome studies, resigned. In his place came Dr. John R. Venable, who began a series of new studies, beginning with office workers who had not been exposed to toxic chemicals. This study was necessary, explained Dow, to test normal persons, designed "to improve our knowledge of chromosome damage." Others, however, such as Dr. Marvin Legator of the University of Texas Medical Branch—who had helped Dow conduct the tests as a consultant in the 1970s—said background levels on normal chromosomes already existed.[10]

By 1983, Dow decided to stop its chromosome studies, claiming the earlier results were not all that revealing. "Neither of the studies revealed chromosome damage," said Dow's Dr. Venable in April 1983. He explained that of 52 benzene workers surveyed, only two revealed a high amount of chromosome breakage. The other tests on epichlorohydrin, proved incorrect because of scientific mistakes, he said. A re-examination of exposed workers' chromosomes showed normal breakage levels. Dow concluded then that it did not have enough knowledge of chromosome breakage to use the data and method as a practical test of exposure. Instead, Dow said it would use what it had traditionally used to gauge potential ill effects on workers—the annual blood test, which it had used since 1960. In any case, by the early 1980s, Dow did have genetic dossiers on a number of its workers, but did not share the results with them "for fear of alarming them prematurely."[11]

---

*In 1977, it also appears there were some excess cases of leukemia among the benzene-exposed employees surveyed by Dow—"prompting Dow to announce a new corporate ceiling limit [for benzene] of 10 ppm in 1977," observes Barry Castleman. "Dow epidemiologists have now [as of 1986, citing Dow ref.] seen 4 deaths from myelogenous leukemia in this work force, versus 0.9 expected; a fifth worker with leukemia was listed as dying with pneumonia." An OSHA researcher further noted that average benzene exposure of these workers was 5.5 ppm. See Barry I. Castleman, ScD, and Grace E. Ziem, MD, DrPH, "Corporate Influence on Threshold Limit Values," *American Journal of Industrial Medicine*, Vol. 13, 1988, p. 550.

The Jack Kilian Affair

In the 1970s, Jack Kilian would take his sail boat out for long rides on the Gulf of Mexico off Freeport, Texas. Kilian loved the outdoors and enjoyed sharing his boat with friends. In his day job, Kilian was a scientist at Dow Chemical. Kilian, in fact, was Dow's medical director at Freeport, and had been since the mid-1960s. But Jack Kilian was also in the vanguard of a handful of industrial scientists charting some new techniques for monitoring the health of workers. Kilian's specialty was cytogenetics, a branch of genetics focused on changes in chromosomes, the rod-shaped bodies in cells that carry genes. The stable population of workers at Dow's Texas operations provided Kilian with a good source of continuing data to study chemical exposure and its effects on workers. Dow then professed it wanted a safe workplace for its employees, and Kilian believed his monitoring of workers could help Dow meet that goal. He soon had major studies underway at Freeport involving nearly 3,000 Dow workers, computers to help analyze his data, and a research building to house his staff. Dow touted the program as state-of-the-art. Kilian came to believe that changes observed in the workers' chromosomes due to chemical exposure could be used by the company as a tool for protecting workers—or at least moving them out of harm's way.

Kilian, and scientists working with him, had complied data on Dow workers exposed to a number of chemicals. In one study of vinyl chloride workers, the scientists had found no negative effects in workers. Dow management was ecstatic about these findings, and encouraged the scientists to publish them. According to Dr. Dante Picciano—one of the Dow scientists who worked under Kilian—Dow allowed the scientists to "go around the country, beating our own drum" about the vinyl chloride findings. But other studies that Kilian and Picciano undertook—those of workers exposed to benzene and epichlorohydrin—had distinctly different results. Kilian found that workers exposed to epichlorohydrin—a solvent used in paints and varnishes—had a doubling of chromosome breakage compared to a control group of workers who had not been exposed. Kilian became convinced more than ever that the studies pointed to a need for a new company policy whereby workers with such breakage would be notified candidly about their problem, and transferred away from the chemicals, to others jobs. But the policy was never adopted. In fact, after the benzene and epichlorohydrin results, Kilian and his associates found that Dow officials grew distant, hostile, and defensive about the studies.

In June 1977, after Picciano had found 52 workers exposed to benzene with high chromosome breakage, he reported his findings and soon met resistance from the company. "They started dragging their feet," he explained to *New York Times* reporter Richard Severo in 1980. "We wanted them to tell the workers what we had found, reduce the levels of benzene to which the workers were exposed, and inform the appropriate government agencies and the rest of the petrochemical industry." Dow did not agree. "As soon as I got positive results," explained Picciano, "everything turned against me, and at no time did anybody ever say to me 'What are we going to do about the workers?'" When asked what he would have told workers if he could have, Picciano replied: "I would have told them: 'Look, you have an increased level of chromosome damage. If it's persistent, it means you have a higher risk of cancer, higher risk of having children with birth defects and a higher risk of spontaneous abortions.' I think we have an ethical responsibility to tell them to avoid exposure to the chemical they've been working with, and I think the chemical company must move to lower the exposures."

Dow, meanwhile, began to question the validity of the studies and Jack Kilian's work, suggesting the controls were weak, or that the Kilian and Picciano studies did not take account of other factors such as viruses workers might have had, medications they used, lab-test methodology and techniques, and even the seasons of the year. By the late 1970s, Kilian and Picciano had quit Dow. Kilian took a job with the University of Texas and Picciano became a consultant in Virginia. In any case, by 1978, relations between Kilian and the new medical director at Dow had become strained. One exchange of letters between the two in February 1978 indicated Kilian's clear displeasure with Dow's refusal to continue testing workers in the Epoxy Resin group (epichlorohydrin). Dow eventually shut down Kilian's labs in Freeport, making the building into a cafeteria. Kilian's files appear to have vanished in the process or went into very deep storage in Dow's medical archive.

New York Times reporter Richard Severo, who wrote about the Kilian projects in 1980, explained his difficulty in pursuing the story:

> In an effort to learn what happened to cytogenetics at Dow, *The New York Times* interviewed past and present employees of the company's Texas Divisions, as well as various professionals who acted as consultants.
>
> There was considerable reluctance to talk unless identities were concealed. With Dr. Kilian's departure, cytogenetics has become a sensitive subject at Dow and some of those approached for opinions said they feared the company would somehow impair their future chances to find work in the chemical industry if they were openly critical.
>
> What emerged from their perceptions is a program surrounded by uncertainty, rumor, even mystery in an industry that has become sensitive about what it sees as a poor public image.

Dr. Marvin Legator, a former Dow consultant, and by 1983, director of the Division of Environmental Toxicology at the University of Texas Medical School, did speak on the record. "It would seem to me that from a moral and legal standpoint, industry should be held accountable for not doing these procedures and informing their workers They should be held liable for having the procedures and not using them to protect the workers."

Sources: Richard Severo, "Dispute Arises Over Dow Studies On Genetic Damage in Workers," *New York Times*, February 5, 1980, p. A-1; Marvin S. Legator, "The Experiment That Failed," pp. 465–86; and, letter of Jack Kilian, MD, Regional Director, Occupational Health and Medical Research, B-1222 Building, Dow Chemical, Texas Division, Freeport, Texas, to J. R. Venable, MD, Medical Director, Texas Division, Dow Chemical, B-101 Building, March 23, 1978.

"Dead Peasants"

When Delores Baker of Freeport, Texas discovered that Dow Chemical Company had a secret life insurance policy on her dead husband, and that the company planned to collect the death benefit for itself, not her, she decided to sue. In fact, it turned out that Dow Chemical had thousands of such policies on its workers; policies it opened in the 1980s in a bit of creative financial management that some found to be downright morbid and unethical. Known broadly as Corporate Owned Insurance Policies, it is not unusual for corporations to take out life insurance policies on key executives, whose untimely demise might adversely affect the company's business and future. But for companies to take out such policies on everyday workers—known as "dead peasant" or "dead janitor" policies—and to cash in on those policies for financial gain, is quite something else. Charlie Singletary, business manager for the International Union of Operating Engineers Local 564—which represents 1,000 Dow employees in Freeport, Texas—said he was shocked to hear Dow bought life insurance on its employees. After learning about the policies, Singletary queried Dow about the practice and was told by company officials Dow had no such policies on union workers in Freeport.[12]

But in 1988, Dow did buy insurance polices on 4,051 of its management-level employees, and three years later, another 17,061 policies for some of its full-time employees—though Dow didn't say just where at the time. According to Dow, the company purchased the latter group of policies in Michigan, relying on a 1991 state law that gives employers an "insurable interest" in all their employees. Amazingly, the practice, even with secret policies, is legal in most states. Texas, California, Ohio, Illinois, Minnesota, and Michigan allow the policies, but require employee consent. And Dow is not alone in the practice. An attorney for Hartford Life Insurance Co. has estimated that nearly one-fourth of the *Fortune 500* companies have invested millions in the policies, covering between 5 and 6 million employees. If a company paid $10,000 a year in policy premiums, the estimated death benefits to covered employees could be worth as much as $300,000 each. But for the companies, there's more than just a death benefit at issue.

Companies using the practice, it was discovered, were also getting tax benefits on the increased value generated from the policies' investments. They were also receiving tax-free benefits when the policies paid off. Some companies used the revenues from death benefits to fund other programs, or to create trusts within the company that could be used for practically anything. Enron-owned Portland General Electric, for example, used the insurance pay-offs from its employee policies to generate nearly $80 million in a special trust fund it then used to fund benefits for the company's managers, directors, and executives. According to PACE, the union for Paper Allied-Industrial Chemical & Energy Workers, the policies can be hidden in corporate coffers, as some companies have buried the policies "so deeply and ambiguously on their books that even the firms' own accounting departments are unaware of their existence."[13]

The policies in Dow's case would not have come into the public limelight were it not for the Internal Revenue Service (IRS) investigating some of Dow's accounting practices on its corporate income taxes. The IRS found that between 1989 and 1991, Dow was deducting a $30.3 million loan used to pay the premiums on the policies, and another $2.7 million in administrative expenses. The IRS ruled that this was an improper deduction. Dow then sued the IRS, claiming the deduction was proper, bringing the practice into public light and to the attention of Delores Baker and others. Baker's husband worked at Dow's Freeport plant as a security supervisor for many years, retiring in 1993 and passing away six years later. Baker filed her suit in U.S. District Court in Houston, claiming that if the company had a life insurance policy on her husband, she should receive the benefit, not the company. Baker also sought class-action status for 21,000 other Dow employees with such policies.[14]

While Texas law allows the policies with employee notice, it also specifies those with "an insurable interest"—close relatives, a creditor, or a company wanting to insure a top executive. In an earlier case involving Texas employees of Wal-Mart, U.S. District Judge Nancy Atlas in Houston ruled that Wal-Mart improperly used a Georgia state law when it bought secret life insurance policies on 350,000 employees. Wal-Mart's Texas employees lived in Texas, worked in Texas, and died in Texas, wrote the judge, and at the time the policies were written, Texas employers did not have an "insurable interest" in the lives of their employees. When the beneficiary doesn't have a legitimate interest, the insurance proceeds revert back to the employee's estate under Texas law. Judge Atlas' decision on Wal-Mart, as well as other Texas cases, opened the door for survivors like Delores Baker to recover any insurance proceeds Dow Chemical may have received for deceased Texas employees.

Meanwhile, in the U.S. Congress, at least one bill has been introduced, by Rep. Gene Green (D-TX), to require companies to inform employees, former employees, and their families when companies take out insurance policies on workers, and also to disclose the policy amount and name of the insurer. The bill—titled the Life Insurance Employee Notification Act—would be retroactive to January 1, 1985 and would require companies taking out new policies to notify employees within 30 days. Under this law, nondisclosure of employer-owned life insurance coverage on employees would be an unfair trade practice and a violation of the Federal Trade Commission Act. In December 2002, Houston's KPCR-TV station offered its support to Congressman Green and his bill, observing with one web-posted editorial that "corporations profiting from workers' deaths is unseemly and to do so without the families' knowledge unconscionable."[15] Green's bill is still pending in Congress, where it has been bottled up with the help of the insurance industry.

Workers Burned

On March 3, 1998, an explosion and fire at an ethylbenzene plant at Dow's Freeport, Texas operations badly injured two workers and demolished a nearby maintenance building. The two workers—Marcus Martinez and Danny Bell—were both hospitalized. The explosion occurred, it was later learned, after a light hydrocarbon vapor cloud had silently formed in a maintenance building near the ethylbenzene plant for some ten hours before the blast. The vapor cloud was created when a utility water line was incorrectly tied into a hydrocarbon line, contaminating the plant's process water with "pygas," or pyrolysis gas. The vapor cloud ignited while the men

Union leaders were concerned with the company's plan to use "unskilled contract labor" to fill the gaps of more experienced people let go.

were in the maintenance building, causing an explosion and fireball, destroying the building and severely burning the two men. They were taken to the burn unit of Galveston's John Sealy Hospital, where they remained for several weeks. Although the mishap closed the ethylbenzene plant at Freeport, a Dow spokesperson indicated the shutdown would not likely affect the plant's ability to meet orders.

As the incident came under investigation to determine the precise cause and sequence of events, some union officials raised the question of whether earlier labor cut-backs by Dow had left the plant short-handed. "The company told us last month that we are six weeks behind on a backlog of maintenance," said Jack Brown, business manager for the pipefitters union, Local 390. However, he emphasized he had no way of knowing if the cut-backs were to blame for the latest mishap. Union leaders in Freeport had worried about possible safety lapses at the plant from job cuts ever since Dow began announcing the cuts in 1997. Brown added that he and other union leaders were also concerned with the company's plan to use "unskilled contract labor" to fill the gaps of more experienced people let go. Outside contractors aren't always the best trained or most knowledgeable about local plant conditions and safety procedures. According to Brown, Dow had expressed some disappointment with the work done by contractors. In the plant's polyethylene section, he had heard that Dow had banned one particular contractor from that area because of previous repairs that left high pressure leaks. Rick Thomas, with Local 564 of the operating engineers, said he hoped the reason for the accident wasn't "that the contractors tied the systems," referring to the mix-up on the lines, if that was determined to be the cause. "That's normally our work," Thomas said, referring to safety-qualified union workers, "and I don't know why we weren't involved. If it is a man-

power issue the company has a lot of questions to answer." Added the Pipefitters' Jack Brown: "When Dow announced the layoffs I was concerned.
But they told us they had made studies to determine that they had enough
craftsmen left for the appropri-

Danny Bell and Marcos Martinez entered the maintenance building to correct the problem just before the explosion.

ate safety levels."[16]

Two days later, Dow
responded that no contract
workers were involved in the
incident. Said the company in a
statement: "... initial findings are
that no contractor employees were involved in the incident and the cause
was not plant maintenance related. Dow continues to believe that its
Freeport facility is appropriately staffed to safely, effectively, and efficiently
operate the site and to keep the facility well maintained."[17]

Meanwhile, Dow investigators confirmed in a preliminary assessment
that a mix-up on lines had occurred and played a significant role in the
explosion. The hydrocarbon-tainted water line was being used to flush out
another system that was to be taken out of service and demolished. Workers at the site became concerned when they smelled hydrocarbon odors
downwind and tried to isolate the source. They soon discovered the incorrectly tied lines. Workers Danny Bell and Marcos Martinez entered the maintenance building to correct the problem just before the explosion and fire
erupted. The two men remained in the hospital burn unit as Dow conducted its early findings. "We are gravely concerned about their condition," said
John Barksdale, vice president of Latin American and Texan operations.
"These are two well-thought-of professionals and co-workers. They will
need our thoughts and prayers throughout their recovery."[18]

Following Dow's preliminary investigation, representatives from the U.S.
Occupational Safety and Hazard Administration (OSHA) arrived to conduct
their investigation. At the plant meanwhile, some 70 workers were tested by
Dow for benzene exposure. The workers had requested the tests as a precautionary measure, under OSHA
standards, following the incident.

In mid-July 1998, OSHA cited Dow for safety violations in the incident and fined the company $10,000.

Dow reported that all the results
registered "well below the OSHA
guidelines, indicating no overex-
posures." Dow said it would
issue letters to all those workers
certifying the results.[19]

In mid-July 1998, OSHA cited Dow for safety violations in the incident and
fined the company $10,000. OSHA's citations related to the inadequacy of
Dow's training of employees handling pyrolysis gas, and required Dow to
develop and submit to OSHA a pygas safety plan for the Freeport plant to
ensure that a similar incident would not occur in the future.[20] "While this was

an unfortunate incident," explained Dow's Christian Erle, vice president of Texas Operations, upon receiving the OSHA citations, "we learned a great deal from it. We have had an OSHA and internal investigation of the incident. What we have learned from these investigations is being shared around the Dow world to aid in preventing a similar incident from reoccurring. We will not be satisfied until we have a work site free from injuries. We are pleased that the employees who were injured in the incident continue to make progress, and it is anticipated that they will return to work in the near future. However, we must continue to focus on safety to prevent any injuries to Dow people."[21]

The two hospitalized Dow workers, having undergone extensive skin grafting to treat their burns, were now recovering at home, wearing tight-fitting pressure garments to protect the medical treatments and skin grafts. While both men were thankful for the treatment they and their families had received from the hospital and Dow in the aftermath of the accident, at least one of the workers, Danny Bell, told a reporter at *The Brazosport Facts* that he never wanted to work in a chemical plant again.[22]

Busting Unions

Although it professes to work with organized labor, Dow Chemical has not been an especially union-friendly company. In fact, it was only under pressure from the federal government during World War II that Dow reluctantly invited unions to organize at all. Since then, Dow has regularly fought to decertify its unions. In 1967, unions represented almost all of Dow's production workers. But through the late 1960s and 1970s, according to the Metal Trades Department of the AFL-CIO, Dow undertook an "unapologetic campaign to rid itself of unions." Dow schooled its plant managers in how to deal with labor malcontents, how to pick apart union contracts, and how to turn the union's grievance procedures against the workers by eating away at union resources. In February 1969, one Dow official warned his plant managers that headquarters would view union election wins as "failures" by local managers, and that such failures would not be repeated. Dow decertification campaigns and various other activities resulted in the loss of 15 labor units at Dow in a period of 6 years.[23] Says the Metal Trades Department:

> The history of union-busting by Dow Chemical Company goes back almost a half century when workers at Dow plants around the nation were represented by an assortment of unions including the Metal Trades Department, Oil Chemical and Atomic Workers, International Chemical Workers Union, United Steelworkers, United Mine Workers, Teamsters,

various craft unions and independent company-oriented unions.

Labor relations were markedly paternalistic and condescending in keeping with the Dow family domination of company management through the 1950s. The tradition established by Herbert Dow in the company's earliest days was to expect employees to be loyal and totally dedicated.... In return, the company encouraged them to buy stock to tighten the connection between the worker and Dow.

In the 1960s and early 70s, Dow officials reacted strongly to a series of strikes and began to develop a company-wide policy to combat union activity through an opportunistic "divide and conquer" system that had evolved into what the company today refers to as its "Basic Principles of Salaried Operations."

The company "discovered" the effectiveness of its "Salaried Operations" sometime in the late 1950s when it opened a major operation in Plaquemine, Louisiana and went on line using untrained and unskilled workers in order to avoid hiring union help.... [24]

By 1981, only one-third of Dow's workers were unionized. And Dow management would take the opportunity of strikes to help further weaken unions, running the plants with its own people during strikes, and driving tough deals at the bargaining table. As a result, very few of Dow's chemical plants today are represented by union workers. As of the mid-1990s, only four plants among the dozens Dow operated were unionized.[25] Two of Dow's biggest operations—at Midland, Michigan and Freeport, Texas—are unionized. But Dow fights with labor regularly at these plants.

Dow's latest battle with union representatives—and another attempt at decertifying local unions—came in 2001 in Texas following Dow's acquisition of Union Carbide. At Carbide's Texas City plant, a collective bargaining agreement was scheduled to expire. Workers in 12 local unions there are represented through the Texas City Metal Trades Council (TCMTC). Dow moved to withdraw recognition of three of the local unions. However in December 2001, the National Labor Relations Board (NLRB) concluded that Dow's moves were illegal, and later approved the holding of an election for workers at the Texas City site to vote on the matter of keeping or decertifying their union.[26]

Taking On Dow

Organized labor, meanwhile, had begun to focus on Dow operations in a new way—company-wide, through all Dow plants and ventures nationally and internationally, as well as across all the various unions representing Dow workers. In July 2002, seven unions representing approximately 5,000 workers in the United States and Canada employed at Dow Chemical, Dow Corning, and DuPont Dow Elastomers, came together in Midland, Michigan at a meeting sponsored by ICEM—the International Federation of Chemical,

Energy, Mine and General Workers' Unions.* The purpose of the meeting was to discuss common problems at Dow operations and forge a common agenda for Dow workers. The unions formed a Dow network to support union activity across Dow operations. "We heard reports from several local unions that Dow is taking an aggressively anti-union approach at their factories," said Harry Lester, of the United Steelworkers, chairman of the newly formed network "and we collectively decided that we would not allow the company to pick us off one

Organized labor is building something of a "super union" at Dow: bringing Dow workers together nationally and internationally, as well as across multiple unions.

by one." When Dow takes on one union, Lester said, "they will be taking us all on at one time." Organized labor, it appears, is building something of a "super union" at Dow.

Among the network's first tasks was to rally behind the Texas City workers to keep their union in place. Union leaders at Dow facilities from across North America began writing to the Texas City workers, urging them to back their union. The Steelworkers' Harry Lester led a delegation of the Dow network that traveled to Texas City for a rally against the decertification attempt. Lester was joined in Texas City by local union leaders from Dow and Dow Corning operations in Midland, Michigan, as well as Dow Chemical workers from Sarnia, Ontario and Freeport, Texas. Kenneth Zinn, ICEM North American Regional Coordinator, added a message from Dow chemical workers in Brazil and Argentina. The Latin American unionists urged the Texas City workers to maintain their union and pledged to back them up in their ongoing struggle for a new contract. "Dow workers around the world are watching what is happening in Texas City and we're mobilizing to back each other up in times of need," said Zinn.[27]

The Texas workers beat back the decertification attempt, with 69 percent of the workers voting to keep the TCMTC as their bargaining agent. The union and the company then returned to the bargaining table, with the new Dow union network pledging its continued backing to the Texas City workers. In December 2002, a new agreement was reached and ratified by the union's membership.

---

*The unions represented were the Communications, Energy and Paperworkers (CEP), International Association of Machinists and Aerospace Workers, International Union of Operating Engineers (IUOE), Paper, Allied-Industrial, Chemical and Energy Workers (PACE), United Association of Journeymen and Apprentices of the Plumbing, Pipefitting, Sprinkler Fitting Industry, United Food and Commercial Workers (UFCW), United Steelworkers of America (USWA), as well as the Metal Trades Department of the AFL-CIO.

14.
The DBCP Saga

*One doctor in Berkeley who saw the test
results thought the men had had vasectomies.*

Cathy Trost, *Elements of Risk*

In 1952, a chemical called dibromochloropropane, or DBCP, was being tested as a promising new pesticide. The chemical had shown good results in California against tiny worms called nematodes that ravaged the roots of fruit trees and vegetable crops in the state's multi-million dollar agricultural regions. Such chemicals, used as soil fumigants, were injected into the soil to kill the worms. Dow had previously been successful with another bromine-derived chemical, ethylene dibromide, or EDB, which researchers at the company's Seal Beach, California lab had adapted for agriculture in 1942. By 1945, *Dowfume W-10*, Dow's new EDB nematicide, hit the market in a big way, allowing yields of some crops like sweet potatoes to double and triple. *Dowfume* soon crushed a rival product made by Shell Chemical Co. But *Dowfume* had its limits; it had to be applied weeks before crops were planted, and could not be used with many other living crops, such as citrus trees and vineyards.

It happened that scientists in Hawaii, at the Pineapple Research Institute, were experimenting with other compounds, some of which built on Dow's EDB line. One of these was dibromochloropropane, DBCP, which showed good results. Shell Chemical had a man in Hawaii, Clyde McBeth, who reported the promising results back to Shell's Modesto, California research center. "DBCP would knock 'em [nematodes] down to a very low population in the field," said McBeth. "It took 'em four years to build up again." Shell soon embarked on a program to develop the chemical. As did Dow. Both companies also began doing some basic toxicology on the chemical, to satisfy the Interstate Commerce Commission and the U.S. Department of Agriculture, which by law required certain testing and labeling requirements for protecting transport workers, pesticide applicators, and farmers handling the chemical. Shell's tests were performed as "directed research," paid for by Shell, at the University of California Medical School laboratory by toxicologist Dr. Charles Hine. The results of Hine's animal tests were presented to Shell in 1954. Dow's testing was done about the same

"These data also show that liver, lung and kidney effects might be expected," said Dow's 1958 DBCP animal testing report. "Testicular atrophy may result from prolonged, repeated exposure."

time, under the direction of Dr. Theodore Torkelson.[1]

Dow's report on its DBCP testing, prepared in July 1958, was circulated only within the company. Skin and inhalation tests on rats, rabbits, guinea pigs, and monkeys showed that DBCP was "readily absorbed through the skin" and "high in toxicity by inhalation." Nearly half of the test animals died after breathing 12 parts per million (ppm)—the equivalent of what workers might face in three months of seven-hour days if the chemical's concentration in the air were at the level. The lab animals also exhibited abnormally small testicles and had a reduced number of sperm cells, some malformed. Rats showed liver and kidney damage. Two monkeys in the experiment grew ill, weak, and listless after chronic DBCP exposure, and were also susceptible to infection. "These data also show that liver, lung and kidney effects might be expected," said the Dow report. "Testicular atrophy may result from prolonged, repeated exposure."[2]

On the Market

By the time of Dow's report, however, both Shell and Dow were already producing and selling their respective DBCP products, named *Nemagon* in Shell's case, and *Fumazone* for Dow.

Dow began making *Fumazone* in 1957; Shell had been producing its version since 1956. Both companies also produced marketing aids. Dow produced a ten-minute, full color film—*Thief in the Soil*—featuring crop damaging nematodes and Dow's saving product. A 1958 Dow brochure, *Plunder Underground*, stated: "Farmers no longer have to watch their prize acreage sapped of its profit by nematodes and other soil borne pests. They can fight back—and win astonishing profits—with the new soil fumigants." With the discovery that the chemical was more toxic than previously thought, Dow had expressed some concerns privately in the back-and-forth with Shell researchers, advocating a tough warning label. At one point, Dow noted to Shell that DBCP levels as low as 5 ppm in the air "were a hazard to exposed persons." Some internal memos at Shell would suggest reducing air levels to 1 ppm. Yet in the early marketing, Dow and Shell issued only mild advisories, suggesting that applicators wear gloves, shoes and garments made of resistant material, and avoid breathing the vapor or fumes.[3]

In September 1961, the earlier findings of the Shell and Dow DBCP animal tests were combined into one report and published for the first time in the *Journal of Toxicological and Applied Pharmacology*. This report indicated that "excessive exposure to the vapors [of DBCP] resulted in damage to the liver, kidneys, and various tissues, including sperm cells..." This report repeated the finding that 40 to 50 percent of the rats exposed to DBCP vapors at 12 ppm had died. The report also emphasized the damage to the animal's testicles. "The most striking observation at autopsy," reported the authors, "was severe atrophy and degeneration of the testes of all species [rats, guinea pigs, rabbits, and monkeys]..."

By this time, Dow and Shell had become the chief manufacturers of DBCP, and were supplying the chemical to a number of users, distributors, and formulators in the United States and around the world. One such customer was Occidental Chemical (Oxy), which operated a formulating plant near Lathrop, California. As a formulator, Oxy bought DBCP from Shell or Dow in bulk, prepared it in various strength formulations, and sold those products under their own label or shipped it out to farm supply stores as a Dow or Shell product. Oxy's predecessor at the site, Best Fertilizers, had bought technical-grade DBCP from both Shell and Dow. By 1964, after Oxy became the operator, Dow became the sole supplier, sending rail cars filled with concentrated DBCP to the Lathrop plant regularly. Oxy, in fact, had signed a contract with Dow in 1964 to bag and ship finished *Fumazone* for Dow—about a half a million pounds worth. Workers at the Lathrop plant, like those at formulation and packaging centers elsewhere, often worked around huge holding tanks, and smaller 1,000 gallon batch tanks where solvents and emulsifiers would be added to make various formulations of the chemical. Other workers, down the line, would do the canning as the formulations were made. Workers, standing on platforms over the tanks, were regularly inhaling vapors or dust, with splashing liquid and/or dust making contact with skin and clothing. Protective clothing and goggles were available, but not always worn. Workers would handle and pour barrels of material into the tanks, lines carrying the liquid would sometimes leak, and there was no ventilation system to draw the fumes away.[4]

Card Games

Back in Midland, meanwhile, Dow's toxicologists were keeping files on the company's various chemicals. The effects of each chemical, in fact, were dutifully entered on medical cards used by company doctors in case of accidents and spills. But as author Cathy Trost reports, the entries made in some categories were altered after 1964:

...*Fumazone's* medical card noted "moderately irritating" eye effects, "slightly irritating" skin effects (although small amounts could be absorbed through the skin and could produce systemic injury, even death), and testicular degeneration, which "may result from chronic exposure to active material." Liver and kidney injury was a possible consequence of excessive exposure from ingestion or inhalation of vapors. The vapors were capable of producing anesthesia.

After 1964 the medical cards on *Fumazone* were slightly modified. "The cards addressed single exposures, and you don't see testicular changes on single exposures," said [Dow's] Dr. Torkelson. "It was put on some of the cards because whoever wrote it knew about it and thought it was important enough to put on there along with liver and kidney effects. When it was retested, the testes didn't show an effect from a single exposure, and a new card was made out."

On the new cards, all of the possible effects were essentially the same as before 1964, save for one: Warnings about testicular effects were removed.*[5]

USDA had given the o.k. to formally register DBCP in 1964 after the companies pointed to their track record of safe sale and use since the late 1950s, and Shell produced worker health exams that showed no problems. Out in ag country, meanwhile, farmers and orchard owners loved DBCP. From Georgia peach growers to California grape growers, sales boomed. Demand for DBCP soared during the 1960s and 1970. By then there were at least 35 formulations containing some DBCP.

More Studies

By 1971, however, Russian studies had confirmed what Dow and Shell had discovered earlier about DBCP—male rats fed DBCP for two and half months could not fertilize female rats. And scientists at the National Cancer Institute (NCI), then looking at various chemicals, found that rats and mice fed DBCP developed cancer. The NCI results were published in December 1973, and also included EDB, the earlier Dow nematicide, which was found to cause cancer in lab animals. "These results show that chronic exposure to either DBCP or EDB could be a health hazard," said the report. "Anyone exposed to DBCP or EDB should...use protective clothing, masks and other means to avoid absorptions of either material."[6] The NCI tests were later followed up by tests at EPA in the spring of 1976, in which 60 percent of the rats and 90 percent of the mice developed stomach cancer. Female rats had a

---

*Dow's Dr. John Lanham later testified in court that the company changed the medical cards in 1966, removing the testicular effects warning because no reproductive problems had surfaced in workers.

high incidence of breast cancer. EPA began a formal review of the chemical in a procedure that might challenge its continued registration and use. Shell, as the largest supplier, began sending new data to EPA to keep the chemical on the market. But both Shell and Dow notified their own workers about the EPA animal studies, though downgrading the studies because of the way they were done. However, neither Dow nor Shell passed the new information on to Occidental, and the workers there never heard about the 1976 cancer findings.[7] Nor had anything been passed on about the testicular and fertility findings. Dow undertook follow-up tests to check EPA's results, but Dow's tests also produced cancer in rats and mice similar to earlier findings. Rats that breathed DBCP in doses of 0.6 and 3.0 ppm in EPA-backed chronic tests developed nasal cavity tumors.[8]

"No Sperm Seen"

At the Oxy plant in Lathrop, meanwhile, some of the workers discovered they were sterile. One, Richard Perez, who had worked in Oxy's Ag Chem section since 1967, knew from tests dating to 1974 that he was sterile. Another, Wesley Jones, had testing done in July 1976 and no sperm was found. Jones' doctor advised him to quit. He filed compensation claims. By the summer of 1976, Oxy's management at Lathrop knew they had a problem: at least 4 of 35 workers had fertility problems. Oxy brought in some experts to go over the plant and by May 1977, DBCP was high on the

One doctor in Berkeley who saw the results thought the men had had vasectomies.

list of suspect chemicals. Workers at the plant had been talking about the problem in a jocular way in the lunchroom, noting their inability to make their wives pregnant. In June 1977, seven of the workers at Oxy volunteered to have their sperm counts tested after an independent filmmaker researching a documentary on industrial hazards, heard about the lunchroom banter and offered to pay for the testing. All seven of the Lathrop workers tested produced abnormally low sperm counts, or "no sperm seen." One doctor in Berkeley who saw the results thought the men had had vasectomies. In mid-July 1977, the union told Oxy's management of the test results, and Oxy met with a doctor to hear the interpretation, and shortly thereafter began consulting with Dow and others. DBCP still wasn't specifically fingered as the culprit, but Dow and others had suspicions. Dow sent Oxy its 1961 Dow-Shell DBCP report. The seven Oxy workers were retested with similar results; four of the men again showed no sperm. Oxy then ordered tests for all who worked in the Ag Chem area and notified the state OSHA of the tests. After those tests showed more sterile men, Oxy shut down pesticide production in the Ag Chem area.

By mid-July 1977, Dow wrote a letter to its formulator customers advising them to adhere to a 1 ppm worker exposure limit which Dow believed to be safe. But when Dow initially tested 14 workers at its own DBCP plant in Magnolia, Arkansas, it found 12 of them with abnormal, depressed sperm counts. Later, in further tests, some 50 of 86 workers at Magnolia were found to be sterile or had low sperm counts.*

Meanwhile, by late July 1977, the story of the sterile workers at Oxy's plant in California had broken locally and nationally. TV crews from ABC and CBS affiliates in San Francisco had camped out at the Lathrop plant and began interviewing workers. An Associated Press story, quoting plant workers, including one intend-

> **"Dow continued to hold to the theory that it took more than one part per million...to cause depressed sperm counts, even though no animal tests had been done to prove it."**
>
> Cathy Trost, *Elements of Risk*

ing to sue, made front page news in California and soon went out to papers all across the country. The news focus was predominantly on the Oxy plant, and Occidental's Hooker Ag Chem staff back in New York had helped prepare the company's California people for the media frenzy. Cal-OSHA, the federal OSHA, and its advisory arm, the National Institute of Occupational Safety and Health, were also involved by this time.

Back in Magnolia, Arkansas, Dow put the best face possible on its operations there, noting it used and enforced a 1 ppm exposure standard, and that its workers wore neoprene gloves, jackets, and boots. Further, Dow had told its workers that DBCP was a carcinogen. Yet it had not told them about the chemical's testicular effects. Soon newspaper reporters began piecing things together and asking Dow scientists and the company's Magnolia workers some questions. If safe exposure levels had been maintained at Magnolia, with workers in protective garb, why were half of them infertile? And why hadn't Dow included reproductive warnings on its own safety information? "I guess at the time we weren't all that concerned about it," explained Dow's vice president Dr. Etcyl Blair to Arkansas reporters in 1977. "That's hindsight. Our concern was the effect on these other organs more than it was that [i.e., testicular effects]." Regarding DBCP and cancer, Blair said DBCP "probably is not going to have an effect. The things that are real-

---

*Other DBCP plants were also tested. At a Velsicol Company plant in El Dorado, Arkansas, about half of the 24 workers who handled DBCP were found to have abnormally low sperm counts. At the Shell plant in Alabama, sterility was also found among workers who handled DBCP. And further tests at the Lathrop plant would reveal that 35 of 114 workers exposed to DBCP were infertile. See also Ronald L. Taylor, "DBCP Still Used Despite Dangers," *Los Angeles Times*, June 28, 1979, and Lewis Regenstein, *America The Poisoned*, pp. 317, 321.

Dead At 27

In 1970, Mike Trout, a recent high school graduate in Manteca, California, took a local job pumping gas. Manteca is an agricultural town in the San Joaquin Valley—the kind of town that has an annual Pumpkin Festival. Mike's parents had wanted him to go to college, but he didn't want college. By January 1971, he had taken a job at the Occidental Chemical Company warehouse not far from his parents' home where he lived until he was about 21. By the spring of 1974, he was transferred to Oxy's Ag Chem division in Lathrop, where the money was better. There he worked with other men who mixed and canned chemicals, including DBCP.

Mike Trout loved kids, and was especially fond of his younger brothers and sisters while growing up. He was also passionate about baseball, even as a young adult, at one point playing about 90 games a season for four different teams. In February 1974, at St. Anthony's Roman Catholic Church in Manteca, Mike married Marta, four years younger. The couple soon had a modest suburban home and a new son, Michael, Jr. But in late 1975, things started to change for the young Trout family. That's when Mike Trout started feeling sick and wasn't quite himself. He had headaches and flu-like symptoms. In February 1976, after a series of tests, a brain tumor was discovered, and Mike had surgery to remove it followed by six months of radiation treatment. Mike took a six-month leave from his job at Oxy. His prognosis for recovery was good, but the ordeal and radiation treatment had taken its toll, diminishing Mike's vitality and, among other things, his much cherished baseball prowess.

By September 1976, Mike Trout had returned to his job at Oxy and was recovering from his brain surgery, but another problem began stalking him, for he was among those at Oxy who had trouble getting their wives pregnant. In fact, for two years or so, he and Marta had been trying to have a second child without success. Mike was one of the seven workers at Oxy who first volunteered to have their sperm counts tested. All seven of the men tested produced abnormally low or no sperm. Mike Trout had a sperm count of less than one million, severely low.

By July 1977, the sterility story at the Oxy plant had become front page news. Mike by then had been removed from the DBCP exposure since Oxy's production was shut down. And as a result, his sperm count had shown some improvement. Marta, in fact, had become pregnant, though Mike at first dismissed her discovery as a false, "hysterical pregnancy." But it proved to be the real thing. Later though, he and Marta worried their child could suffer birth defects, due to Mike's damaged sperm. In November 1978, after Mike was tested again, his sperm count had improved dramatically, as had several of the other Oxy workers that had previously shown low sperm counts. These results suggested that if DBCP exposure were stopped before it caused complete degeneration of sperm cells, the damaged cells might recover. However, workers who suffered total sterilization would not recover. Mike and Marta soon had a healthy second son, Matthew. Other Oxy families weren't so lucky. The wives of two other Oxy workers gave birth to children with birth defects, one in October 1978 and the other, in April 1979.

Meanwhile, Mike Trout's brain cancer, thought to be in retreat, returned in

October 1979. Mike was back at work by this time in the Ag Chem section, but his doctor had found a shadow in a brain scan made during a check up. Things got worse soon thereafter. Headaches, mood swings, depression, and related problems all gradually returned. He was having a harder time at work too, but persevered, even while being harassed by management as a slacker. One night in mid-December 1979, he woke up vomiting, and by morning had begun to have extreme head pain. When the ambulance arrived to take him to the hospital he was kicking and screaming with pain and had to be tied down on the gurney. When the surgeons cut through his skull in the operating room, they found an enormous tumor and so much pressure, "it just kind of shot out" when they cut into his skull, his wife explained. Although breathing on his own after surgery, and still with a good strong heart, doctors could not control the hemorrhaging in his brain. Mike Trout died the next day. He was 27 years old.

As Cathy Trost recounts in her book, *Elements of Risk*, Cal-OSHA received two staff medical reports on Mike Trout's death in January 1980. Both suggested there was an association between brain cancer and his exposure to DBCP, although there were some caveats. "Excessive brain cancer does occur in some industries, particularly chemical, but the causative agents have not been identified to date with one exception, vinyl chloride," wrote Dr. Ira Monosson. "Although conclusive evidence that DBCP causes brain cancer is lacking, there also is no evidence to the contrary. Further, the possibility that DBCP indeed can cause neoplasms of the brain is far from remote and certainly does exist." Dr. Lawrence Rose described the "well documented" carcinogenicity of DBCP but said, "In this particular case, one would have to go over all of the chemical exposures, work history, health history, personal habits, etc. to develop a list of possible substances."

In February 1980, Marta Trout changed her husband's workman's compensation claim to a death case and refiled a pending lawsuit as a wrongful death action. In a court declaration, she described Mike's work as "loading, unloading, packaging, and preparation of the dangerous chemical known as DBCP....He was not the least bit apprehensive of the exposure by reason of the fact that no one had ever warned him of any danger or hazards in connection with the product, which he believed to be 100 percent safe." When presented with a separate settlement from Occidental in November 1982, Marta did not want to settle, but did so to help finance a further trial. She also reluctantly accepted a second settlement from Dow and Shell—a modest amount by all accounts. She had thought about the prospect of a long trial and what effect that might have on her boys. "They understand about the poisoning and what was done at Oxy," she said, "but they're so young, they don't remember the suffering."

Source: Adapted from Cathy Trost, *Elements of Risk: The Chemical Industry and its Threat to America*, New York: Times Books, 1984.

ly going to cause cancer," he said, "are going to be: do they smoke cigarettes, do they eat a lot of fatty substances, these kinds of issues from a physician's point of view or from a scientist's point of view are the things that are going to cause cancer." Yet the same week that Blair made these remarks,

Cathy Trost observed, "the trade journal *Chemical Week* ran a story saying that DBCP produced the earliest tumors ever seen in laboratory animals." Some of Dow's Magnolia workers began talking too, explaining to the press that the Dow plant was shrouded in the smell of DBCP; that workers didn't wear protective gear or masks during hot weather; and that they got the chemical "all over" their hands and boots, sometimes splashing on them or catching in their clothing. Yes, they had been told about DBCP causing cancer in lab animals, but the company downplayed those findings. As for neoprene garb, one newspaper reported that Dow had studies showing neoprene did not provide adequate skin protection against DBCP.[9]

As the DBCP story broke, Dow's Dr. V. K. Rowe, who had conducted some of the early research on DBCP, told reporters the DBCP situation "came as a total surprise to us." Asked why Dow hadn't told workers about the possibility that DBCP could affect sperm counts and why the company hadn't periodically tested workers, Rowe replied, "I think our medical people would have to agree, in retrospect, this would have been a nice thing, a good thing to do."[10]

Oxy, Dow, and Shell had all shut down or suspended their DBCP operations on or before August 11, 1977, the day when the director of California's Department of Public Health received the following analysis from one of its investigators:

> The effect of DBCP in producing sterility in human males has been firmly established from studies done by physicians at UC [University of California] and at the Dow Chemical plant. Animal studies have shown DBCP is also a very potent carcinogen, producing not only primary cancer, but rapidly spreading metastatic lesions as well. In my opinion, it is imperative that this material should no longer be manufactured, formulated or applied for agricultural use, effective immediately.

The next day, California issued an emergency order suspending all uses of pesticides containing DBCP.

At the federal level, OSHA had already asked all manufacturers of DBCP to halt production voluntarily. In early September 1977, OSHA and EPA took further actions on DBCP. OSHA issued an emergency temporary exposure standard of 10 parts per billion (ppb), and later 1 ppb—a standard still 1,000 times more stringent than Dow's favored 1 part per million.

Dow's public relations department had prepared a brochure, *Dow's Reaction to DBCP*, in response to the controversy. In it, Dow defended its testing and explained that although it had tested the chemical down to the 5 ppm level, and was comfortable recommending and using a 1 ppm standard since the "odds of a problem at 1 part per million" were small. "Dow continued to hold to the theory that it took more than one part per million exposure level to DBCP to cause depressed sperm counts," observes Cathy Trost, "even though no animal tests had been done to prove it."[11]

In October 1977, at hearings conducted by the California Department of Industrial Relations, department head Don Vial asked, if Dow was supposed to be "the chemist for the chemical industry," and if the company's commitment to product stewardship was so strong, why had its own workers not been warned about DBCP? Answering for Dow was Dr. Etcyl Blair: "It's rather like teaching your children...don't get in front of the car," he explained. "...You don't spend your time talking all about the various things that can happen to you if you get hit by a car... Our contention [on DBCP] is that if you have exposures greater than 1 part per million you are going to have a problem, so our efforts have been directed in that line."[12]

Cancer Tutorial

The California DBCP hearings went on for four days, with one segment becoming something of a public tutorial on how synthetic chemicals could affect future generations. DBCP, in fact, was the first chemical pesticide found to have reproductive effects. And witnesses at the hearings explained that they were learning much about how modern chemistry invaded the body and what it did once inside. Most carcinogens, one scientist explained, were also mutagens, substances that could cause problems, or mutations, in the germ-line cells—the sperm and eggs that carried hereditary material. Carcinogens, on the other hand, targeted regular body cells, called somatic cells, and once lodged therein, caused tumors to grow 20 years or so later. Scientists were also learning that when a particular chemical entered the body it sometimes converted, or "metabolized," into another, more potent chemical inside the body, becoming the ultimate carcinogen.

At the hearings, during these scientific exchanges, Dow and its scientists stood out as somewhere between rigid and glib. Dow's Dr. Gehring told the hearing that fewer than 3 percent of all cancers were caused by synthetic chemicals, and he suggested that attempts to estimate the risk of cancer from DBCP and other pesticides were "an exercise in futility." Gehring explained, "It is high time that the public recognizes there are numerous compounds capable of producing cancer when given in high amounts. Nature has contributed as many of them as has the ingenuity of man." Dow's scientists also took issue with the theory that every dose of a chemical, no matter how tiny, might have a cumulative effect. In DBCP's case, however, as some scientists explained, it wasn't just a matter of dosages; the body's enzymes were being overwhelmed by synthetic compounds they could not detoxify and excrete. "These enzymes see these particular sorts of chemicals which they have never seen before," explained scientist Arlene Blum, "and they make them into an active form where they are carcinogens....The DBCP incident points out that in addition to somatic cells being affected, the germinal cells—the hereditary cells—are also being affected. At high doses, we get effects like sterility. At low doses, there is the potential for genetic birth defects. I think this is really one of the most frightening things about all these chemicals."[13]

In late October 1977, EPA Administrator Doug Costle had announced a widespread ban and or severe restrictions on most uses of DBCP, then registered for use on some 19 food crops, as well as lawns and golf courses. "The DBCP calamity again dramatizes the need for vigilant, responsible regulation of chemical production and

> "At high doses, we get effects like sterility. At low doses, there is the potential for genetic birth defects. I think this is really one of the most frightening things about all these chemicals."
>
> Dr. Arlene Blum

use," he said. EPA predicted 21 cancer cases for every 1 million people who ate average amounts of foods contaminated with DBCP over a two-year period. But the DBCP saga wasn't over yet.

Legal Wars

A total of 57 DBCP workers had filed lawsuits against Occidental, Dow, Shell, and the University of California. Most of these cases, which had been consolidated, were settled in October 1982 when Occidental paid various claims and one wrongful death action. But one case, with seven workers—*Arnett v. Dow*—continued until only Dow and Shell remained. In that case, the plaintiffs charged that both companies had known about the toxic effects of DBCP on lab animals, including its testicular effects, since the 1950s, but failed to warn workers of the hazards. Plaintiffs also charged that the companies had conspired to suppress the test results by convincing the government of the adequacy of watered-down labels.

During a five-month trial, lawyers for Dow and Shell offered a number of defenses. They argued the two chemical companies had performed extensive tests on DBCP that were widely available though industry journals. Health problems, Dow and Shell scientists believed, would emerge first in the target organs—the kidneys, liver, and lung—before anything would occur in the testes. Dow had more exposure in the trial than did Shell since Dow had the prevailing contract with Oxy. So Dow tried to pin the blame on Oxy. Oxy had signed the contract and was fully warned, argued Dow, and so assumed all responsibility for the workers. Dow said it had sent Oxy a formulator's manual with the safety information on DBCP. Oxy, however, said it never received the manual. Oxy was also blamed for shoddy safety programs. Workers were blamed, too, and said to cause their own exposures through careless handling and not following safety recommendations. They bore responsibility for any fertility problems themselves, said the attorneys. In addition, fertility problems could spring from many causes, argued Dow and Shell, in fact from a wide variety of influences in modern life. Dow and Shell also tried to include the government as culpable, saying the federal agencies knew as much about DBCP's hazards as the companies did: they pointed to the Dow-Shell 1961 report submit-

In April 1983, a jury convicted Dow of failure to warn about the hazards of DBCP. ted as part of their first pesticide registration. Trying to weaken or discredit workers' claims, Dow and Shell also raised other factors, from workers' medical problems and

marijuana use, to cigarette smoking, use of alcohol, or even venereal disease—all of which had been shown to depress fertility in varying degrees, but with full recovery once exposure ended. However, one doctor who had tested the Oxy workers, said that lifestyle factors were "overwhelmed" by the effects of DBCP. Dow and Shell also tried to peel away two of the claimants who had not worked directly on the formulating lines. But the workers' attorneys explained that these workers had been sprayed with the chemical at times, used rags to wipe up DBCP spills, and had often spent hours at a time with their hands covered with chemicals from pallets they handled.[14]

Workers' claims for "fear of cancer and birth defects" were more tricky, with the judge ruling that the science of predicting who might develop cancer was too speculative for consideration in court, but still extracted a commitment from Dow and Shell protecting each worker's right to sue in the future should they contract cancer then. Dow and Shell attorneys tried to argue that fear claims should be rejected on grounds that exposure to chemicals was not an injury at all, but an everyday event or experience by anyone who drank a soda or smoked a cigarette. However, the workers' fertility injury, the judge ruled, coupled with the publicity about DBCP's link to cancer, could cause them anxiety, and he allowed such claims. But the workers would have to show that the DBCP had physically injured them and that their subsequent cancer fears were based on information from doctors and news reports. Workers also claimed birth defect fears for their families given DBCP's genetic injury to their bodies and examples of known birth defects.

In early April 1983, the jury announced the first part of its verdict. Dow was convicted of failure to warn about the hazards of DBCP and acquitted of concealment. Both Dow and Shell were also found innocent of concealment, and the jury could not reach a required 9–3 majority on punitive damages. In mid-April the jury reached agreement on damages, awarding the workers and some of their wives a total $4.9 million in damages. One worker received $2 million for sterility and $25,000 for fear of cancer. His wife received $350,000 for loss of consortium and $250,000 for fear her husband would get cancer. Another received $1 million for sterility, $37,500 for fear of cancer, and $10,000 for fear of birth defects. His wife received $100,000 for loss of consortium and $20,000 for fear of birth defects. Two others also received somewhat lesser damages, with one worker not awarded any damages. Most of the awards were also adjusted modestly for "comparative fault," with damages reduced somewhat for the worker's share of fault for their own injuries. Still, Dow's attorney was surprised at the total amount of the verdict, especially for the fertility injury, but thought the fear claims about cancer—i.e., "this will be a lifelong affliction" kind of thinking—might have caused jurors to push the awards even higher. Dow's Dr. Ted Torkelson, however, wasn't happy: "I don't think we were guilty. I think we

> **"I don't think we were guilty. I think we did everything that was necessary and responsible that we should have done."**
>
> Dr. Ted Torkelson, Dow Chemical

did everything that was necessary and responsible that we should have done. Anything short of an acquittal to me was a loss.

"We made a mistake on DBCP," Torkelson said. "You can't win 'em all. I think everybody is allowed to make a mistake. It's only when you don't learn from your mistakes that you're in trouble. I think our mistake here was that somehow there was a communications goof. I think now we're going to be more careful to make sure that we don't get into the same situation. In terms of what we would do over again, I'm not sure it would be a lot different, given what we knew at that point it time."[15]

Bad Water

By 1990, Dow and the other DBCP producers began facing a variety of other lawsuits, some stemming from DBCP water contamination and others involving foreign workers also exposed to the pesticide. Before being banned, DBCP was a widely used pesticide throughout U.S. agriculture— applied at an estimated 10 to 12 million pounds per year on crops in Arizona, Florida, Hawaii, South Carolina, Texas, and California. In California alone, about 800,000 pounds were used each year. But in 1979, two years after it was banned, California health officials began finding DBCP in half the irrigation and drinking wells tested in the San Joaquin Valley. High levels were also found in the state's vast Central Valley, a region roughly the size of New York state. More than 200 wells in California were found to have DBCP, including some at Riverside, Anaheim, and even Disneyland. At least 16 wineries were found to be producing wine with dangerous levels of DBCP. By fall of 1979, more than 950,000 Californians were drinking water from sources with unsafe levels of DBCP—greater than one part per billion.

In January 1990, the city of Fresno, California filed a $650 million lawsuit against Dow and other DBCP makers for contaminating the city's water supply. At least 35 wells the city relied upon for drinking water were found to be contaminated with unhealthy levels of DBCP and were closed. Fresno sued the manufacturers and distributors to recover the cost of remediation and water treatment. That case was settled in May 1995, with the three companies paying a combined $21 million to help clean up the contaminated wells.[16] Then came the banana worker suits.

Banana Workers Sue

Although initially banned in the United States in 1977, DBCP continued to be shipped abroad and used on agricultural and plantation crops for a number of years. In some countries, there were charges that use of the pesticide continued at least through 1985.[17] Banana workers, claiming they were never told about the pesticide's health effects, began suing their employers and the chemical companies, alleging that the companies knew about the pesticide's harmful effects even before the U.S. ban. At first, the lawsuits came from banana workers in Costa Rica who worked on a plantation run by the Standard Fruit Company. But by September 1995, Dow, Shell, and Occidental were facing lawsuits from 16,000 workers in 11 countries. Dole and Chiquita operations were also involved in some of the suits. The plaintiffs charged that regardless of whether the DBCP supplies came from the distributors' stocks, or from production by the multinationals' subsidiaries abroad, the producers still acted with gross negligence. "They knew of the product's health hazard and should have recalled it," said Texas lawyer Scott Hendler in September 1995, who was then representing 1,500 Ecuadorean banana workers.[18]

In 1997, all of the companies except Dole settled with 26,000 former banana workers in Central America, Africa, and the Philippines for $41 million. The injured workers—after lawyer fees—received an average of $1,500 each. Still, by 2001, tens of thousands of other workers had suits pending in Central America, the Philippines, and the United States.[19] The companies have argued they have no further responsibility after settling claims years ago. They also say many of the workers now suing were never exposed to the chemical, and that the pesticides at issue have not been proved to cause the cancers, birth defects, or organ damage claimed. Dow disputes its liability and says that its product had warning labels with appropriate safety precautions. Dow also says the companies using DBCP did not always communicate proper warnings to their employees.[20]

Legally, Dow and the other companies once argued that the cases should be heard in the country where the purported injuries occurred—a tactic that for years effectively put the litigation in limbo, since many foreign courts were not up to dealing with technical class-action cases involving thousands of workers. But after a few countries became more aggressive in their legislatures and courts on DBCP, the companies changed their tune.

Nicaragua, pushed by its labor unions, passed a law in 2000 for DBCP victims that requires corporate defendants to put up a bond of $100,000 with each case, and do so within three months of being served. Over 400 cases on behalf of some 7,000 workers and other plaintiffs have been filed in Nicaragua—cases seeking more than $9.6 billion in total damages. In December 2002, one Managua court ordered Shell, Dole, and Dow to pay $489.4 million to 450 workers. The

Over 400 cases on behalf of some 7,000 workers have been filed in Nicaragua—cases seeking more than $9.6 billion in total damages.

companies, however, didn't participate in that trial nor have they acknowledged the ruling, arguing that foreign courts have no jurisdiction on U.S.-headquartered companies.[21]

Dow officials have said the Nicaraguan law "offends virtually every notion Americans have of fair play and substantial justice," adding that the company will seek to have the Nicaraguan cases retried in the United States. Lawyers for the banana workers have set their sights on American courts as well—to enforce the judgment and bring other actions. Some workers filed suit in Los Angeles to have the Nicaraguan judgment enforced in the United States, but Dow and Shell requested the case be transferred from state to federal court, a move calculated to have the suit heard without a jury.[22]

Meanwhile, in Central America and elsewhere, alleged injuries abound, with some villages bearing numbers of sterile men, others with cancer, and children with birth defects. "Walking through the plantations, we breathed in the vapors," says Manuel Guido Montoya, who says he and co-workers were drenched in the chemical when they worked the plantations. "I'd get headaches, a bloody nose, stomachaches," he said. "You put up with a lot of pain." Montoya has never had children, and at least one woman left him when she discovered he was sterile. Many of his neighbors are childless too, something of a social stigma in Central America where large families are

One Managua court ordered Shell, Dole and Dow to pay $489.4 million to 450 workers.

not only expected but necessary for economic survival. Other neighbors of Montoya's have children born ill or with birth defects. In Costa Rica, a similar pattern has been found in some villages. U.S. lawyers with plaintiffs there have screened dozens of middle-aged banana workers who provided detailed medical and work histories. They claim they were never told that DBCP was harmful, noting that any warning labels on the chemical drums were useless, since they do not read English. In 2003, Dow spokesman Scot Wheeler acknowledged the company supplied DBCP to Standard Fruit in Costa Rica after it was initially banned by EPA, but that Dow was indemnified against damages. The agreement between the companies, according to Dow, listed numerous safety and health precautions. Yet on the ground in Costa Rica, the plantations ignored safety requirements or failed to provide protective gear. And local authorities, reluctant to challenge the growers, did little or nothing to protect workers. But recently, a federal court in Louisiana has agreed to hear one Costa Rican case being brought on behalf of 3,000 banana workers.[23]

In Nicaragua, meanwhile, the companies have begun a round of political hardball. Dow, Shell, and Dole have hired former Clinton and Reagan administration officials to do some international lobbying. They want the Bush Administration to lean on Nicaragua to repeal that country's recently passed DBCP victims law. Similar laws have passed in Ecuador and Guatemala, but have been found unconstitutional.

Dow, Shell, and Dole have hired former Clinton and Reagan administration officials in an effort to repeal Nicaragua's DBCP victims law.

The Bush Administration reportedly agrees that the Nicaraguan law unfairly aims at a few companies. Secretary of State Colin L. Powell is said to have raised the issue with Nicaragua's foreign minister. In March 2003, Oliver Garza, U.S. ambassador in Managua, conveyed his reservations to the Nicaraguan foreign ministry on the matter, according to the State Department. Otto Reich, the State Department official who was in charge of Western Hemisphere affairs, also raised the issue during a visit to Nicaragua in September 2003. Carlos Ulvert, Nicaragua's U.S. ambassador, reports officials from the State Department saying: "You have some large American companies that have an interest in this; it is in your interest to find a solution." Dow, Shell, and Dole are also talking tough, and have repeatedly told senior Nicaraguan officials that the law hurts the foreign investment climate in the country. The companies "implied that they would do everything short of declaring war," one senior Nicaraguan official said. "These companies come with a lot of stick and very little carrot. I am perfectly aware of the two-by-four they hold over our heads." Ambassador Ulvert said his government favored an out-of-court settlement of the DBCP suits, but that any compromise needed to provide fair compensation to the workers. In November 2002, thousands of workers alleging DBCP harms marched five days to Managua calling on the government to provide financial or medical help.[24] Again, in February 2004, protesting workers camped out in Managua in front of the National Assembly threatened to take their case to the Inter-American Human Rights Commission.

15.

"Dow Water"

"Thirteen," she said. "That many women [having miscarriages] on one street? Something is wrong."

Tammy Green, May 2003,
Myrtle Grove, Louisiana[1]

Plaquemine—pronounced "Plack-uh-mun"—is a French-Cajun word meaning persimmon. It is also the name of the Mississippi River town just south of Baton Rouge, Louisiana where the Dow Chemical Company operates a sprawling, 1,500-acre chemical plant. Dow's site is framed on two sides by the Mississippi River—by one of the river's big meandering loops, a course by river of about 12 miles. The big loop also creates a "peninsula" of land known as Australia Point. Today, the web of tanks and pipes that is the Dow chemical works dominates the area. The plant turns out 19 billion pounds of material and 50 different chemical products every year, making it one of the biggest chemical plants in the world.

More than 100 years ago, well before Dow arrived, the land at this location was known as the Union Plantation, a sugarcane operation run by Andrew H. Gay, and later his descendants. The Gay family had purchased the plantation at a tax sale during the Civil War, and between 1875 and 1928, it produced cane sugar with 600 employees, mostly freed slaves. There was once also a small town here called Morrisonville. But Dow later bought out the town and moved its residents. More on that later.

In the 1950s, when Dow came to build the plant, the old plantation house was still standing, later restored as a Dow social center. But in September 1956, as a bulldozer turned up the loamy land at groundbreaking, Dow promised a $20 million investment. That quickly ballooned to $45 million, and by opening day, it had become a $75 million investment—the company's largest undertaking at the time. By July 1958, Dow was producing vinyl chloride and propylene glycol at the new plant.[2] The July 31, 1958 edition of the *Dow Louisiane* newsletter featuring the new Plaquemine operation showed photographs of Dow managers standing beside outgoing rail cars loaded with vinyl chloride and hydrochloric acid. The vinyl chloride was headed to the Pottstown, Pennsylvania plant of Firestone Plastics Company, a division of Firestone Tire & Rubber Company. The hydrochloric acid was going to Dow's own Dowell oil well servicing subsidiary in El Dorado, Arkansas.[3] Plaquemine would soon add production lines for caustic, chlorine, ethylene, and chlorinated solvents, plus 35 other "minor" undertakings, from brine pipelines to river wharves. By the late 1950s, Dow's president, Lee Doan, and other company executives had already met with Louisiana governor Robert F. Kennon in Baton Rouge to discuss the project and "open up communication channels with the state government."[4]

Before Progress Came

Louisiana along the Mississippi River in the early 1950s was in many ways an undiscovered place—a place passed by and spared the depredations of 19th century industrial "progress" common in the north. Some called

Louisiana between Baton Rouge and New Orleans became something less than a sportsman's paradise.

Louisiana a "sportsman's paradise"—a tag line that survives today on state-issued license plates. In the 1950s, Louisiana was a place with clean air, good fishing, and good food. Back then, people took from the rivers, trapped game in the bayous, and grew vegetables in big gardens. But the 1960s and 1970s changed that. The petrochemical industry, drawn to Louisiana with the help of state tax incentives, cheap labor, and plentiful natural resources such as oil, gas, brine, and water soon transformed the Mississippi River corridor. Louisiana between Baton Rouge and New Orleans along the Mississippi became something less than a sportsman's paradise. Today, that stretch of river—populated with more than 100 chemical and oil companies of one kind or another—is known as "Cancer Alley." The Louisiana parishes that run along that part of the river are among the highest in the nation in deaths caused by cancers of the lung, stomach, gallbladder, intestine, liver, pancreas, bladder, thyroid, esophagus, and skin.[5] But the cancer came after the boom times.

The 1950s and 1960s found Louisiana building plants everywhere. A decade later, Dow Plaquemine was still expanding: 2,000 construction workers swarmed over the site in the early 1970s, adding $165 million in new capacity. By 1974, there were 14 more production plants and 500 new employees, doubling the plant's size. Dow's operation at Plaquemine became a beehive of activity. By the mid-1980s, an average of 1,482 railroad tank cars were rolling through the plant each month, and at least 325 trucks. More than 21,600 vehicles annually moved in and out of Plaquemine each year.[6] By the early 1990s, Plaquemine alone was generating about 10 percent of Dow's worldwide sales—then about $19 billion a year.[7] But Plaquemine continued to expand through the late 1990s, adding a $140 million plant for the DuPont-Dow Elastomers joint venture, an operation to make rubber for tires, belts, and hoses.

Labor & Civil Rights

In the late1950s, Dow prided itself on opening the Plaquemine plant without the help of hourly workers. A couple hundred salaried personnel ran the plant during the lean times of the 1958 recession and gave Dow the idea for a new labor model. "The experiment was such a rousing success that it became a general template for the company, although most major divisions of the company still have (and enjoy good relations with) unionized employees," explains Dow historian, E. N. Brandt. When the Dow Badische Company was formed in 1959 with BASF, it also became a salaried operation. So did the Oyster Creek Division established at Freeport, Texas in 1967. Dow plants at Pevely, Missouri; Dalton, Georgia; Magnolia and Russellville, Arkansas; Allyn's Point, Connecticut; Fresno, California; Licking River, Ohio, and others were also salaried operations. "Following the Dow lead of 1958," continues Brandt, "other companies moved into the Baton Rouge area with salaried operation plants."[8] But there was also something else going on at Plaquemine—and in the south generally.

> **"Dow was counting on the fact that Louisiana remained a segregated state . . . "**
>
> Gerald Markowitz & David Rosner

"Dow was counting on the fact that Louisiana remained a segregated state, populated in part by poor blacks so desperate for work and feeling so powerless that they could be counted on not to cause the kind of labor unrest that Dow had experienced in Texas," observe industrial historians Gerald Markowitz and David Rosner in their book *Deceit and Denial.* "But just as the new Dow plant opened, the civil rights struggle intensified in Louisiana and changed a situation that had seemed so propitious for Dow."[9] When the Congress on Racial Equality (CORE) sent volunteers to Iberville Parish in the early 1960s to help challenge the forces of segregation, it found that no African Americans had been allowed to register to vote since 1960. Northern volunteers who visited Plaquemine proper were appalled by the poverty and squalid housing conditions they found in the black communities. Two black neighborhoods had been gerrymandered out of the town's boundaries; many residents there relied on hand-pumped wells and used outhouses. In June 1963, civil rights activists in Plaquemine demanded a wide range of reforms, including an end to segregation of public facilities and employment discrimination. CORE's national director, James Farmer, was asked to come to Plaquemine by local black activists to lead what would become the city's largest civil rights demonstration in August 1963 when 1,000 people marched on city hall. Two hundred people were arrested, including Farmer, who remained in jeopardy even after release, as deputized white vigilantes were then targeting demonstrators. Farmer safely left town by hiding in a casket headed to New Orleans.[10]

Meanwhile, chemical companies such as Dow were watching a dramatic change unfold before their eyes. "Imagine the situation in Louisiana," observe Markowitz and Rosner. "The chemical industry had built massive chemical plants across the state and was planning for the development of more plants. A huge civil rights struggle was playing itself out, and the consciousness of local citizens was being raised. Citizens were becoming more attuned to the environmental impact of the petrochemical industry and more vigilant about the damage it was doing."[11]

Plaquemine Pollution

In the Plaquemine area, exotic and caustic odors, polluted water, and toxic waste all came with Dow's new plant. At first, the smoke and waste were seen as emblems of industrial progress. Plaquemine was booming. But from the day the plant opened, toxic wastes were buried onsite—a practice which ran from roughly 1958 to 1973. Dow's dumps consisted of a series of unlined pits about 15 feet deep that received more than 50 kinds of chemicals as liquid, sludges, and solid waste. Each successive layer of waste was covered with a few feet of dirt. By the 1980s, Dow discovered its landfills were leaking. A company inventory of the toxic wastes released in the dumps soon revealed they included: heavy tars containing PCBs, polyethylene and methyl cellulose waste, waste oil, asbestos, mercury-contaminated soils, and wastes from the chlorine process. Dow's rough estimate as of 1991, was that 121,800 tons of chemicals were dumped in the area—many known to be human carcinogens with others known to be extremely toxic at very low levels. Over time, the chemicals in the dumps eventually spread, oozing into the ground below. By the early 1990s, the leaking wastes occupied a 30-acre underground toxic mass. Soon the worry became the Plaquemine Aquifer, an underground layer of drinking water. Dow's huge mass of toxic liquid and sludge—some 275 million pounds of it—was on the move, creeping inch by inch, an out-of-sight time bomb, spreading downward toward the aquifer. Some feared the water source would become contaminated. Dow officials said that would never happen, and installed more than 200 pump-and-treat wells to insure that the toxic waste would not reach the aquifer.[12]

By the early 1990s, Dow was using a computer model to predict the movement of the underground chemicals, which had moved about 50 feet in 30 years. Dow's computer was projecting the material would not move at all for the next 100 years. But others weren't so sure. "If we believed the computer models we wouldn't have any contamination at all," said consultant Joey Hebert in February 1991. Hebert had previously worked in the groundwater division of Louisiana's Department of Environmental Quality (DEQ). "The wastes we are encountering are moving much faster than any of the models predicted," he said.[13]

Dow's huge underground mass of toxic liquid and sludge— some 275 million pounds of it—was on the move.

As of 1993, Dow's Guy Barone reported that the treatment method was working. The underground contamination, he said, "has been contained." Yet others found that Dow's own test data in 1993 indicated the huge underground toxic blob hadn't been contained. Instead, it had moved into the clay layer that was supposed to be the last line of defense before hitting the aquifer.[14] In fact, the theory of clay as containment was much over-rated and just plain wrong. Those who studied Louisiana's subsurface found that clay layers would not stand up well to the onslaught of heavy organic chemicals such as those found in Dow's and other companies' dumps. Still, at Plaquemine, there appears to be no finality in cleaning up the underground contamination. The process just goes on and on, using whatever means are available, typically "pump-and-treat." When asked in the early 1990s how long it would take to clean up the underground contamination at Plaquemine, Dow officials told the *Times-Picayune* they expected the cleanup would last "forever."[15]

Petro Processors, 1

In addition to the wastes Dow buried onsite at Plaquemine, the company also used the services of local chemical waste disposal companies, one of which was named Petro Processors. Created in the mid-1960s, Petro Processors began hauling away chemical and oil refinery wastes for Louisiana clients and dumping the material into earthen pits and lagoons at various locations north of Baton Rouge along the east bank of the Mississippi River. In fact, from 1964 to 1980, Petro Processors accepted chemical wastes from nearly a dozen companies, Dow Chemical being among the major contributors. Before long, however, Petro Processors wastes—and some with Dow Chemical's specific tell-tale signature—began to manifest themselves in the local environment in the most unpleasant of ways. Local property owners and those frequenting some out-of-the-way backwoods and bayous began reporting changes in wildlife and domestic farm animals

near areas where Petro Processors was dumping its clients' wastes. One of
the local landowners, David Ewell, who, with his brothers and sisters, inherited a 1,150-acre ranch his father had pieced together in the 1940s through
hard work, found that Petro Processors waste, dumped near his land, was
polluting it, sickening his
livestock, and killing off
fish and wildlife in an area
known as Devil's Swamp,
much loved by hunters
and fishermen. Ewell's sis-
ter-in-law, Catherine, once
spent an entire day in 1969
counting the truckloads
dumped, recording an average of one every three minutes or so.[16]

"When you own your own property, no one is supposed to kick you off, no one can ruin it for you. That's my idea of what 'property' means."

David Ewell

After more than 150 of his cows and calves died in 1969, Ewell had his
land tested. Soil samples showed the land had been poisoned with chlorinated hydrocarbons, including trichloromethane, tetrachloroethane, carbon
tetrachloride, hexachlor-1,3-butadiene, and other persistent chemical
wastes—most at levels ranging from 180 ppm to as high as 25,000 ppm (or
2.5 percent). Ewell and his family sued Petro Processors and their chemical
industry clients for damages. A settlement of $90,000 came, accepted by
Ewell's brothers and sisters, but declined by Ewell himself, who wanted the
land restored to its former un-contaminated state. "When you own your
own property," he was fond of saying, "no one is supposed to kick you off,
no one can ruin it for you. That's my idea of what 'property' means." So,
Ewell persisted in the courts, continuing to sue Petro Processors and the
companies that sent their waste to Devil's Swamp—Dow Chemical, Exxon,
Ethyl, Shell, and others. That case went to trial in civil court, in one of the
longest proceedings in East Baton Rouge history. It concluded in 1975, finding all of the chemical company defendants liable. Yet Ewell was only
awarded damages at the fair market value of the land, which amounted to
about $375 an acre, or $25,000 total, for Ewell's share of the family's land,
plus another $5,000 for mental anguish. Nor was restoration of the land
ordered as Ewell had hoped. Author Michael Brown, reporting on the case
in his book, *Laying Waste*, noted the irony, citing the Louisiana Civil Code
that states: "Every act whatever of man that causes damage to another oblig-
es him by whose fault it happened to repair it."[17] Petro Processors and their
chemical company clients, including Dow, had not made Dave Ewell, or his
land, whole again. But there was still more to come.

In July 1980, the U.S. Justice Department, on behalf of EPA, filed a lawsuit against some of the same chemical companies—Dow among them—for
their involvement at the two Petro Processors waste dumps. The two sites—
the Brooklawn area site and the Scenic Highway site—operated north of
Baton Rouge, separated by about a mile and a half. Wastes were dumped in

"Worse Than Love Canal"

At the Petro Processors sites in the early 1980s, EPA had hired the engineering firm of Ecology and Environment to do site testing and chemical analysis. By 1982, preliminary tests were completed and the results were stunning. A number of wells had been drilled across the dump sites to take soil and water samples. One of these, known as well BL-3, was very contaminated. A water sample taken more than 40 feet below the surface showed chlorinated hydrocarbons at more than 732,000 parts per million—meaning 73 percent of the sample was toxic waste. At the time, this was the most contaminated sample EPA had ever found anywhere in the country. In the 1970s, Dave Ewell, a nearby property owner, had found 100,000 ppm hexachlorobutadiene (HCBD) in samples he'd taken just south of Petro Processors. EPA found HCBD, too. Their 1981–82 samples found, among other things, more than 90,000 ppm of HCBD in well BL-3. HCBD was an important chemical for EPA, as it became a "marker chemical" for identifying waste from the Petro Processors site. Although there were a number of waste sites and industrial facilities in that region at the time, only Dow generated HCBD. EPA knew this because HCBD was the signature waste generated in the production of perchloroethylene, which was only manufactured by Dow at Plaquemine. And Dow was the only company sending this particular waste to the Petro Processors site. HCBD was thoroughly mixed with the other wastes dumped at Petro. Therefore, EPA knew that whenever they found HCBD in the swamp, crawfish, fish, birds, deer, raccoons, vegetation, water or soil they were definitely dealing with waste from Dow and Petro Processors. Also called perchlorobutadiene, HCBD is not found naturally in the environment. Harmful by inhalation, ingestion, and through skin contact, animal studies suggest that HCBD can damage the kidneys and liver and may cause kidney tumors. In addition to HCBD, other toxic chemicals, including trichloroethylene and ethylene dichloride, were also found at high levels—200,000 to 300,000 ppm—in the test samples. In fact, the Petro Processors sites were so contaminated, one Louisiana official, Attorney General William J. Guste, made a comment to a CBS television reporter in September 1982 that the sites "could be worse than Love Canal." After CBS aired the segment, "near hysteria" broke out in the Baton Rouge area over the safety of drinking water, according to the *Times-Picayune*. Guste's comment, meanwhile, got the attention of the governor, David Treen, who assured the public he would not let the hazardous waste sites endanger public health. Guste, meanwhile, was called to a closed door meeting. The mayors of Baton Rouge, Zachary, and Baker, along with Louisiana Department of Natural Resources officials, moved to assure the public that drinking water was safe, with some officials calling Guste's statement "irresponsible." Guste later explained at a follow-up news conference that "there is absolutely no evidence...that the drinking water in this area—Baton Rouge—is contaminated." Regarding Love Canal, Guste explained, "I'm saying that if these allegations are true [the U.S. Justice Department by then had amended their lawsuit against the companies, citing the highly-contaminated test samples], there is no question that this situation is a horrible situation equal to Love Canal."[18]

pits and lagoons at the two sites. For years, there had been complaints of pollution and leakage at the sites, and groundwater contamination was also feared. Both sites were also located in the Mississippi River floodplain. When the river would flood, and occasionally break through river levees, as it did north of Baton Rouge in April

> **"Every act whatever of man that causes damage to another obliges him by whose fault it happened to repair it."**
>
> Louisiana Civil Code

and June of 1983, it would wash over part of the Petro Processors sites, spreading toxic waste through the area.[19]

The federal government brought its lawsuit under the Clean Water Act, alleging that toxic chemicals and heavy metals had been released into local waterways and the Mississippi River, and were posing a threat to underground drinking water. An EPA official at the time of the lawsuit indicated that the Petro Processors case was chosen as an important test case, and one to set precedent, as the government was going after waste generators as well as waste site operators. The set of facts in the case, explained the official, "clearly established a chain" between the chemical companies and the dump site. In addition, the government noted that the Ewell suit, filed in 1969, should have made the companies fully aware of the problems at the sites. According to the government, Dow, Allied Chemical, Shell Chemical, Ethyl, and at least eight other companies, "knew or should have known" that their toxic wastes were being stored unsafely at the Petro Processors operations. The lawsuit charged violations of the Clean Water Act and asked for a $10,000 civil fine against each defendant and for an order to halt the dumping and to clean up the site.[20]

In mid-February 1984, a federal judge approved a consent decree in the government's case, requiring the chemical company "generators" to clean up the site, conduct ongoing monitoring, and determine the nature, extent, and likelihood of future additional contamination. The parties were deemed responsible for perpetual maintenance with no monetary limit placed on the cleanup, with starting estimates then at $50 million. By May, the companies submitted a work plan for a remedial cleanup, which included the purchase of 60 to 90 acres of nearby land where an in-ground "vault" would be constructed capable of accommodating a million cubic yards of toxic material. At the waste sites, however, no cleanup work had started, but the wastes were festering and causing problems. In April 1985, one Louisiana DEQ official described the Brooklawn site containing areas where the ground bulges "like a boil" in summertime heat. Firefighters that year had come to the sites at least three times to put out fires.[21] Dow and the other companies, meanwhile, had formed a corporation, named NPC Services—with Dow and Exxon executives at its head—to handle the Petro Processors cleanup.

By October 1985, Dow Chemical proposed to incinerate a portion of the hazardous Petro Processors clean-up wastes at Dow's plant in Plaquemine, south of Baton Rouge. The clean–up wastes were originally intended for a nearby Rollins Environmental Services incinerator, which had problems and was shut down by the state. NPC Services wrote EPA describing the material to be burned at Dow as "free-phase organics," a mixture of highly chlorinated organic chemicals. NPC claimed the wastes were "nearly identical" to liquid wastes Dow was already incinerating at Plaquemine. Prior to March 1971, Dow disposed of its chlorinated chemical wastes through Petro Processors. Some DEQ officials favored Dow's proposal at the time, saying burning of liquid wastes was better than burying it in the ground. Dow officials said they were "very comfortable" that the material could be handled by their incinerator, which they described as "state-of-the-art," with numerous safeguards if problems occurred.

According to the government, Dow and at least eight other companies "knew or should have known" their toxic wastes were being stored unsafely at Petro Processors.

Shift to Incineration

Facing various toxic waste dump problems around Plaquemine and Baton Rouge, Dow by the mid-1980s had already begun moving more toward incinerating its wastes in high temperature burners rather than burying them in landfills. This appears to have been a corporate-wide shift within Dow, born of problems with land-filled waste not only in Louisiana, but also with brine field wastes re-injected into the ground in Michigan and other locations, and pollution caused by that practice (see Chapter 19). "We look at landfill as the last option and believe strongly that liquid should not be land filled," said Dow's Gary Veurink to *Washington Post* reporter Martha Hamilton in October 1984. EPA at the time was also endorsing incineration as a preferred method of dealing with toxic wastes. Dow, for its part at Plaquemine, had installed a rotary kiln burner and also had eight other incinerators that burned various wastes, scrubbed out gases, and converted some material into reusable substances. The rotary kiln unit at Plaquemine was then fed a diet of plastic drums filled with contaminated materials and burned about 1,000 tons of hazardous waste a month. Still in the end, each 1,000 tons of hazardous waste burned—in addition to toxic emissions from the incineration—also produced about 150 tons of ash and other wastes that went to an onsite landfill.[22] But Dow wanted to burn more.

In fact, the company began looking at its Plaquemine waste incinerators as a potential business opportunity, and began petitioning the Louisiana DEQ to burn other companies' chemical wastes, including that from out-of-state Dow facilities. By 1986, Dow had three burners at Plaquemine with excess capacity—enough to burn nearly 60 million pounds more hazardous waste. That would mean an increase in out-of-state truck traffic hauling hazardous wastes into Plaquemine. Dow then had 21 trucks per month hauling hazardous waste into Plaquemine from out-of-state Dow operations. As a commercial burner, as Dow proposed, 135 trucks per month would haul hazardous waste into Plaquemine. Dow's plan met vigorous protest, and the company backed off, proposing instead in January 1987 to increase its rotary kiln burn rate by one-third, to about 30,000 tons a year, and also expand its full capacity to 42,000 tons per year. Dow also requested that additional types of wastes be burned, a move that would change its emission profile to include ash, nitrogen, halogens, and sulfur. Dow's proposal, which was approved, included increasing emissions to the following levels:

"Prove It's Safe"

When Dow proposed to go commercial with its incinerators at Plaquemine in the spring of 1986, citizens raised concerns about pollution. Abel Daigle, Jr., who lived near Dow's plant and had sought help from DEQ, wanted to know why DEQ had not tested the incinerators for dioxin emissions, and why testing around the perimeter of Dow's plant had not been done. "It's up to Dow to prove to the people that this is safe, instead of us having to prove we have cancer to them," he said at one public hearing. Others, including select woman Etta Lee Gulotta of Iberville Parish, speaking at an April 1986 hearing, pointed to local cancer cases, noting that five people on her street had cancer and that her husband died from it. "It's all over," she said, referring to rising disease rates. "Every week we hear of another person in Plaquemine who has cancer." Les Ann Kirkland charged that Dow's incineration, in Louisiana and elsewhere, was already producing the most toxic form of dioxin, known to cause birth defects.

Sources: "Speakers Hit Dow, DEQ at Incinerator Hearing," *Post/South*, March 20, 1986, p. 5-A, and Candace Lee, "Selectmen Agree To Study Dow Incinerators Conflict," *Post/South*, April 10, 1986.

carbon monoxide	from 15.48 tons	to 46.43 tons per year
nitrogen oxide	from 18 tons	to 131.40 tons per year
sulfur dioxide	from 11.16 tons	to 50.81 tons per year
particulate matter	from 7.20 tons	to 56.94 tons per year
VOCs	from .36 tons	to 4.38 tons per year
hydrogen chloride	from 4.32 tons	to 17.52 tons per year
chlorine	from 14.40 tons	to 17.52 tons per year.[23]

Petro Processors, 2

By November 1985, the clean-up plans at the Petro Processors site put forward by the companies received stinging criticism from state and federal officials and community and environmental organizations, some arguing they had been shut out of the process while others charged the plan would not protect the environment from further contamination. In May 1986, three more fires had erupted at the sites, becoming something of a yearly event with warmer temperatures and hot weather. In July 1986, EPA found the Devil's Swamp area south of the Petro Processors site to have contamination as much as 17 times that of the waste sites themselves, with some officials urging the area be closed to the public for hunting, fishing, and recreation. A spokesman for the chemical companies claimed the Devil's Swamp contamination posed no threat to human health.[24]

In July 1987, about seven years after the Justice Department first brought its lawsuit, clean-up activity began at the Petro Processors sites with some clearing and a plan to build an in-ground waste vault. During excavation of the wastes, volatile contaminants were released into the air, hexachlorobutadiene (HCBD) in particular. Residents in the nearby town of Alsen, as well as workers at other local industrial plants, began complaining of sickening odors.* In fact, the emissions from the site exceeded allowable concentrations of HCBD for that location. In December 1987, all waste handling activities were stopped and the waste excavation was also discontinued. However, the complaints kept coming through March 1988, at which point the NPC Services suspended the clean-up. Not long afterward, a new remedy for the site was developed—pumping and treating of groundwater, with the liquid waste designated for incineration. Soon there were 130 recovery wells, 27 monitoring wells, and 98 French drains at the sites. Still, as of 1988, the plan forecast it would take at least another 50 years to drain

---

*Workers at Schuylkill Metals and the Reynolds Aluminum coke plant, near the Petro Processors Brooklawn Drive site, were among those breathing bad air and toxic fumes that drifted into their workplace and lunchrooms in the summer of 1987. Three workers from these plants—Ray Arnette, Gerald Tillman, and Darnell Dunn, local union leaders—became especially active in the dispute over these fumes. In league with Richard Miller of the Oil, Chemical, and Atomic Workers Union, they soon focused on the fumes problem. First, they tried talking with DEQ, EPA, and NPC officials. Although some pollution monitors were installed, the workers were told essentially that the Petro Processors site work was an EPA-supervised, court-ordered clean-up, and they would just have to put up with the foul air. The workers started talking to an attorney, and soon filed a lawsuit under the state's nuisance laws. They charged the waste clean-up at Petro was causing an unacceptable hazard to nearby workers and facilities. In court, the judge agreed and ordered the clean-up stopped. Recalls Willie Fontenot of the Louisiana Attorney General's Public Protection Division: "This new court order stunned all of the big shots and really empowered the workers and local residents."

the wastes.[25] U.S. District Court Judge Frank Polozola, involved with the case since the mid-1980s, appointed two Louisiana State University professors and LSU's Hazardous Waste Research Center as court-appointed advisors to help expedite the clean-up. Some experts then worried that the pump-and-treat strategy might not get all of the toxins, and that underground clays interwoven with sand channels could still be allowing the contamination to spread. According to EPA documents, more than 75 substances, all believed to be toxic, had been found in boreholes drilled into the Petro Processors dumps.[26]

The Petro Processors sites became national symbols. . . . Jesse Jackson used them in April 1990 as a backdrop to illustrate how industry was poisoning poor communities.

A two-inch clay cap was constructed over some portions of the sites. However, citizen and nearby worker concerns and complaints about site vapors and other clean-up problems continued, including worries about health effects, lack of an evacuation plan, and movement of the contamination to off-site properties. The Petro Processors sites became national symbols of the toxic waste problem. Jesse Jackson used them in April 1990 as a backdrop to illustrate how industry was poisoning poor communities.[27]

In 1993, the Louisiana DEQ and the Department of Health and Hospitals, Office of Public Health (LOPH), expanded a 1987 health advisory against swimming, sediment contact, and fish consumption to include Devil's Swamp and Bayou Baton Rouge. By 1996, the Petro Processors sites were considered public health hazards. Chlorinated hydrocarbons and toxic contaminants were still being detected in soil, groundwater, air, and some surface water. Offsite locations, too, recorded contaminants in water, sediments, and fish.

In the late 1990s, the U.S. Agency for Toxic Substances and Disease Registry (ATSDR) released a preliminary public health assessment and concluded that the site represented a public health hazard. ATSDR pointed to potential public exposures by way of inhaling volatilized contaminants, skin contact with surface water and sediments, ingesting contaminated groundwater, and eating contaminated fish and wildlife. ATSDR recommended continued investigation and monitoring of groundwater, surface water runoff, biota sampling, and air sampling. It also recommended a demographic review of the surrounding residential area.

As this book goes to press, the Petro Processors sites are still contaminated, with some activists fearing the sites will be declared "cleaned up," when in fact, they remain contaminated.

Air & Water

Over the years, Dow's Plaquemine plant has also had its share of everyday pollution problems, with continued toxic emissions and water pollution. Between 1988 and 1991, the plant was cited several times by the state for releasing toxic chemicals into the Mississippi River. During that period, Dow paid a total of $80,000 in fines for such violations. EPA also cited the plant for air quality violations during the same period. The toxic dangers at the plant—and the liability associated with a potential catastrophic event—were among the factors that figured into Dow's buy-out of the town of Morrisonville (see sidebar). Pollution complaints from that community and other locations came in regularly to Louisiana officials, as Willie Fontenot, an environmental specialist in the Louisiana attorney general's office, explained in 1993: "For years I've gotten complaints from people who live three to four miles from the plant about improper emissions from Dow and inadequate response from the plant management. The onus should be on the company to clean up its act, not just to move people out the way." Paul Templet, a former head of Louisiana's DEQ, says moving Morrisonville was a dollars-and-cents thing for Dow: "It was cheaper than pollution-control equipment."[28]

Dow's Plaquemine officials pushed for and received further air pollution allowances

Dow Plaquemine
Sample Production, 1993

Chemical	Annual production
Benzene	200 million gallons
Carbontetrachloride	100 million pounds
Chlorine	1.16 million short tons
Chloroform	120 million pounds
Diethylene glycol	45 million pounds
Dipropylene glycol	15 million pounds
Ethanolamines	185 million pounds
Ethylene	2.3 billion pounds
Ethylene dichloride	1.1 billion pounds
Ethylene glycol	450 million pounds
Ethylene oxide	600 million pounds
Glycol ethers	185 million pounds
Hydrochloric acid	790,000 short tons
Methyl chloride	174 million pounds
Methylene chloride	150 million pounds
Perchloroethylene	90 million pounds
Propylene	775 million pounds
Propylene glycol	150 million pounds
Propylene oxide	400 million pounds
Sodium hydroxide	1.27 million short tons
Toluene	10 million gallons
Triethylene glycol	45 million pounds
Vinyl chloride mon.	1.3 million pounds
Polyethylene resins	1.7 billion pounds

In addition to these chemicals, Dow Plaquemine in 1993 also produced: alkanolamines, chlorinated polyethylene, hydroxybutylcellulose, hydroxtproplycellulose, isoprene, methyl cellulose, propylene dichloride, tripropylene glycol, chlorinated polyethylene, and high-density, linear low-density, and low-density polyethylene resins.

Source: *1993 Directory of Chemical Producers*, SRI International, Menlo Park, CA, 1993.

in the mid-1990s. Under the rubric of production equipment modifications, Dow also sought increases in toxic emissions, over the objections of local citizens and environmental groups including AWARE and the Louisiana Environmental Action Network (LEAN). Spills and other problems also continued to dog the plant.

In May 1998, the DEQ charged that Dow's Plaquemine plant spilled approximately 12 million pounds of brine "from an unpermitted location" into a nearby swamp, polluting state waters and violating state law. The spill was caused by a leak in a high-pressure brine line that serviced some hydrocarbon storage wells.[29] In 1999, Dow's Plaquemine plant was also contributing to the Baton Rouge smog problem as a major generator of the polluting chemicals that make ground-level ozone. The plant that year was in the 90th-and-above percentile of dirtiest facilities nationally for nitrogen oxides (NOx) and volatile organic compounds (VOCs), as well as "soot" pollution, also known as particulate matter, with two sizes of culprits, known as PM-2.5 and PM-10. Plaquemine in 1999 spewed more than 11,580 tons of NOx; 1,670 tons of VOCs, 295 tons of PM-2.5, and 394 tons of PM-10. In mid-October 2001, the DEQ initiated an administrative enforcement action against Dow, seeking a civil penalty of $1.6 million. DEQ alleged that Dow failed to monitor valves at its Plaquemine benzene plant for fugitive emissions during two separate time periods. Dow had requested a hearing and expected the fine would be reduced, but likely remain more than $100,000.[30] But a bigger problem for Dow was brewing in a community southwest of its plant—a community named Myrtle Grove.

Poison at Myrtle Grove

It was in March 2001 that the 300 or so residents of the Myrtle Grove Trailer Park first heard from the Louisiana Department of Health and Hospitals (DHH) that they were drinking contaminated water. In fact, state tests more than four years earlier, in 1997 and 1998, had found vinyl chloride in the Myrtle Grove wells at levels exceeding safe drinking water standards, but not a single resident was then notified. At the time, DHH wanted to run more tests. When DHH completed the tests in June 2001—this being the third set of tests—it found that nine of the 12 wells sampled were contaminated with vinyl chloride.[31] The residents of the 60-unit trailer park by then had been warned not to drink, cook, or wash with the water.

State tests more than four years earlier had found vinyl chloride in the Myrtle Grove wells, but not a single resident was notified.

Samples of underground water in the general area had been taken by

Morrisonville

In the late 1980s, the residents of a small town named Morrisonville were bought out and moved by Dow. Morrisonville, however, had long roots on Australia Point, established well before Dow made the site its chemical home in the 1950s. In fact, Morrisonville—named after minister Robert Morrison—was built in the 1870s by freed slaves who had worked at the Australia Plantation. Generations had lived and died there; many worshiped in the Nazerene Baptist Church and were buried in its cemetery. For a time, Dow and Morrisonville co-existed. The community persevered through all the expansions and general nuisance associated with being a chemical plant neighbor—for more than three decades. Its people rarely complained, though they had reason to. Sometime around 1963, former resident Ernest Young recalled, there was a chemical leak from the Dow plant that caught fire in a Morrisonville drainage ditch. "Some kind of chemical got loose in that ditch and it blew up," he said. "It blew out the picture window. And it burned up my dogs." By the 1970s, Morrisonville had more than 250 residents, black and white. But soon, the plant had grown right up to the doorstep of Morrisonville, with residents complaining of the odors and bright flares that kept some awake at night. "They moved outwards slowly," explained lifelong Morrisonville resident Earline Badon. "They weren't always this close. But before you realized it, they were building right outside your door." In December 1984, the entire chemical industry had been rocked by the catastrophic events of Bhopal, India, where a horrific gas leak had killed more than 3,000 people. Dow and others began reassessing their operations' safety and the situation regarding surrounding communities. One Dow official, while traveling on the land through Morrisonville out toward the river, saw the risks facing the residents there if a chemical accident occurred. There was no way out; the residents were sandwiched in between the plant and the river. Elsewhere along the Mississippi River's chemical corridor, there had been a general awakening of chemical dangers, with some local neighbors rising up in protest. Corporate liability was a factor, too. In 1987, more than 100 residents of Reveilltown, Louisiana filed a $1 billion lawsuit against Georgia-Pacific and the plant's new owner, Georgia Gulf, alleging a variety of health problems and property damage caused by that chemical plant. The lawsuit was settled out of court, but Georgia Gulf relocated the residents and tore down the town. At Norco, Louisiana, a Shell Oil refinery had exploded in May 1988 resulting in numerous lawsuits and a $43 million payout in more than 5,000 claims. These developments and others, it is believed, influenced Dow in its decisions to initiate a pre-emptive buy-out of Morrisonville in May 1989. Dow said it needed a safety buffer. But Dow said that before, in 1959, claimed some residents, and then built right over the buffer with more plant. "Companies are reducing their problems by moving people instead of reducing accidents and pollution," charged Mary Lee Orr, executive director of Louisiana Environmental Action Network in November 1990. But Dow proceeded with its buy-out methodically and persistently, and even built a small subdivision several miles away with a dozen brick homes called Morrisonville Estates. In the end, by 1991, the company paid out more than $10 million in a voluntary buy-out program, under which nearly 250 residents moved to other locations. "We haven't had a catastrophic accident here," said Carroll J. Macalusa, Dow's director of the Morrisonville Plan in February 1991, "but this is a big industrial facility and there are risks inherent in that. We wanted to end up acquiring the property and we wanted the thing to end up happily. We didn't want to be perceived as brutes or bad guys." Although Dow's buy-outs were generous in monetary terms, some residents who were the great-grandsons or great-granddaughters of plantation slaves had deep roots in Morrisonville that no level of compensation could account for.

"My dad walked across this yard. My grandfather walked across this yard. This is a special spot," said Earline Badon, reflecting on her loss in 1991. "My people are in this place, and there are some things you can't put a dollar value on..." Suddenly, she said, "every blade of grass is important to me. My husband planted these pine trees in the yard. You have to live another lifetime to get all this back." But Dow completed its buy-out in 1991 when the last Morrisonville resident moved out. Though some of the town's people continued returning to the Nazerene Baptist Church for a time, that ended too. The history of the land had changed for good. "Dow is the new plantation now," explained Rosa Martin to the *Times-Picayune* in 1991. "It used to be the plantations that owned and controlled everything in our lives. Now Dow does that. They own this town."

Sources: Keith Schneider, "Safety Fears Prompt Plants to Buy Out Neighbors," *New York Times*, November 28, 1991, p. A-1; James O'Byrne, The Death of A Town," *Times-Picayune*, February 20, 1991, p. A-1, and Jon Bowermaster, "A Town Called Morrisonville," *Audubon*, July–August 1993.

both Louisiana DEQ and Dow during May, June, and July of 2001. In May, several wells not being used for drinking water were sampled by DEQ. Two of these—both south of Dow and near the Plaquemine city limits—contained vinyl chloride at 42 parts per billion (ppb) and 6 ppb, levels well above the federal standard.[32] Federal regulations allow a level of 2 ppb of vinyl chloride in drinking water. In June, nine more wells tested positive for vinyl chloride, again ranging from four to 10 times the federal standard.[33] In July, borings taken by Dow at the plant's southeast edge showed contamination levels at 4.1 to 19.2 ppb vinyl chloride. Other Dow borings on property northwest of the trailer park showed vinyl chloride levels at 39.4 ppb and 22.4 ppb.[34] The samples were leading to a pattern of an underground plume of contamination; a plume moving south to southwest of the Dow complex. By late summer, LEAN was beginning to wonder how big a problem the contamination might be, possibly stretching beyond the Myrtle Grove site. "While LEAN is trying to determine the number of residents with houses located over the plume, we know it's in the hundreds," the group said. "If any of these residents living with the plume were to sell their homes, they would be required to reveal to the purchasers that the houses sit on top of an area with vinyl chloride contamination."[35]

Although the contaminated groundwater stretched more than a mile from Bayou Jacob to the Dow Chemical site, appearing to implicate Dow, it had not been proved that the contamination was Dow's. Investigations in 2001 were still underway. Some scientists said they thought the contamination might be the residue of a spill that could have occurred up to 40 years ago.[36] By January 2002, a Louisiana grand jury investigation had been authorized in Iberville Parish to investigate pollution problems.

By March 2002, at least 2,000 Myrtle Grove Trailer Park residents and visitors who drank the water had signed on to a class-action lawsuit.

The panel was created by Judicial District Attorney Ricky Ward to specifically look into the groundwater contamination in north Plaquemine. Ward also appointed Beau Brock, legal counsel for EPA's criminal investigation unit, to assist with the investigation.[37] One of the investigation's first actions was to subpoena documents from Dow Chemical for a September meeting of the grand jury.

By March 2002, at least 2,000 Myrtle Grove Trailer Park residents and visitors who drank the water there had signed on to a class action lawsuit naming the state, the trailer park owners, and Dow Chemical. Another 200 people had filed a separate action against Dow in U.S. District Court in Baton Rouge, claiming the company illegally released vinyl chloride and other chemicals in their water and that the company knew about and covered up the contamination. Both suits allege health damages and increased risk to cancer. In reply to the federal lawsuit, Dow said it "denies that any of its chemicals or degraded products or any air emissions from any of its operations are causing or have caused any harm to [the] plaintiffs and specifically denies that any of its chemicals or products have caused any damage whatsoever to the aquifer that serves Myrtle Grove Trailer Park and/or plaintiffs' drinking water supply." One of the attorneys for the plaintiffs, state senator Rob Marrionneaux (D-Maringouin) explained that Louisiana's courts had been made less powerful in recent years, noting that citizens in the state could only sue for actual damages, not punitive damages. "The stupidest thing the government and the Legislature have ever done is eliminate punitive damages from industry-caused contamination," he said. "There's no fear of the courthouse."[38] Dow meanwhile, began running paid advertisements in local newspapers restating its assertion that the company was not the source of the Myrtle Grove contamination.

Toxic Washings

Then in mid-June 2002, a former Dow supervisor named Glynn Smith told a local television station, WBRZ-TV in Baton Rouge, that he had supervised employees who dumped thousands of gallons of vinyl chloride mixed with water onto the ground at the Dow plant. The dumped mixture came from railroad tank cars that the workers cleaned. Smith said the dumping was standard practice at the plant for three decades, ending in 1992. Some said Smith had an axe to grind, as he had filed a lawsuit against Dow blaming health problems on the company. A judge ruled Smith's problems were probably caused by exposure to the chemicals, and ruled in his favor. Dow then appealed, but the matter was settled out of court. But Smith's story to the TV station received a lot of continuing coverage and appeared to be based on correct information.[39]

Up until 1992, Dow cleaned out hundreds of rail tanker cars each year, dumping the vinyl chloride washings at the siding or on the tracks.

In the railroad-car cleaning operation, 25,000-gallon tank cars were handled in a step-wise fashion, as Smith and others would explain. First, any fumes in the tank cars were burned off. Then they were filled with water for cleaning. After that, the wash water was siphoned from the cars, but then simply dumped at the rail siding or on the tracks. Smith, who supervised the operation at the Dow plant between 1984 and 1987, estimated the operation cleaned an average of two rail cars a day. LSU chemistry professor Louis Thibodeaux estimated up to 200 pounds of vinyl chloride would be released into the ground with each washed-out tank car—and as much as 11,000 pounds during the time Smith was supervising.[40] In its broadcast of this account, WBRZ also stated that Dow did not have a permit to do such dumping.

After the program aired, Dow issued a statement saying that "based on the limited information provided recently by WBRZ-TV, we instituted an investigation of the allegations as we understood them. To date, Dow has found no evidence that it has violated federal or state regulations with regard to this matter, however, our investigation is still ongoing." A few days later, Dow's David Graham told the Associated Press the company had found shallow groundwater contamination at a rail car area in the 1980s, but disposal practices since then had changed and a groundwater cleanup was underway. Dow also issued a press statement to dispel any suggestion that the rail-car washings might be related to the contamination problems at the Myrtle Grove Trailer Park. "To date, there is no data to indicate that Dow's operations are a source" of the vinyl chloride groundwater contamination at Myrtle Grove.[41] In the days ahead, Dow continued to deny the rail-car dumping allegations. "At this point—and we have interviewed over 30 employees—we cannot corroborate the story told on Channel 2. If it happened, it certainly didn't follow procedure," said Dow spokesperson, Donna Carville. WBRZ, on the other hand, said Smith's story was corroborated by three other employees.[42]

Smith said he had never thought much about the practice in the rail-car cleaning area, until he saw the news reports about the contamination of the Plaquemine Aquifer. In the mid-1980s, he explained, there were 300 rail cars that needed to be inspected and there was a big push to clean them and move them out. "Water was going everywhere," outside the tank car cleaning shed, Smith recalled. Another employee, Herbie Walker (who also had a family member suing Dow), said, "We did it all the time. It was a routine thing...water on the ground. It was like a flood" at times.[43] Walker and another former Dow employee, Edward Dominique, would spend hours testifying behind closed doors, telling the grand jury their stories. Dow soon launched a local public relations campaign to make its case to the community. Dow plant manager Earl Shipp spoke several times on a local talk radio station. "I want to reassure the public our current operations are best in class, best industry practices, and this is in no way related to the operations we have going on today." As to the allegations of Smith, Shipp replied, "I don't know if they're true at this time. If they are true, and he was wronged, and if that's the case, we will say that publicly, we will make sure everybody is aware of that." Meanwhile, back at the Myrtle Grove Trailer Park—where a number of residents had become parties to lawsuits aimed at the state agencies and Dow Chemical—the chief worry was health effects.

Vinyl Time Bomb?

Most of what is known about the health effects of vinyl chloride comes from occupational exposures. The U.S. Occupational Safety and Health Administration (OSHA), has set the maximum allowable level of vinyl chloride in a workroom during an 8-hour day at 1 part vinyl chloride per million parts of air, or 1 ppm. "Breathing high levels of vinyl chloride for short periods of time can cause dizziness, sleepiness, unconsciousness, and at extremely high levels can cause death," says the Agency for Toxic Substances and Disease Registry (ATSDR). "Breathing vinyl chloride for long periods of time can result in permanent liver damage, immune reactions, nerve damage, and liver cancer." Animal studies have shown that long-term exposure to vinyl chloride—365 days or longer—can damage the sperm and testes. It has not been proven that vinyl chloride causes birth defects in humans, but animal studies have shown that breathing vinyl chloride can harm unborn offspring and may also cause increases in early miscarriages.[43] However, little is known about vinyl chloride in water. Finding the chemical in drinking water is so rare it has never been studied, according to Sharon Wilbur, an environmental health scientist with the Centers for Disease Control. No one knows what happens when someone drinks water tainted with vinyl chloride, or how much a person would need to consume before showing health effects.[45]

However, by 2003, the residents of Myrtle Grove thought they had a pretty good idea of the harms and damages that might occur from vinyl chloride in water. Miscarriages, for one, had increased in the community. Tammy Green had one in 2000, before anyone had told the residents about the vinyl chloride in their wells. Faye Robertson had one in June 2001. Green and other women in Myrtle Grove, after learning about the vinyl chloride, began to count the number of recent miscarriages in

Myrtle Grove residents now call the poisoned water they unknowingly lived with "Dow water," and say Dow is responsible.

their community. They found there had been a total of 13 in their own neighborhood. "Thirteen," said Green. "That many women on one street? Something is wrong." The women also reported that their children burned and itched from bath water and wading pools—a common form of backyard recreation for children throughout Myrtle Grove. The residents now call the poisoned water they unknowingly lived with "Dow water," and say Dow is responsible. Wilma Subra, a scientist working with LEAN says, "It appears to be originating from the area where Dow has its production facilities. They produce vinyl chloride. They sell it." The Louisiana DEQ, though reluctant to name Dow as the certain source, agrees that the company is the prime suspect. Dow's Rebecca Bentley, however, explains that tests in the aquifer underneath the plant itself have shown no vinyl chloride. Dow's tests, she says, show the aquifer flowing primarily to the west, not southwest, toward the trailer park. In contrast, EPA's tests indicate a south-to-southwest flow, which would carry it under the trailer park.[46] Wilma Subra has also suggested that Dow's monitoring wells may be located in such a way that they are missing the migrating contaminants.[47]

Few residents of Myrtle Grove, however, feel confident the state of Louisiana will finally make Dow accountable, even if the pollution is pinned on the company. Dow employs too many people, they say, holds too much sway over the local economy. The state will back off, they believe. Still, Dow faces a number of lawsuits as well as ongoing federal criminal investigation. Attorney's representing hundreds of Myrtle Grove residents have already begun taking depositions of former Dow employees trying to learn more about the history of the site. Pat Pendley, one of the attorneys, says they've already learned about one 1993 spill of 700,000 pounds of perchloroethylene, a precursor to vinyl chloride. They've also pinpointed the location of a pond on the Mississippi River side of the levee on Dow property that was used as a catch-all waste dump in the 1970s. EPA's Criminal Investigation Division in New Orleans, working with the state, has already convened one grand jury over the last 18 months on the case, and may impanel another if reports turn up more evidence. Some trial dates may be scheduled for 2004.[48] But it is the Myrtle Grove residents who have borne the brunt of the problem so far. In addition to the possibility of future health risks, the Myrtle Grove residents have had their lives severely stressed and repeatedly disrupted throughout the long pollution-discovery odyssey. In the end, they were forced to move from their homes when the trailer park was closed down. It remains to be seen whether, and on what terms, their harms will be righted.

EPA's Criminal Investigation Division in New Orleans has already convened one grand jury in the case.

In December 2003, a construction company began building the first of 82 homes on the property formerly known as Myrtle Grove Trailer Park. The new development will be known as Iberville Trace. According to the construction company, the site is a beautiful piece of property lined with trees. The first homes will be completed in early 2004.

Coddling Polluters

When Dow came to Louisiana in the 1950s, it did so in part because it saw receptive state politics and welcoming communities. While some of that bloom has faded among particular communities in recent years, state regulators still seem to be extending Dow and others the benefit of the doubt—and then some—especially when it comes to toxic pollution and risky operations.

In April 2003, for example, Dow reached agreement with DEQ to pay $2.4 million to settle previous environmental violations occurring at its Plaquemine plant—air, water, and hazardous waste violations. Although some of the violations were minor or "paperwork violations," others involved major spills or failures by the company to maintain pollution controls, such as the failure between October 1999 and April 2000 to conduct required semi-annual air quality testing at some 5,600 pipe junctures at its chemical plant.[49] Dow called that one "a misinterpretation of the regulations regarding monitoring frequency."

In making this settlement, however, Dow was quick to go to the community and explain itself, especially since it was very much in the news on the Myrtle Grove case. Company spokesmen said they wanted to assure the community that Dow was committed to environmental stewardship. They said Dow had a fugitive emissions system in place that was now a model program. They also explained that more than half of the $2.4 million "fine" was being paid in something called Beneficial Environmental Projects, or BEPs—environmental improvement projects that substitute for hard-money penalties. As part of its BEP, Dow was making a $1 million contribution for coastal restoration initiatives, a waterfront park in Plaquemine, and a public awareness program concerning the smog problem in the Baton Rouge area.

But the editors of the Baton Rouge newspaper, *The Advocate,* took the opportunity on the same day of Dow's settlement agreement—without mentioning Dow per se—to offer an editorial on the sad state of environmental enforcement in Louisiana. *The Advocate's* editors pointed to an EPA analysis that had found only 4.2 percent of some 5,000 companies violating environmental laws were fined. In 2002, only 1.7 percent were fined. A state auditor found that 73 percent of the state's solid waste facilities were operating on expired permits, as were 55 percent of hazardous waste facilities. The practice of using BEPs in settlements rather than fines was also noted by *The Advocate,* explaining that the BEPs included often had nothing to do with repairing damage to the environment. Said the editors in their April 2003 comment:

> **"Make no mistake about it: Polluting the environment with harmful chemicals is criminal."**
>
> Editors, *The Advocate*

> ... Chronic polluters do not dump harmful chemicals into the air and water out of simple misunderstandings. They do so because operating cleanly is more expensive. They profit from destroying Louisiana's environment—endangering the health of our children, elderly, and those suffering from respiratory illnesses...
>
> Make no mistake about it: Polluting the environment with harmful chemicals is criminal. And despite some improvements, Louisiana's reputation as an industrial dumping ground willing to turn a blind eye to polluters remains a serious problem...
>
> Failing to punish lawbreakers gives them an unfair competitive advantage against responsible companies that abide by the rules. Punishing only 4 percent of violators creates an incentive to pollute.
>
> If tightly enforcing Louisiana's environmental laws scares some chronic polluters way from Louisiana, good riddance... [50]

16.
Danger Zones

We believe all community residents should be informed about any risks and what safety measures are taken every day to protect people and property.

Dow Chemical Company[1]

"When it first happened, I could feel it," said Captain Pat Yoes of the St. Charles Parish Sheriff's Office describing the explosion that occurred at Dow Chemical's St. Charles, Louisiana plant. It was Tuesday morning, January 8, 2002, about 11:00 a.m. Yoes was sitting in his Hahnville, Louisiana office about four miles away. "It shook the building," he said. Nearby communities, including St. Rose and Luling, also felt the blast, which caused buildings to shudder. At the scene, an ensuing fire was extinguished by plant workers in eight to ten minutes. An alarm had sounded in the Olefins I cracker unit minutes before the explosion, alerting nearby workers. Stanley Dufrene, a Dow spokesman, assured the community that things were under control, and that no one was injured. It appeared that naphtha somehow leaked out, or was released from a pipe, and touched a nearby furnace's flames. Naphtha is a flammable liquid Dow uses to make ethylene, which in turn is used to make plastics. St. Charles Emergency Operations Director, Tab Troxler, said Dow reported that no chemicals were released in the explosion. "All safety systems worked as designed and prevented the incident from escalating to a more serious event," reported the *St. Charles Herald-Guide*.[2]

In March 2001, near Houston, Texas, hydrogen cyanide gas was released at Dow's glycine facility at its Hampshire Chemical Co. subsidiary in Deer Park, Texas. No injuries were reported, but minute amounts of the acutely poisonous gas were detected at the Hampshire fence line. The population of Deer Park and Houston were just beyond the plant gates. Workers at a nearby Rohm and Haas plant were confined to their building for two hours. Company officials believed at the time an unexpected reaction had occurred while making glycolonitrile, causing a rapid rise in temperature and pressure.[3]

In November 2002, a half a world away from Houston, a fire at a Dow's polyurethane plant in the Porto Marghera industrial complex northwest of Venice, Italy, injured four people and released a dark cloud of dense smoke. The intense fire and smoke created some difficulty for firefighters battling the blaze. The mayor asked residents in the city of 500,000 to stay indoors, as the composition of the smoke was unclear, although it was known that phosgene was used at the plant in some processes.[4]

In February 2003, back in the U.S., police and emergency workers in Kanawha County, West Virginia shut down traffic along West Virginia Route 25 for about an hour after Dow Chemical reported a leak of ethylene diamine. The leak occurred at the former Union Carbide-owned Institute, West Virginia chemical plant. Dow, the new owner, reported that about 75 pounds of the chemical escaped from a vent on a storage tank and had moved in a ground-hugging cloud in southwesterly direction across the plant grounds. Dow issued a shelter-in-place order for plant workers and asked the county to block traffic from passing on Route 25, the road adjacent to the plant. State police, Kanawha County police, and area firefighters worked to divert traffic from the area. Emergency workers sprayed the cloud with a fire hose to help eliminate the vapors. The leak was contained at the plant site and Dow reported there were no injuries.[5]

These four incidents at Dow chemical plants illustrate the volatile and dangerous nature of Dow's business. They suggest that accidents and chemical releases do happen at Dow facilities which Dow, for the most part, says it can handle and bring under control. But there are other possibilities; accidents that might not be so routine—what the government calls "worst case scenarios"—potentially catastrophic accidents that Dow and other companies are required by law to be prepared for and plan emergency response.

Worst-Case Scenarios

A "worst-case" hydrogen chloride release at Dow Chemical's Plaquemine plant near Baton Rouge, Louisiana, could endanger an estimated 370,000 people living within a 25-mile radius of the plant (see map, opposite). Another Dow Plaquemine scenario projects a smaller danger zone for a chlorine leak, putting 31,000 people at risk within 6.9 miles of the plant.[6] The worst-case accident for Dow's plant in Pittsburg, California in the San Francisco Bay area, where Dow produces chemical pesticides, shows 180,000 pounds of chlorine escaping from a ruptured rail tank car, potentially putting a large population at risk in Contra Costa and southern Solano counties.[7] In Dalton, Georgia, a catastrophic release of 682,500 pounds of the chemical 1,3-butadiene at a Dow plant there would cause a vapor cloud explosion that would break windows and cause structural damage to buildings within a radius of about a half-mile.[8]

A 1999 pamphlet from Dow's Michigan Operations includes an "Alternative Case Scenario Map"—not the worst case—depicting four circles within

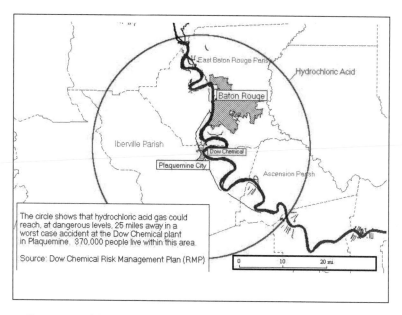

The circle shows that hydrochloric acid gas could reach, at dangerous levels, 25 miles away in a worst case accident at the Dow Chemical plant in Plaquemine, 370,000 people live within this area.

Source: Dow Chemical Risk Management Plan (RMP)

various distances of Dow's Midland plant (see page 334). The circles represent computer modeling from Dow showing the distances that various accidentally-released chemicals might travel from Dow facilities "under typical weather conditions and a partial failure of plant safety systems." Within Circle I, including areas of a half-mile or less, are the chemicals acrylonitrile, isopropyl chloroformate, methyl chloride, and unspecified "flammables." Within Circle II, encompassing an area 0.5 to 1 mile of Dow facilities, are allyl alcohol, ammonia, aqueous hydrochloric acid, propylene oxide, and dimethyldichlorosilane. Circle III, covering distances of 1.1 mile to 2 miles of the Dow facilities, include possible releases of chlorine, chloromethylmethylether, ethylene oxide, anhydrous hydrochloric acid, methacrylonitrile, oleum, phosphorous trichloride, and phosphorus oxychloride. Circle IV, 2.1 to 3.0 miles from Dow facilities, cover possible accidents of bromine and sulfur dioxide.[9]

Dow also revealed worst-case accidents for its Michigan operations—noting that EPA modeling asks that such incidents assume failure of all applicable safety systems, except for a dike or containment pit. "Scenarios like this are extremely unlikely but not impossible," explained Dow in its 1999 pamphlet, "and truly represent the worst case conceivable." For Dow Michigan there were two worst-case sketches. The first—for a toxic material—would involve the release of the entire contents of a chlorine rail car in 10 minutes without the aid of safety systems. Such a release, explained Dow, "could potentially impact an area of a size greater than 25 miles from our plant." The second, for a flammable material, would involve the release of about 1.5 million pounds of butadiene from a storage tank. This release, said Dow, "would

Ten Million At Risk

Hypothetical "Worst-Case" Chemical Accidents At 49 Dow Chemical U.S. Locations, 2000–2003

Company	Facility Location	"Worst Case" Chemical	Pounds	Danger Zone (miles)	At-Risk Population
Dow Chemical	Ironton, OH	Acrylonitrile	375,000	0.54	100
Dow Corning	Midland, MI	Hydrogen chloride (anhydrous)	151,450	19.60	330,000
Dow Chemical	Dalton, GA	1,3-Butadiene	682,500	0.70	150
Dow AgroSciences	Harbor Beach, MI	Ammonia (anhydrous)	70,000	4.00	4,000
Dow Chemical	Channahon, IL	Propylene oxide	29,507	2.60	2,000
Dow Chemical	Freeport, TX	Phosgene	24,750	20.50	105,952
Dow Chemical	Ludington, MI	Chlorine	180,000	19.00	20,000
Hampshire Chem. Corp.	Nashua, NH	Hydrocyanic acid	115,787	16.00	655,400
Dow Chemical*	Torrance, CA	Acrylonitrile	274,000	1.10	15,319
Dow Chemical	Gales Ferry, CT	Acrylonitrile	86,853	2.50	8,100
Dow Chemical	Paincourtville, LA	Chlorine	2,000	5.60	5,500
Angus Chemical Co.	Sterlington, LA	Sulfur dioxide (anhydrous)	100,000	25.00	191,000
Dow Chemical	La Porte, TX	Phosgene	17,346	25.00	1,960,000
Dow Chemical	Plaquemine, LA	Hydrogen chloride (anhydrous)	800,000	25.00	370,000
Dow Chemical*	Pevely, MO	Ethyl chloride	200,000	0.36	130
Dow Chemical	Midland, MI	Chlorine	175,000	34.20	320,000
Dow Chemical	Pittsburg, CA	Chlorine	180,000	25.00	910,000
Hampshire Chem. Corp.	Deer Park, TX	Hydrocyanic acid	106,140	15.00	862,164
Dow Chemical	Charleston, IL	Isopentane	96,000	0.37	0
Dow Corning	Carrollton, KY	Dimethyldichlorosilane	893,000	25.00	141,665
Dow Chemical	Texarkana, AR	Flammable mixture	96,000	0.37	110
Hampshire Chem. Corp.	Owensboro, KY	Vinyl acetate monomer	467,374	1.90	6,000
Hemlock Semiconductor Corp.	Hemlock, MI	Hydrogen chloride (anhydrous)	149,000	20.00	350,000

DuPont Dow Elastomers	Beaumont, TX	Sulfur dioxide (anhydrous)	180,000	16.00	424,000
DuPont Dow Elastomers	Louisville, KY	Chlorine	180,000	14.00	720,000
DuPont Dow Elastomers	Laplace, LA	Chlorine	250,000	16.00	114,000
DuPont Dow Elastomers	Deepwater, NJ	Hydrogen chloride (anhydrous)	43,000	13.00	500,000
Evans Chemetics	Waterloo, NY	Acrylonitrile	99,810	0.70	1,500
Union Carbide	North Seadrift, TX	Ethylene oxide	294,000	12.00	12,400
Union Carbide	Tucker, GA	Acrylonitrile	73,900	0.24	651
Union Carbide	Somerset, NJ	Acrylonitrile	67,600	0.62	300
Union Carbide	Charleston, WV	Vinyl acetate monomer	190,000	5.20	44,678
Union Carbide	Garland, TX	Acrylonitrile	67,600	0.46	398
Union Carbide	Texas City, TX	Vinyl acetate monomer	10,700,000	3.80	19,800
Union Carbide	Institute, WV	Ethylene oxide	354,000	11.00	155,245
Union Carbide (marshaling yard)	Institute, WV	Ethylene oxide	180,000	10.00	105,891
Union Carbide	So. Charleston, WV	Allyl alcohol	39,000	8.40	98,406
Union Carbide (Tech Center)	So. Charleston, WV	Propylene	69,500	0.33	495
Union Carbide	Torrance, CA	Acrylonitrile	67,600	0.55	3,284
Union Carbide	Alsip, IL	Vinyl acetate monomer	195,000	5.30	424,127
Union Carbide	Norco, LA	Titanium tetrachloride	199,000	0.41	84
Union Carbide	Norco, LA	Propylene	300,000	0.54	24
Amerchol Corp.*	Edison, NJ	Ethylene oxide	93,650	7.60	509,204
UCAR Resinas	Bayamon, PR	Vinyl acetate monomer	78,200	0.35	683
Union Carbide	Pequelas, PR	Vinyl acetate monomer	708,000	2.90	23,732
Union Carbide	Texas City, TX	Vinyl acetate monomer	23,000,000	5.00	35,000
Union Carbide	Torrance, CA	Vinyl acetate monomer	1,445,220	1.20	30,689
Union Carbide	Taft, LA	Acrolein	186,000	22.00	608,605

Total at-risk population 2000–2003   **10,090,786**

Source: Data derived from U.S. Environmental Protection Agency, Risk Management Plan Information, 2003. Table and data include U.S. facilities only. Note: Total at-risk population in the 2000-2003 period may be lower in certain years given those facilities that have deregistered (*) from the RMP program, meaning that hazards once identified at those locations have been removed, either temporarily or permanently.

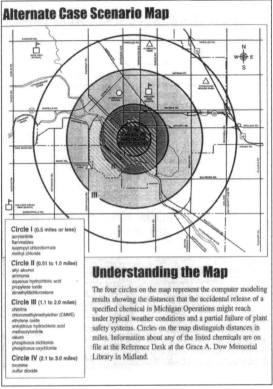

Alternate Case Scenario Map

Circle I (0.5 miles or less)
acrylonitrile
flammables
isopropyl chloroformate
methyl chloride

Circle II (0.51 to 1.0 miles)
allyl alcohol
ammonia
aqueous hydrochloric acid
propylene oxide
dimethyldichlorosilane

Circle III (1.1 to 2.0 miles)
chlorine
chloromethylmethylether (CMME)
ethylene oxide
anhydrous hydrochloric acid
methacrylonitrile
oleum
phosphorus trichloride
phosphorus oxychloride

Circle IV (2.1 to 3.0 miles)
bromine
sulfur dioxide

Understanding the Map

The four circles on the map represent the computer modeling results showing the distances that the accidental release of a specified chemical in Michigan Operations might reach under typical weather conditions and a partial failure of plant safety systems. Circles on the map distinguish distances in miles. Information about any of the listed chemicals are on file at the Reference Desk at the Grace A. Dow Memorial Library in Midland.

Dow's zones of chemical release for a selected scenario, Midland, Michigan, 1990s.

potentially impact an area of little more than 1 mile from our plant."

These estimates of "unthinkable events," were they to happen, are part of the planning and emergency preparedness exercises that many chemical companies have gone through since the 1990 Clean Air Act required something called "risk management plans," or RMPs. Dow Chemical has RMPs on record for plants at 49 U.S. locations—including its various joint ventures and subsidiaries, ranging from Dow Corning and DuPont Dow Elastomers, to its recently-acquired Union Carbide and Hampshire Chemical properties. Taken together, as shown in the table on pages 332–33, more than 10 million people in the United States living near these Dow plants in the 2000–2003 period, comprise the theoretical "at risk" population for worst-case accident scenarios.

Although Dow Chemical has fortunately not had a worst-case accident become a reality, it has had its share of lesser incidents—accidents, toxic leaks, spills, and near misses. Some of that history, stretching over the last 30 years or more—including that of Dow Corning, DuPont Dow Elastomers, and other Dow-related ventures—is recounted below. As this record shows, chemical plant and chemical transportation accidents can and do happen at Dow facilities—as do chronic low-level releases of toxic substances. Reducing the risk of these events must involve more than just emergency planning or new layers of pollution control technology. Dow strategies and planning must increasingly move toward preventing the possibility of such events by removing the chemical threat or toxic release in the first place. This means either replacing the volatile, reactive, and/or extremely hazardous chemicals now used with less dangerous ones, installing fail-safe technology that will unconditionally contain them, or eliminating the need to use such chemicals in the first place.

Chronic Chlorine

Chlorine has been a perennial problem at Dow from its very earliest days. As a key ingredient chemical used in making thousands of other chemicals, from plastics to solvents, chlorine and its derivatives are found in huge quantities throughout Dow's operations. As it has done for more than 100 years, Dow uses electrolysis to form chlorine gas by passing a powerful electric current through a solution of sodium chloride. Chlorine is a heavy, violently reactive greenish gas that does not occur in nature. It can also be deadly, which is one reason it was used as a weapon in the trench warfare of World War I. Once chlorine gas is inhaled, it saps the fluids in the lungs and blood and starts a chain reaction that can end in slow suffocation. Herbert Dow himself, before he came to Midland, had narrowly escaped an explosion of chlorine gas at one experimental location in Ohio. In the late 1890s in Midland, Dow's plant, with virtually no pollution controls, frequently leaked chlorine into the surrounding area, including "Paddy Hollow," the Irish neighborhood across the railroad tracks. Recounts Dow historian, E. N. Brandt:

> Any time a cow died in the vicinity, the owner wanted to believe the cause was chlorine gas, and the company was constantly involved in lawsuits...people in the neighborhood frequently claimed their yard and shrubbery was being blighted and killed by chlorine...Herbert Dow finally planted some bushes and shrubbery inside the company fence to prove they would grow there and that stray chlorine wasn't hurting anything...
> ...[T]he general reasoning of the suits was that chlorine escaping from the Dow plant combined with moisture in the air to form hydrochloric acid, and the acid precipitated out of the air onto trees, plants, screens, and the like, damaging them. The suits were finally decided in favor of the company..., but to clear up all questions about it Herbert Dow bought the land along the plant fences [what is Bay City Road in Midland today] and leased it back to people who wanted to live there, with a proviso in the lease that the company was not responsible for damage caused by escape of chemicals from the plant.

Chlorine escaping from Dow operations in Midland was not only a concern in the early years, as releases of chlorine and related materials have continued to plague Dow operations wherever chlorine is used, as well as in its transport. Countless rail cars, for example, full of chlorine, typically move in and out of Dow operations regularly. Chlorine releases, large and small, involving Dow products or Dow facilities have occurred repeatedly in the U.S., Canada, and other locations over the last 25 years or so. Among some of the more notable reported incidents involving chlorine, hydrochloric acid, and/or hydrogen chloride in which evacuations, exposed or hospitalized workers, and/or officially alerted communities were involved, include the

Chlorine in Germany

In the 1960s, Dow began looking for a site to build a major chlor-alkali complex in Europe. It wanted a site near a salt deposit and close to a large waterway. It also preferred locating near a small- to modest-size town—something of a Dow tradition modeled on Midland, Michigan. After a search in England, Holland, France and Germany, Dow settled on a site in northern Germany on the Elbe River near the town of Stade (pronounced "Stahd - duh"). The government of Lower Saxony at the time was welcoming new industry to the area, and Dow was one of the first to arrive, breaking ground at Stade in October 1969. Not long after the first chlorine plant came on line in 1972, Dow had its first test with the local population.

"We burned a big hole in a chlorine line and released a bunch of chlorine," recounts Bernhard Brummer, one of Dow's managers at Stade. The gas wafted over the Elbe River and Brummer moved to call authorities to "stop traffic on the Elbe River," as he was unsure what might happen. With the boat traffic brought to a halt because of the incident, Dow's operations at Stade began to receive much more public attention. Dow, however, made no public response at the time, and that became a serious failing. At Stade, there were mostly engineers on site, doing what they thought best. "We had not advanced to the degree that we thought we owed anything to the public except building safe plants—that we were convinced we had done," explained Brummer, "and that this is what we thought the public would expect. [B]ut we didn't think we needed to inform our neighbors about what we were doing or to explain to them the hazards involved."

> "We didn't think we needed to inform our neighbors about what we were doing or to explain the hazards involved."

After the chlorine release, "we thought if we fixed the pipe, that was the main thing," said Brummer "We didn't respond [to the public], and the criticism was pretty severe. There was something in the paper very often, until we realized...we had to speak out. We were busy working on the plant, but we were not busy explaining to people what we were doing to get things under control...." Dow eventually began explaining its operations more frequently. "It was a bitter experience we went through," recalled Brummer in 1989, "and we had to struggle for many years for more acceptance by the public. Today I believe we have it. It took us a long time." According to Brummer, Dow worked to improve its environmental performance at Stade and "reduced emissions and spills, improved our safety record, [and] presented it all in public." By 1990, he said, Stade had slashed its waste to practically zero. Stade also developed a giant containment unit to completely house its phosgene equipment, as Dow used phosgene in the production of polycarbonate plastic. However, over the years, Stade had other incidents, including a May 1993 explosion at the chlorine plant that killed one worker and injured another.

Sources: E. N. Brandt, *Growth Company*, pp. 411–15, and Agency France-Presse, "Dow Chemical Blast Kills Worker in Germany," May 3, 1993, and *Chemical Week*, May 1993.

following: a chlorine tank rupture following a February 1977 explosion at Dow's Plaquemine, Louisiana operations that forced 50 families to evacuate, with 17 treated for chlorine inhalation;[10] an April 1978 release of chlorine gas from Dow's Sarnia, Ontario plant that sent 22 construction workers at the neighboring Sunoco refinery to the hospital;[11] a major train derailment at Mississauga, Canada in November 1979 involving the release of chlorine from Dow tank cars resulting in one of the largest evacuations ever in North America (see Chapter 10); repeated incidents of escaping chlorine at Dow's Pittsburg, California plant, including those in July 1988, May 1991, June 1991, October 1995, and February 1998;[12] an October 1994 fire at Dow Chemical's Plaquemine, Louisiana plant that released 7,000 to 8,000 pounds of chlorine prompting shelter-in-place warnings;[13] incidents at Dow Corning plants in Midland and Freeland, Michigan occurring in December 1996 and August 1997;[14] and incidents at Dow's Saskatchewan plant in Alberta Canada, including one leak in June 1997 that caused more than three dozen construction workers to be treated for chlorine inhalation.[15] Other smaller releases of chlorine and related chemicals occur on a more frequent basis. Typical of those, for example, is one that occurred on July 3, 1994, when a worker was injured at Dow Corning's Midland plant after 230 pounds of hydrogen chloride leaked during transfer of material from a rail car to a chemical plant.[16] Or another that occurred in Freeport, Texas in late September 2003, after a malfunction of a Dow incinerator. That release, which only involved a few pounds of chlorine in the early morning, sent a cloud across one part of the nearby Freeport Municipal Golf Course. "It was scary," said Pinkey Hardline, director of the course. "It kind of burnt your throat and made you feel like you had a sore throat." Pinkey also thought his club was lucky that day. "It might have been a different situation if golfers were actually out there playing on the back nine when it was happening."[17]

Accidents Do Happen

In addition to chlorine, Dow facilities handle a variety of other volatile and toxic materials, any number of which can and do cause problems. Below is a sampling of some Dow accidents and chemical releases that have occurred in the last 25 years or so:*

June 1976 Explosion at Dow Chemical's King Lynn plant in England, kills one man and causes extensive damage to the plant and adjacent buildings. The explosion involved a detonation of a chemical known as zoalene, which was used at the time as a poultry feed additive. "The fundamental reason for this incident was a general

---

*Some of these incidents are described elsewhere in this book in more detail; most are offered here in abbreviated form.

lack of knowledge of the destructive potential of zoalene at adiabatic conditions," wrote the U.K. Health and Safety Executive (HSE) in a report on the accident. Adiabatic conditions describe a thermodynamic process in which heat is held constant, without loss or gain. HSE also found that the existing process at the plant was changed to incorporate a drying stage "without fully assessing the implications."[18]

July 1978 A rail tank car carrying Dow Chemical anhydrous hydrochloric acid, ruptures in Jacksonville, Florida, sending a gray plume of toxic hydrogen chloride gas over the northwest part of the city. According to news reports at the time, 34 people were sent to local hospitals and about 2,000 residents were evacuated. Civil defense authorities on the scene kept evacuees away from their homes for at least 24 hours while firefighters and others attempted to deal with the gas. A team of experts from Dow Chemical was unable to patch the hole in the tanker, and concluded the estimated 13,000 gallons remaining in the tanker would be allowed to dissipate. Dow's anhydrous hydrochloric acid was destined for the perfume industry, which used the chemical in its manufacturing.[19]

Oct. 1981 An explosion touched off by a fire at Dow Chemical's Freeport, Texas plant kills five workers and injures seven others, one critically.[20]

May 1986 A violent explosion rips through one of Dow's Central Research labs in Midland, Michigan. No one is injured in the blast, involving a small 10-gallon test reactor containing ethylene glycol and oxygen. However, a sizeable portion of the structure is blown out and about 250 people are evacuated. The lab was conducting a remote-control, pilot-plant test. Technicians in a nearby room were performing a dry-run, "pressure cooker" test with a new vessel.[21]

July 1989 About 3,000 people living within 18-square miles of Freeland, Michigan, are evacuated for at least two days—and some for more than a week—after a 32-car long CSX freight train carrying five Dow Chemical and Dow Corning tank cars derailed (see more detailed account of this incident below).[22]

Jan. 1990 An explosion and fire at a Dow Chemical plant in Russellville, Arkansas forces the evacuation of 100 workers. No injuries are reported.[23]

May 1990 Fear of an explosion and chemical release from an overheating marine cargo tanker at Dow's Freeport, Texas plant leads to an evacuation order and the closing of the Intracoastal Waterway. Nearly 1,900 schoolchildren and about 200 other residents are evacuated and emergency responders are called to the scene. Fortunately, no incident occurred and the evacuation ended in less than 24 hours.[24]

Jan. 1992 An explosion at Dow's 703 rotary kiln incinerator in Midland, Michigan injures one worker and causes major damage to one building and equipment. Human error was later reported to have been a contributing factor, as a natural gas valve was left open. One of the two injured Dow workers in the incident suffered burns on his face and hands. In February 1993, a second explosion occurred at the company's 703 hazardous waste incinerator, this one involving nitroglycerin waste. In this incident, no one was injured, but there was some release of material to the

Two Killed In California

On May 26, 1979, an explosion ripped through Dow Chemical's Pittsburg, California plant killing two workers and injuring more than 45 others, most of whom were taken to area hospitals. The explosion occurred during the third test of a 600-gallon vessel in which iron powder and chlorine were being mixed to make ferric chloride, a catalyst used in the manufacture of a pesticide. The California Industrial Relations Department later charged Dow as partly responsible for the incident, saying the explosion might have been prevented. At least one union official, Monte Manwill of the International Association of Heat and Frost Insulators and Asbestos Workers, Local 16, charged that Dow's alarm system was inadequate and that a poorly-tested chemical mixture caused the explosion. A state investigation showed the accident was caused by a runaway heat-producing reaction within the vessel. Experts concluded that while Dow developed its chemical process to make ferric chloride in a logical, careful, and orderly manner, the company didn't exercise similar care in its design of the equipment to carry out this process. "Furthermore, (Dow) didn't analyze correctly or, in our opinion, respond cautiously to signals of potential hazards in the production stages,"said Don Vial, Director of the California Department of Industrial Relations. Since specific standards of the state safety and health code at the time weren't violated, there could not be any criminal prosecution or fines assessed. But a special order aimed at Dow was issued providing for documentation of operations and potential hazards in the future design of any new process equipment. That order also provided protection for employees by forbidding them to work in areas where the start-up of new operations involving chemical reactions in closed vessels is being conducted. A Dow spokesman at the time said the company had "no quarrel" with the state's order. As for the state's observation on the company's procedure, the spokesman said, "we don't disagree with all their observations. If we knew [then] what we know now, the accident wouldn't have happened."

Sources: "Chemical Blast Kills 2," *Washington Post*, May 27, 1979, p. A-13; "Dow Chemical Co. Officials Say Unanticipated Side Effects to Chemical Caused Explosion," *New York Times*, June 8, 1979; "California Industrial Relations Department Says Dow Was Partly Responsible for Explosion," *New York Times*, November 22, 1979; and "Calif. Aide Scores Dow Chemical On Explosion At Plant In May," *Wall Street Journal*, November 23, 1979.

environment. "The fact that it exploded unexpectedly," explained Michigan DNR enforcement analyst, Phil Schrantz, "suggests the possibility that it was an inaccurate characterization" of the waste. "That means the wastes shouldn't have been incinerated or that it was burned at the wrong temperature or in the wrong quantity." In April 1993, Dow was fined $68,5000 for the two explosions as part of an enforcement action by the Michigan DNR. Both incidents could have been prevented, explained DNR's Phil Schrantz at the time of the fine. "We're very concerned that this kind of operation be conducted in as safe a manner as possible," he said. "This constituted a failure on Dow's part to meet conditions of their permit."[25]

April 1994 A train derailment at the Lausanne, Switzerland central railway station carrying tank cars from Dow Chemical's Stade, Germany plant, causes a spill of 300kg of epichlorohydrin from one of two tank cars. The spill reaches an adjacent canal system, resulting in the evacuation of about 1,200 residents in the immediate area, 200 of whom were kept away from their homes over 24 hours after the accident.[26]

April 1995 External corrosion on a tube in a cooling system at Dow's vinyl plant in Plaquemine, Louisiana results in the release of 7,700 pounds of vinyl chloride, 4,420 pounds of hydrogen chloride, 70 pounds of benzene, 10,930 pounds of ethylene bichloride, and 10 pounds of carbon tetrachloride. Initially discovered by two workers starting a furnace who heard a hissing sound, the incident becomes serious enough to notify emergency officials. Louisiana Route 1 near the plant is closed to traffic and area residents are notified by the Community Alert Network to shelter in place. At the site, Dow takes the system pressure down to isolate the problem, and eventually shuts down the whole vinyl plant to retool all the coolers. No chemicals from the incident were detected off-site, according to Dow officials.[27]

Dec. 1996 Fire and explosion at Dow Chemical's Fort Saskatchewan, Alberta plant in Canada results in the shutdown of the ethylene oxide/ethylene glycol complex through early January 1997.[28]

Aug. 1997 A leak of styrene monomer from a railroad tank car sitting on a siding at the Dow Chemical plant in Midland prompts a shelter-in-place warning for about 4,000 area residents. Inside the tank car, the chemical had begun reacting with itself and was converting from a liquid to a plastic form, creating a build-up of heat and pressure. A warning siren was sounded and television and radio reports were used to notify residents of the leak. Residents within a mile of the plant were told to stay indoors, close all windows, extinguish any open flames, and shut off ventilation systems. Firefighters and Dow workers at the scene poured water on the car to keep the reaction from occurring too quickly. The reaction eventually completed itself with the pressure in the tanker returning to atmospheric levels. The rail car was owned by GATX, a rail company, and the tanker was insulated to handle the chemical. However, Dow officials were initially at a loss to explain the cause of the reaction inside the tanker. After detection monitors later showed the release to be below hazardous levels, the emergency orders were lifted a few hours after the incident.[29]

March 1998 An explosion and fire at Dow Chemical's ethylbenzene plant in Freeport, Texas badly injures two workers and demolishes a nearby maintenance building. The two workers are hospitalized and treated for severe burns and take months to recover, with extensive skin grafting and physical therapy. OSHA later cites Dow for safety violations in the incident and fines the company $10,000.[30] (More detail on this incident in Chapter 13.)

Sept. 2003 The divinylbenzene process operation at Dow's Midland, Michigan plant reports a release of toxic chemicals to the air involving four substances: 8,000 pounds of divinylbenzene, 4,600 pounds of ehtylvinylbenzene, 8 pounds of diethylbenzene, and 3 pounds of naphthalene. According to sources in the Michigan DEQ, a chemical

Worst Case in Nashua?

Hampshire Chemical is the name of a company Dow acquired in 1997. Hampshire is a speciality chemical company with operations in several locations, among them, Nashua, New Hampshire and Deer Park, Texas. At both the Nashua and Deer Park plants, Hampshire handles a chemical named hydrocyanic acid, also known as hydrogen cyanide. Identified as an extremely hazardous substance by EPA under the Clean Air Act, hydrocyanic acid is a flammable and reactive pale blue liquid with a bitter, almond-like odor. The gas is used in industry to kill rodents and insects. The liquid is used in making other chemicals such as acrylates and acrylonitrile. Acute exposure can irritate and burn the skin, eyes, and throat, and can cause dizziness, headache and nausea. High levels can lead rapidly to convulsions or sudden death. Chronic exposure damages the thyroid gland and the nervous system. In Nashua, Hampshire Chemical reported in 1999 it had more than 900,000 pounds of hydrocyanic acid on hand for its operations. A worst-case accident there involving the release of more than 100,000 pounds hydrocyanic acid would put a residential population of more than 650,000 people at risk. Such an accident has never occurred there, and company officials assure the community it never will. But in August 1988, some 1,700 people were evacuated from their homes in Nashua after a pre-dawn release of a toxic cloud following the mixing of phosphorous trichloride. Nine people were treated in that incident, and residents were kept from their homes for some time, as a second cloud of residual materials spread from the plant about eight hours later. In Texas, however, Hampshire has had a more recent episode involving hydrogen cyanide. In August 2002, Hampshire agreed to pay $103,500 in fines and rectify violations found by OSHA inspectors following a March 7, 2002 release of hydrogen cyanide at the company's Deer Park plant near Houston. At the time of that incident, Hampshire had 69 employees on site. Beyond the plant gates, however, was the population of Deer Park and Houston. Among the violations OSHA cited in the 2002 incident were: failure to adequately resolve recommendations of a hazard analysis, failure to ensure that written operating procedures reflected actual practices, and failure to provide adequate refresher training for operators of the glycine unit.

Sources: Reuters, "1,700 Evacuated in New Hampshire Chemical Spill," August 5, 1988; Jeremiah Baumann, Paul Orum & Richard Puchalsky, *Accidents Waiting to Happen*, U.S. PIRG Education Fund and Working Group on Community Right-To-Know, Washington, DC, December 1999, and "Chemical Plant Agrees to Pay $103,500 in Fines," *Houston Chronicle*, August 1, 2002, p. A-22.

cloud of the material did leave the Dow plant site, as residents along Miller Road near the plant reported strong odors with some complaining to the Midland County Emergency Planning Department of adverse health effects. The chemicals, it was later learned, had been in reaction for 10 days without adequate temperature monitoring due to malfunctioning equipment. The mixture overpressured in reaction, releasing the cloud. DEQ sent an Order of Violation to Dow for the incident.[31]

Leaks, Breaks & Spills
At Selected Dow Chemical Locations

Location	1994	1995	1996	1997	1998	1999	2000	2001	1994–2001
Texas Operations	640	508	489	453	329	280	276	246	3,221
Michigan Operations	247	168	155	167	173	170	169	174	1,423
Louisiana Operations	130	114	119	136	112	82	104	94	891
Fort Saskatchewan	59	41	43	79	53	30	29	21	355
Sarnia, Ontario	62	68	64	36	51	35	19	20	355
Corporate	2,381	2,170	1,996	1,980	1,812	1,573	1,499	1,337	

Explanation and sources: "Leaks, Breaks & Spills" is a Dow-defined category, reported annually by Dow Chemical plants at various company locations. Says Dow: "Leaks, Breaks and Spills from our processing equipment and facilities include those that are captured in various backup systems and therefore, do not usually cause environmental impact. However, we track this data because Leaks, Breaks and Spills are often early warning indicators of more severe incidents...." Dow Chemical Co., *The Dow Global Public Report 2001*, Section 4, Environmental Stewardship.

Residents Flee

In July 1989, more than 2,000 people living within five-square miles of Freeland, Michigan, were kept away from their homes for at least two days—and some for more than a week—after a CSX freight train carrying toxic chemicals derailed. The accident occurred about 11:20 a.m. on July 22, about ten miles north of Saginaw and just southeast of Midland. Involved in the wreck of the 32-car train were five chemical tank cars from Dow Corning and Dow Chemical. Two of the cars began burning after the derailment and continued burning for at least two days—one containing chlorosilane and the other, acrylic acid. The fire and spilled chemicals released dangerous fumes into the air. At least 36 people were treated at local hospitals for exposure to toxic fumes. On the first day of the derailment, about 3,000 people were evacuated from an 18 square-mile area.[32]

Earlier that day, the CSX train had departed Port Huron, Michigan on its journey to Midland. At Flint, the train added 23 cars, including 11 with hazardous materials. Just as the train began passing through Freeland, some of the crew members felt a "slight lurch or tug" on the train followed by an emergency application of the air brakes. When they looked back, they saw some of the train's cars derailing, followed by a large fireball and a dense cloud of smoke rising into the air. More than a dozen freight cars had derailed, six of which were tank cars that sustained damage, resulting in either the partial or total loss of their chemical contents. A flatbed car loaded with a large steam generator overturned, and one nearby residence was engulfed by fire following the release of chemicals. As the locomotive and front portion of the train had pulled away from the accident, the conductor and other crew members left the train and began going house-to-house in the immediate area advising residents to leave immediately. The brakeman on the south side of the site did the same. Crew members also went to nearby Highway 47 to warn motorists. Emergency response personnel soon arrived on the scene as evacuations were ordered and a command post for fighting the fire was established. News photos and TV footage from the next few days, including some aerial shots, showed the fireball and smoke rising from the accident site. Others showed the derailed cars at the scene scattered across the landscape still burning.[33]

On the first day of the derailment, about 3,000 people were evacuated from an 18 square-mile area.

Days later, residents and journalists complained they were still having difficulty obtaining a full list of all the chemicals on the train—from both the companies and state authorities. One list cobbled together from local news sources indicated the chemicals on board included: styrene, acrylonitrile, chlorine, styrene monomer, methylchlorosilanes, acrylic acid, petroleum naphtha, paraformaldehyde, and ethyl chloride. But this was not an official list. When local journalist Bob Martin at *Review* magazine in Saginaw couldn't get information from Dow Chemical or Dow Corning, he started phoning around for other sources. He found Fred Millar, a specialist on hazardous chemical transport at the Environmental Policy Institute in Washington, D.C. Millar proceeded to tell Martin about silanes, a family of about a dozen chemicals, one of which, methylchlorosilane, which had burned in the wreck, was among the most dangerous. It turns out that silanes were not a favorite chemical of the rail industry. Conrail, for one, Millar explained, didn't want to carry them as a normal transportation freight. They wanted the chemicals treated as special freight—or as a "flagout," as it's called in the industry—which means using a special train traveling at speeds under 30 mph, using buffer cars around the chemical car, and taking special routing around rail yards to avoid bouncing and rough track. Conrail, in fact, went to the Interstate Commerce Commission, the entity that regulates railroads, and said they didn't want to be forced to carry silanes in regular cars. They also wanted to charge special rates if they were required to carry such chemicals. But Conrail lost that fight in the political arena. "The chemical manufacturers beat the railway," said Millar, and in effect, forced the rail carriers to transport the chemicals as regular freight.[34]

Millar also advised that Michigan citizens ask their Local Emergency Planning Commission—a body empowered by federal law—to request from Dow Chemical, Dow Corning, and CSX "worst-case accident scenarios" for the chemicals being hauled. Chlorine, he noted, was an especially dangerous chemical, citing the earlier train wreck and mass evacuation that had occurred ten years earlier in Canada at Mississauga (see Chapter 10). "In Washington, when the FBI sat down with the Association of American Railroads to do what they call a worst-case terrorist, non-nuclear scenario," Millar explained to *Review* magazine, "they chose a situation where a terrorist would seize a chlorine car or a car with chlorinated compounds, and threaten to blow it up." But Scott Seeburger of Dow Corning told *Review*: "There were no cars with chlorine in them.* Dow Chemical had a car and it had 20,000 gallons of chlorosilane, which is the car that burned. When chlorosilane burns or mixes with water it forms hydrogen chloride fumes, which are known as hydrochloric acid. I personally don't know if there are any synergistic effects with these chemicals."[35]

Conrail didn't want to be forced to carry silanes in regular cars.

In early August 1989, at a town hall meeting at Delta College following the derailment, *Review* magazine interviewed Dr. Vaughan E. Wagner, a toxicologist for the Center for Environmental Health Sciences in the Michigan Department of Public Health. Wagner was asked about potential for toxic synergy in the rail incident, and he provided the following explanation:

> The synergistic effects per se basically say that the effects of a mixture of chemicals are going to be greater than each one taken separately. It *potentiates* it [emphasis added] and makes it more serious from a toxic standpoint. That condition could have very well existed when the first explosion went up, and essentially that cloud and those thermal conditions resulted in a mixture of chemicals or decomposition products that could have resulted in a synergistic effect. However, that condition did not last long and essentially it existed in a state of complete evacuation.
>
> As it settled down, you're looking at HCL and basically silicone, which for these two there really is no documented synergistic effect.... One is rather inert. So yes, there was potential right at the beginning, but in many instances no one was there to begin with [because of the evacuations]. Thereafter, as the situation settled down, synergism became less and less of a problem. The case we're dealing with now which is mixture per se, is HCL converting and combining with silica.

---

*The NTSB final accident report of July 1991, however, did indicate there was one tank car in the train that contained chlorine—DOWX #8065. See NTSB report of July 1991; citation in endnotes.

In the end, we had tanks of acrylonitrostyrene, but they were basically pretty much contained and were shipped off site. We did have acrylic acid, but that was pretty much contained. This is not to dismiss the concept of *potentiation* [emphasis added]. If all three or four of those chemicals went up and continued to go up for the whole time, then I'd say potentiation would be a serious consideration."[36]

Following the derailment, the Michigan DNR hired independent scientists to analyze gas chromatographs of soil and air samples taken at the accident scene by DNR and Dow Corning. EDI Engineering & Science of Grand Rapids, Michigan was hired. The EDI report, despite having some difficulty with Dow Corning in obtaining samples, did turn up a few chemicals that were not reported elsewhere—namely, 1-decene and "three hydrolysis products of trichlorosilane," as well as 90 different volatile and semi-volatile chemical fractions, many of which were not detectable at the detection limits specified in the report. DNR was also focusing on some styrene and acrylic that were spilled at the site. CSX, meanwhile, which during the rail car fire was required to set up monitors around the site and sample what was coming off the gaseous plume, still hadn't sent any of its data to DNR by mid-September, three weeks after the incident.[37]

A year following the derailment, a group of Freeland citizens and environmentalists organized a small protest rally at the accident site. "One year later, after our emergency," said Kathy Garthoff, chairperson of Tri-City Residents for Alternatives to Chemical Contamination (TRACC), "we find ourselves with a contaminated site in our backyards; unfenced, unposted, which yet remains to be cleaned up, and no one knows for how long." By then, there was litigation too. A class action lawsuit had been filed in state courts under *Connie Mason et al. vs. CTX Transportation, et al.* Part of the suit had already been thrown out, but the remaining claims were still being determined. Back at the accident scene, the clean-up was complicated by the fact that beneath the tracks, lots of chemicals had been spilled over the years, and pinning down blame and liability was becoming a major piece of detective work. Still, citizens were frustrated and angry. "Why, one year later, does this 'cleaned up area' still have 60,000 times the safe level of acrylic in the ground?" asked Kim Maxwell at a citizen gathering and press conference at Saint Mathews Church in Freeland. The chemistry brewed at Dow Corning and Dow Chemical, and many other locations around Michigan and the United States, was indeed being moved through communities like Freeland each and every day. And as the Freeland derailment had shown, these materials weren't always safely transported. One study by the Federal Railroad Administration had found that 13 percent of all rail tanker cars tested in Michigan were shown to be leaking.[38]

In July 1991, the National Transportation Safety Board (NTSB) released its final report on the Freeland accident. It identified the probable cause of the incident as "inadequate car inspection" combined with other factors including track conditions and train handling. NTSB also noted that "contributing to the severity of the accident were the release of hazardous material from tank cars that were not equipped with head-shield protection and the lack of effective fire fighting techniques for responding to large trimethylchlorosilane fires." Safety recommendations involving these and other issues were made to the Federal Railroad Administration, the association of American Railroads, CSX, Dow Corning, and others. Dow Corning was charged, in conjunction with the Silicon Health Council, to develop "effective emergency procedures, including the best fire fighting procedures for handling the releases of chlorosilanes in transportation accidents." NTSB also recommended that Dow Corning "modify the Material Safety Data Sheets for chlorosilanes to include the most effective emergency response procedures and to clarify or correct any conflicting information regarding the use of water to extinguish fires and warnings to avoid contact between the product and water."[39]

> **"Why, one year later, does this 'cleaned up area' still have 60,000 times the safe level of acrylic in the ground?"**
>
> Kim Maxwell, July 1990

Back in court, meanwhile, all was not lost for Freeland citizens. On September 11, 1992, a Michigan circuit court judge ruled that certain members of the class action lawsuit, including those evacuated or in the vicinity of the July 22, 1989 derailment, were entitled to damages, and issued a procedure for filing claims.[40]

Right To Know

Community, labor, and environmental activists, as well as some chemical industry safety leaders, have been advocating increased industry responsibility for chemical plant safety and hazardous chemical transport for more than 50 years. But in the early to mid-1980s, and spurred by the 1984 Bhopal tragedy, legislative forces were set in motion that produced new kinds of public information. Formed under a "right-to-know" banner, citizens and communities were entitled to have the latest information about what was produced and emitted by their industrial neighbors. By the late 1980s, U.S. companies were required to annually report toxic chemical releases. Later, in the 1990s, they were required to divulge the amounts of dangerous chemicals stored at their plants and publish "worst-case" accident scenarios. These instruments of public policy were designed to help local communities and the general public understand chemical risks and to prod chemical companies to reduce those risks. The response of the chemical industry to these laws, however, has been mixed and troubling. On the one hand, they have created voluntary internal industry principles such as Responsible Care (see Chapter 11), and say that they are improving industry standards and safety. Yet, on the other hand, industry leaders have also fought to make worst-case scenario accident information extremely difficult for the public to obtain.

Even before RMPs and worst-case accident scenarios began to be published in 1999, the chemical industry moved to limit their publication under the claim that terrorists would use the information to target certain chemical facilities. But environmental and community activists argued that industry was using the issue as a smokescreen to keep the public from having access to information that would help citizens bring pressure on the companies to improve chemical plant safety. The hazardous chemicals were the issue, not the information about the chemicals, argued the activists, who pointed out that there were often safer chemicals and processes available that didn't put people in danger. None of the information divulged provided "how-to" recipes for creating an incident. The activists also noted that of the 600,000 reported chemical accidents in the U.S. between 1987 and 1996, none was the result of terrorism.[41] Moreover, security at some of the plants, was found to be quite lax. Greenpeace activists, for example, were able to gain access to Dow's Plaquemine, Louisiana plant in March 2001. By then, the chemical industry had succeeded in convincing the government to restrict photocopying and internet publication of worst-case accident scenarios that had already been published. Greenpeace, however, posted some of the scenarios on its website, believing the information was vital for pubic safety. "Dow and other chemical industry lobbyists are using security issues as a smoke screen to keep the public from knowing the full extent of worst-case accident scenarios," said Greenpeace spokesman Rick Hind at the time.[42] Further, the activists recommended—in June 1999—that chemical companies claiming their plants were at risk to terrorism should register them with the government and prepare a security program based on a "multiple barriers" hierarchy: take practical steps to reduce hazards, improve site security, harden facilities against potential attack, and establish buffer zones.[43] Then came 9-11.

Homeland Security

Since September 11, 2001, the U.S. government has taken a new look at the U.S. chemical industry. Top government officials, including George Tenet of the CIA and Bush Administration officials, have discussed publicly the possibility that chemical plants could be targeted by terrorists. The U.S. General Accounting Office has pointed to already compiled worst-case accident scenarios as leading indicators of national risk in the chemical industry.

In Congress, even before 9-11, Senator John Corzine (D-NJ) had been working on legislation to require chemical plants, where possible, to reduce dangerous substances they store on site. In July 2002, his bill, then named the Chemical Security Act of 2001, received unanimous approval from the Senate Environment and Public Work Committee. But by August 2002, some 30 chemical and oil company representatives—Dow's among them—had sent a formal letter to key Republicans denouncing the bill, including its provisions for requiring EPA to oversee facility security, and another requiring the industry to use *inherently safer* technologies that would help minimize and eliminate hazardous risks. Seven Republican senators who had voted for the bill in committee, now raised objections and worked to prevent further consideration. The Republicans involved had received generous political contributions from the American Chemistry Council that summer—$850,000 worth. And George Bush's presidential campaign in 2000 was notified that the American Chemistry Council head Frederick Weber agreed to raise $100,000 and was recruiting 25 other chemical industry executives to be Bush fundraisers. Corzine's bill, when it was offered as an amendment to the Homeland Security bill in November 2002, was blocked and was not included in the final act. Also withdrawn from possible Congressional consideration was EPA's attempt to expand its authority under the Clean Air Act for chemical plants. In that package was a key provision to broaden the "general duty" clause on preventing accidents to include chemical industry responsibility for reducing the potential danger of criminal attacks, including those of terrorists. In fact, EPA and the Office of Homeland Security were poised in June 2002 to announce a new "Strategy for Chemical Facility Site Security," which was to begin with government officials visiting chemical plants to highlight needed security improvements. But the announcement never came as the American Chemistry Council and the American Petroleum Institute turned up the heat on the Bush Administration.[44]

> **"Our chemical facilities represent a clear vulnerability in our war against terrorism. "**
>
> U.S. Senator John Corzine

> **Dow lobbied against key provisions of the Chemical Security Act, including one to require inherently safer technologies to help minimize and eliminate hazardous risks.**

"Our chemical facilities represent a clear vulnerability in our war against terrorism," says Senator Corzine. "Yet, as common sense security measures stall in Congress, this appears to be a classic instance of special interests trumping the public interest." Former Senator Gary Hart (D-CO), who has chaired or co-chaired at least two recent panels on national security, agrees. The nation's chemical plants, he says, "are among the potentially most dangerous components of our critical infrastructure. Securing them requires urgent action."[45]

Although 9-11 has rightly drawn attention to the vulnerable state of the nation's chemical infrastructure to terrorist attack—and the lack of national policy on such matters—"chemical terrorism" has existed in America for many years. It is found in both chronic and potentially catastrophic forms, from accidents waiting to happen, to the daily chemical trespass on workers and neighboring communities from leaks, spills, deferred maintenance, and excessive emissions. As the record shows in this book and elsewhere, Dow Chemical's plants have been, and continue to be, part of that problem. Terrorism is only one more good reason to examine the whole of America's toxic and hazardous chemical base anew, and to move quickly to safer alternatives.

17.
Big in Texas

*Forty-two percent of everything Dow sells
in the U.S. is produced in Texas, and more
than 22 percent of what it sells globally.*

Dow brochure, 2001

The Dow Chemical Company is a big deal in Texas—the biggest chemical producer in a state known for its powerful petrochemical industry. Since 2001, with the acquisition of Union Carbide, Dow's position in the state has only grown stronger. With a half dozen or more plants, labs, and offices in and around Houston—including those at Deer Park and La Porte, and south of there, and big plants along the Gulf Coast—Dow is clearly a major player in that region. It also has smaller operations at numerous locations throughout the state. However, Dow's operations in southern Brazoria County, south of Houston, in the Freeport-Brazosport area on the Gulf Coast, comprise one of the largest complexes of its kind in the world. Occupying close to 15,000 acres when all the pipelines, canals, reservoirs, docks and deep-water ports are added up, Dow's 75 plants there turn out 40 billion pounds of chemicals a year. Not far away are two big Carbide operations—one in Texas City and another at Port Lavaca, also known as Seadrift. Dow employs about 11 percent of the state's chemical workers, generating a $400 million local payroll and spreads another $600 million around annually in secondary business outlays. It also pays 17 percent of Texas' corporate property taxes. Dow's influence is felt keenly throughout state and local government. In fact, in some areas of the state, Dow has been the dominant player for decades.

In the 1930s, when Willard Dow and his associates first came to Texas, what they wanted was the seawater of the Gulf of Mexico—to extract bromine and magnesium. Dow and his team had made several trips to the Gulf Coast in search of a good location to set up an extraction plant. Freeport, Texas—about 60 miles south of Houston—got the nod from Dow and his board. "Freeport was a small village surrounded by a sea of salt grass, herds of roaming goats, and marshland," wrote Don Whitehead in *The Dow Story* describing the place in Willard Dow's time. "Yet Freeport's location on a peninsula, having sources of raw materials nearby, and easy disposal of waste brine, was an attraction."[1] Freeport, in fact, was perfect. It had lots of cheap natural gas, salt domes, and sulfur all within easy reach; abundant fresh water from the Brazos River; low-priced land stretching to the horizon; and a local community eager to have new industry. In addition, a new channel of the Brazos River had been dug in 1932 and there was also opportunity for ocean port facilities."[2]

Dow and his company initially bought 800 acres in Freeport, and by the fall of 1940, a construction frenzy ensued. Power lines were strung, a gas pipeline was laid, and a huge intake pipe was extended into the Gulf. Giant pumps were also installed to draw 300 million gallons of water a day into the plant for processing. Dow's first bromine-from-seawater plant was completed in the 1940s, as was a chlorine-caustic plant. A magnesium-from-seawater plant was finished in January 1941.

Dow's investments at Freeport were well timed for World War II. Even before the Japanese attack on Pearl Harbor in December 1941, and America's full involvement in the war, Dow was delivering millions of pounds of magnesium to the British to make fighter planes and bombers. Soon it was doing the same for the U.S. government. The Dow Magnesium Corporation was formed to administer wartime magnesium contracts. By the time of the attack on Pearl Harbor, Dow's Freeport plants were producing bromine, magnesium, chlorine, caustic soda, ethylene, ethylene dichloride, ethylene glycol, and propylene glycol.

Dow's Brazoria

Brazoria County stretches long and flat along Route 288 south from the fringes of Houston's metropolitan area. It extends through the Gulf Coast prairie to the mouth of the Brazos River, just south of Freeport, where land and river meet the Gulf of Mexico. The Brazos divides the county into two sections: the western one third, covered by hardwoods, and the rest, generally prairie land, where cordgrasses, bunchgrasses, and sedges fill out the coastal marshes. It is in this prairieland coastal region, especially along the Gulf, that the industrial minarets of Dow Chemical and partners are seen practically everywhere on the horizon. Brazoria County, in fact, is something of "a company county," with Dow the reigning power.

Life was good. Dow's payroll was flowing fat throughout the region. There was rarely a contrarian view or hint of protest.

During WWII, Dow had built a temporary, barracks-like town for workers dubbed "camp chemical," which became the largest town in Brazoria

County for a time. It was later bulldozed and replaced with an expanded Dow chemical complex. Willard Dow's brother, Alden B. Dow, an architect of some renown and charged with tackling Dow's housing problem, set formal plans to build an entire new city. By the 1950s, the town of Lake Jackson had 5,000 residents, including a section for Dow executives, Lake Jackson Farms. Dow's chemical operations grew as well. By the 1950s and 1960s, Dow marine vessels were hauling chemicals via the Gulf of Mexico to Dow plants and others on the east coast, the Great Lakes, and California. In the early 1970s, Dow added new plants at Freeport and Oyster Creek, building the world's largest phenol plant in 1971, followed a year later by the world's largest chlorine plant.

Freeport grew to include a collection of small towns and municipalities, becoming known as "the Brazosport area," a 214-square-mile urbanized industrial and port area. Dow facilities, Dow affiliated businesses, and Dow customers—ranging from polyvinyl chloride maker Shintech to Hoffman-LaRoche and BASF—are found scattered through the Brazosport area. For many years in this community, life was good. Dow's payroll flowed fat throughout the region,

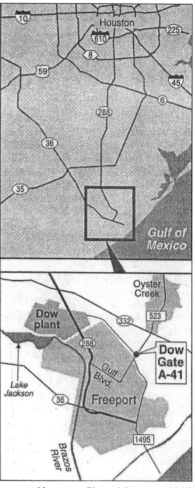

Houston Chronicle map, 1997

and the company became the biggest employer, the biggest spender, and the main player. There was rarely a contrarian view or hint of protest over what Dow wanted. But that began to change in the late 1960s and early 1970s.

"Brazos River is Dead"

Glenn Heath, former editor of *The Brazosport Facts*, remembers the headline well. It appeared one morning in February 1971 in the *Houston Post*. It read: "Brazos River is Dead," and it ran across the front page in big, bold, banner-headline type. It was a story by reporter Harold Scarlett, the first in a series reporting on the pollution of the sprawling Dow Chemical complex in Freeport. The state of Texas at the time made a somewhat obscure report on pollution along the Brazos—the second largest U.S. river flowing into the Gulf of Mexico. Scarlett brought that report to life. What the Texas authorities had found was a river below Dow's wastewater discharge that was essentially devoid of all biological life.[3]

"Preliminary water quality results indicated basically inorganic contamination of the [lower Brazos River] estuary by the Dow Chemical Company at Freeport," wrote biologist Jeffery S. Kirkpatrick in a memo to his superiors at the Texas Water Quality Board in February 1971. "No living organisms could be found in the river...below Dow's discharges..."[4]

In 1970–71, Dow's operations were sending more than 4.5 *billion* **gallons of wastewater** *per day* **into the Brazos and the Gulf of Mexico.**

The Brazos is the longest river in Texas, forming in west Texas east of Lubbock and winding some 840 miles across the state in a southeasterly direction to the Gulf of Mexico. Dow's problem with the Brazos River arose from its dumping of more than 450,000 pounds of magnesium salts *per day* into the river, alkaline wastes which altered the river's ecological balance. "This is what is keeping the fish out," explained Bob Clark in April 1971, then an aide to state senator A. R. "Babe" Schwartz. Dow was also dumping, among other things, glycol and other toxic compounds into the river. But the company said it would fix this—in a few years—by treating the wastes before they were released. Dow had historically relied on dilution by the Brazos's water volume to dispose of its pollutants, releasing materials into a river flow of 5,000 cubic feet per second. But the Brazos's flow by the time it got to Dow's waste pipes was not always at that volume, and in fact, was often flowing at 500 cubic feet per second. Dow's pollutants were not being diluted, and in any case, were flowing into the Gulf of Mexico. Some of the pollutants were sinking to the river bottom, and depleting the river's oxygen.

Dow's discharge to the Brazos was regulated by a 1962 state water permit—a permit that by 1971 was nearly a decade old and had not once been reviewed by regulators. "The Water Quality Board allows Dow to operate and maintain its own testing system and to file its own reports with regard to the amount of effluent discharged and the BOD level [biological oxygen demand]," observed Lake Jackson attorney, Vaughan Stewart. BOD, in fact, was specified in the permit not to exceed 12 ppm, and was vital to the river's health. But Dow's pollution was more or less wiping out the oxygen—or at least creating the conditions to prevent its formation. In 1970–71, Dow's operations were sending more than 4.5 *billion* gallons of wastewater *per day* into the Brazos and the Gulf of Mexico. The salt wastes going into the river, chiefly magnesium hydroxide and calcium carbonate, were settling on the river bottom, preventing normal aquatic life from growing, contributing to the river's lack of oxygen. Dow reported the BOD level in the Brazos at averages in the 4 to 8 ppm range, but others who had taken samples from the Brazos, found it to be as high as 60 ppm. In 1971, despite requests for action on the pollution permit by citizens and Texas politicians—pointing to repeated fish kills along the Brazos, among other problems—the Texas Water Quality Board (TWQB) formally found the company blameless for the pollution.[5] Dow had also proposed to increase the volume of wastes it injected underground into deep wells. There were already five deep wells operating in the area within a five-mile radius of each other, some reaching depths of 5,000 feet or more. But despite the objections and appeals of citizen groups and a local politician, the TWQB approved a new 13-million-gallon-per-month deep well in September 1971.[6] Meanwhile, the activism aimed at Dow began to focus on another issue.

Taking On Dow

It was organized labor that helped raise the visibility of environmental issues in Brazoria County, and it was the local labor unions that helped form one of the first citizen/environmental organizations in the county—a group called the Citizens Survival Committee (CSC). The Texas AFL-CIO helped get the CSC started at the suggestion of two local labor leaders, O. D. Kenemore and Kenneth Koch. The CSC became the lead activist group in raising questions about air and water pollution, focusing initially on the Brazos River and the deep-well injection of wastes.

The unions began to see pollution as a community issue, and a way to leverage Dow on other matters.

The unions began to see pollution as a community issue, and a way to leverage Dow on other matters. One union worker speaking at an April 1971 CSC-sponsored forum on the environment put it this way: "For many years, organized labor had good relations with Dow. We saw the pollution, but we were as greedy as any, and didn't do anything. Now our relations are not so good. My motive now is that all the [worker] benefits in the world are unimportant if we don't have air and water. I don't intend to stop anti-pollution efforts: it's just as big a need as income...."[7]

In its early years, during the time when A. P. "Dutch" Beutel was the general manager of the Texas Division, Dow worked with the unions and needed their talents to build and operate its plants. Prior to about 1970, construction and contract work at the plant had been union too, performed primarily through the Houston Metal Trades Council, representing various craft unions. By the 1970s, Dow was also involved with nearly a dozen unions at its Freeport operations, variously represented by affiliates and locals of the AFL-CIO. The Freeport Metal Trades Council, made up of 10 craft unions all recognized by Dow, included pipefitters, bricklayers, asbestos workers, carpenters, painters, and others. Among the emerging union leaders in the 1970s was pipefitter O. D. Kenemore, who had worked at Dow since 1951. He had secretly brought Harold Scarlett of the *Houston Post* into the Dow complex for a look around, pointing out leaks and other internal problems. That material became grist for Scarlett's stories—stories which became one of the first times Dow had really been confronted publicly on its safety and environmental performance. Scarlett's stories, and an emerging national grassroots concern about the environment generally, helped raise the visibility and activities of the CSC. The group was soon holding community meetings that drew more than 1,200 people at some events, and also began filing formal comments and petitions in state regulatory proceedings and working with state legislators.[8] But in 1972, the CSC and the Freeport community began focusing on something else: the Dow labor strike.

The 1972 Strike

In the late 1960s, as Dow expanded its production units in Brazoria County, it opened a new complex at Oyster Creek as a separate unit and specified it as an "open shop," seeking non-union workers. The existing unions wanted the new unit to be treated as an extension of Dow's current operations—as a union operation. They tried bargaining and negotiating with Dow, but Dow resisted. The union filed an unfair labor practices suit in 1969, and a 14-day court hearing followed, but the union lost. By 1970 and 1971, Dow was hiring more non-union contractors, and the unions saw Dow's practices as a clear threat. "It was obvious they were trying to get rid of organized labor," says O. D. Kenemore, "and then those unions that continued to be strong and fighting them [Dow], they were tripping 'em out; getting rid of them.... If they could get one they could coax into it, that would take a salary job, they'd move them over on a salary job out from under the bargaining unit. Pipefitters were way down at the time... They were out to break the union, is what it really amounted to...."[9]

As Dow continued contracting out repairs to non-union workers, more than 3,000 members of eight unions at Dow Freeport—led by Kenemore of the Freeport Metal Trades and Tommy Crow of the Operating Engineers—walked off the job in June 1972. The unions wanted Dow to limit the amount of non-union maintenance work. Dow would not agree, so the union saw its strike as a survival issue. Pickets soon went up at all the Dow gates, and a full-fledged strike was underway. Brazoria County had not seen anything like it. The strike persisted for four long months, with arrests, picketing workers hit by cars, dynamiting incidents, court injunctions, federal mediation, and hard times for striking workers and their families. But the workers held their ground. And union leaders such as Kenemore improvised along the way.

Kenemore went to the banks to ask leniency for workers' mortgage payments; to local grocery stores to collect day-old bread and buy wholesale quantities of eggs and bologna at discount; and to local merchants for their moral and financial support.[10]

One high point in the strike came on Wednesday, June 28, 1972, as the wives of striking workers organized and marched on Dow headquarters building—with more than 1,100 participants—waving homemade hand-lettered placards, some

"They were out to break the union, is what it really amounted to."

of which read: "Dow is Unfair," "Unskilled Labor Results in—BOOM!!", "Stay Safe, Stay Union," "Stop Pollution," "My Dad is a Craft Man," and others. The wives formed United Wives for Organized Labor and continued to be a factor in the strike, mounting other demonstrations, with some traveling to nearby cities such as Galveston to urge shoppers to boycott Dow consumer products.[11]

After a bitter and confrontational four months, Dow and the eight striking unions reached agreement on a new three-year contract. Dow agreed to a hiring plan and formula designed to keep union workers at 75 percent of the total in any given craft. It also agreed to selected wage increases, though money had never been the main issue in the strike. "We were successful in putting a cap on the type and amount of contract work for the first time," said Kenemore. But Dow's plant manager, David Rooke, boasted that production records were set during the strike, and that salaried workers were able to run the complex safely and without incident.[12]

Dow didn't anticipate community support for striking union workers at Freeport, Texas.   *The Brazosport Facts, June 29, 1972*

Dangerous Places

Dow's operations in Freeport, however, had a number of chemical plant accidents and toxic gas releases—both before the 1972 strike, and in years thereafter. Workers were typically in the front lines; the first to suffer ill effects, severe injury, or loss of life. O. D. Kenemore witnessed or learned about several incidents during his more than 20 years at Dow's plants, and also had some first-hand toxic exposures. In 1953–54, Kenemore remembers that working near allyl alcohol all day made it difficult for him to breathe at night when he went home to bed. By 1958, he was told that one needed full protective gear to work directly with allyl alcohol, with some fellow workers warning him, "that stuff will kill you." Still, Dow's medical staff at the Industrial Medicine Center told Kenemore and others "not to worry" about allyl alcohol, that it "can't hurt you." If a worker had a heavy exposure, Kenemore recalls one Dow doctor saying, "he could be dragged out by his heels into the air" and would recover.[13]

"We breathed chlorine daily."

O. D. Kenemore

Kenemore also recalls explosions that killed workers: one in March 1960 at the glycerine No. 1 unit; another "in the 1900 block of glycerine No. 1, Plant B" in November 1960 that killed four pipefitters and two riggers. In 1964—also in the glycerine block—Dow was trying to develop a new kind of pesticide for the tobacco industry, and conducted an experimental mixing of two chemicals with unknown results. Dow used a railroad tank car with one part of the mixture and a tank truck containing another chemical. Dow rolled the rail tanker "out into the prairie" away from its main operations, recalls Kenemore. The truck containing the other chemical was driven out to the rail car's location where the mixing began. During the course of the experiment, the rail car exploded, killing one worker.[14]

Chlorine releases at the Freeport operations were common in the 1950s and 1960s. "There were numbers and numbers of them," according to Kenemore. "We breathed chlorine daily," he says. And once a week or so "somebody would get too much chlorine," and they would be "loaded into an ambulance and taken to the Industrial Medical Lab" for treatment. "Chlorine pills" were readily available onsite for workers to take whenever they felt the need, says Kenemore—pills which "kept the throat from swelling."[15] In 1973, there was a chlorine blow-out from a Dow pipeline at the Chlorine No. 3 lab in Freeport. A yellow cloud and worker evacuation followed. Vinyl chloride gas leaks from bad gaskets and valve packings were also common at Freeport, according to Kenemore. He remembers such leaks occurring "all the time" from the 1950s through 1970–71, especially at the vinylidene plants (plant V-1 and V-2 within Dow's larger Plant A complex). By the early

1970s, Dow began to acknowledge the vinyl chloride leakage, which had become a chronic exposure problem for pipefitters and other workers.[16]

In October 1981, another incident involving what some believe was an untested catalyst, resulted in a fire and explosion at Dow's Freeport plant that killed six workers and injured seven others.[17] The incident occurred in the polyethylene plant. Kenemore remembers the containment area around the chemical reactor in the plant; it was made of heavy concrete walls about 20 to 25 feet tall with an open roof. In the middle of this containment structure was a reactor about 12 feet tall. The only entrance and exit into the structure was through a thick steel door right by the reactor. In this particular October, Dow had an order for a heavy-gauge plastic bag, and had been experimenting with a new catalyst to make this particular

The reactor heated up and exploded, violently killing five workers instantly, leaving others burned and injured.

line of plastic. In another block of the plant, Dow had been testing the new catalyst under controlled conditions, during which there had been some smaller explosions. But the new material, whatever it was, was always handled carefully. A special cylinder with the material was transferred regularly and always after normal work hours, with firemen and safety personnel on site. One evening that October, however, after the polyethylene reactor had been shut down and cooled, with some repair work occurring on it and other equipment, the reactor heated up and exploded, violently killing five workers instantly, leaving others burned and injured. Another worker later died at Houston Hospital. Rescuers were hindered at the scene since the steel door to the unit was too hot to open. One rescuer who pulled an injured worker from the scene later reported the victim's brains "leaking onto my shoulder."

Kenemore, who was part of the investigative team to visit the accident scene, noted there was a heavy syrup-like material left in the reactor that clung to the walls. It was later determined that the soupy material was the catalyst, which had not completely drained from the reactor when shut down. At the accident scene, Kenemore also observed there was no route of escape for workers in the reactor building, as workers had to exit past the reactor and out the one steel door. Kenemore proposed that a ladder be built inside of all such reactor buildings throughout the Dow complex so that workers could at least have a better route of escape, up the wall and through the open roof. "You have to have a ladder out the top," he remembers explaining. An OSHA investigator, also participating in the follow-up study of the accident, agreed with Kenemore—at least initially. However, by the time the final report came to pass, Dow objected to the escape-ladder idea and it was not included in the final report of post-accident recommendations.[18]

Dioxin in Fish

Back on the Brazos River, meanwhile, there had also been some new developments. EPA had conducted a survey in 1987 called the National Bioaccumulation Study, collecting fish samples at 100 locations across the United States. One of the Texas sites sampled was near a Dow Chemical wastewater discharge on the Brazos River. Dioxin was found in six catfish and six black drum taken at the location. In the catfish, TCDD dioxin was found at 2 parts per trillion (ppt), and hexachlorobenzene at 913 parts per billion (ppb). In the black drum, the TCDD dioxin level was less than 1 ppt with no hexachlorobenzene detected.

In 1990, a fish consumption advisory was posted for the Brazos River, with special attention to the river below Dow's Freeport operations.

"We don't know how to interpret it—we are relying on EPA and they have said there is no need for fishing advisories," explained Dow's environmental manager John Harrison, providing the company's views at a February 1990 press conference. "We know these are extremely low numbers...," said Harrison. "At this point it is too early to understand what these numbers mean, whether they are coming from our Dow facilities...," he continued. "If there are sources of contaminants from our plant site, we will take care of it," he assured. But Harrison went on to say that the fish could have come from offshore or down the river. He also explained that Dow had 15 outfalls to the Brazos, discharging 1 billion gallons of seawater every day. "We have never produced a product associated with the dioxin-furan issue," he said. Nevertheless, the state required that Dow make a study of the matter as a condition of renewing its pollution discharge permit.[19]

By September 1990, the Texas Health Department (TDH) posted a fish consumption advisory for the Brazos River, with special attention to the river below Dow's Freeport discharges. TDH advised that consumption levels of all finfish from the river be curtailed to one meal of eight ounces each month. The advisory also suggested that women of childbearing age and children should not eat any fish from the river. The Texas Water Commission, meanwhile, ordered Dow to find out where the dioxin found in Brazos River fish was coming from.

By April 1991, part of the dioxin contamination found in Brazos River fish was traced to Dow furnaces used in the manufacture of magnesium chloride. "We have confirmed that we are discharging dioxin at extremely low levels," said Dow's John Harrison. "This is the first time we've seen a significant source." But at the time, the hunt for dioxin sources was still ongoing, and several other areas of the plant were yet to be examined.[20] By April 1992, it was determined that Dow's magnesium operation was indeed a major part of the problem. Most of the dioxin was released as a byproduct of magnesium extraction from seawater, a process that had been going on at Freeport since the mid-1940s. Solid wastes created by the manufacture of magnesium containing traces of dioxin had been pumped into the river during that time. But by April 1992, Dow claimed it had eliminated up to 85 percent of the dioxin being released to the Brazos River. David Graham, environmental manager for Dow's Texas operations, explained that Dow now captured the solids in settling ponds and disposed of them at an on-site landfill. Still, the fish consumption advisory remained in effect. The Texas Water Commission recommended that Dow reduce its dioxin discharges to 0.00004 pounds per day. Dow's Graham said the company could reach that goal on some days, but the average discharges were somewhat higher. Dow was then using about 365 billion gallons of water annually at the plant. The amount of dioxin still being discharged amounted to 0.02 pounds per year, Graham said, reduced from a higher level of 0.093 pounds per year.[21] Dow claimed it had cut almost all of its discharges, but a small volume still remained. "It is going to be extremely difficult to define (the remaining dioxin's) exact sources," said Graham. "This is quite a large site—some 80 plants on a 5,000 acre site." But the discharges were only part of the problem. "Even though dioxin may be eliminated from the discharge," said Kirk Wiles, an official of the Texas Health Department in May 1992, "it's not necessarily eliminated from the river."[22]

In March 1995, Greenpeace reported they had taken samples from Dow's Freeport site that showed potentially higher levels of dioxin being released from other sources at the complex, namely Dow's vinyl chloride operations. "If they ever got any samples from our facility, we're certainly not aware of it," said Ed Rainwater, vice president of Dow Texas Operations. "I'd say it's not possible." Greenpeace claimed the samples were from Dow's vinyl chloride feedstock wastes, which Dow makes at the Oyster Creek plant near Freeport and ships by pipeline to nearby vinyl chloride manufacturers. Greenpeace, in this case, was concerned about dioxin emissions from the burned wastes. "There are detectable quantities at very, very low levels....," acknowledged Dow's Rainwater. "You get into parts-per-trillion levels," he said. "In the last few years, we just developed techniques that can even improve our analytical ability to detect levels

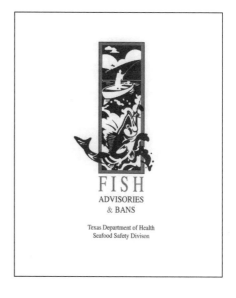

FISH
ADVISORIES
& BANS

Texas Department of Health
Seafood Safety Division

that low... [W]e at this point are convinced there is no public risk. That doesn't mean we are not dedicated to continually reducing (those emissions)." Rainwater also acknowledged at the time that Dow Freeport was still working to remove the Brazos River fish advisory. "Our commitment is to do whatever's necessary to lift that fish advisory," he said. "And we think we're very close to that right now."[23]

In 2001, Dow's Freeport operations released 708.5 grams of dioxin and dioxin-like compounds into local surface waters.

Two years later, in July 1997, the Texas Department of Health (TDH) lifted the fish advisory for the lower Brazos River. "The bottom line is that people fishing the lower Brazos River can now eat their fish without wondering if they're safe," said Kirk Wiles with TDH's Seafood Safety Division. The reevaluation tests that TDH conducted showed negligible dioxin levels in the fish, said TDH. At the time, the tests also found no other chemicals that would make the fish unsafe for consumption.[24] Yet in 2001, according to the Toxic Release Inventory, Dow's Freeport operations released 708.5 grams of dioxin and dioxin-like compounds into local surface waters, with another 13,000 grams or more going into onsite landfills.[25] In the company's Texas Division environmental report for 2001, Dow says there has been a 25–30 percent reduction in dioxin emissions at Freeport since 1995, and the goal for 2005 is a further 90 percent reduction from 1995.[26]

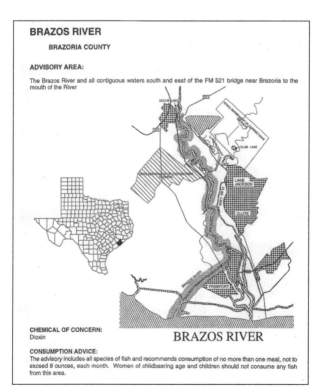

BRAZOS RIVER

BRAZORIA COUNTY

ADVISORY AREA:

The Brazos River and all contiguous waters south and east of the FM 521 bridge near Brazoria to the mouth of the River

BRAZOS RIVER

CHEMICAL OF CONCERN:
Dioxin

CONSUMPTION ADVICE:
The advisory includes all species of fish and recommends consumption of no more than one meal, not to exceed 8 ounces, each month. Women of childbearing age and children should not consume any fish from this area.

Dioxin isn't Dow's only problem, however. In 2001, according to EPA, Dow discharged more than 15 times the legal limit of 1,2-dichloroethane into the Brazos. A probable carcinogen, 1,2 dichloroethane may also damage the liver and kidneys for those exposed to it through drinking water. According to Luke Metzger of the Texas Public Interest Research Group in Austin, Dow continued to violate the law for this pollutant "in eight out of eight quarters from April 2001 to March 2003." And even though "Dow clearly violated the law," explains Metzger, "the company paid no fine for these permit violations."[27]

Chronic Pollution

In the late 1980s, when the first results of the Toxic Release Inventory (TRI) were published for U.S. industrial pollution for the reporting year 1987, Dow Freeport was identified as the 30th worst facility nationally for the release of known and probable carcinogens. Dow Freeport was then releasing nearly 2 million pounds of such substances, among them: 1,2-dichloroethane at nearly 460,000 pounds; tetrachloroethylene at more than 400,000 pounds; carbon tetrachloride at more than 318,000 pounds; dichloromethane at more than 260,000 pounds; benzene at more than 242,000 pounds; and chloroform at nearly 70,000 pounds. By 1995, Brazoria County was the fifth worst county in the nation for TRI releases[28]—a distinction not solely due to Dow, though a number of petrochemical operations there rely on Dow as key supplier or partner. Since the 1980s, Dow has made progress in reducing many of its pollutants. Yet, according to the 2001 TRI, Dow's Freeport operations are still ranked among the "dirtiest or worst" of all U.S. facilities for several categories of pollutants: total environmental release; cancer risk score for air and water releases; air releases of recognized carcinogens; air releases of recognized developmental toxicants; and air releases of recognized reproductive toxicant.[29]

In December 2001, the Texas Natural Resource Conservation Commission (TNRCC) fined Dow $433,388 for air pollution violations at Freeport. The violations included Dow's failure to submit reports on 29 unexplained emission releases, the release of unauthorized emissions on more than two dozen occasions, and the failure to control emissions from a benzene tank, a reactor, and a distillation tower. The state discovered the violations during inspections conducted between August 1999 and October 2000. The Associated Press also reported at the time that Dow had received 22 enforcement orders from the TNRCC during the past 15 years.[30]

Old Wastes Never Die

Dow also has its hands full in Texas cleaning up and/or containing old waste dumps found in and around its operating locations. In 1989, Dow announced it would begin cleaning up 25 areas in Freeport that were contaminated for as long as four decades. The wastes, buried 30 feet or so

Toxic Chemical Release
Dow Chemical, Freeport, Texas, 2001

Chemical Name	Total Release*
	(lbs.)
Ethylene	1,048,544
Propylene	708,035
Picloram (g)	232,885
Chlorodifluoromethane (e,g)	131,727
Copper compounds	98,192
Styrene (d,e,f,g)	77,219
Ammonia (f)	69,549
Benzene (a,b,c,g)	63,676
Hydrochloric acid	60,227
1,1,2-trichloroethane (a)	52,506
Ethylbenzene (d,e,f,g)	47,699
Chlorine	45,990
Epichlorohydrin (a,c,g)	42,511
Toluene (b,f)	39,765
Xylene (mixed isomers) (e,f)	38,551
Cumene	26,463
Dichlorodifluoromethane	23,769
Dichloromethane (a,f,g)	21,352
1,3-butadiene (a,e,f)	19,562
Phenol (e,f)	16,972
1,2-dichloroethane (a,e,f,g)	16,683
Methyl isobutyl ketone (e)	16,544
N-hexane (e,f)	15,390
Trichloroethylene (a,e,f)	13,828
Nickel (a,e,f)	12,411
1,2-dichloropropane (a,f,g)	11,461
1,1-dichloro-1-fluoroethane	10,467
Methyl ethyl ketone (e,f)	9,894
Tetrachloroethylene (a,e,f)	9,441
Propylene oxide (a,e,f)	9,376
Biphenyl (e)	7,955
Vinyl chloride (a,e,f)	7,889
N-butyl alcohol	7,324
Chloroform (a,e,f,g)	6,864
Carbon tetrachloride (a,e,f,g)	5,847

(table cont'd)

Table Key: a) recognized carcinogen; b) recognized developmental toxicant; c) recognized reproductive toxicant; d) suspected carcinogen; e) suspected developmental toxicant; f) suspected reproductive toxicant; g) suspected endocrine toxicant.
*to air, water, land

underground, were the result of plastics production. Core samples taken at the time indicated various chlorinated hydrocarbons, with some samples containing as much as 20 percent contaminants. "Some of what we'll be cleaning up here is what took place in the 1940s and '50s," explained R. C. Dipprey, a Dow spokesman. "We're going to go back and review our past practices and do the appropriate things to clean it up."[31]

Brazoria County Health Department Director Dr. Leo O'Gorman said he didn't see any health dangers and praised Dow for trying to take care of its problems. Dow officials also said there was no chance that the contaminants would migrate into nearby residential wells. A thick layer of clay below the contaminated soil acts as a barrier, said the Dow spokesman, preventing any seepage into drinking water sands more than 100 feet below. A cost estimate on the overall cleanup project was not given at the time, but Dow project manager John Harrison, said it might take as long as a decade.[32] That was in 1989.

More than a decade later, Dow's Freeport operation was confronted with seeping wastes from another Dow dump site—one at the Plant B area. Here, for nearly 60 years, Dow dumped all manner of chlorinated hydrocarbons, such as phenol, benzene, and acetone into an open pit. Dow said the wastes were no problem, and would remain on site. But they didn't. Not far underground, Dow's contaminants were on the move. First, they seeped into the brackish groundwater 20 to 80 feet below the dump site. Then they began to spread outward, beyond the site, moving south in a large underground plume. The plume seeped beneath the Brazos River, and under homes in a small residential area known as the Slaughter Road community. It also ran under the Freeport Municipal Golf Course. Most of the Slaughter Road residents drew their water from a 200-foot city well separated from the contaminated area by a dense layer of clay, which some thought protected them. By early October 2000, however, Dow was distributing letters door-to-door in the neighborhood, explaining its plans to monitor and contain the plume. Dow had first revealed the problem in 1994, when it closed the pit and began capping it with clay. The entire waste site was then encircled with a steel-and-clay barrier wall that extended for some distance.[33]

One Dow spokesman on the project, Harry Engelhardt, explained that Dow's waste disposal into an open pit 50 years ago was considered progressive, and especially for a company to use its own land. "Back then that was very proactive, because you were consuming some of your own land that you could have used for something else. Inside the fence line, that property was very, very valuable," he said. Engelhardt also explained, "these were regulated, legal, best practice, state-of-the-art ways of dealing with waste back in the

Chemical Name	Total Release*
	(lbs.)
4,4'-isopropylidenediphenol (f,g)	5,453
Methanol (e)	5,361
1,3-dichloropropene (a,f)	4,862
Sulfuric acid (d)	4,674
Acrylic acid	4,581
Propionaldehyde	4,479
1,1-dichloroethylene (d,e,f)	3,926
Zinc (e,f)	3,669
1,1,1-trichloroethane (e,f)	3,023
Manganese compounds	2,972
1,2,4-trimethylbenzene	2,810
Ethylene oxide (a,c,e)	2,708
1,1,2,2-tetrachloroethane (a,e)	2,373
Nitrate compounds	2,239
1,2-dichloroethylene	2,054
Allyl chloride (d,e)	1,966
Chloromethane (b,d,f)	1,862
1,2-butylene oxide (d)	1,800
Cyclohexane	1,797
Glycol ethers (e,f)	1,599
Sodium nitrite (e)	1,524
1,1,1,2-tetrachloroethane (d)	1,380
1,2-dichlorobenzene (g)	1,251
1,2,3-trichloropropane (a,f)	1,225
Formaldehyde (a,f)	1,002
Toluene -2,4-diisocyanate (a)	892
Chloroethane (a,e)	822
Toluene diisocyanate (a)	803
2,3-dichloropropene	772
Acetaldehyde (a,e)	673
Naphthalene (a,e)	569
Acrolein (d,e)	545
Mercury (b,f,g)	520
Dicyclopentadiene	509
Ethylene glycol (e,f)	438
Bis(2-chloro-1-methylethyl) ether (a)	423
Hexachloroethane (a,e,f)	355
Hexachloro-1,3-butadiene (d,e,f,g)	323
Phosgene	288
Acrylonitrile (a,e,f)	241
Formic acid	181
Pentachloroethane	139
Anthracene (g)	84
	(table cont'd)

Chemical Name	Total Release*
	(lbs.)
Hydrogen cyanide (f,g)	65
Toluene-2,6-diisocyanate (a)	64
Lead (a, b, c, g)	52
Hexachlorobenzene (a,b,f,g)	41
Bromine (g)	27
Cyanide compounds	23
Triethylamine	19
Polycyclic aromatic compounds (d,f)	14
Cumene hydroperoxide	9
Methyl tert-butyl ether (d,e)	8
Vinyl acetate (d)	2
2,2', 6,6'- tetrabromo-4,4'-isopropylidenediphenol (g)	2
Zinc compounds	2
1,4-dichloro-2-butene (a)	2
Aniline (a,e)	2
Chlorobenzene (e,f)	1
N-methyl-2-pyrrolidone (b,f)	1
Styrene oxide (a,e,f)	1
Dioxin & dioxin-like compounds (a,e)	14,270 grams

Source: Environmental Defense, *www.scorecard.org*.

1940s and '50s. If you impound waste—and that was the way everybody did it—today you know there are some longer term consequences that nobody understood back then."[34]

But residents of Slaughter Road were now worried about the effects of the contamination. Mary Dunnahoe, 58, a resident of Slaughter Road all her life, was wondering about the fair market value of her house. And she was most concerned about the health of her community. "Marie Kitchen and I sat down one day," said Dunnahoe, "and counted 57 people in this neighborhood who had cancer over the last 50 years…I had a mother and an uncle both have cancer in the same house. The people who owned the house before us, she had it and died, and her mother and father before her in that house, they died. The man on the side of me, he died. The people across the street—four in one family—died…. There's not a house that hasn't hardly been affected out here but two or three or four." Dunnahoe indicated that liver and pancreatic cancer seemed to be especially prominent. And her neighbor, Louie Kitchen, agreed. Liver cancer seemed more common, but he wondered if the cancer rates in the Slaughter Road area were really higher than they were in the Brazosport area generally. "There's a lot of cancer here," he said, "but if you did a survey of people anywhere in this area, you'd probably find the same amount."[35]

For nearly 60 years, Dow dumped all manner of chlorinated hydrocarbons, such as phenol, benzene, acetone and others into an open pit.

Still, Dow's problem in the Slaughter Road area, in part, was made quite visible at times by the shallow water table, found as close as 20 feet below the surface. Dow found contamination at the 20- to 40-foot level on the one part of the Municipal Golf Course, and at 60 to 90 feet in one part of the Slaughter Road community. But local resident Ralph Warren explains: "Around here, when we get a wet spring, the water table rises. You can dig a hole at night and come back the next day (without rain) and it's half full of water."

When Dow began buying up residential properties in the community, however, that piqued the interest of more residents and caused others to worry more about the contamination. By October 2000, Dow had bought four homes in the area, and said it wasn't actively seeking any others. However, if sellers initiated the action, Dow would consider their offers. "From the standpoint that we've got monitoring wells out there" explained Dow's public affairs leader, Kanina Blanchard, "if the property becomes available at fair market value and there's some benefit to us—such as increasing our ability to do the monitoring—we would consider buying."[36] However, Dow has also been pushed on the matter recently by residents threatening to sue.

> **"Marie Kitchen and I sat down one day and counted 57 people in this neighborhood who had cancer over the last 50 years."**
>
> Mary Dunnahoe, 58
> Slaughter Road, Freeport, Texas

Leaking Caverns

In Clute, Texas—another Brazosport municipality—residents have had suspicions about some underground leakage that may be coming from one of Dow's huge underground salt domes. At the Oyster Creek operation, Dow has a huge network of salt-dome caverns it uses to store hydrocarbons, much like the government does with the Strategic Petroleum Reserve (a portion which Dow runs for the government at another dome). But to the south of Dow's dome caverns—the Stratton Ridge dome—lies the community of Clute. And on one edge of this town, along East Kyle Road, residents have become concerned. In an area with about 60 homes, there are at least 32 people who either suffer from cancer, have survived cancer, or have already died. "When you see 30-something tumors and cancers," said Billy Mariam, 63, who was diagnosed with kidney cancer in August 2000, "you get to thinking." A Dow retiree, Mariam wasn't ready to blame Dow for his cancer, and he was also a smoker. Still, a number of other people in the community who were non-smokers had problems. Phyllis Strong, an accountant, survived a bout of thyroid cancer in 1995. Her father died of colon cancer that year and her mother had a thyroid tumor removed that was thought to be benign.

In September 2000, the Austin, Texas law firm of Tomblin, Carnes & McCormick had placed a local newspaper ad soliciting screening for asbestosis clients. However, the firm was also contacted by some Kyle Road residents.

The lawyers subsequently held a neighborhood meeting on the problem that brought out about 70 people, with a few dozen signing up as prospective clients. The lawyers also had samples taken from 15 of the Clute water wells. But the Kyle Road community is filled with Dow retirees, many of whom did not sign up with the lawyers—at least initially. "We're not pointing fingers," said Bruce Lowry who lived on East Kyle Road for 22 years. "We're not after nobody. We just want to find out if we've got good water." Wrote *Houston Chronicle* reporter Steve Olafson, covering this story in mid-October 2000: "The people here, by and large, are reluctant to openly accuse the chemical industry for their neighborhood's woes. Many are retired from Dow and receive pension checks from the company, the largest employer in the area."[37]

> "We're not pointing fingers. We just want to find out if we've got good water."

Phosgene Scares

Not far from Houston, Dow's plant at La Porte, Texas is a leader in producing polyurethane chemicals which are used to make a wide variety of products such as pantyhose and ski boots. One of the ingredient chemicals Dow uses at La Porte is phosgene. Phosgene, however, is deadly stuff. A bare whiff of a few ounces or so is enough to kill a man. Made from chlorine and feared in WWI as a vicious chemical warfare agent, today it remains one of the most dangerous substances around. Phosgene is used in the production of pharmaceuticals, agricultural chemicals, plastic additives, and artificial sweeteners. Dow produces about 475 million pounds of phosgene every year at the 140-acre La Porte plant where about 450 workers are employed.

Phosgene is a liquid below 47 degrees Fahrenheit and becomes a colorless gas above that—a gas which can be inhaled in fatal amounts without a person realizing it. When released, the gas, which weighs about the same as air, travels along the ground, much like chlorine. Phosgene breaks down into carbon monoxide and hydrochloric acid when it meets water. But in human lungs, it can produce excessive fluid causing a condition called pulmonary edema. Damage is usually delayed, sometimes not beginning for 24 hours after exposure. A 5,000-pound release can kill or seriously injure people more than 12 miles away under worst-case weather conditions, according to the EPA. A leak as small as a half-pound can be dangerous up to 200 feet away.

Following the deadly December 1984 Bhopal gas leak, OSHA began a series of special inspections at U.S. chemical plants then handling highly toxic substances. OSHA chose its chemicals one at a time, and in the Houston area it chose phosgene because it was the most hazardous substance

Friend of Nature?

In recent years, Dow Chemical, as a good corporate citizen in the Freeport-Brazosport area, has made some highly visible commitments and land donations to signify its concern for the environment and nature. Dow lays claim to hosting the largest Gulf Coast nesting location of gull-like Black Skimmers, who return to the same Dow parking lot of crushed sea shells every year to nest. The crushed limestone shells make good material for the birds to dig a depression, or scrape. The area also has marshes nearby, and the open lot protects the Skimmers from predators. The birds have been coming to the Dow site since the mid-1980s, perhaps owed more to the birds' nesting criteria and accidental ecology than Dow's generosity. Dow, however, is quite hospitable and glad to have the attention, welcoming visitors to the site each year with an open house, when typically more than 200 people come out. Dow has also worked with the Coast Conservation Association and Texas Parks and Wildlife Department to create a 75-acre marine-life education center and fish hatchery named Sea Center Texas in Lake Jackson. And occasionally, Dow takes out some full-page, paid advertisements in local and regional newspapers to tout its good works and environmental commitment. One such ad, appearing in the March 1996 *Brazosport Facts,* showed a coastal scene of blue skies, puffy white clouds over an ocean horizon, and waves lapping onshore. Also pictured in the scene was a modern office chair on the beach at the surf's edge. The ad also included a photo inlay of a popular Gulf of Mexico fish, the redfish. The headline, just below the fish read: "When the Gulf Redfish Population Needed Help, We Expanded Our Home Office." Dow's text explained:

> In 1985, when overfishing threatened the local redfish population, the Texas Parks and Wildlife Department and the Gulf Coast Conservation Association asked Dow for help. We set aside the acreage necessary and worked as partners to create a highly successful hatchery. Today, that hatchery project has spawned the opening of a living museum, Sea Center Texas. You can see, at Dow, we'll go the distance to work with our community. Even if it means leaving our labs to expand our home office.

Many environmentalists, however, found the Dow ad somewhat ironic, especially with the Brazos River dioxin fish advisory still in place and Dow pollution periodically blamed for some very visible fish kills in the area. "Dead Fish Are Removed," was the headline on a *Houston Chronicle* story from February 1994, reporting on Dow workers cleaning up a fish kill "caused by an above-normal discharge of hazardous chemicals into a canal leading into the Brazos River." Local fishers also blamed Dow pollution and its marine operations for contributing to declining fish and shrimp populations, as well as habitat destruction. In the Gulf of Mexico too, the comings and goings of various vessels hauling chemicals and petrochemicals in and out of Freeport to Dow and related operations had their share of spills and other incidents.

In April 1996, for example, a Norwegian tanker, the *Bow Sun,* released

nearly 25,000 gallons of the toxic solvent perchloroethylene into the Gulf of Mexico off the Texas coast near Matagorda Island, a prime shrimping area. Perchloroethylene, a chemical used in dry-cleaning fluid, as a nail polish remover,
and as a degreasing solvent, was being delivered to Dow's Freeport chemical
plant. The tanker, which originated in Brazil, was apparently departing from
Freeport after its delivery, heading to Corpus Christi when the spill occurred. Officials from the *Bow Sun* explained that crew workers—flushing out the ship's
cargo tanks—assumed the tanks were empty, but they weren't. An incorrect
valve was opened, releasing the material into the Gulf. "It will kill any organism
it comes in direct contact with," said Allan Strand of the U.S. Fish and Wildlife
Service (USFWS) in Corpus Christi of the chemical spill—"and because it maintains its consistency it also will basically smother things (at the bottom of the
ocean) for some time." The chemical, heavier than water, sank to the bottom as
the tanker was passing Matagorda Island. Wilma Anderson, executive director of
the Texas Shrimp Association, said that if the spill drifted into the nearby bay systems, it could hurt young shrimp. Sea turtles, such as the endangered Kemp's
ridley, could also be affected, she said. Allan Strand of the USFWS said there was
nothing that could be done to clean up the chemical, and he expected it would
remain on the Gulf and ocean floor for at least 25 days. The Texas Shrimp Association was not happy with the spill, and sought to raise a number of issues with
the chemical industry and government officials—including chemical carrier
accountability, destruction of shrimp habitat, timely notification procedures,
industry responsibility in tracking the fate of materials, and industry follow-up
monitoring of marine-life effects. Some environmental organizations, such as
Greenpeace, thought the incident raised a larger, unreported problem—that of
chemical tankers regularly carrying chlorinated compounds and flushing out
their holds at sea, "legally" dumping such material into the world's oceans.

Sources: "Dow Schedules Black Skimmer Open House," *The Brazorian News*, June 15, 1997, p. A-3;
Steve Olafson, "Skimmers Come Back To Dow," *Houston Chronicle*, June 1997, p. 25-A; Dow Chemical
Co. advertisement, "When the Gulf Redfish Population Needed Help, We Expanded Our Home Office,"
Brazosport Facts, Sea Center, March 6, 1996, p. 5; Eric Brown and Dan Parker, *Corpus Christi Caller-
Times*, "Tanker Spills Chemical: Marine Life Within 20 Miles in Danger," April 5, 1996; Memorandum of
Deyaun Boudreaux, Environmental Director, to Wilma Anderson, Executive Director, Texas Shrimp
Association, Port Isabel, Texas, April 8, 1996, 3 pp.; and Charlie Cray, Greenpeace U.S., "They Lie and
Deny, Part I: Chemical Dependency and Memory Loss," April 17, 1996.

produced there. One of chemical plants inspected at the time was Dow's La
Porte plant—with OSHA agents at the site from late January through early
March 1986. In the end, Dow was cited for two "serious" violations in the
production of phosgene. In one violation, a "quick-opening" valve was being
used improperly. OSHA found that if the valve had been closed accidentally
with a quarter-turn, it could have caused an explosion and lethal release of
chlorine in the area. Chlorine is a main ingredient used in making phosgene.
In addition, OSHA found that Dow failed to comply with a number of "right-
to-know" requirements for providing plant workers with access to their

medical records and information about chemical hazards. Dow officials balked at the citations, which also included some minor fines, and requested a conference with OSHA officials to present its view of the regulations.[38] But two years later, Dow began having "minor" releases of phosgene, with some reported incidents occurring on January 7, 1988; June 23, 1989; January 8, 1990; and January 12, 1992.[39]

In January 1990, a small cloud of phosgene spewed from a 10-foot chemical tank at Dow's La Porte plant while a maintenance crew employed

Phosgene can be inhaled in fatal amounts without a person realizing it; a 5,000-pound release can kill or seriously injure people more than 12 miles away.

by Dowell Schlumberger was cleaning the empty tank with a high-pressure hose. "While hydro-blasting the vessel," explained Dow plant manager Gene Newton at the time, "the water hit a scale and released a pocket of phosgene." A community emergency warning system activated after the phosgene showed up on monitors near the plant's boundaries. Some 40 workers in the immediate area of the leak temporarily sought refuge upwind. The total workforce at the La Porte plant that day included about 500 workers. At the neighboring Quantum Chemical plant, also near the leak, workers stayed indoors. Homes and businesses on the north side of La Porte received computer-generated telephone calls warning them to stay indoors for about 30 minutes. Local police had closed the Miller Cut-Off and Strang Road for about an hour and a half. There were no injuries. But had more phosgene leaked out, plant officials acknowledged, winds from the southwest could have carried the poisonous fumes over the plant at the Miller Cut-Off Road.[40]

In January 1992, on an early Sunday morning about 3:30 a.m., a failed gasket inside the La Porte plant along Texas Route 134 resulted in a leak of phosgene. About 15 pounds of the gas formed a ground-hugging cloud. Although there were no injuries or human exposures, according to a company spokesman, phosgene was measured at 0.4 parts per million outside the area where the leak occurred—about four times the safe threshold level. Along the plant's entrance road, about a quarter mile from the leak site, the gas was measured at 0.19 ppm, about double the

La Porte Worksite	
Loss-of-Containment Incidents	
1992	51
1993	39
1994	55
1995	55
1996	23
1997	32
1998	39
1999	28

Source: Dow Chemical, "La Porte and Deer Park Sites,"Public Report, 1999, p. 5.

amount at which a person can be exposed for an extended time period without health damage. Nose and eye irritation occur at 3 ppm, while lung damage is possible in one minute of exposure at 50 ppm. After the leak occurred, an operator at the plant released a "steam ammonia curtain" to surround the area where the gas had leaked—one of the plant's planned responses to phosgene releases—causing a chemical reaction that neutralizes the gas. The phosgene in the incident dissipated without requiring an evacuation of workers.[41]

Phosgene releases have also occurred at Dow plants in Freeport, as one did in June 1997 when 730 pounds of the gas leaked from a damaged valve. Two workers exposed to the gas were taken to Brazosport Memorial Hospital for treatment and then released. Managers at the Freeport plant thought they had initially contained the leak shortly after its discovery, but a containment device failed. Workers returned in protective suits and finally stopped the leak a few hours later. Dow spokeswoman Cindy Suggs said the company "never discussed" raising the situation from a Level 1 event—which means contained on site—to Level 2, when local residents are alerted that an incident could affect the community. Dow did notify the Texas Natural Resources Conservation Commission and the Brazoria County Sheriff's Office of the event, but according to Dow's Suggs, "it was never at a point where we felt it was going to impact the community."[42]

Fact is, though, for several decades now, Dow's chemicals have been regularly infiltrating Texas communities—crossing boundary lines, visible and invisible.

18.
Trouble in New Zealand

A 58-year-old woman lived in the New Plymouth area between 1969 and 1976. When foamy liquid bubbled out from the ground in her garden she was told by Ivon Watkins-Dow "not to worry."

"Agent Orange: 'We Buried it Under New Plymouth,'"
Investigate, 2001[1]

In 1944, Dan Watkins and his brother founded an agricultural products company in New Plymouth, New Zealand which they named Ivon Watkins, Ltd. The company did well, supplying various agricultural products, including pesticides, to New Zealand's farmers. Some 20 years later, in 1963, the Watkins brothers sought to expand their business. They doubled their capital outlay and floated some new stock. That's when the Dow Chemical Company came on the scene. Dow bought up all the new shares offered by Ivon Watkins, and with that leverage, Dow began a joint venture named Ivon Watkins-Dow.[2]

Dow hadn't done much business in that part of the world until the late 1950s, when it began selling some animal health products, mostly in Australia, to sheep and cattle ranchers. For a time, Dow's pesticidal sheep dip—one of the first anthelmintics, to rid intestinal worms—was a big hit in Australia. In fact, according to Colin Goodchild, Dow's man in the Pacific region at the time, the ag-chem people back home at the Michigan office couldn't believe how much of the stuff Dow was selling in Australia. Dow eventually lost out in the animal health market to drug company competitors and better products. But other Dow products, namely its *Tordon* herbicide, did much better. *Tordon*—used in formulations that combined 2,4-D and picloram, also the basis for Agent White in Vietnam—was sold by Dow throughout Australia. *Tordon* was used there to kill eucalyptus trees to open up more pasture for grazing. Recalls Goodchild: "In the big cattle territories, in the northern territory in Queensland in particular, you could develop more pastures if you could just kill the trees. You didn't necessarily have to fell them.... We found that small amounts of *Tordon* introduced into ax cuts would kill the tree. The growth of the leaves would stop, you'd let in more light, pastures would grow, and you could carry more cattle."[3]

Meanwhile, by November 1963 in New Zealand, the new Ivon Watkins-Dow (IWD) was being managed by Dan Watkins. Over the years, however, Dan Watkins did not move the company according to Dow's plan. Described as a man whose ideas "were too big for his geography," Dan Watkins was soon replaced by Dow's managers. Dow also acquired majority ownership of the company. By 1981, Dow had offices and distribution centers at Hamilton, Palmerston, North Wellington, Christchurch, and Dunedin. "It was a very happy and close relationship we had in New Zealand," recalled Dow's Goodchild. "Although the market was relatively small, the penetration Dow had in New Zealand was one of the highest of any country in the world." Bernie Butcher, a marketing director at Dow in the Pacific and a board member at Ivon Watkins-Dow, saw "big agricultural opportunities" as IWD's key hallmark. "We've made a lot of money there," he said, "but it's always been difficult because it is small market, and it is still all agricultural." By 1988, Dow had bought out the remaining shares in IWD.[4] But Ivon Watkins-Dow also left a toxic legacy in New Zealand—a story that has only recently begun to emerge. Much of that tale has to do with dioxin and the use and production of 2,4,5-T and 2,4-D.

Buried Drums

In 1966–67, IWD had purchased 400 acres of land to use for agricultural experiments with herbicides and pesticides. The land was in an area south of New Plymouth that would later become a residential area called Paritutu. Acquisitions of land in the area during the 1960s included a 300-acre dairy farm stretching south from IWD's main chemical plant, another 90-acre parcel for a "research farm, and a smaller 12-acre farm at Junction Road in New Plymouth. This was in addition to the 29 acres that the chemical factory originally sat on in Paritutu.[5]

In 1967, Dan Watkins dutifully explained all of this to his shareholders in IWD's annual report. Possession of the new research lands, he said, would help the company "evaluate critically new methods of pasture and crop protection with insecticides and weed control with herbicides." But over the next ten years or so, portions of the acquired lands were used for dumping chemical waste—"large quantities of drums containing chemicals buried in trenches over a period of years," according to one account. The contents of the drums dumped, however, wasn't well known at the time. By the mid-1970s, as IWD proposed to build a subdivision on some of the same land where the dumping had occurred, questions were raised about the chemicals dumped there. Some worried specifically about dioxin, since IWD had produced both 2-4-D and 2,4,5-T. One newspaper, the *Taranaki Herald* reported in 1977:

Drums of chemical waste buried under Ivon Watkins-Dow Ltd.'s proposed housing subdivision are not considered a hazard by its management. The Managing Director, Mr. R. M. Bellen, confirmed that drums of waste had been buried in the land, but said none of the material was dioxin and all was expected to degrade in the ground without any harmful effects. They were also buried in a remote part of the proposed subdivision where they would not cause problems to development.[6]

However, after the subdivision was built, at least one resident dug up a 44-gallon drum of chemicals while gardening. Then came even more worrisome revelations about IWD's chemical practices.

Agent Orange, Too

In 2001, a former Ivon Watkins-Dow executive came forward to "spill the beans," as they say, about the company's past. He confirmed that IWD did indeed own a large piece of land "very close to the chemical plant," called the Experimental Farm. "We bulldozed big pits and dumped thousands of tons of chemicals there." But that wasn't all. For years there had been rumors in New Zealand that IWD was supplying Agent Orange for use in

> "We bulldozed big pits and dumped thousands of tons of chemicals there."

the Vietnam War, but no conclusive proof on that charge had ever materialized. "The allegation is true," said the former IWD official. "I was on the management committee of Ivon Watkins-Dow, and I supported the plan to export Agent Orange. In fact, it went ahead on my casting vote." IWD began manufacturing Agent Orange, "but it didn't meet the international specifications," he said, "and probably had an excess of 'nasties' [i.e., dioxin] in it." The problem at the time, he explained, was that neither IWD nor Dow U.S. considered the product harmful to humans. "Our scientists relied on assurances and technical data provided to them by Dow Chemical...," he explained. "We were led to believe it was safe. The whole reason I supported Agent Orange is because we thought we were giving our boys on the ground a hand." But because the product didn't meet international specifications at the time, and "to avoid detection," he said, "we shipped the Agent Orange to South America [sic]—Mexico if I recall correctly—and it was onshipped to its final destination from there." Later, after IWD had the approval of the New Zealand government to produce Agent Orange's two ingredient herbicides—2,4,5-T and 2,4-D—IWD shipped these chemicals separately to be used in making Agent Orange. "Technically, we shipped the chemicals unmixed," said the former IWD executive, "so technically they weren't Agent Orange until somebody mixed them at the final destination." After the war, however, IWD had surplus product on hand, and these leftover Agent Orange chemicals—complete with "excess nasties"—were re-worked into the 2,4,5-T herbicide for use on farms within New Zealand. Surplus chemicals—including 2,4-D and 2,4,5-T used to make Agent Orange—were also dumped at the Experimental Farm, which is now believed to lie beneath the New Plymouth suburb of Paritutu.[7]

"Our scientists relied on assurances and technical data provided to them by Dow Chemical."

Back at the plant during its production years, there had been some accidents and incidents which helped to spread the chemicals around. In November 1972, there had been an explosion at the plant that blew out the walls and roof, scattering chemical fallout throughout the area. No health alert was issued and no monitoring of the local population followed. Nor did IWD disclose what chemical or what process had caused the explosion.[8] In 1983, IWD had at least two pollution incidents involving spills of 2,4,5-T and 2,4-D—one in February and a second in November. Both spills involved releases of the chemicals from a waste dump on the west coast of New Zealand's North Island near the company's plant in New Plymouth. The chemicals polluted the Tasman Sea, and were also discovered in rock pools along a nearby beach where locals gathered shellfish. The company failed to report the November 1983 incident for two weeks, prompting criticisms from New Zealand Health Minister, Anthony Malcolm. "This particular incident may be minor, "he said, "but given the public concern about these pesticides in particular, Ivon Watkins-Dow's apparent desire for secrecy does not improve my confidence in them." IWD officials maintained the delay was due to the time needed to confirm there had been a leak. IWD was then producing

"To avoid detection we shipped the Agent Orange to South America— Mexico, if I recall correctly—and it was on-shipped to its final destination from there."

about 700 tons of the chemicals, mainly for use by New Zealand's farmers, with about 100 tons exported to Australia, Malaysia, and other countries in the Pacific Basin. IWD, like Dow U.S., maintained that there was no conclusive proof that 2,4,5-T caused environmental or health problems. At the time of the 1983 incidents, the New Zealand Health Department said the concentrations in the leaked material on both occasions were not high enough to harm marine life or pose a public health hazard.[9]

As of April 1985, however, Ivan Watkins-Dow officials insisted 2,4,5-T was safe to use, and defended its use and production. Wrote R. W. Moffat,

IWD Research Director in New Plymouth, in an April 1985 letter to the editor:

> ...There is no evidence that 2,4,5-T as used in New Zealand presents a health hazard to either people or the environment, and there is no good reason whatever why it should not continue to be made and used in this country.
>
> IWD continues to manufacture 2,4,5-T because it is a safe and effective tool in the hands of the New Zealand farmer, and unlike the situation in many other countries where agriculture is of lesser importance, it plays a substantial role in the success of New Zealand's farming economy.[10]

But the same month that Mr. Moffat expressed these views, an equipment failure in the trichlorophenol plant resulted in the release of up to 735 mg of dioxin, according to Greenpeace.[11] IWD had also been incinerating dioxin-contaminated waste: between 1975 and 1979, the company incinerated liquid wastes with a dioxin yield of about 6 kg. Another 85 tons of sludges were incinerated between 1986 to 1996.[12] Then, years later, came the birth defects revelations.

1970s Birth Defects

In April 2002, a retired New Zealand hospital worker, then in her 80s, came forward and made available to *Investigate* magazine a collection of photographs she had taken while working in the New Plymouth Hospital pediatrics ward during the early 1970s. Her photographs recorded some of the world's most horrible birth defects among children then born in the New Plymouth area—birth defects some believe were connected to IWD's production of the phenoxy herbicides 2,4,5-T, and 2,4-D, and Agent Orange. The hospital worker, a veteran of some 29 years in obstetrics, worked with newborns, and began to see a number of deformed babies, many with gross disfigurements. In fact, between 1964 and 1971, the number of birth defects reported in New Plymouth nearly doubled. Little was done at the time to investigate why so many babies in one area—one estimates placed the number at 1 in 30—were being born with birth defects. Frustrated, the nurse began taking photographs—photographs of 167 babies, some born dead, some without a brain, and others with multiple birth defects, ranging from club feet and cleft palate to massive facial deformities, truncated and missing limbs, cerebral palsy, and spina bifida. "Most of these photos," said *Investigate* reporter Hamish Carnachan, "were too graphic to publish"—although the magazine did publish some of them.[13]

Ivan Watkins-Dow produced 2,4-D and 2,4,5-T in New Zealand for nearly 40 years. In 1948, it began importing high-dioxin bearing trichlorophenol from Europe. Through the 1960s and early 1970s, it used the two herbicides to make Agent Orange for the Vietnam War. And even through the 1980s—up until 1987, when it became the last place on earth producing 2,4,5-T—IWD produced both herbicides. And IWD was the only source of that production in New Zealand. Given this history, some believe there is a clear link between what IWD produced and the resulting 1970s birth defects. Andrew Gibbs of the Dioxin Investigation Network, an activist group based in New Zealand, believes the level of dioxin turned out by IWD between 1960 and 1972, in particular, was likely far higher than safety levels today. Production of 2,4,5-T peaked in the 1960s and 1970s, precisely when the

Photographs of the 1970s' babies— some born dead, some without a brain, others with club feet, cleft palate, massive facial deformities, truncated and missing limbs, cerebral palsy, and spina bifida—were taken by the hospital worker.

residents of New Plymouth were forming families, observes Gibbs, and they were exposed to levels of dioxin as high as those in Vietnam.

"We were using it from 1948, so New Zealanders were effectively guinea pigs," says Andrew Gibbs. "The 2,4,5-T that we were using had levels of dioxin just as high as that used in Agent Orange. That's why there was such a noticeable rise in the numbers of birth defects in the 60s and 70s."[14] The 1960s batches of the herbicides formulated in New Zealand and elsewhere had dioxin levels thousands of time higher than in the 1980s. And although the production of 2,4,5-T ended in New Zealand in 1987, surplus Vietnam-era Agent Orange and 2,4,5-T are believed to have been used throughout the country in subsequent years, particularly as the country strove to become an agricultural power. "Drums of the material can still be found in farm sheds around the country," reported *Investigate* magazine in April 2002. The other phenoxy herbicide, 2,4-D, was of course still legal, and was used heavily in New Zealand during the 1980s, and continues to be used there in quantity today, as it does in America and elsewhere. People in New Zealand are still being poisoned by these herbicides, both from past and present use.

One 2,4-D Incident

On July 18, 1995, a 51-year-old former researcher for the New Zealand Ministry of Agriculture, Laurie Newman—a man who lives with his partner, Joanne Searle, in the leafy green hill region of Northland, near the small town of Waiotira—was accidentally sprayed by a passing helicopter with the herbicide 2,4-D. Soon after the incident, everyday chores for Newman became excruciating tasks. He became ill tempered, had blinding headaches, and occasional blackouts. He was told he had developed a fore-runner condition to Parkinson's Disease, known as Parkinsonism. By the year 2000, Newman had to be hospitalized after a blackout sent him tumbling down the stairs. Joanne Searle says her partner began experiencing his health problems almost immediately after the spray. "Nowadays he often acts like a gibbering idiot," she explains. "He is incredibly intolerant to the slight- **"New Zealanders were** est noise and suffers from headaches. I **effectively guinea pigs."** have to tell our children what he was like Andrew Gibbs before this happened. He is a shadow of his former self. He doesn't want to do anything and easily loses his temper." Doctors were initially stumped to explain the cause for Newman's condition. Then one Australian medical expert said Newman's health problems were linked to the 2,4-D exposure. "Mr. Newman's condition is directly linked to 2,4-D exposure," the expert wrote. "I have seen a thousand cases like it." That finding, in a longer report on Newman made by the unnamed Australian expert, helped convince the New Zealand Occupational Safety and Health Department (OSH) to draw a similar conclusion. OSH's registrar on the chemical panel, Louisa Thomas, wrote in a letter to Newman: "It is the opinion of the Chemical Panel that your disease is due to exposure to chemicals, in particular, 2,4-D butyl ester." Those findings also helped persuade New Zealand Agriculture Minister, Jim Sutton, to order the Pesticide Board to evaluate the use of 2,4-D in New Zealand. He called the OSH report on Newman "the first official report that has ever been advised to the Pesticide Board claiming a link between 2,4-D and human health effects."[15]

Still, as of December 2000, there was no legal requirement in New Zealand for pesticide applicators or agricultural helicopter companies to keep records of how much, or of what kind of pesticides they use each year. There are anecdotal accounts, and some advertising boasts, like those of one company in 1996 saying it sprayed 60,000 acres of the Northland region with 2,4-D in one year. Another said it sprayed 20,000 hectares. In any case, a lot of 2,4-D is still used in New Zealand, and Dow AgroSciences/IWD sells a fair share of it. Pesticide spray, of course, doesn't always behave in predictable fashion, and applicators don't always follow the instructions that warn of spraying 2,4-D on pastures. IWD warns New Zealand farmers not to spray while animals are grazing as "residues may be found in milk." In 1997, some 500 children at the Waiotira School had to be moved inside after a nearby farm was sprayed with 2,4-D butyl ester. Tree damage in the area was still visible three years later.[16]

Meanwhile, Newman and partner Searle attempted to sue the helicopter company that unleashed the 2,4-D spray on Newman, but Auckland's High Court rejected the case, with the judge claiming it was too big a case to be considered. Newman and Searle are now taking the case to Auckland

District Court, having already spent $25,000 in costs. "We have to see this through," says Searle. Newman, for his part, believes that the most potent form of dioxin is in the 2,4-D esters. The U.S. EPA has also found 14 other dioxins present in 2,4-D. Newman says the main problem is that no complete toxicological analysis has ever been made of 2,4-D in New Zealand. "I am amazed that the Board accepts without question the data supplied by the manufacturers...," he says. Newman believes the writing is on the wall for 2,4-D, and he blames the government for not acting to protect public health:

> "Mr. Newman's condition is directly linked to 2,4-D exposure," the Australian medical expert wrote. "I have seen a thousand cases like it."

> I hold the Pesticides Board personally responsible for my illness by not banning a product that is known, and has been known for some time, to cause illness and crop damage, not to mention human suffering. We already know the effects of 2,4-D and 2,4,5-T had on Vietnam vets who were exposed to Agent Orange. They have suffered a much higher incidence of disease than the unexposed population, including soft-tissue sarcoma, non-Hodgkin's lymphoma, Hodgkin's disease, and chloracne. It seems incredible that the New Zealand government still allows this product to be used on our farms.[17]

New Testing

Meanwhile, back in the New Plymouth area, at Paritutu, where the IWD factory turned out 2,4,5-T and 2,4-D for years, a number of current and former residents believe their serious illnesses, cancers, and birth defects were the result of having IWD as a neighbor. In April 2003, the New Zealand Ministry of Health announced it would carry out blood-serum testing for dioxin on people who lived near the former IWD chemical factory in Paritutu during the 1960s and 1970s. The serum tests are one of a number of investigations into the health of residents near the former IWD chemical plant. "We know this issue has been weighing on the community for some time and the serum dioxin study is another part of the jigsaw the Government is building on organochlorine chemicals to help address these concerns," said Damien O'Connor, Associate Health Minister.[18]

On its corporate web page, Dow Chemical acknowledges its production of various phenoxy herbicides, including 2,4,5-T, in New Zealand during the years 1960 to 1987. And despite all the various national and local health studies completed thus far, Dow says "none of these studies, at a national or local level, has shown cause for concern." Dow says it is looking forward to the New Zealand government concluding its latest round of blood serum testing near the company's plant. The results are expected to be available sometime in 2004.[19]

Yet in New Zealand and Australia, some activists, scientists, and Vietnam veterans see this testing as a beginning rather than an ending. They are looking at some larger patterns and study results that go well beyond New Zealand. They see

New Zealand and Australian activists see similar findings to their own in today's Vietnamese villages.

similar findings to their own in today's Vietnamese villages—some sprayed areas of which have had a threefold increase in stillbirths and miscarriages. One Vietnam province has recorded 69 of every 10,000 babies born with no brain—the same birth defect that had appeared in New Zealand. Others point to studies from Australia that show their veterans five times more likely to develop prostate cancer. New Zealand's Andrew Gibbs says the evidence has been ignored. "World Health Organization tests in 1988 showed we [New Zealand] have a concentration of 2,3,7,8-TCDD in breast milk second only to South Vietnam," he says. Previous blood serum tests, he continues, "haven't taken into account that dioxin has a half life of 7 1/2 years—that means it has broken down and will only be about six to 12 percent of the concentration when the worst exposure occurred prior to 1970." The government has known since 1992, he says, "that herbicide applicators had high levels of dioxin." He cites a worst-case scenario from a 1986–87 government inquiry that calculated a pesticide sprayer would have a dioxin concentration of 2.96 ppt in his blood after 30 years of use. But in 1992, the government found some sprayers with up to 140 ppt in their blood. However, the government is not warning them of their higher risk for prostate cancer. Gibbs believes that one day—when governments start to do their job and quit shielding liable businesses—Dow Chemical might even be required to pay restitution. "People may not be interested in dead babies and cancer," he says, referring to the New Plymouth horror stories of the 1970s. "It's one thing to be a guinea pig—it's another to have to pick up the tab for it . . ." Since Dow lied, he says, Dow should pay. In the meantime, Gibbs keeps pointing to the government's own findings: "A 2001 report by the Ministry for the Environment stated that dioxin is linked to disruption of the immune system, fertility/reproduction, and neurobehavioral outcomes."[20]

Half a world away from New Zealand, in Midland, Michigan, some folks were thinking that Dow should pay too. They were worried about what was showing up in a river there named the Tittabawassee. That story is next.

Time &
The Tittabawassee

The air of Midland is our air; the Tittabawassee is our river. The vast majority of us don't come from some other community and put in our workday and then go back to that other community.... Midland is home... [W]e want to take pride (and do take pride) in the environmental quality of Midland and its health record and its safety achievements.

Paul Oreffice, President, Dow Chemical, 1987

The citizens who have to live in this contamination will not stand for this. We live here, our children play here, we eat the food grown here. Our health and the health of our children is at stake. We will not rest until we get some justice and this mess is cleaned up.

John Taylor, Tittabawassee River Watch[1]

In 1916, about a year after the Dow Chemical Company began making phenol alongside the Tittabawassee River in central Michigan, the company began to hear from local fisherman. The fish they were catching downstream of the Dow plant, they said, tasted bad. Were the chemical wastes from Dow's plant part of the problem? Phenol and chlorinated phenol dissolve in water and do not settle out by force of gravity. Were these chemicals getting into the river and the fish? Indeed, phenol was getting into the river, a fact which Dow could hardly hide or deny. Dow's first solution to the phenol problem was simply "ponding"—running the wastes into large holding ponds that were later opened to the river at flood stage or high water, allowing dilution by the larger water volumes to "solve" the problem. A dike had also been built around the plant to hold the phenol waste until it was diverted to one of the ponds. But one July night, workers at the plant phoned the company's legal advisor, Gilbert A. Currie, to inform him that the dike around the plant had broken, dumping the entire stock of phenol waste into the Tittabawassee. The incident was no small event, and demanded immediate attention. Currie then called the city of Saginaw, downriver, to warn them they should turn off their water intake until the waste phenol had floated by and gone into Lake Huron. The next morning, Herbert Dow, learning of the incident, called Currie into his office and they walked down to the river. Mr. Dow, looking out on the Tittabawassee, said he didn't understand what all the excitement was about. Surely, with that much phenol in the river, there would have been lots of dead fish floating on the surface, but he didn't see any. So what was the problem? Currie then informed Mr. Dow that four boatloads of men had been following the phenol spill as it floated down the river, picking out the dead fish before anyone could see them. Nevertheless, some newspaper reporters arrived at Dow's offices that morning, and Currie warned Dow that the company's name would surely appear in the resulting newspaper stories. But Mr. Dow instructed Currie to "go out and talk to them anyway."[2]

Downstream from Midland, in Bay City, local residents during World War I complained about the foul taste in their water, which was drawn from Saginaw Bay into which the Tittabawassee and Saginaw rivers drained.* Bay City's municipal chemist at the time, Louis Harrison, and a University of Michigan scientist, traced the problem to Dow, 40 miles upstream. They found that "the company was dumping its chemical wastes directly into the river." The problem, they reported, was due to dichlorobenzol, a heavy, oily liquid. Dow said an explosion at one of its Midland plants had resulted in a significant loss of paradichlorobenzol. But Harrison had also tested fish downstream of Dow's discharge, and found that perch were unable to live there. He also found fish in Saginaw Bay with stunted growth. By 1917, the state of Michigan won an injunction against Dow, with the company agreeing to build a crude settling basin to help treat its wastes. Chemical production also began to slow down with the end of the war, helping to curtail some of Dow's pollution problem.[3]

Still, through the 1920s, Dow had become a world leader in phenol production, and by 1931, the plant at Midland had 600 acres of waste ponds. Soon these ponds, which had once handled about 200,000 gallons of waste a day, were overwhelmed. By the mid-1930s they were facing a waste load ten times that amount—now reaching 2 million gallons a day. "Where Dow had once been a small company on a small river,"observed E. N. Brandt, "it was now a very big company on the same small river." By 1934, the state of Michigan had sent its people to talk with Willard Dow about the problem.

_____

*The Tittabawassee River flows south through the city of Midland where it is joined by the Pine and Chippewa rivers. It then heads southeast toward Saginaw. Just past Saginaw, the Tittabawassee joins the Shiawassee and Flint rivers to form the Saginaw River. The Saginaw then flows north through Saginaw and Bay City, draining into the Saginaw Bay of Lake Huron.

Two years later, in June 1936, Dow hired a full-time pollution control professional and began tackling the problem in its laboratories. In June 1937, Dow
began building a large-scale wastewater treatment plant to help degrade
phenols with the help of bacteria. A large 142-foot diameter trickling filter
system was installed that initially
used cinders and blast furnace slag   **In the 1940s, as a "backup"**
as a cleaning medium through   **to checking its wastewater**
which the phenolic waste passed,
also subject to bacteria that ate   **treatment, Dow employees**
phenol. In 1937, the new system   **were used to "taste test" fish.**
handled about 18 million gallons of
phenolic waste a day. By the 1940s, Dow's wastewater treatment system
was refined and underwent a major expansion, making it equivalent to a
system the size of Albany, New York's. Yet for decades thereafter, this system
remained essentially the same in operating principle, though expanded
incrementally to meet larger and larger volumes of waste.[4]

In the 1940s, as a "backup" to checking the integrity of its wastewater
treatment process, Dow instituted daily taste tests of locally-caught fish, serving portions to a panel of Dow employees. The fish, grown in wastewater
samples, were served twice daily to the panel in the Dow cafeteria, with
each panelists tasting about 20 samples. By 1947, the taste tests were
expanded to include fish brought in from the Saginaw River and Saginaw
Bay, downriver from Dow's Midland plant. Perch was the fish chosen for the
taste testing. "For years, these tests served to tell Dow whether it was doing
a good or bad job on its waste stream," explains Dow biographer,
E. N. Brandt. "The data were later provided to the U.S. Public Health Service
under the first industrial research contract the USPHS ever signed with an
industrial firm."[5] But by the 1970s, Dow employees might not be volunteer-
ing to eat the fish, as public health officials were soon calling on Dow for
other reasons. More on this later.

The Brine Problem

Dow had other water pollution problems beyond its process wastewater, especially those related to its brine operations. In fact, by the 1930s,
one of the reasons Willard Dow became convinced it was time to go to the
ocean to extract bromine and magnesium, was the problem of disposing of
waste brines around Midland. Much of Dow's brine wastes at the time were
being pumped back into the ground, but that strategy had its limitations, and
the process could also alter underlying geology and hydrology, as one
account from Dow's "Dutch" Beutel in the early years makes plain:

> I set up a rig in Midland to pump the waste brine down vertically in what
> they call the Parma sand formation, which is one level higher that the Mar-

shall formation. The Parma sand was in the range of about 900 feet deep. I got some tanks from salvage and some big high-pressure pumps that went up to about 600 pounds of pressure. I hooked up the pumps to the brine-field tanks and began pumping the brine into a well. After a time, the pressure was building up but nothing was happening—the brine wasn't moving out of the tanks. Then suddenly everything let go. The pump started to pump like hell and you could see the brine level going down. I couldn't get enough brine into the tanks. I had to shut off the pumps, and refill the tanks. We left the valve open and brine poured down the well. My first thought was that we might be pushing brine through the sand all the way to the outcroppings at Saginaw Bay. But what I had done with the pressure was to lift the earth and fracture the zone. The brine wasn't being forced into the sand—it was pouring into the fracture. If we had known enough at the time, we could have gotten a patent on this process. Actually, this fracturing of the earth became the basis of Dow's oil field operations with pressures running up to 10,000 pounds.[6]

But not all of the waste brine was going back into the ground. Some of it was spilling out onto the land or seeping into groundwater, and as some believed, contaminating local water wells. In 1952, for example, there was a massive brine spill at Dow's #30 well in Ingersoll Township near Midland. Dow estimated the spill at between 350,000 to 500,000 gallons—a spill which eventually covered five acres of land over a 10-hour period. But some residents in the area say it was bigger—more like 1 million gallons covering 12 acres.[7] In 1956, Dow brine pits overflowed in Larkin Township, Midland County. The brine spilled out on John Schaeffer's farm there, near Mier Road. One report had it that Schaeffer's dairy cows lost their hair and the Caterpillar tractor he drove had its tire treads "eaten through." The locals suspected the brine, or something in it. In the period 1965 through 1968, Robert Piegols, also of Larkin Township on North Eastman Road, reported water out of the tap that was the consistency of thick chocolate milk. He drilled a new well. His neighbor, a Mr. Landowski, had similar well-water problems, but he moved. Piegols also reported cattle with blistered livers as well as his own personal health problems, including the loss of his kidneys.[8]

In 1969, Dow received a federal grant in excess of $500,000 from the Federal Water Pollution Control Administration for a pilot project to decontaminate its brines. The grant was aimed at designing and installing equipment to recondition the wastewater so that it would be reused to manufacture chlorine. At that time, Dow was pumping its waste brines into underground storage areas. A year later, Dow indicated it would build a plant and a treatment method for dealing with its waste brine water—then known to be contaminated with organic chemicals, including phenols, chlorophenols, and phenoxy herbicides.

Meanwhile, the brine spills and related troubles continued. By 1983, Dow was battling some of its own former employees over brine spills. Albert Moore, who retired from Dow in 1970 to a farm on Sasse Road in Midland

County, had brine spills on his land several times. One spill resulted in the loss of ten acres of trees. Moore also claimed that Dow consistently under-reported the amount spilled to the Michigan Department of Natural Resources (DNR). He resorted to taking his own photographs and documenting the incidents that occurred on his land. When he gave this information to Dow, he said, company officials shredded the data, telling him the results were confusing.[9]

One report had it that Schaeffer's dairy cows lost their hair and the Caterpillar tractor he drove had its tire treads "eaten through."

"In January of '83," explained Moore to Diane Hebert, "Dow announced they were discontinuing their practice of disposing chemicals in wells." Dow then had a series of 28 injection wells that sent the spent brine back into the earth. "The reason given," said Moore, was that Dow didn't know where the wastes were going. "If they didn't know where their wastes were going in 1983," observed Moore, "how could they know where they've gone for the past 30 years?" Moore also told Hebert at the time, "we feel that these disposal wells could be responsible for contaminating wells of township residents. We have asked the EPA to consider scoring these wells under Superfund." James Chambers, another resident of Midland County, who lived in the section 7 area of Larkin Township, reported an October 1983 brine spill of between 100,000 and 150,000 gallons, with some residue left on his land. At the time, Chambers said he thought Dow had reported a lower amount.[10]

Brine Spills & DNR

In the mid-1980s, Dow was still dealing with its brine wastes, and by then, an aging system of wells and pipelines. Dow had over 112 brine wells, each on a two-acre site, located throughout Midland, Bay, and Saginaw counties Michigan. These wells, together with the 28 injection wells, were laced together by 150 miles of underground pipeline that years earlier had brought the brine back to Midland for processing. Michigan adopted the Mineral Well Act in 1969, but rarely had the money or manpower to enforce the act or to monitor Dow's wells properly. In the 1980s, responding to complaints from farmers and citizens about brine spills, the Michigan DNR began to monitor Dow's performance more closely. In the first three months of 1984, DNR found 14 major spills from Dow's pipes and wells totaling 100,000 gallons and charged the company with violation of the Mineral Well Act. "By and large, this large number of spills reflected poorly maintained equipment and poor operating practices," said DNR's Allen F. Crabtree, in August 1984. Crabtree, assistant chief of DNR's geological survey, also added that Dow "didn't spend much money to maintain the system, and did things routinely that were just wrong." Dow blamed part of its brine problems on a pipeline company that had poorly installed a four-mile section of pipeline in the 1970s. Still, Crabtree observed that Dow "did not always [conduct] the follow-through checking" to make sure the equipment was in good condition. They failed to perform routine maintenance, he charged. "Just cases of shoddy operating procedures," he said.[11]

In the 1980s, DNR ordered Dow to upgrade its brine system. By 1984, Dow proposed to modernize 88 active wells, repair the 150-mile pipeline system, and build spill containment systems at 60 production wells and 28 injection wells. It also planned to improve its surveillance of the entire system. However, facing that prospect, Dow decided to exit the brine business in Michigan and began negotiating with DNR over a final cleanup process.[12] But the spills contin-

> **DNR compiled a seven-page chronology of some 279 Dow brine spills in a three-county area.**

ued. In 1984 alone, DNR documented 68 Dow brine spills, a number of which resulted in contaminated groundwater that residents in three counties used for drinking, cooking, bathing, and cleaning. "The discharges from Dow's Midland brine system were not authorized by either state or federal permit," charged one DNR document, "and have resulted in contamination of the groundwater and surface waters of the state." The discharges, said DNR, "have also contaminated soils which are ongoing sources of groundwater and surface water contamination." DNR was then preparing a consent order that would require Dow, among other things, to do testing in a three-county area and provide replacement water for residents whose water supply was affected. The order also proposed to make formal Dow's pledge to close its system in an orderly fashion by December 1986, or failing that, have it forcibly closed by DNR. As background for its order, DNR compiled a history of Dow's brine spills over the past 34 years, preparing a seven-page chronology of some 279 spills in a three-county area. Some of the spills occurring in 1984, however, were sizeable and problematic—one in March 1984 of more than 320,000 gallons occurred in Ingersoll Township bordering Midland, and another there of 46,000 gallons in April. In Larkin Township, north of Midland, more than 462,000 gallons of brine spilled in April 1984, causing trees and other foliage to die. Another spill of 52,000 gallons occurred in Larkin in November 1984. Ingersoll Township, however, was hit the hardest in 1984, with 187 brine spills from Dow's system.[13] In May 1985, Dow and DNR entered into a consent order with a phased shutdown of the Dow brine system. In 1986, Dow began capping wells and using a field tile system that collected rain-washed brine residues from saturated areas and fed that material back into its old pipeline system, sending the wastewater to Dow's home plant for treatment.[14]

Dow had processed brine historically for its bromine, chlorine, calcium, and iodine, and waste brine consisted of about 70 percent water and 25 per-

Unhappy Neighbors

It was in 1959 that Erich and Edna Tessin of Saginaw County, Michigan had their first run-in with Dow Chemical's brine system. That's when a brine pipeline began leaking salty fluids across their land, eventually killing some 22 trees. Dow quickly made a settlement with the Tessins for the damage, but the money, in Erich Tessin's view, was not nearly enough to compensate for the replacement and full value of the lost trees, some of which were 150 years old. Then in 1981, 21 years later, it happened again to the Tessins. In February of that year, Edna Tessin, on her return from shopping in Midland, noticed that the ditches bordering their three-acre property were full of water. Although unable to pinpoint a source at the time, she noticed that a white residue had formed along the banks of the ditches. It was soon determined that the source of the water was Dow Chemical's brine system, which had a major spill, releasing between 20,000 and 50,000 gallons of brine on the Tessin property and others in the area. This time the water seeped into the Tessin's well to the point that the Saginaw County Health Department told them the water was unfit to drink. The Tessins then had to haul their water in from a source a half mile away. Once again, trees on their property were killed. The Tessins then took Dow to Saginaw County court, claiming among other things, that Dow's spill had devalued their property. Again, a settlement was reached, and again, in Erich Tessin's view, the deal was inadequate. "We should have got 10 times as much as they gave us," said Erich at the time, then a 60-year-old truck driver for Ryder-PIE. "I wanted Dow to put the trees back in—that would have cost Dow $100,000 to $200,000—and clean up the dirt. But my lawyer told me I probably wouldn't get any more." Dow did drill the Tessins a new well at a cost of more than $3,000, paid for nine trees that the spill destroyed, and planned to re-seed the soil on the Tessin land where the spill had burned up the grass. The Tessins also point to farms in the area that had lost productive land due to Dow spills over the years. In fact, between 1951 and 1985, Dow's brine system pipes had leaked more than 275 times. Dow tried to put the best spin it could on the 1981 spill and property damage. "This is the only well we've had to drill as a result of our brine operations," said Dow spokeswoman Mary Beth Curtis of the Tessin well. DNR officials, however, explained that Dow brine spills had caused widespread groundwater contamination in three counties.

Source: Keith Naughton, "Salt-Water Wounds Still Ache, Rural Pair Says,"*Saginaw News*, February 5, 1985, p. B-1.

cent calcium chloride and sodium chloride, with other organic salts as well. But it also contained small amounts of toxic material. In the mid-1980s, EPA had also been studying the Midland area for dioxin contamination and had looked at the brine system as part of a June 1986 report. Explaining that the Dow brines were similar in composition to oil and gas brines, EPA also noted they included "low levels of benzene, toluene, phenol, and various polynuclear aromatic hydrocarbons." The Dow spent brines "may also contain trace levels of PCDDs and PCDFs [i.e., dioxin and furans]," observed EPA.[15] Under its 1985 agreement with DNR, Dow was expected to restore potable water sources to a drinkable standard, and salt-soaked farmland to a "previous use" standard capable of producing crops. In groundwater, salt could not exceed 250 ppm, although some polluted sources in the area had levels at "several thousand" ppm. During the cleanup years, spills continued. In 1986, for example, one Midland-area brine operation had a 20,000-gallon leak into the Pine River in Homer Township near Prairie and Pine River roads. As of 1993, Dow was still working on the brine cleanup, with "no end in sight," according to one report. [16]

> EPA noted that the brines included "low levels of benzene, toluene, phenol, and various polynuclear aromatic hydrocarbons," and possibly dioxins and furans.

Dumps & Groundwater

The front page news of Love Canal in the late 1970s soon revealed a nationwide problem of old chemical wastes dumps, some long buried and forgotten. As such sites were uncovered, and state and federal clean-up programs began, not only were unknowing or newly-built nearby residential areas endangered, but groundwater flowing through these sites could also be contaminated. In the Midland area, some residents began reporting health problems they associated with one landfill operated by Dow Chemical on the Midland-Bay County border (also known as the Rockwell dump). Linda Kerns of Bus Road, reported to Midland County health officials in August 1980 that there were five cancer cases—including the death of a 9-year-old girl—in a row of eight houses about a half a mile southwest of a Dow landfill on Milner Road east of Mapleton. Dow had used the site in the late 1950s to dispose ethylbenzene tar wastes. Four of the residents with cancer had lived near the dump continuously since the 1950s. Another resident in the area, Clarence Phillips of Bus Road, told the *Midland Daily News* of losing two hunting dogs in 1968 after they fell into the pit, which was then not guarded by a fence. A third dog lost all its hair but later recovered. "They put up signs there later on," said Phillips, "but dogs don't read signs." The state had begun an investigation of the dump site in 1978 when another resident's dog became ill after drinking some nearby surface water. That probe led to an 1979 agreement in which Dow would spend $500,000 to ring the site with an underground clay barrier extending ten feet below the surface. That work was ongoing when Linda Kerns wrote her August 1980 letter to the health authorities informing them of local cancers—which was later discussed at meeting between Dow and DNR officials. E. M. Hgenfritz, a techni-

A sampling of headlines featuring Dow's brine-system pollution during the 1970s and 1980s.

cal specialist in Dow's environmental services division, said he wasn't surprised by claims that leakage from the landfill might be connected with cancers in the area. "The story I saw in the letter didn't excite my curiosity," he said. "The papers are full of this kind of thing." John Hesse, then chairman of the Chemical and Health Center of Michigan's public health department, wasn't optimistic about finding a cause-and-effect linkage, pointing to the small number of people involved and the lack of

Clarence Phillips of Bus Road, told of losing two hunting dogs in 1968 after they fell into the pit. A third dog lost all its hair but later recovered.

data from the site, limiting any scientific findings. "We've had several cases like this where a person looks at these sort of factors and comes to this kind of conclusion," he said referring to the Kerns letter. "The truth is that after-the-fact evaluations of groundwater are virtually impossible." Still, an independent study conducted in 1979 by the Williams and Works consulting firm of Grand Rapids found a "perched aquifer," indicating a small stream of water had moved west from the chemical pit. Benzene had been found as high as 2.2 ppm a few yards west of the site. Traces of benzene in shallow test wells several hundred yards west of the dump site "supported the conclusion that leachate had migrated to the west end of the perched aquifer," according to the study. DNR, meanwhile, claimed that the new clay barrier at the site would assure that contaminants in the aquifer would eventually empty out through dilution.[17] In 1983, the Rockwell site was found to be leaking, and some wells in the area were reported to be contaminated. About that time, Dow began to maintain a pumping system there to collect the liquid material that leached through the dump. The collected "leachate" as it is called, is then discharged into the Tittabawassee River.*

Another Dow landfill in the Midland area, the Poseyville Road Landfill, received toxic and hazardous materials between 1955 and 1981, including incinerator ash, waste treatment sludges, styrene wastes, ethylene wastes, chlorine wastes, and vinyl chloride wastes. During 1981 and 1982, Dow notified DNR that it found contaminated groundwater 1,000 feet from the northeast corner of the site. Although Dow has installed clay barriers, purge wells, and a leachate collection system at this landfill, one Greenpeace report in 1985 noted "the complex geology of the site has made monitoring and containment of these hazardous waste difficult, if not impossible."[18] Worries about the old brine system wastes were still apparent in the 1980s, too. Dow had used a deep-well injection system to dispose of its brine wastes and some hazardous

---

*In the 1980s, Dow also built a 152-acre hazardous waste landfill near Salzburg Road. For some history on that site see, for example, Paul Rau, "Water Topic at Landfill Hearing," *Midland Daily News*, January 9, 1981, p. 1.

wastes, sending, by Dow's accounting, over one trillion gallons of the material into deep underground deposits. But in January 1983, Dow ceased deep-well injection. *Fortune* magazine marked the event in a May 1983 report: "Recently Dow abandoned altogether the use of deep well injection as dumps because the company could not be sure what would eventually happen to the wastes."[19] In addition, some old internal company memos were also coming to light. One from 1967 noted concerns of Dow scientists over a plant building that had been contaminated with dioxin from trichlorophenol production. The plant was later dismantled and its equipment buried. But according to the memo, Dow also dumped some 10,000 gallons of dioxin-contaminated water into its underground well system.[20] Back on the Tittabawassee, meanwhile, Dow had also been drawing more attention from the state.

Bad Water, Bad Fish

By 1969, after the Michigan Water Resources Commission issued a pollution violation notice to Dow for "an unintentional transgression," some state officials grumbled that there had been "too many of these unintentional mishaps," suggesting the state's enforcement measures weren't having much effect. In 1969, one Dow discharge to the Tittabawassee River killed more than 2,000 fish, resulting in a Dow fine of $500 by a district court judge, which the *Detroit News* described as hitting Dow "with all the force of ballerina playing fullback." Michigan Attorney General Frank Kelley soon called for tougher fines.[21] But the pollution continued.

In 1976, native catfish taken from the Tittabawassee River below Dow's wastewater discharge were found to contain from 70 to 230 parts per trillion (ppt) dioxin in the edible portions of those fish— in skinned filets. Dow also reported the following year that various species of Tittabawassee native fish it collected had dioxin levels

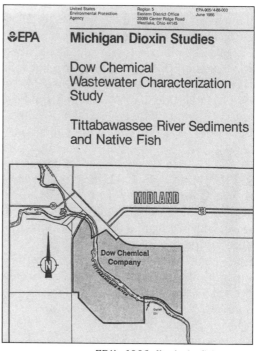

EPA's 1986 dioxin-in-fish report

ranging from not detectible to 240 ppt—most in the 20 to 170 ppt range. Then in June 1978, Dow reported to DNR and the Michigan Department of Public Health that rainbow trout exposed to a mixture of Dow's treated wastewater had accumulated dioxin up to 50 ppt in the edible portion of the fish, and up to 70 ppt in the whole fish. These findings prompted the Michigan Department of Public Health to issue a fish consumption advisory in June 1978 for any fish caught from the Tittabawassee downstream of the Dow Dam at Midland. EPA fol-

> **In June 1978, The Michigan Department of Public Health issued a fish consumption advisory for any Tittabawassee fish caught downstream of the Dow Dam.**

lowed with their own action in September 1978, making a preliminary determination that concentrations of dioxin in Tittabawassee River fish represented a substantial risk to public health. Two months later, in November 1978, Dow released its "Trace Chemistries of Fire" report, Dow's attempt to suggest that dioxin was ubiquitous in the environment, the result of a wide variety of combustion processes, not just Dow manufacturing processes. Follow-up studies by EPA and the U.S. Food and Drug Administration (FDA) in 1979 and 1980 determined that dioxin persisted in native fish at levels of concern in the Tittabawassee and Saginaw rivers, and Saginaw Bay, despite the fact that Dow had closed manufacturing facilities for 2,4,5-T trichlorophenol and the 2,4,5-T herbicide.[22] By the early 1980s, dioxin was front page national news with the evacuations of Love Canal and Times Beach. These events, in turn, brought more attention to Midland and the Tittabawassee's contaminated fish. In addition, a major political controversy would ensue by June 1981 when it was discovered that Dow had special editorial access to one of EPA's dioxin reports (see Chapter 4). But Dow's pollution of the Tittabawassee River continued to bring both regulatory and activist attention.

Greenpeace Plugs Pipes

In the spring of 1985, Greenpeace activists from Toronto and Chicago, along with Michigan environmental groups, were voicing a region-wide concern for the Great Lakes ecosystem. They were tracking Great Lakes pollutants back to their sources, through the region's bays and rivers, which brought them, among other places, to Dow's operations in Midland, along the Tittabawassee. By the 1980s, Dow's wastewater passed from a series of settling ponds and filtered treatment systems to a holding lagoon, after which a portion of the treated material was released into the river. The discharges were legal—for the most part—allowed under DNR permits. Still, toxic substances were being released into the river.

Van Putten v. Dow

Not long after studying at the University of Michigan Law School, Mark Van Putten became the first executive director of the Great Lakes Natural Resources Center, a new regional office of the National Wildlife Federation. It was the early 1980s and Van Putten had targeted Great Lakes water quality as a key issue for his new organization. In law school, Van Putten had studied under Joseph Sax, who advocated using litigation to protect environmental values. Van Putten was of like mind. In one of his first lawsuits, Dow Chemical was charged in a water pollution case. Van Putten recalls he was still a little green around the edges at the time, and admits to making some tactical errors in filing and argument, which improved Dow's chances in negotiations. But Van Putten cared passionately about the environment and was a determined litigator who learned from his mistakes. He soon became expert in practically every nuance of the Clean Water Act, and would leave his mark on Michigan and Great Lakes water law. He would also later become executive director of the National Wildlife Federation in Washington.

In the late 1970s and early 1980s, a major concern of the Michigan Conservation Clubs was Great Lakes water quality. Van Putten and others had played a major role in updating Michigan water standards under something called "Rule 57," which became a model for other states in the Great Lakes region. Dow Chemical, in that process, had also been a contributor. But the bigger issue was dioxin. And it was here that Van Putten made a key discovery: dioxin was entirely unregulated under state or federal water law. Under the federal Clean Water Act, 65 of the most dangerous chemical pollutants were identified as "priority toxic pollutants"—each of which was required by law to have detailed water quality criteria documents compiled before they could be regulated. That was the catch. Dioxin, although identified by name in the list of 65 priority toxic pollutants, was the only chemical in 1982 that didn't have the required documentation. That was not by accident, Van Putten soon discovered. Dioxin by then had become embroiled in the Agent Orange litigation, and whatever might turn up with dioxin in water quality standard documents for a Michigan standard, would also have national ramifications. Dow had its fingers in many dioxin dikes at the time, and this was one of them. Dow had worked to keep the Clean Water Act dioxin water quality criteria from ever emerging. So Van Putten sued to make EPA produce them.

Back in Michigan, meanwhile, Van Putten and his Great Lakes Natural Resources Center decided to go after Dow's water pollution permit. Under the Clean Water Act, "permissions to discharge" under the National Pollution Discharge Elimination System (NPDES), are issued through state agencies in the form of five-year NPDES permits for specific pollutants. The idea behind the five-year time interval is that the permits would become progressively tougher in each five-year period, eventually achieving the goal of "elimination" or zero discharge. That was the theory. In Michigan, however, Dow's previous permit, issued in 1979, had no meaningful limit on dioxin discharge, despite earlier findings of dioxin-contaminated fish. As the state readied its new permit for Dow— with a dioxin limit, as well as first-time limits on several dozen other persistent bioaccumulative toxic chemicals (PBTs)—Dow and allies announced their opposition. Van Putten prepared a lawsuit under state and federal water laws against Dow and the state, charging that Dow's discharge of dioxin at a level of 50 parts per quadrillion was 170 times higher than what was needed to protect fish and wildlife in the river and Saginaw Bay. With the prospect of a long and difficult fight ahead, the parties eventually agreed to a negotiated settlement in 1984. Dow said it would cut its dioxin discharge to the river within two years, reduce the release of 14 other chemicals, and monitor 53 others. Dow also agreed to support the state's new proposed rule to limit the discharge of PBTs. "Without the threatened lawsuit from Van Putten's organization," writes Dave Dempsey in his Michigan environmental history, *Ruin & Recovery*, "the permit and rule would not have happened."

Van Putten, however, still wanted a dioxin water quality standard. Acting in concert with colleagues from the Natural Resources Defense Council and the Environmental Defense Fund, Van Putten and allies filed a petition under the Toxic Substances Control Act to regulate dioxin. That maneuver brought out the heavy guns from the other side, including Dow and the Chemical Manufacturers Association. The chemical industry charged that Van Putten was "putting dioxin on trial." Perhaps he was. Yet legally, all he wanted were the standards promised under the Clean Water Act many years earlier. Van Putten had also tried to use the Food and Drug Act as a way to get at dioxin, petitioning the Food and Drug Administration for its failure to include a warning label on fish containing dioxin. That case went to court, but failed in 1986. The TSCA route however, did bear fruit in the form of a consent decree and a negotiated settlement. Dioxin as a pollutant, the settlement more or less concluded, would be regulated not under TSCA, but under the "media specific" statutes—i.e., air, water, wastes, etc. But on those fronts, too, Dow and the chemical industry proved formidable. On a subsequent NPDES go-round for a new permit in the early 1990s, Dow was more forthcoming with its old adversaries, having been "born again" in the new ways of corporate environmentalism. It went to its adversaries and said, in effect, what can we do? How can we help? How can we make this work? Still, although Dow was changing in the public relations arena, its legal department was still playing hardball. In some near-Orwellian enforcement actions of the 1990s purporting to enforce NPDES permit conditions, Dow actually succeeded in obtaining more favorable terms with permit limits—"limits" that actually turned out to be more generous than they were prior to enforcement.

Looking back on all of this some years later, Van Putten is philosophical, particularly with regard to his experiences with Dow and corporate power. "Dow would move to protect its interests in any number of ways, and on multiple fronts if necessary," he explained. "Whether using science or engineering, or through the agencies—EPA regional, the state agencies, on up to EPA headquarters." Dow did learn from experience, he adds. "They learned that their reputation could be hurt by their arrogance and fighting." In some ways though, "Dow's isolation in Midland and its insular ways hurt them in the policy process, where compromise is needed," he says. "Dow was so used to getting its way," he said— used to being up on a pedestal in Midland and never being challenged on what it said about science or anything else—"they thought they could navigate the same way in the world beyond Midland." That, of course, was not the case, says Van Putten. "Yet it took Dow a long time to realize that."

Sources: Author conversations with Mark Van Putten, 2003, and David Dempsey, *Ruin & Recovery*, Ann Arbor: University of Michigan Press, 2001, pp. 258–59.

In July 1985, a team of three wet-suited Greenpeace divers waded into the Tittabawassee and proceeded to plug 15 of Dow's discharge pipes that normally carried wastewater into the river. Dow, learning of the action the previous day, had temporarily turned off the flow of material from the pipes. Still, the Greenpeace divers did their work, using homemade plywood plugs and long screws. Dow took no immediate action at the scene to remove the activists and allowed the plugging to proceed, as TV cameras rolled and reporters jockeyed for position. "We're not interested in getting involved in any of their publicity stunts," said Dow spokesman Phillip Schneider at the time. "There are a variety of more productive ways they can get involved in the public policy process."[23]

The basis for Greenpeace's concern was founded in part in U.S. law and U.S./Canadian agreements. Put simply, the 1972 and 1977 U.S. Clean Water Acts called for zero discharge of toxic compounds into U.S. waterways. And the 1978 Great Lakes Water Quality Agreement between the United States and Canada had also called for zero discharge of persistent toxic substances. Yet, Dow was discharging millions of gallons of wastewater containing toxic and carcinogenic material into the Tittabawassee. Greenpeace Great Lakes campaign coordinator Helen Perivier had sought a meeting with Dow's president Paul Oreffice and Michigan Division general manager Robert Bumb, but neither would speak with her. Still, Greenpeace got its message out, with newspaper photos and television coverage of the pipe-plugging event, drawing public attention to Dow's continuing pollution of the river, permit or not.[24]

Michigan environmentalists, meanwhile, had been slugging it out with Dow for decades over water pollution. In the 1990s, Dow's Midland operation was again exceeding its pollution discharge permit. Michigan's Lone Tree Council and the Public Interest Researsch Group in Michigan (PIRGM) had discovered pesticide and phosphorus exceedances in 1992, 1994, and 1995. In January 1994, for example, Dow had exceeded its discharge of chlorpyrifos, a pesticide chemical, by 138 percent.* In April 1995, Dow had exceeded its phosphorus discharge by 60 percent. Other exceedances were also registered during those years for 2,4-D and 2,4,6-trichlorophenol. By June 1995, the Lone Tree Council and PIRGM announced their intent to sue Dow under the federal Clean Water Act. "Over the past nine months, Dow has illegally discharged thousands of pounds of phosphorous into the Tittabawassee River

---

*Dow discharged .594 pounds per day of this chemical in violation of its permit.

and ultimately the Saginaw Bay," said PIRGM's campaign director, Caroline Schwarz. "Because these illegal discharges are a serious threat to the health of the river and the bay, we are taking immediate action to stop them."

The phosphorous pollution, while not a public health threat at the time, was promoting the growth of algae which use up oxygen, clog waterways, and kill fish. The Lone Tree Council's Terry Miller reported that algae wash-ups had occurred at Bay City State Park, driving users away because of foul odors and dead fish. The Michigan DNR had served Dow with a noncompliance notice for the infractions, requiring Dow to do additional monitoring.

> **"Over the past nine months, Dow has illegally discharged thousands of pounds of phosphorous into the Tittabawassee River and ultimately the Saginaw Bay."**
>
> PIRGM, June 1995

Dow's Karen Trzcinski, an environmental manager, explained: "We suspect we had a nutrient imbalance in the waste-water treatment plant"—an imbalance that may have altered the diet of the system's waste-eating microbes. In addition, as the microbes die and decay, they contribute phosphorus to the mix, which results in a foul odor. "We have complete faith in our wastewater treatment system," Trzcinski said. The environmentalists, however, were calling into question the effectiveness of Dow's entire treatment system.[25]

By August 1995, the Michigan Attorney General's office also filed a notice of intent to sue Dow over its river pollution. "We're talking about an area where there's been, historically, a lot of pollution," said Marion Gorton, a spokeswoman for the attorney general's office. EPA too, had written to Dow, requiring the company to submit a plan to correct its problems. By then, the Lone Tree Council and the PIRGM had filed their lawsuit in federal district court.[26]

A week later, Michigan's Attorney General, Frank Kelley, joined by DNR and DEQ, formally filed their suit against Dow. "It is unacceptable for Dow to place a tremendous natural resource like the Tittabawassee River at risk," said DNR director Roland Harmes. "Dow needs to accept their environmental responsibilities and come up with a plan to remain in compliance with their permit." Attorney General Kelley said he was seeking a court order to stop the pollution. Dow claimed it was doing all it could, but that solving the problem would take another two to three years.[27]

By September 1995, Dow indicated its discharges were in compliance—at 0.9 ppm phosphorus, just under the allowable 1.0 ppm standard. Yet neither the environmental groups nor the state agencies were backing off their lawsuits, believing the past infractions were still at issue. There was also the matter of long-term compliance. Dow said it had lowered its discharges through the use of chemical additives in the treatment process. But in late December, between the Christmas and New Year holiday, a larger-than-normal release of waste chemicals—and especially several releases of thousands of gallons of methanol—overwhelmed Dow's waste-eating microbes. Normally the methanol, used in making solvents and antifreeze, was discharged into the waste system at 200 gallons an hour, but during several occasions during the holiday period, the methanol wastes came in at 1,000 gallons an hour. Rather than releasing these surges of wastewater to the river, Dow said it was keeping it in holding ponds and also recycling some for process cooling. "It never did get into the river,"

"It is unacceptable for Dow to place a tremendous natural resource like the Tittabawassee River at risk."

Roland Harmes, DNR director, 1995

assured Dow's public relations manger Cindy Newman. Others had their doubts, however, as river samples were lacking. Dow also claimed it didn't understand how the excess methanol got into its system.[28]

By mid-January 1996, Dow did report to the Michigan DEQ that prior to the methanol episode—for the period November 21 to December 20, 1995—its Midland operations exceeded the monthly average permitted release of 1,2,4,5-tetrachlorobenzene to the river. The release level reported was 5.8 ppb vs. the permitted level of 3.2 ppb. Dow said it was installing a carbon adsorption system to fix this problem and comply with its permit.[29]

Groundwater Too

By July 1996, the attention of Michigan regulators turned to Dow's pollution of the Tittabawassee River by way of groundwater. For years, at its sprawling Midland chemical works, Dow had numerous spills and leaks. It also had a variety of makeshift dumps and chemical pits, all of which over time soaked into the ground. Like its dumps in Plaquemine, Louisiana and Freeport, Texas, these wastes and spills eventually reached groundwater below. Some of that underground water moved in the direction of, and fed into, the Tittabawassee River. To prevent this potential source of pollution, Dow had installed something called the Revetment Groundwater Interceptor System, or RGIS for short. The purpose of the RGIS, which runs for 2.5 miles along the Dow site adjacent to the river—is to contain the underground pollution, and keep that pollution out of the Tittabawassee. Over the years, however, it's not clear the system has achieved its goals.

In February 1997, Dow Chemical agreed to pay $800,000 in fines to the state of Michigan and conduct a study of the Tittabawassee to find out if the RGIS was actually doing its job. The Michigan DEQ had conducted an earlier RGIS investigation and reported it had failed on at least five occasions between July 1994 and July 1996, sending pollution into the river. Dow agreed to pay the fines and to conduct fish studies, but did not agree that its system had failed. "We have no indication that there was any material released to the Tittabawassee River during these events," explained Dow's Jeffery Feerer, the environmental health and safety manager at Midland. "We also believe that there is no threat posed to the environment or human health." But Michigan's Attorney General, Frank Kelley, stood firm on the need to improve the RGIS for protecting the river.

In December 1997, Dow agreed to pay $1 million in penalties as part of a settlement in the PIRGM/Lone Tree Council case. "The State of Michigan will continue to insist that companies respect the sanctity of our rivers and streams," he said in February 1997. "Under today's order, Dow will be obligated to take additional steps towards improving the operation of the RGIS in order to protect the quality of the Tittabawassee River or face significant penalties if they don't."[30]

Later that year, in December 1997, Dow agreed to pay $1 million in penalties as part of a settlement in the PIRGM/Lone Tree Council case—the suit brought two years earlier over Dow's phosphorous and pesticide pollution of the Tittabawassee. The settlement also included $100,000 Dow had previously paid to the state of Michigan for a similar lawsuit, and reaffirmed Dow's commitment to improve its wastewater treatment. Both lawsuits were brought against Dow for its 1990s' pollution of the Tittabawassee River in violation of the Clean Water Act.[31]

Under A Cloud

Dow's operations in Central Michigan have not only left their chemical mark on the Tittabawassee, they have also fouled the region by way of air pollution and toxic chemical releases. For decades, chemical particles from Dow's plants have been wafting off into the Michigan skies. In 1979, journalist Michael Brown visited the central Michigan town of Hemlock in Saginaw County and heard anecdotal reports of human health effects ranging from cancer and kidney disease to blackened toenails and teeth broken off at the gumline. There were barnyard curiosities too, such as geese born with their wings on backwards, which Brown saw for himself, and other tales he only heard about—three-legged chickens, mice that ran in circles, and horses and cows that lost their fur. Anecdotal tales, Brown knew, were not worth much in the scientific and regulatory realms. Still, in 1986, Brown returned to the area to further investigate these stories, which some linked to Dow Chemical's Midland operations.[32] Was it the water, or was it something else? Brown had a theory which he presented in his 1987 book, *The Toxic Cloud.* There might be more toxic chemicals in the nation's air than authorities knew about, or had adequately measured, he conjectured. So Brown came to Central Michigan, among other places, to look around.

Dow's plant in Midland—then and now—is huge. By the 1980s, it had 1,950 potential "point sources" of emissions, largely vents and valves, plus regular smokestacks and wastewater systems that also emitted volatile organic compounds, or VOCs, as this category of air pollutants is known. Dow Midland also had an incinerator operating in the 1980s—which in 1983, for example, burned 64.8 million pounds of waste in a rotary kiln, one that rotates while its contents burn. Dow by then had a license from DNR to burn some 88 hazardous compounds.

Journalist Michael Brown found an unusually high rate of birth anomalies that occurred specifically within the 1970–74 period.

One of the nasties that comes with incinerator emissions is dioxin—invisible and in micro amounts, but dioxin, nonetheless. In the 1980s, at least one reading from Dow's Midland incinerator recorded 8.2 parts per trillion dioxin had been found in "particulate matter"—tiny airborne particles—from the incinerator. Another measured dioxin in the incinerator's ash at 280,000 parts per trillion.[33] In addition to the incinerator, Dow also used other burners—at least six of them at different buildings during the 1980s—that were also found to release dioxin in combustion.

In his interviewing and travels in Michigan, Brown more or less followed the geographic footprint of the aerial plume from Dow's plant, a pattern stretching some miles beyond its Midland origin. The plume's movement and reach, he understood, would depend on the prevailing winds of the moment. From Midland outward, Brown ventured into towns such as Hemlock and Alm, collecting an array of anecdotal evidence and stories from people who lived beneath or within range of the plume. He consistently encountered stories about dogs and farm animals with all kinds of maladies.

People were getting sick, too. Brown checked the statistical record and mortality data in the Michigan area to see if there might be some health-effects data that seemed out of the ordinary, or that popped out in a strong pattern. He found an unusually high rate of birth anomalies that occurred in the region during the early 1970s and specifically within the 1970–74 period. This period, he later figured, was just after the surge of Agent Orange production had passed through the Dow complex. "The figures could only be described as jolting ones," he wrote. "In a period that began right around the time EPA announced restrictions on the herbicide 2,4,5-T..., there were fifteen cleft palates among Midlanders when only five would normally be expected." He also found there had been "thirty-four urogenetical defects when only seven should have occurred—nearly five times the expected cases—and heart defects were also exceedingly high."[34]

Brown then asked scientists if a one-shot exposure of dioxin could result in birth defects—his thinking being that a one-time release or unreported incidents at Dow's Midland complex might be implicated in the health effects. The answer he received—at least in laboratory animal testing—was yes. Robert Pratt, head of experimental teratogenesis section at the National Institute of Environmental Health Sciences told him, "...The threshold dose at which we start to see effects in mice with dioxin is around one to two micrograms* per kilogram. For our studies we only give it one time, a single shot during gestation."[35] Single-release chemical events weren't out of the question at Midland or any other chemical plant. Indeed, Brown had discovered in the several week period during his visit in 1986 that there had been accidental releases of sulfur trioxide and hydrogen chloride at Midland, as well as an incinerator flashback that had burned one worker. "When I called a chemical operator at Dow, Thomas D. Dauer," Brown explained, "he told me in his ten years there he had heard about 'quite a few' releases that never had been reported, but they were not intentional ones. He had also heard rumors about documents being destroyed, and about releases at one time from the trichlorophenol plant."[36] Still, local authorities assured Brown that the statistics he found were anomalies, and that if something were wrong in the area, the medical community would know about it. In any case, by 1985, Dow's Midland operation reported it was releasing into the air each year: 76,000 pounds of benzene, 366,000 pounds of toluene, 4.6 million pounds of methyl chloride, and nearly a ton of vinyl chloride. EPA would also soon find dioxin at the parts-per-trillion level in soil of residential areas within 2.5 miles of Dow's Midland operations.[37]

Could a one-shot surge of dioxin production lead to an unexplained rise in birth defects?

Incinerate It

In 1988, Dow proposed to upgrade an existing incinerator at Midland to enable the burning of additional hazardous and toxic wastes. Dow said it needed the newer incinerator because of expanding production, projecting it would produce more wastes in the next several years. Yet two years earlier, Dow had initiated a waste reduction program called WRAP—Waste Reduction Always Pays. The WRAP program, designed to reduce wastes by making chemical processing more efficient and by using recycling to re-use materials, had some success in reducing landfill wastes. Incineration, Dow said, was a major component of its waste reduction program. But Dow was also committed to taking wastes from the Dow Corning operation in Mid-

---

*A microgram is a millionth of a gram.

land, wastes that were also increasing, amounting to about one-third of what Dow Chemical was then burning. Finally, Dow said it needed the new incinerator because the amount of hazardous waste it was generating—and would generate—was on the rise. Dow claimed the new incinerator would be capable of destroying even the most toxic substances it handled, including dioxin, burning the wastes at 2,200 degrees Fahrenheit. That would destroy 99.999 percent of dioxin wastes, Dow said. Not everyone in Midland was convinced. "I don't think they've proven the need," said Diane Hebert, an environmental activist in Midland. "I think it's contradictory to say they need the incinerator

"When we asked them what they will be burning," said DNR's Mike Jury, "they say it could be anything." It turned out Dow wanted to include PCBs and dioxin.

and they say they are reducing their waste. It does not give the company the incentive to reduce waste. In fact, it might work the opposite way."[38]

Permit negotiations with the Michigan DNR for the upgraded incinerator continued through 1989, but ran into some snags when DNR sought to have Dow shut down the unit's power if problems or unreasonable nuisances developed. DNR also wanted to impose some fairly strict emissions limits. "They don't want to be limited as to what they can burn at this facility," explained DNR's Mike Jury in April 1989. "When we asked them what they will be burning they say it could be anything. So in doing the case work on this project, we want to look at everything."[39] It turned out that Dow wanted to include PCBs and dioxin. Dow had 7,000 drums of dioxin-laden wastes that had been in storage at the Midland plant. These wastes—left over from the Agent Orange era—had been held for more than 15 years, and included contaminated soil and contaminated bricks from the chemical plant that Dow had demolished, as well as 350,000 gallons of liquid waste. In total, at both Midland incinerators, Dow was proposing to burn about 100 million pounds of chemical wastes. The plan met with a considerable local protest, including calls from some groups to boycott both Dow Chemical and Dow Corning products.* In addition, by 1992, scientists at the U.S.-Canadian International Joint Commission (IJC) had also voiced concerns about diox-

---

*Among the Dow consumer products targeted at that time, for example, were: *Ziploc* bags—freezer, storage, and sandwich varieties; *Freezloc* freezer wrap; *Dow Bathroom Cleaner* and *Tough Act* bathroom cleaner; *Fantastic* and *Fantastic Lemon Scent*; *Wood Plus* furniture polish; *Glass Plus* glass cleaner, *Handi-Wrap* and *Saran Wrap*; *Spray 'n Wash* (liquid, aerosol, and stain stick varieties); *Spifits* and *Swipes*; *Pine Magic* and *Texsize* pine cleaners; *Vivd* bleach and *Yes* detergent; *Dow Oven Cleaner, Janitor-in-a-Drum; Style, Perma Soft, Apple Pectin, Free Style* and *Textra* shampoos and conditioners; *Lamar* and *Nucleic A* salon shampoos, conditioners, hairsprays, perms, and styling aids; *Dow Corning Bathtub Caulk* and silicone sealants, including products such as *DAP* that use Dow silicone; Merrill Dow pharmaceutical products and *NicoDerm*; and *DowElanco* agricultural chemicals.

in and other persistent chemicals in the Great Lakes region, and specifically the contribution of incinerators. "Incineration facilities in the region should be phased out of use or required to eliminate the production and emission of dioxin, furans, PCBs and inorganic materials, especially mercury and hydrochloric acid," said the IJC.[40]

Greenpeace charged Dow with "cheating" on the incinerator test burn.

Greenpeace had also been monitoring Dow's proposal to incinerate. As Dow moved closer to approval with a test burn in August 1992, Greenpeace found that Dow had used materials in the burn that were not representative of Dow's wastes. "Dow's cheating on the incinerator test burn fits in with what we know about the failure of incineration to deal with dioxin," said Pat Costner, a Greenpeace research director and chemist who had once worked for Shell Oil. "Since the technology won't work," she said "they rigged the test." Costner and Greenpeace then wrote DNR, urging a denial of the permit, submitting their own study of the effects, which projected a huge increase in potential dioxin and furan emissions in the region (ranging between 188 grams and 876 grams of dioxin equivalents.). "This is a major disaster in the making," warned Terry Miller of the Lone Tree Council. "There is already enough dioxin in the Tri-city area, most of it coming from Dow, to justify halting this facility before it emits even one more molecule of dioxin."[41] But Dow's permit request for the upgraded incinerator continued on course through DNR.

Failure to Disclose

Then in November 1993, a new development came to light. An anonymous tip to DNR revealed that Dow's rebuilt incinerator had cracks in the outer steel shell as well as some warping. "If the structural integrity of the kiln is not compromised," said DNR's Phil Schrantz, "this may not be a big deal." However, Schrantz was not happy to learn that Dow kept this information from the agency. "The fact that we learned of this from a source other than Dow is a concern to us." Dow apparently had discovered the cracks in February 1993 when it was doing sonogram testing on the shell, but didn't know for certain until August, it said. DNR meanwhile, had approved the permit in April. "These fractures are not unusual in the steel shells in kilns," said Dow manager Don Berry. "They do not in any way cause a danger to human health or the environment." Nor did holding back the latest data, in Berry's view, constitute a purposeful sleight of hand on Dow's part. Editorial writers at the *Midland Daily News* did not agree. "We believe reporting the information—whether legally required or not—would have been in Dow's, and the public's, best interest," they wrote. "... Dow officials knew the incineration issue was touchy. They knew they faced lengthy regulatory process to get permission to burn the dioxin-contaminated waste.…. This was a time for candor and openness, even if the problem did not warrant any concern."[42] Local activists and community groups were also upset with Dow. The Ecology Center, joined by other Michigan groups, including the Lone Tree Council and Citizens for Alternatives to Chemical Contamination, filed a legal action in Ingrahm County District Court challenging DNR's decision to issue a permit.[43] The citizen groups charged the incinerator had not been proven safe, that Dow improperly tested it, and that it failed to meet regulatory requirements for burning dioxin-contaminated wastes. The suit also noted the permit was open-ended and did not restrict Dow from burning wastes from outside sources, allowing it to become "a commercial dioxin-burning incinerator." Although the suit failed, DNR did not permit Dow to burn its dioxin-laden wastes.[44]

> **"We believe reporting the information—whether legally required or not—would have been in Dow's, and the public's, best interest."**
>
> Editors, *Midland Daily News*

Failing to obtain DNR approval for incinerating its dioxin wastes in Midland, Dow then moved to plan B: shipping the waste to a Westinghouse-owned company named Aptus that operated an incinerator in Coffeyville, Kansas. The Aptus incinerator, by April 1993, had become the first in the United States to burn dioxin wastes. By June 1994, when Dow decided to begin shipping its dioxin waste there, Aptus had burned about 4 million pounds of waste containing dioxin from 100 customers nationwide. Dow planned to ship 5 million pounds to Aptus between 1994 and 1995, about 150 truckloads in all, making it Aptus' single largest dioxin customer. Kansas officials did not seem concerned at the time. "It's no big deal," said Greg Crawford, spokesman for the Kansas Department of Health and Environment, "It's another two to three truckloads a week.… " Some Kansas environmentalists, however, weren't very happy about taking Michigan's waste. "The people in Midland, Michigan have raised so much cain over this, they are sending it to Kansas, where we don't do anything about it, expect to say, 'Come on down,'" said Lauri Maddy of Rose Hill, Kansas.[45] But sending dioxin wastes from Midland, Michigan to Coffeyville, Kansas in the 1990s didn't solve Dow's dioxin problem. More on that later. Chemical problems of another variety, however, would occasionally occur for Dow Chemical and its sister company, Dow Corning, within Michigan.

Clouds Over Midland

On Sunday morning, August 17, 1997, a few residents of Midland noticed it on their way home from church. A white cloud floating above the neighborhood near the Dow Corning and Dow Chemical plants along Salzburg Road. Soon the cloud had grown, stretching over a two-mile section of Midland southwest of the plants. Later that morning, an order had been issued to residents in the area to "shelter in place," close their windows, and stay indoors. The white cloud was hydrogen chloride, a corrosive gas and irritant that can cause the eyes to smart and the lungs to burn. It was coming from the Dow Corning plant. The toxic cloud had formed after a pipeline carrying trichlorosilane—a silicon-based material used in making semiconductors—leaked into the air, forming hydrogen chloride vapor. Hydrogen chloride is toxic and flammable; in contact with moisture, it becomes hydrochloric acid. Local roads were blocked to keep traffic away from the plant. The pipe that leaked the toxic gas was in a group of about 10 to 20 chemical supply pipes running through the plant. Dow Corning safety personnel had to shut off several of the lines before they found the line that had the leak. Midland firefighters, meanwhile, sprayed water into the air above the plant to "scrub" the substance out of the air. "We can scrub a fair amount of it," explained Verne Jacobson, Dow Corning's site manager, "but we can't scrub it all out, and some of it escaped as a white fog." The day following the leak, more than 30 workers were onsite hosing off residue that had fallen on plant equipment. On neighboring Dow Chemical property, some truck trailers were also dusted with a white residue. "Our security cameras showed a white plume was on Dow Chemical property as a result of the Dow Corning release," reported Dow Chemical's Cindy Newman. A Dow Chemical security guard had been taken to the Dow Chemical Medical Center after complaining about a burning sensation on his hands. But generally, there were no serious injuries, and the cool, wet weather helped too. "If this kind of incident had to happen," explained Midland Fire Chief, Dan Hargarten, "yesterday's weather was the best for it. It being cool and wet, that also helped to keep the effects confined. If it had been warm and dry and the winds were higher, it could have (affected a larger area)." Hargarten, in fact, had determined not to sound warning sirens in the city of Midland. "Given the wind direction and speed, sounding the sirens wouldn't have accomplished anything," he said. "Since the conditions were as they were, we decided not to sound the sirens. If there had been any chance that anybody in the city of Midland would have been impacted we would have sounded the sirens." Hydrogen chloride was detected in the air at 0.5 ppm, while danger levels would be at 5.0 ppm, according to Hargarten.[46]

But some of the people returning from church the morning of the incident, seeing the cloud near their neighborhood, decided not to return to their homes until it dissipated. Once it did, some ten hours later, the leak was ruled officially contained. Residents in the affected area were told they might see some white residue on their lawns, gardens, and outside structures. About

360 homes were included in the affected area, according Roger Garner, director of the Midland County emergency services. People with residue on their property were told not to eat fruits or vegetables grown in their yards without calling Dow Corning first. "We prefer they call us so we can assess their individual situation," said Dow Corning's Jacobson. "Each situation is kind of unique."[47] The trichlorosilane line that leaked was moving the chemical to another production process. Trichlorosilane, when refined, is then sent to the Hemlock Semiconductor Corp., a partly-owned Dow Corning venture in the nearby town of Hemlock. That plant used the chemical in making polycystalline silicon, used in turn to make integrated circuits for the electronics industry.

Residents in the affected area were told they might see some white residue on their lawns, gardens, and outside structures.

Two weeks after Dow Corning's trichlorosilane leak, the company issued the results of its investigation of the accident and found that a plastic label marking the 2-inch pipe had corroded it. "The label was collecting moisture underneath...," explained Dow Corning's Verne Jacobson "and the moisture was not getting away. There was a small amount of acid there, as well," he added. Together, the moisture and the acid succeeded in corroding the pipe. Dow Corning used the labeling system on hundreds of pipes throughout its operation. As a result, the company began exploring new ways of labeling the contents of its pipes, from direct lettering them with paint to the use of adhesive labels.

Although there were no injuries in the August 1997 incident, the release did get the attention of area residents and the local media. Questions were raised about some shortcomings in the community's emergency warning capability. Most troubling was the fact that none of the 16 townships surrounding the plant had outdoor warning sirens. Dow Corning's report suggested that a system of indoor alert monitors—essentially, a radio-type system tuned to a specific frequency—could be installed in homes. An emergency tone would then prompt residents to tune in for emergency instructions. Such a system explained the Dow Corning report, "may be more economical and effective than sirens."[48]

Just as the town of Midland was getting over the trichlorosilane incident at the Dow Corning plant in August 1997, another chemical leak occurred about 3:30 a.m. on Saturday, August 30—this time of styrene monomer from a railroad tank car sitting on a siding at the Dow Chemical plant. This leak prompted another shelter-in-place warning for about 4,000 Midland residents. This time, a warning siren was sounded and television and radio reports were also used to notify residents of the leak. Residents within a mile of the plant were told to stay indoors, close all windows, extinguish any open flames, and shut off ventilation systems.

The 1997 incidents at the Dow Corning and Dow Chemical Midland plants, of course, weren't the first. Numerous chronic releases and smaller events occur regularly. Two of these, for example, occurred in December 1996—one, on December 7, involved a 600-pound vapor release of methylchloride, hydrogen chloride, and methanol. Another, occurring nine days later on December 16, involved about 60 pounds of methyl chloride and hydrogen chloride vapor. In this incident, plant officials believed that a quarter-inch stainless steel pipe had vibrated loose during a start-up process, causing the release. A small haze was observed at the source of the leak, but no detectable levels of material left the plant site, according to Dow Corning officials.[49] Another vapor release in June 1996, involving hydrogen chloride from Hemlock Semiconductor, resulted in the evacuation of between 10 and 20 families in the Hemlock area.[50]

Dioxin in The River

In April 2000, General Motors (GM), the giant automaker, was doing some soil testing in a wetland near Saginaw, Michigan. However, the wetland GM happened to be sampling was in the Tittabawassee River flood plain, about 20 miles south of Midland where the Tittabawassee joins the Saginaw River.* There, GM made a surprising discovery: dioxin was present in the soil at very high levels—indeed, way above safe exposure levels at some locations. GM notified the Michigan Department of Community Health of its findings, which proceeded to do its own testing. Between December 2000 and June 2001, new soil samples were tested and analyzed. All but five contained dioxin concentrations above the state's acceptable residential cleanup standard. Some had dioxin concentrations as high as 80 times that level. Alarmed because some of the dioxin was found near homes and parks, DEQ began an internal debate over what to do. The findings, meanwhile, were not released to the public, but stayed under wraps within the health department and DEQ.

By November 2001, the deputies of three state agencies agreed that a "next level" of testing was in order, given the findings. However, DEQ's director, Russell Harding, opted for a slower process and more review first. But there was also something else. Michigan was then weighing whether it should soften its dioxin standard, moving it from 90 parts per trillion (ppt) to 150 ppt. Within DEQ, some scientists and staff opposed the change. EPA, it was noted, had been moving in the opposite direction, and was closer to

---

*GM needed to use the site as a wetland in compensation for another it would damage with contaminants from another project. The replacement, or mitigation site GM would use to offset the other loss was the site at the confluence of the Tittabawassee and Saginaw rivers. GM's testing there was to ensure that it would be a suitable replacement; that it would be safe for terrestrial and aquatic organisms expected to inhabit the new wetland.

tightening its dioxin standard after years of review. "The more I think about it, the more uncomfortable I get," offered one DEQ toxicologist about the prospect of softening Michigan's standard. "Although I agree in principle that the criteria for all hazardous substances should incorporate the same generic exposure assumptions, dioxin is so unique and of such significant public health concern that making it an exception [i.e., giving it a more rigorous standard] is reasonable." Others added that a less stringent dioxin standard would not protect the public health. But Harding wasn't listening to just his own scientists. He had held closed-door meetings with Dow officials, and Dow favored the softer approach.

Soil samples revealed dioxin above the state's acceptable residential clean-up standard—some with concentrations 80 times that level.

Some Michigan environmental groups, meanwhile, including the Michigan Environmental Council, Environmental Health Watch, Lone Tree Council, and the Ecology Center, heard rumors of "something big" in the works at the DEQ. The groups soon filed a Freedom of Information Act request seeking documents related to dioxin contamination in Midland. What they received in return was a highly censored document with blacked-out pages. Michigan health officials told them it was still in draft form. A subsequent DEQ report revealed that high levels of dioxin were found in the Tittabawassee River floodplain. But what upset the environmental groups was that the state was sitting on the findings. Michigan DEQ director, Russell Harding, they charged, was blocking further testing and suppressing a state health assessment. Said the Michigan Environmental Council's Dave Dempsey, who had served as environmental advisor to former Governor James Blanchard: "Director Harding is seeking to ignore the preponderance of scientific evidence, which is driving EPA to toughen standards to protect the public, in order to benefit Dow Chemical Company."[51]

As Michigan officials grappled with what to do on dioxin, EPA was working toward completion of a 12-year reassessment of dioxin risks nationally. Although it was long known that at least one dioxin compound was a confirmed carcinogen, an emerging body of scientific evidence was showing that many dioxin compounds could cause birth defects, neurological effects, and chronic ailments. And this was precisely why some in Michigan's DEQ believed tougher federal standards were on the way. A few documents at DEQ had in fact noted that EPA's dioxin reassessment would "present a cancer potency for dioxin and dioxin-like compounds 25- to 100-times greater than the value previously used in risk assessment for these compounds." Further, the dioxin reassessment by EPA would also indicate that "current dioxin intake from diet alone is greater than the acceptable daily dose," observed DEQ. This meant additional exposures from other sources would more than likely be "unacceptable." In this context, Midland's existing levels of dioxin in the soil would stand out, and likely far exceed any new criterion forthcoming from EPA, not to mention the sky-high levels found down river.

Michigan, in other words, was going in completely the wrong direction with its latest proposal—a near-doubling of the exposure amount, considered by many to be incomprehensible. They saw the move as Michigan doing Dow's bidding. "With a wave of the wand, Harding is trying to 'declare' some areas clean instead of actually removing dioxin," said the Ecology Center's Tracey Easthope. "This

DEQ's Director held closed-door meetings with officials from Dow Chemical.

could save Dow millions of dollars but cost the people of Michigan tens or hundreds of millions of dollars in cleanup and health care costs." Midland activist Diane Hebert noted that many dioxin hot spots in Midland and elsewhere in the region just happened to be in the 90-ppt to 150-ppt range.[52] If the less stringent standard were put in place, Dow would be relieved of a lot of potential liability. Unmoved by his critics, Harding by February 2002 had already set in motion the proposed rule changes that would lead to the softer 150 ppt dioxin standard.

In March 2002, a report released by state and federal health officials only further verified what local environmentalists had long known—that a potential source of the dioxin contamination in the Tittabawassee floodplain was Dow's Midland plant. The report cited a 1986 flood that overwhelmed Dow's containment systems allowing untreated or partially-treated chemical wastes to enter the river. Dow spokesman Jeff Freer denied that such a breech had occurred, and that in any case, floodwaters would have diluted dioxin to concentrations below the high levels being detected downstream. But whatever the source, he said, it wasn't Dow. DEQ, meanwhile, finally released its findings on the down-

An emerging body of scientific evidence was showing that many dioxin compounds could cause birth defects, neurological effects, and chronic ailments.

stream dioxin, and verified that dioxin was in soil near parks and residential areas in a range between 39 ppt to more than 7,200 ppt. Only nine of the initial 35 samples came back below the state standard of 90 ppt. The levels found in some of the samples exceeded both the federal action standard of 1 part per billion (ppb) set by the Agency for Toxic Substances and Disease Registry (ATSDR) and EPA's threshold for action—action, in fact, the agency had already taken elsewhere. In October 2001, EPA said it would relocate some residents of Pensacola, Florida whose residential soil levels reached or exceeded 200 ppt dioxin.

Michigan Activism

The battle with Dow Chemical over dioxin and other issues has involved a long and distinguished line of Michigan activists. For nearly 50 years, conservationists, public health officials, lawyers, environmentalists, politicians, state regulators, housewives, and even Dow employees have kept after the company to clean up its act. Fred Brown, a Dow research and development scientist in the 1950s, became president of the Michigan United Conservation Clubs in the 1960s. Brown, appointed by the governor in the 1980s to the state Water Resources Commission, did battle with his employer over pollution issues well into the 1990s. Mary Sinclair of Midland rose to national prominence in the 1970s fighting Dow and the Michigan utility, Consumers Power Company, when the two companies tried to build a nuclear power plant in Midland that was shown to be flawed and a public safety risk. Wayne Schmidt and others at the Michigan United Conservation Clubs worked on Dow-related water pollution issues in the early 1980s. Diane Hebert, a former flight attendant and Midland, Michigan homemaker, began fighting Dow over 25 years ago when she and Andrea Wilson formed the Environmental Congress of Mid-Michigan to stop Dow's toxic pollution and dioxin contamination. Hebert remains one of Dow's most knowledgeable adversaries. Larry Fink, initially a government regulator turned activist, formed the Foresight Society in the 1980s, and became an important voice in calling for more thorough state and federal scientific study of the dioxin matter. Tracey Easthope, a trained public health professional, has been battling Dow over toxic chemicals since 1990 for the Ann Arbor-based Ecology Center, becoming an effective citizens' advocate and political infighter. Dave Dempsey, a former environmental advisor to Michigan Governor James Blanchard, now with the Michigan Environmental Council, does battle with Dow on regulatory and legal issues. Terry Miller, a founder of the Bay City-based Lone Tree Council in 1978, has become one the Michigan stalwarts on Dow Chemical issues, while working on a host of other local matters. In recent years, Michelle Hurd Riddick, also with the Lone Tree Council, has become a key citizen leader on the Tittabawassee River fight over dioxin contamination. Added to these are numerous Michigan citizens, labor leaders, farmers, local public officials, Dow investors, scientists, and area college students who have also become involved with Dow Chemical on particular issues. National environmental groups—among them, Greenpeace and the Natural Resources Defense Council—have also come to Michigan on Dow matters. But increasingly, Dow issues are becoming international, and Michigan's activists are joining with other Dow activists, whether over Bhopal, India, union issues in Canada, or Agent Orange questions in Vietnam.

Sources: Dave Dempsey, *Ruin & Recovery: Michigan's Rise As A Conservation Leader*, Ann Arbor: University of Michigan Press, 2001; Mark Van Putten, "Frederick L. Brown: The Courage To Speak Out," People Who Make a Difference, *National Wildlife*, National Wildlife Federation, Washington, DC; Terry R. Miller, "Lone Tree Council: A Better World, That's What It's About," *Midland Daily News*, April 16, 1995, p. A-5; and author conversations with various Michigan citizens and environmentalists.

Along the Tittabawassee, however, it soon became apparent that the latest dioxin revelations were potentially an enormous problem for Dow and Michigan. In all, more than 2,000 properties were thought to be contaminated along both sides of the Tittabawassee River, stretching some 22 miles downstream. The contaminated land included homes, parks, churches, schools, farms, a national wildlife refuge, and a number of small businesses. Contaminated river sediment had also been hauled throughout the area and used for landscaping and fill. By October 2002, Michigan environmentalists released documents they said showed collusion between the state and Dow Chemical to create a "dioxin zone" as a way to limit Dow's potential clean-up liability.[53]

DEQ verified dioxin in soil near parks and residential areas in a range between 39 ppt to more than 7,200 ppt.

As the November 2002 elections approached, Michigan's gubernatorial office was up for grabs, and the state's Attorney General, Jennifer M. Granholm (D), appeared on her way becoming the state's next governor. That was not good news for Dow, especially since Granholm was sounding tougher on the environment than her predecessor, Republican John Engler. In fact, DEQ's Russell Harding was quite up front about Dow's pre-election position on the dioxin standard. He told *Chemical Policy Alert* in late October 2002: "Frankly, Dow would like to get this done with our administration here," he said, adding: "The statements that the attorney general [Granholm] made in this campaign scare 'em to death." After Granholm was elected in November, the process to push the new dioxin standard through by the lame-duck Engler administration was put on a fast track.

In December 2002, in one of his final acts as governor, Engler tried to deliver a big Christmas present to Dow by adopting the softer dioxin standard, then packaged in a consent order. Engler's proposed rule change soon drew fire from Governor-elect Granholm as well EPA's regional officials, charging the move as illegal or precipitous. Karl E. Bremer, chief of the EPA's Region 5 toxics division, said in a letter to the state that "it does not appear that U.S. EPA guidance has been considered or followed in developing" the new standard or risk assessment models. Michigan officials and Dow executives said they were merely trying to put in place a long-discussed plan to study the extent and possible health implications of public exposure to dioxin along the Tittabawassee. Michigan environmental groups, however, knew this was a long-standing problem throughout the

In one of his final acts as Michigan's governor, John Engler tried to deliver a big Christmas present to Dow by adopting the softer dioxin standard.

Sowing Dioxin Seed

Some of those present in Michigan during the 1970s and 1980s, believe that Dow had the technological capability to detect dioxin in the environment at very minute levels. By the 1970s, as shown above, the company was finding dioxin in Tittabawassee River fish. But there was little public dioxin monitoring at the time; few government entities had the detection capability that only Dow and a handful of laboratories had. No dioxin monitoring was required by the Clean Water Act or the NPDES permit process, and there were no dioxin standards. Dow's dioxin strategy became one of announcing reductions in its current emissions and discharges, but essentially sitting back on the matter of past contamination—i.e., dioxin already released into the environment. Dow believed that this contamination, over time, would degrade and the environment would cleanse itself naturally. The company could simply outlast any imposed remedy that might emerge for this old contamination. But a few observers say that Dow made a fatal miscalculation with this approach, badly misjudging the persistence of dioxin. True, dioxin will "photodegrade" on leaves in sunlight in the mixtures used in 2,4,5-T and 2,4-D. However, dioxin will not biodegrade, or degrades only very slowly, when bound to ash, soil, or sediment. Moreover, some scientists would find that it was not only the 2,3,7,8-TCDD form of dioxin that was the problem, but that higher chlorinated forms of dioxins in soils, ash, and sediment could photodegrade to 2,3,7,8-TCDD. This meant potentially, that estimates of dioxin in the environment—Tittabawassee River or globally—were likely low, as TCDD-dioxin was being continually formed in the environment by the ongoing degradation of other chemical products bearing the higher-chlorinated varieties of the dioxin molecule. And one of those dioxin-bearing chemicals—produced by Dow in copious quantities over the years—is pentachlorophenol, or PCP, still a widely used wood preservative globally. In pentachlorophenol, the octa-version dioxin molecule is degraded by sunlight, and converted to the deadly 2,3,7,8-TCDD. At Midland, Dow manufactured tens of millions of pounds of PCP for decades, contaminating the soils and Tittabawassee River sediments far and wide—in effect, "sowing the seeds" of future TCDD dioxin for many decades to come. "This source of dioxin," observes one former Michigan scientist and regulatory player, "could have continuously replenished the 2,3,7,8-TCDD in Midland soils and Tittabawassee sediments long after Dow reduced its dioxin emissions from air and water." His conclusion: "Instead of taking a decade for Dow's dioxin fingerprints to disappear from the scene of the crime, it will take more like a century." And still others, such as Pat Costner of Greenpeace, believe that other non-TCDD forms of dioxin released by Dow processes at Midland—some nearly as toxic as TCDD itself—far surpass that of TCDD in terms of total contribution to dioxin-like toxicity.

Saginaw basin watershed, and that most of the dioxin was a chemical byproduct of the last half-century or more of Dow's manufacture of chlorophenol, chlorinated pesticides, mustard gas, and Agent Orange. In December 2002, they went to court in Lansing, the state capital, to block

Engler's move and prevent the softer dioxin standard from taking effect. The governor's rule change proposed to increase, by more than ninefold, the amount of dioxin allowed in Midland's soil—from 90 ppt to 831 ppt. "I think the governor is trying to hand Dow Chemical a sweetheart deal that will essentially relieve them of a large part of their liability for contamination of what is the second-largest watershed in the Great Lakes," said Tracey Easthope of the Ecology Center.[54] Environmentalists also feared the proposed rule change for Midland would become the de facto cleanup standard for the state. But by late December, the deal had fallen apart. Dow had rejected language demanded by the attorney general's office. Russell Harding said he still believed the change was the appropriate solution for addressing dioxin contamination in Midland, but time had run out. The environmental groups dropped their lawsuit but vowed to keep a continuing close watch on the process at DEQ and elsewhere.[55]

Dow's liability, some suggested, was for contamination of the second-largest watershed in the Great Lakes.

Class Action

Meanwhile, the residents downstream of Midland where the high levels of dioxin were found, had been receiving regular bulletins from state agencies about their plight. The first came in late 2001. The message was anything but comforting. Soil samples with dioxin levels as high as 7,261 ppt were found in the area. And the advice—when residents tried to sort out what best to do from various public agencies—was confusing. Soon, official bright yellow signs were popping up at nearby parks and along riverbank land warning the public about dioxin. Residents were told to take precautions, such as wearing face masks when mowing the lawn and showering after doing yard work. Local residents said they wanted to leave the area, but couldn't sell their homes. A new, feisty citizen group sprung to life to help inform the floodplain citizens of their situation: Tittabawassee River Watch, which built a first-class web site and began laying plans for legal action.

Jan Helder, the residents' attorney, suggested parallels to Times Beach and Love Canal; Dow officials predicted a long legal fight.

In March 2003, a lawsuit was filed against Dow Chemical on behalf of 26 residents of the Tittabawassee River flood plain. The suit charged Dow with contaminating the river with dangerous levels of dioxin, sought dam-

Dioxin Hits Homeowners

Along the Tittabawassee River in central Michigan in 2002–03, there were some pretty unhappy homeowners. Real estate values, it seemed, were on the decline. "We listed our house and every time a buyer saw the dioxin warning, they ran like hell," said Wendy Domino, who with her husband Dennis, lived along the river near Saginaw. It was March 2003. The Dominos were among hundreds of families who months earlier had received notices warning them about the dioxin. Soon after, they put their home on the market hoping for a quick sale. "It was frightening," said Wendy. "We were extremely panicked." At one point, Wendy called Dow Chemical on the phone. "I told them, 'Why don't you buy my house. No one else will.'" Dow did send its representatives to visit the Dominos, and the company also paid for two appraisals of their home. But the couple mistakenly believed Dow was actually going to buy their house, as Wendy had suggested. But they were soon advised to sell their home on their own. Dow was not in the real estate business, they were told. To that, Wendy replied: "I'm not in the toxic clean-up business, either." Dow's reps said the appraisal of the Domino home showed that dioxin had not affected the property's value. Wendy and Dennis Domino, who subsequently had five broken deals to buy their home, believe dioxin is the reason. They joined the class action lawsuit against Dow. So did Gary and Kathy Henry, who bought a home along the Tittabawassee near Freeland, Michigan in the early 1980s. "We wanted to be near the water," says Gary Henry, thinking back on the purchase of their ranch style home. "We didn't even look at the house." Nearly 20 years later when the couple should be reaping some appreciation, the river's occasional flood waters have now made the Henry's investment practically worthless, they say. In the course of the dioxin fight, Dennis Domino told one documentary filmmaker in an on-camera interview: "No matter where you are, you always feel home is a safe place to come to. No matter what happens in the rest of your life, the minute you get home, you feel safe. It doesn't really feel safe here anymore." The Dominos did manage to sell their home.

Source: Kathie Marchlewski, "Families Believe Homes Have No Value Due to Dioxin," *Midland Daily News*, March 26, 2003, and Dennis Domino quoted in the film *The Long Shadow*, by Stephen Meador, Little-R Productions in association with Michigan State University School of Journalism, rough cut version, 2003.

ages for lost property values, and called for the establishment of a medical monitoring trust fund for residents. By June 2003, the lawsuit was filed as a class action, seeking relief for all residents on the floodplain. Dow officials questioned whether the high dioxin levels came from its operations, noting that many other facilities discharged into the river over the years. Dow officials said they wanted more sampling and denied that property values declined. But others in the area found no mystery as to the source of the problem. Says Tittabawassee River resident Kathy Henry: "Dow's role seems pretty obvious," pointing to samples showing dioxin levels of 2 ppt upstream from the plant and 3,400 ppt at a park downstream of the plant. Jan P. Helder, the residents' attorney, suggested parallels to other dioxin litigation at Times Beach, Missouri, and Love Canal, New York. Dow officials, meanwhile, predicted a long legal fight.[56] Indeed, within months of the filing, the legal maneuvering on both sides was at full throttle; appeals began to fly, depositions were taken, and a key court date on the plaintiff's class-action status awaited. The stakes in the case, of course, were huge—for Dow, dioxin issues globally, and the lives of the Tittabawassee floodplain citizens and their families. Toxic trespass may soon be coming to trial in a very big way. Stay tuned.

20.
Union Carbide

The new Dow is on its way to a totally new level of performance.

Michael Parker, Dow CEO, 2001[1]

Long before Dow acquired it in 2001, Union Carbide had fully entered the ranks of the world's top chemical corporations. Formed in a merger of five companies that included National Carbon Co., maker of the first dry-cell battery *(Eveready)*, and calcium chloride producer, Union Carbide Co., the new company in 1917 became known as the Union Carbide and Carbon Corporation. Initially engaged in metallurgical and carbon products, Union Carbide soon added gases and chemicals to its repertoire, and by World War II, was even refining uranium and helping to build the atomic bomb. By 1963, Carbide, like Dow, had also become a major plastics producer, shipping more than one billion pounds annually. In the 1970s, as the third largest U.S. chemical company, Carbide became known for consumer products such as *Prestone* antifreeze and *Glad* plastic wrap. But Carbide's largest customer was the steel industry, which it supplied industrial products such as oxygen, chromium, and manganese to stoke its furnaces and feed its mills.[2]

In the 1980s, however, the defining event for Carbide became a catastrophic toxic gas leak: a deadly 1984 incident killing thousands at Bhopal, India (see sidebar). After Bhopal, Carbide became economically vulnerable, and was targeted by Wall Street agents looking to pick up cheap assets. To avoid being taken over entirely, Carbide retrenched. Consumer businesses were sold off, including *Eveready* batteries, *Prestone* antifreeze, *Glad* plastic bags, the ag chem business, and even the company's headquarters in Danbury, Connecticut. By 1989, CEO Robert Kennedy had set up Carbide's remaining parts as a holding company with three primary businesses—chemicals and plastics, industrial gases, and carbon.[3] Although its most notorious legacy became Bhopal, throughout its history—even after Bhopal—Carbide had its share of other environmental problems, workplace woes, and battles with community groups.

Hawk's Nest Silicosis

In the late 1920s, as part of a major hydroelectric project on the New River, the Union Carbide and Carbon Corporation contracted to construct a 3-mile long tunnel. Known as the Hawk's Nest Tunnel at Gauley Bridge, West Virginia, the project included diverting a portion of the New River to a power station to provide electricity for a Union Carbide ferroalloy plant. During the tunnelling, Carbide's contractor had run into a high-content silica deposit; a mineral the company used elsewhere as a raw material. Some 3,000 men had been hired for the tunnelling, three-fourths of whom were African American from the deep South—most working ten-hour days to meet a contracted deadline. During the tunneling, the silica particles became a problem, and a number of the workers developed silicosis, a lung disease caused by inhalation of silica dust. Poor ventilation in the tunnel worsened the problem by creating stagnant air and the need for deeper breathing, but only foremen were provided masks. Management would later claim there was not an officially approved respirator for silicosis. Union Carbide and contractors eventually faced some 538 lawsuits, of which 34 were settled for a total of $200,000, leaving some to draw the conclusion that the courts had determined a tunnel worker's life was worth less than $400.[4] In court, the general manager of the project claimed he never heard his employees complain about the conditions while working in the tunnel, nor had there been any documented case of silicosis reported by any of his workers. Local residents, however, reported seeing the workers leaving the site covered in dust. Wet drilling, a process which would have held down the dangerous dust, was not seen as a viable alternative by management because it would have slowed down the excavation. Estimates of between 700 and 2,000 of the Hawk's Nest workers died of silicosis, though definitive numbers remain in dispute given record keeping at the time. There was also a lag time between exposure and disease, and a number of the dead African American workers were buried in unmarked graves. By the late 1930s, *Time* and *Newsweek*, among others, had run articles about the Hawk's Nest incident, raising national awareness of the problem and alerting other industries to the danger of silicosis. Still, in out-of-court settlements, Union Carbide managed to obtain the rights to some key records and documents, and despite the litigation escaped relatively unharmed. "Union Carbide successfully remained untouched by legal responsibility for all the tragic deaths and injuries at Gauley Bridge," observe authors David Dembo, Ward Morehouse, and Lucinda Wykle, "even though the company determined the design, selected the contractor..., set the deadline..., and remained responsible

Estimates of between 700 and 2,000 of the Hawk's Nest workers died of silicosis.

Bhopal, 1984

In the 1960s, India had begun to embrace the promise of Green Revolution agriculture, with its reliance on new wheat varieties, heavy fertilization, and chemical pesticide use. In central India at that time, a few miles from Bhopal, a city of about 900,000 people, a new pesticide plant was built. By 1969, a company named Union Carbide India, Ltd. (UCIL)—50.9 percent owned by the Union Carbide Corporation of the United States—began producing a pesticide known as *Sevin*, a carbaryl insecticide, and another, *Temik*, an aldicarb pesticide. In making the pesticides, methyl isocyanate, or MIC, was used as an intermediate chemical. For the first decade or so, the Bhopal plant did not make its own MIC, but instead, imported it from a Carbide sister plant located in Institute, West Virginia. By the late 1970s, however, the Bhopal plant added its own MIC production unit, with engineering and design based on Carbide's West Virginia plant. The MIC produced at the Bhopal plant was stored in two of three 15,000 gallon tanks. One tank was kept empty for reserve storage capacity in the event of an emergency. The tanks were partially buried and equipped with safety relief valves. Normally, during the production process, MIC, a dangerous gas, was vented and passed through a sodium hydroxide scrubber and flare towers to prevent any problems. But in early December 1984, something went wrong. At 11:30 p.m. on December 2, workers at the Bhopal plant, with eyes tearing and burning, informed their supervisor they had detected a gas release. By 12:45 a.m. on December 3, a rapid pressure increase occurred inside one of the MIC storage tanks, which opened the safety relief valve, releasing the dangerous methyl isocyanate into the atmosphere. In all, some 40 tons of the gas would be loosed from the plant, rolling southward on gentle winds heading toward the eastern flank of a sleeping Bhopal.

Twice as heavy as air, methyl isocyanate remains close to the ground as an escaping gas cloud. A highly poisonous gas, capable of reacting violently with many substances, including water and some metals, MIC is also particularly lethal to the eyes and respiratory system. On December 3, as the gas left the plant, immediately ahead were densely-populated squatter settlements close to the plant—including Jayaprakash Nagar, Kazi Camp, Chola Kenchi, and the Railway Colony—some of Bhopal's poorest citizens. Thousands were killed in their sleep or as they fled in terror. One journalist who happened to be at the Nalanda Hotel in the old part of the city, woke about 2:30 a.m. trying to tune in a radio station, but then began choking and having a burning sensation in his eyes. "First, I thought it was a hotel problem. When I went out, I was running for some open space where I could get some relief, but I could get no relief nowhere. When I came out I saw hordes of people moving... That was a ghastly experience. I saw ladies almost undressed, straight out of bed, children clinging... all wailing, weeping, some of them vomiting blood, some falling down... The sky was clear... I didn't smell anything... but people were saying it smelt of rotten almonds." The gas had poured out of the plant for nearly two hours, spreading eight kilometers downwind over the city. Hospitals were overwhelmed in the hours and days that followed. "No one is counting the numbers any longer," reported chemical engineer and journalist Praful Bidwai at the Hamidia Hospital three days later. "People are dying like flies. They are brought in, their chests heaving violently, their limbs trembling, their eyes blinking from the photophobia. It will kill them in a few hours, more usually minutes." Although the numbers are still in dispute, more than 3,000 people were killed at Bhopal within a few days of the catastrophe, with another 2,000 or more dying over the next few years. At least 100,000 suffered some injury or impairment from the incident, and as many as 578,000 were somehow adversely affected. Bhopal remains the worst industrial accident in history.

Sources: U.S. Chemical Safety and Hazard Investigation Board, "Bhopal Disaster Spurs U.S. Industry, Legislative Action," Electronic Reading Room, *www.chemsafety.org*, September 1999; Dhiren Bhagat, "A Night in Hell," *Sunday Observer*, reprinted in *Bhopal: Industrial Genocide?* Arena Press, March 1985, p. 23, and "The Poisoned City—Diary From Bhopal," Praful Bidwai, both cited by Russell Mokhiber in *Corporate Crime and Violence*, San Francisco: Sierra Club Books, 1988; Amy Waldman, "Bhopal Seethes, Pained and Poor 18 years Later," *New York Times*, September 21, 2002, p. A-3.

for inspection." In the view of these authors, Carbide was, or should have been, aware of the hazards of silicosis, which were well documented in Britain and the United States at the time, with Canada then taking measures to protect its own workers. The settlements and evasion of responsibility at Hawk's Nest, say Dembo et al., presaged similar maneuvering by Carbide at Bhopal.[5]

Notorious Polluter

By the 1950s, Union Carbide had also developed something of a reputation as a flagrant and recalcitrant polluter. The New Jersey Department of Health ordered the company to cease polluting the Raritan River in 1953.[6] "In the late 1960s and early 1970s," observe Milt Moskowitz, Michael Katz, and Robert Levering in *Everybody's Business*, "Union Carbide was virtually Environmental Enemy number 1. Environmentalists called the company's Alloy, West Virginia iron-alloy plant 'the smokiest factory in the world'..."[7] In 1978, it was learned that *Temik*, a water-soluble Union Carbide pesticide with the active ingredient aldicarb, was contaminating Long Island's single-source underground aquifer. Originally, *Temik* was approved for use on cotton in 1970 based on research paid for by Union Carbide that showed the pesticide would not pose a significant threat to human health. *Temik*'s use soon expanded to other crops, including citrus and Long Island potatoes. When groundwater contamination occurred there, Union Carbide claimed it was due to unique environmental factors. But by 1979, it was also found in the groundwater of Aroostook County, Maine, another potato-growing area. By

Bhopal headlines, past and present. Today, the 20-year-old catastrophe continues to make headlines, and its victims continue to have health problems.

the mid-1980s, it was found contaminating water in a dozen other states, from Rhode Island to Florida. Cornell researchers demonstrated that *Temik* could persist in groundwater for up to 100 years. The chemical was also found to be a neurotoxin, a factor in miscarriages, and an immunological suppressant in lab mice exposed at 1 ppb in water. A metabolite of aldicarb was also found to damage DNA under certain conditions. Carbide initially responded with selective withdrawals of the chemical, new labeling restrictions, and a public relations campaign.[8]

More than 20,000 people were evacuated near Carbide's Taft, Louisiana plant in 1982 after highly toxic acrolein gas spread through the area.

Prior to Bhopal, Carbide had chemical plant incidents in the United States. In December 1982, two huge tanks containing the chemical acrolein exploded at Union Carbide's Taft, Louisiana plant, blowing out windows for a mile and a half and rattling homes as far as seven miles away. More than 20,000 people were evacuated after the highly toxic acrolein gas spread through the area. Claims were later filed against the company for property damage and adverse health effects. A year earlier in West Virginia, Carbide was fined $50,000 for spilling over 25,0000 gallons of propylene oxide, a cancer-causing chemical, into the Kanawha River. In the same year, 402 employees in Union Carbide's *Eveready* battery factory in Indonesia were suffering from kidney diseases due to exposure to mercury. In Texas, Carbide's Texas City plant experienced 14 major upsets during the first four months of 1984, upsets which released significant quantities of toxic materials to the atmosphere—one of the worst performances among chemical companies then tracked by the Texas Air Control Board.[9]

Carbide's Workplace

Union Carbide's record on worker health and safety in the 1970s and 1980s was not always the best either. In 1976, a half dozen vinyl chloride workers at Carbide's plant in south Charleston, West Virginia were found to have rare cases of angiosarcoma. Workers at this plant also exhibited four times the expected rate of leukemia and twice the expected rate of brain cancer. When the workers pursued damages in court, Carbide fought them. In 1977, more than 100 Carbide workers in Massachusetts and Maryland were found to have bladder abnormalities, cancer, and other health problems associated with exposure to the catalyst ESN, produced by Carbide for use in making urethane foam products. OSHA issued a warning on the chemical and the state of California banned it. Carbide's customers soon stopped ordering it and the company eventually withdrew the product from the market. In the late 1970s, Carbide became the leading opponent of strict workplace exposure limits being proposed for ethylene oxide, a major U.S. industrial chemical, then among the 25 highest in production volume. At the time, Carbide was the largest ethylene oxide producer and was also a principal in the Ethylene Oxide Industry Council, which fought the proposed standard and key health studies through the 1980s. However, there was evidence then linking ethylene oxide exposure to cancer, chromosome damage, miscarriages, and possible testicular atrophy. In 1985, workers at the company's Woodbine, Georgia plant were being routinely exposed to oxides of nitrogen, chromium fumes, and high levels of methylene chloride, a widely-used industrial solvent and carcinogen. The workers were being exposed, in part, in the words of one report, because of "poor engineering design and lack of workplace safety controls."[10]

Help from the unions was not an option for most Carbide workers, since less than 20 percent of them were unionized by the mid-1980s. Although not blatantly anti-union, the company would not usually agree to coordinated bargaining, meeting with locals but refusing to recognize union internationals as bargaining agents. In the years immediately following the Bhopal incident, however, Carbide's practices were brought under the spotlight due in part to its poor performance at one plant—Institute, West Virginia.

Institute, West Virginia

At the Institute complex, Carbide produced methyl isocyanate (MIC), the gas that had savaged Bhopal. Carbide officials, however—especially in the aftermath of Bhopal—had promised to focus on safety and leave no stone unturned. Yet federal investigators soon found serious problems at Institute—namely, 190 chemical leaks from the MIC plant in a five-year period. Still, company Chairman Warren Anderson assured the public that Carbide had gone over the complex "with a fine tooth comb" and had determined the plant was "safe to run." The company poured millions into the Institute plant to demonstrate its commitment to safety. But at the very place where the company was making its supposed best effort, another mishap occurred.

On August 11, 1985, the plant released a toxic gas cloud consisting of aldicarb oxime, a chemical used to make the pesticide *Temik*, and methylene chloride, a known neurotoxin and suspected animal carcinogen. At least 135 people were sickened by the gas and taken to local hospitals in what was then the worst chemical leak in Institute's history. The incident soon had the attention of Congress and the nation. "Here we had a company that could not operate in a safe fashion even with a public microscope on it," said U.S. Senator Frank R. Lautenberg (D-NJ). "It casts doubt on the competence and credibility of the whole industry."[11] OSHA found worker health and safety violations at Institute as well. In July 1987, Carbide agreed to pay penalties of $408,500 to settle charges that the company committed hundreds of willful violations of federal worker health and safety rules, many regarding record keeping violations but some involving direct worker threats, such as exposure to deadly phosgene.[12] By the late 1980s, it was not clear that Carbide was making much progress with chemical safety at Institute. It reported, for example, releasing 4,000 pounds more methyl isocyanate into the community in 1988 compared to what it released in 1987.

Federal investigators found there had been 190 chemical leaks from the MIC plant at Institute in a five-year period.

Back in Washington, meanwhile, Congress was spurred to action, particularly in the aftermath of Bhopal and the possibility that similar incidents could occur in the United States, evidenced by Carbide's performance in West Virginia. The 1986 Emergency Planning and Community Right to Know Act was adopted, establishing the Toxic Release Inventory, which improved citizen access to hazardous material information and helped facilitate state and local emergency planning. Chemical plant safety and toxic release questions remained prominent as Congress considered the Clean Air Act Amendments of 1990. One EPA analysis considered during that debate compared the danger of U.S. chemical incidents occurring in the early to mid-1980s to the Bhopal incident. Seventeen U.S. incidents had occurred, the study found, releasing sufficient volumes of chemicals and toxicity, that the potential consequences, with the right set of conditions, could have been *more severe* than in Bhopal. Based on this information and other considerations, more emphasis was placed on chemical plant safety at EPA and OSHA, and new programs were adopted.* The Clean Air Act also established the independent U.S. Chemical Safety and Hazard Investigation Board.[13]

Back in Bhopal**

Back in India, meanwhile, the federal government in 1986 had passed the Bhopal Gas Leak Disaster Act, which made the Indian government the representative for all individuals seeking compensation for damages from

---

*EPA was authorized to develop its Risk Management Program Rule for protection of the public, and OSHA to develop its Process Safety Management Standard to protect workers, with both agencies sharing a responsibility for overseeing the development of accident prevention plans.

**The summary of events recounted here is limited and abbreviated due to space limitations; for more detail see any number of other sources referenced here or online, including the archives of the *Wall Street Journal*, *New York Times*, or activist websites such as *www.bhopal.net*.

the incident. By this time, a slew of court actions had been filed. In fact, when the cases were combined in the U.S. court system, there were approximately 145 actions involving 200,000 plaintiffs. In 1986, the U.S. District Court of Southern New York found in favor of Union Carbide, and directed that the trial be moved to India. As the trial date approached, India contended that Union Carbide was actively involved in finalizing the Bhopal plant's design, and that the company had intentionally reduced or eliminated safety items. Union Carbide was

Some members of Congress questioned the "competence and credibility of the whole industry."

also charged with neglecting oversight and responsibility at the plant, including plant maintenance. Carbide appeared to have neglected recommendations of its own internal audits at the Bhopal plant. But the company, for its part, disputed these claims, and countered that the government of India had prohibited Carbide's active participation in the final plant design. Carbide also asserted it had provided the appropriate training, and charged that the Indian subsidiary, UCIL, was responsible for safety and maintenance, with the government of India as its regulator. Finally, Carbide's investigation had concluded that the MIC storage tank at the heart of the incident was sabotaged, a finding hotly disputed by many others. The case ended in 1989 when the Supreme Court of India authorized Union Carbide and UCIL to pay the agreed-upon sum of $470 million in damages to the government of India.[14] The settlement was challenged in 1990 and 1991, with some advocating pursuit of the $3 billion in damages that had been originally proposed.[15] However, the Indian courts subsequently upheld the civil settlement, but allowed the criminal case to be reopened. The criminal case remains open today.

Back in the United States, through the late 1980s and early 1990s, Union Carbide and its CEO at the time, Robert Kennedy, became very visible players in the move to embrace Responsible Care, the chemical industry's program of self-initiated environmental, health and safety improvement. But the same old Union Carbide seemed to rise from the ashes of the past. On March 12, 1991, for example, an explosion and fire at Union Carbide's Seadrift, Texas plant killed one worker, injured 32 others, and came within minutes of killing hundreds. An OSHA document revealed that Union Carbide's environment, health and safety staff had conducted seven audits at Seadrift over a period of 20 years, at least three of which had warned explicitly of dangers which contributed to the disaster. Four of the audits were conducted after the Bhopal disaster and after Union Carbide's push for Responsible Care. But Union Carbide failed to act on its own EHS staff's recommendations or in accordance with its own Responsible Care rhetoric. Carbide agreed to pay OSHA a $1.5 million fine in November 1992 to settle alleged federal safety violations. OSHA had alleged that Carbide operated the Seadrift plant in a manner that created "the potential for catastrophic explosion involving ethylene oxide—a highly reactive chemical."[16] In India, Carbide sold its interest in the Bhopal plant in 1994. Bhopal victims and activists, meanwhile, continued pursuing Carbide for damages and medical expenses through the 1990s, including filing legal actions in the United States.

Dow Acquires Carbide

Then, in August 1999, Dow Chemical announced it would spend $9.3 billion to acquire Union Carbide, making Dow the world's No. 2 chemical company. The new Dow-Union Carbide company would have $24 billion in annual sales with operations in 168 countries. Dow called the deal a strategic business decision. In early February 2001, when Dow consummated the merger after review by the Federal Trade Commission, the New York Stock Exchange building was wrapped with a giant banner displaying the Dow Diamond. The Carbide deal, after all, was a major event, putting Dow at the top of the world's chemical giants—on the same level as DuPont. "The new Dow is on its way to a totally new level of performance," crowed Michael Parker on page one of a special commemorative magazine Dow published on the merger, touting its upside possibilities.[17] Yet others had wondered why Dow would willingly take on a company with so much unresolved liability, including Bhopal and asbestos.

"When you make an acquisition, you get some pleasant surprises and you get some downside," said Dow CEO William Stavropoulos when asked those questions by a *Midland Daily News* reporter in March 2003. "With Carbide, we got a tremendous upside on the Kuwait and Malaysia operations"— where cheap energy is the prize. "In this world where energy is very expensive," Stavropoulos explained, "we have a source of low-cost energy in Kuwait and Malaysia which we can grow off of."[18] As for Bhopal, Dow claimed all along that the matter was resolved by the Indian courts, and that Dow, at any rate, had insulated itself from Carbide's Bhopal liabilities by virtue of how it structured the acquisition. As for asbestos, Dow has said it would be protected through insurance and/or Congressional action. Dow obviously knew about the potential downsides at Carbide when it first calculated the acquisition, and no doubt believed it could minimize those through a combination of good lawyering, lobbying, and creative public relations. But Dow may have miscalculated.

India's Central Bureau of Investigation is seeking to name Dow instead of Carbide in the pending criminal proceedings. Dow says it has received no formal indication that the Indian government is following through on this threat, and that it doesn't expect any legal action. Some on Wall Street don't like Dow's gamble, and a few have tried to get a closer look at the company's balance sheet. Says David Romero, a litigation manager at a U.S. secu-

Asbestos Liability

Asbestos, the dust of which has long been tied to health problems including lung disease and lung cancer, has been a major problem and huge potential liability for Union Carbide—and now, Dow Chemical. Early recognition of the lung disease asbestosis as an industrial health problem dates to the late 1890s, and to U.K. government reports in the early 1900s. By 1930, asbestosis lung disease was reported in the United States, and by the mid-1930s, working with asbestos was a widely recognized occupational threat. Observes Barry Castleman in his book, *Asbestos: Medical and Legal Aspects*: "Severe disease had occurred even among people who had worked for less than one year with asbestos. It was known that the disease process would not become evident for the first few years of exposure no matter how intense the exposure was. Yet slowly but surely, the lung scarring would develop as the mineral fibers accumulated in the lungs... [B]y the time the disease became evident, cessation of exposure could not halt the inexorable progress of the disease caused by the durable fibers already trapped in the lung tissues." Asbestosis victims also become highly vulnerable to respiratory infections.

Union Carbide owned and operated asbestos mines in California from 1963 to 1985, producing a short-fiber type asbestos used as a filler and reinforcing and thickening agent in plastics, paints, and drywall compounds. In the 1960s, British dockworkers in Liverpool and London refused to handle imported sacks of asbestos, as union officials and government inspectors sought assurances from Carbide that its materials would not endanger workers. Back at corporate headquarters in New York in 1966 and 1967, Union Carbide issued internal reports and memos on asbestos. One explained: "...we are not entitled under any circumstances to state that our material is not a health hazard...," and "...it must surely be our duty to caution [the customer] and point out means whereby he can hold the asbestos air float concentration to a minimum." By June 1968, Union Carbide asbestos sacks did have warning labels, which some believe could have appeared earlier.

Carbide, however, was generally acquainted with the problems emerging around asbestos well before the 1960s. "Even before the purchase of the asbestos mines," says Barry Castleman, "Union Carbide was aware that asbestos dust was hazardous...." Carbide had conducted tests on other companies' insulation products to determine exposures levels. It also had representatives on the boards of both the National Safety Council in the 1930s and the Industrial Hygiene Foundation in the 1940s, with company representatives also attending scientific meetings in the early 1950s where asbestosis and cancer were discussed repeatedly. Still, in the 1970s, after medical experts warned of high levels of airborne asbestos due to the mixing, sanding, and sweeping of drywall spackling material, Carbide moved to fight asbestos restrictions. As consumer groups and others pushed to ban asbestos in products,* Carbide led the industrial opposition, maintaining as it did in late 1977, that consumer exposure to asbestos did not entail an "unreasonable risk." Over the years, however, it soon became clear that many producers of asbestos and asbestos products had major liability on their hands, and a number of firms went into bankruptcy protection. Union Carbide had potential asbestos liability in the billions. That baggage, however, soon became Dow's.

In January 2002, it appeared that Dow might accept Carbide's asbestos liabilities when it settled a Texas asbestos lawsuit previously filed against Carbide. Dow's stock, however, took a beating on the news, falling 30 percent and wiping out $7 billion worth of corporate equity. But a course correction ensued at Dow, with William Stavropoulos coming back in as CEO, assuring nervous investors that insurance would cover the problem. But just in case things went bad, Dow maneuvered to be ready to throw Carbide into bankruptcy if need be, retaining, however, first claim to Carbide's assets should that scenario unfold. On the litigation front too, Dow is prepared for a Dow-Corning/silicone implants-styled siege, sending experienced mass-tort lawyers to help Carbide with its legal strategy. Dow is also hoping—and lobbying—for an asbestos bail-out bill in Congress, working on its own and through a trade group called the Asbestos Study Group that is spending heavily on lobbying. Among other things, the companies want to change the way asbestos lawsuits are handled, most hoping to end them entirely in favor of an industry- and insurer-supported trust fund to pay claims. In November 2003, Carbide lost an appeal to the West Virginia Supreme Court of a jury-verdict case that found the company had exposed workers to asbestos at six plants.

Sources: Barry Castelman, *Asbestos: Medical and Legal Aspects...* pp. 628–29; Phyllis Berman, "Dow Chemical Hits The Trenches," *Forbes*, October 1, 2003; and Brody Mullins, "Asbestos Sparks Big Spending," *Roll Call*, November 18, 2003; and Business News, *Washington Post*, November 4, 2003, p. E-2.

*One of the uses for asbestos that Carbide entertained in the mid-1960s was the possibility of using the material in a sanitary tampon. Southalls Paper Mills, one of Carbide's customers, made such an inquiry in 1966, but it appears the product was never developed. Yet as recently as February 2001, that use is still identified as a possibility in a description of "materials, devices and component fillers" used in connection with a Dow Chemical patent for certain vinyl-derived polymers and fibers. "The fibers of the present invention," explains Dow in the patent abstract, "could have applications such as carpet fibers, elastic fibers, doll hair, personal/feminine hygiene applications, diapers, athletic sportswear, wrinkle free and form-fitting apparel, conductive fibers, upholstery, and medical applications, including but not restricted to, bandages, gamma sterilizable non-woven fibers." See U.S. Patent No. US 6,190,768 B-1,"Fibers Made From a- Olefin/Vinyl or Vinylidene Aromatic and/or Hindered Cycloaliphatic or Aliphatic Vinyl or Vinylidene Interpolymers," Turley et al., assigned to the Dow Chemical Co.

rities law firm that brought an unsuccessful suit challenging the accuracy Dow's liability disclosures: "Union Carbide had simply left India. But Dow is an active presence in the country." Dow has joint ventures there that make adhesives and sealants, as well as agricultural chemicals.

Dow may have also underestimated the tenacity of the Bhopal victims and their allies. Hundreds of U.S. activists, concerned about the continuing plight of Bhopal's victims, are now engaged in the global Bhopal campaign effort. And that campaign is expanding to college campuses, unions, social and religious investors, even involving some members of the U.S. Congress. Bhopal activists, from India and elsewhere, attended Dow's annual shareholders meeting in Midland in 2003, as they have in other years since Dow announced the Carbide acquisition. They come to publicly ask Dow officials and its stockholders to take responsibility for the Bhopal liability. First and foremost, the activists want Dow to face up to longstanding criminal charges against Carbide in India. They also want the company to arrange for long-term medical rehabilitation and monitoring of Bhopal victims. And they want economic rehabilitation and social support for survivors' children, and a clean-up of the toxic wastes and contaminated groundwater still festering at Carbide's old factory site.

Dow may have underestimated the tenacity of the Bhopal victims and their allies.

One major network of Bhopal activists, the International Coalition for Justice in Bhopal (ICJB), has continued to push Dow on multiple fronts since the first announcement of the Dow-Carbide merger. A delegation of Bhopal survivors and ICJB activists took their fight to a number of U.S. cities in the spring of 2003, including New York, Washington, and Houston. Among the protestors were Rashida Bee, 46, and Champa Devi Shukla, 50—two survivors of the Bhopal disaster. Bee lost nine members of her family to the gases and suffers from semi-blindness, breathing difficulties, and other chemical-related illnesses. Shukla and her husband also suffer Bhopal-related health effects. Bee and Shukla also have grandchildren with birth defects common to babies born to gas-affected parents. "If Dow were a truly responsible company, it would have settled the Bhopal issue the day they acquired Union Carbide," said Bee in May 2003 while protesting in New York City.[19] Bee and Shukla, along with longtime Bhopal activist Satinath Sarangi, came to the United States for a 40-day tour of communities affected by Dow, and to raise awareness about Dow and Bhopal.

But the campaign to raise the "full costs" of Dow's Union Carbide acquisition—and bring the company to account for these responsibilities—continues to grow beyond the Indian activists. In August 2003, the Paper, Allied-Industrial, Chemical & Energy Workers International Union (PACE) unanimously passed a resolution on Dow and Bhopal at the union's constitutional convention. The resolution states that just as Dow accepted Carbide's asbestos liabilities in Texas, Dow should also accept the liabilities in Bhopal. The PACE resolution also calls upon the government of India to include Dow in the ongoing criminal case in Bhopal.[20] In October 2003, U.S. Congressman Frank Pallone (D-NJ) and eight other members of Congress filed an amicus brief on behalf of about 20,000 victims of the 1984 Bhopal disaster. The brief, initiated by Pallone—who is co-founder of the Congressional Caucus on India and Indian Americans—came in response to a March 2003 decision by a U.S. District Judge in New York who dismissed all claims against Dow Chemical. Bhopal victims have appealed the judge's ruling. Pallone and his colleagues sent a 23-page brief in the appeal case. It urges the court to hold Dow Chemical responsible. "There is strong support in Congress for holding those responsible for this horrific tragedy accountable for their actions," said Pallone. "It is unacceptable to allow an American company not only the opportunity to exploit international borders and legal jurisdictions, but also the ability to evade civil and criminal liability for environmental pollution and abuses committed overseas."[21]

> **"It is unacceptable to allow an American company...to evade civil and criminal liability for environmental pollution and abuses committed overseas."**
>
> Court brief on behalf of Bhopal victims from nine members of U.S. Congress

In 2004, the 20th anniversary of the Bhopal tragedy, activists promise a year-long roster of actions and continuing protests aimed at Dow Chemical. The planning was well underway by mid-January 2004, as a gathering of more than 25 representatives from various organizations met in Bhopal. They were devising collective strategies to press Dow globally on a range of toxic issues, not just Bhopal. More organizing occurred in late January 2004 at the World Social Forum meeting in Mumbai, India, attended by thousands of activists, some of whom picketed Dow's Mumbai headquarters building. "This is just the beginning of a globally-coordinated fight to expose the toxic skeletons in Dow Chemical's closet...," said the ICJB's Satinath Sarangi, one of the leaders in the Dow campaign, promising to make the fight on a broader palate of issues and with a wider coalition of allies.[22]

With Union Carbide, Dow just might have gotten more than it bargained for.

21.
No Trespassing

If somebody comes onto my land, it's trespassing, but companies can put 85 toxic substances into my body without my permission and tell me there is nothing I can do about it. That can't be right.

Charlotte Brody, Health Care Without Harm[1]

There is no kind definition for the word *trespass*. As a noun, trespass is defined as an encroachment, intrusion, or violation. As a verb, to trespass is to offend, intrude, break into, or generally thrust oneself onto persons or places without permission. In the context of passing beyond limits or boundaries, to trespass is to overstep, to transgress—even to sin or violate moral law. And trespass also means breaking the law or committing a crime, most commonly, a wrongful interference with held property. Trespass, in fact, is a long-standing legal concept, dating to 13th century English common law.

Initially, the law of trespass served as a remedy for injuries to property. In time, trespass was also applied to injuries of persons involving force, such as assault and battery, and became a basis for the law of torts in common-law countries. In present-day usage, however, the term trespass is usually applied to unlawful entry onto private property. If a trespasser refuses a request to leave the premises in question, he may be removed by force. In the United States, hunters and property owners in many states are quite familiar with the bright yellow or red-lettered "no trespassing" signs that abound during hunting season. A violation of such "posted" property by hunters, recreationists, hikers, snowmobilers, etc., is a well-understood concept by most land users, even young children in many rural areas.

At another level, however, trespass has been evolving as a further basis for tort law, and has been used in "toxic trespass" cases. Most of these deal with intrusions of toxic material onto land, as in the aerial spraying of pesticides that damage neighboring property. Some have involved trespass by water, as in the case of a quarry operator found liable in trespass when his quarry operation discharged plumes of silt through a spring that fouled another property owner's pond.[2] In Illinois, a gas station owner was also found liable in trespass after petroleum spilled from his location contaminating an adjoining property.[3] One important 1959 case of toxic trespass is

Martin v. Reynolds Metals Co., in which the court found that fluoride compounds drifting from the Reynolds plant onto a neighbor's property constituted a trespass and awarded the neighbor damages for the reduction in the grazing value of his land. "Although the fluoride compounds were invisible to the naked eye," observes Michael Axline of the University of Oregon School of Law, "the court found the visibility or size of an intruding object to be an artificial distinction, and instead focused on the potential for damage caused by the compounds." Even though relatively few jurisdictions have followed the case, says Axline, "its logic has been uniformly recognized as sound," and it may be only a matter of time before more jurisdictions adopt similar reasoning.[4]

The toxic trespass that has been the subject of this book is in this latter realm of invisible substances crossing boundary lines to do damage. Such transgressions involve both invisible forms of pollution into stream and sky, and the microscopic poisons and mutagens seeping into cells and DNA. This latter trespass, by the errant chemistry of Dow and others, is largely unaccounted for—trespass for which there is huge and continuing cost and consequence; trespass that must be compensated for and ended.

Dow's Trespass

Dow Chemical has been polluting property and poisoning people for nearly a century, locally and globally—trespassing on workers, consumers, communities, and innocent bystanders; on wildlife and wild places; on the global biota and the global genome. Granted, these transgressions were not intentional—at least not initially, as young Herbert Dow pursued his craft in the 1890s. Yet, through the years, as the commercial and legal apparatus of the modern chemical industry evolved, as more was learned about toxic and chemical intrusion, and as businesses like Dow's embedded, rationalized, and defended their practice, the trespass became more intentional and knowing. For the trespass by Dow finds its basis in the harm of chemical molecules crossing into living cells; commercial creations that touch off a cancer, cause a mutation, alter hormonal messaging, or harm reproduction. Such consequence is owed, in part, to the intentional design of chemical molecules to do certain directed things for monetary return—to kill pests, to be durable, to dissolve grease and grime, and mostly, to last for a long time with those traits; i.e., to be persistently toxic. Knowledge of these commercially-valuable and aggressive traits has been around for decades; and so has knowledge about their untoward effects on much of biology.

Lawyers, legislatures, and courts have labored long and hard to design institutional mechanisms for dealing with the explosion of synthetic chemicals in society and the wrongs they have caused. Regulations abound, and all the parties involved seem comfortable with the process that has evolved—save victims and unrepresented life. This regulatory system, supposedly in place to protect public health, is ponderous and slow; essentially a generation behind the carnage. And the burden of proof is wrong; placed on the victims instead of the perpetrators. Chemicals are innocent until proven guilty, even though most have never run a full gauntlet of safety tests. For the last 40 years or more, this process has played out in protracted chemical-by-chemical battles that typically favor "reasonable" phase-out timetables that mostly give businesses more years of marketing time. Public and environmental health are marginally protected, at best. This is not a fair or reasonable system. A better solution is available now.

Dow Chemical, for starters, must end its toxic trespass by disengaging from the production of those chemicals, chemical products, and chemical processes that jeopardize public health. This means the POPs and the PBTs—persistent organic pollutants, and the persistent, bioaccumulative toxic substances. It also means those that cause cancer, birth

Dow Chemical must end its toxic trespass.

defects, and/or genetic damage, and those that disrupt hormonal messaging, cause developmental changes, or affect intelligence. This obviously, is a tall order for any chemical company. It means nothing short of Dow revamping its corporate culture and strategic business plan; adopting a Hippocratic Oath-styled outlook to do no harm; and not to let loose any chemical in the world until all of its toxicological effects have been thoroughly investigated and aired publicly. This will not likely happen voluntarily by Dow's hand, as Dow executives and attorneys will continue to defend their business and practice as they always have. Rather, changing Dow, and the chemical industry, will likely come from the outside.

Gathering Storm

There is a storm building around the Dow Chemical Company; a gathering storm of aggrieved, injured, and angry parties—those who are fighting for harms already done, as well as those tired of chemical intrusion, whether by workplace exposure, factory emissions, product leaching, or toxic legacy. In too many instances, "Dow brand" toxic material has been invasive, harmful, and life-altering. The aggrieved and injured include Dow neighbors from Texas and Louisiana, and fourth generation Vietnamese children suffering Agent Orange's continuing harms. They are joining with labor, investors, lawyers, religious organizations, and everyday moms and dads to make common cause. They are aiming at Dow for specific and continuing harms, but also as corporate symbol and industry surrogate for a process that continues to invent and release synthetic chemicals that are dangerous and archaic. The battle with Dow will be joined on many fronts, by activists and everyday people, who will use whatever tools and avenues of appeal are available—legal, economic, or persuasive.

But on one front there will be more and better information; new knowledge about toxic "body burden"—the hundreds of chemicals seeping into people's blood and body tissue. Although not well understood today, the body burden concept is certain to change people's thinking about toxic chemicals. "In general the public is more aware of chemicals found in the fish they consume or the data from toxic release inventories than they know about the chemicals found in their own bodies," write public health activists Sharyle Patton and Gary Cohen. "But there is a deep psychological significance in knowing that the tissues of one's body are being used as a

> **"There is a deep psychological significance in knowing that the tissues of one's body are being used as a chemical storage site."**

chemical storage site."[5] Indeed, as body burden surveys become more commonplace, and more people realize that their personal space, and that of their children, has been violated by chemical manufacturers like Dow, the politics of public health in the toxic chemicals arena will likely escalate to a new and more powerful level.

And there is another dimension as well. Again, Sharyle Patton and Gary Cohen explain: "Internationally, several United Nations conventions support the human right to freedom from chemical contamination. . . . [T]he United Nations Human Rights Commission has recognized the right to a non-polluted environment as a basic human right. The Convention on the Rights of a Child protect the child's right to integrity of person and right to the highest possible standard of mental and physical health. By anyone's definition of basic human rights, the fact that infants are starting life with a body burden of chemicals represents a gross violation of human rights. . . ."[6]

"Massive Experiment"

One of the results of the Nuremberg Trials after World War II was a universal agreement that civilized nations should not engage in chemical experimentation on humans, even in times of war. "Yet for the last sixty years," argue Patton and Cohen, "the chemical industry has engaged in a massive chemical experiment on the world's human population and the entire web of life. No one has ever given their consent for this experiment. Most people don't even know it is happening."[7]

Dow Chemical is a main player in this experiment; the world's largest manufacturer of some of the most troubling compounds now used in commerce. But Dow is not the kind of company that yields easily. Dow has already had a number of warning shots fired across its bow—from the 1960s with napalm and Agent Orange in Vietnam, through the 1970s with 2,4,5-T and other pesticides, the 1980s with its dioxin-harms cover-up, the 1990s with industrial pollution and the silicone fiasco, to the current battles over dioxin, asbestos, and Bhopal. After each crisis, Dow typically assures the public it has learned a lesson; a new corporate ethic is installed, a new vice president is named, and always, a pledge to do better. But despite the principles, pledges, and new vice presidents, the toxic revelations keep coming, the body burden grows, and the toxic trespass continues. The result, for the most part, is business as usual. But change is coming.

"Billable" Legacy

Corporations like Dow derive their right to operate from the public; their charter to do business is a publicly-given grant of power. Such privileges can and should be redrawn to more adequately reflect expected corporate responsibilities. Revocations should be in order for violations of assumed public goods, public health among them. Within the marketplace as well, shareholders and investment analysts need to adopt more accurate forms of accounting—especially for costs "externalized" on society by corporate products and production. In Dow's case, for example, there is no **Dow's global liabilities are being added up, and they are coming to court.** present accounting for the corporation's full and complete toxic liability, either from the past or the present. Yet that liability, as some observers see it, may soon become an avalanche.

Dow's "billable toxic legacy" is substantial, though not yet acknowledged by Dow. But the adding machines are working, and the liabilities are being tabulated. They are being added up in Vietnam, in New Zealand, and in Brazoria County, Texas. They are found in Bhopal, India; in Plaquemine, Louisiana, and in Brazil, Germany, California, Saskatchewan, South Africa, and Midland, Michigan. All over the globe, in fact, wherever Dow operates, the legacy of harm is being collected and the accountants are busy. Asbestos, dioxins, 2,4,5-T, 2,4-D, chlorpyrifos, perchloroethylene, hexachlorobutadiene, bisphenol-A, vinyl chloride, silicone, picloram. These are the chemicals, with their full costs, that are coming to court.

Wall Street analysts would do well to revise their forecasts on Dow—especially those that look down the road beyond the next quarter or so. For Dow is the lightning rod in a new kind of accountability that is coming to all harmful forms of chemical commerce. People and planet are moving to protect their biological and genetic property. They will no longer tolerate poison in the name of business. No more toxic trespass; that is the message.

Endnotes

Introduction

1. Cathy Trost, *Elements of Risk: The Chemical Industry And Its Threat To America*, New York: Times Books, 1984, p. 32.

2. Ibid., p. 292.

3. E. N. Brandt, *Growth Company: Dow Chemical's First Century*, East Lansing: Michigan State University Press, 1997, p. xiii.

Chapter 1 — In The Blood

1. Jim Carlton and Thaddeus Herrick, "Bhopal Haunts Dow Chemical," *Wall Street Journal*, May 8, 2003, p. B-3.

2. See for example, Dow Chemical Co., chart, "Chlorine Chemistry & End-Product Uses," Form No. 614-00061-92, and *www.eurochlor.org/chlorine/generalinfo/tree.htm*.

3. Joe Thornton, *Pandora's Poison*, Cambridge: MIT Press, 2000, pp. 246, 248.

4. Ibid., pp. 2–5.

5. See for example, Anne Platt McGinn, *Why Poison Ourselves? A Precautionary Approach to Synthetic Chemicals*, Worldwatch Paper 153, November 2000, Washington, DC, and other Worldwatch papers on synthetic chemicals.

6. European Commission, Draft White Paper: Strategy For a Future Chemicals Policy, January 18, 2001.

7. Theo Colborn, Dianne Dumanoski, and John Peterson Myers, *Our Stolen Future*, Dutton: New York, 1996, pp. 137–38.

8. Cathy Trost, *Elements of Risk: The Chemical Industry And Its Threat To America*, New York: Times Books, 1984, p. 53.

9. Ibid.

10. Rachel Carson, *Silent Spring*, Fawcett Crest: New York, 1962, p. 17–18.

11. "Carcinogens: A Review of 20 Major Controversies," *New York Times*, March 20, 1984, p. C-12.

12. Jon R. Luoma, "System Failure," *Mother Jones*, July–August 1999, p. 66.

13. See for example, list prepared by World Wildlife Fund U.S., "Chemicals in The Environment Reported to Have Reproductive and/or Endocrine Disrupting Effects," from Theo Colborn (1998), "Endocrine Disruption From Environmental Toxicants," in W. N. Rom (ed.) *Environmental and Occupational Medicine*, third edition, Lippincott-Raven Publishers, Philadelphia, pp. 807–16; F. Brucker-Davis (1998), "Effects of Environmental Synthetic Chemicals on Thyroid Function," *Thyroid* 8(9): pp. 827–56; and Poly Short and Theo Colborn (1999), "Pesticide Use in the U.S. and Policy Implications: A Focus on Herbicides," *Toxicology and Industrial Health* 15 (1–2): pp. 240–75.

14. Colborn et al., *Our Stolen Future*, p. 81.

15. Gwynne Lyons, *Chemical Trespass: A Toxic Legacy*, Executive Summary, A World Wildlife Fund-UK Report, June 1999, p. 2.

16. Marla Cone, "Human Immune Systems May Be Pollution Victims," *Los Angeles Times*, May 13, 1996, p. A-1.

17. Ruth Rosselson, "Poisons In Your Body," *The Mirror* (London), January 11, 2000, p. 38.

18. Andrew C. Revkin, "F.D.A. Considers New Tests For Environmental Effects," *New York Times*, March 14, 2002, p. A-20.

19. "High Mercury, PCB Levels Found in Some Fish," *Washington Post*, October 30, 2003, p. B-3.

20. Lucy Ament and Phil Zahodiakin, "CDC Releases 'Revolutionary' Exposure Study on Toxic Substances," *Pesticide & Toxic Chemical News*, March 26, 2001, p. 1.

21. See full reports and profiles at *www.pbs.org/tradesecrets/*.

22. Centers for Disease Control and Prevention, National Center for Environmental Health, Atlanta, Georgia, *Second National Report on Human Exposure to Environmental Chemicals*, January 31, 2003, at *www.cdc.gov/exposurereport/*.

23. See Environmental Working Group, Washington, DC, "Body Burden: The Pollution in People," at *www.ewg.org*.

24. Michelle Nijhuis, "What's In Your Body's Chemical Cocktail?" *www.salon.com*, December 10, 2003.

Chapter 2 — House of Wonders

1. Don Whitehead, *The Dow Story: The History of The Dow Chemical Company*, New York: McGraw-Hill, 1968, p. 8.

2. Ibid., p. 43.

3. Murray Campbell and Harrison Hatton, *Herbert H. Dow: Pioneer in Creative Chemistry*, New York: Appleton-Century Crofts, Inc., 1951, p. 84.

4. Whitehead, op. cit. note 1, pp. 97–99.

5. Jamie Lincoln Kitman, "The Secret History of Lead," Special Report, *The Nation*, March 20, 2000. There is a rich literature in the industrial history of TEL and its politics and toxicology. See for example, the background sources cited by Kitman and *The Nation* in their series. Other sources on lead's industrial history and its dangers in the workplace include for example: Gerard Colby, *DuPont Dynasty*, Lyle Stuart: Secaucus, NJ, 1984, pp. 246–50; Jack Lewis, "Lead Poisoning: A Historical Perspective," *EPA Journal*, May 1985; Matthew Purdy, "A Failure To Protect Workers From Lead," *The Philadelphia Inquirer*, Sunday, April 14, 1991, p. A-1; Christopher Scanlan, "U.S. Firms Exporting Lead That's Banned Here," *The Philadelphia Inquirer*, Sunday, June 16, 1991, p. D-1; Kenny Bruno, "Not Getting The Lead Out," *Greenpeace*, October/November 1991, pp. 18–19; Jack Doyle, *Hold The Applause!* A Case Study of Corporate Environmentalism at DuPont, (Friends of the Earth, 1991), see Chapter 5, "Heavy Metal," pp. 34–35; Jack Doyle, *Riding The Dragon: Royal Dutch Shell & The Fossil Fire* (Boston: Environmental Health Fund, 2002), "Leaded Gasoline," in Chapter 3, pp. 53–56; and L. Lombardo, "Get the Lead Out," *Progressive*, August 1974.

6. Whitehead, op. cit. note 1, pp. 106–08.

7. Ibid., pp. 119, 147.

8. Campbell and Hatton, op. cit. note 3, p. 152.

9. Cathy Trost, *Elements of Risk: The Chemical Industry and Its Threat to America*, New York: Times Books, 1984, p. 11.

10. Dow Chemical Co., "Dow and Union Carbide Have Merged," *Around Dow*, Special Commemorative Issue (covering Dow and Union Carbide histories), pp. 1–48.

11. Whitehead, op. cit. note 1, p. 228.

12. E. N. Brandt, *Growth Company: Dow Chemical's First Century*, East Lansing: Michigan State University Press, 1997, pp. 290–92.

13. Harold Schachern, "Dow Opens Its House of Wonders," *Detroit Free Press*, July 28, 1950, in Trost, op. cit. note 9, p. 54.

14. Brandt, op. cit. note 12, pp. 296–97.

15. Doug Henze, "Saran Wrap Wasn't Always A Clear Winner At Dow," *Midland Daily News* and *Detroit Free Press*, January 26, 1994; Brandt, op. cit. note 12, pp. 79, 288–90.

16. Brandt, op. cit. note 12, pp. 374, 375, and 479.

17. Ibid., pp. 381–85.

18. Ibid., pp. 393–95.

19. Ibid., pp. 329–30; and Whitehead, op. cit. note 1, p. 274.

20. Brandt, op. cit. note 12, pp. 399–401.

21. Whitehead, op. cit. note 1, p. 255.

22. Ibid., pp. 254–55.

23. Ibid., p. 258.

24. Ibid., p.226.

25. Brandt, op. cit. note 12, pp. 186–91.

26. Whitehead, op. cit. note 1, pp. 208–09, and Brandt, op. cit. note 12, pp. 186–91.

27. Milton Moskowitz, Robert Levering, and Michael Katz, *Everybody's Business: A Field Guide to the 400 Leading Companies in America*, New York: Doubleday-Currency, 1990, p. 183.

28. Susan Okie, "Study Finds Cholesterol Drug Hazard," *Washington Post*," February 17, 1980, p. A-9.

29. Trost, op. cit. note 9, p. 133.

30. Robert Knight, "Dow Chemical Cultivates a New Image," *Washington Post*, September 21, 1986, p. D-7.

31. John Bussey, "Softer Approach: Dow Chemical Tries to Shed Tough Image and Court the Public," *Wall Street Journal*, November 20, 1987, p. A-1.

32. James Schwartz and Mimi Bluestone, "Dow Dons Velvet Gloves in Its New Round of Ads," *Chemical Week*, October 30, 1995, pp. 36–39.

33. Ibid.

34. Ibid.

35. Ibid.

36. Philip Shabecoff, "Dow Stoops to Calm Congress and Public Opinion," *New York Times*, January 2, 1985.

37. Bussey, op. cit. note 31.

38. Ibid.

39. Dow Chemical Co., 1988 brochure, "Dow At A Glance—Celebrating Ninety-Two Years of Quality Performance," Midland, Michigan.

40. Moskowitz, et al., op. cit. note 27, p. 526.

41. Andrew Wood, "Dow: Back To Basics," *Chemical Week*, August 14, 1996, p. 19.

42. Ibid.

43. Dow Chemical Co., "Three Global Customers Give Dow a Simple Performance Review," *Around Dow*, January/February 1997, p. 4.

44. Paul Wyche and Jim Suhr (*The Saginaw News* and The Associated Press), "Dow Bets Farm on Agroscience," *The Saginaw News*, May 15, 1998.

45. Claudia H. Deutsch, "Dow Chemical Says It Plans to Buy Union Carbide," *The New York Times*, August 5, 1999, p. 1; Martha M. Hamilton, "Chemical Giants Agree to Merger," *Washington Post*, August 5, 1999, p. E-1; and Susan Warren, "Dow Chemical to Acquire

Union Carbide," *Wall Street Journal*, August 5, 1999, p. A-3.

46. *Business Week*, May 29, 2000.

47. Advertisement, Dow Chemical Company, "Today Is A Big Day For Us," *Washington Post*, February 8, 2001, p. A-7.

48. Ibid.

49. Ibid.

50. Chana R. Schoenberger, "Dow Chemical: Weathering The Storm," *Forbes*, January 8, 2001, pp. 114–47.

51. Ellen Licking and Otis Port, "Fields Full of Chemical Factories," *Business Week*, April 3, 2000.

Chapter 3 — Dow Goes to War

1. E. N. Brandt, *Growth Company: Dow Chemical's First Century*, East Lansing: Michigan State University Press, 1997, p. 352.

2. Ibid., pp. 85–93.

3. Ibid., p. 243.

4. Don Whitehead, *The Dow Story: The History of The Dow Chemical Company*, New York: McGraw-Hill, 1968, p. 195.

5. Brandt, op. cit. note 1, p. 242.

6. Ibid., p. 355.

7. Ibid., p. 351.

8. John Bussey, "Softer Approach: Dow Chemical Tries To Shed Tough Image And Court the Public," *Wall Street Journal*, November 20, 1987.

9. These numbers attributed to a 1975 Air Force history of herbicide use in Southeast Asia cited in Ralph Blumenthal, *New York Times*, July 6, 1983.

10. Gale E. Peterson, "The Discovery and Development of 2,4-D," *Agricultural History*, Vol. 41, July 1967, pp. 243–53.

11. D. L. Klingman and G. C. Klingman, "Focus on Herbicides," *Farm Chemicals*, December 1984, pp. 36–37.

12. Rachel Carson, *Silent Spring*, p. 75.

13. Victor Yannacone, Jr., W. Keith Kavenagh, and Margie T. Searcy, "Dioxin—Molecule of Death," *Trial*, February 1982, cited in Cathy Trost, *Elements of Risk: The Chemical Industry And Its Threat To America*, New York: Times Books, 1984, p. 75.

14. Unsealed court files, "Agent Orange," consolidated product liability litigation, U.S. District Court for the Eastern District of New York, cited in Trost, op. cit. note 13, p. 75.

15. Peter Sills, correspondence to Jack Doyle, December 18, 2003.

16. Thomas Whitesides, *The Pendulum and The Toxic Cloud: The Course of Dioxin Contamination*, New Haven: Yale University Press, 1977, p. 5.

17. Carol Van Strum, *A Bitter Fog: Herbicides and Human Rights*, San Francisco: Sierra Club Books, 1983, p. 69; Trost, op. cit. note 13, p. 117, and Sills, op. cit. note 15.

18. Trost, op. cit. note 13, pp. 116–17.

19. Ibid., p. 118–19.

20. Brandt, op. cit. note 1, p. 363.

21. Trost, op. cit. note 13, p. 150–51.

22. Lewis Regenstein, *America The Poisoned*, Washington: Acropolis Books, 1982, p. 61.

23. Whitesides, op. cit. note 16, p. 10.

24. Ibid., p. 10.

25. Ibid., pp. 12–13.

26. Ibid., p. 13.

27. Regenstein, op. cit. note 22, p. 68.

28. Deborah Baldwin, "The War Comes Home," *Environmental Action*, April 1980, p. 3.

29. Ibid.

30. Regenstein, op. cit. note 22, p. 53, and Van Strum, op. cit. note 17, pp. 148–78.

31. Regenstein, op. cit. note 22, p. 53.

32. WGBH-TV, Boston, Massachusetts, "Plague on Our Children," *Nova*, 1979.

33. Baldwin, op. cit. note 28.

34. Ibid.

35. Joanne Omang, "EPA and Dow Negotiating Settlement on Herbicide," *Washington Post*, April 11, 1981, p. A-4.

36. Brandt, op. cit. note 1, pp. 364–65.

37. Margot Hornblower, "A Sinister Drama of Agent Orange Opens In Congress," *Washington Post*, June 27, 1979.

38. Brandt, op. cit. note 1, pp. 364–66.

39. Laura Akgulian, "The Agent Orange Trials," *Multinational Monitor*, July/August 1991, pp. 20–23.

40. Mary Lou Vanest and Associated Press, "Agent Orange Possibly Linked to Birth Defect," *Midland Daily News*, March 14, 1996, p. A-1.

41. Charles Lane, "Supreme Court Allows Agent Orange Suit," *Washington Post*, June 10, 2003, p. A-6, and Associated Press, "High Court Deadlocks on Agent Orange Case," *New York Times*, June 9, 2003.

42. "Leukemia Linked to Herbicide Used During Vietnam War," *Washington Post*, January 24, 2003, p. A-9.

43. Laura Wright "New Study Finds Agent Orange Use Was Underestimated," *Scientific American*, April 17, 2003.

Chapter 4 — Dioxin in the Dark

1. David Burnham, "Dow Says U.S. Knew Dioxin Peril of Agent Orange," *New York Times*, May 5, 1983.

2. Ibid.; "Agent Orange Finally Gets Its Day in Court," *Chemical Week*, May 18, 1983, pp. 44–45; and Ralph Blumenthal, "Files Show Dioxin Makers Knew of Hazards," *New York Times*, July 6, 1983, p. 1.

3. Blumenthal, op. cit. note 2, citing a 1975 Harvard University doctoral dissertation by Robert Baughman.

4. See Robert Baughman dissertation in Thomas Whitesides, *The Pendulum and The Toxic Cloud*, pp. 147–48, and Cathy Trost, *Elements of Risk: The Chemical Industry And Its Threat To America*, New York: Times Books, 1984, p. 16.

5. Blumenthal, op. cit. note 3.

6. Ibid.

7. Trost, op. cit. note 4, pp. 79–80.

8. Ibid., p. 84.

9. Ibid., p. 85.

10. Letter cited in Blumenthal, op. cit. note 2.

11. Trost, op. cit. note 4, p. 87.

12. G. E. Lynn, Director of Registration, Bioproducts Department, Dow Chemical Co., Letter to Brigadier General Fred J. Delmor, U.S. Army Munitions Command, U.S. Department of Defense, Army Chemical Center, Maryland, April 22, 1963, pp. 1–2.

13. Letter cited in Blumenthal, op. cit. note 2.

14. Burnham, op. cit. note 1.

15. Ibid.

16. Letter cited in Blumenthal, op. cit. note 2.

17. U.S. Environmental Protection Agency, *Michigan Dioxin Studies*, "Dow Chemical Wastewater Characterization Study," and "Tittabawassee River Sediments and Native Fish," Region 5, Eastern District Office, Westlake OH, EPA-905/4-88-003, June 1986, p. 1.

18. Ibid.

19. D. Hallett and R. Norstrom, Canadian Wildlife Service, "TCDD in Great Lakes Herring Gulls," December 2, 1980.

20. Joe Thornton, *Pandora's Poison*, Cambridge: MIT Press, 2000, pp. 325–26.

21. U.S. House of Representatives, Washington, DC, Hearing Report No. 78, *Dioxin— The Impact on Human Health*, Committee on Science & Technology, Subcommittee on Natural Resources, Agricultural Research & the Environment, 98th Congress, 1st Session, June 30, July 13, 28, 1983.

22. Iver Peterson, "Michigan Residents Seek Investigation of Dioxins," *New York Times*, March 15, 1983.

23. Ward Sinclair, "Dow Planning $3 Million Program to Allay Fears over Dioxin," *Washington Post*, June 2, 1983, p. A-10.

24. Pete Earley, "Dow Abandons Fight for Two Weedkillers," *Washington Post*, October 15, 1983, p. A-8.

25. Carol Van Strum, "The EPA's Long-Buried Evidence of Human Reproductive Hazards," in Lois Marie Gibbs and the Clearinghouse for Hazardous Waste, *Dying From Dioxin*, Boston: South End Press, 1995, pp. 122–25.

26. Carol Van Strum and Paul Merrell, *No Margin of Safety—A Preliminary Report on Dioxin Pollution and the Need for Emergency Action in the Pulp and Paper Industry*, Washington and Toronto: Greenpeace Great Lakes Campaign, Greenpeace U.S.A., August 1987.

27. "A New Brouhaha Over Dioxin," *Chemical Week*, August 17, 1983, pp. 12–13, and editorial, "A Dioxin Runaround At EPA," *Chemical Week*, August 17, 1983, p. 3.

28. Van Strum, op. cit. note 25.

29. Dow Chemical Co., "Dow Forms Global Chlorine and Chlorine Derivatives Issues Team," *Dow Today*, No. 96, September 10, 1990, pp. 1–2.

30. Thornton, op. cit. note 20, p. 19.

31. International Joint Commission on the Great Lakes, 1992.

32. Joe Thornton, Charlie Cray, Bill Walsh, Bonnie Rice, and Katherine Schultz, *Dow Brand Dioxin*, Greenpeace, Washington, DC, May 1996.

33. Enrique Sosa and Larry Washington, "Speak Out on Chlorine, Before It's Too Late," Forum, *Midland Daily News*, February 27, 1994, p. A-5.

34. Thornton, op. cit. note 20, pp. 344–45.

35. CCC/CMA, 1994.

36. Thornton et al., op. cit. note 32.

Chapter 5 — Dowicides

1. CBS-TV, *Eye to Eye with Connie Chung*, "Lethal Weapon? Government Concerned That the Insecticide Dursban May Be Causing Long-term Health Problems in People," Broadcast, January 12, 1995 (transcript version).

2. Dow Chemical Co., "Dow and Union Carbide Have Merged," *Around Dow*, Special Commemorative Issue, Covering Dow and Union Carbide Histories, p. 18.

3. Don Whitehead, *The Dow Story: The History of The Dow Chemical Company*, New York: McGraw-Hill, 1968, p. 99.

4. Cathy Trost, *Elements of Risk: The Chemical Industry and Its Threat to America*, Times Books: New York, 1984, p. 15.

5. The U.S. patents were issued to L. E. Mills and conveyed to Dow Chemical Co. They were, respectively, U.S. Patent No.#1,991,329 (1935) and No. #2,039,434 (1936). The Dow Chemical prospectus was dated December 16, 1936. See Robert W. Baughman, "TCDD and Industrial Accidents," Excerpt from "Tetrachlorodibenzo-p-dioxin in the Environment: High Resolution Mass Spectrometry at the Picogram Level," PhD dissertation, Harvard University, 1974, cited as Appendix in Thomas Whitesides, *The Pendulum and The Toxic Cloud*, 1977.

6. Trost, op. cit. note 4, p. 30.

7. Ibid., pp. 17–26.

8. Ibid., p. 26.

9. Ibid., p. 33.

10. Jim Morris, "The Stuff in the Backyard Shed," *U.S. News & World Report*, November 8, 1999, p. 64.

11. E. N. Brandt, *Growth Company: Dow Chemical's First Century*, East Lansing: Michigan State University Press, p. 480.

12. Ibid., p. 533.

13. EPA Memorandum, "Chlorpyrifos Poisoning Statistics Summary," From: Jerome Blondell, Health Statistician, Exposure Assessment Branch, To: Henry Jacoby, Science Integration Staff, June 18, 1987, with attachments.

14. Ibid.

15. New Jersey Department of Health, *Hazardous Substance Fact Sheet*—Chlorpyrifos, CAS Number 2921-88-2, New Jersey, 0002-NJDH-86-006, February 1986.

16. Office of Pesticides and Toxic Substances, U.S. Environmental Protection Agency, "Data Call-In Notice—Chlorpyrifos," and "Attachment A: Chlorpyrifos: Data Call-In Chemical Status Sheet," via Certified Mail, sent to all users of chlorpyrifos-containing products, September 19, 1991.

17. National Coalition Against the Misuse of Pesticides, "ChemicalWATCH Factsheet—Chlorpyrifos," compiled April 1989, modified March 1991, 2 pp.

18. Letter and attachments of Edward D. Shive of Kiley, Feldmann, Whalen, Devine, & Patane, P.C., Oneida, New York, to Tracy Frisch, NYCAP Coordinator, Albany, New York, April 29, 1992.

19. Gregory Witcher and Frank E. James, "Dow, Eli Lilly To Join Forces In Agrochemicals," *Wall Street Journal*, April 19, 1989, p. A-8; Milt Freudenheim, "Lilly and Dow to Combine Farm Chemicals Divisions," *New York Times*, April 19, 1989, p. D-1; and Ellen Goldbaum with Langdon Brockinton, "An Ag Venture is Born," *Chemical Week*, April 26, 1989, p. 9.

20. John J. Fried, "Mystery Killer,"*Philadelphia Inquirer*, February 12, 1996.

21. T. Calvin, "Danger on Our Doorstep: The Pesticides Risks Parents Don't Know About," *McCall's*, August 1993, pp. 95–103, cited in Caroline Cox, "Chlorpyrifos, Part I: Toxicology," *Journal of Pesticide Reform*, Winter 1994, Vol. 14, No. 4, p. 18.

22. Morris, op. cit. note 10.

23. "DowElanco Signs Adverse Effects Consent Decree for $732,000, *Pesticide & Toxic Chemical News*, May 3, 1995.

24. See U.S. Environmental Protection Agency, *In the Matter of DowElanco, Inc.*, Docket No. FIFRA 95-H-18, "Amended Complaint and Notice of Opportunity for Hearing," July 22, 1995, also original complaint, filed April 13, 1995.

25. U.S. Environmental Protection Agency, Memorandum, "Review of Chlorpyrifos-Associated Cases of Delayed Neuropathy," to Linda Propst, Section Head, Reregistration Branch, Special Review, and others, from Jerome Blondell, Health Statistician, Health Effects Division, January 19, 1995, pp. 1–37.

26. CBS–TV, op. cit. note 1.

27. Ibid.

28. Ibid.

29. Ibid.

30. Jake Thompson, "Lincoln Lab Is Only One in U.S. to Test Pesticides on Humans," *Omaha World-Herald*, December 19, 1999.

31. John J. Fialka, "EPA Recommends Increased Controls On an Insecticide," *Wall Street Journal*, October 28, 1999, p. A-5.

32. Andrew C. Revkin, "EPA, Citing Risks to Children, Signs Accord to Limit Insecticide," *New York Times*, June 9, 2000, p. A-1.

33. Carol Browner remarks at news conference, "For The Record," *Washington Post*, June 9, 2000, p. A-32.

34. Edward Wong, "In New York's War on Bugs, A Call for New Ammunition," *New York Times*, June 9, 2000, p. A-20.

35. Eric Durr, "Dow AgroSciences Agrees to Pay $2M to State Over Pesticide Ads," *Albany Biz Journal*, December 15, 2003.

36. Michael Gormley, Associated Press, "Dow to Pay $2M for Illegal Safety Claim," December 15, 2003.

37. Durr, op. cit. note 35.

38. Emily Green, "Dow Seeks to Ban Its Own Weedkiller," *Los Angeles Times*, July 27, 2002.

39. Bryan Stuart, "Herbicide Removed; Company Acted Quickly When Clopyralid Found," *Seattle Post-Intelligencer*, January 28, 2002, p. B-3.

40. Green, op. cit. note 38.

41. Karen Dorn Steele, "EPA Accused of Bowing to Dow," *Spokesman-Review*, September 26, 2002.

42. http://action.grrn.org/action/index, November 2003.

Chapter 6 — "Saving" 2,4-D

1. Cathy Trost, *Elements of Risk: The Chemical Industry And Its Threat To America*, New York: Times Books, 1984, pp. 22–24.

2. Keith Schneider, "A New Image for Herbicide," *In These Times*, July 27–August 9, 1983, p. 4.

3. Ibid.

4. Dow Chemical Co. presentation/discussion note page, "III. 1985 Goals and Key Tasks."

5. Robert E. Taylor, "EPA Is Expected To Study Curbs On 2,4-D Herbicide," *Wall Street Journal*, September 3, 1986, p. 58.

6. Kathy Gray, "MSU Researcher Says 2,4-D Linked to Cancer," *Midland Daily News*, March 10, 1987.

7. Emily Green, "Concern Grows In Weed War," *Los Angeles Times*, June 1, 2002, p. A-1.

8. Ibid.

9. Ibid.

10. Ibid.

11. Ibid.

12. Ibid.

13. Carol Van Strum, "The EPA's Long-Buried Evidence of Human Reproductive Hazards," in Lois Gibbs, et al., *Dying From Dioxin*, pp. 122–25.

14. Marcia G. Nishioka, Robert G. Lewis, Marielle C. Brinkman, Hazel M. Burkholder, Charles E. Hines, and John R. Menkedick, "Distribution of 2,4-D in Air and on Surfaces inside Residences after Lawn Applications: Comparing Exposure Estimates from Various Media for Young Children," *Environmental Health Perspectives*, Vol. 109, No. 11, November 2001.

15. *Globe and Mail*, November 10, 2003.

Chapter 7—Plastic

1. E. N. Brandt, *Growth Company: Dow Chemical's First Century*, East Lansing: Michigan State University Press, pp. 227–28.

2. Ibid., pp. 230–35.

3. Don Whitehead, *The Dow Story: The History of The Dow Chemical Company*, New York: McGraw-Hill, 1968, p. 227.

4. Lisa F. Smith, "Styrofoam Celebrates Half Century as Building Material," *Midland Daily News*, February 2, 1998, p. A-1.

5. Whitehead, op. cit. note 3, pp. 227–28.

6. Brandt, op. cit. note 1, pp. 455–56.

7. Associated Press, "Dow Plastics Sees Strong Recovery Continuing," *Midland Daily News*, December 9, 1994, p. 1.

8. Brandt, op. cit. note 1, p. 235.

9. Associated Press, Mariann Caprino "McDonald's Move May Signal Plastic-Shunning Trend," November 2, 1990.

10. See for example, *Modern Plastics*—Annual Report, January 1990, and *Chemical & Engineering News*, October 29, 1990, cited in Susan Birmingham, U.S. PIRG; Marc Osten, PIRG Toxics Action, and Bill Ryan, National Environmental Law Center, *Unmasking Environmental Polluters—A Report on Chemical and Plastics Producers' Opposition to Measure 6*," October 31, 1990.

11. Louis Blumberg and Robert Gottlieb, *War on Wastes*, pp. 267–69.

12. "Sailing the Seas of Trash," *CBS Evening News*, January 7, 2004.

13. Deborah Wallace, *In the Mouth of the Dragon: Toxic Fires in the Age of Plastics*, Garden City Park, NY: 1990, pp. xiii–xvi.

14. Ibid., p. xvi.

15. Ibid., p. xviii.

16. Brandt, op. cit. note 1, p. 218.

17. See for example, Anne Platt McGinn, *"Why Poison Ourselves? A Precautionary Approach to Synthetic Chemicals*, Worldwatch Paper 153, Worldwatch Institute, Washington, DC, November 2000, pp. 49–51, and Joe Thornton, *Pandora's Poison*, Cambridge: MIT Press, 2000, pp. 306–12.

18. Thornton, op. cit. note 17, p. 309.

19. U.S. Agency for Toxic Substances and Disease Registry, Toxicological Profile for DEHP, 1992, cited by Charlie Cray, Greenpeace U.S. Toxics Campaign, "Worldwide PVC Replacement—The Greenpeace Position," Presented at Flexpo '98, Houston, Texas, June 25, 1998, in *Flexpo '98*, Conference Proceedings, Chemical Market Resources, Inc., Houston, Texas, p. 268.

20. Joe Thornton, PhD, *Environmental Impacts of Polyvinyl Chloride Building Materials*, Published by the Healthy Building Network (*www.healthybuilding.net*), Washington, DC, 2002, p. xii.

21. Jim Morris, "Toxic Secrecy," *Houston Chronicle*, 1998.

22. Stephen Fenichell, *Plastic: The Making of A Synthetic Century,* New York: Harper-Collins, 1996, pp. 310–13

23. See for example, Dow Chemical Co., "Evaluation of Vinyl Chloride as a Propellant for Aerosols," July 29, 1959, Papers of the Manufacturing Chemists Association, cited in Gerald Markowitz and David Rosner, *Deceit and Denial: The Deadly Politics of Industrial Pollution,* Berkeley: University of California Press, 2002, p. 184.

24. Author correspondence with Barry Castleman, September 2003; and Barry I. Castleman, ScD, and Grace E. Ziem, MD, DrPH, "Corporate Influence on Threshold Limit Values," *American Journal of Industrial Medicine*, Vol. 13, 1988, p. 548.

25. Markowitz and Rosner, op. cit. note 23, pp. 173–78.

26. D. A. Rausch, Dow Chemical Co., Inorganic Chemicals, "Confidential Treatment of European Study on Vinyl Chloride," December 15, 1972, Papers of the Manufacturing Chemists Association, cited in Markowitz and Rosner, op. cit. note 23, p. 182.

27. Markowitz and Rosner, op. cit. note 23, p. 183.

28. Ibid., p. 191.

29. Fenichell, op. cit. note 22.

30. "Worse Than We Thought," *Environmental Action*, June 22, 1974, p. 9.

31. "High Cancer Rate Found at Plants," *New York Times*, July 24, 1980, p. D-18.

32. Morris, op. cit. note 21.

33. Gwynne Lyons, *Bisphenol-A—A Known Endocrine Disruptor*, A WWF European Toxics Program Report, April 2000.

34. Frederick S. vom Saal, Professor, Division of Biological Sciences, University of Missouri-Columbia, and Wade V. Welshons, Associate Professor, Department of Veterinary Biomedical Sciences, University of Missouri-Columbia, Letter to Lynne Harris, Society of Plastics Industry, Washington, DC, June 12, 1997, pp. 1–6, with attachments.

35. From full interview with Dr. Frederick vom Saal, conducted in February 1998 by Doug Hamilton, producer of *Frontline*'s "Fooling With Nature," Program #1619, WGBH-TV, Public Broadcasting System, air date June 2, 1998.

36. Marc Lappe, *Chemical Deception: The Toxic Threat To Health And The Environment*, San Francisco: Sierra Club Books, 1991, pp. 31–32.

37. Michael Mansur, "Concern About Possible Water Contamination Spreads to Other States," *Kansas City Star*, March 2, 1998.

38. See for example, this Dow web page: *www.dow.com/webapps/lit/litorder. asp?objid=09002f138000ffc5&filepath=/noreg.*

39. Greenpeace, *Chlorine and PVC Restrictions and PVC-Free Policies*—A List Compiled by Greenpeace International, October 1998, pp. 1–51.

40. Beth Daley, "City Adopts Anti-Dioxin Purchasing Policy," *Boston Globe*, October 31, 2003.

Chapter 8 — Taken to the Cleaners

1. K. M. Thompson, "Risk Assessment and the Dry Cleaning Industry," in *The Greening of Industry: A Risk Management Approach*, ed. J. D. Graham, submitted for publication (1996), pp. 3–4, cited in Dan Fagin and Marianne Lavelle, *Toxic Deception*, Monroe, ME: Common Courage Press, 1999, p. 25.

2. Fagin and Lavelle, op. cit. note 1, pp. 25–26, and Dave DeRosa, *Out of Fashion: Moving Beyond Toxic Cleaners in the Fabric Care Industry*, Greenpeace, July 2001, pp. 6–7.

3. Don Whitehead, *The Dow Story: The History of The Dow Chemical Company*, New York: McGraw-Hill, 1968, p. 233.

4. See Cantin, J. (1992), cited in DeRosa, op. cit. note 2; and Bonnie Rice and Jack Weinberg, *Dressed To Kill: The Dangers of Dry Cleaning and The Case for Chlorine-Free Alternatives*, Greenpeace and Pollution Probe, April 1994, pp. 1–41.

5. See Tichenor, B. (1992), cited in DeRosa, op. cit. note 2; and Rice and Weinberg, op. cit. note 4.

6. See ATSDR (1993), cited in DeRosa, op. cit. note 2; and Rice and Weinberg, op. cit. note 4.

7. Fagin and Lavelle, op. cit. note 1, pp. 26–27.

8. Joe Thornton, *Pandora's Poison*, Cambridge: MIT Press, 2000, pp. 302–03.

9. Ibid., p. 305, citing Miller and Uhler, 1988.

10. See for example, Stanley, J. (1986); Pellizzari, E. et al. (1982); Wallace, L. et al. (1984); and others, cited in DeRosa, op. cit. note 2; and Rice and Weinberg, op. cit. note 4.

11. See Strauss, H. (1992), cited in ibid.

12. See for example, RSC (1986); ATSDR (1993); Alexeeff, G. (1991); and others, cited in ibid.

13. See for example, Schreiber, J. (1993); Lutz, S. (1993); Wallace, L. et al. (1995); and others, cited in ibid.

14. Richard C. Paddock, "Firm Settles Complaint on Carcinogen," *Los Angeles Times*, January 17, 1991, p. A-3.

15. See for example, ATSDR (1993); Boettger, A. (1991); NRC (1991); RSC (1986); and others, cited in DeRosa, op. cit. note 2; and Rice and Weinberg, op. cit. note 4.

16. Fagin and Lavelle, op. cit. note 1, pp. 128–29.

17. ICI, 1994.

18. Dow Chemical Co., *Chlorinated Solvents—Still Your Best Choice*, 1997.

19. Jane Kay, "Dow Settles Suit over Tainted Water with Cash, Cleanup—Pittsburg Plant to Treat Aquifer, Pay $3 Million," *San Francisco Chronicle*, April 4, 2002, p. A-18, and "Dow to Use Microbes to Clean up Groundwater Contamination," *U.S. Water News Online*, April 2002.

20. Ibid.

21. John J. Fialka, "EPA Asks Experts To Weigh Danger of Solvent TCE," *Wall Street Journal*, February 23, 2004.

Chapter 9 — Rocky Flats

1. Eileen Welsome, "Bombs Away!" *Westword*, July 20, 2000.

2. Unless otherwise noted, sources for this section include one or more of the following: "Summary of September 1957 Fire," referenced at *www.ohre.doe.gov/ohre/new/findingaids/epidemiologic/rockyfire/intro.html*, citing: The Dow Chemical Company, Rocky Flats Plant, *Report of Investigation of Serious Incident in Building 71 on September 11, 1957* (October 7, 1957), p. 50, 55; United States Atomic Energy Commission, Division of Operational Safety, *Operational Accidents and Radiation Exposure Experience within the United States Atomic Energy Commission 1943–1975* (Washington, DC: U.S. Atomic Energy Commission, WASH 1192), p. 21; ChemRisk, *Reconstruction of Historical Rocky Flats Operations & Identification of Release Points, Project Tasks 3 & 4, Final Draft Report* (August 1992), p. 72; United States Atomic Energy Commission, "Small Metallic Plu-

tonium Fire Leads to Major Property Damage Loss," *Serious Accidents* 130 (November 27, 1957): p. 3; R. J. Walker, "Air Cleaning Operations at the Rocky Flats Plant," *Fifth Atomic Energy Commission Air Cleaning Conference Held at the Harvard Air Cleaning Laboratory, June 24–27, 1957* (Report No. TID-7551); Interview with the Building 771 residue operations manager at Rocky Flats, March 10, 1994. U.S. Atomic Energy Commission, Division of Operational Safety, *Operational Accidents*, p. 21; and Welsome, op. cit. note 1.

3. Welsome, op. cit. note 1.

4. Ibid.

5. E. N. Brandt, *Growth Company: Dow Chemical's First Century*, East Lansing: Michigan State University Press, pp. 290–92; and Welsome, op. cit. note 1.

6. "Summary of September 1957 Fire," op. cit. note 2.

7. Welsome, op. cit. note 1.

8. Ibid.

9. Ibid.

10. Ibid.

11. "Problems Plague Rocky Flats," Physicians for Social Responsibility, *PDR monitor*, June 1991; "Problems Persist at Weapons Plants," Physicians for Social Responsibility, *PDR monitor*, November 1990; Coyle, Dana et al., *Deadly Defense: Military Radioactive Landfills*, Radioactive Waste Campaign, New York, 1988; "Environmental Issues at DOE's Nuclear Defense Facilities," General Accounting Office, Washington, DC, September 1986; "Rocky Flats Plant Site, Final Environmental Impact Statement," Department of Energy, Washington, DC, April 1980.

12. Eileen Welsome, "This Place Is a Dump!" *Westword*, July 27, 2000.

13. Welsome, op. cit. note 1.

14. Welsome, op. cit. note 12.

15. Welsome, op. cit. note 1.

16. "Problems Plague Rocky Flats," Physicians for Social Responsibility, *PDR monitor*, June 1991; "Problems Persist at Weapons Plants," Physicians for Social Responsibility, *PDR monitor*, November 1990; Coyle, Dana et al., *Deadly Defense: Military Radioactive Landfills*, Radioactive Waste Campaign, New York, 1988; "Environmental Issues at DOE's Nuclear Defense Facilities," General Accounting Office, Washington DC, September, 1986; "Rocky Flats Plant Site, Final Environmental Impact Statement," Department of Energy, Washington, DC, April 1980.

17. "Weapons Plant Pressed For Accounting of Toll on Environment and Health," *New York Times*, February 15, 1990.

18. Letter of Ronald J. Pingel, Director of Corporate Operations Environmental Affairs and Responsible Care, Dow Chemical Co., Midland, Michigan, October 24, 1991, to Council on Economic Priorities, New York, NY, and excerpted in "Dow Chemical Company—A Report on the Company's Environmental Policies and Practices," Corporate Environmental Data Clearinghouse, November 1991, pp. 27–28.

19. "Problems Plague Rocky Flats, op. cit. note 16.

20. Associated Press, "Rocky Flats Suit Has Cost Public Millions," *Salt Lake Tribune*, April 9, 1996, p. B-4.

21. "A Rocky Flats Chronology," *Rocky Mountain News*, August 24, 2002.

22. See for example, Eileen Welsome, "Hot Property," *Westword*, August 3, 2000.

23. "Rocky Flats: Locals File $550m Suit for Property, Risks," *Greenwire*, May 6, 1996.

24. Associated Press, op. cit. note 20.

25. Mark Eddy, "Rocky Flats Suit Leaps Forward; Notices in Class Action Mailed to 12,000 Nearby Property Owners," *Denver Post*, October 16, 1999, p. B-1.

26. Berny Morson, "13-Year-Old Flats Suit Gets Judge's Go-Ahead," *Rocky Mountain*

News, July 25, 2003.
    27. Ibid.

Chapter 10 — Poisoning Canada

    1. Gene Schabath, "State to Test Drinking Water—Dredging To Clean St. Clair River at Sarnia Prompts Contaminant Checks at 12 Plants," *The Detroit News*, June 3, 2002.
    2. Ibid.
    3. E. N. Brandt, *Growth Company: Dow Chemical's First Century*, East Lansing: Michigan State University Press, pp. 192–96.
    4. Warner Troyer, *No Safe Place*, Toronto/Vancouver: Clarke, Irwin & Co. Ltd., 1977, p. 13.
    5. Ibid., pp. 22–23.
    6. Ibid., pp. 22–28.
    7. Brandt, op. cit. note 3, pp. 200–01.
    8. Author telephone conversation with Mike Gilbertson, December 17, 2003.
    9. Brandt, op. cit. note 3, pp. 200–01.
    10. Ibid., p. 201.
    11. Dave Dempsey, *Ruin & Recovery: Michigan's Rise as A Conservation Leader*, p. 165.
    12. Brandt, op. cit. note 3, p. 201.
    13. Troyer, op. cit. note 4, pp. 27–28.
    14. Dempsey, op. cit. note 11, pp. 165–67.
    15. Brandt, op. cit. note 3, p. 202.
    16. Ibid., pp. 202–03.
    17. Schabath, op. cit. note 1.
    18. Unless noted otherwise with direct citations, this section is based on web-posted summary and excerpts at: *www.city.mississauga.on.ca/library/history/derail.htm* citing the work, *Derailment: The Mississauga Miracle*. See also, for example: Mississauga *News*, Special Edition, November 12, 1979; Mississauga *Times*—Special Edition, November 14, 1979; "Deserted City Crippled," Mississauga *News*, Special Edition, November 12, 1979; "Welcome Home," Mississauga *Times*—Special Edition, November 14, 1979; Mississauga *News*, November 14, 1979; "The Week They Closed Mississauga," *Sunday Star*, Special Section, November 18, 1979; "Mississauga's Lost Week," *Sunday Sun*, November 18, 1979; "Aftermath," Mississauga *Times*, November 21, 1979; "City In Crisis: Day by Day," Mississauga *News*, November 21, 1979; Insert, Toronto *Sun*, November 12, 1979; "It's Over," *Journal Record* (Oakville), November 14, 1979; "Chlorine Fear After Train Derailment Clears Mississauga...," *Globe and Mail*, November 12, 1979; "Chlorine Leak Plugged, Blaze Dying," *Globe and Mail*, November 13, 1979; Toronto *Star*, November 13, 1979; "Tanker Disaster: The Miracle Is, No One Was Hurt," Toronto *Star*, November 12, 1979; "Mississauga; One Year After," Sunday *Sun*, November 9, 1980; *The Spectator*, November 12, 1979; "Mississauga Nightmare," *Maclean's*, November 26, 1979; "Terror in Mississauga" (the month in pictures), *Photo Life*, April 1980; M. J. Goldstein, *Mississauga Evacuated*, March 1980; Julius Lukasiewicz, "The National Nightmare,"(undated, unnamed newspaper article); "The Mississauga Disaster," *Reader's Digest*, March 1980, pp. 72–79; S. G. M. Grange, Commissioner, *Report of the Mississauga Railway Accident Inquiry*; Toronto *Sun* publication, *Miracle of...Mississauga*; Bob Mitchell, "Mississauga Remembers the Derailment," Toronto *Star*, November 9, 1998; "Remembering The Big One," Mississauga *News*, November 15, 1998; Bob Mitchell, "The Miracle of Mississauga," Toronto *Star*, November 6, 1999; Declan Finucane, "A Night of Memories for First on The Scene, Mississauga *News*, Novem-

ber 10, 1999; John Stewart, "Twenty Years Ago Today Derailment Rocked The City," Mississauga *News*, November 10, 1999; and Diana M. Liverman and John P. Wilson, "The Mississauga Train Derailment and Evacuation," *Canadian Geographer*, 10–16 November 1979, vol. XXV, no. 4, 1981.

19. Robert Macleod, "5th Anniversary of Derailment Mississauga Crash: The Fears Remain," *The Globe and Mail*, November 10, 1984, p. 1.

20. Brandt, op. cit. note 3, p. 208.

21. "Belanger, Father of Responsible Care, Reflects On 35 Years of Contributions," *Chemical & Engineering News*, April 22, 1996, pp. 23–24.

22. David Israelson, "Dow's 'Blob' Incinerator May Not Be Dioxin-Tested," Toronto *Star*, February 15, 1986, p. A-19.

23. David Israelson, "St. Clair River Toxic 'Blob' Lives On," Toronto *Star*, February 17, 1986; and Jane Foy, "Dow Fines Dismissed as 'Mere Pittance'," *The London Free Press*, February 18, 1986, p. D-1.

24. Foy, op. cit. note 23.

25. Israelson, op. cit. note 23.

26. Timothy Palmer-Benson, "The Blobs," *The Amicus Journal*, Spring 1986, p. 11.

27. Jock Ferguson, "Airborne Pollution in Chemical Valley Gets Scant Attention," *The Globe and Mail*, February 15, 1986, p. A-22.

28. Ibid.

29. Ibid.

30. Ibid.

31. Foy, op. cit. note 23.

32. Ibid.

33. Mike Fisher, "Dow Fined $16,000," *The Observer* (Sarnia), February, 18, 1986.

34. Don Tschirhart, "Toxic Vapor Escapes Near Port Huron," *Detroit News*, May 14, 1986.

35. Dow Chemical Co., "Dow Responds to Spill at Sarnia Site (Update)," Press Release, March 23, 2001.

36. Frank Esposito, "38 Workers Treated after Leak at Dow Vinyl Chloride Facility," *Plastics News*, June 30, 1997, p. 26.

37. *www.pollutionwatch.org*, "High Levels of Toxic Chemicals Pollute British Columbia," November 27, 2003, and "Facility Profile—Dow Chemical Canada, Western Canada Operations."

Chapter 11 — Dow Environmentalism

1. Knight Ridder/Tribune Co., "Dow Chemical Vows Effort to Reduce Pollution," *ENN Daily News*, April 29, 1996.

2. Natural Resources Defense Council, "Environmentalists and Dow: Chemical Reduction," *www.nrdc.org*, as of December 2003, last updated July 17, 1999.

3. Cathy Trost, *Elements of Risk: The Chemical Industry And Its Threat To America*, New York: Times Books, 1984, p. 251.

4. E. N. Brandt, *Growth Company: Dow Chemical's First Century*, East Lansing: Michigan State University Press, p. 173.

5. Ibid., pp. 174–75.

6. Dale Russakoff, "Privacy Cases' Unlikely Allies," *Washington Post*, December 9, 1985, p. A-1.

7. Brandt, op. cit. note 4, p. 526.

8. Trost, op. cit. note 3, pp. 253–54.

9. Robert A. Roland, "Toxic Scapegoats," *Washington Post*, April 21, 1979.

10. Ralph Nader and William Taylor, *The Big Boys: Power & Position in American Business*, New York: Pantheon Books, p. 187.

11. Ibid., pp. 187–88.

12. Ibid., pp. 169, 186.

13. "Belanger, Father of Responsible Care, Reflects On 35 Years of Contributions," *Chemical & Engineering News*, April 22, 1996, pp. 23–24.

14. Brandt, op. cit. note 4, p. 208.

15. *Chemical & Engineering News*, op. cit. note 13.

16. Peter Coombes, "Responsible Care: A Journey of Profound Cultural Change," *Chemical Week*, July 17, 1991, pp. 9–14.

17. Ibid.

18. Claudia Deutsch, "Dow Chemical Wants to Be Your Friend," *New York Times*, November 22, 1987.

19. Michael Weisskopf, "EPA Finds Pollution 'Unacceptably High'," *Washington Post*, April 13, 1989, p. A-33, and Philip Shabecoff, "Industrial Pollution Called Startling," *New York Times*, April 13, 1989, p. D-21.

20. Ibid.

21. See for example, Norman L. Dean, Jerry Poje, and Randall J. Burke, *The Toxic 500: The 500 Largest Releases of Toxic Chemicals in the United States, 1987*, Washington, DC: National Wildlife Federation, August 1989.

22. Bradley A. Stertz, "Now, After 91 Years, Dow Chemical Co. May Change Name," *Wall Street Journal*, October 6, 1988, p. C-16.

23. Bradley A. Stertz, "Dow and Chemical Like Love, Marriage Belong Together," *Wall Street Journal*, January 23, 1989, p. B-9.

24. NFO Research, Inc., A National Opinion Research Study on Behalf of the Chemical Manufacturers Association, *The Public and the Chemical Industry: Attitudes, Beliefs, and Opinions*, Report on the Baseline and Diagnostic Study, December 1989, p. 7.

25. "Dow Chemical Names Buzzelli to New Post For Ecology Issues," *Wall Street Journal*, May 7, 1990.

26. Greg Shaw, "Dow Chemical 'Cleanup Czar' Stresses Outreach, Constant Improvement," *Hazmat World*, December 1992, pp. 34–35.

27. Richard Walker, Reuters, "Chemical Industry Must Become Environment Leaders," April 15, 1991.

28. Gary Taylor, "Dow May Link Pricing of Products to Environment," *Journal of Commerce*, October 19, 1992.

29. Elizabeth S. Kiesche, "Dow Chemical: Leading a Quiet Revolution," *Chemical Week*, September 29, 1993, p. 37.

30. See for example, any of Dow's 10-K reports to the U.S. Securities and Exchange Commission during this period, or any of the annual enforcement reports—*Enforcement Accomplishments Report*, by FY—of the U.S. Environmental Protection Agency's Office of Enforcement, such as those filed against or settled with Dow during FY 1991, FY 1992, and FY 1994, among others.

31. Peter N. Kochansky, Hearst News Service, "Gore Wants Ideas, Praises Buzzelli," *Midland Daily News*, July 21, 1993, p. A-1.

32. Tom Barron, "EHS Manager Heads New Clinton E-Panel," *Environment Today*, Vol. 4, No. 7, July 1993, p. 3.

33. "Sign of The Times," *Business Ethics*, September/October, 1995, p. 19.

34. Karl D. Albrecht, "Industry, Activists are On Common Ground," *Bay City Times*,

March 16, 1997.

35. Barnaby J. Feder, "Dialogue on Pollution Is Allowed to Trail Off," *New York Times*, November 23, 2002.

36. Michael Waldholz, "Scientists Debate the Future Threat of Common Chemicals," *Wall Street Journal*, March 7, 1996, p. B-1.

37. Paul Raeburn, "From Silent Spring to Barren Spring?," *Business Week*, March 18, 1996, p. 42.

38. Cynthia Crossen, "Clamorous Pro and Con Campaigns Herald Book's Launch," *Wall Street Journal*, March 7, 1996, p. B-1.

39. Gregory G. Bond, Senior Development Manager, Chemicals TS&D Environmental Affairs, and W. Joseph Stearns, Jr., Director, Chlorine Issues, Dow Chemical Co., Midland, Michigan, Letter to Mary Sinclair, Midland, Michigan, RE: "Response to Concerns Regarding Theo Colborn Article," January 31, 1994, pp. 1–3.

40. Dow Chemical Co., "Position on Endocrine Disruptors," undated, pp. 1–2.

41. See list prepared by WWF-US, "Chemicals in The Environment Reported to Have Reproductive and/or Endocrine Disrupting Effects," from Theo Colborn (1998) "Endocrine Disruption From Environmental Toxicants," in W. N. Rom (ed.) *Environmental and Occupational Medicine*, 3rd edition, Lippincott-Raven Publishers, Philadelphia, pp. 807–16; F. Brucker-Davis (1998) "Effects of Environmental Synthetic Chemicals on Thyroid Function," *Thyroid* 8(9): pp. 827–56; and Poly Short and Theo Colborn (1999), "Pesticide Use in the U.S. and Policy Implications: A Focus on Herbicides," *Toxicology and Industrial Health* 15 (1-2): pp. 240–75.

42. Doug Henze, "Dow Part of Effort to Develop Test for Endocrine Effects," *Midland Daily News*, October 7, 1996, p. A-1.

43. Cass Peterson, "Dow Role Cited in Rebuff to Chemical Testing Plan," *Washington Post*, April 23, 1983, p. A-2.

44. Ibid.

45. Ibid.

46. Dow Chemical Co., "Chemicals Management," *2001 Global Public Report*.

47. Ibid.

48. Thaddeus Herrick, Matthew Newman, and Michael Schroeder, "U.S. Opposes EU Effort to Test Chemicals for Health Hazards," *Wall Street Journal*, September 9, 2003.

49. Andrew N. Liveris, Dow Chemical Co., Business Group President, Performance Chemicals, Speech at Manufacturing Seminar, College of Engineering, University of Michigan,"Improving What's Essential to Human Progress: An Inside Look at Engineers in the Chemical Industry," Ann Arbor, Michigan, February 21, 2002.

50. Michelle Nijhuis, "What's In Your Body's Chemical Cocktail?" www.salon.com. December 10, 2003.

Chapter 12 — Silicone

1. John A. Byrne, "Informed Consent," *Business Week*, October 2, 1995.

2. See for example: Don Whitehead, *The Dow Story: The History of The Dow Chemical Company*, New York: McGraw-Hill, 1968, pp. 192, 272; E. N. Brandt, *Growth Company: Dow Chemical's First Century*, East Lansing: Michigan State University Press, p. 246; Hoover's, Company Profile, Dow Corning Corporation, 2003; and Marc Lappe, *Chemical Deception: The Toxic Threat To Health And The Environment*, San Francisco: Sierra Club Books, 1991, pp. 155–56.

3. Ibid.

4. Joseph Nocera, "Fatal Litigation," *Fortune*, October 16, 1995, p. 64.

5. Susan Zimmerman, *Silicone Survivors: Women's Experience with Breast Implants*, Philadelphia: Temple University Press, 1998, pp. 27–29.

6. John A. Byrne, *Informed Consent*, New York: McGraw-Hill, 1996, p. 46.

7. Zimmerman, op. cit. note 5, p. 28.

8. Lappe, op. cit. note 2, pp. 158, and Zimmerman, op. cit. note 5, p. 29.

9. Ibid.

10. Zimmerman, op. cit. note 5, pp. 32–33.

11. Byrne, op. cit. note 6, p. 82.

12. Public Broadcasting System (PBS) *Frontline*, "Breast Implants on Trial," and related web pages at *www.pbs.org/wgbh/frontline/implants/cron.html*.

13. Byrne, op. cit. note 6, p. 82.

14. PBS, op. cit. note 12.

15. Dow document, dated January 15, 1975, cited in Zimmerman, op. cit. note 5, p. 33.

16. Byrne, op. cit. note 6, p. 183.

17. Zimmerman, op. cit. note 5, p. 36.

18. Ibid.

19. Ibid.

20. Ibid., p. 37.

21. "A Crucial Defeat for Dow Chemical?" *Business Week*, November 13, 1995.

22. Richard Alexander, attorney, Alexander, Hawes & Audet, "Update On Breast Implants: The New Evidence Against Dow Chemical," June 1994, posted at *www.consumerlawpage.com/article/dow.shtml*.

23. Ibid.

24. Ibid.

25. Ibid.

26. Daniel Fisher, Bloomberg News Service, "Implant Silicone Killed Roaches, Tests Revealed," *The Houston Post*, November 5, 1994, p. A-1.

27. Pamela Coyle, "Women Suing Dow Charge Tampering," *The Times-Picayune*, April 30, 1997, p. B-1.

28. Ibid.

29. Ibid.

30. Richard B. Schmidt, "Can Corporate Advertising Sway Juries?" *Wall Street Journal*, March 3 1997, p. B-1.

31. Ibid.

32. "Dow Tries To Overturn Breast Implant Decision: Mahlum vs. Dow Chemical," *The Discoverer Review* (Columbia, MO), May 1997, pp. 15–17.

33. Thomas M. Burton, "Dow Chemical Found Negligent in Silicone Case," *Wall Street Journal*, August 19, 1997, p. A-3.

34. Associated Press, "Judge Refuses to Reconsider Ruling," *Midland Daily News*, January 6, 1998, p. A-1.

35. For the history of this case, see for example, Kara Sissell, "Dow Loses a Skirmish in Breast Implant Case," *Chemical Week*, March 12, 1997, p. 12; Scott Anderson, "Dow Appeals Implant Suit Again," *Midland Daily News*, July 31, 1997, p. A-1; Burton, op. cit. note 33; "Appeals Court: Implant Case Should Not Be Class Action," *Midland Daily News*, February 3, 1998, p. A-1; "Dow: Ruling is 'Significant For Us,'" *Midland Daily News*, April 3, 1998; Associated Press, op. cit. note 34; Associated Press, "Plaintiffs Don't Have to Re-Prove Dow Chemical Negligence," *Midland Daily News*, January 14, 1998, p. A-1; Lisa F. Smith, "Louisiana Implant Trial Against Dow Delayed Indefinitely," *Midland Daily News*, January 14, 1998, p. A-1; Dow Chemical Co., News Release, "Breast Implant Verdict Reversed by Appeals Court," December 9, 2002; and Bloomberg News, "Louisiana: Dismissal in

Implant Suit," National Briefing, *New York Times*, December 10, 2002, p. A-22.

36. Carli Cutchin, "Implants: A Murky Victory," *Reno News & Review*, February 7, 2002.

37. Lappe, op. cit. note 2, pp. 152–53.

38. Ibid., pp. 164–65.

39. Ibid., p. 167.

40. Mary White Stewart, *Silicone Spills: Breast Implants on Trial*, Westport, CT: Praeger, 1998, p. 192.

41. Marc Kaufman, "Silicone Gel Implants Still Banned," *Washington Post*, January 9, 2004, p. A-1.

Chapter 13 — Men At Work

1. E. N. Brandt, *Growth Company: Dow Chemical's First Century*, East Lansing: Michigan State University Press, pp. 141–42.

2. Ibid., p. 37.

3. Robert Gottlieb, Maureen Smith, and Julie Roque, "Greening or Greenwashing? The Evolution of Industry Decision Making," in *Reducing Toxics*, Robert Gottlieb (ed.), Washington: Island Press, 1995, pp. 177–78, citing William Chambless, *Fifty Years of Research and Service: Haskell Laboratory for Toxicology and Industrial Medicine*, Wilmington, Delaware: DuPont, 1985, p. 6, and David A. Hounshell and John Kenley Smith, Jr., *Science & Corporate Strategy: DuPont R&D, 1902–1980*, Cambridge: Cambridge University Press, 1988, pp. 563, 566.

4. Gerald Markowitz and David Rosner, *Deceit and Denial: The Deadly Politics of Industrial Pollution*, Berkeley: University of California Press, 2002, p. 171.

5. Barry I. Castleman, ScD, and Grace E. Ziem, MD, DrPH, "Corporate Influence on Threshold Limit Values," *American Journal of Industrial Medicine*, Vol. 13, 1988, pp. 531–59.

6. Ibid.

7. D. J. Kilian and D. Picciano, "Cytogenetic Surveillance of Industrial Population," in A. Hollaender, ed., *Chemical Mutagens: Principles and Methods for Their Detection*, Vol. 4, New York: Plenum, 1976, pp. 321–40; Richard Severo, "Dispute Arises Over Dow Studies On Genetic Damage in Workers," *New York Times*, February 5, 1980, p. A-1; and "Gene Watching," *New York Times*, September 13, 1981.

8. Samuel Epstein, *The Science and Politics of Cancer*, pp. 130–31.

9. Castleman and Ziem, op. cit. note 5, p. 550.

10. *New York Times*, op. cit. note 7; Susan West, "Genetic Testing on The Job," *Science 82*, p. 16; and "Dow Denies It Quit Testing Chemicals Found Harmful," *Midland Daily News*, April 4, 1983.

11. *Midland Daily News*, op. cit. note 10, and *Environmental Action*, April 1980, p. 11.

12. L. M. Sixel, "Company's Life Policies Draw Suits—Dow Chemical is Accused of 'Dead Peasant' Insurance," *Houston Chronicle*, June 6, 2002, and PACE Union, "Are You Worth More Dead than Alive to Your Employer?" July-August 2002, *www.pacepower.org*.

13. PACE Union, op. cit. note 12.

14. Sixel, op. cit. note 12, and PACE Union, op. cit. note 12.

15. KPCR-TV, Houston, Texas, "Dead Peasant Policies Should Be Stopped; Companies Shouldn't Profit From Worker's Death," *www.kpcr.com*, December 20, 2002.

16. Gary Taylor, "Unions Cite Layoffs in Dow Texas Fire," *Chemical News & Intelligence* (CNI), March 4, 1998.

17. Gary Taylor, "Dow: Texas Plant Appropriately Staffed," *Chemical News & Intelligence* (CNI), March 6, 1998.

18. Gary Taylor, "Dow Eyes Water-Oil Line in Texas Fire," *Chemical News & Intelligence* (CNI), March 6, 1998.

19. Gary Taylor, "Dow Texas Workers Pass Benzene Tests," *Chemical News & Intelligence* (CNI), March 17, 1998.

20. Gary Taylor, "OSHA Fines Dow in Texas Pygas Blast," *Chemical News & Intelligence* (CNI), July 27, 1998.

21. "Plant Blast Injures 2," *Houston Chronicle*, March 4, 1998; "Two Still Hospitalized," *Houston Chronicle*, March 5, 1998; "Ethylene Blast at Dow," *Chemical Week*, March 11, 1998; "Explosion at Dow's Freeport Plant," *Chemical Marketing Reporter*, March 20, 1998; "Dow Fined By OSHA," *Houston Chronicle*, July 17, 1998; and Dow Chemical Co., Press Release, "Dow Receives Report Form OSHA On Explosion," July 16, 1998.

22. Taylor, op. cit. note 20.

23. Metal Trades Department, AFL-CIO, Washington, DC, "Dow's Union Workers— The Forgotten Stakeholders," May 2003, pp. 1–11.

24. Ibid.

25. Peter Fairley, "Labor Reenergized," *Chemical Week*, November 27, 1996, pp. 25–30.

26. "Chemical Unions Unite, Build Power," *ICEM North American Action*, Winter, 2002–03, and Michael Clements, "National Unions Join to Oppose Dow," *The Daily News*, July 17, 2002.

27. *ICEM North American Action*, op. cit. note 26.

Chapter 14 — The DBCP Saga

1. Cathy Trost, *Elements of Risk: The Chemical Industry and its Threat to America*, New York: Times Books, 1984, p. 36.

2. Ibid., p. 37.

3. Ibid., pp. 39–41.

4. Ibid., pp.198–99.

5. Ibid., p. 49.

6. Ibid., p. 205.

7. Ibid., p. 216.

8. Ibid., p. 214.

9. Ibid., pp. 232–33.

10. Ibid., p. 229.

11. Ibid., p. 236.

12. Ibid., p. 240.

13. Ibid., pp. 242–43.

14. Ibid., pp. 282–86.

15. Ibid., pp. 288–90.

16. "3 Firms Sued Over Well Contamination," *Los Angeles Times*, January 1, 1990, and "3 Firms Will Pay To Clean Up Wells; Fresno To Receive $21 Million," *San Francisco Examiner*, May 16, 1995.

17. David Gonzalez with Samuel Lowenberg, "Banana Workers Get Day in Court," *New York Times*, January 18, 2003.

18. "The Cost of Bananas," *The Economist*, September 16, 1995, p. 54.

19. See for example: "Nicaragua Has Enacted a Law That Will Allow Banana Workers and Their Families to Sue," *Pesticide & Toxic Chemical News*, October 12, 2000; and Andrew Hund, "Poisoned Plantations—Ex-Workers in Nicaraguan Banana Fields Sue U.S. Firms Over Illnesses Linked To Toxic Fumigant," *San Francisco Chronicle*, March 15, 2001.

20. Gonzalez, op. cit. note 17.

21. Ibid.

22. Megan Rowling, "Nicaraguan Banana Workers May Finally Get Justice," *In These Times*, August 11, 2003.

23. Gonzalez, op. cit. note 17.

24. Ibid.

Chapter 15 — "Dow Water"

1. Rick Bragg, "Toxic Water Numbers Days of a Trailer Park," *New York Times*, May 5, 2003.

2. E. N. Brandt, *Growth Company: Dow Chemical's First Century*, East Lansing: Michigan State University Press, pp. 285–87.

3. "First Shipments of Products Begin Moving From Division," *Dow Louisiane*, July 31, 1958, Vol. 2, No. 4, p. 1.

4. Brandt, op. cit. note 2.

5. See for example, Jon Bowermaster, "A Town Called Morrisonville," *Audubon*, July-August 1993, p. 44.

6. Ellie Hebert, "Dow Capacity to Incinerate For Others Understated," *Post/South*, March 27, 1986, p. 5-A.

7. Bowermaster, op. cit. note 5, p. 42.

8. Brandt, op. cit. note 2, p. 287.

9. Gerald Markowitz and David Rosner, *Deceit and Denial: The Deadly Politics of Industrial Pollution*, Berkeley: University of California Press, 2002, p. 240.

10. Ibid.

11. Ibid. pp. 241–42.

12. Ellie Hebert, "Kirkland Charges Dow Telling Area Residents 'Drink It or Breathe It'," *Post/South*, January 22, 1987, p. 1-A; "Dow Begins Pumping Up Wastes in Plaquemine," *Post/South*, November 5, 1987, p. 3-A; James O'Byrne and Mark Schleifstein, "Drinking Water in Danger," *Times-Picayune*, February 19, 1991, pp. A-1 and A-5; Doug Henze, "Plaquemine," *Midland Daily News*, May 26, 1996, p. A-6.

13. O'Byrne and Schleifstein, op. cit. note 12.

14. Bowermaster, op. cit. note 5, p. 51.

15. O'Byrne and Schleifstein, op. cit. note 12.

16. Michael Brown, *Laying Waste: The Poisoning of America by Toxic Chemicals*, New York: Pantheon, 1979, 1980, pp. 157–62.

17. Ibid.

18. Charles M. Bargroder, "Guste Is Criticized for Remarks Made About Waste Site," *Times-Picayune*, September 24, 1982, p. 1; telephone conversations and correspondence with Willie Fontenot, Office of the Louisiana Attorney General, Baton Rouge, LA, September 2003 and January 2004; and U.S. Agency for Toxic Substances and Disease Registry.

19. See article on annual flooding of Devil's Swamp, *New York Times*, April 26, 1983.

20. "Agency Names 10 Chemical Firms in Suit Tied to Dump Sites," *Wall Street Journal*, July 16, 1980; "Justice Dept. Sues 11 of Largest American Chemical Corporations to Force Them to Clean Up Toxic Waste," *New York Times*, July 16, 1980; and Samuel Epstein, Lester O. Brown, and Carl Pope, *Hazardous Waste in America*, Sierra Club Books: San Francisco, 1989, p. 238.

21. "Despite Superfund Legislation…Danger Still Lurks at Waste Sites," *Baton Rouge Morning Advocate*, April 25, 1985; "Firefighters Put Out Fire at Waste Dump Near Baker,"

Baton Rouge Morning Advocate, May 7, 1985; and "Waste Dump Catches Fire for Third Time in Year," *Baton Rouge State Times*, May 7, 1985.

22. Martha M. Hamilton, "Dow Tries Burning Its Toxic Waste," *Washington Post*, October 25, 1984, p. B-1.

23. "Speakers Hit Dow, DEQ at Incinerator Hearing," *Post/South*, March 20, 1986, p. 5-A, and Hebert, op. cit. note 6; and Candace Lee, "Selectmen Agree To Study Dow Incinerators Conflict," *Post/South*, April 10, 1986.

24. "Plan to Clean Up Waste Sites Criticized: State, Federal Agencies Fear More Contamination,"*Baton Rouge State Times*, November 21, 1985; Petro Waste Cleanup Plan 'Inadequate'," *Baton Rouge Morning Advocate*, November 21, 1985; Sierra Club Complains About Cleanup Plan, *Baton Rouge Morning Advocate*, November 29, 1985; "Fire At Waste Site a May Event, Says DEQ Official," *Baton Rouge Morning Advocate*, May 7, 1986; "Officials Say Close Down Part of Devil's Swamp,"*Baton Rouge State Times*, July 25, 1986; "EPA Says Devil's Swamp Pollution Worse Than At Petro Processors," *Baton Rouge Morning Advocate*, July 26, 1986; and "Devil's Swamp Poses No Threat, Company Spokesman Says," *Baton Rouge State Times*, September 25, 1986.

25. "Tentative Cleanup Plans Call For Draining Liquid Wastes in 50 Years," *Baton Rouge State Times*, October 7, 1988.

26. Fred Kalmbach, "New Technologies Eyed Cleaning Waste Sites," *Baton Rouge State Times*, March 23, 1990, p. 1-A.

27. "Pollution Protests Start at Waste Site," *Baton Rouge State Times*, November 11, 1988, and "Jackson Says U.S. Firms Poison Poor," *Baton Rouge State Times*, April 3, 1990.

28. Bowermaster, op. cit. note 5, p. 47.

29. Louisiana Department of Environmental Quality, Baton Rouge, LA, *Consolidated Compliance Order and Notice of Potential Penalty*, Enforcement Tracking No. We-CN-00-0085, October 17, 200, p. 4.

30. Dow Chemical Company, U.S. Securities and Exchange Commission, Form 10-K, For Fiscal Year ending December 31, 2001, issued March 1, 2002, p. 12.

31. Mike Dunne, "Samples Fail To Identify Source of Contamination," *The Advocate*, June 27, 2001.

32. "Contaminated Water Source Sought," *The Advocate*, May 18, 2001.

33. "Samples Don't Identify Sources of Contamination," *The Advocate*, June 26, 2001.

34. "Source of Vinyl Chloride Eludes Dow," *The Advocate*, July 27, 2001.

35. Louisiana Environmental Action Network (LEAN), "Myrtle Grove Trailer Park and Iberville Parish Vinyl Chloride Contamination Fact Sheet," July/August 2001, pp. 1–2.

36. Mike Dunne, "Vinyl Chloride Source Still Mystery; Little Known of Chemical's Effects," *The Advocate*, March 10, 2002.

37. Mike Dunne, "Iberville Grand Jury Seeks Records From Dow," *The Advocate*, July 4, 2002.

38. Emily Kern, "Lawsuits Seek Compensation From DHH, Dow and Landlord," *Sunday Advocate*, March 10, 2002, p. 16-A.

39. Staff report, "Ex-Dow Workers Say Cleaning Water Dumped," *The Advocate*, June 13, 2002, and also: "Poison in Plaquemine, Part 2," WBRZ.com, June 14, 2002; Associated Press, "Dow Chemical Denies Charges That Spills Caused Contamination," *The Advocate*, June 14, 2002; Mike Dunne, "Little Change Seen in Chemical Tainting of Wells in WBR," *The Advocate*, June 19, 2002; and Mike Dunne, "Dow Unable To Confirm Allegations," *The Advocate*, June 29, 2002.

40. Staff report, "Ex-Dow Workers Say Cleaning Water Dumped," *The Advocate*, June 13, 2002.

41. Associated Press, "Dow Chemical Denies Charges That Spills Caused Contamina-

tion," *The Advocate*, June 14, 2002.

42. Dunne, op. cit. note 38.

43. Ibid.

44. Agency for Toxic Substances and Disease Registry (ATSDR), "ToxFAQs for Vinyl Chloride," September 1997.

45. Dunne, op. cit. note 35.

46. Bragg, op. cit. note 1.

47. Dunne, op. cit. note 38.

48. Emily Kern, "Myrtle Grove Water-Contamination Suit Developing; Attorney Hoping for Trial in 2004," *The Advocate*, June 30, 2003.

49. Amy Wold, "Dow Settles Complaint With DEQ for $2.4 Million for Plant Violations," *The Advocate*, April 16, 2003, p. 1-B.

50. Editorial, Our Views, "Punish Polluters; Don't Coddle Them," *The Advocate*, April 16, 2003, p. 6-B.

Chapter 16 — Danger Zones

1. Dow Chemical Co., Michigan Operations, "Providing For A Safer and More Informed Community," Risk Management Program, A Cooperative Emergency Planning & Preparedness Effort by Local Industry, Government and Community, 1999, pp. 1–6.

2. Blake M. Petit, "Fire at Dow Disrupts Operations," *St. Charles Herald-Guide*, January 12, 2002.

3. "Gas Leak Strikes Dow," *European Chemical News*, March 18, 2001, and "US: Gas Leak Strikes Dow Chemical," *CBNB*, March 29, 2001.

4. Associated Press News wires, "Fire Breaks Out In Industrial Complex North of Venice," November 28, 2002; Dow Jones International News, "Fire At Industrial Complex Outside Venice Injures Four," November 28, 2002; and e-mail report of Fabrizio Fabbri to Lisa Finaldi, Greenpeace, January 23, 2003.

5. U.S. Chemical Safety and Hazard Investigation Board, Chemical Incident Reports Center, CSB Incident # 2003- 6371, February 21, 2003.

6. Andrew Noyes,"Safety, Security Questioned at Louisiana Chemical Plants," States News Service, March 23, 2001.

7. Jason B. Johnson and Christopher Heredia, "If All Hell Breaks Loose," *San Francisco Chronicle*, May 13,1999, p. A-21.

8. Associated Press, "Catastrophe Threats Outlined for Public," *Augusta Chronicle*, September 27, 1999, p. C-7.

9. Dow Chemical Co., op. cit. note 1.

10. "Reported Chlorine Leak Sends 120 to Hospital," *Morning Advocate*, July 25, 1977.

11. "22 Sent to Hospital After Chlorine Drifts From Plant,"Across Canada, *Globe and Mail*, April 27, 1978.

12. "8 Workers at Dow Treated for Chlorine Inhalation," *Contra Costa Times*, July 7, 1988; "Six Men Injured in Poison Gas Release," *Los Angeles Times*, May 7, 1991; "Chlorine Leak Probed," *San Francisco Chronicle*, June 27, 1991, p. A-19; "Incident Report—Plant #31, Dow Chemical Company, Pittsburg, CA," Compliance and Enforcement Division, Bay Area Air Quality Management District, San Francisco, California, February 2, 1998; and Jason B. Johnson, Christopher Heredia, "If All Hell Broke Loose—Contra Costa Industry Gives Worst-Case Disaster Scenarios," *San Francisco Chronicle*, May 13, 1999, p. A-21.

13. Chris Frank, "Fires At Dow's Plaquemine Plant Cause Release of Chlorine into Air," *The Advocate*, October 4, 1994, p. 1-B.

14. Scott Anderson, "Officials Say Leak Didn't Pose Health Threat, *Midland Daily News*, December 10, 1996; Kelly L. Adams, "Vapor Leaks At DC Plant," *Midland Daily News*, December 17, 1996; Scott Anderson, "Leak Contained—No One Seriously Hurt in Dow Corning Release; Cleanup Continues," *Midland Daily News*, August 18, 1997, p. 1; Scott Anderson, "Leak Contained—About 360 Homes in Affected Area," *Midland Daily News*, August 18, 1997, p. 1; and Scott Anderson and Lisa F. Smith, "Label Helped Cause Dow Corning Leak," *Midland Daily News*, September 3, 1997, p. 1.

15. Frank Esposito, "38 Workers Treated after Leak at Dow Vinyl Chloride Facility," *Plastics News*, June 30, 1997, p. 26.

16. "Spill Releases Gaseous Acid at Dow," *Midland Daily News*, March 21, 1994.

17. Michael Baker, "Chlorine Leak Clouds Freeport," *The Facts*, October 1, 2003.

18. U.K. Health and Safety Executive, "The Explosion at the Dow Chemical Factory, King's Lynn 27 June 1976," HMSO, ISBN 011 8830 03 1, 1976; and F. P. Lees, "Loss prevention in the process industries—Hazard identification, assessment and control," Vol. 3, Appendix 1, Butterworth Heinemann, ISBN 0 7506 1547 8, 1996.

19. "Tank Car Acid Leak Sends 34 To Hospital in Jacksonville," *Washington Post*, July 29, 1978, p. A-7.

20. "Five Killed in Dow Chemical Plant Explosion," *Dow Jones News Service*, October 14, 1981, and "Explosion at Dow Chemical Plant in Freeport (TX) Kills Five Workers and Injures Seven," *New York Times*, October 14, 1981.

21. Kathy Gray, "Dow Lab Damaged By Explosion," *Midland Daily News*, May 15, 1986, p. A-1.

22. Wayne Beissert, Nationline, "Chemical Fire Keeps 2,000 From Homes," *USA Today*, July 24, 1989, p. 3-A.

23. "Arkansas," *USA Today*, January 10, 1990.

24. "Gas Leak Threatens Freeport/Waterway Closed; Some Residents Flee," *Houston Chronicle*, May 31, 1990.

25. Doug Henze, "Dow Fined $68,500," *Midland Daily News*, April 16, 1993, p. A-1.

26. "Derailment Causes Epichlorohydrin Spill," ECN, April 6, 1994.

27. "Industry Reports 15 Spills of 42,000 Pounds in Two Months,"*Post/South*, May 29, 1995, p. 1.

28. "Dow Canada Fire Rattles EO-EG Production," *Chemical Week*, December 11, 1996; *Dow Jones Telerate Energy Service*, "Dow: Alberta Ethylene Glycol Plant Down Until Early Jan.," December 13, 1996; and "Dow Canada Fire Rattles EO-EG Production," *Chemical Business News Base*, January 3, 1997.

29. Associated Press, "Dow Chemical Release Keeps People Penned In," *Bay City Times*, August 31, 1997; Cheryl Wade, "Dow, Firefighters Keeping Close Watch on Problem Tanker," *Midland Daily News*, August 31, 1997, p. A-1; and Cheryl Wade, "Worries, and Pressure in Tanker Subside," *Midland Daily News*, September 1, 1997.

30. "Plant Blast Injures 2," *Houston Chronicle*, March 4, 1998; "Two Still Hospitalized," *Houston Chronicle*, March 5, 1998; "Ethylene Blast at Dow," *Chemical Week*, March 11, 1998; "Explosion at Dow's Freeport Plant," *Chemical Marketing Reporter*, March 20, 1998; "Dow Fined By OSHA," *Houston Chronicle*, July 17, 1998; and Dow Chemical Co., Press Release, "Dow Receives Report From OSHA On Explosion," July 16, 1998.

31. Sources in Midland, Michigan, September 2003 and Michigan DEQ Air Quality Specialist, Jenny Stark. See also WJRT-TV (ABC) *www.abc.local.go.com/wjrt/news/*; and "Dow Says Leak Was Harmless—Gas Escape Was Reported Early this Morning," September 10, 2003.

32. Wayne Beissert, Nationline, "Chemical Fire Keeps 2,000 From Homes," *USA Today*, July 24, 1989, p. 3-A.

33. National Transportation Safety Board (NTSB), Washington, DC, *Derailment of CSX Transportation Inc. Freight Train and Hazardous Materials Release Near Freeland, Michigan July 22, 1989.* NTSB Report Number: RAR-91-04, adopted July 23, 1991, NTIS Report Number: PB91-916304, p. 4; photos, pp. 5, 7.

34. Robert E. Martin, Special Report: "Dow's Rail Disaster—More Questions Loom as the Chemical Smoke Settle," *Review Magazine* (Saginaw, MI), Vol. XI, Issue 219, July 31–August 15, 1989, pp. 2–3.

35. Ibid.

36. Robert E. Martin, Special Feature: "The Freeland Derailment—One Month Later, Questions Still Outnumber Answers," *Review Magazine* (Saginaw, MI), Vol. XI, Issue 220, August 16–30, 1989, pp. 2–3.

37. Robert E. Martin, Special Feature: "Chemicals Not Reported During Derailment—Results From Independent Audit Tell a Different Tale...," *Review Magazine* (Saginaw, MI), Vol. XI, Issue 222, September 21–October 5, 1989, p. 3.

38. Vern A. Pococke, "The Legacy of Our Tortured Tracks," and Robert E. Martin, "Local Media Confuse Issues in CSX Class Action Ruling," *Review Magazine* (Saginaw, MI), Vol. XII, Issue 243, August 20–September 12, 1990, p. 3.

39. NTSB, op. cit. note 36, pp. 47–48.

40. "Court Orders Freeland Train Derailment Class Action Claims Procedures & Deadlines," *Review Magazine* (Saginaw, MI), Vol. XIV, Issue 291, September 24–October 8, 1992, p. 2.

41. Allison LaPlante, U.S. Public Interest Research Group; Paul Orum, Working Group on Community Right-to-Know; and Mike Newman, Sierra Club, *At Risk and in The Dark: Will Companies In Our Communities Reduce Their Chemical Disaster Zones?* Washington, DC, June 1999.

42. Noyes, op. cit. note 6.

43. LaPlante, op. cit. note 41.

44. Anne-Marie Cusac, "Open To Attack," *The Progressive*, November 2003.

45. Ibid.

Chapter 17 — Big in Texas

1. Don Whitehead, *The Dow Story: The History of The Dow Chemical Company*, New York: McGraw-Hill, 1968, p. 159.

2. E. N. Brandt, *Growth Company: Dow Chemical's First Century*, East Lansing: Michigan State University Press, p. 178.

3. Telephone conversation with Glenn Heath, Lake Jackson, Texas, October 2003; interviews and conversations with O. D. Kenemore, Sharron Stewart, Vaughan Stewart, and others, Lake Jackson, Texas, October 24–26, 2003.

4. Jeffrey S. Kirkpatrick, Biologist II, District 7, Texas Water Quality Board, Inter-Office Memorandum to Dick Whittington, P.E., Director of Field Operations, Texas Water Quality Board, Austin, Texas, Subject: "Lower Brazos River Survey: Preliminary Report," February 23, 1971, p. 1.

5. Vaughan Stewart, "Dow Permit Reviewed...After 8 Years," *Ecology in Texas*, Vol. 1, No. 6, March 9, 1971, p. 5.

6. "Objections to Dow Waste Wells Rejected," *Houston Post*, September 18, 1971, and "Injection Well Permit Upheld," *Brazosport Facts*, September 19, 1971.

7. "Panel Explores Waste Efforts for CSC Group," *Brazosport Facts*, April 9, 1971, p. 1.

8. Author's interviews, op. cit. note 3; and *Brazosport Facts*, op. cit. note 7.

9. George Green interview of O. D. Kenemore, Austin, TX, January 17, 1994, from transcribed tape recordings.

10. Ibid., and author interviews and conversations with O. D. Kenemore, Sharron Stewart, Vaughan Stewart, and others, Lake Jackson, Texas, October 24–26, 2003.

11. "Mrs. Fagin Heads Women of Workers," *Brazosport Facts*, August 13, 1972; "Wives, Mothers Are Helping at Freeport," *Brazosport Facts*; Kathy Lewis, "The Others Picket Line in an 11-Week Strike," Woman's World, *Houston Post*, September 8, 1972, p. 1; and "Demonstration," photographs, *Brazosport Facts*, June 29, 1972.

12. "Both Sides Praise Dow Contract," *Houston Post*, September 21, 1972.

13. Author interview with O. D. Kenemore, retired Texas labor leader, Lake Jackson, Texas, October 25, 2003.

14. Ibid.

15. Ibid.

16. Ibid.

17. "Five Killed in Dow Chemical Plant Explosion," *Dow Jones News Service*, October 14, 1981, and "Explosion at Dow Chemical Plant in Freeport (Tex) Kills Five Workers and Injures Seven," *New York Times*, October 14, 1981.

18. Author interview, op. cit. note 13.

19. See for example, Janet Goode, "Dow Asked To Test Brazos River Fish," *Brazosport Facts*, February 27, 1990, p. 1, and "Biologists Plan Study of Dioxin in Fish," *Houston Chronicle*, February 27, 1990.

20. John Toth, "Brazos River Fish Contamination Tied to Dow Dioxin," *Houston Chronicle*, April 12, 1991, p. 28.

21. Associated Press, "Dow Reports Decreasing Dioxin Discharges in River," *Dallas Morning News*, April 30, 1992, p. 34-A.

22. Business Publisher, Inc., State Environment Report, "Texas: Although Dow Chemical Says It Has Slashed Dioxin Discharges From its Freeport Facility by 85 Percent, the Health Department Is Not Ready to Lift its Fish Advisory for the Brazos River," May 20, 1992.

23. Peggy O'Hare, "Dow Downplays Dioxin Report From Greenpeace," *Brazosport Facts*, March 3, 1995.

24. Texas Department of Health, "TDH Lifts Fish Consumption Advisory for Lower Brazos River," July 10, 1997.

25. See Dow Chemical, Freeport Facility, Freeport, TX, at *www.scorecard.org.* for 2001.

26. Dow Chemical Co., Environmental Stewardship, *The Dow Texas Operations Public Report*, 2001.

27. Luke Metzger, "Polluting The Brazos, Sullying Texas' Soul," *Houston Chronicle*, November 9, 2003, p. 1-C.

28. "County Ranked Fifth in Releases," *The Facts*, April 22, 1998, p. 1-A.

29. Environmental Defense, *www.scorecard.org*, U.S. EPA, Toxic Release Inventory data, 2001.

30. Associated Press, "TNRCC Fines Dow Chemical for Air Pollution Violations," December 19, 2001.

31. "Dow To Remove Toxic Wastes Buried 40 Years Ago Inside Freeport Plant," *Houston Chronicle*, October 5, 1989, p. 23.

32. Ibid.

33. Rhonda Moran, "Contamination, Dow Buys Worry Neighbors," *The Facts*, October 15, 2000, p. 1-A.

34. Ibid.

35. Ibid.

36. Ibid.

37. Steve Olafson, "'You Get To Thinking'—A Growing List of Cancer-Stricken Residents Raises Well-Water Concerns in a Clute-Area Neighborhood," *Houston Chronicle*, October 15, 2000, p. 35-A.

38. Bill Dawson, "La Porte Chemical Firm Cited for Violations," *Houston Chronicle*, July 11, 1986, p. 23

39. See U.S. EPA, Region 6, Emergency Response Notification System, for the dates indicated.

40. Bill DiSessa and Mary Ann Kreps, "Phosgene Gas Leak Halts Work at La Porte, Plant; None Injured," *Houston Chronicle*, January 9, 1990, p. 12.

41. "Gas Leak At Dow; No One Hurt," *Houston Chronicle*, January 13, 1992, p. 15.

42. Steve Scheibal, "Dow: Phosgene Gas Leak Contained," *The Facts*, June 17, 1997, p. 1-A.

Chapter 18 — Trouble in New Zealand

1. Ian Wishart and Simon Jones, "Agent Orange: 'We Buried it Under New Plymouth'," *Investigate* (New Zealand magazine), Jan/Feb 2001.

2. E. N. Brandt, *Growth Company: Dow Chemical's First Century*, East Lansing: Michigan State University Press, 1997, pp. 488–89.

3. Ibid., pp. 484–85.

4. Ibid., pp. 488–89.

5. Wishart and Jones, op. cit. note 1.

6. Ibid.

7. Ibid.

8. Hamish Carnachan, "Toxic Waste," *Investigate*, April 2002, p. 33.

9. David Barber, "New Zealand Spotlights Herbicide Leakage," *Christian Science Monitor*, January 20, 1984.

10. R. W. Moffat, Letter to the Editor, "2,4,5-T," *Daily News* (New Zealand), April 19, 1985.

11. According to sources cited by Greenpeace in *Corporate Crimes,* samples taken after this event showed soil levels of 310 ppt. Greenpeace cites: Department of Scientific and Industrial Research, April 18, 1986, released May 20, 1999 under the Official Information Act of 1982, and A Report by a Working Party to the Environmental Council, Commission for the Environment for the Environmental Council (New Zealand), 1986.

12. Greenpeace, *Corporate Crimes*, citing: Report by a Working Party to the Environmental Council, Commission for the Environment for the Environmental Council (New Zealand), 1986.

13. Carnachan, op. cit. note 8, pp. 28–37.

14. Ibid., p. 32.

15. Simon Jones, "The Poisoning of New Zealand II," *Investigate*, December 2000, pp. 26–31.

16. Ibid.

17. Ibid.

18. Rochelle West, "Blood Tests for Former Paritutu Residents," *Daily News* (New Zealand), April 4, 2003.

19. *www.dow.com/environment/dioxin/plymouth.htm.*

20. Carnachan, op. cit. note 8, pp. 28–37.

Chapter 19 — Time & The Tittabawassee

1. "Dow Shalt Not Blight the Earth," *From the Ground Up*, Jan/Feb 2003, pp. 8–9.
2. E. N. Brandt, *Growth Company: Dow Chemical's First Century*, East Lansing: Michigan State University Press, pp. 140–41.
3. Dave Dempsey, *Ruin & Recovery: Michigan's Rise as A Conservation Leader*, University of Michigan Press: Ann Arbor, 2001, p. 257.
4. Brandt, op. cit. note 2, p. 266.
5. Ibid.
6. Don Whitehead, *The Dow Story: The History of The Dow Chemical Company*, New York: McGraw-Hill, 1968, p. 154.
7. Paul Rau, "Brine Spill Debate Heated," *Midland Daily News*, October 4, 1979, p. A-1.
8. Diane Hebert, Midland, MI, Field notes and record of conversations with Michigan residents, 1980s.
9. Ibid.
10. Ibid.
11. "Dow Cleans Up Its Brine Operations," *Chemical Week*, August 29, 1984, p. 30.
12. "Dow Chemical to Close Brine-Products Business Based in Midland, Mich.," *Wall Street Journal*, October 16, 1984.
13. Keith Naughton, "DNR Documents 68 Dow Salt-Water Spills in 1984," *Saginaw News*, January 30, 1985, p. A-1; Julie Morrison, "Dow Cleaning up 50,000 Gallons of Spilled Brine," *Midland Daily News*, November 10, 1984, p. 3; and Keith Naughton, "Daily Inspections of Dow Wells Begin in Seven Townships," *Saginaw News*, January 20, 1984, p. A-1.
14. Doug Henze, "No End In Sight to Cleanup of Dow Brine Spills," *Midland Daily News*, December 19, 1993, p. A-3.
15. U.S. Environmental Protection Agency (EPA), *Michigan Dioxin Studies,* "Dow Chemical Wastewater Characterization Study," and "Tittabawassee River Sediments and Native Fish," Region 5, Eastern District Office, Westlake, OH, EPA-905/4-88-003, June 1986, p. 1.
16. Henze, op. cit. note 14.
17. James Kates, "Dow Dump Checked for Cancer Link, *Saginaw News*, August 28, 1980, p. 1.
18. Greenpeace, "Dow's Chemical Wastes in The Tri-City Area," July 1985.
19. *Fortune*, May 5, 1983.
20. Ward Sinclair, "Chemical Firms 'Hangs Tough'," *Washington Post*, April 24, 1983, p. A-1.
21. "Judges' Laxity Necessitates Tougher Antipollution Law," *Detroit Free Press*, August 6, 1971, cited in Dempsey, op. cit. note 3, p. 257.
22. EPA, op. cit. note 15, p. 1.
23. Kathy Gray, "Media Outnumber Demonstrators as Greenpeace Plugs Dow Pipe," *Midland Daily News*, July 11, 1985.
24. Ibid.
25. Doug Henze, "Groups Sue Dow," *Midland Daily News*, June 29, 1995, p. A-1.
26. Doug Henze, "Activists Sue Dow Over Discharges," *Midland Daily News*, August 17, 1995, p. A-8.
27. Doug Henze, "State Files Pollution Lawsuit Against Dow," *Midland Daily News*, August 21, 1995, p. A-7.
28. Doug Henze, "Dow Working On Wastewater Plant Problem," *Midland Daily News*, January 8, 1996, p. A-1, and Doug Henze, "Dow Says Waste Water Overload Didn't Affect Tittabawassee River," *Midland Daily News*, January 9, 1996, p. A-1.
29. "Dow Exceeds Release Permit," *Midland Daily News*, January 13, 1996, p. A-3.

30. Scott Anderson, "Dow Agrees to DEQ Fines," *Midland Daily News*, February 11, 1997, p. A-1.

31. Lisa F. Smith, "Dow To Pay $1 Million in Penalties," *Midland Daily News*, December 24, 1997, p. A-1.

32. Michael H. Brown, *The Toxic Cloud: The Poisoning of America's Air*, New York: Harper & Row, 1987, pp. 23–25.

33. Ibid., p. 42.

34. Ibid., p. 40.

35. Ibid., p. 39.

36. Ibid., pp. 44–45.

37. Letter from Dow Chemical Company of, March 7, 1985, submitted to Gerald P. Dodson, staff director, U.S. House of Representatives Subcommittee on Health and the Environment, cited in Brown, op. cit. note 32, pp. 26–27.

38. "Environmentalist Questions Need for Dow Incinerator," *Midland Daily News*, October 12, 1988.

39. Jeff Green, "Dow, DNR Disagree Over Permit Provisions," *Midland Daily News*, April 10, 1989.

40. Robert E. Martin, "Will Dow's Toxic Incinerator Be Allowed to Burn?" *Review Magazine*, September 10, 1992, p. 14.

41. Ibid., pp. 7, 14.

42. Editorial—Our View, "Policy of Openness Must Be A Dow Priority," *Midland Daily News*, October 8, 1993.

43. Doug Henze, "Incinerator is Cracked," *Midland Daily News*, November 6, 1993, p. A-1.

44. "Lone Tree Council, Ecology Center, and Citizens for Alternatives to Chemical Contamination, Press Release, "Citizens Appeal Dow Permit to Burn Dioxin," November 4, 1993, pp. 1–2; and Geri Rudolf, "Activists to Fight Incinerator in Court," *Saginaw News*, November 8, 1993.

45. Jean Hays, "Dow Chemical Set to Begin Shipping Contaminated Wastes to Kansas Incinerator," *Wichita Eagle*, June 14, 1994.

46. Scott Anderson, "Leak Contained—No One Seriously Hurt in Dow Corning Release; Cleanup Continues," *Midland Daily News*, August 18, 1997, p. 1.

47. Scott Anderson, "Leak Contained—About 360 Homes in Affected Area," *Midland Daily News*, August 18, 1997, p. 1.

48. Scott Anderson and Lisa F. Smith, "Label Helped Cause Dow Corning Leak," *Midland Daily News*, September 3, 1997, p. 1.

49. Kelly L. Adams, "Vapor Leaks At DC Plant," *Midland Daily News*, December 17, 1996, and Scott Anderson, "Officials Say Leak Didn't Pose Health Threat, *Midland Daily News*, December 10, 1996.

50. Mark Ranzenberger, "Leak Leads to Evacuation at Hemlock," *Midland Daily News*, June 10, 1996.

51. Ecology Center, *From the Ground Up*, Ann Arbor, Michigan, March 2002, p. 4.

52. Curt Guyette, "Questions of Cover-Up," *Metro Times* (Detroit), March 27–April 2, 2002, p. 11.

53. Lone Tree Council, Press Release, "Michigan Environment Agency in Collusion with Dow Chemical to Create 'Dioxin Zone'," October 22, 2002, pp. 1–2.

54. Eric Pianin, "Mich. Weighs Lower Dioxin Standards," *Washington Post*, December 6, 2002, p. A-2.

55. Eric Pianin, "Michigan and Dow Drop Dioxin Pact," *Washington Post*, December 31, 2002.

56. Jeff Johnson, "Dow Sued Over Dioxin in Soil," *Chemical & Engineering News*, June 8, 2003.

Chapter 20 — Union Carbide

1. Dow Chemical Co., "Dow and Union Carbide Have Merged," *Around Dow*, Special Commemorative Issue, p. 1.

2. Company Profile, Union Carbide Corporation, *Hoover's*, December 2000; Milt Moskowitz, Michael Katz, and Robert Levering, *Everybody's Business*, Harper & Row: San Francisco, 1990, pp. 526–27; David Dembo, Ward Morehouse, Lucinda Wykle, *Abuse of Power: Social Performance of Multinational Corporations: The Case of Union Carbide*, New York: New Horizons Press, 1990, pp. 12–19.

3. Milt Moskowitz, Michael Katz, and Robert Levering, *Everybody's Business*, Harper & Row: San Francisco, 1990, pp. 526–27.

4. David Dembo, Ward Morehouse, Lucinda Wykle, *Abuse of Power: Social Performance of Multinational Corporations: The Case of Union Carbide*, New York: New Horizons Press, 1990.

5. Cherniak, Martin, *The Hawk's Nest Incident: America's Worst Industrial Disaster*, New Haven: Yale University Press, 1986; Council on Economic Priorities, *Union Carbide: A Report on the Company's Environmental Policies and Practices*, New York: CEP, December 1992 and 1994; and Dembo et al., op. cit. note 4, pp. 21–31.

6. "Pollution Law Enforced," *New York Times*, May 14, 1953.

7. Moskowitz et al., op. cit. note 3, p. 616.

8. "Corporate Profile—Union Carbide Corporation," The Chemical Industry Responsibility Project, Cambridge, Massachusetts, November 1985, pp. 30–31.

9. Ibid., pp. 28–32.

10. Ibid., pp. 28–29.

11. Anndee Hochman, "Faulty Valve Blamed For Leak at Second Union Carbide Plant," *Washington Post*, August 15, 1985, p. A-3; Stuart Diamond, "Credibility a Casualty in West Virginia," *New York Times*, August 18, 1985, p. 1-E; Associated Press, "Carbide Details Poison Leak," *Washington Post*, August 24, 1985, p. A-5; and W. Joseph Campbell, "Toxic Leak Still Haunts W. Va., Despite Carbide's Efforts," *Philadelphia Inquirer*, December 27, 1985.

12. Philip Shabecoff, "Union Carbide Agrees to Pay $408,500 Fine for Safety Violations," *New York Times*, July 25, 1987, p. 8.

13. U.S. Chemical Safety and Hazard Investigation Board, "Bhopal Disaster Spurs U.S. Industry, Legislative Action," Electronic Reading Room, *www.chemsafety.org*, September 1999.

14. Sanjoy Hazarika, "Bhopal Payments Set At $470 Million For Union Carbide," *New York Times*, February 15, 1989, p. A-1.

15. See for example, Associated Press, "India Seeks To Reopen Bhopal Case," *New York Times*, January 22, 1990, p. D-1.

16. "Union Carbide to Pay A $1.5 Million Fine To Settle U.S. Charges," *Wall Street Journal*, November 4, 1992, p. A-16.

17. Dow Chemical Co., op. cit. note 1, p. 1.

18. Kathie Marchlewski, "Stavropoulos Speaks: Dow CEO Answers Questions from Michigan Ops to Union Carbide and More," *Midland Daily News*, March 23, 2003.

19. Jim Carlton and Thaddeus Herrick, "Bhopal Haunts Dow Chemical," *Wall Street Journal*, May 8, 2003, p. B-3.

20. Paper, Allied-Industrial, Chemical & Energy Workers International Union (PACE), "Bhopal/Dow Chemical," Resolution No. 49, Adopted August 18–23, 2003, Las Vegas, Nevada.

21. "Congressman Pallone Fights for Bhopal Gas Victims," *Times of India*, October 18, 2003.

22. International Coalition for Justice in Bhopal (ICJB), Press Release, "Activists Mount Global Challenge To Dow," January 16, 2004.

Chapter 21 — No Trespassing

1. Stacy Malkan, "Pollution of the People," *Multinational Monitor*, May 8, 2003.

2. See *Gill v. LDI*, 19 F. Supp. 2d 1188 (W.D. Wash. 1998), cited in Chapter 3, "Theories of Liability," *Guide to Toxic Torts*, Matthew Bender & Co., 2003.

3. See *Mondry v. Speedway Superamerica* LLC, No. 96 C 2159, 1999 U.S. Dist. LEXIS 9095, at 21 (N.D. Ill. May 13, 1999), cited in Chapter 3, "Theories of Liability," *Guide to Toxic Torts*, Matthew Bender & Co., 2003.

4. See *Martin v. Reynolds Metals Co.*, 221 Or. 86, 342 P.2d 790, 792 (1959), and also, generally, F. M. Powell, *Trespass, Nuisance, and the Evolution of Common Law In Modern Pollution Cases*, 21 Real Estate L.J. 182 (1992), cited in Chapter 3, "Theories of Liability," *Guide to Toxic Torts*, Matthew Bender & Co., 2003.

5. Sharyle Patton and Gary Cohen, "Building the Right to Know About Chemical Body Burden and Stopping the Chemical Industry's Toxic Trespass," at *www.ombwatch.org/ rtkconference/ body_burden.html*.

6. Ibid.

7. Ibid.

Index

About the Author

Jack Doyle is director of J.D. Associates, a Washington, D.C. investigative research firm specializing in business and environmental issues. He has been writing about technology, business, and the environment for more than 20 years. *Publisher's Weekly* called his June 2000 book on the U.S. auto industry, *Taken for a Ride* (Four Walls Eight Windows, Inc.) "a valuable source for...partisans on all sides of the debate." At Friends of the Earth in the 1990s, Doyle wrote *Crude Awakening*, a book on the U.S. oil industry, and *Hold The Applause!*, a critique of DuPont's "corporate environmentalism." A 1985 book on agricultural biotechnology, *Altered Harvest* (Viking-Penguin), is regarded as a pioneering work on the subject. In the 1970s, working as a lobbyist and policy analyst at the Environmental Policy Institute, Doyle wrote reports on the coal mining industry that helped moved strip mining legislation in Congress. *Lines Across The Land*, a 1979 exposé of the U.S. rural electric cooperative system, was used by liberals and conservatives to push reforms at the U.S. Rural Electrification Administration. Doyle's writing has appeared in the *New York Times, Washington Post, Newsday, Boston Globe, Atlanta Journal-Constitution, Des Moines Register, San Francisco Chronicle,* and *TomPaine.com,* among others. He has consulted with various public agencies and private clients, including the President's Council on Environmental Quality, the former Congressional Office of Technology Assessment, the AFL-CIO, several national environmental organizations, and *Fortune 500* companies. He has also appeared as an expert witness before U.S. Congressional committees and has served on the board of the Coalition for Environmentally Responsible Economies in Boston. He holds degrees from Millersville University and the Pennsylvania State University.